Microsoft

Microsoft® Visual Basic® .NET Programming Essentials

Textbook

Bernie O'Brien
Catherine Seaver

PUBLISHED BY
Microsoft Press
A Division of Microsoft Corporation
One Microsoft Way
Redmond, Washington 98052-6399

Library of Congress Cataloging-in-Publication Data pending.
    ISBN 0-7356-2118-7
    (Microsoft Press)
    ISBN 0-07-225621-4
    (McGraw-Hill)

Printed and bound in the United States of America.

1 2 3 4 5 6 7 8 9   QWE   9 8 7 6 5 4

Distributed in Canada by H.B. Fenn and Company Ltd.

A CIP catalogue record for this book is available from the British Library.

Microsoft Press books are available through booksellers and distributors worldwide. For further information about international editions, contact your local Microsoft Corporation office or contact Microsoft Press International directly at fax (425) 936-7329. Visit our Web site at www.microsoft.com/learning/. Send comments to *mspinput@microsoft.com*.

Acquisitions Editor: Linda Engleman
Project Editor: Barbara Moreland
Technical Editor: Robert Brunner
Indexer: Lynn Armstrong

Body Part No. X10-58454

CONTENTS AT A GLANCE

CONTENTS

ABOUT THIS BOOK

Welcome to *Microsoft Visual Basic .NET Programming Essentials*. Through lectures, discussions, demonstrations, textbook exercises, and classroom labs, this course teaches students the skills and knowledge necessary to create Windows- and Web-based applications using the Visual Basic .NET programming language. The fourteen chapters in this book walk you through key concepts of the Visual Basic .NET language used within the Visual Studio .NET integrated development environment.

TARGET AUDIENCE

This textbook was developed for students with little or no programming experience. Although no prior programming experience is assumed, students should be sufficiently knowledgeable in the use of a Windows-based computer. More advanced students migrating from a different programming language would also benefit greatly from this book because it covers many of the concepts they are already familiar with and introduces many new concepts that they may not yet have seen.

PREREQUISITES

This textbook requires that students meet the following prerequisites:

- Proficiency with using a Windows-based computer.
- Ability to create files and folders using Windows Explorer or the command window utility.
- Ability to perform standard tasks such as application installation.
- Prerequisite knowledge and course work as defined by the learning institution and the instructor.

THE TEXTBOOK

The textbook content has been crafted to provide a meaningful learning experience to students in an academic classroom setting.

Key features of the Academic Learning Series textbooks include the following:

- Learning objectives for each chapter that prepare the student for the topic areas covered in that chapter.
- Chapter introductions that explain why the information is important.
- An inviting design with screen shots, diagrams, tables, bulleted lists, and other graphical formats that makes the book easy to comprehend and supports a number of different learning styles.

- Clear explanations of concepts and principles, and frequent exposition of step-by-step procedures.

- A variety of reader aids that highlight a wealth of additional information, including:

  - ❑ Note—Additional explanations of complex procedures and concepts, and real-world application insights.

  - ❑ Tip—Explanations of possible results or alternative methods for performing tasks.

- End-of-chapter exercises that assess knowledge and can serve as homework, quizzes, and review activities before or after lectures. Additional exercises within the chapter serve as periodic checks on students' understanding of the material. (Answers to the textbook questions are available from the instructor.)

- Chapter summaries that distill the main ideas in a chapter and reinforce learning.

- A comprehensive glossary that defines key terms introduced in the book.

THE SUPPLEMENTAL COURSE MATERIALS CD-ROM

This book comes with a Supplemental Course Materials CD-ROM, which contains a variety of informational aids to complement the book content:

- An electronic version of this textbook (eBook). For information about using the eBook, see the section titled "eBook Setup Instructions" in this introduction.

- Microsoft PowerPoint slides based on textbook chapters, for note-taking.

- Microsoft PowerPoint Viewer.

- Code files required to complete the exercises in the textbook.

eBook Setup Instructions

The eBook is in Portable Document Format (PDF) and must be viewed using Adobe Acrobat Reader.

▶ Using the eBooks

1. Insert the Supplemental Course Materials CD into your CD-ROM drive.

   If AutoRun is disabled on your machine, refer to the Readme.txt file on the CD.

2. On the user interface menu, select eBook.

   You must have the Supplemental Course Materials CD in your CD-ROM drive to run the eBook.

NOTATIONAL CONVENTIONS

The following conventions are used throughout this textbook:

- Characters or commands that you type appear in **bold** type.

- Terms that appear in the glossary also appear in **bold** type.

- *Italic* in syntax statements indicates placeholders for variable information. Italic is also used for book titles and terms defined in the text.

- Names of files and folders appear in Title caps, except when you are to type them directly. Unless otherwise indicated, you can use all lowercase letters when you type a filename in a dialog box or at a command prompt.

- Filename extensions appear in all lowercase.

- Acronyms appear in all uppercase.

- `Monospace` type represents code samples or entries that you might type at a command prompt or in initialization files.

- Square brackets [ ] are used in syntax statements to enclose optional items. For example, *[filename]* in command syntax indicates that you can type a filename with the command. Type only the information within the brackets, not the brackets themselves.

- Braces { } are used in syntax statements to enclose required items. Type only the information within the braces, not the braces themselves.

KEYBOARD CONVENTIONS

- A plus sign (+) between two key names means that you must press those keys at the same time. For example, "Press ALT+TAB" means that you hold down ALT while you press TAB.

- A comma (,) between two or more key names means that you must press the keys consecutively, not at the same time. For example, "Press ALT, F, X" means that you press and release each key in sequence. "Press ALT+W, L" means that you first press ALT and W at the same time, and then you release them and press L.

THE MICROSOFT CERTIFIED PROFESSIONAL PROGRAM

The MCP program is one way to prove your proficiency with current Microsoft products and technologies. These exams and corresponding certifications are developed to validate your mastery of critical competencies as you design and develop, or implement and support, solutions using Microsoft products and technologies. Computer professionals who become Microsoft certified are recognized as experts and are sought after industrywide. Certification brings a variety of benefits to the individual and to employers and organizations.

For a full list of MCP benefits, go to *http://www.microsoft.com/learning/mcp /default.asp*.

Certifications

The MCP program offers multiple certifications, based on specific areas of technical expertise:

- **Microsoft Certified Professional (MCP)**   In-depth knowledge of at least one Windows operating system or architecturally significant platform. An MCP is qualified to implement a Microsoft product or technology as part of a business solution for an organization.

- **Microsoft Certified Solution Developer (MCSD)**   Qualified to develop, test, and deploy enterprise and business solutions with Microsoft development tools and technologies, including the Microsoft .NET Framework.

- **Microsoft Certified Application Developer (MCAD)**   Qualified to develop, test, deploy, and maintain powerful applications using Microsoft tools and technologies, including Microsoft Visual Studio .NET.

- **Microsoft Certified Systems Engineer (MCSE)**   Qualified to effectively analyze the business requirements for business solutions and design and implement the infrastructure based on the Windows and Windows Server 2003 operating systems.

- **Microsoft Certified Systems Administrator (MCSA)**   Qualified to manage and troubleshoot existing network and system environments based on the Windows and Windows Server 2003 operating systems.

- **Microsoft Certified Database Administrator (MCDBA)**   Qualified to design, implement, and administer Microsoft SQL Server databases.

- **Microsoft Certified Desktop Support Technician (MCDST)**   Qualified to support end users and to troubleshoot desktop environments on the Microsoft Windows operating system.

MCP Requirements

Requirements differ for each certification and are specific to the products and job functions addressed by the certification. To become an MCP, you must pass rigorous certification exams that provide a valid and reliable measure of technical proficiency and expertise. These exams are designed to test your expertise and ability to perform a role or task with a product, and they are developed with the input of industry professionals. Exam questions reflect how Microsoft products are used in actual organizations, giving them real-world relevance.

- Microsoft Certified Professional (MCP) candidates are required to pass one current Microsoft certification exam. Candidates can pass additional Microsoft certification exams to validate their skills with other Microsoft products, development tools, or desktop applications.

- Microsoft Certified Solutions Developer (MCSD) candidates are required to pass three core exams and one elective exam. (MCSD for Microsoft .NET candidates are required to pass four core exams and one elective.)

- Microsoft Certified Application Developer (MCAD) candidates are required to pass two core exams and one elective exam in an area of specialization.

- Microsoft Certified Systems Engineer (MCSE) candidates are required to pass five core exams and two elective exams.

- Microsoft Certified Systems Administrator (MCSA) candidates are required to pass three core exams and one elective exam.

- Microsoft Certified Database Administrator (MCDBA) candidates are required to pass three core exams and one elective exam.

- Microsoft Certified Desktop Support Technician (MCDST) candidates are required to pass two core exams.

ABOUT THE AUTHORS

The textbook, pretest, testbank, and PowerPoint slides were written by instructors and developed exclusively for an academic, instructor-led classroom environment.

Bernie O'Brien works as a Technical Specialist/Scientist for Southern California Edison (SCE). His working knowledge of computers and business software—including analysis, design, and development—and his keen sense of what is important in using and developing business software have enabled him to develop many instructional manuals, procedures, and user guides used within the corporation. In addition to working full time for SCE, Bernie also teaches beginning and advanced Visual Basic .NET, Visual C# .NET, and Visual Basic for Applications at Saddleback College in Mission Viejo, California. Working in the industry has allowed Bernie to provide his students with real-world knowledge of software design and development, which has enabled many of his students to advance rapidly into program development.

Catherine Seaver is an Assistant Professor of Computer Science at Manchester Community College (MCC) in Manchester, Connecticut. She has been working with and teaching programming using Visual Basic for over ten years. Catherine has created supplemental instructional materials for several programming books and has helped to develop programming courses for various organizations. In addition to programming, Catherine teaches networking, operating systems, and basic engineering courses at MCC. She holds the MCSD certification and several networking certifications; in the past she was a Microsoft Certified Trainer.

FOR MICROSOFT ACADEMIC LEARNING SERIES SUPPORT

Every effort has been made to ensure the accuracy of the material in this book and the contents of the CD-ROM. Microsoft Learning provides corrections for books through the World Wide Web at the following address:

http://www.microsoft.com/learning/support/

If you have comments, questions, or ideas regarding this book or the companion CD-ROM, please send them to Microsoft Learning using either of the following methods:

Postal Mail:
Microsoft Learning
Attn: *Microsoft Visual Basic .NET Programming Essentials* Editor
One Microsoft Way
Redmond, WA 98052-6399

E-mail: moac@microsoft.com

Please note that product support is not offered through the above addresses.

For online support information relating to any Microsoft software, go to *http://support.microsoft.com*. For information about ordering any Microsoft software, call Microsoft Sales at (800) 426-9400 or visit *http://www.microsoft.com*.

CHAPTER 1
AN INTRODUCTION TO VISUAL BASIC .NET PROGRAMMING

Welcome to Microsoft Visual Basic .NET. Don't worry if you have never programmed before and don't have a clue as to what Visual Basic .NET is all about. In this chapter we will walk you through a short introduction to Visual Basic .NET, Microsoft Visual Studio .NET, and the integrated development environment. Then we'll jump into creating two simple Visual Basic .NET applications so you can see how easy it really is. Finally, we'll talk about what kind of help is available to answer any questions you might have along the way.

Upon completion of this chapter, you will be able to:

■ Get an overview of what Visual Basic .NET is and what you can do with it.

■ Learn how to open the Visual Studio .NET integrated development environment.

■ Practice setting up the integrated development environment.

■ Use the menu and toolbars in the integrated development environment.

■ Create a simple program by using Visual Studio .NET.

■ Open and work with an existing Visual Basic .NET project.

■ Save and store your Visual Basic .NET projects.

INTRODUCTION TO VISUAL BASIC .NET AND VISUAL STUDIO .NET

Visual Basic .NET is the seventh generation of the most popular programming language produced by Microsoft. Visual Basic .NET is used to create applications for business, engineering, medicine, education, entertainment, and many other fields. Visual Basic .NET is easy to learn yet powerful enough to meet the needs of most programmers and the specifications they use to develop applications.

Visual Basic .NET is a part of **Visual Studio .NET**. Visual Studio .NET is a professional development environment that supports various programming languages, such as Visual Basic, C++, C#, and J#. In addition to the extensive language support, Visual Studio .NET also contains a host of tools that can be used when developing Microsoft Windows–based and Web-based applications. In this textbook, we will talk about Visual Basic .NET and how it works within Visual Studio .NET.

The Origins of Visual Basic

Visual Basic has its roots in BASIC (Beginners All-purpose Symbolic Instruction Code). BASIC was introduced in 1964, and, for the first time, users could create programs by using common English syntax rather than a more cryptic low-level language such as FORTRAN. In 1985, Microsoft introduced its own version of BASIC, called QBASIC, and packaged it with the MS-DOS 5.0 operating system.

Later in this chapter, we will create a simple program by using Visual Basic .NET. The program will display a greeting in a console window. A *console window* is a DOS-style window that is used to print text characters to the screen. To see how similar Visual Basic .NET is to BASIC, look at the line of BASIC code that is used to print text to the screen.

```
PRINT "Hello World"
```

In Visual Basic .NET, the line of code to do the same thing would look like this:

```
WriteLine("Hello World")
```

Although much has changed since 1964, you can see that the conceptual simplicity of the BASIC language has been retained. Of course this is not BASIC; this is Visual Basic, so the question is what makes Visual Basic *visual*? The answer lies in the fact that Visual Basic is really made up of two distinct parts. The first part is one or more code modules that contain the source code that will eventually be compiled and run. The second part is the visual designer that allows the programmer to use many prebuilt design templates to quickly create the visual components that will be used in the program.

Although Visual Basic has been around since 1991, when version 1.0 was introduced, Visual Basic .NET is the first version of Visual Basic that supports all the features of object-oriented design (OOD). Incorporating these features into your programs is known as object-oriented programming (OOP).

Object-Oriented Programming

Before we discuss **object-oriented programming (OOP)**, you should know what came before OOP and why OOP is a better way of programming.

Prior to OOP, there was a procedural-based or process-based programming methodology. A process would have a starting point and an ending point. Each code statement would be executed in turn until the process was complete. To provide some intelligence and decision-making capabilities, programmers used special *GOTO* statements that would allow code execution to skip several code statements or go back to other code statements previously executed. Adding functionality to any process required increasing use of special coding statements such as *GOTO*, and these produced complex code structures that became increasingly difficult to follow and even more difficult to maintain. Process coding structures such as this were commonly referred to as *spaghetti* code because the code intertwined so much.

OOP is not only a different way of programming, it is a different way of thinking. An **object** is an abstraction of a real-world entity. If you were to create a program that allowed a student to enroll in a course at a local college, the two objects that would immediately come to mind would be the Student object and the Course object. In programming terms, the Student object would have attributes such as *name* and *studentNumber*, and the Course object would have attributes such as *title* and *courseNumber*. The Course object would also have **methods** (procedures that perform an action on the object) to enroll a student in the course and to drop or withdraw a student from the course.

Visual Basic .NET supports the philosophy and components of OOP, as you will see throughout this textbook.

The Visual Studio .NET Integrated Development Environment

The **integrated development environment (IDE)** is a comprehensive work area in Visual Studio .NET that allows the developer to design, configure, and code an application without having to switch to other tools outside of Visual Studio .NET. You cannot do everything from within Visual Studio .NET, but, for the most part, the IDE does an admirable job of allowing the creation, control, and maintenance of all aspects of your applications without having to step outside of the Visual Studio .NET IDE or start another tool or program.

Let's take a look at the IDE. To do so, we need to start Visual Studio .NET because Visual Basic .NET is part of Visual Studio .NET.

Starting Visual Studio .NET

If you don't have an icon for Visual Studio .NET on your desktop, click Start and then select Programs. Locate the Microsoft Visual Studio .NET program folder icon, and then select Microsoft Visual Studio .NET. This will only work if you have installed Visual Studio .NET in the default location. Because Visual Studio .NET is rather large, it might take several seconds to start. Be patient; it will load eventually.

NOTE   The default location to use when saving your Visual Basic .NET projects is \My Documents\Visual Studio Projects. If you are working through this textbook as part of a structured class, your instructor might suggest an alternative location in which to store your projects. It is important to always be aware of where you are saving your projects and what you call them so you can find them again at a later time.

IDE Components

Let's start by looking at the various parts of the IDE. Figure 1-1 illustrates each facet of the IDE in the following discussion.

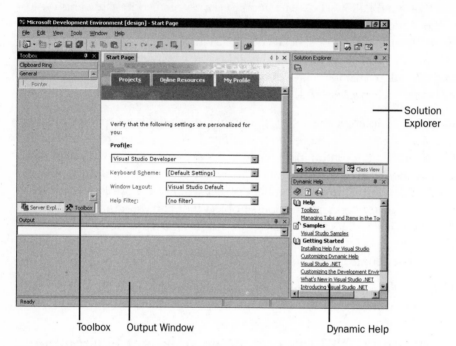

Figure 1-1   The major components of the Visual Studio .NET IDE

Toolbox   This window displays a number of controls that you will use when developing a Windows-based or a Web-based application. The Toolbox (like many of the windows, menus, and toolbars) is *context-sensitive*. This means that the contents generally are not visible until it makes sense to display them. If a Windows form is not visible in the design window, the controls in the Toolbox that are used to create a Windows-based form will be hidden.

Output Window   The information that appears in this window depends on what is going on in the IDE. The types of information that can be displayed here include details about the project when it is compiled and any errors that might have been generated. Note that the list of actual errors that occur when you run a program will be displayed in a different window called the *Task List*.

Recently Opened Projects   This is a list of recently opened Visual Studio .NET projects. The default number of projects that are listed is four. You can quickly open a project you have been working on by selecting it from this list.

Start Page   This is the main window that appears when you start Visual Studio .NET. Later you will find that you don't have to use this as your default starting point. You have a number of options, and you can change them at any time.

Solution Explorer   This window displays the current solution. It is empty at this time because there is no open solution. We will go into more detail about this window and talk about what a solution is after we have a project loaded.

Dynamic Help   This is a powerful window that is especially useful for people new to Visual Studio .NET. Dynamic Help follows what you are doing when you are developing an application. It is also considered to be context sensitive because Help is aware of what type of solution you are developing and whether you are currently designing a form or a Web page or are writing code. Help then displays the appropriate Help topics for the task you are trying to complete. One disadvantage of this kind of Help is that it takes up a lot of process time when you are running your application from within the IDE.

The Visual Studio .NET Menu

The Visual Studio .NET menu, shown in Figure 1-2, is similar to the Windows menus that you have used in many other applications. Most of the new menu items are self-explanatory. In this section, we will cover the most important menu items that you need to get started. We will cover the other menu items when it is appropriate for a particular topic.

File   Edit   View   Tools   Window   Help

Figure 1-2   The Visual Studio .NET menu

Figure 1-3   The File menu

Most applications have a File menu, as shown in Figure 1-3, to get you started. Use the New menu item to create a new project, the Open menu item to open an existing project or file, or the Open Solution menu item to open an existing solution. Although many of the menu items are probably familiar to you, the File menu in Visual Studio .NET has one menu item that is not quite so obvious. The Source Control menu allows you to select a project or file that is located in a central repository called Microsoft Visual SourceSafe (VSS). VSS is most useful when you are working on a team and several developers need access to the same files. VSS acts as a library from which you can "check out" files to work on them without the fear of someone else making different changes to another copy of the same file.

Figure 1-4 The View menu

The View menu, shown in Figure 1-4, allows you to locate the various windows that make up the Visual Studio .NET IDE. Because many windows are available, it is sometimes hard to know which is which. The View menu makes it easy for you to keep track of all these windows. As you gain more experience, you will find it convenient to close many of these supporting windows to gain additional work-space on the screen. When you need a particular window that is not already available on the screen, just click View and then click the name of that window. If you don't see the window you want on the View menu, it might be located on the next level, under the menu item Other Windows.

Many of the windows have shortcut keys associated with them, such as CTRL+ALT+L for the Solution Explorer. These keys are used to open a particular window without having to navigate around the menus with the mouse.

The Tools menu, shown in Figure 1-5, has several menu items that will enable you to use some of the more advanced features of Visual Studio .NET. The discussion of many of these menu items is beyond the scope of this textbook, but there is one that we will be using later in this chapter: the Options menu item, which is located at the bottom of the Tools menu. The Options menu item will allow you to cus-tomize the Visual Studio .NET IDE. You might never change many of these options, but it is nice to know that the IDE is flexible enough to provide a working envi-ronment that can be customized to the developer.

Figure 1-5   The Tools menu

The Window menu, shown in Figure 1-6, allows you to select how you want a window to behave or appear. The following menu items found on the Window menu determine how and where a particular window appears on the screen.

- **Dockable**   You can attach a dockable window to the side, top, or bottom of the IDE.

- **Hide**   This will hide the selected window. Use the View menu to display it again.

- **Floating**   This will undock a window so that it can be moved freely on the screen.

Figure 1-6   The Window menu

Figure 1-7 shows the Dynamic Help window displayed as a **floating window**. You can place a floating window anywhere on the screen by clicking on the title bar and dragging the window to a new position.

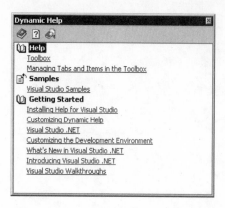

Figure 1-7   A floating Dynamic Help window

Play around with the windows to get comfortable with manipulating them. If you ever want to reset the layout of the screen to the original format, just click Tools and then Options to open the Options dialog box, and then click Reset Window Layout. We will look at the Options dialog box shortly and show you how you can further customize the IDE to make your experience with Visual Studio .NET an even better one.

Toolbars   The Visual Studio .NET toolbars contain buttons that are shortcuts to the various menu items. You can display or hide each of the toolbars at any time by right-clicking the menu area at the top of the IDE and selecting one of the toolbars from the extensive list that appears.

The Standard toolbar, shown in Figure 1-8, is the most important and most used toolbar in the Visual Studio .NET IDE. Two other toolbars will be quite useful when you start developing applications: Layout and Text Editor. Figures 1-9 and 1-10 show the Layout and the Text Editor toolbars.

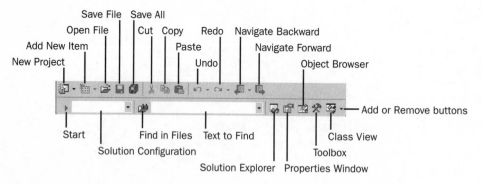

Figure 1-8   The Standard toolbar

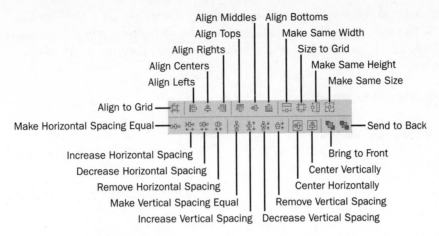

Figure 1-9   The Layout toolbar

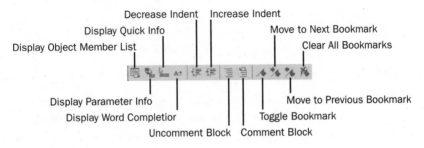

Figure 1-10   The Text Editor toolbar

My Profile

The My Profile settings can be viewed and modified from the Start Page. If the Start Page is not visible, click the Help menu and then select Show Start Page.

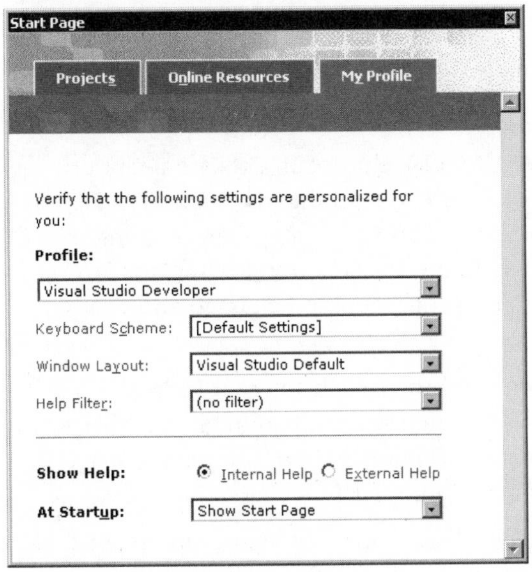

Figure 1-11   The My Profile screen

In this textbook, we will use the default layout for Visual Studio .NET, as shown in Figure 1-11. You can change the layout at any time by changing the Profile setting to Visual Basic Developer. If you make this change, notice that the layout of the screen automatically changes.

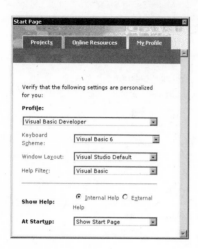

Figure 1-12   Changing the Profile setting on the Start Page

Notice in Figure 1-12 that when the profile was changed, the Keyboard Scheme and Window Layout options also changed. The Keyboard Scheme shows Visual Basic 6, and the Window Layout shows Visual Studio Default. The reason for this is that many thousands of developers have been using Visual Basic for years and are accustomed to the standard layout that was used in Visual Basic 6.0.

If you later decide that you want to program in one of the other languages supported by Visual Studio .NET, such as C++ or C#, you might decide to change the profile at that time. As you can see, it's easy to do.

Other Settings in My Profile

Besides profile information, the Start Page has several other settings, as shown in Figure 1-13.

- **Help Filter**   As you can imagine, a lot of Help documents are included when you install Visual Studio .NET. You can filter the information to just those topics related to Visual Basic .NET. This is definitely a good thing to do because it can be a little overwhelming to see all of the information available for every Visual Studio .NET programming language and tool each time you use Help.

- **Show Help**   Show Help will normally be left with Internal Help selected. If you have constant access to the Internet, you might decide to choose External Help, which provides additional Help information available from resources outside of Visual Studio .NET.

- **At Startup**   The last thing is to decide how you want Visual Studio .NET to load at startup. Click the down arrow to display the At Startup options and make your selection.

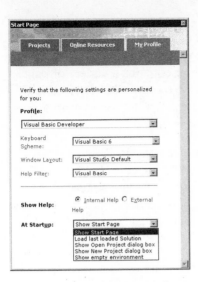

Figure 1-13   Changing the At Startup option on the Start Page

You can see from Figure 1-13 that you have several choices as to what happens each time Visual Studio .NET starts. For consistency, leave At Startup at the default Show Start Page option.

The Options Dialog Box

You can change many of the settings that affect the IDE in the Options dialog box. You can display this dialog box by selecting Tools and then Options, which is shown in Figure 1-14. For example, you can change the default location that is used to save your projects. You can also alter the default appearance and behavior of the IDE windows and create shortcuts for commonly used commands. In addition, the Options dialog box contains a variety of other language-specific, platform-specific, and product-specific options.

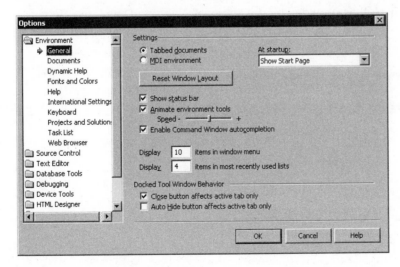

Figure 1-14   The Options dialog box

Layout of the Options Dialog Box

The Options dialog box is divided into two parts: a navigation pane on the left and a page display area on the right. The navigation pane contains folders such as Environment, Source Control, and Text Editor. Each folder contains a variety of pages. For example, the HTML Designer folder contains two pages called General and Display. When you select a page under a folder on the left, its contents appear in the page display area on the right side of the Options dialog box.

Clicking OK in the Options dialog box saves all option settings, including settings made on pages other than the one currently displayed. Clicking Cancel on any Options dialog page cancels all change requests, including those made on other pages. After the changes have been saved, some options, such as those made on the Font And Colors page, will take effect only after you close and reopen Visual Studio .NET.

Specific IDE feature options do not appear in the Options dialog box until the feature is loaded into memory. Therefore, you might not see the same options each time you open the Options dialog box. When you create a project or use a command from a particular application, the options related to that command will appear in the Options dialog box and remain available as long as that IDE feature remains in memory. The most frequently used options will always be available in the Options dialog box.

> **NOTE**   Clicking Cancel will cancel all changes in all pages of the Options dialog box. No changes will be saved from any page.

Obtaining Help in the Options Dialog Box

A full explanation of all the settings in the Options dialog box is beyond the scope of this book. For a more detailed explanation of these settings, open the Options dialog box, select any of the main topics you are interested in, and then press F1. This will display the Help window containing information about that topic. You can also click Help, click Index, and then type **options dialog box** for more information.

Visual Studio .NET Help is provided by the Microsoft Solution Developer Network (MSDN). Figure 1-15 shows an example of a typical Help window displayed in MSDN Help.

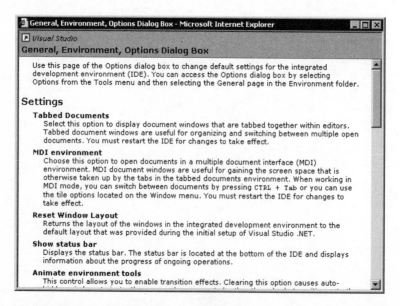

Figure 1-15   A typical MSDN Help window

Windows, Windows, and More Windows

As we said previously, many different windows make up the IDE. Keeping track of them is sometimes difficult. For the most part, you should keep the following IDE windows open and available on the screen at all times:

- **Start Page**   Located on the Help menu
- **Solution Explorer**   Open with the View menu
- **Properties window**   Open with the View menu
- **Toolbox**   Open with the View menu
- **Dynamic Help**   Located on the Help menu
- **Output window**   Located on Other Windows on the View menu

Docking Windows

In our introduction to the Window menu, we mentioned that all of the windows in the Visual Studio .NET IDE can be **docked**. If the window is marked as Dockable, as soon as it gets close to a docking position (the edge of the screen), it will be drawn immediately into that position as if by magnetism. If you want a window to float, mark it as Floating by right-clicking the title bar of that window and selecting Floating from the context menu. If you have undocked a window and it is floating on the screen, you can return it to its previous docked location by double-clicking its title bar. You can undock a window by clicking the title bar and dragging it away from its current location. A window cannot be both floating and docked at the same time.

Auto Hide

Screen workspace is often at a premium in Visual Studio .NET, so Microsoft included a feature that lets you have windows immediately available but tucked away until needed. This feature is called **Auto Hide**. If Auto Hide is turned on (selected) for a window, the window is available but is shown only as a tab on the side of the IDE. When the window is "hidden," you can move the mouse pointer over its tab and the window will slide open. Once you have finished with the window, move the mouse pointer away from the window and it will retract back into hiding.

Keeping the window open when you need to use it is easy. If you look at one of the windows (the Toolbox, for example), notice that there is a small pushpin button displayed on the right side of the title bar for that window. If the pushpin is pointing to the left, the Auto Hide feature is turned on for that window. If the pushpin is pointing down, the window is "pinned" and will stay open when you move the mouse pointer away.

We've talked about Auto Hide, but we haven't mentioned that you can also hide a window by selecting the Hide option from the context menu. Right-click the title bar of the window to display the context menu. Selecting Hide completely removes the window from view and does not leave a tab. You can display the window again by selecting it from the View menu.

Auto Hide All

On the Window menu, an item called Auto Hide All allows you to unpin all the windows at one time. When Auto Hide All is selected, all the windows retract immediately and are displayed as tabs on the side of the IDE. If any window does not retract, make sure that the mouse pointer isn't hovering over it.

Although we have looked at a lot, we have really only scratched the surface of what you can do to set up the Visual Studio .NET IDE. In the next sections, you will create two Visual Basic .NET projects. Although these projects have limited functionality, they provide you with an opportunity to explore more of the many tools that are available in Visual Studio .NET.

Try It

Open Visual Studio .NET, select Tools, and then select Options. Answer the following questions using the information found on the various screens of the Options dialog box. You might have to open different folders on the left side of the Options dialog box or use Help to answer these questions.

1. Can you configure Visual Studio .NET to automatically display the last loaded solution upon startup? If so, how?

2. How can you change the foreground color for selected text in the IDE?

What Do You Think?

1. How are Visual Basic .NET and Visual Studio .NET related?

2. What are the major components of the Visual Studio .NET IDE, and what is each used for?

3. What menu items are on the Visual Studio .NET menu, and what is each used for?

4. How is the information in the Options dialog box laid out on the screen, and what is the potential impact of clicking the Cancel button when making changes to this screen?

5. What are the advantages of having the ability to customize your IDE by using the Start Page and Options in Visual Studio .NET?

CREATING THE HELLO WORLD CONSOLE APPLICATION

It wouldn't be Microsoft programming if we didn't start off with the tradition of developing a Hello World program. We are actually going to demonstrate two different versions of the Hello World program. First we will introduce it as a console application and, later in the chapter, we will create a Windows-based Hello World application.

You will find it easier to understand console applications if we tell you what they do rather than what they are. A **console application** is designed to display text, perhaps a result of some calculation, in a DOS-style window. For example, you might have an application that should display to the user a series of executed instructions. Console applications are also handy if you want to test code, such as a complex mathematical routine, but do not need to create fancy forms and controls to display the results to the user.

You might be wondering what a DOS-style window is. In the early days of computers, the operating system was disk operating system (DOS). Programs running on DOS were capable of displaying only text (white text on a black background).

The New Project Dialog Box

Before we begin creating our first project, let's look at the New Project dialog box. If you haven't done so already, start Visual Studio .NET. Click the New Project button on the Start Page, or, on the File menu, select New, and then select Project. The dialog box shown in Figure 1-16 will appear, with the information on the screen organized into the following two areas:

- **Project Types**   This pane displays the various project types available in Visual Studio .NET. You can select a type of project, depending on the language you are programming in, or you can create a Setup And Deployment Project. For now, we will select Visual Basic Projects as the Project Type.

- **Templates**   The list of templates displayed will vary depending on the particular version of Visual Studio .NET you are using and the project type you have selected. Because we are using Visual Studio .NET Professional, we generally will have several more templates available for use than someone using the Standard version. Figure 1-17 shows a full list of the Visual Basic project templates that are available to us.

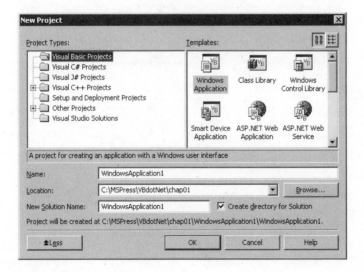

Figure 1-16   The New Project dialog box

Figure 1-17   The Visual Basic project templates

We will be using a few of these templates in this book, and we will explain them in more detail when it is appropriate.

▶ **Creating the Hello World program as a console application**

This DOS-style application will display a simple "Hello World" message to the user.

1. Click Visual Basic Projects in the Project Types pane of the New Project dialog box.

2. Click Console Application in the Templates pane. If you don't see Console Application in your list of templates, scroll down to locate it in the list.

3. In the Name box, type **HelloWorldConsole**, as shown in Figure 1-18. Notice that we have used Pascal-casing for the name.

   NOTE   *Pascal-casing is a convention in which the first letter of each significant word in a name is uppercase and the rest of the letters are lowercase.*

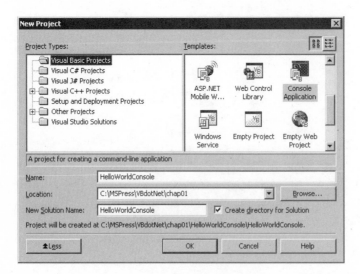

Figure 1-18   Name your new project HelloWorldConsole

4. In the Location box, type the location (the folder) in which you want to save the new project, or click the Browse button and navigate to the folder you want to use.

5. Click OK. After a moment, a basic console application will be created for you.

6. Look at the Solution Explorer, shown in Figure 1-19, and notice the list of files and references that has been created. We will discuss them in detail later in the chapter. For now, click once on Module1.vb in Solution Explorer to select it.

Figure 1-19   Solution Explorer

7. Locate the *FileName* property in the Properties window. Change the *File-Name* property from Module1.vb to **HelloWorld.vb**.

   TIP   You can also change the name of Module1.vb by right-clicking it in Solution Explorer and then selecting Rename from the context menu.

   The Properties window should look like Figure 1-20.

Figure 1-20   The Properties window

Before you actually code the application, you must change the module name in the Code Editor. The **Code Editor** is the window you will use to type the actual lines of Visual Basic .NET code.

8. If the Code Editor is not visible, click the module that is now named HelloWorld.vb to select it, and then click the View Code button at the top of Solution Explorer, as shown in Figure 1-21.

Figure 1-21   The View Code button on Solution Explorer

9. In the Code Editor, change Module Module1 to read **Module HelloWorld**. The code should now look like this:

```
Module HelloWorld
    Sub Main()
    End Sub
End Module
```

Now we will make the application do something useful by typing code into the *Sub Main* procedure. After we have done that, we will explain what we have done and why it works the way it does.

10. Click between Sub Main() and End Sub, and type the word **Console** followed by a period.

You might have noticed something after you typed the word *Console*. As soon as you typed the period, a list of names appeared, as shown in Figure 1-22. These names are the members of the *Console* class. The appearance of this list is a result of IntelliSense, a helpful feature provided by Visual Studio .NET. The IDE knows what the *Console* class is, and it displays the members that belong to its family. To enter the code properly, scroll down the list to locate the *WriteLine* member, select it, and then press TAB. We haven't really discussed classes yet, so don't worry if you're not sure what they are. We discuss them in great detail later in the book.

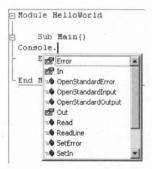

Figure 1-22   IntelliSense displays the members of the *Console* class

11. The parentheses after *WriteLine* will be automatically added for you if you click on another line of code or press the ENTER key. Now type the words **Hello World** inside the parentheses and inside the double quotation marks, as shown here:

```
Module HelloWorld
    Sub Main()
        Console.WriteLine("Hello World")
    End Sub
End Module
```

WriteLine is known as a method, and it is a predefined procedure associated with the *Console* class. The *WriteLine* method expects a value to be provided to it whenever it is used. The value you placed inside the parentheses is called a *string*, and it must be enclosed in double quotation marks. The *WriteLine* method's job is to write a line of text (a string) in the console window.

Everything looks good, so let's run the application and see what happens.

12. On the Debug menu, click Start, or press the F5 function key to run the application.

We've got our first error. Figure 1-23 shows the message that appears. Let's identify and correct the error, and then we'll explain why it was introduced.

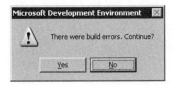

Figure 1-23   A build error message box

13. Click No. (We cannot run the application with the error, so clicking Yes would be a waste of time.)

14. Now, in Solution Explorer, right-click the project name HelloWorld-Console (not the solution name). Select Properties from the context menu. This will open the dialog box shown in Figure 1-24.

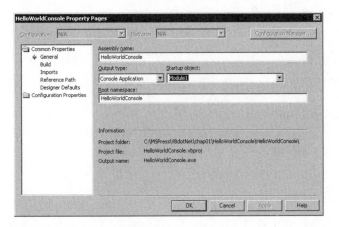

Figure 1-24   The HelloWorldConsole Property Pages dialog box

Locate the Startup Object list. Notice that it says Module1. Remember that earlier you changed the name from Module1 to HelloWorld? Well, that name change wasn't made here, so now you have to change it manually.

15. Click the down arrow for the startup object and select HelloWorld from the list, as shown in Figure 1-25. Click the OK button.

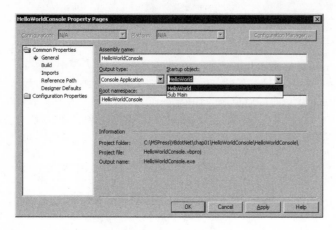

Figure 1-25   Changing the startup object

16. Now run the program again by pressing F5 or by clicking Debug and then Start.

17. The application should run successfully, assuming no other errors are found. Even though no error was generated, there is still a problem with the application. The problem is that the console window flashes on the screen momentarily and then disappears without giving you a chance to read the message. You need some way to freeze the window open until you read the message and decide to close it. For this you will add one more line of code to your procedure to tell the window to stay open until you read the line and close the window. The method of the *Console* class that you use to keep the window open is called *ReadLine*. Enter the statement **Console.ReadLine()** below the existing `Console.Write-Line("Hello World")` statement, as shown in the following code:

```
Module HelloWorld
    Sub Main()
        Console.WriteLine("Hello World")
        Console.ReadLine()
    End Sub
End Module
```

18. Press F5 to run the application again. The console window will appear, display the "Hello World" message, and remain on the screen, as shown in Figure 1-26, until you press ENTER or close the window by clicking X (the Close button) in the upper right corner of the window. Both of these actions will stop the program.

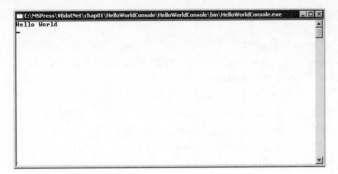

Figure 1-26 The console window displayed when the application is running

19. The last step is to save your project and close it. On the File menu, select Save All to save all of the changes you have made. On the File menu, select Close Solution to close the current solution, or select Exit to close Visual Studio .NET.

Congratulations! You have just completed your first application. You really have achieved a milestone.

Step-by-Step Summary

To summarize, here are the steps you took to create the Hello World console application:

1. Created a Visual Basic .NET console application.

2. Changed the name of the module from Module1 to HelloWorld. Actually, you changed the module name and the file name. You changed the module name in the Code Editor, and you changed the file name in the Properties window.

3. Entered Visual Basic code into the Code Editor to make the application do something useful.

4. Ran the application and received an error message.

5. Corrected the error by selecting the correct startup object on the Start Page.

6. Ran the program successfully but found that the console window went away as soon as it appeared.

7. Corrected that anomaly by adding another line of code that kept the window on the screen so you could read the line.

8. Ran the program again, and this time the console window remained on the screen until you closed it by pressing ENTER or by clicking the Close button on the title bar.

Inside the Solution

Now that you have a working solution open in our IDE, let's take a closer look at Solution Explorer. (You might want to refer back to Figure 1-19.) You can see a tree-view display of items. The topmost item is the **solution**. The solution has the same name as the project because Visual Studio .NET automatically gave it that name. A solution is really a grouping of projects. In forthcoming chapters, you will find that you can have multiple projects in a single solution. This is a convenience because you might have to work on multiple projects that are related, and this saves you from having to open multiple instances of Visual Studio .NET to look at each project.

Below the solution is the **project**. A project is also called an *assembly*. We will talk more about assemblies in later chapters. Under normal circumstances, a project will have two or more files and a reference folder displayed in Solution Explorer. In our Hello World console application, there are two files. We will not discuss references in detail right now, but all projects must have them, and Visual Studio .NET automatically provides many references for you when you select a particular template.

For the console application, Visual Basic .NET created the two files you see in Solution Explorer. They are the AssemblyInfo.vb file and the HelloWorld.vb file.

Each project must have one (and only one) AssemblyInfo.vb file. AssemblyInfo.vb is a text file that describes the assembly. A project becomes an assembly when it is compiled into an .exe file (a standard executable file) or a .dll file (an internal executable file commonly referred to as a dynamic-link library). The second file in this project is the HelloWorld.vb file. This file contains the code that you wrote, along with the code that was automatically generated by Visual Studio .NET.

You might be surprised to find out that all of the files that make up a project can be opened and viewed in a text editor such as Notepad. Even more surprising is that, if you wanted to, you could create an entire Visual Basic .NET application by using only Notepad and a special Visual Basic compiler that is available for free from Microsoft.

Back to the Error

Remember the error that was generated when you first tried to run the application? The reason the error was introduced is really quite simple. When you first created the application, Visual Basic .NET created a standard module and named it Module1. You saw that in the Code Editor and in Solution Explorer. Changing the file name to HelloWorld.vb in the Properties window did not produce the error; that only changed the name of the file. However, when you changed the name in the Code Editor, you introduced the error.

You see, when a project is first created, the startup object must be established. Every project must have either a startup object specified or a reference to *Sub Main*. The startup object becomes the starting point (sometimes referred to as the point at which the execution of code begins) of the application. When you changed the name in code, you essentially broke the link between the project and the module selected to be used as the startup object.

In order to re-establish that link, you went back to the project's Properties dialog box and selected the new name for the file from the list. When you selected the new name for Module1 from the list, you might have also noticed the name Sub Main in the list. This is a special entry point for applications. If you had selected Sub Main instead of HelloWorld, the application would have worked just as well. The reason for this is that the compiler expects either the startup object to be specified explicitly by name or it requires a *Sub Main* procedure to be present.

> **NOTE**   To avoid the error in the first place, whenever the name of the module is changed in the Code Editor, open the Project Properties dialog box and select the new name from the Startup Object list.

Try It

Let's make a change to the message that is displayed in our Hello World console application. Instead of displaying the message "Hello World," let's display the message "What a Beautiful Day!"

1. If your Hello World console application is not open, click Open Project on the Start Page. Browse to the location of the HelloWorld-Console project file that you created earlier. Select the file and then click Open.

2. In Solution Explorer, double-click the HelloWorld.vb file to open it in the Code Editor.

3. Change the `Console.WriteLine("Hello World")` statement to `Console.WriteLine("What a Beautiful Day!")`.

4. On the Debug menu, select Start, or press F5 to run the program with the change.

5. Close the console window and save your changes by selecting File and then selecting Save All.

6. Close the solution by selecting File and then selecting Close Solution.

What Do You Think?

1. Describe the kind of window used to display the output of a console application.

2. What kind of information is contained in Solution Explorer?

3. Where can you change the name of the startup object for your project?

4. What is a method?

5. What is the difference between the `Console.ReadLine` and `Console.WriteLine` methods?

6. Describe the relationship between a solution and a project in Visual Studio .NET.

CREATING THE HELLO WORLD WINDOWS APPLICATION

Now that you have built a console application that will display the message "Hello World" on the screen, it is time to create a Windows application that will do the same thing. A **Windows application** is an application that uses visual objects such as forms, labels, and text boxes to display information to the user and allows for user interaction through the keyboard and mouse. Most Windows applications use some form of the standard Windows design guidelines to maintain consistency. This means that users of Windows applications can expect certain things to be the same from one program to the next. For example, they expect the File menu to be the leftmost menu item, and if they click a Cancel button, they expect any changes they have made to be discarded.

For this application, you will use a Windows form, and you will add a Label control and a Button control to the form. A **form** is a window that you create to display information and provide the user interface for your Windows application. **Controls** are the objects that you place on a form to display information and interact with the user.

▶ Providing Visual Basic implementation code

In the following exercise, you will provide code that makes the application do something useful; specifically, it will display the "Hello World" message when the user clicks a button. As will be the custom in this textbook, we will guide you all the way through the process and then go back later and look more closely at what we have done so you will have a good understanding of how everything happens.

1. Start Visual Studio .NET if it is not already running.

2. If the Start Page is not displayed, on the File menu, point to New and then select Project. If the Start Page is displayed, click New Project.

   Visual Studio .NET will display the New Project dialog box, as shown in Figure 1-27. Here you will specify the name, location, type, and template for the new project.

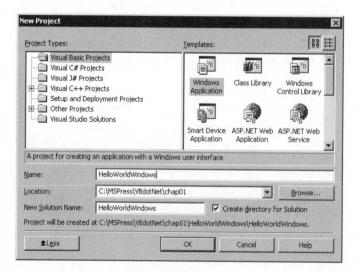

Figure 1-27   The New Project dialog box

3. In the New Project dialog box, select Visual Basic Projects for the Project Type.

4. Select Windows Application for the Template.

5. Type the name of the program, **HelloWorldWindows**, in the Name box.

6. In the Location box, type the location (the folder) where you want to save your project, or browse to the location.

7. Click OK. The wizard will now create and initialize the project, including all the files necessary for a basic Windows application.

Figure 1-28   Clicking Form1.vb in Solution Explorer

8. Click Form1.vb in Solution Explorer to select it, as shown in Figure 1-28, and then change the *File Name* property in the Properties window from Form1.vb to **HelloWorld.vb**, as shown in Figure 1-29. The Properties window should be displayed below Solution Explorer. If it isn't, on the View menu, select Properties Window, or press F4.

Figure 1-29   Changing the File Name property in the Properties window

9. Select the form in the designer window by clicking its title bar. The *designer window* is the window that contains the form you are working with. The tab at the top of the window says HelloWorld.vb (Design).

Now look at the Properties window, shown in Figure 1-30, and notice that it has changed. You are now seeing the properties of the form, not the properties of the file.

Figure 1-30   The form properties shown in the Properties window

Change the *(Name)* property of the selected form from Form1 to **frmHelloWorld**, and then press ENTER to complete the change.

The new name of the form includes a special prefix that you typed in lowercase letters. This is known as *Modified Hungarian Notation*. It is designed to clarify the type of object the name is referring to. In this case, the prefix *frm* refers to a form object.

10. You are now at the point at which you know you will generate an error when the application is run for the first time because your startup object is invalid. Let's fix that situation before you go any further. Right-click the project name HelloWorldWindows in Solution Explorer, and then select Properties. Notice that the Startup Object box still shows Form1.

11. Click the down arrow next to the Startup Object box, and then select frm-HelloWorld. Click OK.

Now that you have fixed that pesky problem, the only errors you should get are those you cause yourself by writing bad code.

Unlike in the console application, selecting *Sub Main* in this application would not have been a good choice and would have generated an error. Although our console module actually had a *Sub Main* procedure, as you will soon see, our Windows application does not have a *Sub Main* procedure.

12. Click the title bar of the form in the designer window to select it, and scroll down in the Properties window to locate the *Text* property for the form. Change this property's value from Form1 to **Hello World**, as shown in Figure 1-31, and then press ENTER. Notice that we have put a space between the words "Hello" and "World" this time. The *Text* property holds the text that will appear in the title bar of the form.

Figure 1-31   Changing the *Text* property of the form in the Properties window

Look at the form. Notice that there are small white squares on all of its corners and sides. These are called **sizing handles** and, as you might have guessed, they are used to change the size of the form.

Before you resize the form, look at the *Size* property for the form in the Properties window. It should be set to 300, 300, which is the default size of the form.

Now you will make the form a little bigger by placing the mouse pointer over the sizing handle in the lower right corner of the form and then pressing and holding down the left mouse button while dragging the window to the right and down a little. The new size doesn't matter all that much for this application, but for a professional application, the form size can be critical. After resizing the form, check the values in the *Size* property. Our form is now 460, 350, but yours might be different. You might be eager to add some controls, but, before you do that, you need to change one more property of the form. You will need to change the *Font* property from the default size of 8 points to 10 points.

13. Look for the *Font* property in the Properties window, and click it once to select it. Notice that the default font size is actually 8.25 points.

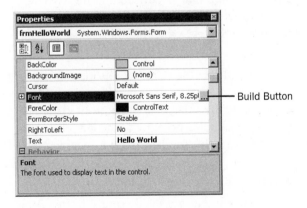

Figure 1-32   The Build button, located to the right of the existing value in the *Font* property

14. Click the Build button located to the right of the existing value of the *Font* property, as shown in Figure 1-32. This will display the Font dialog box shown in Figure 1-33.

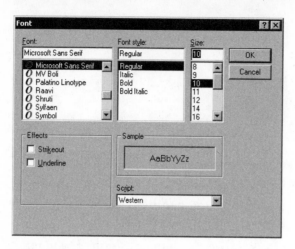

Figure 1-33   The Font dialog box

15. Select 10 for the Size and leave the Font and Font Style values as they are. Click OK.

When you return to the Properties window, you will notice that the value of the font size is now 9.75 points. The actual size of a font will vary depending on the font that is selected.

Why did we change the font size? Eight-point font is generally too small for most Windows controls. By changing the font size of the form before you add controls, all text on the controls will default to the new font size of the form when we add them. You can still change the individual font sizes of any of the controls that are added to the form. Doing so will not have an effect on the font size of any other controls you add to the form.

16. Now you will add a Button control from the Toolbox to the form. A Button control will display a command like OK or Cancel, and the user will click the Button control to select that command. If your Toolbox is not visible, on the View menu, select Toolbox. Notice that the Toolbox is one of several windows that can use the Auto Hide feature.

As we discussed earlier, this feature allows the window to slide out of the way when it is not in use. We will be covering all the windows in more detail in Chapter 3, but for now, locate the small pushpin button on the title bar of the Toolbox window. If the pushpin is pointing to the left, click it so that it points downward. This will make the Toolbox window stay in place.

17. Click the Button control in the Toolbox once to select it. You should be able to see that it has been clicked. If you aren't sure which control is the Button control, hover your mouse pointer over each control in the Toolbox and read the ToolTips that appear.

18. Move the mouse pointer over to the form. Press and hold down the left mouse button anywhere on the form and then drag the mouse to the right and down. You should now see the button being "drawn" onto the form.

19. When the button looks large enough, release the mouse button.

The Button control has the default name (and text) of Button1. You will change these values now.

20. Make sure that the Button1 control on the form is still selected, and change its *(Name)* and *Text* properties to **btnHelloWorld** and **Hello World**, respectively. After you modify each property value, make sure to press ENTER to correctly enter the changes.

   NOTE If you inadvertently double-clicked the button and found yourself in the Code Editor, just click the HelloWorld [Design] tab located at the top of the Code Editor. This will return you to the display of the form in design view.

21. Using the same techniques, add a Label control to the form. A Label control is used to display information or messages to the user. Change the Label's *(Name)* property to **lblHelloWorld**. The *Text* property value will be provided in code, so leave the default value there for now. You will erase the default value later, after you have formatted the label the way you want it.

22. With the label still selected, locate and select the *TextAlign* property in the Properties window.

23. Click the down arrow to the right of the existing value in the *TextAlign* property. The window shown in Figure 1-34 will appear.

Figure 1-34   The TextAlign property selection window

24. Click the center button. The window will disappear, and the value displayed should be MiddleCenter.

25. Change the font size of the label to 24 points. (Locate the *Font* property and then click the build button.) Select 24 for the size and then click OK in the Font dialog box.

If everything has worked out up to this point, the form should look similar to Figure 1-35. If it doesn't, you can move a control by clicking it once to select it then dragging it to a new position. You can also resize the controls by using their sizing handles.

Figure 1-35   Hello World form with Label and Button controls

Coding the Application

To complete the application, you need to provide code to tell Visual Basic .NET to display your "Hello World" message. To have your code run when you want it to, you must wait for an **event** to occur. An event is a predefined action for an object, such as the *Click* event for a Button control or the *Paint* event for a form.

▶ Displaying the message when the *Click* event occurs

1. Double-click the Hello World Button control in the designer.

   After a moment, the current window will change and you will see the Code Editor, which contains some code already provided for us.

   The event procedure *btnHelloWorld_Click* (called an event handler) that you want to use has been created for you. All you have to do now is add the code you want to run when the user clicks on this button, and the application will be ready for testing.

2. Type the boldface statement exactly as shown in the following code:

```
Private Sub btnHelloWorld_Click(ByVal sender As System.Object, _
        ByVal e As _System.EventArgs) Handles btnHelloWorld.Click

    lblHelloWorld.Text = "Hello World"
End Sub
```

   A **procedure** is a group of lines of code that run starting at the first line (in this case `Private Sub`) and ending at the last line (`End Sub`). Any code that you want to run in our application must be placed inside a procedure, just as we have shown here.

   Notice that, in the previous example, the first line of code is actually broken up into two lines. We have added a space followed by the underscore character to tell the compiler that these two lines should be treated as one line of code. The space followed by an underscore is called the *line continuation character*, and it should be used whenever you want to break up long lines of code. In Chapter 3, we will discuss the line continuation character in more detail and show you how you can use it to format your code and make it easier to read.

3. Let's run the application to test it. Click the Start button on the toolbar (or press F5, or, on the Start menu, select Debug).

4. When the form loads, click the Hello World button on the form, as shown in Figure 1-36, to display the message in the Label control.

Figure 1-36   The Hello World form

This looks good, and it works as you expected, although there are two minor problems you should fix.

The first problem should be obvious. The Label control displays Label1 when the program starts running, and Label1 is meaningless to the user. The second problem is really a matter of preference. Each time you run the program, the form appears at a different location on the screen. You really want to make the form appear in the center of the screen every time the application runs.

You could fix these two problems by changing the appropriate property values in the Properties window, or you could write Visual Basic code to set the required properties to the correct values when the application starts running. (Remember how you set the *Text* property of the label to display our "Hello World" message in Visual Basic code.) Actually, you will do both. You will set the *StartPosition* property of the form by using the Properties window and set the label's *Text* property with Visual Basic code.

5. First, make sure the application is not running by selecting the Debug menu and then selecting Stop Debugging.

6. Select the form in the designer window by clicking its title bar once.

7. Locate and select the *StartPosition* property in the Properties window.

8. Click the down arrow and then select CenterScreen.

9. Test the application again to make sure that the form is displayed in the center of the screen.

The last thing to do is to clear the label so that it doesn't display the string *Label1* when the form is first loaded.

10. Make sure the application is not running, and then double-click a free area of the form. A *free area* is defined as any area not occupied by any control.

The IDE will switch back to the Code Editor, and the form's *Load* event handler will be created.

11. Type the boldface statement shown in here into the *frmHelloWorld_Load* event handler.

```
Private Sub frmHelloWorld_Load(ByVal sender As System.Object, _
        ByVal e As _System.EventArgs) Handles MyBase.Load
    lblHelloWorld.Text = ""
End Sub
```

12. Run the application once more to be sure everything works as designed. Test the program and verify each of the changes you just made, and then close the program. Save your changes and then close the solution.

Step-by-Step Summary

Here is a summary of how you created the Hello World Windows application:

1. Created a basic Windows application.

2. Changed the *File Name* property of the form to HelloWorld and the *(Name)* property to frmHelloWorld.

3. After changing the *(Name)* property, you opened the project Properties window and changed the startup object to eliminate the error that you anticipated.

4. Changed the form's *Text* property to Hello World.

5. Changed the font size of the form from 8.25 points to 9.75 points.

6. Added a Button control to the form and changed its *(Name)* property to btnHelloWorld, and then changed its *Text* property to Hello World.

7. Added a Label control to the form and changed its *(Name)* property to lblHelloWorld. However, you did not change (or erase) the default value in the label's *Text* property.

8. Changed the *TextAlign* property of the Label control to MiddleCenter so that the message would appear in the center of the label.

9. Set the font size of the Label control to 24 points.

10. After completing the user interface, you provided implementation code to display the message when the user clicks the button. You did this by using the button's *Click* event handler.

11. Set the *StartPosition* of the form in the Properties window and then provided code in the form's *Load* event handler to ensure that the label does not display the default text when the form is loaded.

Getting Help

If someone is not guiding you every step of the way, where do you get help? So much help is available that you might find yourself suffering from help overload. Discriminating between the various sources of help improves with persistence and experience. You will gain experience with using Help as you progress through this textbook.

You probably installed all the MSDN Help files when you installed Visual Studio .NET. If you did, you are well ahead of the game. If you didn't, check to see that you have plenty of disk space. If you do, install all the Help files now. You will find that it is a great timesaver. If you cannot install all the Help files, each time you look for Help, you will be prompted to insert one of the MSDN CDs.

You can access Help information in several ways, as summarized in Table 1-1.

Table 1-1 **Accessing Help Information**

To get Help information	Do this
About the task you're currently working on	Click the Dynamic Help tab in the development environment to see a list of Help topics related to the features you're using, or, on the Visual Studio Help menu, select Dynamic Help.
By topic or activity	On the Visual Studio Help menu, select Contents.
While working in the Code Editor	Click to select the keyword or program statement you're interested in, and then press F1.
While working in a dialog box	Click the Help button in the dialog box.
By searching for a specific keyword	On the Help menu, select Search, and then type the term you're looking for.
In a window outside of Visual Studio .NET	On the Windows taskbar, click the Start button, point to Programs, point to Microsoft Visual Studio .NET, and then select Microsoft Visual Studio .NET Documentation. Use the Contents, Index, and Search tabs to find information.
From Visual Studio websites and newsgroups	On the Visual Studio Start Page, click Online Community and then the website or newsgroup you're interested in.
About contacting Microsoft for product support	On the Help menu, select Technical Support.

Try It

Let's go back to the Hello World Windows application you just created and add another Label control that will display the message "What a Beautiful Day!" when the user clicks the Hello World button.

1. Click the Open Project button on the Start Page.

2. Browse to the location of the HelloWorldWindows.sln solution file that you created earlier. Select the file and then click the Open button.

3. If the HelloWorld.vb form is not displayed in design view, click Hello-World.vb [Design] at the top of the window.

4. Add another Label control to the form. Add the new label under the lblHelloWorld Label control.

5. Set the *(Name)* property of the new Label control to **lblBeautifulDay**, and then set the *TextAlign* property to MiddleCenter.

6. Double-click the Hello World button to open the Code Editor.

7. Add the line `lblBeautifulDay.Text = "What a Beautiful Day!"` after the code that sets the other label to "Hello World."

8. Scroll to the *HelloWorld_Load* event handler and add the line of code `lblBeautifulDay.Text = ""` to set the new label to display an empty string when the form loads.

9. On the Debug menu, select Start, or press F5, to run the program with the changes. Test the program by clicking the Hello World button.

10. Close the application window and save your changes.

11. Close the solution.

What Do You Think?

1. How is a Windows application different from a console application?

2. What are forms and controls used for in Visual Basic .NET?

3. What are sizing handles used for?

4. What is a Button control typically used for?

5. When is an event?

6. What is a procedure in Visual Basic .NET?

Q&A

Q. Why didn't you just enter the values in the *Size* property of the form rather than resizing the form by using the mouse?

A. You used the mouse because dragging the form by using the sizing handles was more fun, wasn't it? But you can also type in the values for the *Size* property if you prefer that method or have a specific size you need to use.

Q. Why did you have to name the controls?

A. Part of your objective here is to make your code as easy to read and understand as possible. If you had an application that incorporated many controls of the same type, and you left them all with their default names (such as Label1 and Label2) you would have a difficult time figuring out which control was which when reading and debugging your code. In addition, if you were to turn our project over to someone else for maintenance, they would have a much harder time deciphering our code, and they wouldn't be too happy.

Q. Why was it important to name the controls before you started coding?

A. If you had started coding first, the event handlers that were created would refer to the default names. After you changed the names in the *(Name)* property, these event handlers would have the wrong names and you would have had additional syntax errors to deal with.

Q. When you double-clicked the button, an event handler was created. What is an event handler, and why would you use one?

An event handler is a special method that is linked to one of a control's events. Whenever the user clicks a button, a *Click* event is raised (the event is triggered). The event handler allows you to trap that event and use it to run some code. The event will be raised regardless of whether you have coded the event handler. You know that the event will fire, and you are just using it to run your code at the right time.

Q.   What is the purpose of the code that is inside the parentheses following an event handler name?

A.   We will cover that in more detail in a later chapter. For now, just know that this code is required and that it is basically the same for all event handlers.

Q.   In the *Load* event for the form, you set the *Text* property of the label to two double quotation marks with nothing between them. Why?

A.   The pair of double quotation marks provides what is called an *empty string*. Before going any further, we should explain that a string is a grouping of one or more text characters that represents a literal value. When the program is compiled and executed, you do not want the compiler to treat these characters as programming code and, as such, you will place them inside double quotation marks. Returning to the question, remember that in the button's *Click* event handler, you placed the words "Hello World" inside double quotation marks. This allowed the value to be passed to the *Text* property of the label and subsequently displayed. The *Text* property of any control requires a value of type *String*, and the value must be placed inside double quotation marks. If you want the label to be blank, provide the pair of double quotation marks without specifying any text value between them.

Q.   Could you have set all of the property values by using code rather than the Properties window?

A.   For the most part, yes. There are a few controls whose properties cannot be set in code. Likewise, there are a few controls whose properties cannot be set in the Properties window. Generally speaking, if the value of a property needs to change at run time (when the application is running), it is best to set it in code. If the value of a property stays the same throughout the life of the application, it is probably better to set it in the Properties window.

Q.   Can you explain the other code that you saw in the Code Editor, specifically the Windows Form Designer–generated code?

A.   Take a look at the Code Editor again (Figure 1-37).

```
Public Class frmHelloWorld
    Inherits System.Windows.Forms.Form

   Windows Form Designer generated code

    Private Sub frmHelloWorld_Load(ByVal sender As System.Object, _
        ByVal e As System.EventArgs) Handles MyBase.Load
        lblHelloWorld.Text = "Hello World"
        lblBeautifulDay.Text = ""
    End Sub

    Private Sub btnHelloWorld_Click(ByVal sender As System.Object, _
        ByVal e As System.EventArgs) Handles btnHelloWorld.Click
        lblHelloWorld.Text = "Hello World"
        lblBeautifulDay.Text = "What a Beautiful Day!"
    End Sub
End Class
```

Figure 1-37   The Code Editor showing outlining

Notice that there are + (plus) and – (minus) signs to the left of some of the lines of code. This is known as **outlining**. If you click any of the minus signs, you will notice that the procedure collapses and shows just the top line of code for the procedure. When a procedure is collapsed, the – changes to a + and the Code Editor looks like Figure 1-38.

```
Public Class frmHelloWorld
    Inherits System.Windows.Forms.Form

    Windows Form Designer generated code

    Private Sub frmHelloWorld_Load(ByVal sender As System.Object, _
        ByVal e As System.EventArgs) Handles MyBase.Load...

    Private Sub btnHelloWorld_Click(ByVal sender As System.Object, _
        ByVal e As System.EventArgs) Handles btnHelloWorld.Click...
End Class
```

Figure 1-38   The Code Editor with collapsed procedures

The code in the Windows Form Designer–generated code region is the code that Visual Studio .NET created for you when you created the project, added controls to the form, and set some property values. This region is critical and at this point should not be changed. If you want to change a property value, it might be tempting to go to this region and make the change there, but this would be the wrong thing to do. All changes should be made in the designer window; Visual Studio .NET will take care of updating this region whenever it is necessary.

WRAPPING UP

- Visual Basic .NET is a programming language that comes with Visual Studio .NET. Visual Studio .NET provides an integrated development environment (IDE) containing many tools that are used to create an application using one of the supported languages, such as Visual Basic .NET. You can use the Start Page to determine how you want your IDE to look and work when Visual Studio .NET starts. Use the Options dialog box to further configure the many options available in Visual Studio .NET.

- A console application runs in an MS-DOS window and is used when there is no need for a Graphical User Interface (GUI). A Windows application uses forms and controls to build a GUI that allows the user to interact with the application. Console and Windows applications can both be created with the Visual Studio .NET IDE.

- In a Windows application, controls from the Toolbox are added to forms. The properties of the form and controls can be modified in the Properties window or by writing Visual Basic .NET code in the Code Editor. Code is written in the event handlers that are created by Visual Studio .NET.

- Many different types of Help are available when you are using Visual Basic .NET. Visual Studio .NET provides Help through MSDN, which is installed with Visual Studio .NET.

KEYWORDS

Auto Hide

console application

docked

floating window

integrated development environment (IDE)

method

object-oriented programming (OOP)

procedure

sizing handles

Visual Basic .NET

Windows application

Code Editor

controls

event

form

IntelliSense

object

outlining

project

solution

Visual Studio .NET

REVIEW QUESTIONS

1. The _____ is the working area provided by Visual Studio .NET that is used to design, configure, and code an application.

   a. Toolbox

   b. Code Editor

   c. IDE

   d. Output window

2. A window that can be dragged to any location on the screen is a _____ window.

   a. docked

   b. floating

   c. hidden

   d. visible

3. The main window that is displayed when you start Visual Studio .NET is the _____ .

   a. Start Page

   b. Options dialog box

   c. Visual Basic .NET editor

   d. Designer window

4. Many of the settings that affect the IDE can be modified from the _____ dialog box.

   a. Design

   b. Open Project

   c. Options

   d. Edit

5. If Auto Hide is turned on for a window and the mouse pointer is not in that window, the window will be shown as a(n) _____ on the side of the IDE.

   a. tab

   b. button

   c. list

   d. icon

6. A console application is different from a Windows application because it runs or executes in a _____ window.

   a. Designer

   b. DOS-style

   c. Form

   d. Property

7. The naming convention that uses a capital letter for each significant word in the name is called _____.

  a. Pascal-casing

  b. Camel-casing

  c. Hungarian Notation

  d. Class-casing

8. Which of the following is not a type of project that can be created in Visual Studio .NET?

  a. Visual C# Projects

  b. Visual Basic Projects

  c. Visual C++ Projects

  d. Visual D+ Projects

9. The small white squares that appear on all four corners and sides of a selected form are called _____.

  a. sizing handles

  b. dragging handles

  c. control squares

  d. sizing squares

10. Code that should run when an event is raised for an object should be placed in a(n) _____.

  a. object handler

  b. method

  c. event handler

  d. property

11. Visual Studio .NET is part of the Visual Basic .NET suite of programming languages and tools. True or false?

12. Dynamic Help will display appropriate Help topics depending on what you are doing in the Visual Studio .NET IDE. True or false?

13. The Toolbox, Output window, Start Page, and Solution Explorer are all part of the Visual Studio .NET IDE. True or false?

14. The Auto Hide All item on the Window menu is used to "unpin" all windows at the same time. True or false?

15. IntelliSense is the ability of Visual Studio .NET to create the forms you need for your project after you have typed the code. True or false?

16. The _____ menu is the menu that is used to locate the windows that make up the Visual Studio .NET IDE.

17. The most commonly used toolbar in Visual Studio .NET is the _____ toolbar.

18. The default location used to save your projects, in addition to other settings, can be configured in the _____ dialog box.

19. The Visual Studio .NET window that displays a list of the files and references in a Visual Basic .NET project is called _____.

20. A grouping of projects in Visual Studio .NET is called a(n) _____.

STEP BY STEP

In the Step by Step exercises in this textbook, you will create programs for the fictitious Baldwin Museum of Science. The museum is setting up a special exhibit about household pets and would like you to create some applications that they can use. In this exercise, you will create a new project and add controls to the form. You will be given step-by-step instructions for completing this exercise. The completed form should look like Figure 1-39. When you click the Click Here button, the message "A healthy pet is a happy pet" will appear in the label.

Figure 1-39   The Pet Exhibit form

▶ Creating a new project

1. Open Visual Studio .NET if it isn't already open.

2. Click the New Project button on the Start Page.

3. Click Visual Basic Projects under Project Types and Windows Application under Templates.

4. Type **PetsCh1** in the Name box.

5. Browse to the location where you are storing your projects.

6. Click the OK button.

▶ Configuring the form and changing the startup object

1. Right-click Form1.vb in Solution Explorer, and rename Form1.vb as **Pets.vb**. Press ENTER.

2. Click the title bar of the form and change the *(Name)* property of the form to **frmPets**.

3. Change the *Text* property of the form to **Pet Exhibit**, and then press ENTER.

4. Right-click the PetsCh1 project name in Solution Explorer and then click Properties.

5. Change the startup object to frmPets, and then click OK.

6. Click the title bar of the form and use the sizing handles to make the form a little bit smaller.

▶ Adding a Label control to the form

1. Click the Label control in the Toolbox to select it.

2. Drag and draw a Label control in the center of the form, near the top of the form.

3. In the Properties window, set the *(Name)* property of the Label control to **lblPet**.

4. Click the *Font* property and then use the build button to change the font size to 12. Click OK.

5. Change the *TextAlign* property to MiddleCenter.

▶ Adding a Button control to the form

1. Click the Button control in the Toolbox to select it.

2. Drag and draw a Button control in the center of the form, under the label.

3. In the Properties window, set the *(Name)* property of the Button control to **btnPet**.

4. Change the *Text* property of the Button control to **Click Here**.

▶ Adding the Visual Basic code to the project

1. Double-click any free space on the form to open the Code Editor.

2. Type the following line of code in the *Pet_Load* event handler, which will clear the contents of the *lblPet.Text* property when the form first loads.

```
lblPet.Text = ""
```

3. Click the Pets.vb [Design] tab at the top of the window to return to the design view of the form.

4. Double-click the Click Here Button control to open the Code Editor.

5. Type the following line of code in the *btnPet_Click* event handler, which will display the message in the lblPet control:

```
lblPet.Text = "A healthy pet is a happy pet"
```

▶ Saving and testing your project

1. On the File menu, select Save All to save your work.

2. On the Debug menu, select Start to run your project.

3. Click Click Here to make sure that the label displays the correct message.

4. On the Debug menu, select Stop Debugging to end the program.

5. On the File menu, select Close Solution to close your project.

6. Close Visual Studio .NET.

FINISH THE CODE

In the Finish the Code exercises in this textbook, you will write programs for the fictitious Woodgrove Bank. To complete this exercise, you will open the project WoodgroveBankCh1 that came in your student file.

This project is not complete, and your task is to finish it and then test the project to make sure it works correctly.

1. Open the project WoodgroveBankCh1.

2. Change the Label control named lblBankName to display "Woodgrove Bank" when the form loads.

3. Change the Label control named lblBankMotto to display "The Best Little Bank in the West!" when the form loads.

4. Change the *Text* property of the btnOpenAccount button to **Open Account**.

5. When the user clicks btnOpenAccount, the Label control named lblMoneyMessage should display "We will take care of your money."

6. Run the project and test the form.

7. Save the solution.

8. Close the solution.

JUST HINTS

In the Just Hints exercises in this textbook, you will write programs for the fictitious company Fabrikam, Inc., which is a company that makes tools. In this exercise, you will create a new project for Fabrikam, Inc. The project will contain one form that looks like Figure 1-40. When the user clicks the Sales Phone Number button, the phone number will be displayed below the button.

Figure 1-40   The Fabrikam, Inc., form

▶ Creating a new project

Here are some hints for what you need to do to complete this exercise.

1. Create a new project and name it **FabrikamCh1**.

2. Change the name of the form to **frmFabrikam** and the name of the file to **Fabrikam.vb**.

3. Change the startup object for the project to frmFabrikam.

4. Resize the form to make it bigger.

5. Change the *Text* property of the form to **Fabrikam, Inc.**

6. Change the *Font Size* property of the form to 10.

7. Add three Label controls and one Button control to the form.

8. Rename the Label controls and the Button control to use meaningful names.

9. In the form *Load* event, change the *Text* properties of the two Label controls on the left side of the form to display the text shown in Figure 1-40.

10. In the form *Load* event, change the *Text* property of the third Label control to an empty string.

11. Modify the *Text* property of the Button control to contain **Sales Phone Number**.

12. Add code to the *Click* event of the Button control to display the number 1-555-555-0199 in the third Label control.

13. Run the project and test the form.

14. Save the solution.

15. Close the solution.

ON YOUR OWN

In the On Your Own exercises in this textbook, you will create programs for the fictitious company Tailspin Toys, which distributes toys and games over the Internet. In this exercise, you will create a new project and call it TailspinToysCh1. The form should look like Figure 1-41 when all labels are showing. After you have created the project, run it, test it, save it, and close the solution.

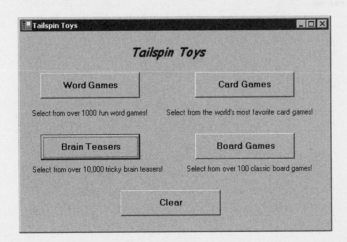

Figure 1-41   The Tailspin Toys form

■ The project should contain one form that contains five Button controls and five Label controls.

■ All four of the labels under the buttons should be blank when the form first loads. See Figure 1-41.

■ When the user clicks the Clear button, all of the labels on the screen should be cleared.

■ When the user clicks any of the four buttons on the screen, the appropriate messages listed in Table 1-2 should be displayed in the label under the button, as shown in Figure 1-41.

Table 1-2   **Messages To Display**

Button clicked	Label message
Word Games	Select from over 1000 fun word games!
Brain Teasers	Select from over 10,000 tricky brain teasers!
Card Games	Select from the world's most favorite card games!
Board Games	Select from over 100 classic board games!

MORE PRACTICE

1. Write a Visual Basic .NET statement that would display the numbers 0 through 9 on a console screen, all on the same line, with one space between each number.

2. Write a Visual Basic .NET statement that would display the numbers 0 through 9 on a Label control called lblNumbers.

3. A bakery would like you to develop a Visual Basic .NET program that will display on a form the prices of the various types of items they sell. The names of each item type should be displayed on buttons on the form, one name per button. When the user clicks a button, the price of that item should appear in a label next to that button. Make sure to include simple instructions on the screen to tell users how to use the program.

   The bakery items and their prices, shown in Table 1-3, should be included on the form.

Table 1-3   **Bakery Items and Prices**

Item type	Price
Donuts	$.50 each
Bagels	$1.00 each
Muffins	$.50 each
Bread	$2.50 a loaf
Cookies	$.25 each

4. A nursery would like you to develop a Visual Basic .NET program that will display the various types of plants they sell. The program should contain a form that lists the types of plants on buttons. When the user clicks a button, the program should display a list of examples of that type of plant in a label under the button. Use the information in Table 1-4 to complete this program.

Table 1-4   **Plant Types and Examples**

Plant type	Plant examples
Annuals	Pansy, impatien, larkspur, snapdragon
Perennials	Astilbe, coneflower, hollyhock, sedum
Bulbs	Daffodil, freesia, lily, tulip

5. Create a Visual Basic .NET program that will allow a user to click a button that represents the grade a student is in. When a button is clicked, the subjects studied by students in the grades listed on the button should appear in a label at the bottom of the page. In other words, all buttons should display their subjects in the same Label control when they are clicked. Use the information in Table 1-5 to determine the subjects to display.

Table 1-5 **Grades and Subjects Studied**

Grade	Subjects
Kindergarten	Letters, numbers, art, music, gym
Grades 1–3	Reading, math, science, art, music, gym
Grades 4–6	Reading, math, science, social studies, health, art, music, gym
Grades 7–12	English, math, history, science, foreign language, elective

6. Many people have a hard time remembering nursery rhymes, songs, and stories from their childhood. Create a Visual Basic .NET program that will allow a user to click a button that contains the title of a nursery rhyme, song, or story. The program should then display the first line of that rhyme, song, or story on a label at the bottom of the screen. Be sure to group the buttons by their type (nursery rhyme, song, or story) on the form. Use the information in Table 1-6 to complete this program.

Table 1-6 **Nursery Rhyme Types, Titles, and First Lines**

Type	Title	First line
Nursery rhyme	Hickory Dickory Dock	Hickory dickory dock, the mouse ran up the clock.
Nursery rhyme	Jack and Jill	Jack and Jill went up the hill to fetch a pail of water.
Nursery rhyme	Hey Diddle Diddle	Hey diddle diddle, the cat and the fiddle.
Song	Baa, Baa, Black Sheep	Baa, baa, black sheep, have you any wool?
Song	Hush-A-Bye Baby	Hush-a-bye baby, on the tree top.
Song	Eensy Weensy Spider	The eensy weensy spider went up the water spout.
Story	The Three Little Pigs	Once upon a time there were three little pigs.
Story	Little Red Riding Hood	Once upon a time there was a dear little girl who was loved by everyone who looked at her.
Story	Goldilocks and the Three Bears	Little Goldilocks was a pretty girl who lived once upon a time in a far-off country.

CHAPTER 2

DEVELOPING A VISUAL BASIC .NET APPLICATION

In Chapter 1, we developed two simple applications—one as a console application and the other as a Microsoft Windows application. In this chapter, we will look at the process of developing an application and include the steps that occur before you ever write any code or create any forms. We will see what tools can be used to define the program's requirements, and we will explore the steps required for the entire development process. We will also talk about the development of the user interface, which is an important component of a well-made application.

Upon completion of this chapter, you will be able to:

- Recognize the basic steps of the application development process.

- Create a flowchart.

- Write some simple pseudocode.

- Create an easy-to-use GUI.

THE APPLICATION DEVELOPMENT PROCESS

In this section, we will look at the general tools and approaches used in application development. One of these is a three-step development cycle that can be applied to most projects. Other tools include flowcharts and pseudocode, which help you to plan the logic of the application before beginning to write code. Yet another tool is comments, which allow you to document the purpose of your code in plain language for future reference and revision.

The Development Cycle

Sometimes the hardest part of developing a new application is getting started. Following a consistent process helps at the beginning and throughout the development process. In essence, three steps make up the process, and we will look at them more closely in the following sections. The steps are design, code, and test.

The Ideal Development Cycle

Much of the time, the person who writes a program is not the same person who decides what the program should do. The requirements for a program are generally written down in a **specification** by those responsible for designing the program. This specification is given to the developer, who creates the program by using tools such as Microsoft Visual Studio .NET. The amount of detail in the specification will vary from program to program and from company to company.

Sometimes several specifications are written for one program. If this is the case, one specification might define the functional requirements of the application, a second might define the technologies that will be used to create the application, and a third might describe exactly how the application will be implemented. Other times, there might be no one to write a specification, and the software analyst or developer will meet directly with the future users of the program to define how the program should look and work. Although the specification documentation still might need to be created and maintained, including the users in the design process greatly increases the likelihood that you will produce a quality product the first time around.

The specification step of the development cycle is called the **design** phase. At this point, we would consider design to include the functional requirements of the application (how the program will work) and not the visual components of the application (the GUI). In general, the more time you spend in the design phase of the project development process, the less time you will spend in the second phase of the development cycle, which is when you **code** the application.

During coding, the GUI is created and the code (Microsoft Visual Basic .NET code, in our case) is written. Often the developer is asked to provide an estimate of the amount of time that will be needed to code a program. This can be difficult to do, especially if the developer is inexperienced or the specifications for the program are vague. Many developers underestimate the time it will take to write the code for a program, and they sometimes find that the actual time it takes to code a program is two or three times their original estimate.

After coding is complete, it is time to **test** the program. Testing is the third part of the development cycle, and it might be the most important part. During testing, the GUI and all of the code that was written are exercised to make sure that everything works as it should. A test specification might be written to define exactly what is to be tested and how the testing will take place. Test data might also be created, and end users might be involved to make sure the software works the way they expect it to.

Testing a complex program so well that all of the bugs and flaws are found can be difficult and time-consuming. An important point to remember is that the cost of fixing software is much lower before the software is released to users than it is after. Thorough testing before release is definitely worthwhile.

Figure 2-1   The design, code, and test process

This process of designing, coding, and testing shown in Figure 2-1 is a simplified version of the actual software development process. Large projects might be broken down into hundreds of smaller steps that might or might not fall into one of the three steps we have defined here. Often, when an error is found, changes must take place in the code and testing must start again. Because of this, the design, code, and test cycle shown in Figure 2-2 is probably more realistic. You will find that various companies have their own ways of breaking down the development of a project into manageable steps.

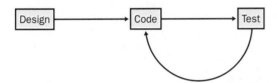

Figure 2-2   A more realistic design, code, and test process

The Real Process

Now that we've filled your head with a finite three-step process (design, code, and test), we need to disclose that it isn't like that in the real world. What we have described so far is considered in the industry to be a *waterfall* process. You write the specification first. This specification would include the functional requirements and the design specifications. The next step would be to actually design the program (identify the types to be used, create the form or forms, and add the necessary controls). Following the design phase would be the coding and, finally, the testing. From this process we can see a flow of work and, theoretically, we can predict the completion date of the project. Now for the surprise.

In reality, we will use these three steps, but they do not always flow one after the other. We actually design a little, code a little, and then test a little. Then we recode and retest. These steps are repeated until we are satisfied that each piece of the program is working as it should—this is known as *unit testing*. After that's done, we can put all the pieces together and perform *integrated testing*. Another level of testing, called *system testing*, might also be necessary if the program must interact with other systems or programs on the computer or on the network. Recoding and even redesign might occur several times throughout the development cycle.

Flowcharts

You've probably heard the phrase "a picture is worth a thousand words." This is also true when you are developing software. The pictures we create to show how a program or process should work are called **flowcharts**. A flowchart uses a set of standard symbols to define each step in a process and the flow of execution through these steps.

Although flowcharts are not always required when developing software, they can help everyone on the team to better understand the overall design and functionality of the software.

This section on the use of flowcharts is not a tutorial on how to create them for software development. If you have little or no experience in flowcharting but want to explore the topic further, you might investigate many of the resources available on the Internet or at a local library or bookstore.

There are several rules that you should follow when creating a flowchart:

- Always begin with a Start and finish with an End in a terminal symbol.

- Use only one Start and one End symbol.

- Use arrowheads on all connectors to indicate the direction of the flow of execution.

- Only one step or task should be represented by each symbol.

- Include text in each symbol that briefly describes what takes place during that step.

Standard symbols are widely accepted for use in creating flowcharts. Flowcharts can be created by hand by using a template or with a program such as Microsoft Word or Microsoft Visio. Figure 2-3 shows the standard flowchart symbols that are provided in Word.

Figure 2-3   Standard flowchart symbols in Word

Some of the most commonly used flowchart symbols are shown and described in Table 2-1.

Table 2-1 **Common Flowchart Symbols**

Name	Description	Symbol
Process	Contains a processing task to be performed	
Decision	Contains a condition that must be evaluated	
Data	Data is input to or output from the program	
Document	The report generates a printed or hard copy report	
Terminator	Indicates where the program begins and ends	
Preparation	Used to initialize a variable or condition	
Connector	Used to show connections in the flowchart without using lines	

As an example, let's look at the steps required to create a new project in Visual Studio .NET. Basically, you need to perform the six steps in the following list to complete this operation. Figure 2-4 shows an example of a flowchart that describes the same process using the standard flowchart symbols.

1. Click the Visual Studio .NET icon.
2. Click New Project in the Start box.
3. Click the type of project.
4. Type a name for the project.
5. Type the location for the project.
6. Click OK.

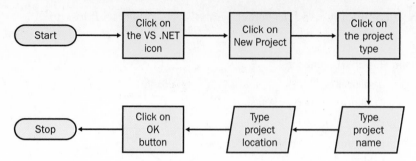

Figure 2-4   Flowchart showing process to create a new Visual Studio .NET project

In this flowchart, we used the terminator, process, and data symbols to represent the six steps in the process. If we wanted to integrate the use of a decision symbol into our flowchart, we might improve on the process by checking to see whether the user has an icon for Visual Studio .NET on the desktop. The flowchart in Figure 2-4 was created based on the assumption that users do have a Visual Studio .NET icon, and they probably do, but what if they don't? We should find out at the beginning of the process and branch to different tasks depending on the user's desktop configuration. Figure 2-5 shows this updated flowchart.

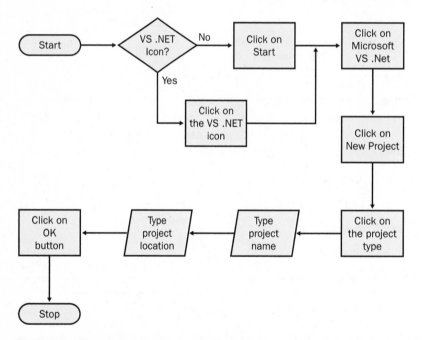

Figure 2-5   Flowchart to create a new Visual Studio .NET project with branch depending on desktop configuration

The decision symbol is used when a process requires the evaluation of a condition to determine the direction of the flow of execution through the flowchart. In this case, we ask whether or not the user has an icon for Visual Studio .NET on the desktop. If the answer is yes, the user completes the original set of steps. If the answer is no, we have to tell the user how to open Visual Studio .NET by using the Start menu before we can continue with the original set of steps.

There are a few more important things to remember when using a decision symbol in a flowchart:

- The condition or question inside the decision symbol must be able to be answered with a Boolean (true or false) response such as Yes or No or True or False.

- All decision symbols must show what to do when either of the two possible answers is selected.

- Each connecting line that comes out of the decision symbol must be labeled with the appropriate response.

Pseudocode

Another way to design and represent the steps required to complete a process is to write **pseudocode**. Simply put, pseudocode is a plain-language representation of the steps that need to be taken to complete a process. When you use pseudocode, you do not have to be concerned with the specific rules and syntax of the programming language you will be using to develop the program. There are no rules for writing pseudocode, and pseudocode is not compiled or executed, or even entered into the computer.

> NOTE Sometimes programmers will type their pseudocode into the Visual Basic .NET Code Editor as comments to document their code and make it easier to read and understand.

Perhaps the best way to learn about pseudocode is to look at an example. Let's look at the pseudocode that describes the steps required to get two numbers from the user, add them together, and display their sum on the screen.

1. Get the first number from the user.
2. Get the second number from the user.
3. Add the two numbers together.
4. Display the sum of the two numbers on the screen.

From these four simple steps, it would be easy to create a simple Visual Basic .NET application to perform this process. We would look at each step in our pseudocode and decide how to get this done in our program. There isn't always a one-to-one relationship between the steps in the pseudocode and the lines of code we write in Visual Basic .NET. Sometimes a step in our pseudocode requires adding a control to the form instead of writing code. For instance, the first step above, *Get the first number from the user*, will likely require us to add a TextBox control to our form. The second step will require the same action. The third step will require writing at least one line of code and perhaps creating a variable to store the result of the addition operation. (Variables will be covered in Chapter 4.) The fourth step can be performed by either adding a control such as a label to display the result, or perhaps by displaying the result in a message box.

Writing pseudocode is a good way to get started on a new project. We will write pseudocode at times during this textbook to show how it is used, and you should feel free to write pseudocode for any programming projects you work on.

Comments

Sometimes well-placed **comments** in code can make all the difference when it comes to understanding what a block of code does, especially when you aren't the person who wrote the code in the first place. Visual Basic .NET lets you add comments anywhere in your code, as long as you begin them with a single quotation mark ('). Comments are used to describe what is going on in your code. Think of them as notes to yourself and others who might read the code at a later date. You might also want to include comments when you make changes to code, so that you know where and when the changes were made.

By default, any comments you add to your code will be displayed in the color green. You can change the color of the comments you add by selecting Tools and then selecting Options to display the Options window, and then selecting Comment from the Display Items box. You can then set the item foreground color to any color you like.

Try It

1. For practice, write pseudocode that reflects the steps required to go to the grocery store, buy everything on your grocery list, drive home, and unpack the groceries. Make sure to include everything you do during this process. The more detail you add to your pseudocode, the easier it will be to turn it into real code.

2. Using the Drawing toolbar in Word, create a flowchart that contains the steps you follow to log on to your e-mail application, check your e-mail, read any new e-mail messages, close your e-mail application, and then shut down your computer.

What Do You Think?

1. What are the three steps in the application development cycle?

2. What are the standard symbols used in a programming flowchart?

3. What are the five rules that should be followed when creating a flowchart?

4. What rules should be followed when writing pseudocode to describe a process?

5. What kind of information would be included as comments in your code?

DESIGNING THE GRAPHICAL USER INTERFACE (GUI)

In some ways, the GUI might be the most important thing you develop in your application. No matter how complex or impressive the code you write might be, what is on the screen is what the user will see. If the GUI for your application is sloppy and difficult to use, the user will probably wonder how much care was put into the code. The credibility of your application might be in question.

With the advent of the Windows design influence on most applications, users have come to expect certain things to be true about all Windows-based applications. The same thing is true for Web applications. Maintaining consistency within your application and adhering to the tried and true GUI design conventions is important. In this section, we will look at some of the factors involved in designing and developing a good GUI for your user.

If you stop and think about it, there are many standard GUI design conventions that you have come to expect when you open a Windows-based application. You expect the first menu to be File and the last menu to be Help. You expect to have the ability to click a button called Cancel to discard any changes you have made in a window without saving them. You expect to see the Cut, Copy, and Paste commands on the Edit menu. And, when you press TAB, you expect the cursor to move through the fields in a window in a logical order.

> **NOTE**   Several good books have been written on how to create a GUI that
> adheres to standard conventions. These books cover everything from menus to
> buttons to colors and fonts. Although we will cover some of the major GUI design
> items here and make other suggestions throughout the textbook, you should
> investigate other resources for more information on GUI design.

Menus

In general, you should include a menu item for every user-executed task in your program, and, if necessary, you can also provide a button or other control on the form for the most significant tasks. There are exceptions to this rule, especially for simple programs that might not include a menu. Keeping this in mind, you should strive to provide at least two ways to perform each task in your applications, especially the important tasks like saving data.

For instance, if the user is to save changes they have made on a form, you might place a Button control with the caption *Save* on the form. You might also have a Save menu item on the File menu. Visual Basic .NET provides a wonderful tool that makes it easy to create menus for your forms. We will be using this tool to create menus for our programs later in this textbook.

Shortcut and Access Keys

Make sure that everything you can do with your mouse can also be done with the keyboard. What if your mouse stops working while you are in the middle of entering a lot of data? You would want the ability to save the data by using just the keyboard. We incorporate shortcut keys such as CTRL+S (save) and access keys such as

ALT+X (exit) to run these commands. At times, users might be busy typing information into a form and might prefer to keep their hands on the keyboard to run the commands rather than having to use the mouse to click controls or menu items.

Shortcut keys are defined by setting the *Shortcut* property of the menu item and are shown next to the menu item on the menu. Access keys are defined by placing the ampersand character prior to the letter that you want to use as the access key. The letter defined by the access key is displayed as underlined on the user interface.

We'll look at how we can add shortcut keys to a menu when we develop menus later. For now, let's look at how you can add an access key to the text displayed on a control. It's easy. All you have to do is put an ampersand (&) character before the letter that should be used with the ALT key to run the command. For example, if you want the caption of a command button to appear as Exit, you would type **&Exit** into the command button's *Text* property.

Tab Order

Nothing is more annoying than an improper **tab order** for a form. The tab order is the order in which the cursor moves through the controls on a form when you press TAB. When your form is first loaded and displayed on the screen, the cursor typically will be in the control at the top-left corner of the window, or wherever you want the user to start entering data. When the user presses the TAB key, the cursor will move down the left side of the window from control to control to the bottom of the window, and then up to the top of the next column.

Another term you should become familiar with is **focus**. A control is said to have focus when any data input or any action taken by the mouse or selected keys will affect that control. So, to pull it all together, the tab order that you set for the controls on your form will also determine the order in which the controls receive focus. Not all controls can receive focus, though they will show up in the tab order. For example, a label cannot receive focus and a text box can, but both will show up in the tab order.

Let's look at how you set the tab order for a form. By default, the tab order for the controls on a form will be the order in which the controls were added to the form. This might work if you put all of the controls you need on the form in perfect order, but if you have to go back and add another control to the middle of the form later, the tab order will not be correct. You can change the tab order by using either the properties of the control or the Tab Order window from the menu.

Open the HelloWorldWindows solution in Visual Studio .NET. Display the form in the designer window, select View, and then select Tab Order. This will turn on the tab order selection mode of the form. A number will be displayed next to each control on the form. This number is the value of the *Tab Index* property for each control. To change the tab order, simply click the controls in the order you want them to receive focus. Their *Tab Index* values will change automatically to show the new order. When you are finished, select View and then select Tab Order to exit the tab order mode.

You can also change the tab order for controls on a form by manually changing the *Tab Index* property for each control on the form. If there is a control that you want to skip in the tab order, you can set that control's *Tab Stop* property to False.

Interacting with the User

Most applications require some interaction with the user, such as entering one or more pieces of information. There are several ways to get information from the user, and the method that you select depends on how much information is needed, what kind of information the user will be entering, and what your program is going to do with it. Let's look at a couple of the easiest ways to get information to and from the user. We will cover other methods of interacting with the user in later chapters.

TextBox Control

A TextBox control is added to a form from the Toolbox, either to allow the user to enter information or to display information to the user. Forms that allow users to enter several pieces of information, such as their name and address, often use Text-Box controls. Figure 2-6 shows an example of a Visual Basic .NET form with several TextBox controls used to collect information about the user. The information that is entered by the user is available in the *Text* property of the TextBox control. The *Text* property is also used to display information to the user. We'll try this out later in the chapter.

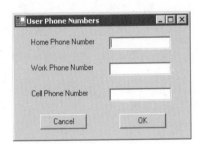

Figure 2-6   A Visual Basic .NET form with TextBox controls for entering information

MsgBox Function

By using the *MsgBox* function, you can display a message to the user and enable the user to click a button to indicate a response. When the *MsgBox* function is executed in Visual Basic .NET code, a message box appears on the screen. When the user clicks a button in the message box, the program will use this information to proceed accordingly. Figure 2-7 shows an example of a message box that is prompting the user to click Yes or No.

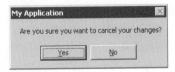

Figure 2-7   A message box

Here is the code that displays the message box shown in Figure 2-7:

```
Dim strResponse As String
' Display a message to verify canceling of changes
strResponse = MsgBox("Are you sure you want to cancel your changes?", _
    MsgBoxStyle.YesNo, "My Application")
```

The *MsgBox* function takes three parameters when it is used: *Prompt*, *[Buttons]*, and *[Title]*. The *Prompt* parameter contains the message to be displayed to the user. The *Buttons* parameter contains an indication of which buttons to display in the message box (for example, OK, Cancel, Yes, or No). The *Title* parameter contains the title to be displayed in the title bar of the message box. The *Buttons* and *Title* parameters are optional, but the *Prompt* parameter is required. When you type the *MsgBox* function in your code, IntelliSense will display a list of the valid options for the parameters where required.

Although the *MsgBox* function is available to use in our programs, we will be using the *MessageBox* class to display a message box on the screen in most of our examples. The *MessageBox* class will be covered in Chapter 4.

InputBox Function

If you need the user to type a piece of information as text for input, you can use the *InputBox* function. Like the *MsgBox* function, when the *InputBox* function is executed in code, it will display a dialog box on the screen. Figure 2-8 shows an example of an input dialog box.

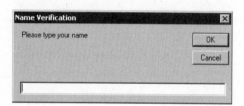

Figure 2-8   An input dialog box

Following is the code that displays the input dialog box in Figure 2-8:

```
Dim strResponse As String
' Ask the user to enter their name
strResponse = InputBox("Please type your name", "Name Verification")
```

The *InputBox* function provides five parameters when it is used: *Prompt*, *[Title]*, *[DefaultResponse]*, *[XPos]*, and *[YPos]*. The *Prompt* parameter is required and contains the message to be displayed to the user in the input dialog box. The *Title* parameter is optional and contains the title to be displayed in the title bar of the input dialog box. The *DefaultResponse* parameter is also optional and contains the information to be displayed in the text box in the input dialog box if no other information is entered. The *XPos* and *YPos* parameters are optional and determine where the input dialog box appears on the screen. Notice that all optional parameters are enclosed in square brackets. This is typical in Visual Studio .NET.

Car Information Application

Now we are going to build a Windows application to try out some of the things we have been talking about. The purpose of this application is to gather information about the user's car. The user will enter the make, model, color, and year of the car into TextBox controls. The user will then click a button to use an input dialog box to enter the VIN (vehicle identification number) of the car. A second button, when clicked, will display all of the information about the car in a message box. A third button will be used to close the form and exit the application. We will not do anything with the information; we will just collect it.

▶ **Creating the car information application**

1. Start Visual Studio .NET if it is not already running.

2. If the Start page is not displayed, on the File menu, point to New and then select Project. If the Start page is displayed, click the New Project button.

3. In the New Project dialog box, select Visual Basic Projects for the Project Type.

4. Select Windows Application for the Template.

5. Type the name of the program, **CarInformation**, in the Name box.

6. In the Location box, type or browse to the location where you want to save your project.

7. Click OK. The wizard will create and initialize the project, including all of the files necessary for a basic Windows application.

8. Click Form1.vb in Solution Explorer to select it, and change the *File Name* property in the Properties window from Form1.vb to **CarInformation.vb**.

9. Click the form to select it, and change the *(Name)* property in the Properties window from Form1 to **frmCarInformation**.

10. Change the *Text* property of the form to **User's Car Information**.

11. Right-click the project name, CarInformation, in Solution Explorer, and then select Properties.

12. Click the arrow next to the Startup Object box, and then select frmCarInformation. Click OK.

    Now we are ready to start adding controls to the form. Figure 2-9 shows what the completed form will look like. We will build it step by step together and talk about what we are doing along the way.

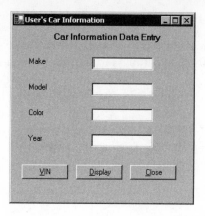

Figure 2-9   The completed CarInformation form

First let's add a Label control to display a title at the top of the form. Assuming you have enough space on the form, it is good to provide this additional information so that the user is fully aware of the purpose of the form and application.

13. Add a Label control to the top center of your form by double-clicking the Label control in the Toolbox. Drag the Label control to the desired position.

14. Change the *Text* property of the Label control to **Car Information Data Entry**. Use the sizing handles on the Label control to make it wider, so that it will fit all of the words on one line.

15. Still working with this Label control, click the plus sign (+) next to the *Font* property in the Properties window. We want to make the text in this Label control bold. Double-click the word False next to the *Bold* property to change it to True.

16. Change the *Size* property of the font to 10. This will help the title stand out at the top of the form. If necessary, resize the Label control again.

    Now we are ready to add the Label controls that identify the TextBox controls that the user will use to enter information.

17. Add four more Label controls, and line them up on the left side of the form. Change their *Text* properties to **Make**, **Model**, **Color**, and **Year**, as shown in Figure 2-9.

18. Add four TextBox controls to the form, and place one next to each of the Label controls.

19. Add three Button controls to the bottom of the form.

20. Set the properties of the TextBox and Button controls as shown in Table 2-2. Notice that we prefix each button's text with the ampersand character. This is known as an access key. It allows the user to click the button by using the keyboard. The user presses and holds down the ALT key while pressing the letter defined by the access key. The letter defined as the access key will be underlined on the user interface.

Table 2-2   **TextBox and Button Control Properties**

Control	(Name) property	Text property
TextBox	**txtMake**	\<blank\>
TextBox	**txtModel**	\<blank\>
TextBox	**txtColor**	\<blank\>
TextBox	**txtYear**	\<blank\>
Button	**btnVIN**	**&VIN**
Button	**btnDisplay**	**&Display**
Button	**btnClose**	**&Close**

21. At this point, your form should look like the form in Figure 2-9. Click the Save button on the toolbar at the top of the screen to save the work you have done so far.

    If you were to run your application right now, you would be able to enter information into the four text boxes, but nothing would happen if you clicked any of the three buttons. Let's add the code so that the buttons will do something.

22. Double-click the Close button to open the Code Editor.

23. Type the boldface statement shown in the following code:

```
Private Sub btnClose_Click(ByVal sender As System.Object, _
      ByVal e As System.EventArgs) Handles btnClose.Click
   Me.Close()
End Sub
```

IMPORTANT Be careful to type the code exactly as it appears in the examples, including any spaces, or the words in the message might run together or the code might not run properly.

Now, when the user clicks the Close button, the CarInformation application will close. Next we will add code to prompt the user to enter a VIN into an input dialog box.

1. Click the CarInformation.vb [Design] tab to return to the design view of the form.

2. Double-click the VIN button to open the Code Editor.

3. Type the boldface statements shown in the following code sample:

```
Private Sub btnVIN_Click(ByVal sender As System.Object, _
      ByVal e As System.EventArgs) Handles btnVIN.Click

   Dim strVIN As String
   strVIN = InputBox("Please enter your VIN", _
"Vehicle Identification Number")
End Sub
```

When the user enters the VIN by using the input dialog box, it is stored temporarily in the variable *strVIN*. We are not saving the VIN anywhere else right now. We will talk more about variables and how they are used in Chapter 4.

There is one more thing to do before we test this program. When users click the Display button, we want to display a message in a message box telling them what model of car they have and what color it is.

4. Click the CarInformation.vb [Design] tab to return to the design view of the form.

5. Double-click the Display button to open the Code Editor.

6. Type the boldface statement shown in the following code sample:

```
Private Sub btnDisplay_Click(ByVal sender As System.Object, _
        ByVal e As System.EventArgs) Handles btnDisplay.Click

    MsgBox("You have a " & txtColor.Text & " " & txtModel.Text & _
        " car", MsgBoxStyle.OKOnly, "Your Car")
End Sub
```

7. Let's run the application to test it. Click the Start button on the toolbar.

8. First make sure that all of the buttons work as we want them to. Type information about a car into the text boxes, and then click Display. Then click VIN and enter any number. When you are done, click Close to exit the application.

9. Now we need to go back and verify the tab order of the GUI. Run the application again and make sure that the Make box has focus and that, when you press TAB, the focus moves from top to bottom through the text boxes. If it doesn't, close the application, select View, and then select Tab Order to make changes to the Tab Index values of the controls.

10. When you are through making sure everything works in your CarInformation application, return to Design view.

Colors and Fonts

Visual Basic .NET gives you the ability to modify the foreground and background colors used for the various visual components in your application, including the form and the controls you place on the form. Although varying the colors used in a program can make the windows more interesting and easier to use, be careful not to use too many colors, or you might end up creating an overwhelming, circus-like interface. Most companies have visual design standards that determine what and how many colors can be used when developing software.

The same rule goes for using multiple font types and sizes on your forms. Multiple font types and sizes can be used successfully to differentiate types of information and areas of the form, but too many variations in the fonts can make the interface difficult to read and understand.

We have already looked at how to modify the font type and size used for the controls on a form, so let's look at how to change the colors. We will use two properties to modify the colors used on our form: *BackColor* and *ForeColor*.

The *BackColor* property is used to set the background color, and the *ForeColor* property sets the color of the text on the control or form.

▶ Changing colors in the Car Information application

1. If your CarInformation project is not already open, click the Open Project button on the Start page, and then browse to the location of the CarInformation project file that you created earlier. Select the file, and then click Open.

2. If the CarInformation.vb form is not displayed in design view, click the CarInformation.vb [Design] tab at the top of the window.

3. Click the frmCarInformation form to select it.

4. Click the *BackColor* property in the Properties window, and then click the down arrow to open the Color dialog box.

5. Click the Custom tab to display the color palette, and then click a color you would like to use as the background color for the form.

   The background color of your form should have changed. Next, we will select the four TextBox controls on the form and change their *ForeColor* properties all at once.

6. Click the Make TextBox. Hold down the SHIFT key and click the other three TextBoxes, so that all four TextBox controls are selected.

7. Click the *ForeColor* property in the Properties window, and then click the down arrow to open the Color dialog box.

8. Click the Custom tab to display the color palette, and then click a color you would like to use as the foreground color for the text in the TextBox controls.

9. Click the Save button on the toolbar, and then run the application to verify that the changes to the colors have occurred.

Pictures

Another way to make your forms more interesting and to make your applications easier for users to understand is to add one or more pictures to your forms by using the PictureBox control from the Toolbox. All you have to do is add a PictureBox control to the form and then set the *Image* property to the location and name of the file that contains the image you want to display on the form. The image file can be in bitmap, GIF, JPEG, metafile, or icon format.

You can use the *SizeMode* property to control how the image will be displayed in the PictureBox. There are four options available for the *SizeMode* property:

- **Normal** The image is placed in the upper-left corner of the control. This is the default setting.

- **AutoSize** The size of the control is adjusted to the size of the image in the file.

■ **CenterImage**   The image is centered inside the control. If the image is larger than the control, the outside edges of the image are clipped.

■ **StretchImage**   The size of the image is adjusted to fit completely inside the control.

Let's add a picture of a car to our form in the CarInformation project to make the screen more attractive.

▶ **Adding a picture to the Car Information application**

1. If your CarInformation project is not already open, click the Open Project button on the Start page and then browse to the location of the CarInformation project file that you created earlier. Select the file and then click Open.

2. If the CarInformation.vb form is not displayed in design view, click the CarInformation.vb [Design] tab at the top of the window.

3. Add a PictureBox control to the right side of the form. You will probably need to resize the form to make it large enough to display an image.

4. Click the PictureBox control to select it, and then set the *(Name)* property to **picCar** in the Properties window.

5. Click the *Image* property for the PictureBox control, and then click the Build button. Browse to find a picture of a car. Visual Studio .NET has quite a selection of images located at C:\Program Files\Microsoft Visual Studio .NET 2003\Common7\Graphics (assuming you have installed Visual Studio .NET in the default location on your computer).

6. By default, the *SizeMode* property will be set to Normal. Go ahead and change *SizeMode* to other values to see how this changes the way the image is displayed in the PictureBox control.

   Figure 2-10 shows the CarInformation application displaying a picture of a car.

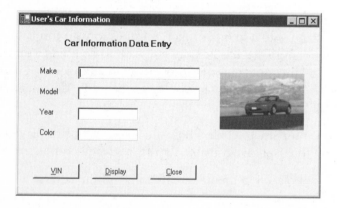

Figure 2-10   The CarInformation form displaying a picture of a car

When you are ready, save your changes and run the program to see how the form looks with the image added.

Splash Screens

Some applications you develop might take a bit of time to load, especially if they have to establish a connection to a database or perform other initialization tasks. In these cases, a **splash screen** can be added to your project. A splash screen is a form that is displayed when the project is starting up to give the user something interesting and perhaps informative to look at while they wait for other background processing to occur. Not every application requires a splash screen. If nothing much happens when your application starts, the splash screen would be displayed for such a short period of time that the user would not have time to see it.

You can create a splash screen by adding a new form to your project and then setting it as the startup object for the project. Make the splash screen colorful and interesting, and perhaps display information like the program name, the version, copyright information, and related logos. To make this work for your application, you also need to provide a control, such as a button to display the application's main form and close the splash screen, or use a Timer control to close it automatically.

Try It

1. Use Help to find information about the *InputBox* function. Read about the various parameters, and then scroll down to find the namespace and class information about this function.

2. Open the CarInformation application and change the position of the Color and Year boxes on the form so that the year comes before the color. Fix the tab order so it is correct for the new layout.

What Do You Think?

1. Why is it a good idea to include shortcut and access keys in a form's GUI?

2. What is the tab order of a form?

3. What is the purpose of a TextBox control?

4. How is the *MsgBox* function different from the *InputBox* function?

5. What properties of a Form object are used to modify its colors?

6. Which control should you use to display a picture on a form?

7. What is the purpose of a splash screen?

Q&A

Q. Do I always have to create a flowchart and write pseudocode before I can begin creating a GUI and writing Visual Basic .NET code for my application?

A. No. You should use your judgment when given a programming assignment as to what you need to do to understand and document the process. Keep in mind, though, that some companies might have specific requirements about what must be created as documentation for each application.

Q. Should I create a splash screen for every application that I write?

A. Whether or not a splash screen is required usually depends on the amount of time it takes the application to load into memory, initialize, and establish any database connections it needs. This might not be an issue in some applications, but in other applications it might be. Splash screens advertise the program and provide some comfort to the user that something is happening when an application takes a relatively long time to initialize and load the main form.

Q. Where do I find the images to display in PictureBox controls in my application?

A. That will depend on what the application is and what you want to display. Your marketing department might give you image files that contain logos and photographs of products to include in the application. You might also find pictures that you can use on the Internet, although you have to make sure there are no copyright issues to deal with before you can use them in your application.

WRAPPING UP

- The process of developing an application consists of three steps: designing, coding, and testing. A specification is often written that defines the requirements for the application. The developer is given this specification to work with when writing the program.

- A flowchart is used to provide a visual representation of a process. There are standard symbols that are commonly used to create flowcharts that represent processes. Writing pseudocode is another way to represent the logic of a process without writing the actual code in a programming language. Pseudocode has no rules and is not processed by the computer. The developer will analyze each step of the pseudocode and write the appropriate programming code for each step.

- It's important to use standard Windows design conventions when creating the GUI for an application. Several of the easiest ways to exchange data with the user in a GUI are to use TextBox controls, message boxes, and input boxes. It's also important to add a menu system to your application to back up the actions that users can take by using the mouse and the controls on the form. Developing a proper tab order is another important factor in creating an easy-to-use GUI.

■ You can use multiple colors and fonts to dress up your forms, although you should be careful not to have too many colors and fonts on any one form. The background and foreground colors of forms and most controls can be modified to display various colors. Splash screens also incorporate the use of color and graphics in a form that the user can look at when an application takes a relatively long time to load and initialize.

KEYWORDS

code	comment
design	flowchart
focus	pseudocode
specification	splash screen
tab order	test

REVIEW QUESTIONS

1. Designing, coding, and testing make up an application's _____ cycle.

   a. coding

   b. compiling

   c. definition

   d. development

2. The document that is written to define the requirements for an application is called a _____.

   a. specification

   b. namespace

   c. code sample

   d. reference

3. The process symbol that is used when creating a flowchart is in the shape of a _____.

   a. rectangle

   b. circle

   c. diamond

   d. hexagon

4. If you want a line of Visual Basic .NET code to be a comment that will be ignored by the compiler, you should put a(n) _____ at the beginning of that line.

   a. period

   b. comma

   c. single quote

   d. exclamation point

5. When you use CTRL+S to perform a save operation, you are using a(n) _____ key.

   a. access

   b. shortcut

   c. function

   d. alternative

6. What do you call the order in which focus moves through the controls on a form when TAB is pressed?

   a. Focus order

   b. Tab order

    c. Control order

    d. User order

7. Which function could you use if you wanted users to type in the name of the town they live in?

    a. *MsgBox*

    b. *TextBox*

    c. *InputBox*

    d. *TypeBox*

8. Which property is used to modify the color of the text displayed in a control?

    a. *TextColor*

    b. *BackColor*

    c. *LetterColor*

    d. *ForeColor*

9. Which property is used to specify the name of the file that contains the image to be displayed in a PictureBox control?

    a. *Picture*

    b. *File*

    c. *Image*

    d. *Graphic*

10. What do you call a form that is used to display information about a program, like the program name, version number, and copyright information, when the application is starting up?

    a. Startup screen

    b. Information screen

    c. Load screen

    d. Splash screen

11. It is acceptable to skip the testing phase of the development cycle if the developer is sure there are no errors in the program. True or false?

12. A flowchart must have one Start symbol and, optionally, it can also have an End symbol. True or false?

13. A decision symbol is used in a flowchart when there are three or more possible outcomes of the evaluation of a condition. True or false?

14. There are no specific rules to follow when writing pseudocode. True or false?

15. It is not always necessary to design an application's GUI to provide more than one way for a user to perform a task, but it is recommended. True or false?

16. A(n) _____ is created by using standard symbols to define each step in a process.

17. _____ is often written to provide a plain-language representation of the steps in a process.

18. The _____ control is used to allow the user to enter information or to display information to the user.

19. The _____ function provides an easy way to prompt the user to enter text needed by the program.

20. You should add a(n) _____ control from the Toolbox if you want to display a picture on a form.

STEP BY STEP

In this project for the Baldwin Museum of Science, you will create a form in which visitors to the pets display at the museum can enter the names of their pets in a text box and then click a button that will prompt them to enter the type of their pet in an input dialog box. The pet's name and type will be displayed back to them in a message box when they click the Message button. The form for this application will look like Figure 2-11.

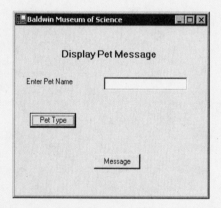

Figure 2-11   The completed frmPetMessage form

▶ Creating a new project

1. Open Visual Studio .NET if it isn't already open.

2. Click the New Project button on the Start page.

3. Click Visual Basic Projects under Project Types, and then click Windows Application under Templates.

4. Type **PetsCh2** in the Name box.

5. Browse to the location where you are storing your projects.

6. Click OK.

▶ Configuring the form and changing the startup object

1. Right-click Form1.vb in Solution Explorer, and rename Form1.vb as **Pet-Message.vb**. Press ENTER.

2. Click the title bar of the form and change the *(Name)* property of the form to **frmPetMessage**.

3. Change the *Text* property of the form to **Baldwin Museum of Science**, and then press ENTER.

4. Right-click the PetsCh2 project name in Solution Explorer, and then click Properties.

5. Change the startup object to frmPetMessage, and then click OK.

▶ Setting up the form

1. Click the form to select it. Change the *BackColor* property of the form to a light blue color.

2. Change the *ForeColor* property to a dark purple color.

3. Add a Label control to the top of the form from the Toolbox. Change the *Text* property of the label to **Display Pet Message**. Because we will not be referencing this label in our code, we do not need to change its *(Name)* property.

4. Click the *Font* property, and then change the Size to 11 and set Bold to True.

5. Click the *TextAlign* property, and then click the center alignment block.

6. Add another Label control to the left side of the form, and change the *Text* property of this label to **Enter Pet Name**.

7. Add a TextBox control to the right of the label, and then set its *(Name)* property to **txtName** and its *Text* property to <blank>.

8. Add a Button control to the left side of the form, and then set its *(Name)* property to **btnType** and its *Text* property to **Pet Type**.

9. Add a Label control to the right of the button, and then set its *(Name)* property to **lblType** and its *Text* property to <blank>.

10. Add another Button control to the bottom of the form, and then set its *(Name)* property to **btnMessage** and its *Text* property to **Message**.

▶ Adding code to the form

1. Double-click the Pet Type button on the form to open the Code Editor in the button's *Click* event handler.

2. We will need to display an input dialog box so the user can enter the type of pet and display the input in the label next to the button. Type the following line of code in the Pet Type button's *Click* event handler:

```
lblType.Text = InputBox("Please enter the type of pet", "Pet Type")
```

3. Return to the form design view and double-click the Message button.

4. We want to display a message box that contains the pet's name and type when the user clicks the Message button. Type the following line of code in the Message button's *Click* event handler:

```
MsgBox("You have a " & lblType.Text & " called " & txtName.Text)
```

▶ Saving and testing your project

1. On the File menu, select Save All to save your work.

2. On the Debug menu, select Start to run your project.

3. Test the program by typing a name into the text box and then clicking Pet Type to enter a pet type, such as cat or dog. Click Message to verify that the appropriate message is displayed.

4. On the Debug menu, select Stop Debugging to end the program.

5. On the File menu, select Close Solution to close your project.

6. Exit Visual Studio .NET.

FINISH THE CODE

To complete this exercise, open the WoodgroveBankCh2 project that came in your student file. This project contains a form for Woodgrove Bank that is used to set up a new customer. Although the form has been created for you with all of the required controls, it doesn't look nice or work very well. Finish the project by incorporating the following requirements:

- The tab order should move through all of the controls by starting on the top left side of the form, going down, and then moving up to the top of the second column and moving down.

- The same font should be used for all controls. The font size should also be the same for all controls, except for the label at the top center of the form.

- The background color should be light blue for the form and light yellow for the TextBox controls.

- The foreground color should be dark blue for all controls.

- All controls should line up neatly, with their left sides justified.

JUST HINTS

In this exercise, you will make a form that customers of Fabrikam, Inc., can use to select an item they want to order. You will create a new project containing one form that looks like Figure 2-12.

Figure 2-12   The Fabrikam, Inc., order form

If users click a picture of an item, an input box should appear that prompts them to enter the quantity they want to order. The order quantity should be displayed in a label under the picture of the item, as shown in Figure 2-13. There should also be a Clear button that clears the contents of all of the quantity labels under the pictures.

Figure 2-13   The Fabrikam, Inc., order form input box

Use the following information to complete this exercise.

1. Create a new project and name it **FabrikamCh2**.

2. Change the name of the form to **frmOrder** and the name of the file to **Order.vb**.

3. Change the startup object for the project to frmOrder.

4. Resize the form to make it similar to Figure 2-12 above.

5. Add a Label control to the top of the form. The label should display the words Order Form. Center the label on the form and make sure the font is bold. You might also want to increase the font size.

6. Add six PictureBox controls and change the *(Name)* properties of these six controls appropriately. Set the *Image* property of each PictureBox control to one of the file names containing a picture of a tool. (The image files to use on the form are either included in your student file or will be provided by your instructor.)

7. Add a Label control under each PictureBox. When users click a picture, an input dialog box should appear asking them how many items they want to order. The Label control under that picture should be updated with the quantity entered by the user.

8. Add a Button control to the bottom of the form. Set the *(Name)* and *Text* properties appropriately. In the *Click* event for this button, clear the *Text* properties of the labels that display quantities.

9. Run the project and test the form. Figure 2-13 shows the form with an input box displayed.

10. Save the project.

11. Close the solution.

ON YOUR OWN

In this exercise, you will document the process flow for the game of solitaire by using both a flowchart and pseudocode. First open the solitaire game that came with your Window's operating system and play a hand or two. Then, in pseudocode, write the steps that you follow to open the application, start a new game, and so on. Provide as much detail as possible. After the pseudocode is complete, create a flowchart for this same process.

MORE PRACTICE

1. Create a flowchart for a program that will prompt the user to enter two numbers, add the numbers together, and then display the result on the screen.

2. Write the pseudocode for a program that will prompt users to enter their name, calculate how many characters are in the name, and then display this value on the screen.

3. Write pseudocode and create a flowchart for a program that will prompt users to enter the number of miles they drive to work each day, the number of miles per gallon they get from their vehicle, and the current price per gallon of gasoline. The program should calculate the user's gasoline cost for one trip to work and back, and then display this value on the screen.

4. Write pseudocode and create a flowchart for a program that will prompt users to enter their age. If the age is less than 18, the program should display the message "You are not old enough to vote." Otherwise, the program should display the message "You can vote."

5. Create a Visual Basic .NET application that contains a form that displays four images indicating four types of weather (sunny, rainy, snowy, and windy). If the user clicks any one of these four images, the program should display a message box that displays a message such as "It is a sunny day." or "It is a rainy day." You will find graphics files that you can use for the weather images in your student file under Chapter2.

6. Create a Visual Basic .NET application that contains a button labeled Birthday on a form. When users click this button, an input dialog box should appear prompting them to enter their name. This name should be displayed in a label on the form. Next, users should be prompted to enter their birthday into another input dialog box. A sentence displaying the birthday should be added to the end of the label that contains the user's name.

7. Create a splash screen in a Visual Basic .NET application for a new online card game called Zwizee-Zway. The splash screen should be colorful and should contain a message that says "Please wait while game is loading." The splash screen should also contain the information in the following list:

   ❑ Created by Tailspin Toys

   ❑ September 2003

   ❑ Version 1.017

8. Create a flowchart and write pseudocode to represent the process used to create an application that would allow users to enter the dollar amount of an item they want to purchase and the sales tax rate for that item. The application should calculate the amount of the sales tax and the total amount of the purchase and then display these two values on the screen.

CHAPTER 3
FORMS AND CONTROLS

In Chapter 1, you learned about the Microsoft Visual Studio .NET integrated development environment (IDE) and used several of the windows available to you when you created the Hello World programs. In this chapter, we will concentrate more on the Windows Forms Designer, with particular emphasis on the Toolbox, which is one of the important windows that you will use when creating a Microsoft Windows application. You will also learn about several of the more popular controls used to create friendly GUIs, including the ListBox, the ComboBox, the CheckBox, and the RadioButton controls.

Upon completion of this chapter, you will be able to:

■ Learn more about the Windows Forms Designer and the Toolbox.

■ Get more experience updating property values.

■ Learn to align controls on a form.

■ Use ListBox and ComboBox controls.

■ Use CheckBox and RadioButton controls.

■ Use the line continuation character to format long lines of code.

■ Learn more about the *Load*, *Click*, and *CheckedChanged* events.

THE WINDOWS FORMS DESIGNER AND TOOLBOX

The **Windows Forms Designer**, shown in Figure 3-1, is a graphical area in the Visual Studio .NET IDE that was designed to reduce the time needed to create Windows applications.

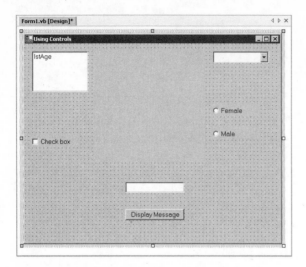

Figure 3-1   The Windows Forms Designer

Visual Studio .NET is a **Rapid Application Development (RAD)** tool. One of the key requirements for developing applications rapidly is to have the ability to put controls together quickly and easily to create a GUI. To create a GUI back in the old days, a programmer had to write several hundred lines of code just to display a screen and its constituent controls. Then the programmer still had to write code to make the controls do something useful. Because of tools such as Visual Studio .NET, development time has been greatly reduced, and the number of skilled developers has increased dramatically. Well-designed visual development tools allow developers to concentrate more of their time on the functional requirements of a program rather than on writing the code required to create the user interface.

Visual Studio .NET provides a rich set of tools and an intuitive environment to work in. The basic form that you see in Figure 3-1 is created automatically for you when you start a new project using a Windows Application template. Adding a control to the form takes nothing more than a simple double-click on the desired control in the Toolbox. What used to take hours or days now takes literally seconds or minutes.

Using a RAD tool will allow you to give your customers a glimpse of what the application will look like early in the development cycle. They can then provide feedback at a time when it is relatively easy for you to make changes to the application. This is a good thing, but be forewarned! Some of your customers might mistakenly think that the application is nearly finished when you demonstrate the GUI to them. Note the saddened look on their faces when you tell them that you have just scratched the surface of the application's development!

The Visual Studio .NET Toolbox contains a standard set of the most commonly used controls. These are called **intrinsic controls**, and they are shown in the Toolbox in Figure 3-2. There are many other controls that can be added to the Toolbox, some from Microsoft and others available from other developers.

The Toolbox is typically docked on the left side of the IDE. The controls will be displayed in and are selected from the Toolbox whenever a form is displayed in the designer window. If you do not see the Toolbox on your screen, on the View menu, select Toolbox to bring up the Toolbox. If you would rather use the keyboard shortcut, press ALT+CTRL+X to do the same thing.

Figure 3-2   Intrinsic controls in the Visual Studio .NET Toolbox

Beginning the UsingControls Program

In this section, you are going to begin creating a Windows application that is designed to teach you how to use several of the most widely used controls in the Toolbox. We could spend the entire book covering all the controls and their properties, but instead we will cover a couple of the more important controls now to get you started and introduce others later, when it is appropriate. As you work through this exercise and the others in this textbook, remember that all controls have a *(Name)* property that should be set as soon as you add the control to the form. In addition, many controls have a *Text* property that can be set at design time or at run time. The decision of whether to set the *Text* property at design time depends on whether the text should be displayed to the user as soon as the form is loaded or if it should be displayed at a later time.

▶ Initializing the project

Let's get started. Our simple UsingControls program is going to use several types of controls to let users select options such as their age range, their gender, and the type of clothing they are wearing. The program will then display a message on the screen containing the selections.

1. Start Visual Studio .NET if it is not already running.

2. If the Start Page is not displayed, on the File menu, point to New and then click Project. If the Start Page is displayed, just click the New Project button located at the bottom of the Start Page.

   Visual Studio .NET will display the New Project dialog box, as shown in Figure 3-3. In this dialog box, you will specify the project type, the template, the name, and the location for the new project.

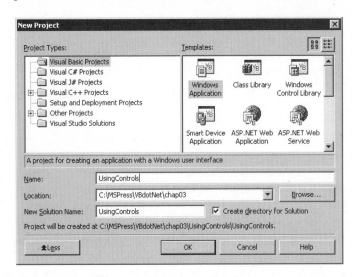

Figure 3-3   Specifying the project type, template, name, and location in the New Project dialog box

3. In the New Project dialog box, select Visual Basic Projects for the Project Type.

4. Select Windows Application for the Template.

5. **UsingControls** will be the name of the project, so type that into the Name box.

6. Type the location or click Browse to find the location in which you want to save your project.

7. Replace the text in the New Solution Name box with the name **Controls**, as shown in Figure 3-4. The default name for the solution is always the same as the name you give the project, and in many cases it is fine to accept the default. For this exercise, you will change the solution name from UsingControls to Controls, just so you can see that it can be done.

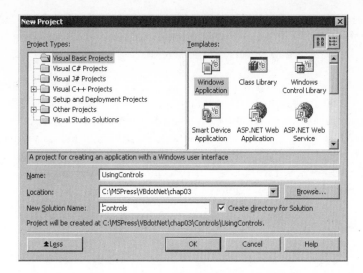

Figure 3-4   Typing Controls for the New Solution Name in the New Project dialog box

TIP   It is not necessary to manually create a folder for your project because Visual Studio .NET will create one for you and give it the same name as the project. However, if you already have a folder that you want to use, clear the check box located next to the New Solution Name box in the New Project dialog box (Figure 3-4), and make sure to update the path in the Location list to include the name of the folder.

8. Click OK.

The wizard will now create and initialize the project and include all the files necessary for a basic Windows application, as shown in Figure 3-5.

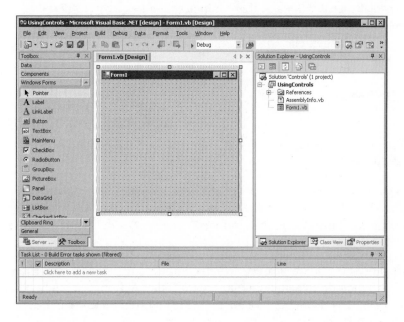

Figure 3-5   A basic Windows application displayed in the IDE

Before you continue with the application, let's take a closer look at the IDE. Your IDE might look a little different from ours if you have different windows open or if your windows are in different locations on the screen.

The Toolbox

The main window (the designer window) contains the form. To the left of the form is the Toolbox. The controls in the Toolbox are sorted alphabetically. If your controls are not sorted this way and you would like them to be, right-click anywhere inside the Toolbox (except on the title bar) and select Sort Items Alphabetically from the context menu, as shown in Figure 3-6. Another way to perform this sort is to press ALT+O when the Toolbox is selected.

Figure 3-6   Sorting the list alphabetically

Notice the Pointer control at the very top of the Toolbox. The Pointer is not actually a control, and it is not sorted along with the rest of the controls. The Pointer control is a special selection area in the Toolbox that allows you to deselect the previously selected control. If you select a control and then decide that you don't want it selected any longer, clicking the Pointer in the Toolbox will reset the current control selection.

Solution Explorer

To the right of the form are two other special windows: Solution Explorer and the Properties window. Solution Explorer, shown in Figure 3-7, shows the name of the solution, the name of the project in that solution, and a list of all the files and references that make up the project.

In the References section of Solution Explorer, you will see a list of namespaces. These namespaces refer to various class libraries that are available to you when you code an application. We briefly mentioned namespaces in Chapter 2, but we will cover some of them in a little more depth in Chapter 13.

Each individual project is an **assembly**. When compiled, an assembly becomes an executable (.exe) file or a dynamic-link library (.dll) file. Although it might be a little simplistic, for now you can think of an .exe file as a program that can be started directly by the user. A .dll file cannot be started by the user. A .dll file is used to provide additional functionality for the .exe file, and, as such, can only be called by the .exe file. Each project has one and only one *AssemblyInfo.vb* file. The AssemblyInfo.vb file contains information about the assembly, such as its title, a description, the company that created it, and a version number. Each assembly file in a project is essentially just a plain text file that can be viewed with Notepad or any text editing application.

Figure 3-7   Form1.vb in Solution Explorer

Form1.vb, shown in Figure 3-7, is the form file for our project. Think of this file as having two sides to it. The front side is the canvas on which the controls are placed, and the back side is the **code module** where you will write code to provide functionality to your application.

The Properties window, shown in Figure 3-8, is typically located below Solution Explorer. It displays a list of properties for the form or for the control that is selected on the form. If the Properties window is not visible, on the View menu, select Properties Window, or press F4.

Figure 3-8   The Properties window

Notice in Figure 3-8 that the properties for the form are sorted in alphabetical order. This is not the default sort order for the Properties window. If you want to sort the properties alphabetically, you must click the AZ button at the top of the Properties window. The default sort order is by category. In the category sort, properties are grouped into various categories, such as appearance, behavior, data, design, and layout.

When you return to the UsingControls program, we'll pick out a few properties to change as you continue developing the GUI. In a typical project, you would have been given a specification defining the requirements for the GUI. A specification might include requirements for such property values as the font size (*Font*), the width and height of the form (*Size*), the name of the form (*Name*), and the text that will be displayed in the title bar of the form (*Text*).

> **NOTE** When you named the form, you used a three-letter (lowercase) prefix fol-
> lowed by the name of the form (and the first letter of the name of the form is in
> uppercase). As we mentioned earlier, this is a standard convention known as Mod-
> ified Hungarian Notation. Although many books discuss this convention and might
> even tell you that Microsoft (and others) is discouraging its use, many others
> continue to promote its use. The truth of the matter is that you should always
> use a standard notation because this will provide consistency in your code. You
> might eventually be using your programming skills professionally, and you might
> work for a company that has set its own standards for coding. In this textbook,
> we will use Modified Hungarian Notation because it is a good standard that makes
> perfectly clear the type of object and control we are referring to in our code.

Continuing the UsingControls Program

Let's get back to the UsingControls program.

▶ Configuring the properties of the form and controls

1. Given the form requirements specified in Table 3-1, modify the appropriate properties of the form in your UsingControls project. You will have to scroll up or down in the Properties window to locate each of the properties.

Table 3-1 **UsingControls Form Properties**

Form property	Value
(Name)	**frmControls**
Font	**10**
Size	**560, 440**
Text	**Using Controls**

2. After you have renamed the form, remember to change the startup object in the Project Properties window. If you don't remember how to do this, refer back to the section "Providing Visual Basic implementation code" in Chapter 1 for instructions.

3. Add the controls listed in the first column of Table 3-2 to the form, changing the *(Name)* property of each control as you add it. Make sure that you're modifying the properties of the correct control.

> **NOTE**   It's important that you name your controls as you add them to the form. If you don't do this, you will have a harder time understanding which control is which when you're working with a complex project that has many similar controls. It's also important to name the form, because you will soon be working with projects that have multiple forms. See the discussion on naming conventions above.

There are several ways to add new controls to a form. Try these methods when you add the required controls to the form:

❑   Click the control in the Toolbox to select it, and then "drag and draw" the control on the form.

❑   Double-click the control in the Toolbox. This will place the control at its default location on the form, which is the upper-left corner of the form.

❑   Click the control in the Toolbox to select it, and then click anywhere on the form to place it at that location.

Table 3-2   **UsingControls Controls and Properties**

Control	Name	Text
Button	**btnDisplayMessage**	**Display Message**
ComboBox	**cboClothes**	<blank>
CheckBox	**chkHuman**	**Check box**
Label	**lblMessage**	<blank>
ListBox	**LstAge**	**Not applicable**
RadioButton	**radFemale**	**Female**
RadioButton	**RadMale**	**Male**
TextBox	**txtFirstName**	<blank>

4. Still using Table 3-2, update the *Text* property of each of the controls to the appropriate value.

You can update several controls at the same time if they have one or more properties in common. For example, the ComboBox, Label, and TextBox controls all have a *Text* property, and if you want to blank out the value of the *Text* property for each of these controls, it makes sense to do all of them at the same time. To select more than one control at a time, click the first control to select it and then hold down the CTRL key while you click the other controls you want to select. You can see that the TextBox, Label, and ComboBox controls are all selected in Figure 3-9.

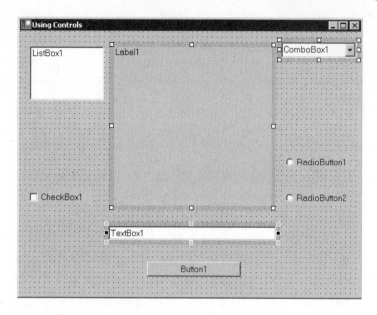

Figure 3-9   Form with three selected controls

5. With the three controls selected, scroll down to the *Text* property in the Properties window. Notice that the *Text* property is already blank. In this case, the designer cannot determine a value to display, so it displays nothing. Because you cannot delete something that is not there, you actually have to replace the value with something. Press the Spacebar once and then press ENTER. You will notice that all the controls are blank, although they each actually have a single space in their *Text* properties. You will need to remove that.

6. Select the *Text* property again, press the Backspace key, and then press ENTER. This will remove the space from the *Text* property of all three selected controls.

   TIP   Changing common property values for multiple controls at the same time is very useful and is a great timesaver. If you select multiple controls and do not find the property you are looking for, it's safe to assume that one of the selected controls does not support that property.

   Let's go ahead and change the font size for all of the controls on the form by using this technique. Instead of holding down the CTRL key and selecting each control one by one, you will select them by drawing a marquee selection around all the controls.

7. Place the mouse pointer on a free area of the form, to the left of and above the ListBox control.

   TIP   The free area of a form is any area on the form that is not being taken up by a control.

8. Press the left mouse button and hold it down while you drag the mouse down and to the right while staying on the form. While you drag, you will notice a rectangle displayed. This rectangle shows you what will be included in the selection. When all the controls have been included in the rectangle, release the left mouse button. All the controls are now selected, as shown in Figure 3-10.

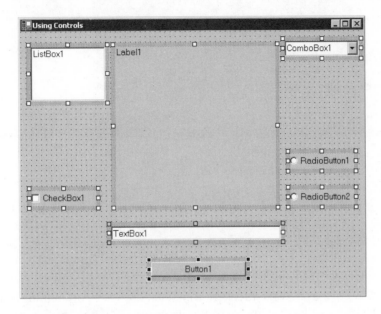

Figure 3-10   Form with all controls selected

9. Click the *Font* property in the Properties window, and then click the build button. When the Font dialog box appears, as shown in Figure 3-11, select 11 for the Size and then click OK. The font size for all the controls is now 11 points.

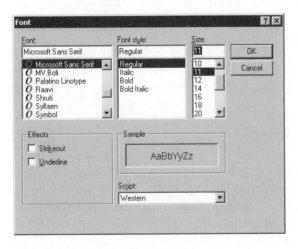

Figure 3-11   The Font dialog box

10. Resize each control as necessary, and then adjust their positions on the form so that everything aligns properly. After you have added and named all the controls, the form should look like Figure 3-12.

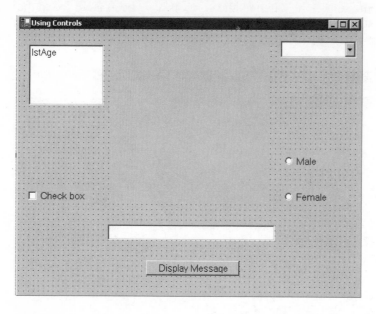

Figure 3-12   The form with all controls resized and aligned neatly

Visual Studio .NET provides several excellent tools that are used for aligning and sizing controls. These tools include the **grid** that is displayed when the form is in design view, and the **Format menu**. You can also lock the controls down once you have sized and placed them.

> **TIP**   The Layout toolbar contains much of the functionality of the Format menu. If you prefer to use the Layout toolbar and it is not already displayed, right-click the toolbar area of the IDE and select Layout from the list of available toolbars.

The Grid

In the form designer, notice that the form displays dots in a grid pattern on the background of the form. Although you can see the grid in the form designer, you cannot see the grid on the form at run time. The grid is used to help you align your controls so that the screen appears neat and orderly. By default, the grid is set to 8, which means that the dots on the grid are placed 8 pixels apart (down and across). If you want to set these dots closer together, which will allow you to have more precision when placing controls on the form, you can change the value of the *Grid* property for the form. To try this out, select the form in the form designer and click the *Grid* property in the Properties window. Type **4, 4** and then press ENTER. The dots on the grid are now only 4 pixels apart. They appear much closer together, giving you more precision over where the controls are placed on the form.

By default, all controls added to the form will snap to the grid, which means that every control will automatically be lined up against a row of dots. By setting the *Grid* property to a lower value, you will have tighter control over the positioning of the controls. If you do not want to be restricted and would rather freely position your controls on the form, you can turn off the "snap to" function. Locate the form's *Snap To Grid* property in the Properties window, and set the value to False.

If you do not want to display the grid on the form at all, you can turn it off by setting the form's *DrawGrid* property to False.

The Format Menu

Rather than trying to manually size and position controls on the form, it is much easier to use the tools provided and allow the designer to do it for you. The Format menu has a selection of menu items that will do this with ease.

To use the Format menu, display the form in design view and select the controls that you want to align or size. You can select multiple controls by holding down the CTRL key while you click each control. Notice, as you click each additional control, that only one of them will have black sizing handles. This is important because that is the control that is used as the reference, and the other controls will align or size to that reference control.

After all the controls are selected, on the Format menu, point to Align and then select Lefts to align the left side of all the selected controls. This would be useful if you had multiple TextBox controls positioned vertically below each other on a form and you wanted to have them all align. To make multiple controls the same width, on the Format menu, point to Make Same Size and then select Width.

The Horizontal Spacing and Vertical Spacing menu items on the Format menu are used to make changes to the vertical or horizontal spaces between the selected controls. The Center In Form menu item is used to place one selected control in either the horizontal or vertical center of the form. The Order menu item is used when you are layering controls on a form. We will talk more about layering controls on a form later.

Lock Controls

After you have added all of your controls to the form and positioned them so that the form is laid out just the way you want it, you don't want to accidentally move any controls out of their position. To keep this from happening, you can use the Lock Controls menu item on the Format menu to lock all of the controls on the form into their current positions. This command also locks the form's size so that it cannot be changed.

The Lock Controls menu item sets the *Locked* properties of the form and all of its controls to True. If you click the Lock Controls menu item again, the *Locked* properties of the form and its controls will return to False. If you only want to lock one control, select the control and set its *Locked* property to True. If you want to unlock an individual control, select the control and set its *Locked* property to False.

Completing the UsingControls Program

Let's get back to our UsingControls program and straighten up the form a bit so that the controls look neat and orderly.

▶ **Aligning the controls using the Format menu items**

1. In the form designer, click the CheckBox control to select it.

2. Hold down the CTRL key and click the ListBox so that it is also selected. The ListBox will become the reference control. (Note the black sizing handles.)

3. On the Format menu, point to Align and then select Lefts, as shown in Figure 3-13.

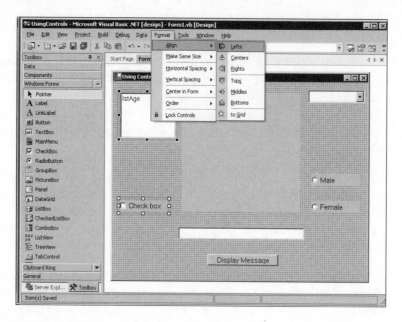

Figure 3-13   Using the Format menu to align controls

After completing these steps, you will notice that the left side of the CheckBox is now positioned to align with the left side of the ListBox. Because the ListBox was the reference control, the CheckBox was moved to complete the command and the ListBox stayed in its original position.

As you can see, after you have added all the controls to a form, properly aligning, sizing, and positioning them is easy. A neat and orderly form makes for a professional appearance and enhances the credibility of the programs you create. If you present a messy form to your customers, they will wonder if your code is also messy and full of errors.

4. The GUI is finished, but, before you go any further, let's run the program and see what it looks like at run time. On the Debug menu, select Start, or click the Start button on the toolbar, and make sure your form looks like Figure 3-14.

5. Return to design view by closing the running form. Because this is the only form in the program, closing the form will terminate the program.

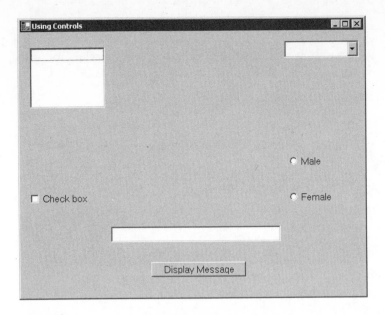

Figure 3-14   The UsingControls form displayed at run time

Try It

Let's do a few more things to line up the controls on your form by using the Format menu. First, make sure the width of the Label control is the same as the width of the TextBox control.

1. Click a blank area of the form to deselect any previously selected controls.

2. Hold down the CTRL key while you click the Label control and then the TextBox control.

3. On the Format menu, point to Make Same Size and then select Width.

Second, make sure the left side of the ComboBox control lines up with the left sides of the two RadioButton controls.

1. Click the ComboBox control and then hold down the CTRL key while you click each of the two RadioButton controls.

2. On the Format menu, point to Align and then select Lefts.

Next, make sure the Label, TextBox, and Button controls are in the center of the form.

1. Click the Label control and then hold down the CTRL key and click the TextBox control and the Button control.

2. On the Format menu, point to Center In Form and then select Horizontally.

Now see if you can use the Format menu to make sure the top edge of the ListBox, Label, and ComboBox controls are all neatly aligned. Use the same sequence of steps you used to make the other format changes, only this time use the Tops submenu item of the Align menu item.

What do you think?

1. Describe RAD and how it affects the development of software applications.

2. What are intrinsic controls?

3. What is the default solution name used for a new project?

4. How can you sort the controls displayed in the Toolbox in alphabetical order?

5. What is the Pointer control used for?

6. Describe three different methods that can be used to add a control to a form.

7. What is the purpose of having a grid on the design view of a form?

8. What kinds of sizing and positioning tasks can you accomplish by using the items on the Format menu?

CODING THE USINGCONTROLS APPLICATION

Now that you have finished creating the user interface for the UsingControls program, you can start thinking about adding some Microsoft Visual Basic .NET code. At this point you need to decide how to add the required functionality to the application. Because this is a lesson in the use of the common controls, our application does not have any lofty purpose other than to attempt to give you some insight as to what controls you might choose when designing your own applications, and why you might choose one type of control over another. Before getting directly into the code, let's talk a bit more about properties and each of the types of controls used in this application.

More About Properties

Properties are the attributes that describe an object (a control). They define the state, behavior, and appearance of the object. Most graphical controls have properties that can be changed to define how the control appears to the user. You have already seen several properties and have even set the values of some of them. Let's look at a real-life example of the use of properties. A person has a *Name* property, and you might set that property to Bill. That person will also have a *Hair Color* property, and that is set to Brown. You can see that properties *describe the object*. There are many other properties, but don't be alarmed when you see them and don't understand what they are for. Many of these properties are rarely used in normal day-to-day programming. You will learn the more common properties in this textbook and can easily pick up on others when needed.

Properties for all controls are **strongly typed**, which means that they will only accept an entry that conforms to the value type assigned to that property. For example, the *Text* property will accept any text character, but the *Enabled* property will accept only one of two predefined Boolean values (True or False). Some other properties require the entry of a numerical value and will not accept text characters.

Remember these points when setting the value of a property by using the Properties window:

- If a property has a limited number of valid entries, they will be available in a drop-down list in the Properties window. Click the property and then click the down arrow on the right of the property to see the list of valid entries.

- If a property accepts either True or False as a valid entry, you can type the word *True* or *False*, select the word from a drop-down list, or double-click the property to toggle the value between True and False.

- If the property uses a dialog box to set one or more property values, a build button will be displayed next to the property in the Properties window. Click the build button to see the dialog box. The build button is shown in Figure 3-15.

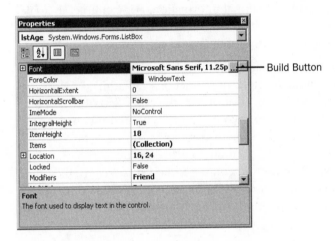

Figure 3-15   The build button displayed next to a property

More About Controls

You have been working with controls since Chapter 1, so you are already familiar with some of them. Here is a summary of the controls you have used so far:

- **Form**   A form is also a control, albeit a very special one. It is a container control, which is a control that is used to host or organize groups of other controls.

- **Button**   A Button control allows the user to interact with the program. The user can click a Button control to run a command represented by the text displayed on the button. These are easy controls to work with; users need very little training to understand what they do.

- **ComboBox**   A ComboBox control allows the user to make a selection from a predetermined list of items. You can also configure the application you are creating to give the user the ability to add items to the list in the ComboBox control.

- **Label**   A Label control is used to display information that you do not want the user to change. You would typically place a Label control next to a TextBox control and set the *Text* property of the Label to something that tells the user what type of data is expected in the TextBox. Labels can also be used to display messages to the user.

- **ListBox**   A ListBox control is similar to a ComboBox control in that it provides a predetermined list of items, although it takes up more space on the form because it doesn't collapse. The ListBox control doesn't allow the user to add additional items to the list. The benefit of the ListBox control is that it provides users with an immediate view of the items so that they don't have to click to expand the list. With the ListBox control, you can also set the number of items that will normally be displayed and, if there are more items in the list, the user can scroll through the list by using the scrollbars or the up and down arrow keys.

- **CheckBox**   A CheckBox control is used to allow the user to select an option and also to provide additional information. For example, in a File Properties dialog box, you might select a CheckBox control to specify that the file is read-only or that the file should be hidden.

- **RadioButton**   Although similar to the CheckBox control, the RadioButton control is quite unique in the way it functions. What makes it so special is the fact that it has to share control with the other RadioButtons that are in the same container. When two or more RadioButton controls are placed directly on a form, they share a common container (the form). Therefore, only one of the RadioButton controls can be selected at any given time. When one RadioButton control is clicked (*selected*), the other one will be *deselected*. A group of RadioButton controls would be appropriate to use if you wanted the user to select only one of several available options.

  RadioButtons are often placed inside a GroupBox control instead of directly on a form. The GroupBox control acts as a container, which means that all of the RadioButtons that are contained within one Group-Box control will work together. You will be working with the GroupBox control in Chapter 13.

- **TextBox**   The TextBox control is probably the most common and versatile control used on forms. The TextBox control can be used to display information and also to allow the user to enter or change information. You can set properties to limit the number of characters a user can enter into a TextBox control. You can also easily use the TextBox control to allow the user to enter a password. Setting the *PasswordChar* property of the TextBox control will allow the TextBox to display a special character such as an asterisk (*) rather than the actual character that the user typed in. This will protect the entry of sensitive information such as a password.

Planning and Writing Code

Now that you have the user interface for the UsingControls program, you need to provide some functionality. In other words, let's make it do something! Before adding code, though, you have to decide what should happen when the user does something. Perhaps the user will click a button or select an item in a list box. For example, if the user enters a first name in a text box and then clicks the button, you could display the name in a label. When the user selects an item in a list box, you could display the selected value in a label. This type of planning is sometimes referred to as writing pseudocode.

Commenting the Code Module

Before discussing pseudocode, we need to discuss commenting the code module. Commenting is more than just jotting down a few notes to yourself while you code a program. It is used to document what you have done and what you are going to do. Comments should be inserted at the top of the code module (prior to any code or declarations) and should include such information as the name of the program, the name of the programmer or programmers who coded the module, the date the module was created, and a brief description of the program. Here is an example:

```
' UsingControls Program
' Programmer(s): Judy Lew & Paul West
' Date: 06/25/2003
' Description of Program: This program will allow the user to interact with
' several of the most commonly used controls available in the Toolbox.
```

> **NOTE** If multiple code modules are included in the project, add similar comments to each code module. The description should be limited to just that code module, but you should also include how that code module relates to the project as a whole.

If you update a module, you should add additional comments to the code. These additional comments should include a reference to the procedures that were changed or added, the programmer or programmers who made the changes, and the date the changes were made.

To add a comment to a code module, start a new line and type a single quotation mark. Now type your comments. All comment lines should be preceded by a single quotation mark to differentiate them from code. To assist you, the IDE automatically displays comments in green text. The keyword *REM*—which stands for remark—can be used instead of the single quotation mark, but, although it is supported, it is rarely used these days.

Comments can also be added to the end of a code statement, but no additional code can be added after the comment on the same physical line. Additionally, if you break up a long code statement into two or more lines by using the line continuation character, comments can only be added at the end of the last line of that code. The line continuation character is discussed below.

TIP Any text that follows a single quotation mark is considered a comment and will be ignored by the compiler. This is not true when the single quotation mark is placed inside double quotation marks; it is then treated as a literal character.

Comments are not limited to a description of the code module. Each procedure should include comments that describe the function of the procedure. In addition, comments should be inserted above each code block or statement to clarify what the code is supposed to do.

While commenting code might seem tedious, it can be a big timesaver when you have to come back to the code several months later to make changes. It can be even more important when you have to work on someone else's code and you're not quite sure what the code is doing. As you improve your skills, you will find that some code is "self-describing" and warrants no additional clarification. For now, you should comment your code to help you understand what you are writing and why you are coding it that way.

Pseudocode

You can easily get into hot water if you dive right into coding without giving some thought to how you will implement the functionality your application requires. You need to take the requirements for your program and begin turning them into the steps that must be programmed with code. As you saw in Chapter 2, writing pseudocode is a good way to make the transition from a description of your application's requirements to lines of code. The pseudocode that you write now can be used as comments when you convert it to real code. This not only provides good documentation for your code modules; the comments can be reviewed later when you need to check to make sure that all the functional requirements of the program have been met.

Table 3-3 shows the requirements of the UsingControls program, written in pseudocode.

Table 3-3   Pseudocode for UsingControls

Step	Pseudocode
1	Add items to the combo box
2	Add items to the list box
3	Type text into the text box
4	Click button
5	Display text in the label
6	Select an item in the list box
7	Display the selected list box item in the label
8	Select an item in the combo box
9	Display the selected combo box item in the label

Next you need to add a description of what the program must do to perform each step in the pseudocode, as shown in Table 3-4. This will help you move from the pseudocode to the appropriate Visual Basic .NET code. In some cases, you will find that a step actually represents an action by the user and does not require any code.

Table 3-4   **Pseudocode and Code Descriptions for UsingControls**

Step	Pseudocode	Code description
1	Add items to the combo box	Add values to the *Items* collection of the ComboBox by using the *Add* method.
2	Add items to the list box	Add values to the *Items* collection of the ListBox by using the *Add* method.
3	Enter text into the text box	Set the *Text* property of the TextBox.
4	Click button	No code is needed here. The *Click* event of the Button control will be raised automatically when the user clicks the button.
5	Display text in the label	Set the *Text* property of the Label.
6	Select an item in the list box	No code is needed here. The *Selected-IndexChanged* event of the ListBox control will be raised automatically when the user clicks a selection.
7	Display the selected list box item in the label	Set the *Text* property of the Label to the value selected in the list box.
8	Select an item in the combo box	No code is needed here. The *SelectedIndexChanged* event of the ComboBox control will be raised automatically when the user clicks a selection.
9	Display the selected combo box item in the label	Set the *Text* property of the Label to the value selected in the combo box.

Now you have an idea as to what code you need to write based on the steps that must occur. Next you need to decide where to write this code.

Where to Write the Code

Knowing where to place code is one of the more difficult questions to answer and, typically, this is where many new programmers get stuck and become frustrated. Using the pseudocode and the code descriptions you wrote, we will show you how to determine where each code statement should be placed and why it should be placed there.

Getting back to your pseudocode, let's look at the first and second steps in the table: *Add items to the combo box and list box*. We want these two controls to be populated when the form is first displayed. The *Load* event of the form will be a good place to include that code. The third step refers to an action taken by the user (typing text into the text box control) so you do not have to provide any code here. The fourth step will automatically occur when the user clicks the button, so the *Click* event handler of the button would be an appropriate place to grab the value that the user entered into the text box (in step 3) and place it in the label (step 5).

> **TIP**   Although the *Load* event is the most common event for a form, it is not always the event you want to choose for implementing your code. We will later discuss selecting a different event and why you would choose one event over another.

Code Layout—Using the Line Continuation Character

Before we go much further, we should also talk about proper code layout and, more specifically, the **line continuation character**. The line continuation character is used in Visual Basic .NET to break up long lines of code so they appear on more than one line. All you have to do is type a space followed by an underscore character to break one line of code into two lines. When breaking up literal strings (text placed inside double quotation marks), you must ensure that each part of the literal string is started and ended on the same line. The following two code samples do exactly the same thing: they display a literal string. The first example uses the line continuation character, whereas the second example does not. Also notice that, when you break a literal string into two or more strings, you must include the ampersand (&) symbol to join the strings. By concatenating two or more literal strings, you are informing the compiler that they should be treated as one string.

```
lblMessage.Text = "I am a brown cat, my name is Fluffy," & _
    " and I like to chase butterflies."

lblMessage.Text = _
    "I am a brown cat, my name is Fluffy, and I like to chase butterflies."
```

If you break up long code statements by using line continuation characters, your code will be much easier to read, understand, and debug. The Visual Studio .NET IDE does a great job of indenting and wrapping code, but this is only an aid to coding. For professional results, you need to apply some additional manual formatting. In the following examples, we will break up code by using the line continuation character, and then explain exactly why we choose to do so.

▶ Converting the pseudocode into Visual Basic .NET code

Let's go back to the UsingControls program and add the Visual Basic .NET code required for the first five steps of pseudocode.

1. Make sure that your application is not running. Display the form in the designer and double-click a free area of the form.

    The Code Editor should appear and, more importantly, the *frmControls_Load* event handler has been added for you. Each control has a default event. The default event is generally the most commonly used event for that control. When you double-click a control in the design window, the Code Editor will open with the event handler for that default event already created.

2. Type the boldface code shown below into the *frmControls_Load* event handler. You should also write comments prior to each block of code that describe what the code will do. For now, you can use our comments or feel free to make up your own.

```
Private Sub frmControls_Load(ByVal sender As System.Object, _
        ByVal e As System.EventArgs) Handles MyBase.Load
    ' Add items to the ListBox
    lstAge.Items.Add("0 - 19")
    lstAge.Items.Add("20 - 39")
```

```
        lstAge.Items.Add("40 - 69")
        lstAge.Items.Add("60 - 79")
        ' Add items to the ComboBox
        cboClothes.Items.Add("Jacket")
        cboClothes.Items.Add("Sweatshirt")
        cboClothes.Items.Add("Raincoat")
        cboClothes.Items.Add("Parka")
End Sub
```

The two code statements that Visual Studio .NET provided for you are called the event handler **wrapper lines**. The top wrapper line begins with Private Sub, and the bottom wrapper line is End Sub. You can see that the top wrapper line is rolling over to the next line using the line continuation character. This is not done for you automatically; you will need to do this yourself. Where you place the line continuation character is important for readability.

3. Now run your application again and correct any errors that might have occurred. When your program is running, it should look like Figure 3-16. You should see a list of age range items in the list box, and if you click the down arrow on the combo box, a list of clothing items will appear.

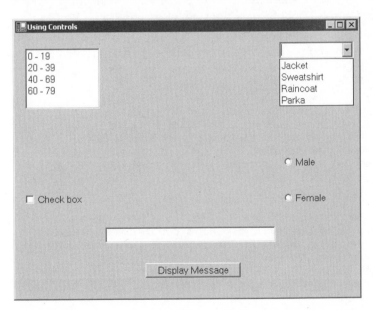

Figure 3-16   The UsingControls form displaying data in list box and combo box controls

4. The *SelectedIndexChanged* event is the default event for the ListBox and the ComboBox controls. Return to design view, double-click the ListBox control, and then type in the first line of boldface code (the line after the comment) exactly as shown in the following code sample. Repeat these steps for the ComboBox control, typing in the second line of boldface code shown in the following code sample. Once again, notice the appropriate use of the line continuation character for formatting the code.

```
Private Sub lstAge_SelectedIndexChanged(ByVal sender As System.Object, _
        ByVal e As System.EventArgs) Handles lstAge.SelectedIndexChanged
```

```
        ' Assign the string and the ListBox's selected item to the
        ' Text property of the Label
        lblMessage.Text = "My age is between: " & lstAge.SelectedItem
    End Sub

    Private Sub cboClothes_SelectedIndexChanged(ByVal sender As System.Object, _
        ByVal e As System.EventArgs) Handles cboCLothes.SelectedIndexChanged
        ' Assign the string and the ComboBox's selected item to the
        ' Text property of the Label
        lblMessage.Text = "I am wearing a " & cboClothes.SelectedItem
    End Sub
```

5. Run your program again and test it by selecting items in the list box and the combo box. Make sure the label changes to display your selection. When you are done testing, close your program and return to design view.

   TIP   It's a good idea to test your application often so you don't have to debug too much code at a time. It's easy to run your application in Visual Studio .NET, so there's no excuse for not testing, and testing often!

6. The *CheckedChanged* event is the default event for the CheckBox and RadioButton controls. Double-click the CheckBox control in the form's design view, type in the first line of boldface code in the following code sample, exactly as shown, and then repeat the steps for each of the two RadioButton controls on the form. Make sure you type the correct line of code for each control's *CheckedChanged* event.

```
    Private Sub chkHuman_CheckedChanged(ByVal sender As System.Object, _
        ByVal e As System.EventArgs) Handles chkHuman.CheckedChanged
        ' Assign the string and the CheckBox's checked value to the
        ' Text property of the Label
        lblMessage.Text = "I am a CheckBox and my Checked value is " & _
            chkHuman.Checked
    End Sub

    Private Sub radMale_CheckedChanged(ByVal sender As System.Object, _
        ByVal e As System.EventArgs) Handles radMale.CheckedChanged
        ' Assign the string and the RadioButton's name and checked value to the
        ' Text property of the Label
        lblMessage.Text = "I am a RadioButton, my Name is " & radMale.Name & _
            " and my Checked value is " & radMale.Checked
    End Sub

    Private Sub radFemale_CheckedChanged(ByVal sender As System.Object, _
        ByVal e As System.EventArgs) Handles radFemale.CheckedChanged
        ' Assign the string and the RadioButton's name and checked value to the
        ' Text property of the Label
        lblMessage.Text = "I am a RadioButton, my Name is " & radFemale.Name & _
            " and my Checked value is " & radFemale.Checked
    End Sub
```

   Let's finish writing the rest of the code for the application, and then we can discuss the merits of your labor and dissect some of the code you have written.

7. Double-click the Button control and then type in the boldface code shown in the following sample.

```
    Private Sub btnDisplayMessage_Clicked(ByVal sender As System.Object, _
        ByVal e As System.EventArgs) Handles btnDisplayMessage.Clicked
```

```
        ' Assign the string along with the TextBox's Text value to the
        ' Text property of the Label
        lblMessage.Text = "Hello, my Name is " & txtFirstName.Text
    End Sub
```

8. That's it. You have finished. Now you need to test your application thoroughly to make sure everything works as designed and to verify that your application satisfies the requirements that have been specified.

Working in accordance with the requirements for your application is an important concept. For some developers, giving users what they ask for is a novel concept. They sometimes think they know better what the program should do than the user does (and in some cases that might be true, but that isn't the point). Consider this: If you walked into a restaurant and ordered a pizza and the waiter or waitress brought you back a plate of pancakes instead, you might be somewhat perturbed. It might be true that the pancakes actually taste better, will fill you up, and, in some cases, might be cheaper, but that isn't what you asked for. If the waiter had said that the pizza wasn't good that day and highly recommended the pancakes, you might have been enticed into changing your order. As a developer, at times you might need to explain to users that their requirements are either technically unsound or impossible to implement with the current technology, or that there might be a better way to get the same result.

With that sermon concluded, we can start dissecting the code and perhaps learn a few more things about Visual Basic .NET.

Inside the Code

Let's look in detail at the lines of code you typed, beginning with the code to populate the ListBox and ComboBox controls:

```
lstAge.Items.Add("0 - 19")
```

A ListBox (or ComboBox) has an *Items* collection property. This *Items* property has a method called *Add* that takes an argument of type *Object*. An **argument** is a value that is required by a method. Arguments are always placed inside parentheses after the method name. Not all methods require arguments, but, in this case, one argument is required. Some methods require more than one argument. It should be clear, if you think about it, that if you didn't provide the value to be added to the list, it would be pointless to run the *Add* method for the list.

Earlier we said that methods are actions on an object. Perhaps this is a little clearer now that you have seen a method in action. You are performing an action on an object by adding an item to the ListBox's *Items* collection.

One more thing about this particular argument. The required argument is an object, but you are adding a string. Well, a string actually is an object and, as you will find out later, practically everything in Microsoft .NET is derived from objects.

The code to display the list box item information in the label is as follows:

```
lblMessage.Text = "My age is between: " & lstAge.SelectedItem
```

When you typed the name of the control and followed it by a period, Visual Studio .NET displayed a list of properties and methods to select from. You can ignore many of these for now, but remember how you got there? You started to type in the word *Text*, and the IntelliSense feature automatically displayed the list and scrolled to that property. The IDE knows what type of object lblMessage is, and IntelliSense automatically displayed the properties and methods for that type of object.

You then typed an equals sign (=), which means that you are assigning a value to the property. You made the property *equal to the value*. Visual Basic .NET always takes the value on the right side of an equals sign and assigns it to whatever is on the left side of the equals sign.

The *Text* property of the ListBox control holds strings of alphanumeric characters that are typed as text characters surrounded by double quotation marks. What you are doing here is passing a string of alphanumeric characters to the *Text* property. In this case, the value is the text (in quotation marks) joined with the value of the item that is selected in the ListBox. Just like when you joined two literal strings, this time the ampersand (&) character is used to concatenate a literal string with the value of the selected item.

Concatenation refers to the amalgamation of two or more entities. How about calling it the joining of two string values? It might be a complex word, but this is a fairly simple concept.

Next, let's look at the code to display combo box item information in the label:

```
lblMessage.Text = "I am wearing a " & cboClothes.SelectedItem
```

As you can see, the syntax and purpose of this line of code is the same as what you wrote for the list box.

To display check box information in the label, you wrote the following:

```
lblMessage.Text = "I am a CheckBox and my Checked value is " & _
    chkHuman.Checked
```

When users click the check box, they are just adding a check mark or removing it. In this code snippet, you are displaying a message about the control concatenated with the value of the *Checked* property of the CheckBox control, which will be either True or False. True will appear if the check box is selected; False will appear if it is not selected.

Finally, the following code displays radio button information in the label:

```
lblMessage.Text = "I am a RadioButton, my Name is " & _
    radMale.Name & " and my Checked value is " & radMale.Checked
```

Although this code is similar to what you used for the CheckBox control in concept, it differs in functionality. A RadioButton that coexists with other RadioButton controls in the same container takes priority when selected. This means that when any RadioButton is selected, all the others in that same container are automatically cleared.

As we mentioned earlier, the default event is not always the one you should be using. Many times you will want to select a different event that will run your code at a different time or when something different happens. In the UsingControls program, you used the *CheckedChanged* event, which is raised whenever the *Checked* property of a CheckBox or RadioButton control changes.

In the program we are discussing, this means that if *radMale* is selected and we click *radFemale*, we would expect that the *radFemale.CheckedChanged* event would be raised, and it is. However, what we didn't expect was that the same event for *radMale* will also be raised just before the *CheckedChanged* event is raised for *radFemale*. Remember, the *CheckedChanged* event is raised when the *Checked* property value has changed from Checked (True) to Unchecked (False), or vice-versa. When a user selects *radFemale*, the *Checked* property of *radFemale* changes to True, and the *Checked* property of *radMale* also changes, to False.

You should also know that, although you cannot prevent an event from being raised, if no code is in the event handler for that event, nothing will happen when the event is raised.

Sometimes you can provide the same functionality by using different code in different events. For example, you could have used the *Click* event of the Radio-Button control instead of the *CheckedChanged* event to display a message. If you had used the *Click* event, the event handler for radMale would look like the following code.

```
Private Sub radMale_Click(ByVal sender As Object, _
        ByVal e As System.EventArgs) Handles radMale.Click
    ' Set the RadioButton's checked property to true
    radMale.Checked = True
    ' Assign the string and the RadioButton's name and checked value to the
    ' Text property of the Label
    lblMessage.Text = "I am a RadioButton, my Name is " & radMale.Name & _
        " and my Checked value is " & radMale.Checked
End Sub
```

Try It

Why don't we add a few more clothing items to those already loaded into the ComboBox control? To do this, you need to go back to the form's *Load* event handler and add the lines for the new clothing items.

1. Make sure you are in the form designer window, and double-click any empty space on the form to open the Code Editor.

2. You should find yourself in the *frmControls_Load* event hander. Add the following lines of code after the line that adds *Parka* to the list of ComboBox items.

```
cboClothes.Items.Add("Gloves")
cboClothes.Items.Add("Boots")
cboClothes.Items.Add("Scarf")
```

3. Run your program, and make sure the three new items are now appearing in the combo box when you click the list. Stop the program and return to design view.

Now add a new Button control to the form that will display the results of all the selections at one time in the Label control. This means you are going to have a pretty long line of code, so you will want to use the line continuation character several times to break it into multiple lines.

1. Make sure you are in the form designer window, and add a new Button control to the form. Place this new Button control under the existing Button control at the bottom of the form.

2. Change the *(Name)* property of the new button to **btnDisplayAll**, and change the *Text* property to **Display All**.

3. On the Format menu, use the Make Same Size command to make both of the button controls the same width.

4. Double-click the new Button control to open the *btnDisplayAll_Click* event handler. Add the following lines of code inside the event handler wrapper lines.

```
lblMessage.Text = "My name is " & txtFirstName.Text & _
    " and I am between the ages " & lstAge.SelectedItem & _
    " and I am wearing a " & cboClothes.SelectedItem
```

5. Test your program again. Make sure you enter your first name and select an age range and an item of clothing before clicking Display All. If the message in the label doesn't look right, make sure you put spaces where they are required so the strings don't run together.

What Do You Think?

1. What are an object's properties used for?

2. Describe the difference between a CheckBox control and a RadioButton control.

3. When would you want to use the line continuation character?

4. How and where are arguments used in Visual Basic .NET code?

5. What does concatenation mean?

Q&A

Q. Why do I need to learn about debugging? If I write code correctly the first time, I won't need to debug my programs.

A. Well, we all plan on winning the lottery one of these days, but until then, we will continue to work so we can feed ourselves. We all also plan on writing bug-free code, but occasionally everyone makes mistakes. The obvious mistakes in the code are generally caught by the compiler, but the not-so-obvious errors might slip through unless you test your code thoroughly. In Chapter 5, we will talk about debugging in depth.

Q. When I coded the *Add* method of the ListBox and ComboBox controls, I noticed an *AddRange* method listed. What is *AddRange* used for?

A. The *AddRange* method is a very cool technique that allows you to add multiple values to a ListBox or ComboBox control at one time. If you wanted to add all the clothing items to the ComboBox by using the *AddRange* method instead of adding each item one at a time, the code would look like the following:

```
Private Sub frmControls_Load(ByVal sender As Object, _
      ByVal e As System.EventArgs) Handles MyBase.Load
    ' Using the AddRange method
    cboClothes.Items.AddRange(New Object() _
      {"Jacket", "Sweatshirt", "Raincoat", "Parka"})
End Sub
```

This routine might look a little strange to you because it uses an array of values and we haven't talked about arrays yet. Don't worry; we will be covering arrays and collections in Chapter 11. In the meantime, you can use this code, but remember that the values are added to the *Object* array and all the items are specified inside curly braces.

WRAPPING UP

- The Windows Forms Designer and the many functions on the Format menu allow you to quickly design a GUI that represents the front end of your application. The grid helps you to align and size the controls on a form so that you can create neat and orderly forms. You can select more than one control at a time and then format them as a group and set the properties that these controls have in common.

- The process of writing pseudocode is a good way to begin developing the Visual Basic .NET code that is required for an application. Pseudocode describes the functionality of the application in plain language, and the pseudocode you write now can be used as part of your built-in documentation when writing your comments.

- Most of the code you write will reside within event handlers that allow you to take advantage of the events that will occur naturally in your program. Sometimes more than one event can be used to accomplish the same task.

- You can make your code easier to read and more professional looking by using the line continuation character (a single space followed by an underscore) to break long lines of code into shorter, logical pieces.

KEYWORDS

argument	assembly
code module	concatenation
container control	grid
intrinsic controls	line continuation character
Rapid Application Development (RAD)	strongly typed
Windows Forms Designer	wrapper lines

REVIEW QUESTIONS

1. The Label control is a member of the standard set of _____ controls that are included in the Toolbox.

   a. intrinsic

   b. exterior

   c. interior

   d. literal

2. The default name used for the solution when you create a new project is always the same as the name of the _____.

   a. computer

   b. developer

   c. project

   d. form

3. The _____ control located at the top of the Toolbox is a special selection area that allows you to reset the currently selected control.

   a. Label

   b. TextBox

   c. ComboBox

   d. Pointer

4. The name of the file in a project that contains information about the assembly, such as its title, a description, the company that created it, and a version number, is _____.

   a. Form1.vb

   b. AssemblyInfo.vb

   c. System.vb

   d. Project.vb

5. The default sort order of the items in the Properties window is _____.

   a. by category

   b. by behavior

   c. alphabetical

   d. numerical

6. The _____ property of a form is used to determine how close together the dots are placed on the form in design view.

   a. Grid

   b. Grid Spacing

   c. Snap To Grid

   d. Draw Grid

7. Which menu contains the Align, Make Same Size, Horizontal Spacing, Vertical Spacing, Center In Form, Order, and Lock Controls menu items?

   a. Edit

   b. Tools

   c. View

   d. Format

8. If you want to let the user select only one of several options on a form, what type of control should you use?

   a. CheckBox

   b. RadioButton

   c. Button

   d. Label

9. _____ is a plain language representation of the code that you need to write to give your program the required functionality.

   a. Pseudocode

   b. Visual Basic code

   c. C++ code

   d. Fake code

10. To use the line continuation character to wrap one line of code onto the next line, type a space followed by a(n) _____.

   a. exclamation point

   b. period

   c. comma

   d. underscore

11. You must always manually create a new folder for each new project to keep it separate from other projects. True or false?

12. The controls in the Toolbox cannot be sorted alphabetically. True or false?

13. If the Properties window is not displayed when you open an application, you must close Visual Studio .NET and reopen it in order to view the Properties window. True or false?

14. The only way to add a control to a form is to double-click the control in the Toolbox. True or false?

15. A strongly typed property will accept the entry of only values that conform to the value type assigned to that property. True or false?

16. The graphical area in the Visual Studio .NET IDE that is used to create applications for Windows is called the _____.

17. The code that you write to make your program do something resides in a(n) _____.

18. If you want to make sure you don't accidentally move any controls on your form, you should use the _____ menu item on the Format menu to lock them in place.

19. The _____ is an example of a container control because it can host or organize other controls.

20. The values placed in parentheses after a method name are called _____.

STEP BY STEP

You are going to create a form for the Baldwin Museum of Science. On this form, visitors to the pets display can enter the type of pet they have, the color of the pet, and the name of the pet. There will also be a check box to let users indicate whether they have other pets. Figure 3-17 shows what the form will look like when it is complete.

Figure 3-17   The completed PetsCh3 form

▶ Creating a new project

1. Open Visual Studio .NET if it isn't already open.

2. Click New Project on the Start Page.

3. Click Visual Basic Projects under Project Types and Windows Application under Templates.

4. Type **PetsCh3** in the Name box.

5. Browse to the location where you are storing your projects.

6. Click OK.

▶ Configuring the form and changing the startup object

1. Right-click Form1.vb in Solution Explorer, and rename Form1.vb as **Pets.vb**.

2. Press ENTER.

3. Click once in the title bar of the form, and change the *(Name)* property of the form to **frmPets**.

4. Change the *Text* property of the form to **Baldwin Museum of Science**, and then press ENTER.

5. Right-click the PetsCh3 project name in Solution Explorer and then click Properties.

6. Change the startup object to frmPets, and then click OK.

7. Click once in the title bar of the form, and then use the sizing handles to make the form a little bit bigger.

▶ Adding the pet type RadioButtons

1. Click the RadioButton control in the Toolbox once to select it.

2. Click the form in the upper-left corner to drop the RadioButton.

3. Repeat the previous two steps to add another RadioButton control below the first.

4. Click the top RadioButton to select it.

5. In the Properties window, set the *(Name)* property of the RadioButton to **radCat**.

6. Scroll down and change the *Text* property to **Cat**.

7. Click the bottom RadioButton control to select it.

8. In the Properties window, set the *(Name)* property of the RadioButton to **radDog**.

9. Scroll down and change the *Text* property to **Dog**.

▶ Adding the color ListBox

1. Click the ListBox control in the Toolbox once to select it.

2. Drag and draw a ListBox on the form in the center, near the top.

3. In the Properties window, set the *(Name)* property of the ListBox to **lst-Color**.

▶ Adding the pet name TextBox and Label

1. Click the Label control in the Toolbox once to select it.

2. Drag and draw a Label on the form, below the RadioButtons.

3. In the Properties window, set the *(Name)* property of the Label to **lblPet-Name**.

4. Scroll down and change the *Text* property to **Pet Name**.

5. Click the TextBox control in the Toolbox once to select it.

6. Drag and draw a TextBox on the form just to the right of the Label.

7. In the Properties window, set the *(Name)* property of the TextBox to **txt-PetName**.

8. Scroll down and delete the contents of the *Text* property.

▶ Adding the other pets CheckBox

1. Click the CheckBox control in the Toolbox once to select it.

2. Drag and draw a CheckBox control on the form, below the pet name controls.

3. In the Properties window, set the *(Name)* property of the CheckBox to **chkOtherPets**.

4. Scroll down and change the *Text* property to **Do you have other pets?**.

▶ Changing the font for all controls

We forgot to change the font for the form and the controls while we were adding the controls, so let's select all of the controls at once and change their font size.

1. Hold down the CTRL key and click all of the controls that you added to the form.

2. In the Properties window, find the *Font* property and click the build button.

3. Change the Size to 10 and then click OK.

4. You might have to resize some of your controls to fit the larger text. Go ahead and do that now. You might also want to use some of the commands on the Format menu to arrange the controls neatly on the form.

▶ Adding the Visual Basic code to the project

1. Double-click in any free space on the form to open the Code Editor.

2. Type the following lines of code into the *frmCustPets_Load* event handler to add the colors to the ListBox control when the form first loads.

```
lstColor.Items.Add("Brown")
lstColor.Items.Add("White")
lstColor.Items.Add("Black")
lstColor.Items.Add("Orange")
lstColor.Items.Add("Mixed")
```

▶ Saving and testing your project

1. On the File menu, select Save All to save your work.

2. On the Debug menu, select Start to run your project.

3. Try each control to make sure they are working correctly.

4. On the Debug menu, select Stop Debugging to end the program.

5. On the File menu, select Close Solution to close your project.

6. Exit Visual Studio .NET.

FINISH THE CODE

We have started a customer survey form that you need to finish for the Woodgrove Bank. This form will be used to find out if the bank's customers are satisfied with the service they are receiving. To complete this form, open the project WoodgroveBankCh3 that came in your student file. This project is not complete; your task is to finish it as described below.

1. All of the required controls have been added to the form, and their *(Name)* properties have been set correctly. Change the *Text* property of each control to the value required, based on what appears in Figure 3-18.

2. Display the appropriate message in the Label control when the user clicks each of the satisfaction options:

   ❏ Option "Very Satisfied": Display the message "We are happy that you are happy!"

   ❏ Option "Somewhat Satisfied": Display the message "What can we do to make things better?"

   ❏ Option "Not Satisfied At All": Display the message "We are sorry! We will fix everything!"

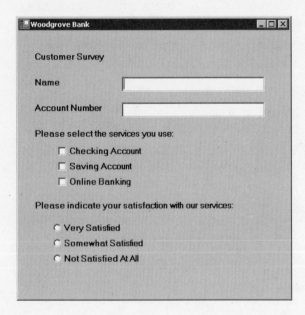

Figure 3-18   The WoodgroveBankCh3 form

JUST HINTS

Your job is to create a form for Fabrikam, Inc., that can be used to select a type of lawn equipment, the type of warranty, and the quantity desired. There should be an Order Summary button on the form that will display a message summarizing the order.

Use the following information to complete this exercise.

1. Create a new project and name it FabrikamCh3.

2. Change the name of the form and the name of the file to something more appropriate and meaningful. Then change the startup object so that it correctly refers to the new name of the form.

3. Resize the form if necessary, and add three RadioButton controls to represent the Lawn Mower, Weed Wacker, and Hedge Trimmer options. Also, add a Label control that instructs users to select the type of lawn equipment they are interested in.

4. Add a ComboBox control to display the three types of warranties that are available. Also, add a Label control that instructs users to select the warranty they want. The possible warranty types are:

   ❑ 5 Year Extended Warranty

   ❑ 3 Year Extended Warranty

   ❑ 1 Year Extended Warranty

   ❑ No additional warranty

5. Add another Label control that identifies the quantity to be ordered and a TextBox control that users will use to enter the quantity. The text box should not display anything when the form first loads.

6. Add a Button control displaying the label "Order Summary."

7. Under the Button control, add two more Label controls that will be used to display messages to the user.

8. Now you need to program the three RadioButtons to update the first Label with a message indicating what type of lawn equipment was selected. For instance, if the user clicks Lawn Mower, the message "You would like to buy a Lawn Mower" should appear at the bottom of the screen.

9. When users click Order Summary, a message should appear in the second label at the bottom of the screen that displays the warranty they selected in the combo box and the quantity they specified. See Figure 3-19 for an example of the messages that should appear.

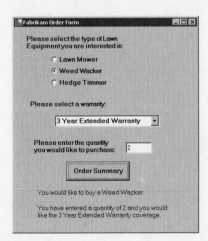

Figure 3-19   The FabrikamCh3 form showing messages

10. Run the project and test the form.

11. Save the solution.

12. Close the solution.

ON YOUR OWN

Tailspin Toys would like you to develop a games inventory update request form that their online customers can fill out and submit to request an update of the games that are in their inventory. Create a form that looks like Figure 3-20.

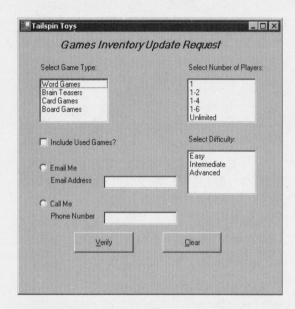

Figure 3-20   The Games Inventory Update Request form

Write code to program the Verify button to display a message that concatenates the game type selected, the number of players selected, and the difficulty selected into a message displayed at the bottom of the form, as shown in Figure 3-21. The Clear button should clear the contents of the Label and TextBox controls on the form. After you have created the project, run it, test it, save it, and close the solution.

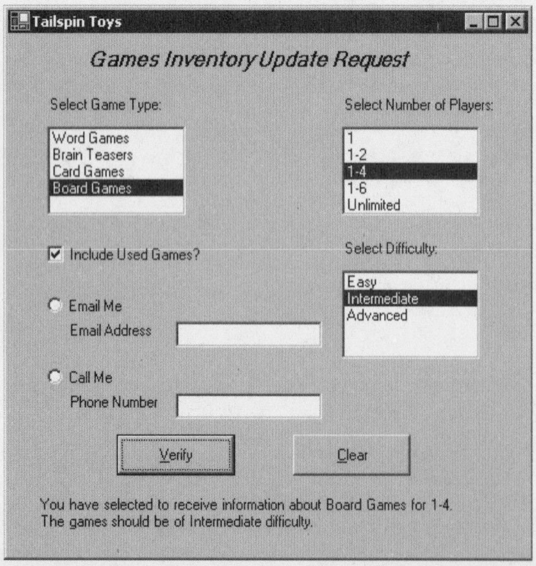

Figure 3-21   The Games Inventory Update Request form and message

MORE PRACTICE

1. Write the Visual Basic .NET statement that will display the message "Your account is overdue" in a Label control named lblAccountStatus.

2. Write the Visual Basic .NET statement that will display the message "Your sales representative's name is" followed by the contents of the txtRepName TextBox control's *Text* property in the text box called txtRepResponse.

3. Write the Visual Basic .NET statement that will add the item "Silverware" to the ListBox named lstHousewares.

4. Write the Visual Basic .NET statement that will display the item selected in the ComboBox named cboIngredients in the Label control named lblDisplayIngredients.

5. A pet boarding kennel would like you to design a form that will be used to enter a reservation for a pet that will boarding at the kennel. There should be a Cancel button and a Save button at the bottom of the form. Users should be able to enter the information dictated by the fields listed in Table 3-5 on the form. Determine the correct type of control to use for each input field.

Table 3-5 **Input Fields**

Input fields	Control
Pet Name	
Pet Type (Select one from dog, cat, bird, reptile, hamster, guinea pig, and fish.)	
Owner Name	
Emergency Phone Number	
Start Date	
Number of Days	
Feeding Instructions	
Special Needs	
Playtime (Select yes or no.)	
Medication (Select yes or no.)	

6. A beauty salon would like you to develop a Visual Basic .NET application containing a form that customers can use to sign in when they come for a haircut. The form should be attractive and display the name of the salon (make up a name) at the top. Customers should be prompted to enter the information listed in Table 3-6. There should be two buttons at the bottom of the form: Sign In and Clear. If customers click the Sign In button, a message should appear thanking them for signing in and instructing them to take a seat in the waiting area. The Sign In button should also automatically clear all input fields on the form. If the customer clicks the Clear button, all of the input fields on the form should be cleared.

Table 3-6 **Input fields**

Input fields	Control
First Name	
Adult/Child (Customer can select only one of these two options.)	
Wash/Cut/Color/Perm (Customer can select any or all of these options.)	
Preferred Stylist (Customer can select only one of the following names: Brenda, Caroline, Dave, Ellen, Frank, and Gale.)	

7. A dry cleaning shop would like you to create a form in a Visual Basic .NET application that is used by employees of the store to enter a customer's drop-off order. There should be four buttons at the bottom of the form, as described in Table 3-7, and seven input fields above these fields, as described in Table 3-8.

Table 3-7 **Buttons**

Button	Purpose
Clear	Clear the contents of all fields on the form
Next	Display the message "Item saved" and clear the contents of all fields on the form except for Name and Phone Number
Cancel	Display the message "All items will be deleted from this order" and clear the contents of all fields on the form
Save	Display the message "Order saved" and clear the contents of all fields on the form

Table 3-8 **Input Fields**

Input field	Control
Name	
Phone Number	
Clothing Item Type (Select one from Dress, Suit, Pants, Shirt, Skirt, Coat, and Other.)	
Service Required (Select one from Press Only, Dry Clean, and Hand Wash.)	
Pickup Date	
Cost	
Special Instructions	

8. Create a registration form in Visual Basic .NET that students can use to register for a class. The students should be able to enter their first name, last name, and student ID at the top of the screen. Next they should select the semester (Fall, Spring, or Summer) they are registering for. When they select a department from a list (Chemistry, Computer Science, English, Math, Other), a list of courses that department is offering should appear. The student should be able to select one course from the list. When they click the Complete button at the bottom of the form, a message should appear on the form confirming the name of the course they have registered for. Use the list of courses, categorized by department, shown in Table 3-9.

Table 3-9 **Course Information**

Chemistry	Computer Science	English	Math	Other
Chemistry I	Visual Basic I	American Literature	Calculus I	Art Appreciation
Chemistry II	Visual Basic II	Poetry Writing	Calculus II	Music
Organic Chemistry	Databases I	Writing Nonfiction	Trigonometry	Psychology
Inorganic Chemistry	Algorithm Design	Modern Literature	Geometry	Tap Dancing

CHAPTER 4

WRITING VISUAL BASIC .NET CODE

It's one thing to be able to create a professional user interface, but soon enough you actually have to write code to make the program do something useful. This is really where the "rubber meets the road." Remember that project managers manage projects, analysts analyze business processes, and programmers write code, plain and simple.

In this chapter, you will learn more about using the Code Editor and become familiar with many of the ways to code routines. We'll talk about writing various types of procedures and how to create and use variables and constants. These are all important concepts that you need to understand to start writing useful and powerful programs.

Upon completion of this chapter, you will be able to:

■ Gain more experience with using the Code Editor.

■ Learn about modules and procedures.

■ Create and use methods (Sub and Function procedures).

■ Understand what scope is and how it defines the accessibility of code elements.

■ Create variables.

■ Use operators.

TOOLS AND COMPONENTS FOR WRITING CODE

In this section, we will look at several important tools for writing code and several fundamental components of code in Microsoft Visual Basic .NET. We will consider:

- **The Code Editor**   The primary tool for writing code.

- **Modules and procedures**   Two of the fundamental components of Visual Basic .NET code.

- **Methods and their subcategories (Sub procedures and Function procedures)**   The basic unit of execution. Methods contain code that will be run when the method is called. Sub procedures do not return a value; Function procedures do return a value.

- **Scope**   The factor that determines when an object, method, or variable in your code can be seen and used by other objects, methods, or variables.

- **Event handlers**   The code that generates the appropriate response to an event.

The Code Editor

The Code Editor in Microsoft Visual Studio .NET is an extremely intelligent plain text editor. It uses IntelliSense to determine what you are typing and changes the color of the text depending on whether you have typed a keyword, a comment, or a program statement.

In the Code Editor (see Figure 4-1), keywords are blue, comments are green, and general program statements are black. You can change the colors used for the various types of statements with the Options dialog box by selecting the Environment folder and the Fonts And Colors page.

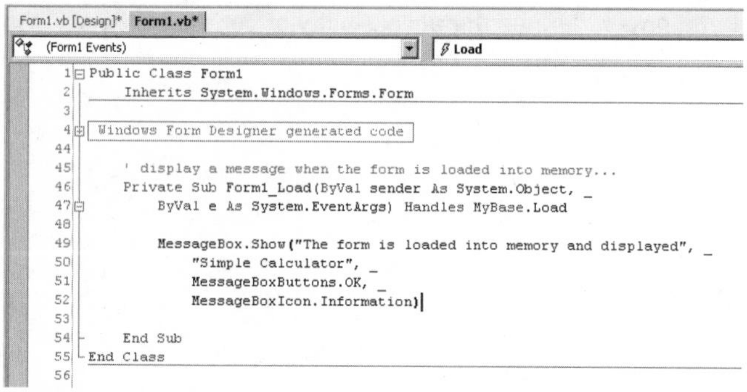

```
Form1.vb [Design]*  Form1.vb*
(Form1 Events)                              ▼  ƒ Load
  1 ⊟ Public Class Form1
  2       Inherits System.Windows.Forms.Form
  3
  4 ⊞  Windows Form Designer generated code
 44
 45       ' display a message when the form is loaded into memory...
 46       Private Sub Form1_Load(ByVal sender As System.Object, _
 47 ⊟        ByVal e As System.EventArgs) Handles MyBase.Load
 48
 49         MessageBox.Show("The form is loaded into memory and displayed", _
 50              "Simple Calculator", _
 51              MessageBoxButtons.OK, _
 52              MessageBoxIcon.Information)|
 53
 54  -    End Sub
 55  └ End Class
 56
```

Figure 4-1   The Visual Basic .NET Code Editor

Statements, Keywords, and Comments

Statements are Visual Basic .NET instructions that contain keywords, operators, variables, constants, and expressions. The default color for statements in the Code Editor is black, and they are displayed as normal text.

Keywords are language-specific words that have special meaning in Visual Basic .NET. You should never use keywords when naming controls and variables. By default, keywords are displayed in the color blue.

As you already know, any text following a single quotation mark is handled as a **comment** (unless the single quotation mark is placed inside double quotation marks). By default, words that make up comments are displayed in green in the Code Editor. Comments are used to describe your code to make it clear to the reader what the code is supposed to do. Remember that the compiler will ignore any comments in your code at run time.

Invalid Syntax

The Code Editor includes a convention for indicating invalid words or statements in your code: they are displayed with a wavy underline beneath them. Notice that in Figure 4-2 the words *The* and *form* are underlined with a wavy line. This shows you that these words are invalid in the current context. In other words, something in your code is wrong at this spot and must be fixed.

```
(Form1 Events)                                      ƒ Load
 1 ⊟ Public Class Form1
 2      Inherits System.Windows.Forms.Form
 3
 4 ⊞  Windows Form Designer generated code
44
45      ' display a message when the form is loaded into memory...
46      Private Sub Form1_Load(ByVal sender As System.Object, _
47 ⊟       ByVal e As System.EventArgs) Handles MyBase.Load
48 |
49      MessageBox.Show(The form is loaded into memory and displayed, _
50          "Simple Calculator", _
51          MessageBoxButtons.OK, _
52          MessageBoxIcon.Information)
53
54      End Sub
55 └ End Class
56
```

Figure 4-2   Invalid words and statements displayed with a wavy line underneath them

If you hover your mouse pointer over the word *The*, a brief message appears to tell you what the problem is, as shown in Figure 4-3. Well, sort of. The message actually tells you that the word *The* is not declared.

```
Form1.vb [Design]*  Form1.vb*
(Form1 Events)                                      ƒ Load
 1 ⊟ Public Class Form1
 2      Inherits System.Windows.Forms.Form
 3
 4 ⊞  Windows Form Designer generated code
44
45      ' display a message when the form is loaded into memory...
46      Private Sub Form1_Load(ByVal sender As System.Object, _
47 ⊟       ByVal e As System.EventArgs) Handles MyBase.Load
48
49      MessageBox.Show(The form is loaded into memory and displayed, _
50          "Simple Calcul  Name 'The' is not declared.
51          MessageBoxButtons.OK, _
52          MessageBoxIcon.Information)
53
54      End Sub
55 └ End Class
56
```

Figure 4-3   Hover mouse pointer over underlined word to display explanation of error

Although the explanation of the error might not be totally clear at this point, it does tell you that something is wrong and that the code must be corrected before it can be compiled.

So what's wrong with the statement? The *Show* method of the *MessageBox* class requires a text value as the first argument. Text must be placed inside double quotation marks, and we did not include the double quotation marks before and after the words *The form*. Visual Basic .NET is treating the word *The* as a variable that has not been declared. To correct the problem, place the entire line of text inside double quotation marks. The wavy lines will disappear.

Before we move on, let's look at how IntelliSense is used to make the *MessageBox* class much easier to understand and use.

MessageBox

The *MessageBox* class is used extensively in Windows applications. You will use it primarily to provide significant information to users when they navigate their way through your programs. It works very much like the *MsgBox* function that we covered in Chapter 2.

> **NOTE**   The MessageBox class is the preferred method for displaying a message box to users, and we will use it instead of the MsgBox function in the future.

Although the *MessageBox* has several methods, we are going to be using the *Show* method for our discussion. In the *Form1_Load* event handler, type the word *MessageBox* followed by a period. IntelliSense will immediately display a list of the methods available to the *MessageBox* class. Select the *Show* method by clicking it once. After the word *Show* is displayed, type an opening parenthesis, and look at the next tip that appears (Figure 4-4).

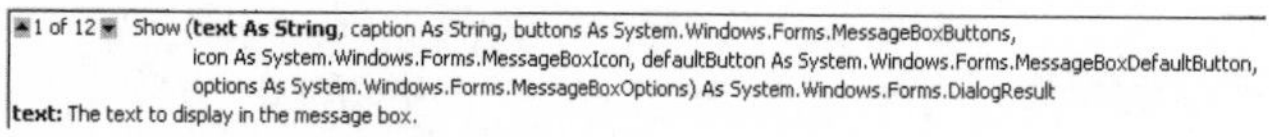

```
▲1 of 12 ▼  Show (text As String, caption As String, buttons As System.Windows.Forms.MessageBoxButtons,
            icon As System.Windows.Forms.MessageBoxIcon, defaultButton As System.Windows.Forms.MessageBoxDefaultButton,
            options As System.Windows.Forms.MessageBoxOptions) As System.Windows.Forms.DialogResult
text: The text to display in the message box.
```

Figure 4-4   The Show method IntelliSense tip

This tip provides hints about the arguments required by the *Show* method. The arguments are separated by commas, and you can see that the first and second arguments require text values. The third and fourth arguments require constants that specify the type of buttons and the type of icon that are to be displayed in the message box. The fifth and sixth arguments require constant values that specify the default button (if more than one button is displayed) and the options. The options determine whether the message box is displayed normally, whether the caption is right aligned, whether the display is from right to left, and whether it is a service notification.

This is a lot of arguments, but fortunately the only arguments that are required are those displayed in bold. So, in the case of the *MessageBox* class, you are only required to specify one argument: the text that will be displayed in the message box. The rest of the arguments are optional.

Notice, in Figure 4-5, that at the beginning of the tip there are up and down arrows and the text "1 of 12."

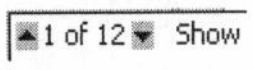

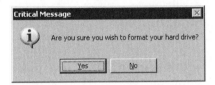

Figure 4-5   Arrows displayed in IntelliSense tip

This just tells you that you can code the *Show* method in 12 different ways by using various combinations of the available arguments. For the most part, you will use the most common way of coding this method, which is the first way.

Now that you've learned how to use the *MessageBox* class, don't go crazy with it! For the most part, users hate message boxes, especially message boxes that provide no added value to the program. Message boxes should be used whenever it is critical to the application, such as when displaying a confirmation warning before deleting a record or file. Given that, what we have demonstrated here is an example of the incorrect use of a message box. It does not provide any useful function; its only purpose here is to annoy the user. Figure 4-6 shows an example of a critical and much more useful message.

Figure 4-6   Message box with the Yes button as the default button

Notice that the Yes button is the **default button**. If the user presses Enter when the message box appears on the screen, it simulates the Yes button being clicked. Of course, you have to provide code that performs the task of formatting the hard drive when the user clicks Yes.

Modules and Procedures

Modules, sometimes referred to as *code modules*, are files that are part of the assembly. A module is simply a physical file that is stored on a disk. Each module's file name has the extension .vb when saved to disk. When coding, you can think of this file as one modular unit of code.

So far, you have worked with very simple programs that create only one file when they are compiled. This one file is known as the **application file**. Application files are executable files that have the file name extension .exe. More complex programs can consist of many files.

Several types of modules are used in Visual Basic .NET:

- **Class module** A class module is used to create objects. We will be covering class modules in Chapter 13.

- **Form module** A form module is a special type of class module that has a visual interface. This interface enables users to interact with the application. A form module will contain code applicable to a form. Each form in your project will have its own form module.

- **Module** A module, sometimes referred to as a *base module* or a *standard module*, can be used to code common routines that are typically global (available to the entire application). A module can also be used as the main entry point for an application. Back in Chapter 1, you used a module when you created the HelloWorldConsole application. Modules are not linked to any particular form; they contain code that can be used just about anywhere in the project.

All of these types of files have the .vb extension at the end of their names, so there might be some initial confusion as to which file is which, but you will get used to it. To make things a little simpler, the word *module* will always refer to a base module, the word *class* will always refer to a class module, and the word *form* will always refer to a form module.

All of these files are very much alike, which is why Microsoft decided to give them all the same file extension. If you open up the HelloWorldConsole program, you will see that the module contains the code shown in Figure 4-7.

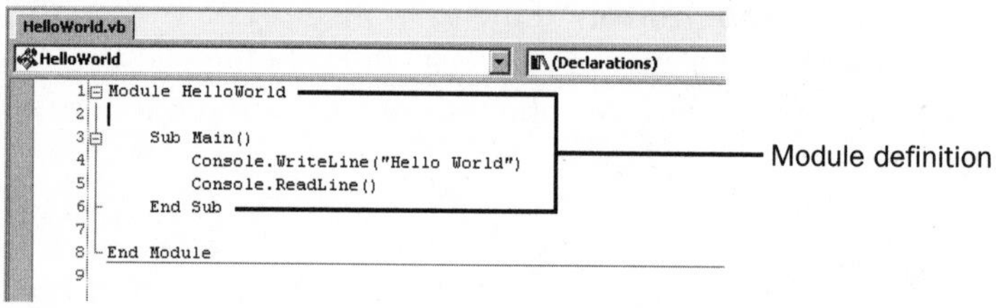

Figure 4-7　The HelloWorldConsole code module

If you open the HelloWorldWindows program, as shown in Figure 4-8, you can see the difference in the definition.

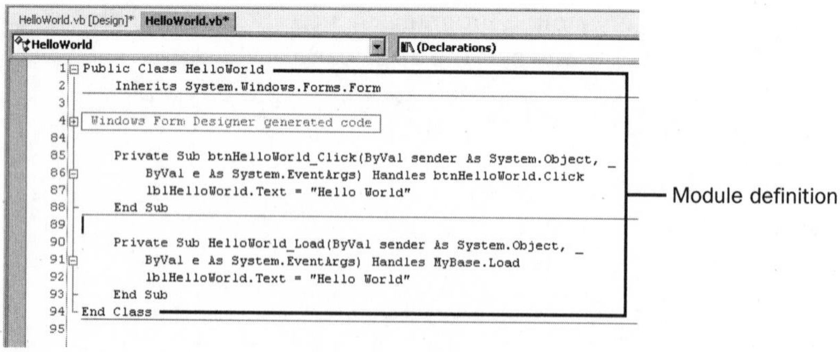

Figure 4-8　The HelloWorldWindows code module

As you can see when you compare a standard module to a form module, both permit the writing of code. The difference is that the form module is also a class that is associated with a designer and, as such, has a *design time* visual interface that can be opened, viewed, and worked on in Visual Studio .NET.

Procedures are the smallest units of executable code in Visual Basic .NET. Procedures are run to provide functionality to your program. In this chapter we will be looking at two types of procedures: *Sub* and *Function procedures*. Sub and Function procedures are referred to as *methods* and are used to run code. The difference between them is that a Sub procedure runs code but does not return a value when it is called, whereas a Function procedure runs code and will return a value when it is called.

A procedure is used to run one or more code statements when that procedure is called. Procedures can be called by code statements inside other procedures. In this section, we will be discussing special Sub procedures known as **event handlers**, and then we will move on to discuss other uses of Sub and Function procedures.

Creating and Using Methods (Sub and Function Procedures)

Look at the Code Editor in Figure 4-9. Notice the tabs at the top of the window. When you are in tabbed view you can have multiple windows available to you. Each tab represents either a code module or a forms designer window. Below the tabs, there are two list boxes. The list box on the left side is called the Class Name list box, and it contains a list of all the classes (objects and controls) that you are currently using in your application. You haven't added any controls to this form yet, so you only see Form1 in the list, in addition to three other items: (General), (Overrides), and (Form1 Events). In this chapter we will be working with procedures listed under Form1 and (Form1 Events).

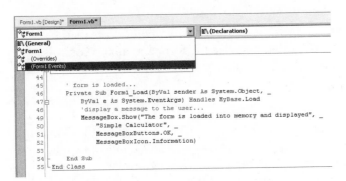

Figure 4-9   The Class Name list in the Code Editor

The list box on the right side is called Method Name (Figure 4-10), and, as you might guess, this list shows all the methods available for the currently selected class.

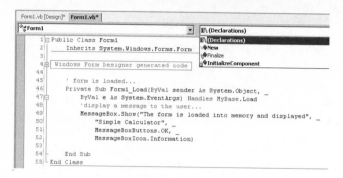

Figure 4-10   The Method Name list in the Code Editor

Let's take a look at the methods that are already included in the form when you create a new Microsoft Windows application. When you select Form1 in the Class Name list and then click the Method Name list, you can see the following methods in the list:

- **New.**   The *New* method is called a *constructor*. Every class has a constructor method. When a form class is instantiated—meaning that the form is loaded into memory—its constructor is called and any code inside the constructor is run at that time. Notice that this item appears in boldface type. This tells you that the method is already included in the form's code module.

- **Finalize.**   The *Finalize* method is called when the form is disposed. A form is disposed when it is no longer needed and it is ready to be destroyed. This item does not appear in boldface type, which means that it has not been included in the form's code module.

- **Initialize Component.**   The *Initialize Component* method is called from the constructor and is used to initialize the form and all the controls that are added to the form. This item also appears in boldface.

Where are these methods? They generally are not touched by the programmer and as such are hidden inside a collapsible code area known as a *code region*. This particular region is created for you by Visual Studio .NET and is called the *Windows Form Designer–generated code*. Open the Code Editor of any Windows application and click the (+) sign next to that region directive. The region will expand and enable you to see the code that has been placed there. After you have finished browsing, click the (–) sign to collapse the region.

Event Handler

An event handler is a special Sub procedure that is linked to an event. When the event is raised, the code inside the event handler runs. An event is raised when something significant occurs in the program. For example, if the user clicks a button on the form, the button's *Click* event is raised. If the event handler associated with that event is included in the code form's code module, the code inside that event handler will run.

You saw this in Chapter 1 when you created the HelloWorldWindows program, and you saw it again in Chapter 3 when you created the UsingControls program. Although an event handler is a Sub procedure, we generally do not refer to them as such to avoid confusing them with regular Sub procedures. We will be discussing regular Sub procedures next.

In the example in Figure 4-11, the form's *Load* event handler has been coded. The *Load* event is raised when the form is loaded into memory and the form is displayed. In this event handler, we are running code that will display a message box to the user. Although this might not be a practical use of the *Load* event, it shows how code runs when an event is raised. Figure 4-11 also shows some of the events associated with the *Form* class. To display the list of events, select (Form1_Events) in the Class Name list and then click the Method Name list.

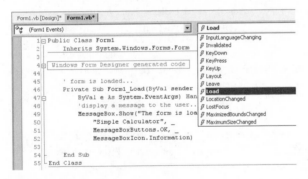

Figure 4-11   The Method Name list

Sub Procedure

A **Sub procedure** is a method that runs one or more code statements and does not return a value to the calling statement. The following is an example of a Sub procedure:

```
Private Sub NameOfSubProcedure()
```

A Sub procedure cannot run on its own; it must be *called* from another procedure. Taking our current example, we can call a Sub procedure from the *Form1_Load* event handler, as shown in Figure 4-12.

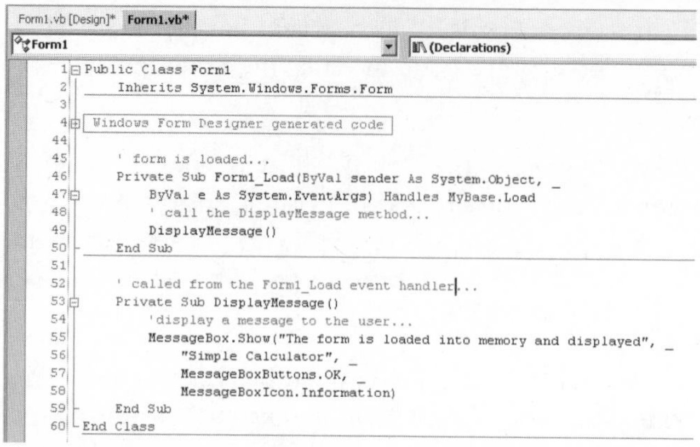

```
Form1.vb [Design]*   Form1.vb*
Form1                                              (Declarations)
 1  Public Class Form1
 2      Inherits System.Windows.Forms.Form
 3
 4      Windows Form Designer generated code
44
45      ' form is loaded...
46      Private Sub Form1_Load(ByVal sender As System.Object, _
47          ByVal e As System.EventArgs) Handles MyBase.Load
48          ' call the DisplayMessage method...
49          DisplayMessage()
50      End Sub
51
52      ' called from the Form1_Load event handler...
53      Private Sub DisplayMessage()
54          'display a message to the user...
55          MessageBox.Show("The form is loaded into memory and displayed", _
56              "Simple Calculator", _
57              MessageBoxButtons.OK, _
58              MessageBoxIcon.Information)
59      End Sub
60  End Class
```

Figure 4-12   Calling a procedure named DisplayMessage

Let's look at the steps required to create a Sub procedure.

▶ **Creating a Sub procedure**

1. Click anywhere inside the class declaration area below the Windows Form Designer–generated code region (but not inside any existing procedure).

2. Type the following line of code and then press ENTER. You will notice that the End Sub is automatically added for you.

   ```
   Private Sub DisplayMessage()
   ```

3. Now you can type the code that you want to be executed between the Private Sub DisplayMessage() and End Sub lines of code. This code will run whenever the *DisplayMessage* procedure is called.

Function Procedure

A **Function procedure** is a method that runs one or more code statements and returns a value. The value that is returned to the calling code statement must have a return data type. What this means is that you must declare the data type when you create the Function procedure. The following is an example of a Function procedure:

```
Private Function NameOfFunctionProcedure() As DataType
```

For example, if the function is designed to return a text value, the return type would be *String*. If the function is designed to return a whole number, the return type would be *Integer*.

Like general procedures, Function procedures cannot run by themselves. They must be called from another procedure. The process of creating a Function procedure is called a **declaration**. You must declare the procedure in the Code Editor, just as you would for a Sub procedure, but replace the word Sub with the word Function.

Let's look at the steps required to create a Function procedure.

▶ Creating a Function procedure

1. Click anywhere inside the class declaration area below the Windows Form Designer–generated code region (but not inside any existing procedure).

2. Type the following line of code and then press ENTER. This time you will notice that End Function, rather than End Sub, *is automatically added*.

```
Private Function GetMessage() As String
```

You replaced the word Sub with the word Function, but you also changed the name of the procedure and added the words As String at the end of the declaration. Why did you need to that? Well, for this procedure you are going to return the message that will be displayed in the message box. The name of the procedure should reflect what it is going to do. Because it is *getting a message* rather than *displaying a message*, it is appropriate to change the name. The addition of As String to the end of the declaration tells the compiler what type of value you are returning. Figure 4-13 shows how this was implemented.

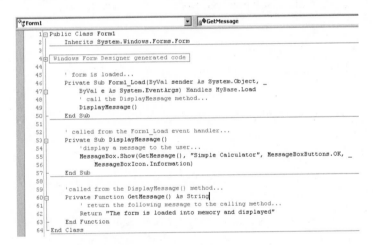

```
 1  Public Class Form1
 2      Inherits System.Windows.Forms.Form
 3
 4      Windows Form Designer generated code
44
45      ' form is loaded...
46      Private Sub Form1_Load(ByVal sender As System.Object, _
47          ByVal e As System.EventArgs) Handles MyBase.Load
48          ' call the DisplayMessage method...
49          DisplayMessage()
50      End Sub
51
52      ' called from the Form1_Load event handler...
53      Private Sub DisplayMessage()
54          'display a message to the user...
55          MessageBox.Show(GetMessage(), "Simple Calculator", MessageBoxButtons.OK, _
56              MessageBoxIcon.Information)
57      End Sub
58
59      'called from the DisplayMessage() method...
60      Private Function GetMessage() As String
61          ' return the following message to the calling method...
62          Return "The form is loaded into memory and displayed"
63      End Function
64  End Class
```

Figure 4-13   The *GetMessage* function

There are a few things that we did here that you need to be aware of:

■ The *MessageBox.Show* method calls the *GetMessage* function to retrieve the string that will be displayed in the message box. In other words, *GetMessage* is being used as the first argument for the *MessageBox.Show* method. When the *MessageBox.Show* method runs, the first thing it will do is call the *GetMessage* function. When the call is completed, *GetMessage* will hold the value that was returned.

■ The *GetMessage* function uses the *Return* keyword to return the value to the calling statement, which is the *MessageBox.Show* method.

■ The *GetMessage* function uses the return type *String*, which informs the compiler what type of value is being returned.

Scope: Public or Private

Scope determines whether an object, method, or variable can be accessed by other objects, methods, or variables. (Variables will be discussed a little later in this chapter.)

So far in our example, you have seen that the scope of the class definition for the form is public, but the method declarations are private. In this case, an external object or program can reference the form but would not be able to refer to any of the methods.

Why would you want to make anything private? That's a good question, but a better one is, "Why would I want to make anything public?" Scoping is used to determine the access level of an object. The more you restrict access to an object, the more secure it is and the easier it will be to control what's going on in your program. You should only expand the access level when you really have a good reason to do so.

Although you have seen only two levels of scope (access), there are actually five levels of scope that can be used:

- **Public** Accessible to any object or process that can reference the current class or process

- **Private** Accessible only to the current class

- **Protected** Accessible to the current class and any class that inherits from the current class

- **Friend** Accessible to the class and any other file in the assembly

- **Protected Friend** Accessible to the current class, any other file in the assembly, and any class that inherits from the current class

Implementing Event Handlers

Although we have talked about events already, it is worth reviewing them before we dive into event handlers. Events occur or are raised when something happens to an object. For example, a car has a *Crash* event that is raised when you don't pay attention and run into another car. The car might also have a *Stopped* event that is raised along with the *Crash* event. There might come a time when you want to raise the *Stopped* event without running the *Crash* event. This can be done by running the *Stop* method of the Car object.

Events are created by component developers and are *raised* when something significant happens to the object. (We use the word *raise* rather than *fire* because the word *fire* implies that there is code to handle the event.) In the case of a button on a form, the significant action that occurs could be the clicking of the button (*Button1_Click*) or the movement of the mouse over the button (*Button1_MouseEnter*, *Button1_MouseMove*, or *Button1_MouseLeave*).

If you don't provide implementation code, the event is still raised, but nothing will happen. Consider the following example, which might help to explain this further. Have you ever been to a supermarket and heard a special announcement over an intercom? Did you decide to rush to the aisle and purchase the product, or did you make a conscious decision not to purchase it? If you did either, you *handled* the event. If you ignored the announcement completely, you didn't handle the event and the announcement was wasted on you.

To implement an event handler, you take advantage of the fact that the event was raised. When a button is clicked, you can provide code in the *Button1_Click* event handler that will run in response to the event.

Each object (each form or control) has what is known as a **default event**. This event is typically the one that is most commonly used among all of the events that can be raised by that object or control. For example, a form's default event is the *Load* event, and a button's default event is the *Click* event. Double-clicking the control in the design window will automatically take you to the Code Editor and create the wrapper lines of the default event handler for you. Then all you have to do is add the code you want to run.

If you want to code the event handler for any event other than the default event, switch to the Code Editor, select the control from the Class Name list on the left, and then select the event from the Method Name list on the right. After you select the event (the method), the event handler for that event will be created in the Code Editor.

Try It

Let's create a quick project with a Button control that calls the *MessageBox* class.

1. Create a new project in Visual Studio .NET that is a Visual Basic .NET Windows application.

2. Name the project **Ch4MessageBox**.

3. Add a Button control to the form. Change the (*Name*) property of the Button control to **btnMessage**, and change the *Text* property to **Click for Message**.

4. Double-click the button to open the *btnMessage_Click* event handler.

5. Type the following line of code in the event handler:

```
MessageBox.Show("Do you like programming?","My First Message Box", _
    MessageBoxButtons.YesNo)
```

6. Run the program, and click the button to test the code.

What Do You Think?

1. What is the difference between a statement and a keyword?

2. How does the Code Editor let you know that you typed an invalid word or statement in your code?

3. What types of modules are available in Visual Basic .NET?

4. What are declaration statements used for?

5. How are Sub procedures and Function procedures different, and how are they the same?

6. What types of scope are available in Visual Basic .NET?

7. What do we mean by the *default event* for an object?

VARIABLES AND OPERATORS

Nearly every program you write will require the declaration of variables to hold pieces of information that are used in the program. You are also likely to use operators in mathematical expressions at some point in your programming career. This section includes a discussion of variables and operators and presents a coding example that uses variables and operators in addition to the other coding components introduced in this chapter.

Variables

Visual Basic .NET, like most programming languages, uses variables for the temporary storage of values. A **variable** is simply a temporary location in memory that is used to store a piece of data or a reference. Virtually every program you write will require the use of variables, so it is important that you understand how and where to declare variables.

Each variable you want to use in your program must be defined with a name and a data type.

- **Variable name**   The word or identifier you use to refer to the piece of data the variable will be storing

- **Variable data type**   The type of data the variable can store (string or number, for example)

Rules for Naming Variables

The name you assign to a variable should be meaningful and represent the values stored in that variable. There are a couple of basic rules that must be followed when determining the name of a variable:

- All variables names must start with a letter or the underscore character

- Variable names cannot exceed 255 characters

Typically, the first three characters of the variable name are lowercase and indicate the data type assigned to that variable. This notation is known as *Modified Hungarian Notation*. We discussed this convention in previous chapters when you were naming your forms and controls. Although this convention isn't required, it makes the code easier to read and understand. Additionally, some programmers like to precede the data type prefix with another lowercase character to represent the scope when declaring module-level or global variables.

For example, a variable declared inside a procedure would have local scope (accessible only to code within the procedure) and would be declared like this:

```
Dim strName As String
```

A variable declared at the modular level (outside a procedure) would have scope throughout the code module (accessible to any code in the module) and would be declared like this:

```
Private m_strName As String
```

A variable declared at the global level (accessible to any code in the project) would be declared like this:

```
Public g_strName As String
```

Primitive Types

Primitive data types (usually referred to as *Primitives*) are the basic data types used by most programming languages. Table 4-1 shows the primitive data types used in Visual Basic .NET. Note the Prefix column. These are the suggested prefixes to use when declaring variables of each type.

Table 4-1   **Primitive Data Types Used in Visual Basic .NET**

Data type	Size (in bytes)	Value range	System mapping	Prefix
Byte	1	0 to 255	*System.Byte*	byt
Short	2	–32,768 to 32,767	*System.Int16*	sht
Integer	4	–2,147,483,648 to 2,147,483,647	*System.Int32*	int
Long	8	–9,223,372,036,854,775,808 to 9,223,372,036,854,775,808	*System.Int64*	lng
Single	4	–3.402823E38 to –1.401298E–45 for negative values; 1.401298E–45 to 3.402823E38 for positive values	*System.Single*	sng
Double	8	–1.79,769,313486,231E308 to –4.940,656,458,441,247E–324 for negative values; 4.940,656,458,441,247E–324 to 1.79,769,313,486,231E308 for positive values	*System.Double*	dbl

Table 4-1   **Primitive Data Types Used in Visual Basic .NET (Continued)**

Data type	Size (in bytes)	Value range	System mapping	Prefix
Decimal	12	+/–79,228,162,154,264,337,593, 543,950,335 with no decimal point; +/–79,228,162,154,264,337,593, 543,950,335 with 28 places to the right of the decimal point	System.Decimal	dec
Boolean	4	True or False	System.Boolean	bln
Date	8	January 1,1 to December 31, 9999	System.DateTime	dte
Char	2	0 to 65,535	System.Char	chr
String	10 + (2 * string length)	0 to approximately 2 billion Unicode characters	System.String	str

Scoping of Variables

Each variable that you declare will have scope (accessibility). Variables are declared with one of four possible levels of scope, as shown in Table 4-2.

Table 4-2   **Variable Scopes**

Scope modifier	Scope	Declaration location
Public	Global. Accessible to any module or program that can reference the current module.	At the module level
Private	Module/Class. Accessible only to other code in the module in which the variable is declared.	At the module level
Dim	Local/Procedure. Accessible only to code inside the procedure in which the variable is declared. Additionally, the variable must be declared before any other code within the procedure can refer to it.	At the procedural level
Dim	Local/Block. Accessible only to code within the block of code in which the variable is declared. Additionally, the variable must be declared before any other code within the procedure can refer to it.	At the block level

Examples of Variable Declarations

With that said, let's look at a few examples in Table 4-3 to explain the declaration of variables a bit better.

Table 4-3   **Variable Declaration Examples**

Variable declaration	Allowed or not allowed?
`Dim strFirstName As String`	Allowed. Using the Hungarian Notation as a prefix is an acceptable coding convention.
`Dim _name As String`	Allowed. Not widely used.
`Dim 2number As Integer`	Not allowed. The name cannot start with a number.
`Dim @Date As Date`	Not allowed. The name cannot start with an @ symbol.
`Private m_intNumber As Integer`	Allowed. The m_ prefix along with the data type prefix helps to clarify the declaration by showing that it is declared at the modular level.
`Dim strFN As String`	Allowed. Not recommended because the intended use of the data is not clear.
`Public g_intNumber As Integer`	Allowed. The g_ prefix is generally used when declaring global variables.

Initializing Variables

You can declare variables without explicitly initializing them. Although you can assign an initial value to a variable when it is declared, it is not required. The following two declarations are both valid in Visual Basic .NET:

```
' This variable is explicitly initialized with the value of 0
Dim intNumber As Integer = 0

' This variable is implicitly initialized
Dim intNumber As Integer
```

When a variable is declared, Visual Basic .NET takes care of initialization and provides a default value. The default value for a numeric type is always *0*; the default value for a string type is a *null* reference; the default value for a Boolean type is *False*; and the default value for the date type is *1/1/0001 12:00:00 AM*.

It is nice to be able to see the default, minimum, and maximum values for various variable types. In the next example, we have created a console application that will display all of these values. Create a new Visual Basic .NET project as a console application (you can accept the default project name), using the same process you used in Chapter 1. Replace the generated code with the code shown here, and run the application when you are finished.

```
Module Module1
    Sub Main()
        ' Declare a variable of type Byte and display its default,
        ' minimum, and maximum values...
        Dim bytNumber As Byte
        Console.WriteLine("The default value for a Byte is {0}", _
            bytNumber.ToString())
        Console.WriteLine("The minimum value for a Byte is {0}", _
            bytNumber.MinValue.ToString())
        Console.WriteLine("The maximum value for a Byte is {0}", _
            bytNumber.MaxValue.ToString())
```

```vbnet
' Declare a variable of type Short and display its default,
' minimum, and maximum values...
Dim shtNumber As Short
Console.WriteLine("The default value for a Short is {0}", _
    shtNumber.ToString())
Console.WriteLine("The minimum value for a Short is {0}", _
    shtNumber.MinValue.ToString())
Console.WriteLine("The maximum value for a Short is {0}", _
    shtNumber.MaxValue.ToString())

' Declare a variable of type Integer and display its default,
' minimum, and maximum values...
Dim intNumber As Integer
Console.WriteLine("The default value for an Integer is {0}", _
    intNumber.ToString())
Console.WriteLine("The minimum value for an Integer is {0}", _
    intNumber.MinValue.ToString())
Console.WriteLine("The maximum value for an Integer is {0}", _
    intNumber.MaxValue.ToString())

' Declare a variable of type Long and display its default,
' minimum, and maximum values...
Dim lngNumber As Long
Console.WriteLine("The default value for a Long is {0}", _
    lngNumber.ToString())
Console.WriteLine("The minimum value for a Long is {0}", _
    lngNumber.MinValue.ToString())
Console.WriteLine("The maximum value for a Long is {0}", _
    lngNumber.MaxValue.ToString())
' Declare a variable of type Single and display its default,
' minimum, and maximum values...
Dim sngNumber As Single
Console.WriteLine("The default value for a Single is {0}", _
    sngNumber.ToString())
Console.WriteLine("The minimum value for a Single is {0}", _
    sngNumber.MinValue.ToString())
Console.WriteLine("The maximum value for a Single is {0}", _
    sngNumber.MaxValue.ToString())

' Declare a variable of type Double and display its default,
' minimum, and maximum values...
Dim dblNumber As Double
Console.WriteLine("The default value for a Double is {0}", _
    dblNumber.ToString())
Console.WriteLine("The minimum value for a Double is {0}", _
    dblNumber.MinValue.ToString())
Console.WriteLine("The maximum value for a Double is {0}", _
    dblNumber.MaxValue.ToString())

' Declare a variable of type Decimal and display its default,
' minimum, and maximum values...
Dim decNumber As Decimal
Console.WriteLine("The default value for a Decimal is {0}", _
    decNumber.ToString())
Console.WriteLine("The minimum value for a Decimal is {0}", _
    decNumber.MinValue.ToString())
Console.WriteLine("The maximum value for a Decimal is {0}", _
    decNumber.MaxValue.ToString())

' Declare a variable of type Boolean and display its default value...
Dim blnChar As Boolean
Console.WriteLine("The default value for a Boolean is {0}", _
    blnChar.ToString())
```

```
                      ' Declare a variable of type Date and display it's default,
                      ' minimum, and maximum values...
                      Dim dteDate As Date
                      Console.WriteLine("The default value for a Date is {0}", _
                           dteDate.ToString)
                      Console.WriteLine("The minimum value for a Date is {0}", _
                           dteDate.MinValue.ToString())
                      Console.WriteLine("The maximum value for a Date is {0}", _
                           dteDate.MaxValue.ToString())

                      ' Declare a variable of type Char and display it's default value...
                      Dim chrString As Char
                      Console.WriteLine("The default value for a Char is {0}", _
                           chrString.ToString())

                      ' Verify that the default value of chrString is equal to
                      ' a similar variable explicitly initialized to ChrW(0)...
                      Dim chrInitialized As Char = ChrW(0)
                      Console.WriteLine("The default value for chrString " & _
                           "is equal to ChrW(0) : {0}", _
                               chrString.ToString().Equals(chrInitialized.ToString()))

                      ' Declare a variable of type String and display it's default value...
                      Dim strName As String
                      Console.WriteLine("The default value for a String is {0}", strName)
                      Console.ReadLine()
                  End Sub
              End Module
```

The results from the execution of this code are displayed in a console, as shown in Figure 4-14.

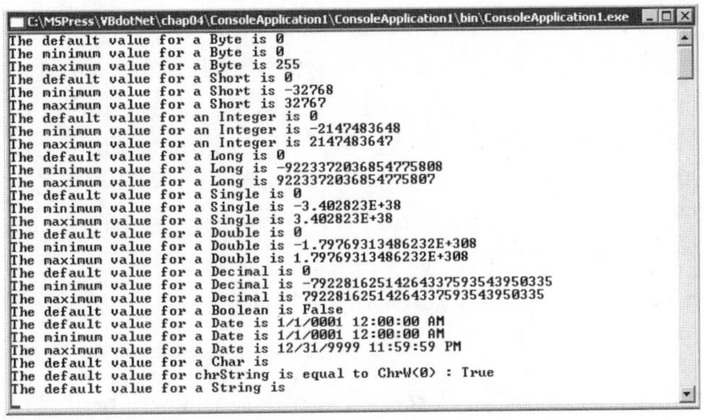

Figure 4-14   Output of the ConsoleApplication1 program

As you can see from Figure 4-14, the default, minimum, and maximum values are retrieved. Notice that you don't see any values for *Char* and *String*. Actually, there is a value for *Char*, but you can't see it. You could demonstrate the presence of the default value by checking its length, which is 1. The *String* variable has not been explicitly initialized, so its default value will be a *null* reference. This is not visible in the output either. Attempting to use any of the *String* variable's methods will result in an Unhandled Exception Of Type Null Reference, which really means that, although the space in memory is reserved for the variable, the initialized default value was set to *null*, as shown in Figure 4-15.

You can cause this exception to occur (in other words, *throw* this exception) by modifying the code just a little. Locate the following line of code:

```
Console.WriteLine("The default value for a String is {0}", strName)
```

Now add the *ToString* method to the end of *strName* so that the code looks like this:

```
Console.WriteLine("The default value for a String is {0}", strName.ToString())
```

Now run the program again to see the results. Click the Continue button to close the program.

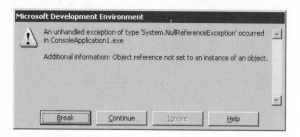

Figure 4-15   Error Message Box received when using a variable initialized to *null*

Why did you get the exception when you added the *ToString* method and not when you left it off? The answer is really not so simple, and this explanation should help you to understand what happened.

A *String* variable doesn't actually hold the value that you assign to it. Instead, it holds a reference to the value. A string can be any size from a single character to up to 2 billion characters. As such, you need a memory location large enough to handle that amount of data. When you assign a value to a *String* variable, a reference pointing to the location in memory where the actual value is stored is placed in the variable. As we explained earlier, the default value for a *String* variable is a *null* reference. If you attempt to explicitly convert a null reference to an actual string by using the *ToString* method, an exception is thrown because there is no value to convert. When you omitted the *ToString* method, there was no exception thrown because you just asked it to return the contents of the variable, which was *null*.

In Figure 4-15, you can see that the Unhandled Exception message is quite informative because, in addition to telling you the file and the module and procedure from which the exception was thrown, it also tells you the line number of the line of code that threw the exception. If this looks a little odd to you, don't worry because we will be covering *structured exception handling* in Chapter 5.

In the previous code sample, we used syntax that might look a little strange. Let's take one line of code as an example and explain it in detail:

```
Console.WriteLine("The default value for a Byte is {0}", bytNumber.ToString())
```

You already know a little bit about the *Console* class and the *WriteLine* method. You also know that the *WriteLine* method requires an argument—the text that will be displayed in the console window—but what is the {0} for, and why is there a second argument?

The {0} (zero surrounded by curly-braces) is called a **placeholder**, and it will be used to display the value provided in the trailing argument. Placeholders start at 0 (zero) and continue for as many trailing arguments as you want to insert. For example, you could use placeholders in a string to display the words *Visual Basic .NET* like this:

```
Console.WriteLine("The language we are using is {0} {1} {2}", _
    "Visual", "Basic", ".NET")
```

In this example, there are three placeholders and three trailing arguments. Running this code will yield the results shown in Figure 4-16.

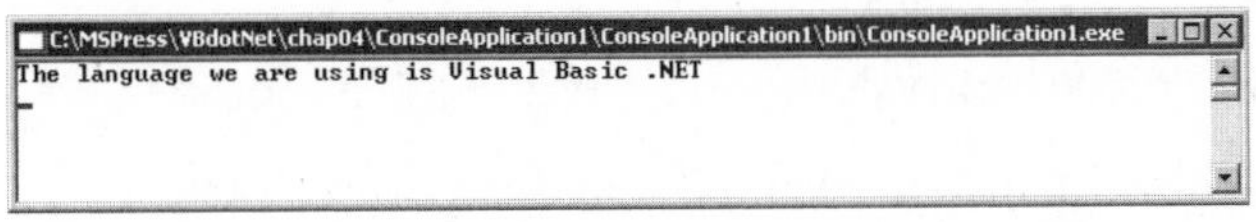

```
C:\MSPress\VBdotNet\chap04\ConsoleApplication1\ConsoleApplication1\bin\ConsoleApplication1.exe
The language we are using is Visual Basic .NET
```

Figure 4-16   Output from the three-placeholder *WriteLine* method

There is one last thing to explain here and to keep in mind when you are coding. You added the *ToString* method at the end of the *bytNumber* variable (following the period). Although this is not always necessary (the number will be implicitly converted to a string by default), it is more professional because you are explicitly telling the compiler that you want to convert the value inside the variable into a string.

Scope Modifiers: When to Use *Public*, *Private*, or *Dim*

In most cases, the scope modifier *Dim* is the same as *Private*, and Visual Basic .NET allows you to use these two modifiers interchangeably when declaring a module-level variable. However, when declaring a variable inside a procedure, the use of the modifier *Private* is not allowed. Notice that in the code you ran earlier, all of the variables are declared using the scope modifier *Dim*. The use of *Dim* is required in this case because all of the variables are declared inside a procedure (*Sub Main*).

Many developers use the scope modifier *Dim* when declaring all variables (except variables that are required to be public). You will find many books and references using this same convention. In this textbook, we will use *Dim* only when declaring variables inside procedures or code blocks. We will use the scope modifier *Private* for all module-level variables. This makes the declarations in the code clearer and more professional.

Variables That Are Constant

This sounds like an oxymoron. How can anything that is variable be constant? If we define the word *variable* as *a temporary storage space in memory*, a **constant** can be defined as a variable. The difference here is that a constant is declared by the keyword *Const*. In addition, a constant must be explicitly initialized with a value when it is declared. Let's look at an example:

```
Private Const m_strTITLE As String = "My Application"
```

You can see in the above declaration that the constant is declared using the scope modifier *Private* in addition to the *Const* keyword, and that it is initialized to "My Application". Notice that the name portion of the constant is uppercase. This is a standard programming convention. Additionally, in most cases programmers will omit the prefix that denotes the scope and data type when declaring a constant. For example, when a prefix is not used, the name of the constant would be TITLE.

After a constant is declared, its value cannot be changed anywhere in your code. If the value of a constant could be changed, it wouldn't be *constant*, would it?

Following are the important rules for declaring constants:

- Like variables, constant names must start with a letter or the underscore character.

- Constant names cannot exceed 255 characters.

- When declaring a constant inside a procedure, do not include a modifier.

- When declaring a module-level constant, use the *Private* modifier. The use of *Dim* is not allowed.

Operators

Like variables, operators are used everywhere in programs. Operators perform important roles in all applications, from simple assignment to complex mathematical equations. You will use operators when building expressions, performing calculations, and assigning and comparing values. You have already used one such operator many times: the equals (=) operator. You used this operator when you assigned values to properties and variables. Table 4-4 lists the most common operators available in Visual Basic .NET.

Table 4-4   **Visual Basic .NET Operators**

Arithmetic operator	Description
+	Addition
–	Subtraction
*	Multiplication
/	Division
\	Integer division (returns whole numbers only)
Mod	Modulus (returns the remainder from a division)
^	Exponentiation (raising to a power)
Concatenation operator	**Description**
&	String concatenation
Comparison operator	**Description**
=	Equal to (also used as the assignment operator for variables and properties)
<>	Not equal to
<	Less than
>	Greater than
<=	Less than or equal to
>=	Greater than or equal to

> **NOTE**   Visual Basic .NET allows the use of the + operator for string concatenation, but this is generally viewed as poor programming. For string concatenation, use the & (ampersand) operator.

Operator Precedence

When an expression, such as a mathematical computation, includes the use of multiple operators, an order of precedence dictates which part of the expression is dealt with first. Table 4-5 shows the order of precedence for each of the aforementioned operators. When two operators have equal precedence, the order of operation occurs from left to right. For example, if we were to calculate the following mathematical expression, what do you think the result would be?

```
2 + 4 * 2 / 4 ^ 2
```

If you knew nothing about precedence, you might guess that the result is 9, but you would be wrong. The actual answer is 2.5. How did we figure that out? The simplest way is to look at each of the operators and see which ones have the highest precedence. After you have done that, you can complete the calculation. Following is the expression rewritten with parentheses to show you how it is really being calculated, according to the rules of precedence.

```
2 + ((4 * 2) / (4 ^ 2))
```

Because the exponent operator has the highest precedence, $4 ^ 2$ is calculated first. The answer to that part is of course 16. Next, the multiplication (4 * 2) is performed, and that result is 8. Remember that multiplication and division have the same precedence, so the calculations are performed from left to right. Next, you divide the result of the multiplication by the result of the exponentiation, the result of which is .5. Finally, you add 2 to get the result.

Table 4-5   Operator Order of Precedence

Order	Operator type	Operator symbols
1	Exponentiation	^
2	Multiplicative	×, /
3	Integer division	\
4	Modulus	*Mod*
5	Additive	+, -
6	Concatenation	&
7	Comparison	=, <>, <, >, <=, >=

You can also use parentheses in expressions to determine the order of operations. All operations inside parentheses are always processed first, although the order of precedence described in Table 4-5 still applies to whatever is inside the parentheses. In practice, many programmers vaguely remember the order of precedence and will not bother to look it up. For this reason, they generally use parentheses to ensure that their calculations are performed correctly. Also, when you use parentheses, the expression is often easier to read and understand.

A Simple Calculator

The following program will help you understand the use of variables and operators. The finished form is shown in Figure 4-17.

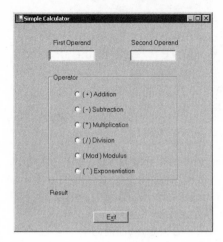

Figure 4-17   The completed Simple Calculator form

▶ **Creating the Simple Calculator form**

1. Open Visual Studio .NET.

2. On the Start Page, click the New Project button. If the Start Page is not visible, on the File menu, point to New and then select Project.

3. Name the project **Simple Calculator**.

4. Select Form1 in Solution Explorer and then change the File Name in the Properties window to **Calculator**.

5. Select the form in the designer window and change the *(Name)* property of the form to **frmCalculator**.

6. After you have changed the name of the form, don't forget to also change the startup object in the Project Properties window.

7. Before adding the controls, set the font size for the form to 10 points. After this is done, all the controls that you add to the form will default to 10 points.

8. Add all the controls listed in the first column of Table 4-6 to the form. Set the *(Name)* and *Text* properties for each control as specified in Table 4-6.

Table 4-6   **Simple Calculator Controls and Properties**

Control type	(Name)	Text
Label	Label1	**First Operand**
Label	Label2	**Second Operand**
TextBox	**TxtFirstOperand**	\<blank\>
TextBox	**TxtSecondOperand**	\<blank\>

Table 4-6 **Simple Calculator Controls and Properties**

Control type	(Name)	Text
GroupBox	**GrpOperator**	**Operator**
RadioButton	**RadAddition**	**(+) Addition**
RadioButton	**RadSubtraction**	**(-) Subtraction**
RadioButton	**RadMultiplication**	**(*) Multiplication**
RadioButton	**RadDivision**	**(/) Division**
RadioButton	**RadModulus**	**(Mod) Modulus**
RadioButton	**RadExponentiation**	**(^) Exponentiation**
Label	Label3	**Result**
Label	**LblResult**	<blank>
Button	**btnExit**	**E&xit**

9. Align and size the controls so that the form looks like Figure 4-17.

10. After the controls are in the proper places, you can lock their positions down by clicking the Format menu and then selecting Lock Controls.

Coding a Simple Calculator

Now that you have finished with the GUI design, it is time to write Visual Basic .NET code that will make the form act like a calculator. To help you with coding, let's talk briefly about how the application is supposed to work. If you don't know how it should work, how will you ever know whether it functions correctly?

Users are expected to type a valid numeric value into each of the two operand boxes. They will then click any of the radio buttons provided to select an operator. The result will be calculated using the two operands and the selected operator, and then displayed in the appropriate label. Now that you have this information, you are ready to write the pseudocode to perform the selected operation.

The pseudocode for this program is as follows:

1. Click the Addition radio button.

2. Calculate the result by using the addition function procedure (this assumes that valid numeric values have been entered into each of the two text boxes).

3. Display the result in a label.

This looks simple enough, so let's return to coding the calculator application.

▶ Coding the addition and subtraction functionality

1. Select the form in Solution Explorer.

2. Open the Code Editor by clicking the Code Editor button at the top of the Solution Explorer window.

   If you look at the first step of the pseudocode, you can see that you want the action to start when a radio button is clicked. This tells you that you should use one of two events. The first event to consider is the default event of the RadioButton control, which is the *CheckedChanged* event.

The second event to consider is the *Click* event. Although the *Checked-Changed* event might look like it would work, remember that it will be raised when the radio button is selected in addition to when it is cleared. Because you don't want to run more code than is absolutely necessary, and because you know that when radio buttons are grouped together only one can be selected at a time, you should probably use the *Click* event. The *Click* event will only be raised once when a radio button is clicked. Any previously selected radio button will be automatically cleared.

3. Select *radAddition* from the Class Name list on the left.

4. Select the *Click* event from the Method Name list on the right.

   When you select the event, the wrapper lines for the *radAddition_Click* event handler will be automatically inserted in the Code Editor.

5. In the *radAddition_Click* event handler, you are going to call a function (*AddOperands*) that will perform the calculation and return the result. Before you code the event handler, you need to create the Function procedure. Below the line End Sub and above End Class, type the following code:

```
' Calculate and return the results to the calling procedure
Private Function AddOperands() As Double
    ' Declare a local variable of type Double
    Dim dblResult As Double

    ' Calculate and store the result in the variable
    dblResult = txtFirstOperand.Text + txtSecondOperand.Text

    ' Return the contents of the variable
    Return dblResult
End Function
```

6. Now you can code the event handler. Enter the boldface code shown here:

```
Private Sub radAddition_Click(ByVal sender As Object, _
        ByVal e As System.EventArgs) Handles radAddition_Click
    ' Call the AddOperands function and pass the result to the Result Label
    lblResult.Text = AddOperands()
End Sub
```

7. Now repeat the same steps for the subtraction calculation by using the *radSubtraction_Click* event. The function will be named *SubtractOperands*. Your code should look like this:

```
' Calculate and return the results to the calling procedure
Private Function SubtractOperands() As Double
    ' Declare a local variable of type Double
    Dim dblResult As Double

    ' Calculate and store the result in the variable
    dblResult = txtFirstOperand.Text - txtSecondOperand.Text

    ' Return the contents of the variable
    Return dblResult
End Function
```

```
Private Sub radSubtraction_Click(ByVal sender As Object, _
        ByVal e As System.EventArgs) Handles radSubtraction_Click
    ' Call the SubtractOperands function and pass the result to the
    ' Result Label
    lblResult.Text = SubtractOperands()
End Sub
```

8. Before you go any further, save your work by clicking the File menu and selecting Save All. After your work is saved, you will need to test the program to make sure you are on the right track.

9. On the Debug menu, select Run, or press F5 to run the program.

10. Type the number **22** in the First Operand box and the number **2** in the Second Operand box.

11. Click the Addition button and look at the result of the calculation.

Houston, I think we have a problem!

The result displayed is 222. The result should have been 24. This is obviously a logic error, so let's figure out what happened and correct it.

Take a look at the following line of code in the *AddOperands* function.

```
dblResult = txtFirstOperand.Text + txtSecondOperand.Text
```

The problem is fairly simple after you understand what is happening. Remember that TextBox controls only hold string values. The value in the txtFirstOperand control is not the number 22; it is the text value "22." The same can be said for the value in txtSecondOperand. When Visual Basic .NET encounters string values and the plus (+) operator, it concatenates the two values; it has no way of knowing that this was supposed to be a mathematical calculation. To ensure that Visual Basic .NET treats this as a calculation using numbers and not a concatenation of strings, you must convert the text values to numeric values before you perform the addition operation.

Casting   Because you are passing the result of the addition to a variable of type *Double*, you will convert each of the two text values to values of type *Double*. You will use a technique known as **casting** (also known as *coercion*) to perform this conversion. You have the option of doing this casting one of four ways:

- **Option 1**   By using the *CDbl* function. Placing the control property *txtFirstOperand.Text* inside the parentheses will convert any valid text to *Double*. In this case, valid text is any text that visually represents a number. For example, the text value 22 is valid, but the text value 22E is not valid. Any attempt to convert 22E to a *Double* will result in an exception being thrown.

  The casting would look like this:

```
dblResult = CDbl(txtFirstOperand.Text) + CDbl(txtSecondOperand.Text)
```

- **Option 2**   By using the *Double.Parse* function.

```
dblResult = Double.Parse(txtFirstOperand.Text) + _
    Double.Parse(txtSecondOperand.Text)
```

- **Option 3** By using the *CType* function.

```
dblResult = CType(txtFirstOperand.Text, Double) + _
    CType(txtSecondOperand.Text, Double)
```

- **Option 4** By using the *Convert.ToDouble* function.

```
dblResult = Convert.ToDouble(txtFirstOperand.Text) + _
    Convert.ToDouble(txtSecondOperand.Text)
```

Let's get back to the code now and finish the program. Feel free to choose any of these options, but for the discussion in the rest of this chapter, we will use option one.

▶ Using a cast to correct the code

1. After you have corrected the code for the addition, test it again to ensure that the result is indeed 24.

2. Now that you have cast the text value in the *AddOperands* method, do the same for the *SubtractOperands* method. This will give you cleaner code and shows consistency in your coding style.

   NOTE   As good programmers, we now know that we need to be explicit when pass-ing data to any object or control that takes a specific value type. With this in mind, again remember that a Label takes a *String* and that you are attempting to pass a value of type *Double* to its *Text* property. You need to clean up your code a little and convert the *Double* back to a *String*. You can do this by using the *ToString* method of the variable when you pass it back in the event handler.

3. Change the code in each of the two event handlers so that the variable uses the *ToString* method when passing the contents of the variable to the Label. Your code for the *radAddition_Click* event handler will look like the following line of code:

```
lblResult.Text = AddOperands().ToString()
```

4. After changing the code for both methods and event handlers, your final code should look like this:

```
' Calculate and return the results to the calling procedure
Private Function AddOperands() As Double
    ' Declare a local variable of type Double
    Dim dblResult As Double

    ' Calculate and store the result in the variable
    dblResult = CDbl(txtFirstOperand.Text) + CDbl(txtSecondOperand.Text)

    ' Return the contents of the variable
    Return dblResult
End Function

Private Sub radAddition_Click(ByVal sender As Object, _
        ByVal e As System.EventArgs) Handles radAddition_Click
    ' Call the AddOperands function and pass the result to the Result Label
    lblResult.Text = AddOperands().ToString()
End Sub
```

```
' Calculate and return the results to the calling procedure
Private Function SubtractOperands() As Double
    ' Declare a local variable of type Double
    Dim dblResult As Double

    ' Calculate and store the result in the variable
    dblResult = CDbl(txtFirstOperand.Text) - CDbl(txtSecondOperand.Text)

    ' Return the contents of the variable
    Return dblResult
End Function

Private Sub radSubtraction_Click(ByVal sender As Object, _
        ByVal e As System.EventArgs) Handles radSubtraction_Click
    ' Call the SubtractOperands function and pass the result to the
    ' Result Label
    lblResult.Text = SubtractOperands().ToString()
End Sub
```

For the rest of the routines, we are going to take a slightly different approach. Rather than having the functions extract the values directly from the TextBoxes containing the two operands, we are going to provide parameters in the methods (Function procedures) and pass in values (arguments) when these methods are called.

Methods can have parameters?

Up until now you have dealt with methods (Sub or Function procedures) that have no parameters. **Parameters** are variables that are declared inside the parentheses following the method name. Now you know that you can call methods by providing arguments (values) when the method is called. You can choose to use the values that are passed into the method when running the code that the method contains.

If a method has parameters, you must provide values for each parameter to complete the call successfully. In fact, if you do not provide the correct type and number of arguments in the calling statement to match the parameters, the code will not compile. Generically, the code will look as follows:

```
Private Sub objectName_Click(ByVal sender As Object, _
        ByVal e As System.EventArgs) Handles objectName.Click
    Label1.Text = functionName(arg1, arg2)
End Sub

Private Function functionName(ByVal param1 As Double, _
        ByVal param2 As Double) As Double
    Dim dblResult As Double
    dblResult = param1 + param2
    Return dblResult
End Function
```

Let's code the routines for the rest of the operators that the user can select, and, while doing so, remember that you want to use our new coding style and ensure that you explicitly cast all of the values you need to pass.

▶ **Coding the multiplication calculation**

Create the multiplication function and implement the *radMultiplication_Click* event handler by typing the following code:

```
Private Sub radMultiplication_Click(ByVal sender As Object, _
        ByVal e As System.EventArgs) Handles radMultiplication_Click
    ' Declare variables of type Double to store the values entered
    ' into the text boxes
    Dim dblFirstOperand As Double = CDbl(txtFirstOperand.Text)
    Dim dblSecondOperand As Double = CDbl(txtSecondOperand.Text)

    ' Call the MultipleOperands function and pass the operands as arguments
    ' Display the result in the Result Label
    lblResult.Text = MultiplyOperands(dblFirstOperand, dblSecondOperand)
End Sub


' Calculate and return the results to the calling procedure
Private Function MultiplyOperands(ByVal firstOperand As Double, _
        ByVal secondOperand As Double) As Double
    Return firstOperand * secondOperand
End Function
```

The code that you entered to perform the multiplication operation looks a little different from the other code you entered, and this warrants some explanation.

The event handler contains code to declare two variables of type *Double* and initialize them to the values entered into the text boxes. The values in the text boxes are cast to *Double* by the *CDbl* function. If you don't pass these values (arguments), the code will not compile.

Looking at the event handler, you can see that the two parameters are separated by a comma and that each parameter is typed as a *Double*, just as if it were a variable. Indeed, it is a variable. The naming convention is slightly different from what you have used before. Here, we are using *camel-casing*, which means that the leading word is in lowercase and the next significant word has its first letter in uppercase. We use this style to provide a more user-friendly name. This is an acceptable practice because it is still clear what the type of the variable is. The function will use the values inside the two parameters to complete the calculation and then return the result to the code in the calling procedure.

Try It

Complete the rest of the Simple Calculator program by adding the code for the division, modulus, and exponentiation operators. The code that needs to be added is listed in the code sample below, in case you need help. Try to complete the program on your own before looking at our code. You will notice that in the rest of the code we did not declare and use variables in the event handlers as you did with the multiplication routine. We did this more to show you what can be done rather than to suggest that one way or the other is right or wrong.

```vbnet
Private Sub radDivision_Click(ByVal sender As Object, _
        ByVal e As System.EventArgs) Handles radDivision_Click

    ' Call the DivideOperands function and pass the operands as arguments
    ' Display the result in the Result Label
    lblResult.Text = DivideOperands(CDbl(txtFirstOperand.Text), _
        CDbl(txtSecondOperand.Text)).ToString()
End Sub

' Calculate and return the results to the calling procedure
Private Function DivideOperands(ByVal firstOperand As Double, _
        ByVal secondOperand As Double) As Double
    Return firstOperand / secondOperand
End Function

Private Sub radModulus_Click(ByVal sender As Object, _
        ByVal e As System.EventArgs) Handles radModulus_Click

    ' Call the ModOperands function and pass the operands as arguments
    ' Display the result in the Result Label
    lblResult.Text = ModOperands(CDbl(txtFirstOperand.Text), _
        CDbl(txtSecondOperand.Text)).ToString()
End Sub

' Calculate and return the results to the calling procedure
Private Function ModOperands(ByVal firstOperand As Double, _
        ByVal secondOperand As Double) As Double
    Return firstOperand Mod secondOperand
End Function

Private Sub radExponentiation_Click(ByVal sender As Object, _
        ByVal e As System.EventArgs) Handles radExponentiation_Click

    ' Call the ExponentiateOperands function and pass the operands
    ' as arguments
    ' Display the result in the Result Label
    lblResult.Text = ExponentiateOperands(CDbl(txtFirstOperand.Text), _
        CDbl(txtSecondOperand.Text)).ToString()
End Sub

' Calculate and return the results to the calling procedure
Private Function ExponentiateOperands(ByVal firstOperand As Double, _
        ByVal secondOperand As Double) As Double
    Return firstOperand ^ secondOperand
End Function
```

Also notice, in the routines shown in this code, that we have cast the values entered into the two text boxes directly inside the method call. These arguments are then passed to the two parameters inside the method declaration. The calculations are performed, and the result is passed to the Label's *Text* property. We included the *ToString* method when we returned the result.

We have not provided code to handle any exceptions. The program will display the Unhandled Exception dialog box shown in Figure 4-18 if a user does not provide valid numeric values in either of the text boxes when attempting to run any of the calculations. (Just click the Continue button for now.) Exception handling is covered in the next chapter.

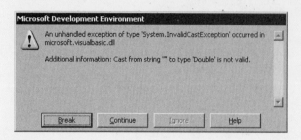

Figure 4-18   The Unhandled Exception dialog box

What Do You Think?

1. What is a variable?

2. List the primitive data types supported by Visual Basic .NET.

3. What modifiers are used to determine the scope of a variable?

4. What is the difference between a constant and a variable?

5. What is the *order of precedence* of operators?

6. What is casting?

7. What is the difference between an argument and a parameter?

Q&A

Q.   Earlier in the chapter you said that procedures are the smallest unit of executable code. Surely a single statement is the smallest unit of executable code. What did you mean?

A.   It is true that a single code statement can be run, but our Visual Basic .NET code (which is compiled to MSIL code) is compiled to executable code one procedure at a time, and then the entire procedure is executed. It is not possible to run just one statement if it is not inside a procedure.

Q.   I'm confused about methods. Can you explain a little more?

A.   A method is a procedure that runs code to perform some action in your program. Other than variable declarations, no executable code can exist outside a procedure. Remember that there are several varieties of methods. A method that runs code but does not return a value is a Sub procedure. A method that runs code and does return a value is a Function procedure.

Q.   Is it good programming practice to explicitly initialize variables when they are declared?

A.   We'll have to answer that by saying "yes and no." Good programmers are as explicit as they can be when writing code. This type of coding generally removes ambiguity and exposes any problems early in the programming cycle. In many of our examples, we have declared variables without explicitly initializing them. Visual Basic .NET will always initialize variables for us, which relieves us of that chore. Other languages, such as C#, are not so kind. If you are in doubt or if there is a chance that the initial value of a variable could be anything other than the default value, you should provide your own initializing value.

Q.   Why are there so many ways of casting?

A.   There is a need for each of these techniques. The *CDbl* function allows you to cast from any convertible type to a *Double*. What we mean by *any convertible type* is that the value you want to convert must be something that can be converted. In this case, you can convert from a *String* to a *Double, but only if the string contains a value that can represent a number*. The other ways of casting provide several overloaded methods that allow customization of the cast. We will discuss casting in more detail in later chapters, but, for now, *CDbl* is the most efficient method of casting a convertible type to a *Double*.

Q.   In the Simple Calculator program, we converted every value entered into the text boxes to *Double*. Is that acceptable, and should I always do that for all numeric conversions?

A.   Absolutely not! It is not acceptable to use *Double* for everything. If you refer to Table 4-1, you can see that a *Double* data type takes up 8 bytes of memory and can store an extremely large number. If you are only dealing with small numbers, it makes sense to store them in a variable that takes up less memory. When choosing a data type for any variable, it is typical to select the smallest data type (in terms of memory usage) that will perform the task. This will generally provide the greatest efficiency. In the Simple Calculator program, and in many of the other examples in this book, we favor technique over efficiency. After you understand the techniques and can produce code that functions as designed, then you can work on efficiency.

Q.   Why did we use functions to perform the calculations? Couldn't we have coded everything in the event handlers of each of the RadioButton controls?

A.   It is more a matter of specialization and reusability than anything else. Our functions are specialized in that they each perform one task and they perform it very well. Although we could have put our calculation code into the event handler, that could lead to unnecessary complexity. If we wanted to run the same code from another event handler, having the code in the event handlers of the Radio-Button controls could force us to create duplicate routines and further complicate things.

WRAPPING UP

- The Code Editor is basically an enhanced Notepad. The Code Editor is a tool in which you can write the code that provides intelligence to your program. IntelliSense provides tips about what to write. It also occasionally completes the code, making programming work much easier.

- Modules are the *pages* in which you write your code. Modules can contain multiple classes, but generally there is only one class inside a module. Procedures (normally referred to as *methods*) are the basic units of execution. Procedures come in several varieties: Sub, Function, and Property. Sub procedures just run code. Function procedures run code and return a value. Property procedures serve as custom properties for your classes.

- You can create methods by typing in the upper wrapper line and specifying the scope (public or private), the type of method (Sub or Function), and the name of the method. If the method is a function, it will return a value, so you need to specify a return data type.

- The scope of a procedure, variable, or constant defines the level of accessibility that an object has. There are five levels of scope: *Public*, *Private*, *Friend*, *Protected*, and *Protected Friend*.

- Variables are temporary storage locations in memory that are given names and referenced in code by that name. They enable you to conveniently and temporarily store data that you need to use in your code. Variables can be declared at the global level (*Public*), at the modular level (*Private*), at the procedural level (*Dim*), and even at the block level (*Dim*). Operators are key characters that allow you to complete expressions, assign values to variables and properties, and perform calculations.

KEYWORDS

application file	casting
comment	constant
declarations	default button
default event	event handlers
Function procedure	keywords
modules	parameters
placeholder	primitive data types
scope	statements
Sub procedure	variable

REVIEW QUESTIONS

1. If you want to change the color scheme that is used in the Code Editor to differentiate between keywords, commands, and comments, you should go to the _____ folder and _____ page of the Options dialog box.

   a. Code Editor, Fonts And Colors

   b. Colors, Code Editor

   c. Environment, Fonts And Colors

   d. Fonts And Colors, Environment

2. Which method of the *MessageBox* class is used to display a message on the screen?

   a. *Show*

   b. *Display*

   c. *Alert*

   d. *Warning*

3. Which of the following is not a valid type of module in Visual Basic .NET?

   a. Form

   b. Class

   c. Option

   d. Base

4. Before a new variable or procedure can be used in your code, it must be _____.

   a. declared

   b. constructed

   c. instantiated

   d. evaluated

5. Which type of procedure returns a value to the calling statement?

   a. Sub

   b. Function

   c. Data

   d. Temporary

6. The _____ determines whether an object, method, or variable can be accessed by other objects, methods, or variables.

   a. environment

   b. scope

   c. data type

   d. name

7. Which of the following is an invalid name for a variable in Visual Basic .NET?

   a. *intMonthlySum*

   b. *m_intMonthlySum*

   c. *Month12Sum*

   d. *12MonthsSum*

8. If you need to store the number 8 in a variable, what data type could you use when you declare the variable?

   a. *Integer*

   b. *Double*

   c. *Boolean*

   d. *Char*

9. What keyword must you use when you are declaring a constant in Visual Basic .NET?

   a. *Constant*

   b. *ConstValue*

   c. *Con*

   d. *Const*

10. Which of the following is not a valid operator in Visual Basic .NET?

    a. *@*

    b. */*

    c. **

    d. *&*

11. Visual Basic .NET indicates invalid words or statements in code by displaying a wavy line under the word or statement. True or false?

12. IntelliSense displays tips with the required arguments for a method shown in bold. True or false?

13. You should use message boxes as much as possible to communicate with the user. True or false?

14. A Sub procedure is a method that performs some action and returns a value. True or false?

15. It's a good idea to use scope to keep the access to objects as restricted as possible. True or false?

16. Keywords, operators, variables, constants, and expressions are all used in Visual Basic .NET _____ that you write in code.

17. _____ are the smallest executable units of code in Visual Basic .NET. They can be one of three types: Sub, Function, or Property.

18. A(n) _____ is a special Sub procedure that is called when an event is raised. It contains the code to be executed in response to the event occurrence.

19. A temporary location in memory used to store a piece of data that can change when the program is running is called a(n) _____.

20. The conversion of a value of one data type to another data type is called _____.

STEP BY STEP

In this project for the Baldwin Museum of Science, you will create a form to enter the number of each type of animal the museum has for a pet exhibition. The program will then display the total number of animals in the pet exhibition. Figure 4-19 shows what the form will look like when it is complete.

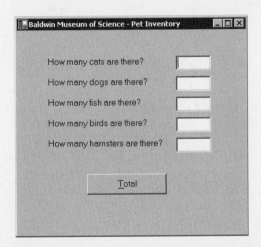

Figure 4-19 The completed PetsCh4 project form

▶ Creating a new project

1. Open Visual Studio .NET, if it isn't already open.

2. Click the New Project button on the Start Page.

3. Click Visual Basic Projects under Project Types and Windows Application under Templates.

4. Type **PetsCh4** in the Name box.

5. Browse to the location in which you are storing your projects.

6. Click OK.

▶ **Configuring the form and changing the startup object**

1. Right-click Form1.vb in Solution Explorer and rename Form1.vb as **Pet-Count.vb**. Press ENTER.

2. Click once in the title bar of the form and change the *(Name)* property of the form to **frmPetCount**.

3. Change the *Text* property of the form to **Baldwin Museum of Science–Pet Inventory** and then press ENTER.

4. Right-click the PetsCh4 project name in Solution Explorer and then click Properties.

5. Change the startup object to frmPetCount and then click OK.

6. Click once in the title bar of the form and use the sizing handles to make the form a little bit bigger.

▶ **Adding controls to the form**

1. Add five Label controls to the form. Change the *Text* property of each Label to what is displayed on the form in Figure 4-19. Because you will not be referencing these Labels in your code, you do not need to change their *(Name)* properties.

2. Use the Format commands to neatly arrange the Labels and change their font size to 10.

3. Add five TextBox controls to the form, placing them next to the Label controls. Change the *(Name)* properties of these controls to the following names:

   ❑ **txtCats**

   ❑ **txtDogs**

   ❑ **txtFish**

   ❑ **txtBirds**

   ❑ **txtHamsters**

4. Clear the contents of the *Text* properties for each of the TextBoxes. Remember that you can select all of the TextBox controls at once to change their *Text* properties together.

5. Add a Button control at the bottom of the screen. Change the *(Name)* property of the Button to **btnTotal**, and then change the *Text* property to **&Total**.

6. Add a Label control under the Button control. Change the *(Name)* property of the Label to **lblTotal**, and then delete the contents of the *Text* property.

▶ Adding code to the form

1. First, you will create a new variable to store the total of all of the counts of animals. Double-click any free space on the form to open the Code Editor.

2. In the left list box at the top of the Code Editor, select (General).

3. Under the line that says "Windows Form Designer generated code," type the following statement to create the variable.

```
Dim intTotalPets as Integer
```

4. Return to form design view and double-click the Total button.

5. In the *btnTotal_Click* event handler, type the following code to add up the pet counts in each of the text boxes on the form.

```
intTotalPets = CInt(txtCats.Text) + CInt(txtDogs.Text) + CInt(txtFish.Text) _
    + CInt(txtBirds.Text) + CInt(txtHamsters.Text)
lblTotal.Text = "There are " & intTotalPets & " pets in the store's inventory"
)
```

▶ Saving and testing your project

1. On the File menu, select Save All to save your work.

2. On the Debug menu, select Start to run your project.

3. Test each control to make sure it is working correctly.

4. On the Debug menu, select Stop Debugging to end the program.

5. On the File menu, select Close Solution to close your project.

6. Close Visual Studio .NET.

FINISH THE CODE

To complete this exercise, open the WoodgroveBankCh4 project that came in your student file. This project contains a form for Woodgrove Bank that customers can use to calculate the average balance of all of their accounts. The form has been created for you with all of the required controls. You just need to add the code required to perform the calculation.

▶ Finishing the project

1. Create a variable that is the *Double* data type. Name it **dblRunning-Balance**.

2. Create another variable that is the *Double* data type, and name it **dblAverage**.

3. Add code to perform the following tasks in the *Click* event of the Totals button.

   a. Add all of the values in the text boxes beside the check boxes to the *dblRunningBalance* variable. Display the *dblRunningBalance* variable in the Total Balance text box.

b. Divide the value in *dblRunningBalance* by the number of accounts, which is 4, and store the result in the variable *dblAverage*. Display the value of *dblAverage* in the Average Balance text box.

4. Add code to close the application to the *Click* event of the Close button. Use the command *End* to close the application in the event handler.

5. Run the project and test the form.

6. Save the project.

7. Close the solution.

JUST HINTS

In this exercise, you will create a form that customers of Fabrikam, Inc., can use to determine how much fertilizer they need for their yards. You will create a new project containing one form that looks like Figure 4-20.

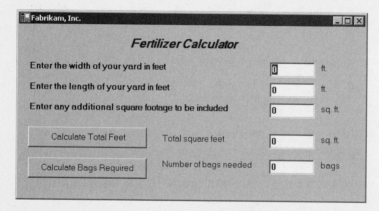

Figure 4-20   The completed frmFertilizerCalc form

Use the following information to complete this exercise.

1. Create a new project and name it **FabrikamCh4**.

2. Change the name of the form to **frmFertilizerCalc** and the name of the file to **FertilizerCalc.vb**.

3. Change the startup object for the project to frmFertilizerCalc.

4. Resize the form to make it similar to the form in Figure 4-20.

5. Add a Label control displaying the text "Fertilizer Calculator" to the top of the form. Center the Label on the form and set the font to bold and italics. You might also want to increase the font size.

6. Add six more Label controls and three TextBox controls that will be used to gather information regarding the size of the property to be fertilized. Change the *(Name)* and *Text* properties of these nine controls appropriately. Set the *Text* properties of the three TextBoxes to zero, as a default.

7. Add two Button controls to the bottom of the form. The top button will be used to calculate and display the total square footage to be fertilized. The bottom button will be used to calculate how many bags of fertilizer are required. Set the *(Name)* and *Text* properties of the two Button controls appropriately.

8. Add two Label controls and two TextBox controls next to the buttons, and set their properties appropriately. These two TextBoxes will be used to display the results of the calculations that occur when either of the two buttons is clicked.

9. In the *Click* event for the top button, calculate the total square footage by multiplying the values in the width and length text boxes and then adding the value in the additional square footage text box to the sum. Display the result in the text box next to the top button.

10. In the *Click* event for the bottom button, calculate the number of fertilizer bags required by dividing the total square footage by 5,000. Use the integer division operator (\) to return only a whole number. Place this whole number in the text box next to the bottom button.

11. Run the project and test the form. Figure 4-21 shows the form with some test data that you can use.

12. Save the project.

13. Close the solution.

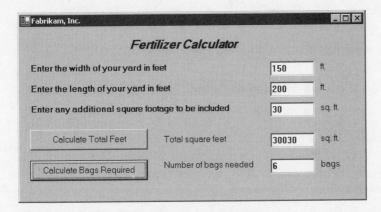

Figure 4-21   The FertilizerCalc project with test data

ON YOUR OWN

In this exercise for Tailspin Toys, you will create a little form that "plays" with a user's age. Create a new project, and call it TailspinToysCh4. The form should look like Figure 4-22. When the user clicks each option, perform the corresponding operation on the user's age. You should do this by writing three functions, one for each option. Display the result of each operation in the text box next to that option.

If the user clicks the Refresh button, call each of the three functions to update the value in the text box for each function. If the user clicks the Clear All button, clear the contents of all four text boxes. If the user clicks the Close button, close the application by using the *End* command.

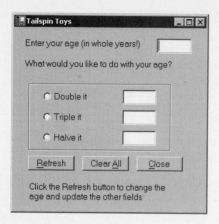

Figure 4-22   The TailspinToysCh4 project form

MORE PRACTICE

1. Write the declaration statement for a new function called *CalcTax* that has one *Single* parameter called *Amount* and returns a *Single* value.

2. Write the declaration statement for a *String* variable called *strCustomer-Name* that has a public scope.

3. Write the declaration statement for an *Integer* constant called *intYears* that has a private scope.

4. What is the value of *intAnswer* after this statement is evaluated?

    ```
    intAnswer = 10 / 2 + (9-7)*4
    ```

5. Write a Visual Basic .NET statement that will call a function named *RaiseValue* that has two *Integer* arguments defined. Pass the *Integer* variables *Number1* and *Number2* to the function. Save the result of *RaiseValue* in a variable called *NewValue*.

6. Create a Visual Basic .NET application with a form that will convert inches into miles and meters. The user should be able to enter a number in inches and then click a button named Convert. The equivalent number of miles and meters should be displayed. Use the equivalencies listed. There should also be a Reset button and a Close button that will clear all fields and close the application, respectively.

    ❑   1 mile = inches / 63,360

    ❑   1 meter = inches / 39.37

7. A store that sells carpeting would like you to create a Visual Basic .NET application with a form that can be used to calculate the cost of installing carpet into a customer's home. Customers should be able to enter information into the following fields on the form:

   ❑ Customer name

   ❑ Street

   ❑ City

   ❑ Phone number

   ❑ Square feet of area to be carpeted

   ❑ Price/square foot of selected carpet

   ❑ Price/square foot of selected padding

   ❑ Sale discount (enter percentage)

   There should also be a box to select if furniture must be moved (add $100 to the total cost) and a Calculate Costs button. When the Calculate Costs button is clicked, the total cost should be calculated, including the total cost of the carpet (square feet of area to carpet * price/square foot of carpet) plus the total cost of padding (square feet of area to carpet * price/square foot of padding) plus the cost to move furniture (if applicable) plus labor (square feet of area to carpet * $2.00). This total should be multiplied by the sale discount, if there is one. The total cost should be displayed in a message box.

8. Create a Visual Basic .NET application with a form that will calculate and display the balance in a savings account after 5 years of saving at a particular rate. The user must enter the amount of the principal (P) and the interest rate (r). The formula to use to calculate the balance in 5 years is: (P * (1 + r))^5. The calculation should be performed and the future balance displayed whenever the user clicks a button labeled Future Balance.

9. Create a form in a Visual Basic .NET application that will calculate a salesperson's commission amount for the four quarters in a year. The salespeople must enter their sales amounts for each of the four quarters (Q1, Q2, Q3, and Q4). They must also enter their commission rates as percentages. There should be three buttons named Calculate, Clear, and Close on the form. If the salesperson clicks the Calculate button, the commission amount for each quarter should be calculated by multiplying each quarter's sales amount by the commission rate. Each quarter's commission amount and the total commission amount for the year should be calculated and displayed on the form. If the salesperson clicks the Clear button, all controls containing sales amounts, the commission rate, and totals should be cleared. The Close button should close the application.

CHAPTER 5
DEBUGGING YOUR APPLICATION

We all would like to think we write perfect code. Unfortunately, that's usually just a dream. Good coding is typically the result of good debugging. In Chapter 8, you will be learning how to handle run-time errors and exceptions through the use of *structured exception handling*, but for now you will learn about the debugging tools available in Microsoft Visual Studio .NET. Mastering these tools to find and fix problems in your code will help you easily build robust and functional applications.

Upon completion of this chapter, you will be able to:

- Use regular and conditional breakpoints to stop execution at just the right time.

- Learn how to use the Debug toolbar to see exactly what's happening while your program is running.

- Set a Watch or Quick Watch to monitor your code while it is running.

- Understand the use of the Immediate, Autos, and Locals windows.

- Use the Call Stack to trace execution.

USING BREAKPOINTS

It might look to you like some of the debugging tools we are going to cover overlap each other and provide similar functionality, and you would be right. The truth is that you don't need to master all of the tools to become proficient at debugging your programs. It's okay to learn to use a few of them now and learn to use others as needs arise.

In this section, we are going to focus on a debugging tool referred to as a *breakpoint*. A **breakpoint** is a location you identify in your code where you want execution of the program to pause so that you can look at what is going on at that moment. You will often need to pause the execution of your program because there is a bug in the code that is adversely affecting the outcome.

What Is a Bug?

Before we look closer at breakpoints, you should understand what a bug is. A **bug** is any unwanted action or reaction in your program. A bug can be just a **compilation error**, which is generally quite easy to locate and fix. Compilation errors occur when you attempt to compile code that the compiler can't read. A bug could also generate a **run-time error** that causes your program to inexplicably stop running when you try to run it. The kinds of bugs that generate run-time errors are usually tougher to locate. A bug could even cause a **logic error**. When you have a logic error, the code runs just fine and no errors are noted, but the result or outcome of the program is not what was expected. Logic errors are sometimes the biggest challenge of all, especially if your program is rather complex.

A bug can be a minor annoyance or a major disaster. For example, a mouse cursor that changes from a standard pointer to an hourglass at an incorrect time would be a minor annoyance, whereas the program crashing and taking the entire contents of the hard drive with it would be a major disaster.

The origin of the term *bug* as it relates to computers reputedly goes back to the early days of computing, when a problem in an electromechanical computer at Harvard University was traced to a moth being caught between the contacts of a relay in the machine. Yes, we know, a moth is technically not a bug, but we are programmers, not entomologists. Perhaps we should call the process of fixing problems in our software *de-mothing*.

Locating the bug is usually the toughest part of debugging; fixing it is often a breeze in comparison. A word of warning though: many times, when a bug is located and fixed, it causes another bug to occur as a result of the bug-fix. Also, be careful that you're not just fixing the symptom rather than the problem.

Project Configuration

When you create a new Microsoft Visual Basic .NET project, Visual Studio .NET can create two types of project configurations: debug and release. The **debug version** is of course designed for debugging the application. When a project is compiled to a debug version, a *.pdb* (Program Database) file is created (along with an .exe or .dll file) and placed in the bin folder of the project. The .pdb file contains debug information for the .exe or .dll file. When the project is compiled to a *release* version, a .pdb file is not produced, and the .exe or .dll file is created without debug information. A **release version** is optimized, meaning that it is smaller and will run faster. You will distribute the release version to end users. For more information on optimization, on the Help menu, select Index and then type **optimization** in the Look For box. Then select About Visual Basic .NET Optimization from the list of available topics.

Setting a Breakpoint

Setting a breakpoint is as simple as clicking in the left margin of the Code Editor next to the line of code on which you would like your program to stop. Note that the line of code marked by the breakpoint will not run; execution stops when that line is the next line to run. This is useful when you have an exception being thrown and you suspect you know where the problem is and want to see what is happening just before the exception is thrown.

> **TIP** An exception object is thrown when an error is encountered while the program is running. The exception object contains information about the error which will assist you in debugging the program. Exception handling will be covered in Chapter 8.

▶ **Setting a breakpoint in code**

1. Open the Code Editor and locate a line of code on which you want the code to break.

2. Click in the left (gray) margin next to the line of code, as shown in Figure 5-1.

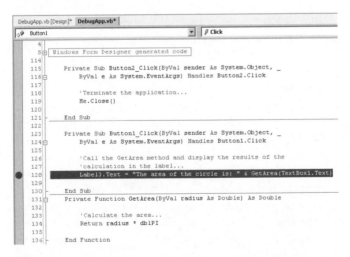

Figure 5-1   Clicking in the gray margin to set a breakpoint

> **TIP** The line of code you select must contain code that can be executed. For example, you cannot set a breakpoint on a line that declares a variable, unless the declaration includes code to initialize the variable. Attempting to set a breakpoint on a line of code that will not execute will result in an error message in the status bar at the bottom of the integrated development environment (IDE). The message will say "This is not a valid location for a breakpoint."

3. Press F5 or, on the Debug menu, select Start to start the program.

   TIP If you inadvertently press CTRL+F5 or, on the Debug menu, select Start Without Debugging, the debugger will not be enabled and the program will ignore any breakpoints.

4. Perform any user actions necessary to run the routine that contains the breakpoint.

The program should now halt at the selected line of code. You should also notice that the line of code that will run next is highlighted.

Using the Debug Toolbar

To use the Debug toolbar, on the View menu, point to Toolbars and then select Debug. Figure 5-2 shows the Debug toolbar. The purpose of each button on the Debug toolbar is as follows:

- **Start** Click the Start button to run the program in Debug mode.

- **Break All** Click Break All to halt execution but remain in break mode. The debugger stops execution of all programs running under the debugger. The programs do not exit and you can resume execution at any time. The debugger and your application are now in break mode.

- **Stop Debugging** Click Stop Debugging to end the debugging session.

- **Restart** Click Restart to stop the current debugging session and start a new one.

- **Step Into** After the program has halted, you can step into the code line by line by pressing the F8 key, clicking Debug, and then selecting Step Into, or clicking the Step Into button on the toolbar. Continue pressing F8 to run each line.

  NOTE In Chapter 1 you set the Visual Studio .NET keyboard mappings to follow the Visual Basic scheme. In this mode, the F8 key is used to step into code. The default Visual Studio .NET keyboard mapping scheme uses the F11 key for stepping into code.

- **Step Over** If you break at a line of code that calls another method and you know there are no problems with the called method, you can choose to bypass stepping through the entire method by clicking the Step Over button. The called method will still run, but you will not have to take the time to step into each line just to get back to the where you started. Continue pressing F8 to run each line.

- **Step Out** If you are stepping through code and you step into a called method, you can click Step Out (SHIFT+F8) at any time to return to the line of code that called the method. This allows you to test some of the code in the called method without having to manually step into every single line in the method. Continue pressing F8 to run each line.

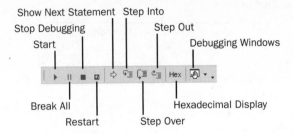

Figure 5-2   The Debug toolbar

Other buttons on the Debug toolbar include the following:

- **Show Next Statement**   This button allows you to return to the line of code that is set to run next.

- **Hexadecimal Display**   This button toggles the display of numeric values in the debugging windows from decimal to hexadecimal and back again.

Clicking the down arrow next to the last button on the Debug toolbar displays a menu for all other debugging windows. Figure 5-3 shows what is available on this menu. Note that you must be in break mode to see the list as shown. If you are not in break mode, only the Immediate and Breakpoints selections will be available.

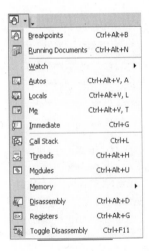

Figure 5-3   The Debug toolbar drop-down menu

The Debugging Windows and Commands

Table 5-1 shows the various debugging windows and commands available in Visual Basic .NET. We will provide details about the windows and commands that you will use most often. Don't be concerned if some of these windows and commands seem alien to you at this point; that is to be expected. You can review them again later when you are more comfortable with debugging your programs.

Table 5-1   **Debugging Windows and Commands**

Debugging window	Purpose
Breakpoints	Lists all the currently set breakpoints.
Running Documents	Lists script code loaded in the current process. You will use this when debugging Web applications or other applications in which scripting is used.
Watch	Shows variables, register contents, and any valid expression recognized by the debugger.
Quick Watch	Much like the Watch window, except it is quicker to use when you want to evaluate a single variable or expression. To display the Quick Watch window, select an expression or variable and then select Quick Watch from the Debug menu.
Autos	Displays variables in the current and previous statements.
Locals	Lists all local variables.
Me	Lists all the properties for the current class.
Immediate	Allows you to enter expressions for evaluation.
Call Stack	Shows names of methods on the Call Stack with parameter types and values.
Threads	Provides information on sequential streams of execution (threads).
Modules	Lists modules (.dll and .exe files).
Memory	Shows memory contents.
Disassembly	Shows assembly code generated by the compiler.
Register	Lists contents of the register.
Toggle Disassembly	Toggles between the Code Editor and the assembly.

Before we get into details about some of these windows, let's open a simple application that you can use to practice debugging. The DebugApp application shown in Figure 5-4 is available in your student file. You will modify this project later in this chapter. Although you can open the project in Visual Studio .NET from the CD, you will not be able to run it from there because you will need to be able to make changes to the project. To complete the exercises, you must copy the entire project to your hard drive and open it from there.

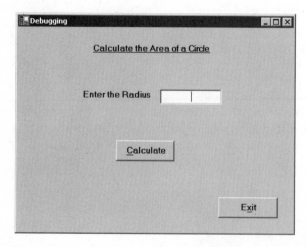

Figure 5-4   The DebugApp application form

With DebugApp open in Visual Studio .NET, let's take a more detailed look at how to use breakpoints. Later in this chapter, we will look at some of the other debugging tools that are available.

Breakpoints

The Breakpoints window is one of two debugging windows that can be viewed and set up when you are not in break mode (the other one being the Immediate window). On the Debug menu, point to Windows and then select Breakpoints to display the Breakpoints window, as shown in Figure 5-5.

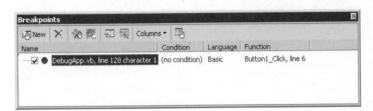

Figure 5-5   The Breakpoints window

Figure 5-5 shows the Breakpoints window with one breakpoint set and a few of the columns displayed. The Breakpoints window toolbar, shown in Figure 5-6, allows you to perform the tasks summarized in Table 5-2.

Table 5-2   **Breakpoints Window Icons and Tasks**

Icon	Task
Add Breakpoint	Adds a new breakpoint
Delete Breakpoint	Deletes the currently selected breakpoint
Clear All Breakpoints	Clears all the breakpoints in the current assembly
Disable All Breakpoints	Disables all breakpoints but maintains them for future use
Go To Source Code	Takes you to the source code for the selected breakpoint
Go To Disassembly	Takes you to the location of the breakpoint in the Disassembly window (only available in break mode)
Columns	Shows a list of columns that can be displayed in the Breakpoints window
Properties	Displays the Properties dialog box for the currently selected breakpoint

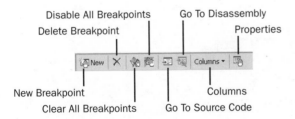

Figure 5-6   The Breakpoints window toolbar

Breakpoint Properties

If you look at the Breakpoint Properties dialog box shown in Figure 5-7, you can see the name and path of the file in which you have set the breakpoint. You can also see the line and the number of the character on which the breakpoint was placed in the code. Notice that there are two buttons: Condition and Hit Count. Clicking either of these buttons will display a dialog box that you can use to further customize the use of the breakpoint in your code. If you click Condition, you can set a condition that must exist before the code will break at the line of code. If you click Hit Count, you can specify the number of times that the line of code must run before execution pauses at the breakpoint.

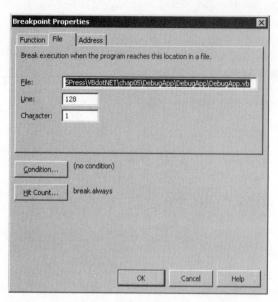

Figure 5-7   The Breakpoint Properties dialog box

▶ Using the hit count

1. Display the Code Editor and clear any existing breakpoints by selecting the Debug menu and then selecting Clear All Breakpoints.

2. Set a breakpoint on the following line of code:

```
Label3.Text = "The area of the circle is: " & GetArea(TextBox1.Text)
```

3. Display the Breakpoints window if it is not already displayed.

4. Select the breakpoint in the Breakpoints window, as shown in Figure 5-5, and then click the Properties button to open the Breakpoints Properties dialog box.

5. Click the Hit Count button to display the Breakpoint Hit Count dialog box, as shown in Figure 5-8.

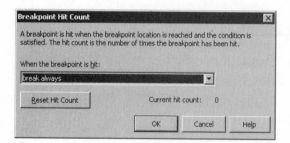

Figure 5-8   The Breakpoint Hit Count dialog box

6. Click the arrow on the list box to display the available options, as shown in Figure 5-9.

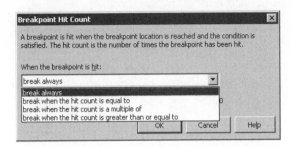

Figure 5-9   Options for when the breakpoint is hit

7. Select "break when the hit count is equal to" from the list and then type the number **2** in the text box next to the list box. The dialog box should now look like Figure 5-10.

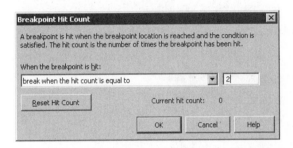

Figure 5-10   The Breakpoint Hit Count dialog box set to break when the hit count is 2

If you set the hit count to 2, the breakpoint will be ignored by the debugger the first time it is encountered, and the application will not break. The second time the breakpoint is encountered, it will break. Let's test that now and see what happens.

If you look at the Breakpoints window now and display the Hit Count column, you should see that the hit count is set as shown in Figure 5-11.

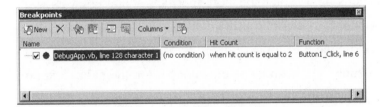

Figure 5-11   The Hit Count column in the Breakpoints window shows current setting

8. On the Debug menu, click Start to start the application.

9. Type the number **3** in the text box to set the radius, and then click Calculate. The calculation will be executed, and the result will be displayed in the label.

10. Type the number **6** in the text box after clearing the existing number, and then click Calculate once more. The application will now break at the line of code you selected, proving that the hit count worked.

You will now set a condition for the breakpoint. Setting a **condition** is simply applying some criteria to a task. For example, you might say to a potential employer "I will work for you on the condition that you pay me." Putting this in the context of our application, the application will break on condition that the radius text box has the value 6 typed into it.

▶ Setting a condition for a breakpoint

1. Display the Breakpoint Properties dialog box.

2. Click the Hit Count button and clear the hit count criteria by resetting the hit count to "break always."

3. Click OK to close the Hit Count dialog box.

4. Click the Condition button to display the Condition dialog box.

   Type the expression **TextBox1.Text = 6** in the Condition box, as shown in Figure 5-12.

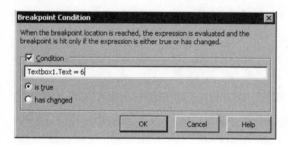

Figure 5-12   The Breakpoint Condition text box

Setting the above condition instructs the debugger to execute a break whenever the number 6 appears in the *Text* property of the TextBox1 control. If any other value is used, no break will occur. You can see how setting conditions allows you to be more specific when testing your code.

5. Click OK to close the Condition dialog box.

6. Click OK to close the Breakpoint Properties dialog box.

7. Run the application again, and type the number **2** in the radius text box.

8. Click Calculate to complete the calculation. The code will not break. The result of the calculation will be displayed in the label.

9. Type the number **6** in the radius text box and click Calculate once more. The code will now break.

Try It

Let's add another breakpoint to the DebugApp program and set it to break when the value in the *TextBox1.Text* property changes.

▶ Set another breakpoint

1. In the DebugApp program, locate the *Click* event handler for the Calculate button and put a breakpoint at the following line of code:

```
Label3.Text = "The area of the circle is: " & GetArea(TextBox1.Text)
```

2. Open the Breakpoint Properties dialog box, and then click the Condition button.

3. Change the breakpoint condition so that the program will enter break mode only when the value of the *Text* property of TextBox1 has changed.

4. Run the program and verify that the program only enters break mode if the value in the radius text box changes. You can do this by clicking the Calculate button more than once without changing the value of the radius.

5. Remove the breakpoint before continuing.

What Do You Think?

1. What is a breakpoint, and why would you use one in your code?

2. List the three types of errors that you might encounter in a program.

3. If you set a regular breakpoint at a line of code and then run the program, but the program runs to completion and never enters break mode, what does that tell you about the line of code on which you set the breakpoint?

4. What are the Condition and Hit Count buttons in the Breakpoint Properties dialog box used for?

USING WATCHES AND THE IMMEDIATE WINDOW

Now that you have a good grasp of how to use breakpoints, we will look at some of the other debugging windows and commands.

Watches

A **watch** is designed to keep track of a variable or expression and display the results in a window. As with most of the debugging windows, you must be in break mode to use a watch. There are two types of watches available: a **Quick Watch** and a *Watch*. Using a Quick Watch is simply a matter of selecting a variable, property, or expression in the Code Editor, selecting the Debug menu, and then selecting Quick Watch. You can also right-click the selected variable, property, or expression and then select Quick Watch from the shortcut menu. This opens the Quick Watch dialog box and allows you to change the value of the selected variable, property, or expression. Local variables that are not in scope cannot be changed because they have no reference in memory and therefore cannot hold values.

A Watch is something a little more permanent than a Quick Watch in that you can set a Watch in the Watch window and check the value as you step through the code. After a Watch is set, it will be saved when you close the project. This is useful when you want to reopen the project to continue debugging and want to use the watches you had previously set. When in break mode, you can open a Watch window (one of four), type in the name of the variable, property, or expression, and monitor the value. After it is in scope, the value will be displayed and can be changed if required.

Right-clicking a selected variable or expression and selecting Add Watch from the shortcut menu will (by default) add it to Watch 1. If you want to add it to a different Watch window (in this example, Watch 2), open Watch 2 by clicking the Debug menu, pointing to Windows, pointing to Watch, selecting Watch 2, and then selecting the variable or expression and dragging it to the Watch 2 window.

▶ **Using a Watch on the DebugApp project**

1. Set a breakpoint so that the code breaks when Calculate is clicked.

2. Run the application, type the number **3** in the radius text box, and then click Calculate. Application execution will pause as soon as Calculate (Button1) is clicked.

3. Open a Watch window by clicking the Debug menu, pointing to Windows, pointing to Watch, and then selecting Watch 1. This will display a Watch window at the bottom of the IDE.

4. Type **radius** in the Name field and then press ENTER, as shown in Figure 5-13. Notice that the Value column tells us that the name *radius* is not declared. This is because the *radius* variable is declared locally as a parameter of the *GetArea* method. When the *radius* variable is in scope, it will receive the value passed to it from the calling statement's argument.

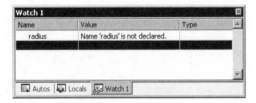

Figure 5-13   Setting up a Watch in the Watch 1 window

5. Step into the code by pressing F8 several times. When the *GetArea* method is highlighted (indicating that it is the next code statement to be executed), notice that the *radius* variable is now in scope and contains the value passed to it from the argument. At this point you can change the value in the Watch window. Let's do that now.

6. Click the number in the Value column twice (two single-clicks, not a double-click) to select the value.

7. Change the value to **4**, as shown in Figure 5-14. You have now changed the contents of the *radius* variable to 4. The value is displayed in red to indicate a change.

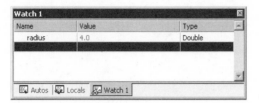

Figure 5-14   Changing the Watch value in the Watch 1 window

8. Press F5 to continue execution. The rest of the code will continue to run without stopping, and the form will display the calculated result. Notice that the value in the text box still shows 3, but the result of the calculation assumes that the multiplier operand is actually 4.

You can have up to four Watch windows open at the same time to monitor several variables or expressions at once.

Autos Window

The Autos window is extremely useful because it automatically displays the variables and properties (and their values) for the current program statement, along with up to three statements on either side of the current statement.

▶ **Using the Autos window**

1. Set a breakpoint so that the code will break when Calculate is clicked.

2. Run the application, type the number **4** in the radius text box, and then click Calculate. Application execution will halt as soon as the button is clicked.

   Open the Autos window by selecting the Debug menu, pointing to Windows, and then selecting Autos. This will display the Autos window at the bottom of the IDE, as shown in Figure 5-15.

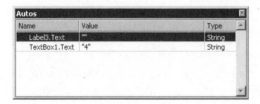

Figure 5-15   The Autos window

3. Step into the code by pressing F8 several times. Notice that when execution reaches the *GetArea* method, the contents of the Autos window changes, as shown in Figure 5-16. You will now see the variables and properties of that method displayed in the Autos window, along with the value (the content) and the type.

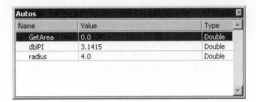

Figure 5-16   The Autos window showing the objects in the *GetArea* method

Locals Window

The Locals window is also quite useful because it is specific to the current method. As with many of the debugging windows, you must be in break mode in order to be able to display and interact with the Locals window.

Figure 5-17 shows the Locals window when execution breaks at the breakpoint. You have set a breakpoint at the same statement as before (when the user clicks the button). You can display the Locals window by selecting the Debug menu, pointing to Windows, and then selecting Locals. (The application must be in break mode.)

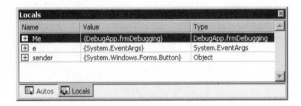

Figure 5-17   The Locals window

What you see in Figure 5-17 might not seem very useful at first, but when you step into the code you will see that the information provided is quite meaningful and helpful. Right now you can see three major items in the list, each with a plus sign (+) to the left of the object name. The plus sign indicates that this is a tree view of the objects. Clicking the plus sign expands the object list and displays the hierarchy of the object.

- *Me* represents the current class, which at this time is the form.

- *e* represents the *EventArgs* argument for the Calculate button. This is a generic argument required for all event handlers. It does not provide any useful information at this time.

- *sender* represents the sending object, which in this case is the Calculate button.

Stepping into the code will bring you to the *GetArea* method. The contents of the Locals window will now change. Figure 5-18 shows the updated contents of the window. Because the calculation has not yet been completed, *GetArea* still shows 0.0, but when you step again, the calculation will be completed and the value column will be updated with the result of the calculation.

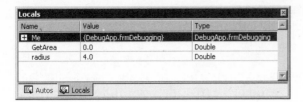

Figure 5-18   The Locals window displaying the objects in the *GetArea* method

Me Window

The Me window allows you to examine the *data members* of the object associated with the current method. In the example, there is one class (the form), so *Me* represents the form. The Me window displays the same information you saw in the Locals window. You can open this window from the Debug menu by pointing to Windows and then selecting Me.

Immediate Window

In earlier versions of Visual Basic, the Immediate window was probably the most used of all the debugging windows. It is still extremely useful, but its importance is now shared with several other windows in our debugging toolbox.

Basically, the Immediate window allows you to examine the contents of variables and properties by typing in the variable or property name preceded by a question mark. You can open this window from the Debug menu by pointing to Windows and then selecting Immediate (or by pressing CTRL+ALT+I). It is available in any mode.

▶ Using the Immediate window for additional debugging

1. Start the application. (You should still have the breakpoint set.)

2. Type the number **3** into the radius text box, and then click Calculate.

3. The application should break as expected. Now display the Immediate window.

4. Type the following statement into the Immediate window and then press ENTER:

```
?Textbox1.Text
```

5. Notice that you typed a question mark (?) followed by `Textbox1.Text`. The question mark informs the Immediate window that you want to print the value in the window. The value of the *Text* property is now displayed, as shown in Figure 5-19.

Figure 5-19   The *Text* property displayed in the Immediate window

6. Next, change the value you entered into the text box by typing the following statement below the current contents of the Immediate window:

```
Textbox1.Text = 4
```

7. Now you can examine the contents to be sure that the value was actually changed. Rather than typing **?Textbox1.Text** again, you can re-execute that statement. Place the cursor at the end of the first line in the Immediate window and press ENTER. You should now see the statement ?Textbox1.Text added to the bottom of the list.

8. Press ENTER one more time to display the contents, as shown in Figure 5-20.

Figure 5-20   Redisplaying the *Text* property in the Immediate window

Remember that, when using the Immediate window, you are running a single program statement at a time. You cannot type in blocks of code to run all together because the Immediate window does not provide the ability to do this. Another thing to remember is that, when you want to examine the contents of a variable or property, you must precede the statement with a question mark, which tells the Immediate window to print the results of the statement when it is executed.

Call Stack

The **Call Stack** allows you to see a list of all the methods in the current sequence. For example, if you have an event handler that calls another method, which in turn calls a third method, you would see all three methods in the Call Stack. In the sample program, there is an event handler that calls the *GetArea* method. When execution reaches the called method, you will see it in the Call Stack.

Figure 5-21 shows the Call Stack with three methods displayed. You will always see the *Main* method because this is the entry point for the class (the form). The top line shows the current method, and the second line shows the method (the event handler) that called the current method.

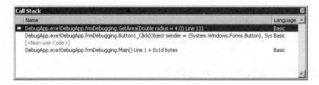

Figure 5-21   The Call Stack window

You can change what is displayed in the Name column by right-clicking the Call Stack window and selecting or clearing the various options on the context menu, as shown in Figure 5-22.

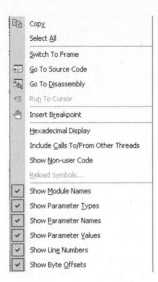

Figure 5-22   The Call Stack window context menu options

As you can see, you can do a lot with the Call Stack window, much of which is beyond the scope of this chapter. As with many of the topics we have covered so far, it's sufficient to learn the basics of each of the tools we're covering, and, as the need arises, you can research further for additional information.

Try It

▶ Changing the value of a control's property using the Immediate window

1. Add the *frmDebug_Load* event handler to the Code Editor. This can be done by double-clicking the form in the design window. At this point it is not necessary to provide any code inside the event handler. Now set a breakpoint so that execution will break when the form starts to load.

2. Run the program. When the program enters break mode, display the Immediate window by selecting the Debug menu, pointing to Windows, and then selecting Immediate.

3. In the Immediate window, type the following line:

   ```
   Label2.Text = "Type the radius here"
   ```

4. Press ENTER.

5. Press F5 to continue running the program. Make sure that the label for the radius text box has changed.

6. Stop the program, remove the breakpoint, and then run the program again. Notice that the radius text box label is back to the original value. Why didn't the change to the property occur again?

What Do You Think?

1. How is a Watch different from a Quick Watch?

2. What is the Autos window used for?

3. How can you examine the contents of a variable or property by using the Immediate window?

4. If you were trying to figure out the order in which several methods called each other, which debugging tool could you use?

5. Why are only the Breakpoints and Immediate menu items available on the Debug menu when you are in design view?

DEBUGGING THE APPLICATION

One thing that we have talked about several times in this textbook is the importance of using proper naming conventions for the objects you create and reference in your code. Specifically, you should name your controls as you add them. In the example we are using in this chapter, we did not do that . . . yet! We did this purposely to demonstrate a point and to show you the kinds of problems that can result when you wait until late in the development of a project to correctly name the controls.

In this section, you will do the following:

- Rename all of the controls

- Test the application

- Discuss each of the bugs you encounter

- Correct the code as necessary

▶ **Renaming the DebugApp project controls**

1. If you don't have the DebugApp project open, open it now so that you can continue to work with it.

2. Display the form in the DebugApp project in design view.

3. Select each of the controls and rename them using the information in Table 5-3.

Table 5-3   **New DebugApp Form Control Values**

Control type	Old control name	New control name
Label	Label3	lblResult
TextBox	TextBox1	txtRadius
Button	Button1	btnCalculate
Button	Button2	btnClose

4. After you have changed the names, run the program. The all-too-familiar error message shown in Figure 5-23 will appear.

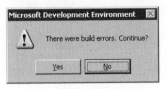

Figure 5-23   The build errors message box

5. Click No to display the Task List window, as shown in Figure 5-24. Clicking Yes would run the last successful build, and the results might not be what you expect. By clicking No, you are prompting the compiler to stop the process and display the errors.

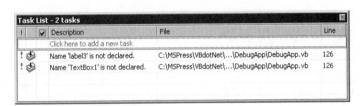

Figure 5-24   The Task List window

Luckily, this is a simple application with very few controls and limited functionality, which is why you didn't get too many errors. You can imagine how long the list would be for a complex application. This is when you might be tempted to pass this project off to someone else and tell them what a satisfying challenge it would be for them to resolve all the errors!

The two errors you see are compilation errors and must be corrected before you can truly debug the program. Fortunately, fixing these errors is fairly easy.

▶ **Fixing the errors**

1. Double-click the first error in the Task List. This will display the Code Editor and take you to the location in the code where the name Label3 is referenced, as shown in Figure 5-25.

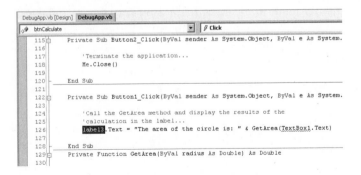

Figure 5-25   The line containing the first error

2. Change the name from Label3 to **lblResult** and compile the program again.

3. Rather than running the application to recompile, on the Build menu, select Rebuild Solution.

> **TIP**   When correcting control or object references in code, you can use Intel-liSense to assist you in selecting the correct value. Erase the highlighted value and type in **lbl**, and then press CTRL+SPACEBAR. If there is only one control with the prefix lbl in your program, IntelliSense will automatically complete the name for you. If there are several label controls, a list from which you can select the correct one will appear.

4. Examine the Task List again. There should now be only one error listed because you have resolved the first one.

5. Double-click the remaining item in the Task List. TextBox1 is now highlighted, showing you where the error is.

6. Change the name from TextBox1 to **txtRadius** and recompile the program. The project should now compile and display information in the Output window, as shown in Figure 5-26.

Figure 5-26   The Output window displaying information from the recompilation

Take a look at the code view window for the DebugApp, which is shown in Figure 5-27. Notice that although the event handlers for btnCalculate and btnClose have been updated, the names of the methods still show as *Button1_Click* and *Button2_Click*. Although this inconsistency does not impair the functionality of the program as designed, it could hurt you later if you need to call either of these two event handlers from another method. Besides that, it isn't very professional to have your code this way, so you should change the names of the event handlers to reflect the new names of the controls.

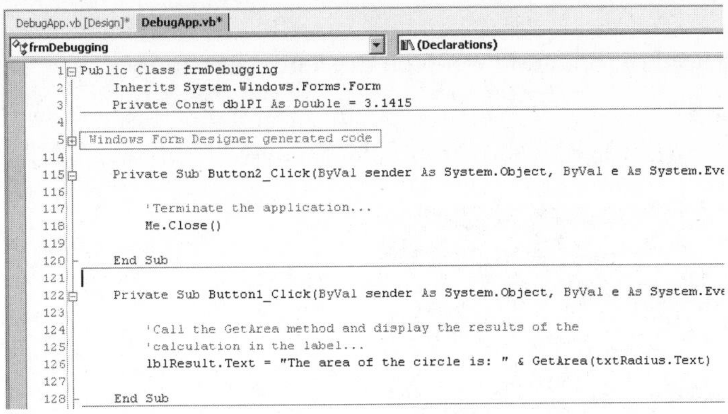

```
DebugApp.vb [Design]*   DebugApp.vb*
frmDebugging                        ▼  (Declarations)
  1 Public Class frmDebugging
  2    Inherits System.Windows.Forms.Form
  3    Private Const dblPI As Double = 3.1415
  4
  5 Windows Form Designer generated code
114
115    Private Sub Button2_Click(ByVal sender As System.Object, ByVal e As System.Eve
116
117       'Terminate the application...
118       Me.Close()
119
120    End Sub
121
122    Private Sub Button1_Click(ByVal sender As System.Object, ByVal e As System.Eve
123
124       'Call the GetArea method and display the results of the
125       'calculation in the label...
126       lblResult.Text = "The area of the circle is: " & GetArea(txtRadius.Text)
127
128    End Sub
```

Figure 5-27   The method names do not match the event handlers

▶ **Cleaning up the code**

1. Change the name of the *Button1_Click* event handler to
   btnCalculate_Click.

2. Change the name of the *Button2_Click* event handler to **btnClose_Click**.

3. Reformat the code to provide a neat appearance. Use the line continuation character to break up long lines of code, and use the TAB key to indent code so that the reader can clearly see what the code represents.

After you make the changes and reformat the code, it should look like the code in Figure 5-28.

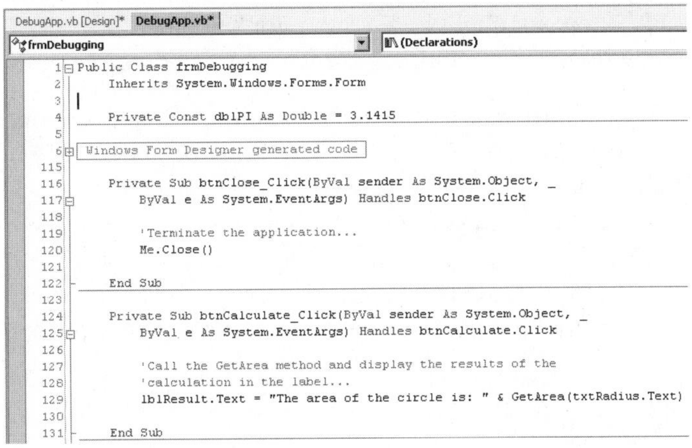

```
DebugApp.vb [Design]*   DebugApp.vb*
frmDebugging                        ▼  (Declarations)
  1 Public Class frmDebugging
  2    Inherits System.Windows.Forms.Form
  3
  4    Private Const dblPI As Double = 3.1415
  5
  6 Windows Form Designer generated code
115
116    Private Sub btnClose_Click(ByVal sender As System.Object, _
117       ByVal e As System.EventArgs) Handles btnClose.Click
118
119       'Terminate the application...
120       Me.Close()
121
122    End Sub
123
124    Private Sub btnCalculate_Click(ByVal sender As System.Object, _
125       ByVal e As System.EventArgs) Handles btnCalculate.Click
126
127       'Call the GetArea method and display the results of the
128       'calculation in the label...
129       lblResult.Text = "The area of the circle is: " & GetArea(txtRadius.Text)
130
131    End Sub
```

Figure 5-28   The method names now match the event handlers

Run-time Errors

Now that you have corrected the syntax to eliminate any compile-time errors and cleaned up naming issues in the code, you need to deal with any run-time errors that might exist. As the name implies, a run-time error is an error that appears while the program is running. In Chapter 8, we will be discussing structured exception handling, but for now let's see what a run-time error is.

▶ Debugging the run-time errors

1. Start the DebugApp application, and then type the letters **abc** in the radius text box.

2. Click Calculate. The error message shown in Figure 5-29 will appear.

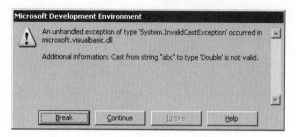

Figure 5-29   A run-time error message box

3. Click Continue to stop the program.

This problem occurred because you typed the characters *abc* rather than numbers in the radius text box. When Visual Basic .NET tried to perform a calculation using the characters, an error was generated. This kind of problem should be avoided, and in the next chapter we will be discussing defensive programming techniques that can be used to prevent this type of exception from being thrown.

Logic Errors

Logic errors are somewhat devious because there is often no visual indication that an error even exists. The only symptom might be that you don't get the correct output for the input provided to the program, and this is often hard to determine.

You might have already noticed that there is a logic error built into our application. If you have spotted it already, good for you! If you have not, don't be alarmed; you have just joined the ranks of the majority. The logic error is in the *GetArea* method. The calculation is not correct because it multiplies pi by the radius to return the area of the circle. If you think back to your days in your high school math class, you might remember that the formula for calculating the area of a circle is r^2 or (PI * (r ^ 2)). Because you are multiplying the radius by pi, your results are definitely incorrect.

▶ Correcting the code logic

1. Change the expression to calculate the area of the circle. Replace

```
Return radius * dblPI
```

with

```
Return (radius ^ 2) * dblPI
```

2. Run the program again.

3. Type the number **3** into the radius text box.

4. Click Calculate.

Now the correct result, 28.2735, should be displayed.

Try It

Let's change the program so that it also calculates the diameter of a circle, which is equal to the radius multiplied by 2. We will give you a line of code to enter into the project, and— what do you know—the code has an error. Even if you see the error right away, enter the code with the error so that you can use the debugging tools to fix the error later.

▶ Modifying the DebugApp application

1. Add another label below lblResult and give it the name **lblDiameter-Result**. The *Text* property should be blank for this new label.

2. Locate the *Click* event handler for the Calculate button, and add the following line of code before the End Sub statement:

```
lblDiameterResult = "The diameter of the circle is: "
& Textbox.Text / 2
```

3. Run the program and fix any compilation errors that prevent the program from running.

4. When the program will run, enter **6** for the radius and then click Calculate. Is the result 12? If not, fix any logic errors in the calculation and retest.

What Do You Think?

1. What problems can occur if you change the name of a control after you have entered code into one of that control's event handlers?

2. How can you use the Task List window to easily locate the line of code in which an error occurred?

3. Why are logic errors sometimes difficult to find?

4. Many programmers find that when they fix one problem in their code, another problem surfaces. Why do you think this happens?

Q&A

Q. You set the value of the constant *dblPI* to 3.1415. Isn't that an incorrect value because it is shortened and could result in some inaccuracies in the answer?

A. You are correct, and you should be as explicit as possible when declaring constants such as this. The Microsoft .NET Framework actually provides a *Math* class that includes a defined constant for pi. If you were using this code in a real application, you would use the built-in value for pi by referring to the *Math* class in your code.

Q.   If I always name my controls correctly when I add them, will I ever have to be concerned with syntax errors?

A.   Yes. Even if you name your controls at the start of the development process, you might decide later in the project that one or more of the control names does not really fit its design function and that you should rename it. Also, you need to take into account your typing accuracy. Extensive use of IntelliSense will help to alleviate problems resulting from typos.

Q.   If I include complex notation in my code but I'm not really sure whether the formulas I'm using are correct, what should I do?

A.   Get help. There are many resources available on the Internet and in libraries to assist you when developing formulas for use in calculations. It might also help to have a subject matter expert available when performing user-acceptance testing. The expert should be able to verify any inputs and validate the results.

Q.   You mentioned defensive programming techniques. What are they?

A.   Because we will be covering them in the next chapter, we will not go into too much detail here. Defensive programming techniques involve coding to prevent the introduction of invalid values. For example, in the DebugApp program, you required the user to enter a valid number in the radius text box. Because you have no direct control over the user, there is nothing to stop them from entering invalid characters. By using defensive programming techniques, you can examine what users enter before you pass the inputted values to the *GetArea* method. If a value is invalid, you can warn the user and not go any further in the calculations without requiring the user to correct the problem.

WRAPPING UP

- The Debug toolbar provides the ability to step through code so you can see exactly what's happening. You can set breakpoints to pause the execution of code at specific locations in your program. You can also customize a breakpoint so that code execution will pause when a certain condition is true, or only when that line of code has executed a specified number of times.

- You can add Watches and Quick Watches to view the values of variables, properties, and expressions. The Autos window will display the values of variables and properties along with the three statements on either side of the current statement. The Locals window displays information specific to the current method. By using the Immediate window, you can examine and change the values of variables and properties while the program is in break mode. You can use the Call Stack to see a list of all called methods and the sequence in which they were called.

- You have to be careful if you change the names of controls after you have referenced them in code or created event handlers for them. Even if a name change does not generate an error, it's a good practice to go back and change any reference to the old name in the code.

KEYWORDS

breakpoint

Call Stack

condition

logic error

release version

Watch

bug

compilation error

debug version

Quick Watch

run-time error

REVIEW QUESTIONS

1. Which of the following types of error occurs when you type code that does not follow the required rules of the programming language?

    a. Run-time error

    b. Logic error

    c. Compilation error

    d. Minor error

2. Which of the following is the type of error that has occurred if your program stops functioning while you're running it?

    a. Run-time error

    b. Logic error

    c. Compilation error

    d. Minor error

3. Which of the following is the type of error that has occurred if your program runs but generates the wrong output for the input provided?

    a. Run-time error

    b. Logic error

    c. Compilation error

    d. Minor error

4. If you set a(n) _____ in your code, the program will enter break mode when the line of code is reached.

    a. bug

    b. breakpoint

    c. exception

    d. release

5. Which of the following buttons appear in the Breakpoint Properties window and are used to customize the use of a breakpoint in your code?

    a. Hit Condition

    b. Condition

    c. Hit Count

    d. Stop Condition

6. Which window can you use to change the value of a property in break mode by placing a question mark at the beginning of a statement?

    a. Immediate

    b. Locals

    c. Autos

    d. Me

7. The Call Stack is used to display a list of all active _____ in their sequence of execution.

    a. variables

    b. events

    c. bugs

    d. methods

8. A Quick Watch is different from a Watch in that a Quick Watch is more _____.

    a. temporary

    b. flexible

    c. powerful

    d. informative

9. If you change the name of a control after an event handler has been created for that control, the _____ name for that control will not automatically change.

    a. method

    b. event

    c. debug

    d. temporary

10. Errors that occur when you build your program are displayed in the _____.

    a. Immediate window

    b. Task List

    c. Me window

    d. Debug toolbar

11. An unwanted action or reaction in your program is called a bug. True or false?

12. The F1 key is used to step into your code and run it line by line. True or false?

13. You can use the Condition button in the Breakpoint Properties window to specify the number of times the code must run before it will pause at a breakpoint. True or false?

14. You can use the Locals window when the program is actively running. True or false?

15. Logic errors in a program often produce no obvious indications or symptoms. True or false?

16. The two types of project configurations available in Visual Basic .NET are the _____ version and the _____ version.

17. A breakpoint can be configured so that a set _____ must exist before the code will break at the breakpoint.

18. The _____ window is used to display the values of the variables and properties for a current program statement, along with the three statements on either side of the current statement.

19. The Me window is used to view the data members of the _____ associated with the current method.

20. A plus sign (+) displayed next to an object name in the Locals window indicates that the window provides a(n) _____ view of the object.

STEP BY STEP

To complete this exercise, you will open the AdmissionsCh5 project in your student file. This application will be used by the Baldwin Museum of Science to calculate daily admission information. There are some errors in this project that you will find and correct.

▶ **Opening the project**

1. Open Visual Studio .NET, if it isn't already open.

2. Click the Open Project button on the Start Page.

3. Browse to find the AdmissionsCh5 project in your student file, and then click Open.

▶ **Fixing syntax errors**

1. Click Start on the toolbar to compile the program.

2. You should receive a message box saying there were build errors. Click No to continue.

3. The Task List should appear at the bottom of the screen. It will contain errors indicating that *txtAdultTotal* is not declared. This means that you used a TextBox control name in your code that is not valid. Return to the form design view and check the *(Name)* property of the adult total TextBox control.

4. You will see that the *(Name)* property of the adult total TextBox control is actually set to txtAdultsTotal. Remove the "s" after "Adult" in the *(Name)* property.

5. Click Start on the toolbar to compile the program again.

▶ **Fixing logic errors**

1. The program should run this time. Type **10** for the number of adult, youth, and group tickets, and then click Calculate.

2. More problems! There is no value displayed for the group total, and the overall total is incorrect. Put a breakpoint in the *Click* event for the Calculate button to see what's wrong. Stop the program and double-click the Calculate button to locate its *Click* event handler.

3. Place a breakpoint next to the first line in the *btnCalculate_Click* event handler and run the program again.

4. Type **10** for the number of adult, youth, and group tickets, and then click Calculate. When the program enters break mode, step into the code by using the F8 key until you reach the line that calculates the group total.

5. If you compare the code that is handling the group totals to the code for the other ticket totals, you'll notice that the line of code required to display the value in the group totals variable has been commented out. Stop the program and remove the comment from the code statement.

6. Restart the program and press F8 to continue stepping into the code until you reach the line of code that assigns a value to the *Text* property of txtTotalCost.

7. Unlike the calculation for the number of tickets, notice that the calculation for the total cost is incomplete. The expression `CDbl(txtGroupTotal.Text)` is missing from the total cost calculation.

8. Stop the program again and add `CDbl(txtGroupTotal.Text)` to the expression that calculates the value for *txtTotalCost.Text*.

9. Click Start on the toolbar to compile and run the program again.

▶ Performing the final test

1. The program should run this time. Type **10** for the number of adult, youth, and group tickets, and then click Calculate. Verify that the values in all fields are correct.

2. Save your changes and close the application.

FINISH THE CODE

Open the WoodgroveBankCh5 project in your student file. This project will calculate the simple interest that would be received for a given amount of principal deposited into a savings account at a specified rate. There are some problems with this project, and your job is to find the errors and fix them. You might want to use breakpoints, watches, and the Immediate window to perform this task. You should also read the comments in the code closely to make sure each line of code is doing what it is supposed to do.

JUST HINTS

Open the FabrikamCh5 project in your student file and use the debugging tools to correct the code that calculates the average daily production for one week. Test the program by calculating the average daily production with your calculator and comparing it to the answer displayed by the program.

ON YOUR OWN

Open the TailspinToysCh5 project in your student file. This file contains a program that will simulate the tossing of three dice and display the odds of receiving that particular combination of numbers, without regard to the order. This program will not generate any compilation or run-time errors when you run it, but the logic does not work correctly. Fix the logic errors and then verify that the program is displaying the correct odds for each throw. Use the information in Table 5-4 to verify the odds.

Table 5-4   **Odds of Throwing Dice Combinations**

Dice combination	Odds
Any triple	31 to 1
Total value of dice equals 4 or 17	62 to 1
Total value of dice equals 5 or 16	31 to 1
Total value of dice equals 6 or 15	18 to 1
Total value of dice equals 7 or 14	12 to 1
Total value of dice equals 8 or 13	8 to 1
Total value of dice equals 9 or 12	7 to 1
Total value of dice equals 10 or 11	6 to 1
Any double	6 to 1

MORE PRACTICE

1. Open the MorePractice1Ch5 project in your student file. The purpose of this project is to calculate the total value and the average of the check amounts entered by the user. Users will enter the word *Done* when they are finished entering check amounts. There are some problems in the code, so the project does not work correctly. Find and fix the problems so that the project runs without errors and displays the correct values. To display the values as currency, use the *FormatCurrency* function. For example, `FormatCurrency(CheckAvg)` will convert the result to a currency format that will return the result with the $ symbol and two decimal places.

2. Open the MorePractice2Ch5 project in your student file. The form in this project contains a list box and a button that can be clicked by the user to add items to the list. Another button displays the number of items in the list in a message box. There are some problems in the code, so the project does not work correctly. Find and fix the problems so that the project runs without errors and displays the correct values.

3. Open the MorePractice3Ch5 project in your student file. This project will calculate the final price of an item, using the discount rate and tax rate entered by the user. There are some problems in the code, so the project does not work correctly. Find and fix the problems so that the project runs without errors and displays the correct final price.

4. Open the MorePractice4Ch5 project in your student file. On this form, users can enter what they eat on any given day and find out how well their diets correspond to recommendations made in the food pyramid. Specifically, the program should tell them whether they need to eat more or less of the foods in each food group. The program should also display a message congratulating them if they ate correctly and do not need to make any changes. There are some problems in the code, so the project does not work correctly. Find and fix the problems so that the project runs without errors and provides the correct feedback to the user. Make sure to read the comments in the code carefully so that you understand what the program is supposed to do.

CHAPTER 6
DECISION MAKING

In the previous chapter, you learned how to debug your programs. As you dive deeper into programming, topics will get more complex, but you will find that you have the ability to create more robust and powerful applications. Remember that bugs are more likely to be introduced into complex routines than simple routines, and that your skills in debugging will continue to be tested more and more as you advance further.

In this chapter, you will learn how to construct blocks of code that will allow your programs to branch off in different directions based on the values stored in variables and properties. In short, your programs will be able to make decisions, and you will essentially be controlling the flow of the programs. We will also be introducing some of the defensive programming techniques that we discussed briefly in Chapter 5.

Upon completion of this chapter, you will be able to:

- Create and use conditional expressions.

- Use the *If...Then* statement.

- Use the *Select* statement.

IF...THEN STATEMENTS

The *If...Then* statement is a special construct that allows you to control the flow of programs. This construct allows you to use conditional expressions and, depending on the outcome, will direct execution appropriately. In this section, we will look at the general characteristics of conditional expressions. We will then look at how we can apply *If...Then* statements.

Conditional Expressions

We all make decisions every day. Shall I go to work or go to the beach? Should I order steak or hamburger? If only life was always that simple. Unfortunately, there are usually conditions that affect our decisions. In programming, we use conditional expressions to determine whether a particular code statement or group of statements runs.

A **conditional expression** is a statement intended to provide an answer of *True* or *False*. This is sometimes referred to as a **Boolean expression**. Using this type of expression in your code allows you to construct a more intelligent code block that can run different code statements depending on the results of the expression.

Let's take a look at a few conditional expressions to understand them better. In the first example, you will start by declaring and initializing a variable. You will then use the variable in a conditional expression to determine the outcome.

```
Dim strWeather As String = "Sunny"
```

If you use the variable *strWeather* in a conditional expression, you are able to provide an answer of True or False when you compare *strWeather* to any value.

In this case, the expression will be `strWeather = "Sunny"`, but to make sense of it you will need to construct it in the form of a question.

Is *strWeather* equal to "Sunny"? If True, go to the beach. If not True, go to work.

In the variable declaration statement, the = (equals) operator is used as an assignment operator. This use of the = operator allows you to assign a value to the variable. When you use the same statement as an expression, the = operator is used as a conditional operator. By including the expression inside a question, you are informing the compiler that you are not attempting to assign a value to the variable but are comparing the value inside the variable with another value.

Let's look at another example to see how you can use a conditional expression to help you make a decision. Again, you will declare and initialize a variable and use that variable when you build the conditional expression.

```
Dim decPriceOfSteak As Decimal = 4.95
```

Looking at the above statement, you can see that the variable *decPriceOfSteak* is initialized to 4.95. Your current budget is $5.95. You have to determine whether the steak is within your budget when you are deciding what to order. Let's pretend that you don't know the value stored in the variable. You do know, however, the name of the variable and the amount of money in your pocket. You will see that you really don't need to know the actual value stored in the variable. You will simply ask a question: "Is the cost of the steak (*decPriceOfSteak*) less than or equal to $5.95 (the amount of money you have)?" You will expect a response of True or False. If the answer is True, you can order the steak; if it is False, you will have to settle for the hamburger. (This assumes that you are not in a fancy restaurant where the price of a hamburger is more than $5.95!)

In this case, the expression will be `decPriceOfSteak <= 5.95`. As before, you will have to put it in the form of a question. Is *decPriceOfSteak* less than or equal to 5.95? If True, order the steak. If not True, order the hamburger.

Let's look at one more example.

```
Dim intAge As Integer = 18
```

In this case, the variable is assigned a value of 18. By comparing the value stored in *intAge* with a person's actual age, you can determine whether the person can vote. Once again, all you need is a result of True or False to determine in which direction the program should go.

Is *intAge* greater than or equal to 18? If True, the person can vote. If not True, the person cannot vote.

A conditional expression must return a value that can be used to make a decision. A conditional expression generally consists of three parts. Two of the three parts are the two values used in the comparison, and the third part is a special operator that defines how to compare the two values. This operator is called a **comparison operator**, and it is used to define the kind of comparison that should be made. Table 6-1 describes the comparison operators that are available in Microsoft Visual Basic .NET.

Table 6-1   **Comparison Operators**

Comparison operator	Definition
=	The right side of the expression equals the left side of the expression
<>	The right side of the expression does not equal the left side of the expression
>	The left side of the expression is greater than the right side of the expression
<	The left side of the expression is less than the right side of the expression
>=	The left side of the expression is greater than or equal to the right side of the expression
<=	The left side of the expression is less than or equal to the right side of the expression

Now that you understand conditional expressions, you can put them in the form of questions and run code based on the answers.

The *If* Statement

The previous examples, although extremely simple, don't make too much sense until they're put in context. Let's ask some questions based on these expressions.

If the weather is sunny, then go to the beach.

If the price of the steak is less than $5.95, then order the steak.

If your age is greater than or equal to 18, then you can vote.

In each of these questions, the result of the expression or condition that is evaluated must be True if the statement or statements following the word *then* are to be executed. In other words, if the condition does not evaluate to True, nothing will happen. You can now construct a code block to see how this is all put together.

The syntax of a basic *If* statement will look like this:

```
If conditional expression Then
    ' code that will run if the conditional expression returns True
End If
```

Notice that the words *If*, *Then*, and *End If* are Visual Basic .NET keywords that must be included in a properly constructed *If* statement.

To see this in action, let's create a new application and try it out.

▶ **Creating the Decisions application**

1. Create a new console application called **Decisions**.

2. Type the boldface code in the following code sample inside the *Main* method.

```
Module Module1
    Sub Main()
        ' Declare and initialize the following variables…
        Dim strWeather As String = "Sunny"
        Dim decPriceOfSteak As Decimal = 4.95
        Dim intAge As Integer = 18

        ' Display a prompt to the user…
        Console.WriteLine("Is it sunny? - " & _
            (strWeather = "Sunny").ToString())

        ' Is the weather Sunny?
        If strWeather = "Sunny" Then
            Console.WriteLine("Go to the Beach")
        End If

        ' Display a prompt to the user…
        Console.WriteLine("Is the price less than 5.95? - " & _
            (decPriceOfSteak < 5.95).ToString())

        ' Is the price of the steak less than 5.95?
        If decPriceOfSteak < 5.95 Then
            Console.WriteLine("Order the Steak")
        End If

        ' Display a prompt to the user…
        Console.WriteLine("Are you 18 or older? - " & _
            (intAge >= 18).ToString())
```

```
        ' Is the person's age greater than or equal to 18?
        If intAge >= 18 Then
            Console.WriteLine("You can vote")
        End If


        ' Pause the screen…
        Console.ReadLine()
    End Sub
End Module
```

3. Press F5 to run the program. Figure 6-1 shows the results that will display when the program is run.

Figure 6-1   The execution results displayed in the console window

So far, everything works as expected in our example, but the decision making remains unfinished. That is, if the result of each of the expressions is True, code is executed, but what happens if the result is False?

Adding an *Else* Block

In many cases, you will need to run different code statements if the result of the evaluation of the condition is False. Including an *Else* block in the *If* statement will allow you to do that.

The syntax of a basic *If…Else* statement will look like this:

```
If conditional expression Then
    ' code that will run if the conditional expression returns True
Else
    ' code that will run if the conditional expression returns False
End If
```

▶ **Updating the Decisions program to include the *Else* block**

1. Open the Code Editor.

2. Update the code in *Sub Main* to match the lines of boldface code in the following code sample.

```
Module Module1
    Sub Main()
        Dim strWeather As String = "Rainy"
        Dim decPriceOfSteak As Decimal = 8.95
        Dim intAge As Integer = 17

        Console.WriteLine("Is it sunny? - " & _
            (strWeather = "Sunny").ToString())

        If strWeather = "Sunny" Then
            Console.WriteLine("Go to the Beach")
        Else
            Console.WriteLine("Go to Work")
        End If
```

```
        Console.WriteLine("Is the price less than 5.95? - " & _
            (decPriceOfSteak < 5.95).ToString())

        If decPriceOfSteak < 5.95 Then
            Console.WriteLine("Order the Steak")
        Else
            Console.WriteLine("Order the Hamburger")
        End If

        Console.WriteLine("Are you 18 or older? - " & _
            (intAge >= 18).ToString())

        If intAge >= 18 Then
            Console.WriteLine("You can vote")
        Else
            Console.WriteLine("Sorry, you cannot vote")
        End If

        Console.ReadLine()
    End Sub
End Module
```

3. You can see that the initialized value of each of the variables has been changed to ensure a different outcome. Run the program to see the results shown in Figure 6-2.

Figure 6-2   Result of changing initialized variables

Although you have improved upon the functionality of the *If* block, it is still somewhat limited. For instance, the weather is only evaluated for *sunny*, and the result of this evaluation determines whether you go to the beach or go to work. You should ask yourself if there are any other values you should be evaluating besides *sunny* and *rainy*. If so, you must construct your code to check the variable for different values. Fortunately, the *If* statement provides another keyword—*ElseIf*—that allows you to evaluate different expressions.

The *ElseIf* Block

You can run code statements by asking different questions. Including an *ElseIf* block in your *If* statement will allow you to do that. Again, remember that the result of each expression must return the value of True in order to run the code within that particular block.

The syntax of a basic *If…ElseIf* statement will look like this:

```
If conditional expression 1 Then
    ' code that will run if conditional expression 1 returns True
ElseIf conditional expression 2 Then
    ' code that will run if conditional expression 2 returns True
ElseIf conditional expression 3 Then
    ' code that will run if conditional expression 3 returns True
```

```
Else
    ' code that will run if all conditional expressions return False
End If
```

There is one important thing to note when creating an *If* code block with multiple *ElseIf* blocks. The first expression in the chain that evaluates to True will determine the code that will run. This means that if the first expression is true, the code inside that block will run, and, once that code is completed, execution falls through to the bottom and no other expression in the block will be evaluated.

▶ **Adding *ElseIf* blocks to the Decisions application**

1. Open the Code Editor.

2. Update the code in *Sub Main* to match the lines of boldface code in the following code sample.

```
Module Module1
    Sub Main()
        Dim strWeather As String = "Rainy"
        Dim decPriceOfSteak As Decimal = 2.25
        Dim intAge As Integer = 18

        Console.WriteLine("Is it sunny? - " & _
            (strWeather = "Sunny").ToString())

        If strWeather = "Sunny" Then
            Console.WriteLine("Go to the Beach")
        ElseIf strWeather = "Cloudy" Then
            Console.WriteLine("Go to the Movies")
        ElseIf strWeather = "Rainy" Then
            Console.WriteLine("Do something else")
        Else
            Console.WriteLine("Go to Work")
        End If

        Console.WriteLine("Is the price less than 5.95? - " & _
            (decPriceOfSteak < 5.95).ToString())

        If decPriceOfSteak < 5.95 Then
            Console.WriteLine("Order the Steak")
        ElseIf decPriceOfSteak < 2.5 Then
            Console.WriteLine("Order two Steaks")
        Else
            Console.WriteLine("Order the Hamburger")
        End If

        Console.WriteLine("Are you 18 or older? - " & _
            (intAge >= 18).ToString())

        If intAge >= 18 Then
            Console.WriteLine("You can vote")
        Else
            Console.WriteLine("Sorry, you cannot vote")
        End If

        Console.ReadLine()
    End Sub
End Module
```

3. Run the program again and test it with different input.

Notice that you have included multiple *ElseIf* blocks and changed the values of two of the variables. Look carefully at the *If* block that evaluates the price of steak. Do you see a potential problem?

Remember that the amount of money you have in your pocket is $5.95. The price of the steak was changed to $2.25. Based on the new price, you can now afford to order two steaks. The problem arises when you evaluate the first expression decPriceOfSteak < 5.95. Because the price of the steak is now $2.25, the result of that expression will be True (2.25 is less than 5.95). The code in that block will run and no other expression will be evaluated.

How can you fix this? The answer is to present each of the conditions in the appropriate order. You must evaluate the most restrictive condition first and then gradually widen the expression. In other words, you want to check the condition that has the least chance of being True first. To do this, change the order of evaluation so that your code now looks like this:

```
If decPriceOfSteak < 2.5 Then
    Console.WriteLine("Order two Steaks")
ElseIf decPriceOfSteak < 5.95 Then
    Console.WriteLine("Order the Steak")
End If
```

Making the Grade

Let's take a look at another example to show what we mean about presenting the conditions in the appropriate order. You will create a simple program that will calculate a letter grade based on the percentage a student receives.

▶ Creating the CalculateGrade application

1. Create a new console application called **CalculateGrade**.

2. Type the boldface lines of code shown here into *Sub Main*. Because you changed the name of the Module from the default, don't forget to change the startup object.

```
Module CalculateGrade
    Sub Main()
        ' Declare variables for percentage and grade...
        Dim intPercentage As Integer
        Dim strGrade As String

        ' Display a prompt...
        Console.WriteLine("Enter the percentage")

        ' Enter the percentage. The ReadLine() method will be used to assign
        ' the value entered by the user to the variable intPercentage
        intPercentage = Console.ReadLine()

        ' Evaluate the percentage to determine the grade...
        If intPercentage > 60 Then
            strGrade = "D"
        ElseIf intPercentage > 70 Then
            strGrade = "C"
        ElseIf intPercentage > 80 Then
            strGrade = "B"
```

```
        ElseIf intPercentage > 90 Then
            strGrade = "A"
        Else
            strGrade = "F"
        End If

        ' Display the percentage and the letter grade on the screen …
        Console.WriteLine("You scored " & intPercentage.ToString() & _
            " and received the letter grade " & strGrade.ToString())
        Console.ReadLine()
    End Sub
End Module
```

3. Press F5 to run the program.

4. Type **98** at the prompt and then press ENTER. Notice the results, which are displayed in Figure 6-3.

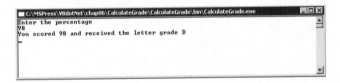

Figure 6-3   Testing the program

Wait a second. The student got 98 on the assignment but received a D. Does that seem fair? As you can see, there is no problem with the code: it ran without any run-time errors. But there is a problem in the logic used in the code. If you evaluate the code from the top down, you can correct the logic error.

5. Modify the code so that it evaluates the most restrictive condition first.

```
If intPercentage > 90 Then
    strGrade = "A"
ElseIf intPercentage > 80 Then
    strGrade = "B"
ElseIf intPercentage > 70 Then
    strGrade = "C"
ElseIf intPercentage > 60 Then
    strGrade = "D"
Else
    strGrade = "F"
End If
```

6. Press F5 to run the program.

7. Type **98** at the prompt and then press ENTER to display the results, which are shown in Figure 6-4.

Figure 6-4   The correct results

Providing User Input—Creating the MenuChoices Application

In our examples so far, you have hard-coded the initializing value for each variable. This makes the outcome predictable and the program less useful. What you need to do is provide a way for the user to enter a value at run time and then allow the program to determine the outcome based on the value entered.

To do this, you will create a Microsoft Windows application with input controls that will allow the user to enter information. The form you are going to create will look like Figure 6-5.

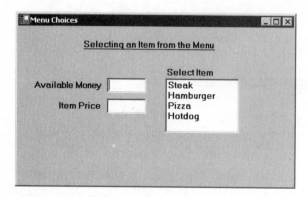

Figure 6-5   The MenuChoices form

Let's use the existing functionality in our console application. The new program will require only minor changes to the code. You can re-create the program as a Windows application and allow the user to enter the values that will be used in the expressions in the code.

▶ **Creating a Windows application**

1. Create a new Windows application named **MenuChoices**.

2. Name the form **frmMenuChoices**, and set the *Text* property of the form to **Menu Choices**. Don't forget to change the startup object after you have changed the name of the form.

3. Refer to Table 6-2 for the information needed to add the controls to the form and name them. Note that the list of items in the list box will be added at run time by the *frmMenuChoices_Load* event handler.

Table 6-2   Controls and Properties for the MenuChoices Application

Control	Name	Text
TextBox	**txtMoney**	<blank>
TextBox	**txtItemPrice**	<blank>
ListBox	**lstItems**	
Label	Label1	**Selecting an Item from the Menu**
Label	Label2	**Available Money**
Label	Label3	**Item Price**

Table 6-2   **Controls and Properties for the MenuChoices Application**

Control	Name	Text
Label	Label4	**Select Item**
Label	**lblChoice**	\<blank\>

4. Size and position all the controls. Use the Format menu for more accurate alignment and positioning.

Coding the Program

After the GUI is complete, you will be adding code to provide the functionality. Let's break the task down to ensure that you cover all the requirements.

You want to add code that will populate the list box when the form is loaded. As with most things in Visual Basic .NET, this can be accomplished in several ways, but for this program you will be using the *Add* method of the ListBox control.

```
ListBox.Add(item)
```

As its name implies, the *Add* method adds a value to the list box. For each item you want to add to the list box, you must run the *Add* method and provide the value inside the parentheses. Because you are actually adding string values to the list box, you must ensure that each value is enclosed in double quotation marks, as shown in the following line of code.

```
ListBox.Add("item1")
```

As you can see in the following code sample, the *Add* method runs four times, once for each item you want to add to the list box.

```
Private Sub frmMenuChoices_Load(ByVal sender As System.Object, _
        ByVal e As System.EventArgs) Handles MyBase.Load

    ' Load the menu items in the combo box…
    lstItems.Items.Add("Steak")
    lstItems.Items.Add("Hamburger")
    lstItems.Items.Add("Pizza")
    lstItems.Items.Add("Hotdog")
End Sub
```

The next thing you need to do is give users a way to enter the amount of money they have available to spend. You have provided a text box for them to use for this purpose. You need to verify two things: First, that they enter a value, and second, that the value they enter is numeric. We will use the *TextChanged* event handler shown in the following code sample to monitor any keystroke for the TextBox control and prevent the user from attempting to evaluate any expression containing an incorrect value.

IsNumeric Function

In the next code sample, we will introduce a special function called *IsNumeric*. This function is used to evaluate a value to determine whether it is a number (or can be converted to a number). The *IsNumeric* function will return *True* if the value is a number and return *False* if the value is not a number. In the code sample, the contents of the text box will be evaluated (assuming there is a value in the *Text* property of the TextBox). If the content of the text box is a number, the result will be True; if the content includes an alphabetical character or any other non-numeric character, the result will be False. The following statements are examples of how the *IsNumeric* function is used as a conditional expression.

```
IsNumeric(42) ' the result of this expression will be True
IsNumeric("42") ' the result of this expression will be True
IsNumeric("Number42") ' the result of this expression will be False
```

If we were to write this out fully, the *If* statement would look like this:

```
If IsNumeric(42) = True Then
```

Including = True in the expression is redundant and, as such, is omitted.

```
Private Sub txtMoney_TextChanged(ByVal sender As System.Object, _
        ByVal e As System.EventArgs) Handles txtMoney.TextChanged

    ' If there is text in the text box and the value entered
    ' is numeric, enable the list box.
    If txtMoney.TextLength > 0 And IsNumeric(txtMoney.Text) Then
        lstItems.Enabled = True
    Else
        ' place the cursor in the text box
        txtMoney.Focus()

        ' highlight the contents of the text box
        txtMoney.SelectAll()

        ' disable the list box
        lstItems.Enabled = False

        ' deselect any selected item in the list box
        lstItems.SelectedIndex = -1
    End If

End Sub
```

Inside the Code

In the preceding code, we have created two expressions joined by the *And* keyword. This is one of six **logical operators** that you can use when evaluating expressions. (See Table 6-3 for a list of all the logical operators used in Visual Basic .NET.) If both expressions evaluate to True, the code inside the block runs. If either of the expressions evaluate to False, the code in the *Else* block will run. This code will do the following:

- Set focus on the Money text box. This places the cursor in the text box so that users can easily input information.

- Select any text already placed in the text box. Because the text is selected, the user can immediately type in a new value without deleting the existing value first.

- Disable the list box. This prevents the user from selecting any item in the list.

- Clear any previously selected item in the list box. Each item in the list box has an index value. The index value of the first item is 0. If we set the *SelectedIndex* to 0, the first item in the list will be selected. By setting the index value to –1, we are ensuring that no item is selected.

Table 6-3 **Logical Operators**

Logical operator	Definition
And	The overall result is True as long as both expressions evaluate to True.
Or	The overall result is True as long as one of the expressions is True.
Not	If the expression evaluates to False, the result is True. The *Not* operator reverses the result of the expression.
Xor	Also known as an *Exclusive Or*. If just one of the expressions evaluates to True, the result is True. If both expressions evaluate to True or both expressions evaluate to False, the overall result is False.
AndAlso	If the first expression evaluates to False, the second expression is ignored and the overall result is False. If the first expression evaluates to True, the second expression is evaluated.
OrElse	If the first expression evaluates to True, the second expression is ignored and the overall result is True. If the first expression evaluates to False, the second expression is evaluated.

Defensive Programming

When programming code requires input from the user or perhaps the existence of an external file, you need to include code that will test the condition first and provide a mechanism to redirect code execution should the condition be evaluated as something other than what was expected.

By using *If* and *Select* statements, you can *defend* against the possibility that the user will enter an invalid value or that the file will not be located as expected.

You can think of defensive programming as a three-step process:

- Know and understand the expected condition.

- Create an appropriate expression to test the condition.

- Run code if the expected condition is false.

We incorporate defensive programming techniques in our programs because we have little control over what users will do when the program is running. We know what we want them to do and, by carefully crafting our code, we can steer users in the right direction or at the very least prevent them from doing something that can produce unwanted results.

Using *TextLength* in a Boolean Expression

You know that a *Boolean* variable can hold the values True or False. What might be surprising is that we can also use an integer value to determine True or False. The number 0 represents False, and any non-zero number represents True. Not all languages allow this use of *Boolean* variables, but it is allowed in Visual Basic .NET.

Knowing this, we could modify the following code, which is from the preceding code sample, by omitting the > 0 in the first expression. If there is no text entered in the text box, the *TextLength* property returns 0. When used in a Boolean expression, the result is False. If there is text in the text box, *TextLength* will return a value greater than 0. When used in a Boolean expression, the result is True.

```
If txtMoney.TextLength And IsNumeric(txtMoney.Text) Then
    lstItems.Enabled = True
```

When we join these two expressions with the *And* operator, we are saying that if one or more characters are in the text box *And* all the characters are numeric, the entire expression should evaluate to True and the list box should be enabled. This will allow the user to select an item in the list box.

Short-Circuiting the Conditional Expressions

Rather than using *And*, we could have used *AndAlso*. *AndAlso* is one of two new logical operators introduced in the latest version of Visual Basic .NET. *AndAlso* is known as a **short-circuiting** operator. It provides some additional efficiency when evaluating expressions. Let's rework the previous code by using the *AndAlso* operator, as shown in the following code sample.

```
Private Sub txtMoney_TextChanged(ByVal sender As System.Object, _
        ByVal e As System.EventArgs) Handles txtMoney.TextChanged

    ' If there is text in the text box and the value entered
    ' is numeric, enable the list box…
    If txtMoney.TextLength > 0 AndAlso IsNumeric(txtMoney.Text) Then
        lstItems.Enabled = True
    Else
        ' place the cursor in the text box
        txtMoney.Focus()

        ' highlight the contents of the text box
        txtMoney.SelectAll()

        ' disable the list box
        lstItems.Enabled = False

        ' deselect any selected item in the list box
        lstItems.SelectedIndex = -1
    End If

End Sub
```

The *AndAlso* operator, much like the *And* operator, joins two conditional expressions. If the first expression evaluates to False, the second expression will not be evaluated. It would be pointless to evaluate it because both expressions would have to evaluate to True in order to run the code in the block. The efficiency comes from not having to evaluate the second expression if the first expression evaluates to False. The improvement in efficiency is quite small and perhaps insignificant in this program, but more complex programs that incorporate many decision constructs could see significant improvement in efficiency as a result of using the short-circuit operators. Regardless of the size or complexity of the program, it is important that you write code that will run as quickly as possible.

The other short-circuiting operator is the *OrElse* operator, which works very much like the *Or* operator. When the *OrElse* operator is used to join two expressions, if the first expression evaluates to True, the second expression is ignored and the code inside the block runs. The reason for this is that only one of the two expressions needs to be True in order to run the code in an *Or* condition, so if the first condition is True, it doesn't matter how the second condition evaluates.

The last thing we need to do is run the code shown in the following code sample to provide the cost of the selected item in the list box and compare that value to the amount entered by the user in the text box provided.

```
Private Sub lstItems_SelectedIndexChanged(ByVal sender As System.Object, _
        ByVal e As System.EventArgs) Handles lstItems.SelectedIndexChanged

    ' If there is no item selected in the list box, then exit the procedure
    If lstItems.SelectedIndex = -1 Then Exit Sub

    ' Test the selected item and set the price based on the selected item
    If lstItems.SelectedItem = "Steak" Then
        txtItemPrice.Text = "5.95"
    ElseIf lstItems.SelectedItem = "Hamburger" Then
        txtItemPrice.Text = "3.50"
    ElseIf lstItems.SelectedItem = "Pizza" Then
        txtItemPrice.Text = "2.50"
    ElseIf lstItems.SelectedItem = "Hotdog" Then
        txtItemPrice.Text = "1.50"
    End If

    If CDec(txtMoney.Text) > CDec(txtItemPrice.Text) Then
        lblChoice.Text = "Order the " & lstItems.SelectedItem.ToString() & "."
    Else
        lblChoice.Text = "Out of your price range."
    End If

    txtMoney.Focus()

End Sub
```

Inside the Code

In the code shown in the preceding code sample, we used the *SelectedIndexChanged* event of the list box to evaluate the expressions and run the code. This event will be raised whenever an item is selected. Note that this event will be raised even when the item selected is the same one that was previously selected. For example, if the first item is selected and the user again clicks the first item, the event is raised again. This seems counter to the name of the event, but the *SelectedIndexChanged* event does not consider what item was selected previously and what item is selected now.

From here we need to explain a little more about the code, starting with the first statement.

Single-Line *If* Statements

In the following line of code, you can see that if no item is selected in the list box, program execution will exit the procedure without running any other code in the procedure.

```
If lstItems.SelectedIndex = -1 Then Exit Sub
```

We could use the *Return* keyword in place of *Exit Sub*. This would essentially do the same thing.

```
If lstItems.SelectedIndex = -1 Then Return
```

Notice that the preceding *If* statement is all on one line, and that there is no *End If*. You should understand that Visual Basic .NET code runs one line at a time. In a normally constructed *If* block (one that is constructed on multiple lines), the compiler understands that the end of the block is defined by the *End If* statement. When the *If* statement starts and finishes on the same line, the *End If* is not required because the entire line is the block and the compiler understands that.

Why was this single-line *If* statement required in the first place? Well, other than to show you an example, we also want to handle a situation in which the user might erase the amount entered in the Available Money text box. If this happens, we want the list box to become disabled and, in doing so, we want to make sure that any selected item is cleared. Remember that the *SelectedIndexChanged* event will be raised any time an item is selected. It also is raised when an item is cleared. Look at the following line of code in the *txtMoney_TextChanged* event handler:

```
lstItems.SelectedIndex = -1
```

We can determine if an item in a list box is selected because the *SelectedIndex* property will always return the index value of the selected item. If no item is selected, the *SelectedIndex* property will always be –1. We can also select an item in the list box by setting the *SelectedIndex* property to any number from 0 to one less than the number of items in the list box. By setting the *SelectedIndex* property to –1, any previously selected item is cleared.

Evaluating Each Item in the List

The second *If* statement in the code above for providing the cost of the selected item in the list box basically evaluates the selected item in the list. When the user selects an item, the program evaluates each of the expressions in turn until it determines the item that was selected. After the program determines the selected item (the first expression that evaluates to True), it will run the code in that *ElseIf* block to assign the price of the selected item to the *Text* property of the text box.

```
If lstItems.SelectedItem = "Steak" Then
    txtItemPrice.Text = "5.95"
ElseIf lstItems.SelectedItem = "Hamburger" Then
    txtItemPrice.Text = "3.50"
ElseIf lstItems.SelectedItem = "Pizza" Then
```

```
    txtItemPrice.Text = "2.50"
ElseIf lstItems.SelectedItem = "Hotdog" Then
    txtItemPrice.Text = "1.50"
End If
```

Comparing the Amounts

The last *If* statement compares the two amounts entered into the text boxes. Notice that we convert each of the amounts to decimal values prior to the comparison by using the *CDec* function. This is good programming practice because we are really comparing numeric values and not string values.

```
If CDec(txtMoney.Text) > CDec(txtItemPrice.Text) Then
    lblChoice.Text = "Order the " & lstItems.SelectedItem.ToString() & "."
Else
    lblChoice.Text = "Out of your price range."
End If
```

Nesting *If* Statements

Sometimes it is necessary to ask another question depending on the answer to the first question. This is quite common and should be expected when coding. Consider a situation in which you are ordering software over the Internet from a company that sells hardware and software. The first question might be "Are you ordering hardware or software?" Based on your answer (you select software), the second question might be "Is this for Mac OS or Windows?" The response to this question might even raise an additional question. Using this example, a nested *If* statement would look like this:

```
If typeOfOrder = software Then
    If typeOfOS = Windows Then
        ' code that will run if OS is Windows
    ElseIf typeOfOS = Mac Then
        ' code that will run if OS is Mac
    End If
ElseIf typeOfOrder = hardware Then
    ' code that will run if order is hardware
End If
```

In any *If* statement, if the conditional expression returns True, the code in that block runs. The block might contain additional *If* statements that can further refine the flow of execution. There is no real limit to the number of levels you can nest *If* statements, but, practically speaking, you should keep the number of levels to four or less.

To demonstrate this, let's take a look at code we have already used. Let's rework the code from above, in the "*IsNumeric* Function" section, to show how we can use a nested *If* statement in place of the *And* operator.

```
Private Sub txtMoney_TextChanged(ByVal sender As System.Object, _
        ByVal e As System.EventArgs) Handles txtMoney.TextChanged

    If txtMoney.TextLength > 0 Then
        ' we will only ask this question if the first If statement returns true
        If IsNumeric(txtMoney.Text) Then
            lstItems.Enabled = True
```

```
        End If
    Else
        txtMoney.Focus()
        txtMoney.SelectAll()
        lstItems.Enabled = False
        lstItems.SelectedIndex = -1
    End If

End Sub
```

Try It

► Modifying the MenuChoices application

1. Add an *If...Then* statement to the code in the MenuChoices application that displays a message box at the end of the *lstItems_SelectedIndexChanged* event handler.

2. If the user has no money (if *txtMoney.Text* is "0"), display a message that says "You are out of cash!" If the user has more than $100, display the message "You have plenty of money!"

What Do You Think?

1. What are the two possible results of the evaluation of a conditional expression?

2. What are the six comparison operators?

3. When would an *If...Then* statement be used in code?

4. When would an *ElseIf* block be used in code?

5. What are the six logical operators?

6. Give two examples of short-circuiting operators.

THE SELECT STATEMENT

When you are evaluating a variable or control property that can contain one of several values, a more elegant way of creating an *If...ElseIf...Else...End If* block is to use a *Select* statement. The *Select* statement construct is generally more efficient and, in many cases, easier to understand.

The syntax of a basic *Select* statement looks like this:

```
Select Case variable
    Case value
        ' code to run if the variable compares to the value and returns True
    Case Else
        ' code to run if no other Case returns True
End Select
```

So how does the *Select* statement work? The variable used in the *Select* statement is compared to the value specified in each of the *Case* blocks. As soon as there is a match, the code statements in that block run. At that point, no other *Case* blocks are evaluated and execution falls through to the *End Select* statement. If none of the specific *Case* values match the variable, the code inside the *Case Else* statement runs. We should note that the *Case Else* statement is optional. If there is no *Case Else* statement and the variable doesn't match any of the *Case* values, no code will run.

A *Select* statement is limited in that it can only be used to compare the content of a variable or control property to any number of different values. In contrast, an *If…ElseIf* construct would allow you to evaluate totally different conditional expressions in the *If* block and in each of the *ElseIf* blocks.

To see this in action, let's rework the code in the *lstItems_SelectedIndexChanged* event handler, replacing the *If* statements with *Select* statements, as shown in the boldface section of the following code sample.

```
Private Sub lstItems_SelectedIndexChanged(ByVal sender As System.Object, _
        ByVal e As System.EventArgs) Handles lstItems.SelectedIndexChanged

    If lstItems.SelectedIndex = -1 Then Exit Sub

    Select Case lstItems.SelectedItem.ToString()
        Case "Steak"
         txtItemPrice.Text = "5.95"
        Case "Hamburger"
            txtItemPrice.Text = "3.50"
        Case "Pizza"
            txtItemPrice.Text = "2.50"
        Case "Hotdog"
            txtItemPrice.Text = "1.50"
    End Select

    Select Case CDec(txtMoney.Text)
        Case Is > CDec(txtItemPrice.Text)
            lblChoice.Text = "Order the " & _
                lstItems.SelectedItem.ToString() & "."
        Case Else
            lblChoice.Text = "Out of your price range."
    End Select

    txtMoney.Focus()
End Sub
```

Inside the Code

We need to explain how the conditional expression works in the *Select* statement because it cannot be directly translated from the *If* statement.

Remember that, in the *If* statement, the conditional expression is evaluated as a whole.

```
lstItems.SelectedItem = "Steak"
```

In a *Select* statement, the variable part of the expression is shown once, at the top the *Select* block, and each possible value is compared to the variable in each of the *Case* blocks.

```
Select Case lstItems.SelectedItem.ToString()
    Case "Steak"
        :
    Case "Hamburger"
        :
    Case "Pizza"
        :
    Case "Hotdog"
        :
End Select
```

In the above code, when we compare for equality, the = operator is implied. If we want to use greater than or less than comparisons, we must include the > or < operators along with the *Is* keyword.

> **TIP** Type **Case > value** and press ENTER. Notice that Visual Basic .NET automatically changes the statement to include the *Is* keyword.

```
Select Case CDec(txtMoney.Text)
    Case Is > CDec(txtItemPrice.Text)
        lblChoice.Text = "Order the " & lstItems.SelectedItem.ToString() & "."
    Case Else
        lblChoice.Text = "Out of your price range."
End Select
```

Multiple Values and Ranges

If you need to run the same code for a number of values, you can list the values in a single *Case* block, separating each value by a comma. For example, if we decided to make hamburger and pizza the same price, we could code it as follows. (Refer to the first code sample in the "The Select Statement" section above to see the original code.)

```
Select Case lstItems.SelectedItem.ToString()
    Case "Steak"
        txtItemPrice.Text = "5.95"
    Case "Hamburger", "Pizza"
        txtItemPrice.Text = "3.50"
    Case "Hotdog"
        txtItemPrice.Text = "1.50"
End Select
```

Just as we can use a *Case* value to determine whether a value matches a variable, we can also specify a range. To start, let's take a look at the code from the CalculateGrade application, in which we evaluated a letter grade for a student based on a percentage. As you might remember, this code produced a logic error that required you to modify the code to test the most restrictive value first.

```
If intPercentage > 60 Then
    strGrade = "D"
ElseIf intPercentage > 70 Then
    strGrade = "C"
ElseIf intPercentage > 80 Then
    strGrade = "B"
ElseIf intPercentage > 90 Then
    strGrade = "A"
Else
    strGrade = "F"
End If
```

We can convert this to a *Select* statement and, if we use a range, it will not be necessary to evaluate the most restrictive value first. To demonstrate this, we will change the *If* statement to a *Select* statement and establish the ranges to determine the outcome.

```
Select Case intPercentage
    Case 60 To 69
        strGrade = "D"
    Case 70 To 79
        strGrade = "C"
    Case 80 To 89
        strGrade = "B"
    Case Is > 90
        strGrade = "A"
    Case Else
        strGrade = "F"
End Select
```

Looking at the code above, you can see that each *Case* block is discrete in that it doesn't have to appear in any particular sequence to get the correct results. Of course, we should keep the list of *Case* blocks in some logical order so that it is easy to read and ensure that we have covered all possible grades.

Try It

Modify the *Select* statement in the MenuChoices application to display the price of french fries as $1.00 and the price of a milk shake as $1.25. Next, change the second *Select* statement, which displays the message "Out of your price range," to include a display of the additional amount of money the user needs to purchase the item.

What Do You Think?

1. What kind of statements can the *Select* statement replace?

2. What is the purpose of a *Case Else* statement in a *Select* block?

3. How can you compare for something other than equality in a *Select* statement?

Q&A

Q. Why is it preferable to create a traditional *If* statement rather than using the single-line version when you do not need an *Else* block?

A. In many circumstances, an *Else* block is not required and might never be. The problem is that requirements change, and you might need to reconfigure the block to provide additional functionality.

Q. If you use a single-line *If* statement, can you run two or more statements if the expression evaluates to True?

A. Yes, but given the considerations noted in the previous answer, it is generally not preferable. Many programmers stay away from this style because it is unusual and harder to understand.

A single-line *If* statement that runs multiple statements requires that each of the statements be separated by a colon. The basic syntax for a single-line *If* statement that runs multiple statements is:

If conditionalexpression Then run *statement 1* : run *statement 2* : run *statement 3*

Q. Can I use a *Select* statement to evaluate the *SelectedIndex* property of a list box or combo box rather than using the *SelectedItem* property?

A. Yes. In fact, many programmers use the *SelectedIndex* property more often than the *SelectedItem* property because the items added to the list box might change at some point, and that would require additional changes to the code. Following is an example of a *Select* statement using the *SelectedIndex* property:

```
Select Case lstItems.SelectedIndex
    Case 0
        txtItemPrice.Text = "5.95"
    Case 1
        txtItemPrice.Text = "3.50"
    Case 2
        txtItemPrice.Text = "2.50"
    Case 3
        txtItemPrice.Text = "1.50"
End Select
```

WRAPPING UP

- You control the flow of code in an *event-driven* language by using expressions and decision structures. Routines that can branch based on user input, system events, and properties form the basis for most functional programs.

- Expressions that compare variables, properties, and other values are used to create programs that require decision making to satisfy their requirements. These comparisons evaluate to either True or False, and the determination of what code to run is based on these results.

- All decision structures, whether *If* statements or *Select* statements, must be able to handle all possible situations. Because you can't provide an *ElseIf* or *Case* block for every possible value, you must cover all the important ones and cover the others with an *Else* or *Case Else* block.

- You can sometimes optimize decision statements by using short-circuit operators that eliminate needless evaluation of some conditions. The *AndAlso* and *OrElse* keywords are examples of short-circuit operators.

KEYWORDS

Boolean expression   conditional expression

comparison operator   logical operator

short-circuiting

REVIEW QUESTIONS

1. Conditional expressions are designed to be evaluated as either
   _____.

   a. Up or Down

   b. True or False

   c. Left or Right

   d. On or Off

2. Which of the following is not a valid comparison operator?

   a. +

   b. =

   c. <

   d. <>

3. Which keyword should be used to evaluate more than one conditional
   expression inside an *If* block?

   a. *End If*

   b. *Then*

   c. *ElseIf*

   d. *Return*

4. What is the name of the method used to load a single item into a list box?

   a. *AddItem*

   b. *LoadItem*

   c. *Add*

   d. *AddObject*

5. *And, Or, Not,* and *Xor* are all examples of _____ operators.

   a. arithmetic

   b. comparison

   c. relational

   d. logical

6. Which logical operator should be used if both expressions that are being
   evaluated must be True in order for the code following the expression to
   run?

   a. *Or*

   b. *Not*

   c. *And*

   d. *Xor*

7. Which of the following are examples of short-circuiting operators? (Choose all correct answers.)

   a. *OrElse*

   b. *IfElse*

   c. *AndAlso*

   d. *AndElse*

8. A complex *If* statement that is evaluating multiple *ElseIf* blocks can often be replaced with a(n) _____ statement to generate code that is more efficient and easier to read.

   a. *Return*

   b. *Evaluate*

   c. *Condition*

   d. *Select*

9. Which of the following is a properly formed *Select* statement that tests to see whether the *Case* variable is less than 5?

   a. `Case Less Than 5`

   b. `Case Is < 5`

   c. `Case > 5`

   d. `Case LT 5`

10. What type of statement should be included in your *Select* statement to handle any value that wasn't specifically covered in one of the cases?

    a. *Else*

    b. *Case Return*

    c. *Case Else*

    d. *Select Else*

11. Conditional expressions are used to control the flow of the statements in code. True or false?

12. <, >, and <> are examples of comparison operators. True or false?

13. When writing an *If* code block containing multiple *ElseIf* blocks, you should evaluate the most restrictive condition first. True or false?

14. The *Or* logical operator requires that either one or both of the expressions be True in order for the entire expression to be True. True or false?

15. If you put an entire *If* statement on one line in the Code Editor, it must still end with *End If*. True or false?

16. A conditional expression is also commonly called a(n) _____ expression because it evaluates to either True or False.

17. *If*, *Then*, and *EndIf* are all examples of Visual Basic .NET _____.

18. You can use a(n) _____ block if there are statements to run when a condition is False in an *If...Then* block.

19. _____ operators are used to join two expressions so they can be evaluated as one expression.

20. _____ operators are new, more efficient operators in Visual Basic .NET that are used to evaluate expressions.

STEP BY STEP

In this project for the Baldwin Museum of Science, you will create a form that will allow the user to click a button to display the current month, day, and time.

The form for this application should look like Figure 6-6.

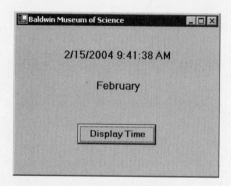

Figure 6-6   The Baldwin Museum of Science date and time form

▶ **Creating a new project**

1. Open Visual Studio .NET if it isn't already open.

2. Click the New Project button on the Start Page.

3. Click Visual Basic Projects under Project Types, and click Windows Application under Templates.

4. Type **TimeCh6** in the Name box.

5. Browse to the location in which you are storing your projects.

6. Click OK.

▶ **Configuring the form and changing the startup object**

1. Right-click Form1.vb in Solution Explorer and rename Form1.vb as **Time.vb**. Press ENTER.

2. Click once in the title bar of the form and change the *(Name)* property of the form to **frmTime**.

3. Change the *Text* property of the form to **Baldwin Museum of Science**, and then press ENTER.

4. Right-click the TimeCh6 project name in Solution Explorer and then click Properties.

5. Change the startup object to **frmTime**, and then click OK.

▶ Setting up the form

1. Add a Button control to the bottom of the form, and name it **btnDisplay-Time**. Change the *Text* property to **Display Time**.

2. Add a Label control to the top of the form, and name it **lblSystemTime**. Delete the contents of its *Text* property. This label will display the system time as it is stored in the computer.

3. Add a second Label control under the first Label, and name it **lblMonth**. Delete the contents of its *Text* property. This label will display the current month in text.

▶ Adding code to the form

1. Double-click the Display Time button on the form to open the Code Editor in the button's *Click* event handler.

2. Type the following code into the *btnDisplayTime_Click* event handler. We are using the *Mid* function to extract or parse the system date so we can figure out what the first one or two characters are and the month that they represent.

```
Dim strMonth As String

'Display the current system time and date
lblSystemTime.Text = Now()

'Use the Mid function to parse the system date and
'get the number representing the month
If Mid(lblSystemTime.Text, 2, 1) = "/" Then
    strMonth = Mid(lblSystemTime.Text, 1, 1)
Else
    strMonth = Mid(lblSystemTime.Text, 1, 2)
End If

'Use a Select statement to determine which month it is
'and display it in the label
Select Case strMonth
    Case 1
        lblMonth.Text = "January"
    Case 2
        lblMonth.Text = "February"
    Case 3
        lblMonth.Text = "March"
    Case 4
        lblMonth.Text = "April"
    Case 5
        lblMonth.Text = "May"
    Case 6
        lblMonth.Text = "June"
    Case 7
        lblMonth.Text = "July"
    Case 8
        lblMonth.Text = "August"
    Case 9
        lblMonth.Text = "September"
    Case 10
        lblMonth.Text = "October"
    Case 11
        lblMonth.Text = "November"
    Case 12
        lblMonth.Text = "December"
End Select
```

▶ Saving and testing your project

1. On the File menu, select Save All to save your work.

2. On the Debug menu, select Start to run your project.

3. Test the program by clicking the Display Time button. The current date and time should be displayed in the top label, and the current month should be displayed in the lower label.

4. On the Debug menu, select Stop Debugging to end the program.

5. On the File menu, select Close Solution to close the project.

6. Close Visual Studio .NET.

FINISH THE CODE

To complete this exercise, open the WoodgroveBankCh6 project that came in your student file. This project contains a form for Woodgrove Bank. The form is used to calculate the fees that should be assessed for an account when given the input information about the average daily balance and other characteristics of the account. Finish the project by referring to the following requirements.

The form has been set up with the required controls, and the *(Name)* and *Text* properties of the controls have been set appropriately. Your task is to write the code for the application. Use the following rules to program the form to calculate the correct total fees. The total fees should be calculated and displayed on the screen in the appropriate label.

- If the average daily balance is less than $500.00, there is a $3.00 fee.

- If the customer is using online bill payment and their average daily balance is less than $500.00, there is an additional $5.00 fee.

- If the customer used an automated teller machine (ATM) more than 10 times during the month, there is an additional fee of $.50 for each ATM use over 10.

- If the customer had any overdrawn checks, there is a $25.00 fee for each overdrawn check.

JUST HINTS

In this exercise, you will create a reorder form for Fabrikam. Inc.. that will show the amount of material that should be reordered, based on the quantity on hand, the quantity on order, and the type of material used in the item.

▶ Creating the application and finishing the form

1. Use the following information to create and finish the form. The completed form is shown in Figure 6-7.

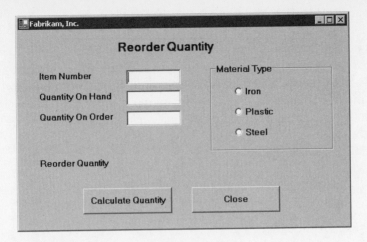

Figure 6-7   The Fabrikam, Inc., reorder form

2. Program the Close button to exit the application.

3. Program the Calculate Quantity button to calculate the amount (in pounds) of material needed. To do this, first subtract the quantity on order from the quantity on hand. If the result is greater than or equal to zero, display the message You do not need to order any material for the item " & txtItemNumber.Text & " at this time in the Reorder Quantity label.

4. If the result is less than zero, multiply the difference by the amount of material needed for each item, as shown in the following list. Display the amount of material that needs to be reordered in the label, along with the item number specified by the user. See Figure 6-8 for an example of the form containing sample data.

- ❏ Iron   5 lbs/Item
- ❏ Plastic   7 lbs/Item
- ❏ Steel   2 lbs/Item

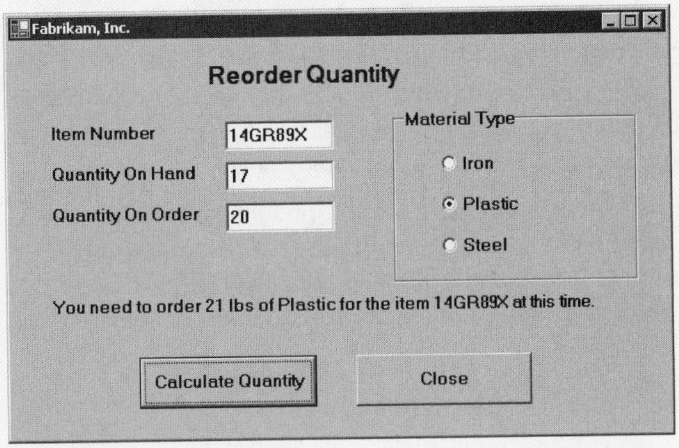

Figure 6-8   The Fabrikam, Inc., reorder form with sample data

ON YOUR OWN

In this exercise, you will create a Visual Basic .NET application for Tailspin Toys that has a form that can be used to select a toy for a child. The user should be able to enter the child's age range and gender and the desired price. The program should use this input data along with the following rules to display a suggestion for an appropriate gift for the child. If, based on the information input by the user, there are no suitable toys, display the message "We have no suggestion for your gift" in a message box. Use the following rules:

- All children under 3 should get a teddy bear.
- Teddy bears cost $5.00.
- All boys over age 10 should get a game.
- All girls over age 2 and under age 10 should get a doll.
- All girls age 10 or over should get a book.
- All boys over age 2 and under or equal to 10 should get a car.
- All cars cost over $10.00.
- All books cost over $8.00.

MORE PRACTICE

1. Write an *If* block that checks to see whether a variable called *intValue* is greater than 150. If it is, display a message box that says "The number is greater than 150."

2. Write an *If...Else* block that checks to see whether *strEntry* is equal to *VOID*. If it is, add one to the variable *intVoidCount*. Otherwise, add one to the variable *intValidCount*.

3. Write the appropriate statements in pseudocode to determine the utensils that should be given to a customer at a restaurant, based on what the customer has ordered. Give salad forks to customers who order salads. Give soup spoons to customers who order soup. Give bibs to customers who order lobster. Give steak knives to customers who order steak. Customers who order both lobster and steak will automatically get salads with their meals, so give them bibs, steak knives, and salad forks. Give pasta spoons to customers who order pasta instead of steak or lobster.

4. Write a *Select* statement that will add the appropriate amount to a variable called *Value*, based on the contents of a variable called *strCoin*. If *strCoin* contains "Penny", add 1 to *Value*. If *strCoin* contains "Nickel", add 5 to *Value*. Add 10 or 25 to *Value* if *strCoin* contains "Dime" or "Quarter", respectively.

5. Write a Visual Basic .NET program that will allow users to enter their age into a text box. If a user enters a number that is less than 1 or greater than 115, display a message box that says the entry is not valid. If the user enters a valid age, display a message box with the appropriate message. Use the information in Table 6-4.

Table 6-4 **Age and Message Information**

Age	Message
1–12	You qualify for the Child discount
13–17	You qualify for the Youth discount
18–25	You qualify for the Young Adult discount
26–54	No discount applies
55–115	You qualify for the Senior Citizen discount

6. Write a Visual Basic .NET program that will calculate the total cost of purchasing a specified number of gallons of a particular type of gasoline. Users should be able to enter the number of gallons they need and the type of gasoline they want to purchase. Determine the price per gallon based on the number of gallons to be purchased and the specified type, using the information in Table 6-5. Calculate the total cost of the gasoline to be purchased and display it in a message box.

Table 6-5 **Gasoline Prices**

Number of gallons	Price per gallon – Regular	Price per gallon – Premium
1–20	$1.70	$1.80
21–30	$1.68	$1.78
31–40	$1.66	$1.76
Over 40	$1.65	$1.75

7. Write a Visual Basic .NET program that will allow the user to enter two numbers and select a calculation type from a list box. The list box should contain the following items: Largest, Smallest, and Average. Use the list box selection and the two numbers entered by the user to display the answer in a label on the form. Display the answer whenever the user clicks an item in the list box.

8. Write a Visual Basic .NET program that will allow the user to enter a word into a text box and then click a button to find out how many vowels (a, e, i, o, u) are in the word. In labels on the screen, display the total number of vowels in the word and how many times each individual vowel appears in the word.

CHAPTER 7
LOOPS AND TIMERS

In the previous chapter, you learned how to run sections of a program based on the decisions made in the code. This allows programs to take various paths through the code and eventually provide different results based on decisions made. In this chapter, we will be discussing the concept and structure of *repetitive execution*, which is the ability to run blocks of code repeatedly.

Upon completion of this chapter, you will be able to:

- Create *For* loops that repeat a fixed number of times.

- Code *While* loops that repeat as long as a condition is True.

- Create *Do loops* that repeat until a condition is True.

- Read the contents of a text file by using a *Do* loop.

- Use a timer that will run code at specified intervals.

FOR...NEXT LOOPS

Before we get into specific types of loops, it might be a good idea to understand how loops work and why you would want to use them in the first place. A little later we will discuss each type of loop in greater detail, but for now let's look at the syntax of a *For...Next* loop. Let's look at an example of a *For...Next* loop:

```
For intIndex As Integer = 0 To 9
    Console.WriteLine(intIndex)
Next intIndex
Console.ReadLine()
```

In the preceding code, you can see that we have declared a variable of type *Integer* that will be used to keep track of the current iteration through the loop. The first line of the loop, `For intIndex As Integer = 0 To 9`, is where we actually declare the variable and set the starting and ending values for the loop. A properly constructed *For...Next* loop must have defined start and end points in order to compile. If you omit either of these values, you will get a syntax error when you attempt to build or run the code.

Note also that *intIndex* (the variable used for the loop counter) only has scope inside the loop. After the loop terminates, *intIndex* will go out of scope and will no longer be accessible. If you need *intIndex* to have scope beyond the boundaries of the loop, you must declare it prior to the loop. Let's look at an example of this:

```
' The counter variable will have scope after the loop has terminated.
Dim intIndex As Integer

For intIndex = 0 To 9
    ' write the current value of the counter variable
    Console.WriteLine(intIndex)
Next intIndex
Console.ReadLine()
```

The second line of code, `Console.WriteLine(intIndex)`, prints the current value of the counter variable *intIndex* to the console window (or to the Output window if you have created a Microsoft Windows application). The last line of code in the loop, `Next intIndex`, automatically adds 1 to the current value of *intIndex*, assuming that the current value is less than or equal to 9. The loop will terminate when the value of *intIndex* is greater than 9.

Now you know how a simple *For...Next* loop works. This is a good time to briefly explain why you might want to use a loop in the first place. Let's say you had a rather long list of items in a list box and you wanted to evaluate each item in turn to see whether it matched another value. It would be rather tedious to write code that would evaluate each item one by one. In the next programming example, we will demonstrate a functional but tedious way of comparing a list of values with another value.

ListColors Application

The ListColors application will allow the user to enter a color and see whether the color exists in a list box.

▶ **Building the ListColors application**

1. Create a new Windows application named **ListColors**.

2. Name the form **frmListColors**, and set the *Text* property of the form to **List Colors**. Don't forget to reset the startup object after you have changed the name of the form.

3. Use the information in Table 7-1 to name the controls and set their *Text* properties appropriately.

Table 7-1   **Controls and Properties for the ListColors Application**

Control	(Name)	Text
TextBox	**txtColor**	<blank>
ListBox	**lstColors**	
Label	Label1	**Type the name of a &color:**
Button	**btnFindColor**	**Find Color**

The completed form should look like Figure 7-1 when it is running. Notice that a limited list of colors is added to the list box when the form loads. The user will enter the color in the text box provided, and that value will be compared with each of the items in the list box.

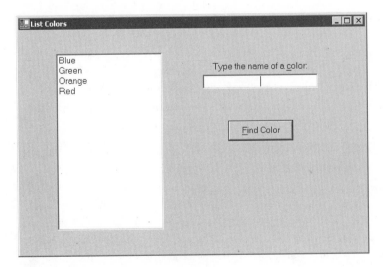

Figure 7-1   The completed ListColors form

You might notice that this program has very little in the way of functionality and that users could just check the list to see if it contains the color they are looking for. This example is designed to show you a couple of ways to iterate through a list of items to locate a value. Later in the chapter we will work with examples that have more practical uses in the real world.

You will add the list of colors to the list box by using the *Form_Load* event handler. When the user enters a value and clicks the Find Color button, the value in the text box will be compared to each list box item in turn until a match is found. When a match is found, you will display a message to the user in the label confirming that the color was found in the list box. If no match is found, an appropriate message will appear.

We will take a look at code that will demonstrate this, but first you want to add the colors to the list box. You will do that by using the *AddRange* method of the list box's *Items* collection. This method allows you to add several items to the *Items* collection of the list box by using a single line of code.

Using the *AddRange* method

In Chapter 6, you saw how to add items to a list box (or a combo box) by using the *Add* method. This method of adding items to a list box works quite well, but when you have a fixed number of items, the coding is repetitive and inefficient.

The *AddRange* method adds a group of objects to the *Items* collection of the list box. This group of objects is known as an *array*. We will discuss arrays in more detail in Chapter 11, but for now you can think of an array as an object that can store a set number of items. In your code, you will create a list of items, add the items to an array, and then pass the array to the *Items* collection of the list box. Although this sounds difficult, it's not. Let's look at the syntax for creating the array, and then you will use this when you implement the *AddRange* method. Look at the following declaration:

```
Dim strItems() As String = {"item1", "item2"}
```

The variable *strItems* is the array that will store the values. We have declared the array as a *String* type and then included the items we wanted to add to the array. The array is declared and initialized with values in one line of code. Because the array is declared as a *String* type, each value is represented inside double quotation marks, and the items are separated by commas. The entire list of items must be surrounded by curly braces (*{}*). Curly braces are used to define the starting and ending points of the list of items that will be added to the array.

Take a look at the following code to see how you can use this array to populate the list box by using the *AddRange* method.

```
Dim strItems() As String = {"item1", "item2"}
ListBox1.Items.AddRange(strItems)
```

We said earlier that you can do this in one line of code, but you can see that the preceding example uses two lines of code. You can create it as one line of code, but you will have to change the syntax a little. The next example shows how you can do this in one line of code.

```
ListBox1.Items.AddRange(New String() {"item1", "item2"})
```

In the preceding example, notice that the array variable *strItems* isn't included. Actually, an array is declared but is not given a specific name. Because you will not be referring to the array in code, you do not need to specify a name. In fact, if you attempted to give the array a name, the code would not compile, and you would get a syntax error.

The list of items is added to a string array as before, but because you do not have a specific name for the array, you also omit the = operator when assigning values to the array because this is done implicitly. As before, if you included the = operator, the code would not compile.

Now that you understand how to use the *AddRange* method, let's implement this method in code.

▶ **Using the *AddRange* method**

1. Double-click a free area of the form to display the Code Editor and create the *Form_Load* event handler. Add the boldface code shown here to the *Form_Load* event handler.

```
Private Sub frmListColors_Load(ByVal sender As System.Object, _
      ByVal e As System.EventArgs) Handles MyBase.Load

    lstColors.Items.AddRange(New String() {"Red", "Green", "Blue", "Orange"})

End Sub
```

2. In the designer window, double-click the Find Color button to display the Code Editor and create the *Click* event handler for the button. Add the boldface code shown in here to the *Form_Load* event handler.

```
Private Sub btnFindColor(ByVal sender As System.Object, _
      ByVal e As System.EventArgs) Handles btnFindColor.Click

    If lstColors.Items(0).ToString() = txtColor.Text Then
        lblColor.Text = txtColor.Text & " is in the list"
    ElseIf lstColors.Items(1).ToString() = txtColor.Text Then
        lblColor.Text = txtColor.Text & " is in the list"
    ElseIf lstColors.Items(2).ToString() = txtColor.Text Then
        lblColor.Text = txtColor.Text & " is in the list"
    ElseIf lstColors.Items(3).ToString() = txtColor.Text Then
        lblColor.Text = txtColor.Text & " is in the list"
    Else
        lblColor.Text = txtColor.Text & " is not in the list."
    End If
End Sub
```

3. Press F5 to run the program.

4. Type **Orange** in the text box and then click the Find Color button. The color is found, and the message in the label confirms this.

5. Now type **Yellow** in the text box and click the Find Color button. The color yellow is not in the list.

   Although this code works, it is a poor solution and is doomed to fail. There are a couple of problems here, the first of which is that each of the *ElseIf* blocks must evaluate each of the items in the list box and, secondly, the code is repetitive and inefficient. Let's rewrite the code using a *For...Next* loop to demonstrate an easier and more efficient way of handling this task.

6. Comment out or delete the original code in the *btnFindColor_Click* event handler, and add the boldface code shown in the following code sample.

```
Private Sub btnFindColor(ByVal sender As System.Object, _
    ByVal e As System.EventArgs) Handles btnFindColor.Click

    For intIndex As Integer = 0 To lstColors.Items.Count - 1
        If lstColors.Items(intIndex).ToString() = txtColor.Text Then
            lblColor.Text = _
                lstColors.Items(intIndex).ToString() & " is in the list"
        Else
            lblColor.Text = txtColor.Text & " is not in the list."
        End If
    Next

End Sub
```

Inside the Code

The counter variable (*intIndex*) keeps track of the current iteration of the loop. This variable is also used to determine the item in the list box that you want to evaluate. You can do this because the starting value for the counter variable is 0 and you know that the index value of the first item in the list box is also 0.

The counter variable has a starting value and an ending value. The starting value is of course 0, and the ending value is a count of the number of items in the list minus 1. You use `Count - 1` because, if the first item has an index value of 0, the last item must have an index value of one less than the total number of items in the list box.

Stepping into this code for the first time, you can see that the value of *intIndex* is 0. The expression `lstColors.Items(intIndex).ToString() = txtColor.Text` is evaluated, and if it returns *True*, the code inside the *If* block runs. If the expression returns *False*, the code inside the block is ignored and the loop continues.

At this point, the value of *intIndex* is incremented and execution returns to the top of the loop. If the value of *intIndex* is less than or equal to the number of items in the list minus 1, the code inside the loop runs. If the value of *intIndex* is greater than the number of items in the list minus 1, execution falls through and the loop is terminated.

Now that you have a better idea of the uses and advantages of looping, let's look more closely at the syntax of a *For...Next* loop and use it in a more practical example.

For...Next Syntax

The basic syntax of a *For...Next* loop looks like this:

```
For counter As Integer  = start To end [ Step step ]
    ' code to run at each iteration
    { Exit For }
Next [ counter ]
```

The *For...Next* looping structure is self-iterating, which means that the construction of the loop includes a starting value and an ending value. The ending value determines when the loop will terminate. Without a way to terminate the loop, you would have what is known as an **infinite loop**.

The loop can be incremented by 1 (the default) or by any other value if you include a *Step* value. The following code provides an example.

```
For intIndex As Integer = 0 To lstColors.Items.Count - 1 Step 2
    If lstColors.Items(intIndex).ToString() = txtColor.Text Then
        lblColor.Text = lstColors.Items(intIndex).ToString() & _
            " is in the list"
    End If
Next intIndex
```

You can also loop backwards by specifying a negative value, as shown in the next example:

```
For intIndex As Integer = lstColors.Items.Count - 1 To 0 Step -1
    If lstColors.Items(intIndex).ToString() = txtColor.Text Then
        lblColor.Text = lstColors.Items(intIndex).ToString() & _
            " is in the list"
    End If
Next intIndex
```

You can terminate the loop early by including an *Exit For* statement, as shown in this example:

```
For intIndex As Integer = 0 To lstColors.Items.Count - 1
    If lstColors.Items(intIndex).ToString() = txtColor.Text Then
        lblColor.Text = lstColors.Items(intIndex).ToString() & _
            " is in the list"
        Exit For
    End If
Next intIndex
```

In the preceding example, terminating the loop early is far more efficient. If the item is found early in the list, it makes no sense to continue looping until the end.

Let's demonstrate the *For...Next* loop in the following Windows application. Note that you will be declaring the counter variable in the loop statement, so the variable will go out of scope when the loop terminates.

▶ Creating the ListNames application

1. Create a new Windows application named **ListNames**. This application will allow the user to compile a list of unique names. This could just as easily be a list of items or ingredients with which you would allow the user to create a shopping list and for which duplication must be avoided.

2. Name the form **frmListNames**, and set the *Text* property of the form to **List Names**. Don't forget to reset the startup object after you have changed the name of the form.

3. Use the information in Table 7-2 to name the controls and set their *(Name)* and *Text* properties appropriately.

Table 7-2   **Controls and Properties for the ListNames Application**

Control	(Name)	Text
TextBox	**txtName**	<blank>
ListBox	**lstNames**	
Label	Label1	**Enter Name:**
Button	**btnFindName**	**Find Name**

The completed form should look like Figure 7-2 when it is running. Notice that there is no functionality to automatically populate the list box when the form is loaded. All names will be manually entered and added to the list box by the user at run time.

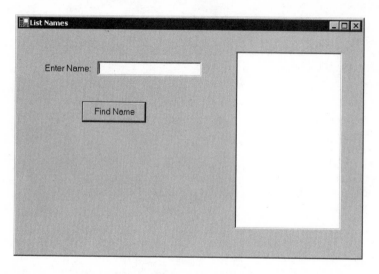

Figure 7-2   The completed ListNames application form

4. In the designer window, double-click the Find Name button to display the Code Editor and create the *Click* event handler. For this example, all the code will be placed inside this event handler.

Pseudocode

Let's write some pseudocode so that you know what functionality to include. This will also give you something to refer to later when you are testing to make sure the program works as designed.

1. Type a name in the text box. The name can be typed in uppercase or lowercase letters, or any combination. The value entered will be converted to proper case before evaluation.

2. Compare the name entered into the text box with each of the items currently in the list box.

3. If the name is not listed, ask the user if he or she wants to add the name to the list.

4. If the user chooses to add the name to the list box, run code to add the name to the *Items* collection of the list box.

5. If the user elects not to add the name to the list box, do nothing.

6. You must scan through the list, but you must also compare the values correctly. By this we mean that both values must be cased the same, in uppercase, lowercase, or proper case. To accomplish this, you will enhance your code slightly to ensure that your comparisons are accurate and will not depend on the user entering the value in any specific case. **Proper casing** is a casing style in which the first letter of the word is uppercase and all subsequent letters are lowercase.

7. Add the boldface code shown here to the *btnFindName_Click* event handler.

```
Private Sub btnFindName_Click(ByVal sender As System.Object, _
        ByVal e As System.EventArgs) Handles btnFindName.Click

    If txtName.TextLength = 0 Then
        txtName.Focus()
        Exit Sub
    End If

    Dim strName As String = StrConv(txtName.Text, VbStrconv.ProperCase)
    Dim blnNameFound As Boolean = False

    For intIndex As Integer = 0 To lstNames.Items.Count - 1
        If lstNames.Items(intIndex).ToString().ToLower() _
            = strName.ToLower() Then
            MessageBox.Show(strName & _
                " was found in the list!", "Name Found", _
                MessageBoxButtons.OK, _
                MessageBoxIcon.Information)

            blnNameFound = True

            lstNames.SelectedIndex = intIndex
            txtName.Clear()
            txtName.Focus()
            Exit For
        End If
    Next

    If blnNameFound = False Then
        If MessageBox.Show(strName & " was not found in the list, " & _
            "do you want to add " & strName & "?", _
            "Add Name?", _
            MessageBoxButtons.YesNo, _
            MessageBoxIcon.Question, _
            MessageBoxDefaultButton.Button1) = DialogResult.Yes Then

            lstNames.Items.Add(StrConv(txtName.Text, VbStrConv.ProperCase))
            txtName.Clear()
            txtName.Focus()
        End If
    End If
End Sub
```

Inside the Code

The first block of code you typed looks like this:

```
If txtName.TextLength = 0 Then
    txtName.Focus()
    Exit Sub
End If
```

The purpose of this code is to test to make sure that a value has been typed into the text box. If nothing has been entered, the value of the *TextLength* property will be 0 and the result of the expression will be True. Focus is then set to the text box, the Sub routine is exited, and the rest of the code is not executed. It is necessary to set focus in code because the user changed the object that has focus when he or she clicked the button.

The next line of code looks like this:

```
Dim strName As String = StrConv(txtName.Text, VbStrConv.ProperCase)
```

This line declares a *String* variable that will store the formatted value from the text box. The value is later compared with each of the values in the list box. The *StrConv* class (sometimes called an *inline function*) takes two arguments: the first is the control (or variable) that is currently storing the value for conversion, and the second is the format that you are converting the value to.

The next line of code is:

```
Dim blnNameFound As Boolean = False
```

Here, you can see that you are declaring a variable of type *Boolean*. This variable will be used a little later in the routine and will allow you the option of adding a name to the list if it is not already there.

After the declarations are complete, you can get to the heart of the code that is the *For...Next* loop. Let's look at that code block now.

```
For intIndex As Integer = 0 To lstNames.Items.Count - 1
    If lstNames.Items(intIndex).ToString().ToLower() = strName.ToLower() Then
        MessageBox.Show(strName & _
            " was found in the list!", "Name Found", _
            MessageBoxButtons.OK, _
            MessageBoxIcon.Information)

        blnNameFound = True
        lstNames.SelectedIndex = intIndex
        txtName.Clear()
        txtName.Focus()
        Exit For
    End If
Next
```

> **NOTE** We have declared the counter variable in the loop. Although the scoping of all variables should be as restrictive as possible, you might have reasons for declaring this variable outside of the loop construct. We suggest that you declare the variable as shown in this example and change the scope only if you have code outside the loop that needs to reference the variable and use its value.

The loop declaration has a starting index of 0 and an ending index that is the last index value in the list box. You can always determine the ending index by getting a count of the items and subtracting 1 from that value.

Inside the body of the loop, you ask the question "Is the value in the text box the same as the value at the position indicated by the counter variable?" The first time through, the counter variable is 0. You will be comparing the value in the text box with the value at the first (technically speaking, the 0th) position of the list box.

Because you currently have no items in the list, what do you think the chances are that you will successfully locate the name? If you said that the chances are good, go to the back of the room.

The thing to note here is that the ending value is actually –1 (subtract 1 from *Count*), so the loop will terminate immediately. Any time the ending value is less than the starting value, the loop will terminate as soon as it is started. This is an important thing to remember when you are debugging your programs.

If you assume that the list box contains some names already, you see that the loop will run. At each iteration, ask the same question "Am I there yet?" or something like that. As soon as the comparison value is found, you will do the following:

1. Display a message to the user, as shown in Figure 7-3.

Figure 7-3   Message displayed to the user

2. Set the *Boolean* variable *blnNameFound* to *True*.

3. Set the *SelectedIndex* property of the list box to the current value of the counter variable. This will highlight the item in the list, as shown in Figure 7-4, and provide visual indication to the user that the value was actually located.

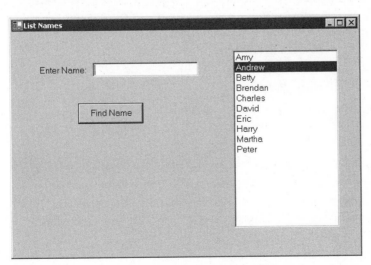

Figure 7-4   The value entered is selected in the list box

4. Clear the text box. This will allow the user to enter a new value without having to select and delete the prior name.

5. Exit the loop.

Now let's take a look at the last block of code:

```
If blnNameFound = False Then
    If MessageBox.Show(strName & " was not found in the list. " & _
        "do you want to add " & strName & "?", _
        "Add Name?", _
        MessageBoxButtons.YesNo, _
        MessageBoxIcon.Question, _
        MessageBoxDefaultButton.Button1) = DialogResult.Yes Then

        lstNames.Items.Add(strName))
        txtName.Clear()
        txtName.Focus()
    End If
End If
```

You can now evaluate whether the name was found in the list. This is done by checking the value of the variable *blnNameFound*. If the value is True, do nothing and exit the procedure. If the value is False, ask the user if he or she wants to add the name to the list. The message box will display the message along with two buttons (Yes and No). You will write the message box code in the form of a question. The result returned by the message box is determined by the button the user clicks when answering the question. If the user clicks Yes, the *DialogResult* will be *Yes* and the code inside the *If* block will run. The name will then be added to the list, the text box will be cleared, and focus will once again be set on the text box to allow users to enter another name if they want to.

Try It

You will now add more functionality to the *btnFindName_Click* event handler to provide more feedback to the user, and also use the *Step* parameter in the *For* statement.

1. If the user clicks the Find Name button without entering a name in the text box, the code will exit out of the *btnFindName_Click* event handler so that no errors will occur, but there is no message displayed to the user explaining what happened. Add a message box to the first *If* statement in the *btnFindName_Click* event handler that reminds users that they must enter a name into the text box before they click the Find Name button.

2. Add Step 1 to the end of the *For* statement in the *btnFindName_Click* event handler. Run the program to see if it performs any differently.

3. Inside the *For* loop in the *btnFindName_Click* event handler, modify the *If* statement so that it will display the index value of the item that was found in the list box. Remember that the index value of the *Items* collection of the list box starts at 0. To make the application more user friendly, add 1 to the index value so that users will know that they are looking at the 1st item and not the 0th item.

What Do You Think?

1. What is the purpose of a counter variable in a *For* loop?

2. How does a *For* loop know when to stop running?

3. What is an infinite loop?

4. How would the performance of the *btnFindName_Click* event handler differ if you added `Step 2` to the end of the `For intIndex As Integer = 0 To lstNames.Items.Count - 1` statement?

WHILE LOOPS

A *While* loop differs from a *For* loop in that it will not run a predetermined number of times. This means that the loop construction does not have predefined starting and ending points. The loop includes an expression that determines how long the loop will keep running. As long as the condition evaluates to True, the loop will stay active. The loop will terminate when the value of the expression changes to False.

The basic syntax for a *While* loop looks as follows:

```
While Boolean expression
    ' code to run at each iteration
End While
```

> **TIP** A *While* loop will continue to run as long as the Boolean expression evaluates to True. It is important to include a way to terminate the loop at some point in time.

Following is a simple example of a *While* loop:

```
While intCounter As Integer < 6
    intCounter += 1
End While
```

Note the use of the += operator in the statement `intCounter += 1`. Remember that += is a shortcut operator. It is used to increment the value *intCounter* by a specified number. If you were to write the longhand version of this statement, it would look like this: `intCounter = intCounter + 1`

The preceding loop will continue to run as long as the value inside the counter variable is less than 6. The expression `intCounter < 6` will return False when the value of *intCounter* is equal to or greater than 6.

You can easily modify the code in the previous application to use a *While* loop rather than a *For* loop. Much of the internal code will remain the same, but the loop syntax will change, and you must also add a statement that increments the value of the counter variable to avoid an infinite loop.

Coding the *While* Loop

Change the existing *For* loop to a *While* loop in the ListName application. After completing the changes, your code should look like the following code:

```
Dim intIndex As Integer

While intIndex <= lstNames.Items.Count - 1
    If lstNames.Items(intIndex).ToString() = strName Then
        MessageBox.Show(strName & " was found in the list!", "Name Found")
        blnNameFound = True
        lstNames.SelectedIndex = intIndex
        txtName.Clear()
        txtName.Focus()
        Exit While
    End If

    intIndex += 1
End While
```

Note that a *While* loop differs from a *For* loop in that the variable used in the conditional expression cannot be declared in the loop construct. It must be declared by using a *Dim* statement before the loop begins.

Do Loops

A *Do* loop is like a *While* loop in that it will not run a predetermined number of times. Instead, the termination of the loop depends on the value of the conditional expression. *Do* loops can be implemented in four different ways, as summarized in Table 7-3. A *Do While* loop is functionally equivalent to a *While* loop, and many programmers prefer to use the *Do While* loop rather than the *While* loop.

Table 7-3 **Do Loops in Visual Basic .NET**

Type of *Do* loop	Description
Do While condition ... Loop	Loop runs while the condition is true
Do Until condition ... Loop	Loop runs until the condition is true
Do ... Loop While condition	Loop runs at least once regardless of the condition, and then continues to run while the condition is true
Do ... Loop Until condition	Loop runs at least once regardless of the condition, and then continues to run until the condition is true

We can use the existing ListNames application to demonstrate the use of these four types of *Do* loops.

Do While...Loop

```
Dim intIndex As Integer
Do While intIndex <= lstNames.Items.Count - 1
    If lstNames.Items(intIndex).ToString() = strName Then
        MessageBox.Show(strName & " was found in the list!", "Name Found", _
            MessageBoxButtons.OK, MessageBoxIcon.Information)
        blnNameFound = True
```

```
            lstNames.SelectedIndex = intIndex
            txtName.Clear()
            txtName.Focus()
            Exit Do
        End If
        intIndex += 1
Loop
```

Do Until...Loop

```
Dim intIndex As Integer
Do Until intIndex > lstNames.Items.Count - 1
    If lstNames.Items(intIndex).ToString() = strName Then
        MessageBox.Show(strName & " was found in the list!", "Name Found", _
            MessageBoxButtons.OK, MessageBoxIcon.Information)
        blnNameFound = True
        lstNames.SelectedIndex = intIndex
        txtName.Clear()
        txtName.Focus()
        Exit Do
    End If
    intIndex += 1
Loop
```

Do...Loop While
This loop will run at least once.

```
Dim intIndex As Integer
Do
    If lstNames.Items(intIndex).ToString() = strName Then
        MessageBox.Show(strName & " was found in the list!", "Name Found", _
            MessageBoxButtons.OK, MessageBoxIcon.Information)
        blnNameFound = True
        lstNames.SelectedIndex = intIndex
        txtName.Clear()
        txtName.Focus()
        Exit Do
    End If
    intIndex += 1
Loop While intIndex <= lstNames.Items.Count - 1
```

Do...Loop Until
This loop will run at least once.

```
Dim intIndex As Integer
Do
    If lstNames.Items(intIndex).ToString() = strName Then
        MessageBox.Show(strName & " was found in the list!", "Name Found", _
            MessageBoxButtons.OK, MessageBoxIcon.Information)
        blnNameFound = True
        lstNames.SelectedIndex = intIndex
        txtName.Clear()
        txtName.Focus()
        Exit Do
    End If
    intIndex += 1
Loop Until intIndex > lstNames.Items.Count - 1
```

File IO Example: Reading a Text File Using a *Do While...Loop*

In this example, we will be introducing a new concept called **File IO** (input/output). We will be using File IO to read a text file located on a disk. You will find that you can just as easily write back to the file and add or update the contents of the file. In order to implement File IO, you will use special class libraries that will allow you to access and interact with files.

File IO is a system-level process that allows you to read and write to files stored on a local hard drive or accessible network server. Although we will not go into great detail about File IO, we will introduce the steps used to provide basic text file access and to read the contents of a file into a text stream.

The FileIO program allows us to populate a ListBox control with a list of names that you extract from a plain text file. The benefit of using an external file is that you can change the list (add, remove, or change names) at any time to suit your needs without having to recode and rebuild the program.

▶ Creating the FileIO application

1. Create a new Windows application named **FileIO**.

2. Use Table 7-4 to set up the form and all the controls. Don't forget to reset the startup object after you have changed the name of the form. The completed form should look like Figure 7-5 when it is running.

Table 7-4   **Controls and Properties for the FileIO Application**

Control	(Name)	Text
Form	**frmFileIO**	**FileIO – Do While...Loop**
ListBox	**lstNames**	
Button	**btnAddNames**	**Add Names**

Figure 7-5   The FileIO application form

3. In the designer window, double-click the Add Names button to display the Code Editor and create the *Click* event handler. In this example, all the code will be placed inside this event handler.

4. Add the boldface code shown here to the *btnAddNames_Click* event handler.

```
Private Sub btnAddNames_Click(ByVal sender As System.Object, _
        ByVal e As System.EventArgs) Handles btnAddNames.Click

        Dim strFilePath As String = Application.StartupPath & "\Names.txt"
        Dim sr as System.IO.StreamReader = System.IO.File.OpenText(strFilePath)
        Dim strName As String = sr.ReadLine()
        Do While Not strName Is Nothing
            lstNames.Items.Add(strName)
            strName = sr.ReadLine()
        Loop

        sr.Close()
End Sub
```

Inside the Code

In the following code statement from the application, you declare a *String* variable that sets the path to the location of the text file and, of course, the name of the file. *Application.StartupPath* is a built-in constant that defines the folder that contains the .exe file.

```
Dim strFilePath As String = Application.StartupPath & "\Names.txt"
```

When the program is built for the first time, the .exe file is created and placed in the *bin* folder. When the text file is placed in the same folder as the .exe file, you can use the *Application.StartupPath* constant to locate the file. Without this, it would be quite tedious to locate the file every time the application was deployed on a different user's computer. The name of the file is concatenated to the end of the path and includes a backslash to denote that the file is located in that folder.

Let's look at the next code statement:

```
Dim sr As System.IO.StreamReader = System.IO.File.OpenText(strFilePath)
```

Here you declare a variable of type *StreamReader*. This is the variable that will store the contents of the text file. Of course you need to open the file (place it in memory), and for this you will use the *OpenText* method of the *File* class.

Next you will declare and initialize a *String* variable called *strName* that will store the first line of text in the text file. To make this happen, you will use the *ReadLine* method of the *StreamReader* object *sr*. After that you will loop through each line of text and add the line that is read to the *Items* collection of the list box.

```
Dim strName As String = sr.ReadLine()
Do While Not strName Is Nothing
    lstNames.Items.Add(strName)
    strName = sr.ReadLine()
Loop
```

This loop will continue to run as long as there is something to read. Note the use of the *Not* operator. This would be frowned upon in standard English because it forces us to use a double negative. (If something is *not nothing*, then it must be something, right?) The loop could be rewritten like this and still provide the same functionality:

```
Dim strName As String = sr.ReadLine()
Do Until strName Is Nothing
    lstNames.Items.Add(strName)
    strName = sr.ReadLine()
Loop
```

Notice the two statements inside the body of the loop:

```
lstNames.Items.Add(strName)
strName = sr.ReadLine()
```

The variable *strName* already holds the first line of text that was read, so you can immediately add that value to the *Items* collection of the list box, and then you can read the next line of text.

Finally, let's look at the last statement:

```
sr.Close()
```

This line of code closes the *StreamReader* object. This is a good programming practice because it releases any resources that the *StreamReader* object is using. Although doing this is not a requirement, it is strongly encouraged.

Using the *Imports* Statement

When you declared and initialized the *StreamReader* object variable, you prefixed the class name *StreamReader* with *System.IO*. The *StreamReader* class belongs to the *System.IO* namespace. To use this class, you must inform the compiler where to locate it.

By adding the Imports System.IO statement to the top of the code module (prior to any other statements), you can effectively eliminate the need to prefix that namespace in code. Let's take a look at the completed code shown in the following code sample. Notice that we have included the *Imports* statement and removed the namespace prefix for the *StreamReader* class.

```
Imports System.IO

Public Class frmFileIO
    Inherits System.Windows.Forms.Form

    ' Windows Form Designer generated code not shown
    Private Sub btnAddNames_Click(ByVal sender As System.Object, _
            ByVal e As System.EventArgs) Handles btnAddNames.Click

        Dim strFilePath As String = Application.StartupPath & "\Names.txt"
        Dim sr As StreamReader = File.OpenText(strFilePath)
        Dim strName As String = sr.ReadLine()
        Do While Not strName Is Nothing
            lstNames.Items.Add(strName)
```

```
        strName = sr.ReadLine()
    Loop

        sr.Close()
    End Sub
End Class
```

▶ **Running and testing the application**

1. Press F5, and click the Add Names button when the form appears. At this point you should receive the error message shown in Figure 7-6. If you read the message closely, you will see that the program could not find the file containing the names. You still need to create it.

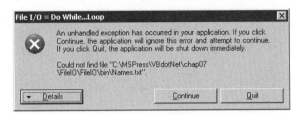

Figure 7-6   Error message displayed when text file is not found

2. Click Quit, closing the message and halting the program.

3. To create the text file, open Notepad and save the file as **Names.txt** in the bin folder of the FileIO application.

4. Type a list of names into the text file. After each name, press ENTER. This ensures that each name will be written on a separate line.

5. After adding the names, save and close the file.

6. Now run the program once again and click the Add Names button. The list box is now populated with the names you added to the text file. For example, see Figure 7-7 for a representative list.

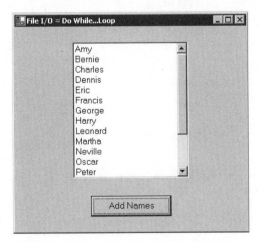

Figure 7-7   The list box populated with names from the file

Defensive Programming

When we introduced debugging in Chapter 5, we mentioned **defensive programming** techniques, which are methods of catching and handling potential error situations before they generate errors. In Chapter 6 we introduced this technique in our decision structures. For the FileIO application, because we are relying on an external file being present in the location we have specified, it makes sense to provide some defensive coding to handle the inevitable run-time exception that will occur if the file isn't found. The defensive code should prevent a run-time exception from being thrown and provide an appropriate message to the user.

Let's write the pseudocode that defines exactly what we want to do.

1. Test to make sure that the file exists in the specified location.

2. If the file is not located, display a message to the user and then exit the procedure.

3. If the file does exist, run the rest of the code in the procedure.

Now that you have pseudocode describing what needs to be done, you can write the code to implement this defensive technique. Insert the following code block after the *strFilePath* variable declaration and before the *StreamReader* variable declaration.

```
If Not File.Exists(strFilePath) Then
    Dim strMessage As String = Chr(34) & _
        strFilePath & Chr(34) & " does not exist."

    MessageBox.Show(strMessage, "File Error", _
        MessageBoxButtons.OK, _
        MessageBoxIcon.Error)
    Return
End If
```

The code for the entire event handler should look as follows:

```
Private Sub btnAddNames_Click(ByVal sender As System.Object, _
        ByVal e As System.EventArgs) Handles btnAddNames.Click
    Dim strFilePath As String = Application.StartupPath & "\Names.txt"

    If Not File.Exists(strFilePath) Then
        Dim strMessage As String = Chr(34) & _
            strFilePath & Chr(34) & " does not exist."
        MessageBox.Show(strMessage, "File Error", _
            MessageBoxButtons.OK, _
            MessageBoxIcon.Error)
        Return
    End If

    Dim sr As StreamReader = File.OpenText(strFilePath)
    Dim strName As String = sr.ReadLine()

    Do While Not strName Is Nothing
        lstNames.Items.Add(strName)
        strName = sr.ReadLine()
    Loop

    sr.Close()
End Sub
```

Inside the Code

To verify that the file has been located, the *File* class has an *Exists* method that takes the file name and path as a string argument. This method will return a *Boolean* value (True if the file exists or False if the file does not exist). You will test the return value and then run the appropriate code.

```
If Not File.Exists(strFilePath) Then
```

Notice that we have again included the *Not* operator in the expression. As always, there is more than one way to code the expression. Remember that, in order to run code statements inside the *If* block, the result of the conditional expression must be True. The *Not* operator reverses the result. If the method returns False, the overall result of the expression is True, allowing the code inside the *If* block to run.

You know that, to run the code in the *If* block, the *File.Exists* method call would have to return False; therefore, you could recode the *If* statement like the following statement:

```
If File.Exists(strFilePath) = False Then
```

The rest of the code should be somewhat familiar to you, perhaps with the exception of *Chr(34)* and *Return*. The purpose of *Chr(34)* is to present the displayed string inside double quotation marks. The ASCII value for a double quotation mark is 34. Using the built-in *Chr* function, you can convert the ASCII value of a double quotation mark to its character representation on the screen.

Rather than using the *Chr* function, you could just type the double quotation mark directly in your string, as long as you include the escape character in front of it. In this case, the escape character is another double quotation mark. Let's look at how that's done.

Take the following code statement:

```
Chr(34) & strFilePath & Chr(34)
```

If we use the escape character, the statement would look like this:

```
"""" & strFilePath & """"
```

The *Return* statement exits the procedure. Technically, the *Return* statement returns execution to the procedure (the method) that called this procedure. The *Return* statement is normally associated with a method call that expects a returned value. Because you are not returning any value, the *Return* statement is used without a value.

Using Nested Loops

Just as you can nest an *If* statement inside another *If* statement, you can nest a loop within another loop. Assuming that you wanted to compare the items in one list box to the items in another list box, you would construct the loop like this:

```
For intOuterLoop As Integer = 0 To ListBox1.Items.Count -1
    For intInnerLoop As Integer = 0 To ListBox2.Items.Count -1
```

```
                If ListBox1.Items(intOuterLoop).ToString() = _
                    ListBox2.Items(intInnerLoop).ToString() Then
                    Label1.Text = ListBox1.Items(intOuterLoop).ToString() & _
                        " was found in the ListBox2."
                    Exit For
                End If
            Next intInnerLoop
    Next intOuterLoop
```

To see this in action, create a new Windows application that will compare the items in one list to the items in a second list.

CompareLists Program

In this example, you are going to create a program named CompareLists that will compare the items in one list box to the items in a second list box. After the comparison has been made, any matched values will be selected in each list box. Figure 7-8 shows the running form for the CompareLists program.

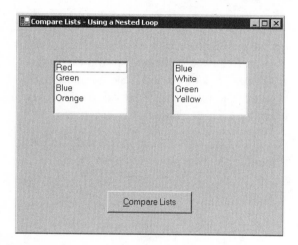

Figure 7-8   The CompareLists program form

▶ **Creating the CompareLists program**

1. Create a new Windows application named **CompareLists**.

2. Use Table 7-5 to set up the form and all the controls. Don't forget to reset the startup object after you have changed the name of the form.

Table 7-5   **Controls for the CompareLists Program**

Control	(Name)	Text
Form	**frmCompareLists**	**Compare Lists – Using a Nested Loop**
Label	**lblResult**	<blank>
ListBox	**lstColors1**	
ListBox	**lstColors2**	
Button	**btnCompareLists**	**&Compare Lists**

3. Following is the pseudocode for the program:

   a. When the form is loaded, both list boxes will display a list of colors.

   b. When the button is clicked, the colors in the first list box will be compared to the colors in the second list box.

   c. If any color in the first list box matches a color in the second list box, both colors will be selected and the label will display the result.

4. Double-click a free area of the form to display the Code Editor and create the *Form_Load* event handler. Add the boldface code shown here to the *Form_Load* event handler.

```
Private Sub frmCompareLists_Load(ByVal sender As System.Object, _
    ByVal e As System.EventArgs) Handles MyBase.Load

    lstColors1.Items.AddRange(New String() _
        {"Red", "Green", "Blue", "Orange"})
    lstColors2.Items.AddRange(New String() _
        {"Blue", "White", "Green", "Yellow"})

End Sub
```

5. Double-click the button to display the Code Editor and create the *btnCompareLists_Click* event handler. Add the boldface code shown here to the *btnCompareLists_Click* event handler.

```
Private Sub btnCompareLists_Click(ByVal sender As System.Object, _
    ByVal e As System.EventArgs) Handles btnCompareLists.Click

    ' This routine will loop through each item in the first list box
    ' and compare each value with each of the items in the second
    ' list box...

    ' Construct the outer loop...
    For intOuterLoop As Integer = 0 To lstColors1.Items.Count - 1
        ' Construct the inner loop...
        For intInnerLoop As Integer = 0 To lstColors2.Items.Count - 1
            ' If the current item in the lstColors2 is equal to the
            ' current item in lstColors1 then display the match in
            ' the label...
            If lstColors1.Items(intOuterLoop).ToString() = _
                lstColors2.Items(intInnerLoop).ToString() Then
                    lblResult.Text &= lstColors1.Items(intOuterLoop).ToString() & _
                        " was found in lstColors2." & ControlChars.CrLf

                ' Highlight (select) the matched items...
                lstColors1.SelectedIndex = intOuterLoop
                lstColors2.SelectedIndex = intInnerLoop

                ' If there is a match, exit the inner loop...
                Exit For
            End If
        Next intInnerLoop
    Next intOuterLoop

End Sub
```

6. Press F5 to run the program. When the form appears, both list boxes will be populated.

7. Click the Compare Lists button. Verify that the label displays the matched items. Also verify that the matched items are selected in each list box. Figure 7-9 shows the results.

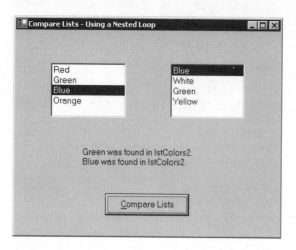

Figure 7-9   Comparing the items in the list boxes

Is there a problem? Well, yes and no. The program runs fine, but there are two colors in the first list box with matches in the second list box. The colors green and blue appear in both list boxes, but only blue is selected. What happened to green? The problem isn't in the code; it's in the setting for the *SelectionMode* property of the list boxes.

▶ Modifying the *SelectionMode* property

1. Display the form in design view, and select both list boxes.

2. Locate the *SelectionMode* property and notice that the default value is One. This means that there can only be one item selected at a time in the list box.

3. Change the value of the *SelectionMode* property to **MultiSimple**.

4. Save the changes and press F5 to run the program again.

5. Click Compare Lists. Verify that the label displays the matched items. Also verify that both green and blue are selected in both list boxes. Figure 7-10 shows the correct results.

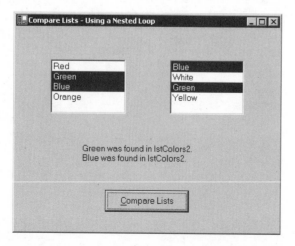

Figure 7-10   The corrected comparison

Inside the Code

When the form is loaded, the list boxes are populated with a number of string values representing colors. The list boxes are populated by the *AddRange* method of the *Items* collection of each list box.

Let's take a look at the code once again:

```
For intOuterLoop As Integer = 0 To lstColors1.Items.Count - 1
    For intInnerLoop As Integer = 0 To lstColors2.Items.Count - 1
        If lstColors1.Items(intOuterLoop).ToString() = _
            lstColors2.Items(intInnerLoop).ToString() Then
            lblResult.Text &= lstColors1.Items(intOuterLoop).ToString() & _
                " was found in lstColors2." & ControlChars.CrLf

            lstColors1.SelectedIndex = intOuterLoop
            lstColors2.SelectedIndex = intInnerLoop
            Exit For
        End If
    Next intInnerLoop
Next intOuterLoop
```

Looking at the code in the *btnCompareLists_Click* event handler, you can see that there are two loops. The outside loop will run and initialize the counter variable *intOuterLoop* to 0. This will provide the value of the first item in *lstColors1*. When the inside loop runs, this value will be compared to each of the items in *lstColors2*. If a match is found, a message will appear and the item will be selected in each of the list boxes. At that point, the inside loop will be exited, the outside loop will be incremented, and the cycle will start again, but this time with a new comparative value from *lstColors1*.

Each successful comparison will result in the message being updated to show all the matches and, of course, the matched items will be selected in their respective list boxes. Take a closer look at the following code:

```
lblResult.Text &= lstColors1.Items(intOuterLoop).ToString() & _
    " was found in lstColors2." & ControlChars.CrLf
```

When more than one match is found, you want to display the information, so you must append any new text to the existing text in the label. By using the &= shortcut operator, you can concatenate the new text to the existing text. If you didn't do that, the new text would overwrite the existing text and you wouldn't know what matches were found unless you looked at the selected items in each of the list boxes.

Appending the text is fine, but you want to write each match on a separate line to make the text more readable. To do that, you have used the constant *CrLf* (carriage return/linefeed). *CrLf* is one of several members belonging to the *ControlChars* module. Table 7-6 shows the useful constants available to you when you reference the *ControlChars* module. The Member column lists the constants that you can use directly. The Equivalent column shows the ASCII values that can be used in place of the constants. The *Chr* function converts the ASCII value to its character representation.

Table 7-6   *ControlChars* **Constants**

Member	Equivalent	Description
CrLf	*Chr(13) & Chr(10)*	Carriage return/linefeed character combination
Cr	*Chr(13)*	Carriage return character
Lf	*Chr(10)*	Linefeed character
NewLine	*Chr(13) + Chr(10)*	New line character
NullChar	*Chr(0)*	Character having value 0
Tab	*Chr(9)*	Tab character
Back	*Chr(8)*	Backspace character
Quote	*Chr(34)*	Quotation mark character (" or ') used to enclose values

From Table 7-6, we can see that *Chr(13) & Chr(10)* would be equivalent to using *ControlChars.CrLf*.

If you want to learn more about the various constants in the *ControlChars* module, select Index from the Help menu and type **ControlChars constants** in the Look For box. To learn more about using the ASCII values to represent characters, type **ASCII** in the Look For box.

Let's step through the code to see what happens in slow motion.

▶ **Stepping into the code**

1. Set a breakpoint next to the *btnCompareLists_Click* event handler declaration.

2. Press F5 to run the program.

3. Click Compare Lists. Code execution will halt at the breakpoint.

4. Add the expressions shown in Figure 7-11 to a Watch window. Remember that you cannot add expressions to the Watch window until the program is in debug mode.

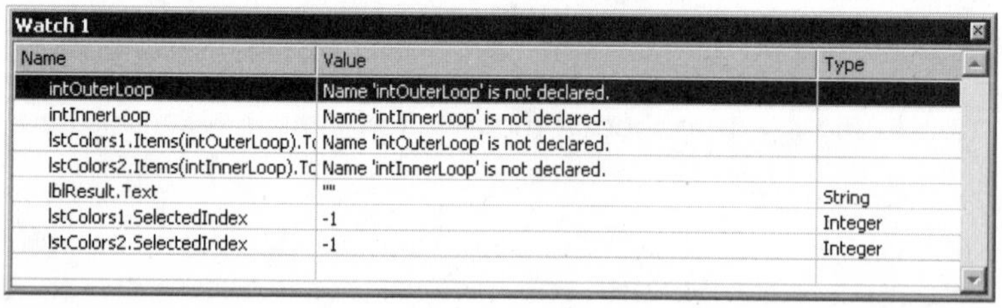

Watch 1		
Name	**Value**	**Type**
intOuterLoop	Name 'intOuterLoop' is not declared.	
intInnerLoop	Name 'intInnerLoop' is not declared.	
lstColors1.Items(intOuterLoop).T(	Name 'intOuterLoop' is not declared.	
lstColors2.Items(intInnerLoop).Tc	Name 'intInnerLoop' is not declared.	
lblResult.Text	""	String
lstColors1.SelectedIndex	-1	Integer
lstColors2.SelectedIndex	-1	Integer

Figure 7-11   The Watch window displaying the expressions to monitor

As you might remember from Chapter 5, this can be done quite easily. Select the expression in the Code Editor, right-click on the expression, and then select Add Watch from the context menu. The expression will be added to a Watch window, and the current value of the expression will be displayed. You can monitor the Watch window as you step into the code to get a better idea of what is happening. Figure 7-11 shows the Watch window listing the expressions that you want to monitor.

Notice that, at this point, the values for each of the counter variables and the current item in each of the list boxes are shown as not declared. This is expected because both counter variables are currently out of scope. The current value for the label is an empty string, and it will remain so until the first match is found. Finally, the *SelectedIndex* value for each list box is shown as −1 because no item is currently selected.

5. Press F11 several times. Monitor the Watch window for changes to the values as you continue to press F11.

6. As you continue pressing F11, the values of the counter variables will be updated for each loop iteration. When there is a match, the label will be updated and the matching items will be selected in the list boxes. Figure 7-12 shows the Watch window after the first match. We have halted execution at the *Exit For* statement to display the results you currently see in Figure 7-12.

Figure 7-12   The Watch window after the first match is found

7. Continue pressing F11 until the second match is found. Look at the Watch window to see the results.

8. Press F5 to continue to the end. The form will now appear, showing the selected matches.

TRY IT

Modify the ListNames application to use the four different types of *Do* loops (*Do While*, *Do Until*, *Do...Loop While*, and *Do...Loop Until*). Which one do you think is the best choice for this application?

What Do You Think?

1. How is a *While* loop different from a *For* loop?

2. If you write a *While* statement with a condition that will never evaluate to False, what will happen?

3. What are the four types of *Do* loops?

4. What is File IO used for?

5. Why would you use the `Imports System.IO` statement?

LOOPING WITH TIMERS

Sometimes you will want your code to run repeatedly based on timing instead of using a conditional loop. Running code at predetermined intervals is a job for a timer. Microsoft Visual Basic .NET provides a Timer component and a *Timer* class that you can use to accomplish this task.

Timer Component

The Timer component is easy to use in your applications. It is available from the Toolbox and can be added to the component tray at design time. The component tray is located below the form and is displayed after you have added a component to it. The component tray is designed to hold components that have no design-time visual interface. The Timer component, besides having a *(Name)* property, has two other properties that we will be interacting with. Additionally, the Timer component has one event.

The properties are:

- **Enabled** The *Enabled* property takes a *Boolean* value and is used to turn the timer on and off.

- **Interval** The *Interval* property takes a numeric value that equates to milliseconds. 1000 milliseconds = 1 second.

The *Tick* event is used to run code at a predetermined interval. Each time the amount of time specified in the *Interval* property elapses, the code in the *Tick* event will run.

DigitalClock Program

In the next example, you are going to create a DigitalClock program that will display the current system time in a label. To always display the current time, you need to periodically refresh the time displayed in the label. To do this, you will use a timer that will raise the *Tick* event at an interval of 500 milliseconds. The timer's *Tick* event handler will contain the code. Figure 7-13 shows the running form for the DigitalClock program.

Figure 7-13   The DigitalClock program form

▶ Creating the DigitalClock program

1. Create a new Windows application named **DigitalClock**.

2. Use Table 7-7 to set up the form and all the controls. Don't forget to reset the startup object after you have changed the name of the form.

3. When you have added the Timer component and renamed it, set its *Interval* property to **500**. The *Enabled* property's default setting is False. We will provide code to change this value at run time.

Table 7-7   **Controls for the *DigitalClock* Program**

Control	(Name)	Text
Form	**frmClock**	**Digital Clock**
Label	**lblClock**	<blank>
Label	**lblClockStatus**	**Clock Running**
Button	**btnClock**	**Start Clock**
Timer	**tmrClock**	

4. Following is the pseudocode for the program:

   a. When the form is loaded, the main label will display midnight (12:00:00 AM), and the secondary label will display the text *Midnight*.

   b. When the button is clicked, the clock will start to run. The time will be updated twice every second to ensure that the time is always current. The button's text will now display *Stop Clock*.

   c. When the button is clicked a second time, the displayed time will freeze and the button's text will display *Start Clock*.

5. Double-click a free area of the form to display the Code Editor and create the *Form_Load* event handler. Add the boldface code shown here to the *Form_Load* event handler.

```
Private Sub frmClock_Load(ByVal sender As System.Object, _
        ByVal e As System.EventArgs) Handles MyBase.Load

    lblClock.Text = FormatDateTime("00:00:00", DateFormat.LongTime)
    lblClockStatus.Text = "Midnight"

End Sub
```

6. In the designer window, double-click the Start Clock button to display the Code Editor and create the *Click* event handler. Add the boldface code shown here to the *btnClock_Click* event handler.

```
Private Sub btnClock_Click(ByVal sender As System.Object, _
        ByVal e As System.EventArgs) Handles btnClock.Click

    If btnClock.Text = "Start Clock" Then
        btnClock.Text = "Stop Clock"
        tmrClock.Enabled = True
        lblClockStatus.Text = "Clock Running"
    Else
        btnClock.Text = "Start Clock"
```

```
            tmrClock.Enabled = False
            lblClockStatus.Text = "Clock Stopped"
        End If

    End Sub
```

7. In the designer window, locate the Timer component in the component tray and double-click it.

8. The *Tick* event handler will be added to the Code Editor. Add the bold-face code shown below to this event handler.

```
Private Sub tmrClock_Tick(ByVal sender As System.Object, _
        ByVal e As System.EventArgs) Handles tmrClock.Tick

    lblClock.Text = Now.ToLongTimeString()

End Sub
```

9. Press F5 to run the program. When the form appears, the main label will display 12:00:00 AM.

10. Click Start Clock. Verify that the clock starts and updates twice every second. Also verify that the button's text now displays Stop Clock.

11. Click Start Clock a second time. Verify that the clock stops and the displayed time freezes. Also verify that the button's text now displays Start Clock.

12. Click the button several more times to toggle the clock on and off.

Inside the Code

When the form is loaded, you want to display 12:00:00 AM. We chose this time because this is the time that the VCR has flashed since it was purchased several years ago. To display the time as shown, we used the *FormatDateTime* function and provided the two arguments required: "*00:00:00*", which represents a time value, and *DateFormat.LongTime*, which is the format we want to use when the time is displayed.

Each time the button is clicked, we need to determine whether we are turning the clock on or turning it off. Although there are several ways to do this, the following method is the easiest to explain and, we hope, to understand.

```
If btnClock.Text = "Start Clock" Then
    btnClock.Text = "Stop Clock"
    tmrClock.Enabled = True
    lblClockStatus.Text = "Clock Running"
Else
    btnClock.Text = "Start Clock"
    tmrClock.Enabled = False
    lblClockStatus.Text = "Clock Stopped"
End If
```

The preceding block of code is a classic switch (sometimes referred to as a *toggle*). Basically, if the clock is on, turn it off. If it is off, turn it on. The expression uses the *Text* property of the button to determine whether we want to enable the timer (start the clock) or disable the timer (stop the clock).

When the button is clicked, check the value of the button's *Text* property. If it's equal to "Start Clock", the result of the expression is True. At this point you can be reasonably sure that the timer is disabled and the clock is not running. You can then change the value of the button's *Text* property to "Stop Clock", change the status label's *Text* property to "Clock Running", and start the timer. The clock is now running, and the controls are set to allow you to stop the clock whenever you want.

When the timer is enabled, the *Tick* event will be raised at regular intervals. The interval is the value that you established at design time (500 milliseconds). This value can also be set at run time. The event is raised when the specified interval has timed out. For example, if the *Interval* is set to 10 seconds (10,000 milliseconds), the first time the *Tick* event is raised would be 10 seconds after the timer was enabled.

```
lblClock.Text = Now.ToLongTimeString()
```

Each time the *Tick* event is raised, the label's *Text* property is updated to display the value of *Now*, a built-in function that represents the current date and time. When you format the output using the *ToLongTimeString* method, the current time will be displayed.

Timer Class

Rather than using the Timer component in your application, you could use the *Timer* class and **instantiate** it at run time. When you say you are going to instantiate a class, you mean that you are going to create an instance, or object, from that class. Using the *Timer* class has an added benefit: you can declare and instantiate it precisely when you want it. This helps to reduce the resources used by the application and provide some additional efficiency.

The *Timer* class is part of the *Timers* collection namespace. This is another handy feature in that it allows you to have several timers running, and you are able to control each one individually or all of them at once through the collection.

To demonstrate the use of the *Timer* class, we will rebuild our digital clock application. Most of the code you wrote for the first clock program can be retained. We'll show you what you'll need to change and add to complete this project by using the *Timer* class instead of the Timer component.

DigitalClock Using the *Timer* Class

Before you update the code, it's worth mentioning that the *Timer* class has more functionality than the Timer component, and as a result it has properties and methods that require a little explanation. The properties, methods, and events are summarized in Table 7-8. With these in mind, you can begin modifying the DigitalClock program.

Table 7-8 *Timer* **Class Properties, Methods, and Events**

Property	Purpose
Enabled	This works the same as the *Enabled* property of the Timer component.
Interval	This works the same as the *Interval* property of the Timer component.
AutoReset	This property takes a Boolean value. When it's set to *False*, it allows the Timer's *Elapsed* event to be raised one time only. When it's set to *True*, the *Elapsed* event will be raised continuously, depending, of course, on the value of the *Interval* property.

Method	Purpose
New	The default constructor. This creates a new instance of the *Timer* class.
New(ByVal Double)	This is an *overloaded* constructor that allows you to set the interval when the instance is created.
Start	This method sets the *Enabled* property of the *Timer* to *True* and turns on the timer.
Stop	This method sets the *Enabled* property of the *Timer* to *False* and turns off the timer.
Close	This method closes the *Timer* and releases the resources (memory).

Event	Purpose
Elapsed	This is the only event available for the *Timer* class. It is functionally equivalent to the *Tick* event of the Timer component.

▶ **Modifying the DigitalClock program**

1. Open the DigitalClock solution in Microsoft Visual Studio .NET and locate the tmrClock Timer component in the component tray.

2. Select the Timer component and press DELETE.

   TIP The code related to the Timer component that you deleted is actually retained, and if you try to compile the code at this point, several syntax errors will be generated.

3. Declare a class-level variable of type *Timer* with events, and name it **tmrClock**. The declaration statement will look like the following line of code:

```
Private WithEvents tmrClock As Timer
```

What is *WithEvents* and why would you use it in the declaration? We don't want to get into too much detail, but consider the following. A class has predefined properties, methods, and events. You know this because you have been dealing with many of them up to this point. Although properties and methods are freely available when you use an object (think form or control), the events are not freely available unless the object variable is explicitly declared with the *WithEvents* keyword.

You didn't know anything about *WithEvents* before, but you were able to use the events of the form and controls. Why? Fortunately, Visual Studio .NET declared the object variables appropriately for you. Each time a control is added to the integrated development environment (IDE), the object variable is declared, and if that object has publicly available events, the declaration includes the *WithEvents* keyword.

After you create an instance of a class or instantiate it, you will be able to use the properties and methods of the class. Because you declared the class with *WithEvents*, you can code for its event.

You can create an instance of tmrClock inside the *frmClock_Load* event handler.

4. Type the boldface statement shown here in the *frmClock_Load* event handler, just below the two statements that assign values to the labels.

```
Private Sub frmClock_Load(ByVal sender As System.Object, _
        ByVal e As System.EventArgs) Handles MyBase.Load

    lblClock.Text = FormatDateTime("00:00:00", DateFormat.LongTime)
    lblClockStatus.Text = "Midnight"

    tmrClock = New Timer(500)

End Sub
```

In the statement you just typed, you have created an instance of the class, and in doing so you have also set the interval for the timer. You could have coded it like this:

```
tmrClock = New Timer()
tmrClock.Interval = 500
```

If you had coded the two statements like this, the overall results would have been the same but a little less elegant and, more importantly, less efficient.

Because the Timer class has an *Elapsed* event rather than a *Tick* event, you must replace the *Tick* event handler with the *Elapsed* event handler. Let's do that now.

5. Select and display the Code Editor for the form and locate the *Tick* event handler.

6. Select the code statement in the body of the event handler and then copy it to the clipboard. (Use the keys CTRL+C.)

7. Select the entire *Tick* event handler and delete it.

8. Select the tmrClock object in the Object Name box (at the top of the Code Editor), and then select the *Elapsed* event from the Method Name box. As expected, the body of the event handler is created.

9. Place the cursor in the body of the event handler, and paste in the code that you copied to the clipboard in step 5. (Use the keys CTRL+V.)

10. Now that you are done with the coding, press F5 to run the program. After the form is loaded, start and stop the clock until you are satisfied that everything works as it should.

Try It

Let's make some modifications to the DigitalClock program to change how often the clock refreshes and how the time is displayed.

1. In the *frmClock_Load* event handler, configure the clock to update (refresh) every 2 seconds. Make sure you correctly convert 2 seconds into milliseconds.

2. Use Help to read more about the *FormatDateTime* function, and then change the format that is used to display the system time.

3. Test the program and make sure the clock now updates every 2 seconds instead of twice every second.

What Do You Think?

1. How do you add a timer to a form?

2. What are the names of the two most commonly used properties of the Timer component?

3. When would you use the *WithEvents* keyword?

Q&A

Q. In a *For* loop, is it better to declare the counter variable inside the loop declaration or to declare it prior to the loop declaration?

A. In most circumstances it is better to declare the counter variable inside the loop declaration. This ensures that the counter variable will not be affected by other code in the body of the procedure. In some cases, you might need to use the ending value of the counter in code that follows the loop. In this situation, it is acceptable to declare the counter variable prior to the loop.

Q. Can I use a *Do While* loop to run code even when the expression is False by using the *Not* operator in the expression?

A. Yes, but why would you want to? (Don't you hate it when the answer to a question is another question?) There are times when the *Not* operator is useful, but this isn't one of those times. For better clarity, use a *Do Until* loop.

Q. Can you explain further why I would want to use a *Timer* class rather than a Timer component?

A. Two reasons, actually. The first reason is that using a *Timer* class enables you to instantiate a timer at any time. You can also create any number of Timer objects, depending on what the user wants to do. For example, let's say you have a program that displays the current time in various parts of the world, but you want the

times to be updated at various intervals. When you use a Timer component, you have to determine exactly how many locations you will allow the users to select from. If they want one more location than your program provides for, you will have to modify the program and redistribute it. By using the *Timer* class, you can instantly create a new Timer object whenever the user selects another location.

The second reason is that the *Timer* class is more efficient than the Timer component. Rather than using the *Enabled* property to start and stop the Timer, you can use the *Start* and *Stop* methods. Although these two methods actually set the *Enabled* property internally, it is more efficient to use a method call than to set a property value.

WRAPPING UP

- When you want to run code more than once to implement the requirements of your program, you can use loops or timers in your routines. This will help you to write code that is more robust and reduce the amount of duplicate code that you have to write and maintain.

- Several types of loops are available in Visual Basic .NET, and many programmers tend to favor one type of loop over another. This is not usually a problem, but you will find (as we all have) that one type of loop might not work for all situations. It is important that you learn how to use all types of loops and that you are able to determine which type of loop works best in each situation.

- A *For...Next* loop has a predefined starting and ending index in the construction of the loop. This type of loop is normally iterated by incrementing the loop counter by 1, but, by using a *Step* value, you can iterate through the loop by incrementing the counter variable by any value. You can also iterate backwards by setting the starting index to something greater than 0 and the ending index at 0 and using the *Step* to decrement the counter variable.

- A *While* loop takes the form *While expression...End While*. It evaluates a Boolean expression and will continue to run while the result of the expression is True.

- A *Do While* loop that takes the form *Do While expression...Loop* will also evaluate a Boolean expression and will continue to run while the result of the expression is True.

- You can use a *Do While* or a *Do Until* loop to read the contents of a text file. In our example, we used the *StreamReader* class to open the file and then used its *ReadLine* method to read each line in the file. The loop continues until there is nothing left to read.

- A *Do...Until* loop that takes the form *Do Until expression...Loop* will evaluate a Boolean expression and continue to run until the result of the expression is True.

■ A *Do...While* loop that takes the form *Do...While expression* will always run the code inside the loop at least once. This is important if the result of the expression going into the loop is False but you still want the code to run once.

■ A *Do...Until* loop that takes the form *Do...Until expression* will always run at least once, but remember that the evaluation of the expression is the opposite of that of the *Do...While* loop.

■ A timer is useful whenever you want code to run at preset intervals. The clock program is a good example of an application for this feature. There are two ways to use a timer in an application: the Timer component and the *Timer* class. The Timer component can be added to your project and configured at design time. This component has a *Tick* event that will be raised when the predefined interval of time has passed. The *Interval* property takes a numeric value that specifies the number of milliseconds (1/1000 seconds). You can turn the timer on or off by using the *Enabled* property.

■ The *Timer* class is declared in code and instantiated at run time. The *Timer* class has an *Elapsed* event that works the same way as the *Tick* event of the Timer component. You can turn the timer on or off by using the *Enabled* property or the *Start* and *Stop* methods.

KEYWORDS

defensive programming

infinite loop

proper casing

File IO

instantiate

REVIEW QUESTIONS

1. A *For* statement that uses a counter that is initialized to 1 with an *End* value of 10 and a *Step* of 2 will run the code inside the *For* statement _____ times.

    a. 4

    b. 5

    c. 6

    d. 10

2. Which of the following statements uses the proper syntax for initializing the counter variable of a *For* loop inside the *For* statement.

    a. `For intCounter As Integer = 0 To 5`

    b. `For intCounter = 0`

    c. `For intCounter = 0 To 5`

    d. `For Dim intCounter As Integer = 0 To 5`

3. How many times will the code inside a *While* loop run?

    a. It will run only once.

    b. It will run an infinite number of times.

    c. It will run the number of times determined by the counter variable.

    d. It depends on when the expression in the *While* statement changes to False.

4. Which statement must be added to the top of your code module so you do not have to explicitly reference the namespace for the *StreamReader* class?

    a. `Imports System.IO`

    b. `Reference System.IO`

    c. `Include System.IO`

    d. `Add System.IO`

5. _____ are used to reduce the occurrence of run-time errors by catching potential problems early, before they can generate run-time errors.

    a. Loops

    b. References

    c. Defensive programming techniques

    d. Variables

6. Which event of the Timer component is used to run code at a predetermined interval?

   a. *Tock*

   b. *Tick*

   c. *Enable*

   d. *Execute*

7. If you want to run code every 2 seconds by using the Timer component, what value should you assign to the *Interval* property of the Timer?

   a. 2

   b. 20

   c. 200

   d. 2000

8. Instead of using a Timer component in your application, you could use the _____ class and instantiate it at run-time.

   a. *Clock*

   b. *Tick*

   c. *Timer*

   d. *Repeat*

9. Which event of the *Timer* class is equivalent to the *Tick* event of the Timer component?

   a. *Elapsed*

   b. *Tock*

   c. *Alarm*

   d. *Execute*

10. Which keyword must be used to declare an object variable if you are going to use the events associated with that object variable?

    a. *WithEvents*

    b. *AllowEvents*

    c. *DoEvents*

    d. *ObjectEvents*

11. Any *For...Next* loop that you use in your code must have a start value, although the end value is optional. True or false?

12. If the ending value used in a *For* loop is less than the starting value, the loop will end as soon as it starts. True or false?

13. A *While* loop has predefined starting and ending points that determine how many times it will run. True or false?

14. The system-level process that is used to read and write to files on a local drive or network share is called File IO. True or false?

15. The Timer component and the *Timer* class have exactly the same properties and events. True or false?

16. The variable that is used to keep track of how many times the loop is run is called a(n) _____ variable.

17. A loop that runs with no way to terminate is called a(n) _____ loop.

18. The capitalization style in which the first letter of a word is capitalized and the rest of the word is left lowercase is called _____ casing.

19. The variable that is used to store the contents of a text file in a program has the type _____.

20. The function that is used to convert the ASCII value of a character to the representation of that character on the screen is _____.

STEP BY STEP

In this project, you will make a countdown screen that will be used in the aerospace display at the Baldwin Museum of Science. Users should be able to enter a number and click a Start button to watch the program count down from the number they entered to "blastoff." When blastoff occurs, a picture of a rocket launching will appear on the screen for 5 seconds before the application ends automatically.

The completed form for this project will look like Figure 7-14.

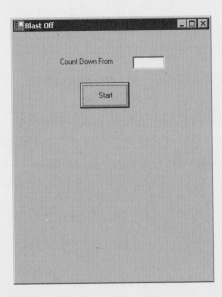

Figure 7-14   Completed project form before execution

When the program is run and the graphic is displayed, the form should look like Figure 7-15.

Figure 7-15   Completed project form after execution

▶ **Creating a new project**

1. Open Visual Studio .NET if it isn't already open.

2. Click the New Project button on the Start page.

3. Click Visual Basic Projects under the Project Types and Windows Application under Templates.

4. Type **BlastOffCh7** in the Name box

5. Browse to the location in which you are storing your projects.

6. Click OK.

▶ **Configuring the form and changing the startup object**

1. Right-click Form1.vb in Solution Explorer and rename it as **BlastOff.vb**. Press ENTER.

2. Click once in the title bar of the form and change the *(Name)* property of the form to **frmBlastOff**.

3. Change the *Text* property of the form to **Blast Off!**, and then press ENTER.

4. Right-click the BlastOffCh7 project name in Solution Explorer, and then click Properties.

5. Change the startup object to **frmBlastOff**, and then click OK.

▶ **Setting up the form**

1. Add a Button control to the form and name it **btnStart**. Change the *Text* property to **Start**.

2. Add a TextBox control to the form and name it **txtCountDownFrom**. Delete the contents of the *Text* property.

3. Add a Label control next to the text box. Change the *Text* property to **Count Down From**.

4. Add to the form another Label control that will be used to display the countdown value. Change the name of this label to **lblCountDown**, and delete the contents of its *Text* property.

5. Add a PictureBox control to the form under the lblCountDown label. Change the name of the PictureBox control to **picBlastOff**.

6. Set the PictureBox control's *Image* property to the BlastOff.jpg file that came with your student file. Set the *Visible* property to False.

7. Add a Timer component to the form. Set the *Interval* property of the Timer component to 1000 so it will count down in 1-second intervals.

▶ **Adding code to the form**

1. Double-click the Start button on the form to open the Code Editor in the button's *Click* event handler.

2. Type the following code in the *btnStart_Click* event handler:

```
If txtCountDownFrom.Text < 0 Or txtCountDownFrom.Text > 10 Then
    MessageBox.Show("Please enter a number between 1 and 10")
    txtCountDownFrom.Focus()
Else
    Timer1.Enabled = True
    pic1BlastOff.Visible = False
    lblCountDown.Text = txtCountDownFrom.Text
End If
```

3. Return to the form's design view, and double-click the Timer1 component in the tray below the form to open the Code Editor in the timer's *Tick* event handler.

4. Type the following code in the *Timer1_Tick* event handler:

```
lblCountDown.Text = lblCountDown.Text - 1
If lblCountDown.Text = 0 Then
    Timer1.Enabled = False
    'display picture of rocket here
    lblCountDown.Text = "Blast Off!"
    picBlastOff.Visible = True
End If
```

▶ **Saving and testing your project**

1. On the File menu, select Save All to save your work.

2. On the Debug menu, select Start to run your project.

3. Test the program by entering a number between 1 and 10 and then clicking the Start button. The countdown should be displayed in the label, and the picture of the blastoff should appear when the countdown reaches 0.

4. Test the program by entering the number **0** and then the number **11** to make sure the code for catching out-of-range values works correctly.

5. On the Debug menu, select Stop Debugging to end the program.

6. On the File menu, select Close Solution to close the project.

7. Close Visual Studio .NET.

FINISH THE CODE

We have started a project that will be used to create an end-of-the-day transaction summary screen for Woodgrove Bank. In this exercise, you will open the project WoodgroveBankCh7 that came in your student file. Users should be able to specify the number of transaction totals they want to enter. Input boxes should be used to prompt for entry of the transaction name and total amount. Check to make sure that the transaction name is not blank and that the amount is greater than or equal to zero. When the transaction information has been entered, display a message thanking the user for entering the data, and then close the application automatically.

JUST HINTS

In this exercise, you will create a form for Fabrikam, Inc. Users will use the form to enter the inventory counts for each of the company's products. Users should be able to enter the product ID and the number of warehouses that store this product ID. Display input boxes prompting users to enter the product counts for each warehouse when they click the Enter Counts button. As the user enters an inventory count for each warehouse, display the warehouse counts for the product in a list box on the screen.

ON YOUR OWN

In this exercise, you will create a computer game for Tailspin Toys. In the game, users will be able to race to see how many times they can click a button on the screen in a specified period of time. Users should be able to select the size of the button (very small, small, medium, or large) and the number of seconds (5, 10, 15, 20, 25, or 30) they want to have to click the button. When the timer expires, display the number of times they clicked during the selected period of time in a message box.

MORE PRACTICE

1. Write a *For...Next* loop that runs six times and displays the counter value in a message box within the loop.

2. Write a *While* loop that will add 5 to a variable called *intAccumulator* as long as the variable *intCounter* is less than 20. Add 2 to *intCounter* inside the loop.

3. Write a Visual Basic .NET statement to declare a variable called *srFileText* that will contain the contents of a text file called Addresses.txt that is located in C:\MyFiles.

4. Write the Visual Basic .NET statements required to set a Timer component called tmrRaceClock to use an interval of 10 seconds and to enable this timer.

5. Write a Visual Basic .NET program that will calculate the factorial of a number entered by the user. The factorial should appear on the screen at the end of the calculation. Hint: The factorial of a number is the product of all of the digits that lead up to that number in sequence. For example, the factorial of 4 is 1 * 2 * 3 * 4, which is equal to 24.

6. Write a Visual Basic .NET program that will calculate and display the number of trays that are needed to hold the donuts made by a bakery. Each tray can hold 20 donuts. The user should be able to enter the number of donuts baked, and the program should then display the number of trays needed. Make sure you handle any extra trays required if the number of donuts is not evenly divisible by 20. Use a *While* loop to complete this program.

7. Write a Visual Basic .NET console application that will display the following pattern of numbers in the console window, each on a separate line. Use the various looping techniques we covered in this chapter to print the digits one number at a time.

    1

    12

    123

    1234

    12345

    1234

    123

    12

    1

8. Open the MorePractice8Ch7 project that came in your student file. This project is a clock program that displays the system time in a label on the screen and refreshes the display every second. Buttons have been included that the user will be able to click to start and stop the refreshing of the time display. A third button will allow the user to change the refresh rate of the clock. This project is not complete, and it has a few errors. Fix the problems and finish the code. Test the application thoroughly.

CHAPTER 8
HANDLING EXCEPTIONS

One of the primary goals of software development is to maintain control of the program regardless of any error conditions that might be encountered. Programmers might introduce errors in their programs but, with good debugging skills and hours of (sometimes) painstaking testing, these errors can be eliminated or at least reduced to a manageable number. Striving to eliminate all possible errors in complex programs is a grand goal but, sad to say, an almost impossible task. Well–thought-out and appropriately implemented exception handling can prevent nasty run-time errors from crashing a program.

As one author so eloquently put it, "Only perfect programmers write perfect code." The rest of us must confess to being less than perfect and provide functionality in our programs to handle our "less than perfect code."

Upon completion of this chapter, you will be able to:

- Learn how to locate and correct syntax, execution, and logic errors.

- Use *Try...Catch...Finally* blocks to handle exceptions.

- Use structured exception handling and defensive programming techniques.

- Understand how exceptions are bubbled-up (passed up the Call Stack) to methods that are equipped to handle the exceptions.

- Learn how to re-throw the original exception and provide a custom message.

- Use the *Finally* block of a *Try...Catch* to run clean-up code that will run regardless of whether an exception was thrown.

ERRORS AND EXCEPTIONS

The terms *error* and *exception* are sometimes used interchangeably. You might hear programmers talking about errors when they really mean exceptions, and the other way around. There is a difference, so first we will explain what each is. We will then transition to structured exception handling to see how you can maintain control of a program whenever you encounter exceptional conditions that could otherwise cause the program to fail. During our discussion of structured exception handling, we will discuss the *Exception* object in more detail.

There are three basic types of errors: syntax, execution, and logic. Each of these error types are explained in the following paragraphs.

Syntax errors occur when the compiler cannot interpret the code you have written. You might have mistakenly provided the wrong type of arguments when calling a procedure with parameters, or you might have simply mistyped a keyword. In any case, this type of error must be corrected before you can compile the code. Syntax errors are generally the easiest errors to locate and fix because, in many cases, the IntelliSense built into Microsoft Visual Studio .NET will identify them when you attempt to compile the code.

Execution errors (frequently called *run-time errors*) are errors that occur while a program is running. They are often caused by something external to the program that the code must interact with. This could be as benign as the user entering the wrong type of value, or perhaps a database that is locked or a file on the local hard drive or a network server that is unavailable. It could also be something a little less obvious, such as an attempt to iterate a loop beyond its defined ending value or a failed attempt to cast (convert) a value from one type to another.

Logic errors (sometimes called *semantic errors*) are errors that produce unexpected or unwanted results. An example of a logic error is a calculation that multiplies two values when it should divide them. The program will appear to work correctly, and the error might go unnoticed until the program is in production. Extra care should be taken to ensure that logic errors are located and fixed. This is especially true when you are producing software that people depend on for making decisions. Given these considerations, you need to be aware that logic errors present a challenge because they are sometimes the hardest type of error to locate and fix.

As you can see from the preceding descriptions, errors are problems in code that can prevent the code from compiling, possibly causing the program to fail or even produce unwanted or unreliable results. OK, that makes sense. So what is an exception and how is it different from an error?

In general terms, an **exception** is a deviation from an expected condition that occurs when code is running. In programming terms, an exception is an object that is created and thrown back to the executing procedure as a result of this deviation.

Let's say that a program attempts to access a file in a specified location and the file is missing. An error occurs, causing an exception to be thrown. Here's another example: If a user enters alphabetical characters instead of numeric characters and attempts to run a mathematical function, an error occurs, causing an exception to be thrown.

Let's look back at our definition. We can see that, in our examples, the expected condition is that the file is there or that the user enters the correct numeric characters. The exceptional condition occurs when the file is missing or the user enters the incorrect characters. The exception object that is thrown contains information about the error that occurred.

At this point you need to be aware that not all errors result in an exception being thrown. Syntax and logic errors will not throw exceptions.

Structured Exception Handling

Structured exception handling is used to isolate specific code statements or blocks of code and catch any exception that is thrown as a result of an error. As we mentioned earlier, when code execution causes an error, an exception object is created and is said to be "thrown" back to the calling procedure. If this exception is handled correctly, the problem can generally be taken care of. However, if the exception is not handled, an unhandled exception is returned. Sometimes the user can continue, but other times the program will halt abruptly. A good programmer will anticipate potential problem areas in code and actions on the part of users that might cause errors and ultimately throw exceptions that could abruptly terminate the program.

The *Exception* Object

The *Exception* object, as defined in the Microsoft .NET Framework, is the base class for all exceptions. Rarely (if ever) will any application, component, or class throw the **base exception object** because it is far too generic to be of much use. In general, the exception that is thrown will be quite specific, and typically we can provide an efficient way to handle it.

To make this point a little clearer, let's say that you are driving your car and it suddenly stops. For the purposes of this analogy, we will assume that you didn't run into the back of another vehicle. You call a service station for help. It would be nice to have a theory about why the car stopped, so they ask you if there is sufficient gasoline in the car's tank. You look at the gauge and tell them that the needle is pointing to E. Now that's a problem they can resolve quite easily. Had you not been able to provide a more specific response, the problem could have taken much longer to resolve. The Exception object that is thrown will provide the information that will assist in pinpointing the problem.

Six main class hierarchies are defined under *System.Exception*, but we will cover just one (*System.SystemException*) in this chapter. After you understand the concept of exception handling, it will be easy for you to dive into other exception object hierarchies.

System.SystemException is quite substantial and provides for the majority of the exceptions you will need to handle. Table 8-1 shows some of the more common exceptions that reside under the *System.SystemException* object. For more information and a complete list of exceptions, select Index from the Help menu, type **System-Exception class** in the Look For list, and then select About *SystemException* class from the list of topics. Click the Derived Classes link at the top of the displayed page.

Table 8-1 **Common *System.SystemException* Exception Classes**

System.ArgumentException	System.ArithmeticException
System.ArrayTypeMismatchException	System.BadImageFormatException
System.Data.DataException	System.Data.Odbc.OdbcException
System.Data.OracleClient.OracleException	System.Data.SqlClient.SqlException
System.Data.SqlServerCe.SqlCeException	System.Data.SqlTypes.SqlTypeException
System.ExecutionEngineException	System.FormatException
System.IndexOutOfRangeException	System.InvalidCastException
System.InvalidOperationException	System.InvalidProgramException
System.IO.InternalBufferOverflowException	System.IO.IOException
System.NotSupportedException	System.NullReferenceException
System.OutOfMemoryException	System.Runtime.Serialization.Serialization-Exception
System.TypeUnloadedException	System.Web.Services.Protocols.Soap-Exception
System.Xml.Schema.XmlSchemaException	System.Xml.XmlException
System.Xml.XPath.XPathException	System.Xml.Xsl.XsltException
System.ArgumentException	System.InvalidOperationException
System.ArithmeticException	System.InvalidProgramException
System.ArrayTypeMismatchException	System.IO.InternalBufferOverflowException
System.BadImageFormatException	System.IO.IOException
System.Data.DataException	System.NotSupportedException
System.Data.Odbc.OdbcException	System.NullReferenceException
System.Data.OracleClient.OracleException	System.OutOfMemoryException
System.Data.SqlClient.SqlException	System.Runtime.Serialization.Serialization-Exception
System.Data.SqlServerCe.SqlCeException	System.TypeUnloadedException
System.Data.SqlTypes.SqlTypeException	System.Web.Services.Protocols.Soap-Exception
System.ExecutionEngineException	System.Xml.Schema.XmlSchemaException
System.FormatException	System.Xml.XmlException
System.IndexOutOfRangeException	System.Xml.XPath.XPathException
System.InvalidCastException	System.Xml.Xsl.XsltException

Because it is beyond the scope of this textbook to explain each of these exception classes, this list is provided for reference only. To get more information on any of the above classes, use the *Object Browser* in the Visual Studio .NET integrated development environment (IDE). As an example, let's use the Object Browser to find more information about *DivideByZeroException*.

▶ Using the Object Browser

1. Assuming you have a project opened in Visual Studio .NET, click on the View menu and select Object Browser.

2. In the Object Browser, click the Find Symbol button located on the Object Browser's toolbar to display the Find Symbol dialog box, which is shown in Figure 8-1.

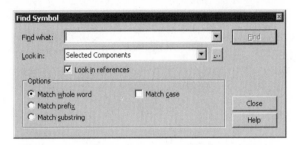

Figure 8-1   The Find Symbol dialog box

3. Type the particular exception class you want to locate in the Find What box. For this example, type **DivideByZeroException**.

4. Click the Find button to the right of the list box. The Find Symbol Results window will now appear in the IDE. It will list the selected class, as shown in Figure 8-2.

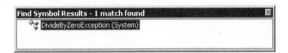

Figure 8-2   The Find Symbol Results window

5. Double-click the item in the list (DivideByZeroException (System)). The Object Browser window will open, as shown in Figure 8-3. The class will be displayed in the Object Browser, and information related to the class you were searching for will appear in the gray section at the bottom of the window. You might have to resize each of the frames in the Object Browser to see all of the information.

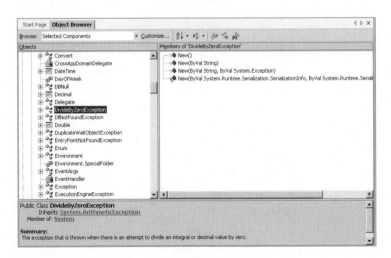

Figure 8-3   Object Browser displaying results of search

Inside the *Exception* Object

Before you can start using any of the exception classes, it would be nice to know what properties and methods will be important to you. In this section, we will explain the most important properties and methods.

Properties of the *Exception* Object

- **Message**   The *Message* property returns the description of the exception. For example, the message for a *DivideByZeroException* is "Attempted to divide by zero." The *Message* property is the most commonly used of all the properties. You will notice that we use the *Message* property in many of the examples in this chapter. When the exception is handled, the *Message* will be displayed to the user or perhaps written to a database or an error log where it can be evaluated later. The *Message* property is read-only.

- **TargetSite**   The *TargetSite* property returns the name and the signature (parameter list) of the procedure that caused the exception to be thrown. As with the *Message* property, the property value for *TargetSite* can be displayed to the user or written to a database or an error log where it can be evaluated later. The *TargetSite* property is read-only.

- **StackTrace**   The *StackTrace* property returns a string that describes the path of execution from the procedure that caused the exception to be thrown to the procedure that ultimately caught the exception. *StackTrace* contains information that should rarely (if ever) be displayed to the user. This information would normally be used by the programmer during testing and debugging. The *StackTrace* property is read-only.

- **HelpLink**   The *HelpLink* property sets or returns a URN (Uniform Resource Name) or URL (Uniform Resource Locator) to the Help file associated with the exception object. This file is not created for you, so you will need to create it yourself. If an exception is thrown and you want to provide a more detailed description of the exception and perhaps provide some instructions to help users understand and correct the problem, create an HTML file and point the link to the location of the file. The following is an example of such a pointer: file://c:/MyApplication/Instructions.html#DivideByZeroException. The *HelpLink* property is read/write.

Methods of the *Exception* Object

The *ToString* method returns the same information as the *Message* property, but if the application's executable file contains debugging information, the *ToString* method also includes information such as the name of the procedure and the exact line number on which the error occurred. If the program is compiled as a release version, debugging information will not be present in the executable file. In this case, *ToString* will return the same information as the *Message* property.

Try It

Close the Object Browser and repeat the steps from the preceding procedure to find information about the following exception classes. Read the results of each search and make sure you understand a bit about each of these exception classes.

- *ArgumentException*
- *DataException*
- *FormatException*

What Do You Think?

1. What is an exception in Microsoft Visual Basic .NET?

2. What is the difference between an error and an exception?

3. Why is structured exception handling used?

4. When would you use the Object Browser?

5. List and describe the properties and methods available for the *Exception* object.

THE *TRY...CATCH* STATEMENT

In this section, we will use the *Try...Catch* statement to provide structure when we attempt to run code. This structure will allow us to trap the errors that result from improperly executed code.

The syntax of a basic *Try...Catch* statement looks like this:

```
Try
    ' code to execute
Catch
    ' code that will execute if an exception is thrown
End Try
```

The terms *Try* and *Catch* are probably new to you, so let's look at what they mean.

- **Try** This defines the block containing the code you want to run.

- **Catch** This defines the block in which the exception will be caught (if one is thrown). You will provide code that will handle the exception. If user interaction is required, you must provide a prompt to users so that they understand what happened and what they can do to correct the error. You might need to gracefully terminate the program at this point if the exception cannot be handled in any other way.

- **End Try** The program will exit the *Try...Catch* block.

Exception Handling vs. Defensive Programming

You can think of exception handling as dealing with an error after it has occurred. Defensive programming, on the other hand, tests for success or failure before you run the code that could cause the error.

For example, when you use exception handling, if the program needs to access an external file and it is missing, the code that is attempting to access the file will fail and an exception will be thrown. You must provide code to handle the exception. When you use defensive programming, you test to verify that the file exists in the specified location and, if it's there, you run the code. If the file is missing, you do not attempt to run the code to access it.

Exception handling and defensive programming are not mutually exclusive. Most programs should include both. A guideline that most experts agree on is as follows: if an error will occur less than 25 percent of the time, use exception handling; if the error is likely to occur more than 25 percent of the time, use defensive programming. This is obviously not a rigid rule. Whether to include one or the other or both depends on the type of program and, of course, the requirements and standards of the company you are working for.

The reasoning behind this guideline is that structured exception handling slows down code execution, which will have a negative effect on program performance. If performance is a priority, you might want to reduce the number of *Try...Catch* blocks that you incorporate into the program and work harder on your defensive programming skills.

Variable Scope

Variables declared inside a *Try* block will be invisible to any code outside that block. If you need to refer to that variable from inside the *Catch* block, the variable must be declared prior to the *Try* block. In the following example, you can assume that the variables *intNumerator* and *intDenominator* are already declared, but the variable *intResult* is declared inside the *Try* block.

```
Try
    Dim intResult As Integer
    intResult = intNumerator / intDenominator
    ' execute other code here
Catch
    If intResult > 0 Then
        ' execute code if expression is True
    Else
        ' execute code is expression is False
    End If
End Try
```

This is invalid. It will not compile because the variable *intResult* declared in the *Try* block goes out of scope after the *Try* block has finished. Attempting to refer to that variable in the *Catch* block will return a syntax error, and the code will not compile. On the other hand, the following block of code will compile without any problems.

```
Dim intResult As Integer
Try
    intResult = intNumerator / intDenominator
    ' execute other code here
Catch
    If intResult > 0 Then
        ' execute code if expression is True
    Else
        ' execute code is expression is False
    End If
End Try
```

The *Catch* Block

The *Catch* block is the key element of the **structured exception handler** because this is where the exception object that is thrown will be caught and handled. The most important part of this block is to identify the possible exceptions. After you know what these exceptions are, it is relatively easy to handle them.

To demonstrate the *Catch* block, we will create a new Windows application named DivideByZero. It will be a simple application consisting up of two text boxes, some labels, and a button. Figure 8-4 shows what the completed form should look like.

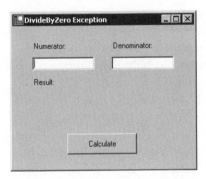

Figure 8-4   The DivideByZero application form

▶ Creating the DivideByZero application

1. Create a new Windows project called **DivideByZero**, add the controls listed in Table 8-2, and set their properties as described in Table 8-2.

Table 8-2   **DivideByZero Controls and Properties**

Control	(Name)	Text
Form	**frmDivideByZero**	**DivideByZero Exception**
TextBox	**txtNumerator**	\<blank\>
TextBox	**txtDenominator**	\<blank\>
Label	**lblResult**	\<blank\>
Label	Label1	**Numerator:**
Label	Label2	**Denominator:**
Label	Label3	**Result:**
Button	**btnCalculate**	**Calculate**

2. Double-click the button in the designer and type the boldface code shown below into the *btnCalculate_Click* event handler.

```
Private Sub btnCalculate_Click(ByVal sender As System.Object, _
        ByVal e As System.EventArgs) Handles btnCalculate.Click
    Try
        Dim intNumerator As Integer = Integer.Parse(txtNumerator.Text)
        Dim intDenominator As Integer = Integer.Parse(txtDenominator.Text)
        Dim intResult As Integer

        intResult = intNumerator \ intDenominator
        lblResult.Text = intResult.ToString()

    Catch ex As System.DivideByZeroException
        lblResult.Text = "A divide by zero exception was thrown: " & _
            ControlChars.CrLf & ex.Message

    Catch ex As ArithmeticException
        lblResult.Text = "An arithmetic exception was thrown: " & _
            ControlChars.CrLf & ex.Message

    Catch ex As Exception
        lblResult.Text = "A general exception was thrown: " & _
            ControlChars.CrLf & ex.Message

    End Try
End Sub
```

3. After you are done entering the code, save your work and run the program. To test the program, enter **42** in the Numerator box and **0** in the Denominator box. A *DivideByZero* exception should be thrown and caught in the appropriate *Catch* block. The message from the *Catch* block should be displayed in the Results label, as shown in Figure 8-5.

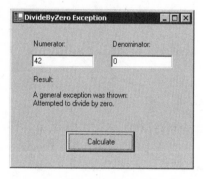

Figure 8-5   The DivideByZero application form with exception error message

Order of Exceptions

As you have probably already noticed, you can have multiple *Catch* blocks in a *Try...Catch* structure. Think of it as a slightly modified *Select Case* structure in which you test several expressions. In a *Try...Catch* structure, the first expression that evaluates to True will be the one that will handle the exception. That being the case, the most specific exception will be caught first. The least specific exception is always placed in the last *Catch* block. Let's look at the sequence of the *Catch* blocks for DivideByZero:

```
Try

    Dim intNumerator As Integer = Integer.Parse(txtNumerator.Text)
    Dim intDenominator As Integer = Integer.Parse(txtDenominator.Text)
    Dim intResult As Integer
    intResult = intNumerator \ intDenominator
    lblResult.Text = intResult.ToString()

Catch ex As System.DivideByZeroException
    lblResult.Text = "A divide by zero exception was thrown: " & _
        ControlChars.CrLf & ex.Message

Catch ex As ArithmeticException
    lblResult.Text = "An arithmetic exception was thrown: " & _
        ControlChars.CrLf & ex.Message

Catch ex As Exception
    lblResult.Text = "A general exception was thrown: " & _
        ControlChars.CrLf & ex.Message

End Try
```

Notice that the first exception (*System.DivideByZeroException*) is the most specific
and is thrown if the user enters a zero in the Denominator text box. The second
Catch block (*ArithmeticException*) catches the exception if the value entered into
the text box is too large for an integer variable to accept. The third *Catch* block
(*Exception*) catches any exception that is not caught by either of the two prior *Catch*
blocks. You can see that, with this structure, if we place `Catch ex As Exception`
first, execution will never reach the other two *Catch* blocks and would not be
evaluated correctly.

To further understand the ordering of exceptions, you can think about the hierarchy of the exception classes. For example, the *DivideByZeroException* class is
derived from the *ArithmeticException* class and, as such, it is more specific than the
ArithmeticException class. If we had placed the *ArithmeticException Catch* block
before the *DivideByZeroException Catch* block and again attempted to divide by
zero, the *ArithmeticException Catch* block would catch the exception, and the
exception would never be caught by the *DivideByZeroException Catch* block.

Using the *When* Keyword

We can include an additional expression in a *Catch* block to further filter when an
exception is caught. We could say, "Catch the exception only when the *additional
expression is true*."

The following is an example of including additional expressions:

```
Try
    Dim intNumerator As Integer = Integer.Parse(txtNumerator.Text)
    Dim intDenominator As Integer = Integer.Parse(txtDenominator.Text)
    Dim intResult As Integer
    intResult = intNumerator \ intDenominator
    lblResult.Text = intResult.ToString()

    Catch ex As System.DivideByZeroException When IsNumeric(txtDenominator.Text)
        lblResult.Text = "A divide by zero exception was thrown: " & _
            ControlChars.CrLf & ex.Message
```

```
Catch When txtDenominator.Text = ""
    lblResult.Text = "Invalid Calculation. The denominator is missing!"
    txtDenominator.Focus()

Catch ex As Exception
    lblResult.Text = "A general exception was thrown" & _
        ControlChars.CrLf & ex.Message

End Try
```

In the preceding code, we provided additional expressions to the first two *Catch* blocks. The first one uses the *IsNumeric* function, which will evaluate to True only if a numeric value is entered into the text box. This *Catch* block would be ignored if the user entered any character that was not numeric. The second *Catch* block omits the exception expression but will still catch the exception if the user does not enter a value in the text box. If this *Catch* block were placed first in the chain, it would actually work just as well.

Using a *Try...Catch* for Defensive Programming

As we mentioned earlier, structured exception handling causes a performance penalty. Because of this penalty, having a single *Catch* block that tests for the absence of a value in a text box, as shown in the following code, would be prohibitive in terms of program performance and should be avoided. However, if this *Catch* block was included along with other, more specific *Catch* blocks, the additional performance penalty would be negligible.

```
Try

    Dim intNumerator As Integer = Integer.Parse(txtNumerator.Text)
    Dim intDenominator As Integer = Integer.Parse(txtDenominator.Text)
    Dim intResult As Integer
    intResult = intNumerator \ intDenominator
    lblResult.Text = intResult.ToString()

Catch When txtDenominator.Text = ""
    lblResult.Text = "Invalid Calculation. The denominator is missing!"
    txtDenominator.Focus()

End Try
```

Throwing Exceptions

All exceptions carry a message that describes the exception being thrown. This message, although it is understandable to the programmer, might be cryptic to the user. For this reason, you might want to specify a more explicit (think reader-friendly) message for the user.

Let's modify our DivideByZero program slightly to include exception messages that will be more meaningful to the user.

▶ **Adding exception messages**

1. Open the DivideByZero program and create a *Calculate* method (Sub procedure) that does not return a value. Cut the code from the *btnCalculate_Click* event handler and paste it into the *Calculate* method. The *Calculate* method should look as follows:

```
Private Sub Calculate()
    Try
        Dim intNumerator As Integer = Integer.Parse(txtNumerator.Text)
        Dim intDenominator As Integer = Integer.Parse(txtDenominator.Text)
        Dim intResult As Integer
        intResult = intNumerator \ intDenominator
        lblResult.Text = intResult.ToString()

    Catch ex As System.DivideByZeroException
        Throw New System.DivideByZeroException("You cannot divide by zero")
    Catch ex As Exception
        lblResult.Text = "A general exception was thrown: " & _
        ControlChars.CrLf & ex.Message
    End Try
End Sub
```

2. Now change the code in the *btnCalculate_Click* event handler to look as follows:

```
Private Sub btnCalculate_Click(ByVal sender As System.Object, _
        ByVal e As System.EventArgs) Handles btnCalculate.Click
    Try
        Calculate()
    Catch ex As Exception
        lblResult.Text = "An exception was thrown: " & _
        ControlChars.CrLf & ex.Message
    End Try
End Sub
```

3. Run the program. Type **42** in the Numerator box and **0** in the Denominator box. A *DivideByZero* exception is thrown and caught in the DivideByZero *Catch* block in the *Calculate* method, but instead of handling it there, we will throw a new exception. This new exception will then be caught in the exception handler in the calling procedure (the *btnCalculate_Click* event handler). The Results label should now display our custom message, as shown in Figure 8-6.

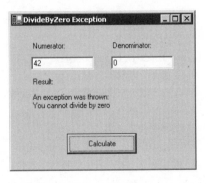

Figure 8-6   *DivideByZero* exception in the DivideByZero application

When you created the new exception, you provided your own custom message. This message is passed back to the calling procedure as part of the new exception and handled there. This is not a custom exception but a custom message for a pre-defined exception.

Re-Throwing the Original Exception

You could have thrown the original exception back by just running a *Throw* statement without an argument. This has an advantage over the `Throw New System.DivideByZeroException` statement in that it re-throws the current exception and doesn't reset the *StackTrace* property of the exception object. The *Throw* statement with the argument resets the *StackTrace* property as if it were a brand new exception and actually masks the source of the original exception.

Exception Bubbling

As you have learned, placing a *Try...Catch* in every procedure will result in a loss of performance that might be unacceptable. How can you provide the necessary protection in your applications and still produce fast code? The answer is to pass the exception back up the Call Stack to any procedure that can handle it.

Let's say you have one procedure that calls a second procedure, which in turn calls a third procedure. Any of these procedures might well throw an exception. At first you might consider providing a *Try...Catch* block in each of the procedures, but this would be inefficient and it would increase the amount of code that you would need to write.

To demonstrate the concept of **exception bubbling**, we will once again turn to a hands-on example. In this program, we will code several methods that are suitable candidates for exception handling. If an error occurs in any of these methods, an exception will be thrown. If the affected procedure does not have an exception handler, the exception will be thrown to the calling procedure. If the calling procedure does not provide a handler, it, in turn, will throw the exception back to the procedure that called it. If no procedure in the Call Stack provides the necessary handler, an **unhandled run-time exception** will be thrown and the program will terminate. Our program will provide an exception handler in the *Main* method, and you will see how an *InvalidCastException* is thrown and eventually handled in that method.

▶   Creating the ExceptionBubbling application

1. Create a new console application, and title it **ExceptionBubbling**. This program will use a chain of several methods that will calculate the total cost of a product, which is the sales tax added to the price of the product. All of the methods are likely candidates for exception handling, but rather than putting *Try...Catch* blocks in each of these procedures, we will instead place one *Try...Catch* block in the original calling procedure that will catch any exception that the called procedures could throw.

   Rather than work from the first method (which is *Main*), you will start at the end and work backwards. This will help you to understand how the program really functions.

2. For now, do not code the *Main* method. Instead, create a new method called *CalculateTotal*, as shown in the following code sample. This method will take two arguments of type *Decimal* and return the result of the calculation, which is also a *Decimal* value.

```
Private Function CalculateTotal(ByVal decPrice As Decimal, _
        ByVal decTax As Decimal) As Decimal
    Return decPrice + decTax
End Function
```

When this method is called, you must provide values (arguments) for the two parameters. These will obviously be the price of the product and the sales tax. These two values are added together and returned to the calling statement.

3. To calculate the tax, you must first get the tax rate. For this method, you must provide the state code and return a rate. The rate will be used to calculate the amount of tax that will be added to the price of the product. Create a method called *GetTaxRate* that will take a *String* argument for the state code and return the tax rate as a *Decimal* value. The code to do this is shown in the following code sample.

```
Private Function GetTaxRate(ByVal strState As String) As Decimal
    Select Case strState
        Case "CA"
            Return 8.25
        Case "NV"
            Return 0.0
        Case Else
            Console.WriteLine("The tax rate for " & strState & " is unknown.")
            Console.Write("Enter the sales tax that you would like to pay: ")
            Return CDec(Console.ReadLine())
    End Select
End Function
```

When this method is called, you must provide the state code. The *Select* statement will evaluate the value entered and return the tax rate for the specified state. Notice that the last *Case* statement is designed to allow users to enter the rate they would like to pay if the state they entered was not in the list. Obviously this method is not very realistic; users who enter anything more than 0.0 are either not paying the bill or have more money than they know what to do with. Either case is unlikely, so please suspend your disbelief throughout this example.

4. Create another method called *CalculateTax*, as shown in the following code sample. This method will take one argument of type *Decimal* and return a value of type *Decimal*.

```
Private Function CalculateTax(ByVal decPrice As Decimal) As Decimal
    Console.Write("Enter the two character code for your state: ")
    Return decPrice * GetTaxRate(Console.ReadLine().ToUpper()) / 100
End Function
```

When calling this method, you will pass the price of the product and display a prompt to the user to have them enter the state code. The *Console.ReadLine* method will take the value entered and pass that to the *GetTaxRate* method. The returned tax rate is then multiplied by the price to get the total amount of tax due. The total tax is then passed back to the calling statement. Nearly done. There is one more method to create before you code the *Main* method.

5. Create the *CalculateTransaction* method, as shown in the following code sample. This method takes no arguments and does not return a value.

```
Private Sub CalculateTransaction()
    Dim decPrice As Decimal
    Dim decTax As Decimal

    Console.Write("Enter the price of the product: ")
    decPrice = CDec(Console.ReadLine())
    decTax = CalculateTax(decPrice)
    Console.WriteLine("The tax on this product is: {0}", _
        FormatCurrency(decTax))
    Console.WriteLine("The total cost for this product is : {0}", _
        FormatCurrency(CalculateTotal(decPrice, decTax)))
End Sub
```

For this method, you will ask the user to enter the price of the product. The value the user enters is actually a *String* and, as such, you must convert it to a *Decimal*. The converted value will be stored in a local variable, *decPrice*, and will be used to call the *CalculateTax* and *CalculateTotal* methods. The tax is calculated and passed back to the variable *decTax*. Because the *CalculateTax* method returns a *Decimal* value, you do not need to convert this value. You can then display the tax and the total cost in the console window by using the *WriteLine* method of the *Console* class. One more procedure to code and you are done. Coding the *Main* method is as simple as calling the *CalculateTransaction* method, but this is where you must provide the exception handling.

6. Program the *Main* method by using the code shown in the following code sample.

```
Sub Main()
    Try
        CalculateTransaction()
    Catch ex As InvalidCastException
        Console.Write("The following exception was thrown: {0}: {1}", _
            ControlChars.CrLf & ex.Message, _
            ex.StackTrace().ToString())
    Catch ex As Exception
        Console.Write("The exception was thrown in " & _
            Ex.StackTrace().ToString() & " and was caught in Main")
    End Try
    Console.ReadLine()
End Sub
```

The *Main* method is where the *Try...Catch* block is placed. As you can see from the preceding code, you are calling the *CalculateTransaction* method. In turn, this will cause a chain of methods to be called. Because you are converting several *String* values to *Decimal* by using the *CDec* function in several of the called methods, you need to provide exception handling for each conversion. If the user fails to provide a value that can logically be converted, a run-time exception will be thrown. The *Try...Catch* block in the *Main* method will provide the required protection for such a situation.

The expected exception would be *InvalidCastException*, but just in case there could be another exception thrown, you have provided a second *Catch* block that will catch any other exception. This is a good practice, and it should be incorporated in any exception handler that you create.

To test the program, you must create a situation that will cause the initial exception to be thrown.

7. Click the Start button or press F5 to run the program.

8. Type **42** when asked to enter the price of the product.

9. Enter **IL** for the state code.

10. Enter **none** when asked to enter the tax rate. Note the exception that is finally caught and handled in the *Main* method, as shown in Figure 8-7.

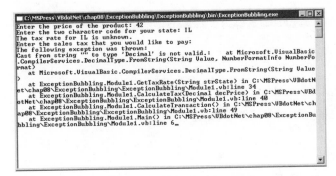

Figure 8-7   Handling of an exception by the *Main* method

By reading the details of the exception, you can see that the error initially occurred at line 34, as shown in Figure 8-8. Note that the line numbers in your program might be different from ours, depending on how you formatted your code.

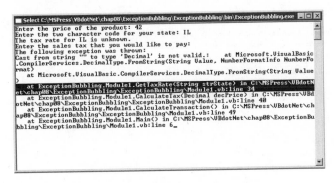

Figure 8-8   The first exception occurs at line 34

This exception was bubbled up to the calling method, so the next time you see the exception it is at line 40, as shown in Figure 8-9.

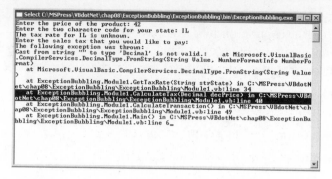

Figure 8-9 Exception appears again at line 40

Once again, the exception was thrown back and appears again at line 49, as shown in Figure 8-10.

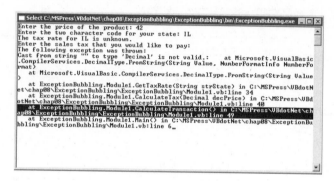

Figure 8-10 Exception appears again at line 49

Finally, the exception was thrown at line 6 and handled in that method, as shown in Figure 8-11.

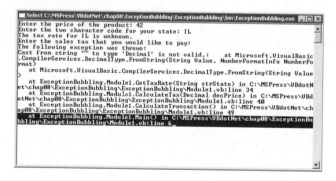

Figure 8-11 Exception appears again at line 6 and is handled

Exiting a *Try...Catch* Early

If you need to, you can exit a *Try...Catch* at any time by running an *Exit Try* statement. This statement can be placed in the *Try* block or any of the *Catch* blocks.

The *Finally* Block

Using a *Finally* block is perfect for cleanup code in any procedure that uses a *Try...Catch* block. Many programs have routines that access a database or perhaps a file on disk. When you have finished with the file or need to disconnect from the database, you will need to run code to do that. The problem is that if an exception is thrown while the file is open or while there is an active open connection to the database, the code to close the file or disconnect from the database might never run. The *Finally* block will provide the means to run the cleanup code and take care of these situations. The great thing about the *Finally* block is that it is guaranteed to run no matter what happens. This is true regardless of whether an exception is thrown.

> **TIP** It is acceptable to have a *Try...Finally...End Try* without a *Catch* block, but you cannot have a *Try...End Try* without either a *Catch* block or a *Finally* block.

▶ **Testing the console application**

1. Add a *Finally* block to the exception handler in the *Main* method, as shown in the following code sample.

```
Sub Main()
    Dim blnThrownException As Boolean = False
    Try
        CalculateTransaction()
    Catch ex As InvalidCastException
        Console.Write("The following exception was thrown: {0}: {1}", _
            ControlChars.CrLf & ex.Message, _
            ex.StackTrace().ToString())
        blnThrownException = True
    Catch ex As Exception
        Console.Write("The exception was thrown in " & _
            Ex.StackTrace().ToString() & " and was caught in Main")
        blnThrownException = True
    Finally
        If blnThrownException Then
            Console.WriteLine ("The finally block has been executed after " & _
                "an exception was thrown")
        Else
            Console.WriteLine("The finally block has been executed when " & _
                "no exception was thrown")
        End If
    End Try
    Console.ReadLine()
End Sub
```

2. Retest the program and generate an exception to see how the handling occurs.

The following changes were made to the *Main* method:

- A *Boolean* variable (*blnThrownException*) was added. This variable will be set to True if an exception is thrown.

- An *If...Then...Else* block was added to the *Finally* block to evaluate the variable *blnThrownException*. If `blnThrownException = True`, we know that an exception was thrown. If `blnThrownException = False`, we know that no exception was thrown. Testing both cases proves that the *Finally* block always runs.

Try It

Remove all exception handling code from the ExceptionBubbling application you just created. Retest the program and observe the errors that are generated. Are the errors harder or easier to understand than the errors that were generated by the application with the *Try...Catch* statements?

What Do You Think?

1. What is the *Try...Catch* block used for?

2. How do you decide whether to use exception handling or defensive programming for a particular section of your code?

3. What is the scope of a variable declared inside a *Try* block?

4. What statement block actually catches and handles the exception object that is thrown when an error occurs?

5. If you have multiple *Catch* blocks in a *Try...Catch* structure, how do you determine the order of the *Catch* blocks?

6. In what situation would you use the *When* keyword in a *Catch* block?

7. Describe exception bubbling.

8. What is the purpose of the code that is typically put in a *Finally* block?

Q&A

Q. I heard that it's okay to use the old Visual Basic error handling in Visual Basic .NET. Is this true?

A. Yes, the *On Error* statement is still valid in Visual Basic .NET, and there might be times when it is more practical to use that type of error handling in your code. The *Err* object allows you to raise a custom error quite easily by using *Err.Raise*. It also allows the use of `Resume Next` (`On Error Resume Next`) to allow execution of code to continue at the line of code that follows the line that raised the error. There is no equivalent to the *On Error* statement in any of the other languages supported by Visual Studio .NET.

One important thing to note is that an *On Error* statement and a *Try...Catch* cannot coexist in the same procedure. We have chosen not to provide details about the *Err* object and using the *On Error* statement because this is not the preferred method of dealing with errors in Visual Basic .NET. For more information on the *Err* object and the *On Error* statement, select Index from the Help menu, type **On Error** in the Look For box, and then select On Error Statement from the list of available topics.

Q. If I use the integer division operator (\ ) and divide a number by zero, a *DivideByZeroException* is thrown. If I use the normal division operator (/) and divide a number by zero, an *OverflowException* is thrown. Why is that?

A. When using the / operator, you are actually performing a floating point division calculation. Per Institute of Electrical and Electronics Engineers (IEEE) 754 Arithmetic standards, a floating point division calculation can never be allowed to throw an exception. When you use the / operator to divide a number by 0, the result will always be positive infinity, negative infinity, or a special result called NaN (Not a Number). Remember that, with the calculation you are performing, you are dividing one number by another number and passing the result to another variable. It is the variable that receives the calculated value that is causing the *OverflowException* because that variable can only hold an integer value. Remember that an *Integer* variable can only hold a value between -2,147,483,648 and 2,147,483,647. If you attempt to pass in a value greater than what is allowed, an *OverflowException* is thrown. Because positive infinity or negative infinity is greater than what is allowed for an *Integer*, an *OverflowException* will always be thrown.

WRAPPING UP

- An exception is an exceptional condition that deviates from what was expected. In programming terms, an exception is an object that is created and thrown as the result of a run-time error that occurs while a program is running.

- An exception handler is used to catch an exception after the error has occurred; defensive programming is used to prevent the error from occurring in the first place. When using defensive programming, test for success or failure and then run the appropriate code based on the results of the test.

- Although structured exception handling is not always very flexible, it is fully Microsoft .NET compliant and will work consistently across all the languages supported by the common language runtime.

- You can use *Try...Catch* blocks to handle the various types of exceptions that can be thrown when something out of the ordinary happens in your programs. However, you should use *Try...Catch* blocks sparingly because too many can degrade the performance of your application.

- When including multiple *Catch* blocks in a *Try...Catch*, make sure that the order of the *Catch* blocks is correct. The more specific the exception is, the higher in the order it should be.

- When displaying information to the user, it is essential that the information provided be clear and concise. Users should either be able to understand error messages so that they can correct the problems themselves, or they should be able to provide this information to the help desk. Remember that user-friendly messages will reduce the number of post-midnight phone calls that you might receive if your programs fail.

KEYWORDS

base exception object

exception bubbling

logic errors

structured exception handler

unhandled run-time exception

exception

execution errors

structured exception handling

syntax errors

REVIEW QUESTIONS

1. Structured exception handling is used to handle which type of errors in your applications?

   a. Syntax

   b. Logic

   c. Execution

   d. None of the above

2. An exception is actually a(n) _____ that is created when an error occurs at run time and is thrown back to the calling procedure.

   a. message

   b. event

   c. object

   d. property

3. What is the name of the utility in the Visual Studio .NET IDE that you can use to find information about any class in Visual Studio .NET?

   a. Object Browser

   b. Reference Browser

   c. Class Browser

   d. Detail Browser

4. As a general rule of thumb, if an error will occur less than 25 percent of the time, you should use _____.

   a. defensive programming

   b. exception handling

   c. the *Error* object

   d. no error handling

5. Variables that are declared inside a *Try* block are _____ to any code outside of that *Try* block.

   a. inaccessible

   b. accessible but read only

   c. accessible

   d. None of the above

6. The _____ block in a program will catch the exception object that is thrown and handle it as defined in its code.

   a. *Try*

   b. *Finally*

   c. *When*

   d. *Catch*

7. If you have multiple *Catch* blocks in your *Try...Catch* structure, you should put the *Catch* block that handles the exception that is most likely to occur _____.

   a. first

   b. in the middle of the *Catch* blocks

   c. last

   d. in a separate *Try...Catch* structure

8. You should use a(n) _____ statement to further define (or filter) when an exception is caught in a *Catch* block.

   a. *If*

   b. *Only*

   c. *When*

   d. *AND*

9. Handling exceptions by using the Call Stack to minimize the amount of code written is called _____.

   a. casting exceptions

   b. exception bubbling

   c. exception passing

   d. defensive programming

10. Code that is written in a(n) _____ block is guaranteed to run no matter what happens when your program runs.

    a. *Finally*

    b. *Catch*

    c. *Try*

    d. *When*

11. If a user types the word *dog* in a text box that requires a numeric value that will be used in a calculation, an exception will be thrown when the calculation is attempted. True or false?

12. *System.Exception* contains only one class, *System.SystemException*, which provides all of the exceptions supported by the .NET Framework. True or false?

13. All *Try...Catch* blocks must contain a *Try* statement, an *End Try* statement, and at least one *Catch* block or a *Finally* block. True or false?

14. It is a good idea to display the message associated with any exception that is thrown, because the messages are always easy to understand. True or false?

15. The *Throw* statement can be executed without an argument if you want to re-throw the current exception. True or false?

16. _____ uses code that will catch any exception that is thrown when an error occurs to handle the exception appropriately.

17. The base class for all exceptions in the .NET Framework is the _____ object.

18. The _____ property of the Exception object returns the description of the exception that has occurred.

19. The _____ block in a *Try...Catch* block contains the code that you want to run to catch any exception that is thrown.

20. If an exception occurs and there is no procedure in the Call Stack with an exception handler to handle it, a(n) _____ exception will be thrown and the program will terminate.

STEP BY STEP

In this exercise, you will create a program for the Baldwin Museum of Science health exhibit that will display the number of days a person has been alive. Users will enter their date of birth on the form and click a button labeled Display Days. The program will determine how many days they have been alive (including the current day) and display the result on the screen. The program will use structured exception handling to catch and handle any errors that might occur. Figure 8-12 shows what the completed form will look like.

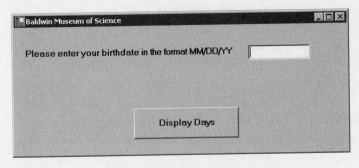

Figure 8-12   Form to calculate days since birth

▶ Creating a new project

1. Open Visual Studio .NET if it isn't already open.

2. Click the New Project button on the Start page.

3. Click Visual Basic Projects under Project Types and Windows Application under Templates.

4. Type **DaysAliveCh8** in the Name box.

5. Browse to the location in which you are storing your projects.

6. Click OK.

▶ Configuring the form and changing the startup object

1. Right-click Form1.vb in Solution Explorer, and rename Form1.vb as **Days.vb**. Press ENTER.

2. Click once in the title bar of the form, and change the *(Name)* property of the form to **frmDays**.

3. Change the *Text* property of the form to **Baldwin Museum of Science**, and then press ENTER.

4. Right-click the DaysAliveCh8 project name in Solution Explorer, and then click Properties.

5. Change the startup object to frmDays, and then click OK.

▶ Setting up the form

1. Add a Label control to the top of the form on the left side, and change the *Text* property to **Please enter your birthdate in the format MM/DD/YY**.

2. Add a TextBox control next to the Label, and name it **txtBirthdate**. Delete the contents of its *Text* property.

3. Add a second Label control to the middle of the form, and name it **lbl-DaysAlive**. Delete the contents of its *Text* property. This label will display the number of days the user has been alive.

4. Add a Button control to the bottom of the form, and name it **btnDisplay-Days**. Change the *Text* property to **Display Days**.

▶ Adding code to the form

1. Double-click the Display Days button on the form to open the Code Editor in the button's *Click* event handler.

2. Type the following code in the *btnDisplayDays_Click* event handler. You are using the *DateDiff* function to calculate the difference between the two dates, and you will handle two of the three exceptions that are listed in Help for the *DateDiff* function. You are not handling the exception that occurs as a result of an invalid interval because you have hard coded the interval.

```
Dim datBirthDate As Date
Dim intDaysAlive As Integer

' Clear the contents of the label
lblDaysAlive.Text = ""

Try
    ' Convert the date they entered as a string into a date field
    datBirthDate = CDate(txtBirthdate.Text)

    ' Calculate the days alive
    intDaysAlive = DateDiff(DateInterval.Day, datBirthDate, Now())

    ' Display the result on the form
    lblDaysAlive.Text = "You have been alive for " & intDaysAlive & " days!"
```

```
Catch ex As ArgumentException
    MessageBox.Show("Please enter a valid date")
    txtBirthdate.Text = ""
    txtBirthdate.Focus()

Catch ex As InvalidCastException
    MessageBox.Show("Please enter a correctly formatted date")
    txtBirthdate.Text = ""
    txtBirthdate.Focus()

End Try
```

▶ **Saving and testing your project**

1. On the File menu, select Save All to save your work.

2. On the Debug menu, select Start to run your project.

3. Test the program by entering your birthdate and clicking the Display Days button. The number of days you have been alive should appear in the label.

4. Test the program by entering the birthdate **00/00/00**. You should receive the message "Please enter a valid date."

5. Test the program by entering the birthdate **6**. You should receive the message "Please enter a correctly formatted date."

6. On the Debug menu, select Stop Debugging to end the program.

7. On the File menu, select Close Solution to close the project.

8. Close Visual Studio .NET.

FINISH THE CODE

Open the project file called WoodgroveBankCh8 that came with your student file. The purpose of this program is to calculate a monthly mortgage payment when the amount of the principal, the time period of the loan (in months), and the interest rate are entered. Add the necessary code to handle the exception that would be thrown if the user left any one of the three text boxes empty. The message displayed when the exception is caught should display the system description of the error followed by instructions to the user to enter a value into each of the text boxes. Figure 8-13 shows an example of the error message that should appear.

Figure 8-13 **Exception message displayed to user**

JUST HINTS

Open the project you created for Fabrikam, Inc., in Chapter 6. If you did not complete this project in Chapter 6, you can open the project called FabrikamCh8 that came in your student file and use it for this exercise. In this exercise, you will add some additional code to the project to handle any possible errors that could occur.

▶ Use the following hints to add error handling to the project

1. Use defensive programming to check the value entered in the Quantity On Hand box. If users enter a value that is less than zero, display an error message and set the focus to that box so they can reenter a valid number. Do not continue with the rest of the calculation until a valid value has been entered.

2. Add the same defensive programming to handle the entry of a negative value in the Quantity On Order box.

3. Do not use any defensive programming code to check whether the user entered a numeric value into the Quantity On Hand and Quantity On Order boxes. Instead, catch the exception that is thrown when the attempt is made to convert the *String* value to an *Integer*, and display an appropriate message to the user.

ON YOUR OWN

In this exercise, you will open the project you created for Tailspin Toys in Chapter 6. If you did not complete this project in Chapter 6, you can open the project called TailspinToysCh8 that came in your student file and use it for this exercise. In this exercise, you will add the appropriate defensive programming techniques and exception handling to create an application that can handle the entry of any information and the selection of any combination of the available parameters. Carefully test your final program to make sure that all possible combinations of entry into the form have been handled correctly. Also, make sure that all messages displayed to users clearly explain what they did wrong and what they need to change.

MORE PRACTICE

1. Write a *Try...Catch* block that will prompt the user to enter a whole number with the *InputBox* function and place this value in an *Integer* variable called *intNewNumber*. Write a *Catch* block that will catch any exception that is thrown and display the message "An error has occurred" to the user.

2. Write a *While* statement that will prompt the user to enter a word that contains more than three characters with the *InputBox* function and place this value in a *String* variable called *strWord*. If the length of the word entered is fewer than four characters, display the message "This word is too short" to the user and keep prompting them to enter a word.

3. Write a Visual Basic .NET program that will convert all of the characters in a sentence entered by the user to either uppercase or lowercase letters, as directed by the user. Use your defensive programming skills to handle the situation in which the user does not enter a sentence or does not specify whether to convert to uppercase or lowercase.

4. Write a Visual Basic .NET program that will calculate the amount of time it would take to fly from one city to another. The user should be able to enter two city names, the distance between the cities in miles, and the speed the plane will fly in miles per hour. Calculate the flying time and display it on the form. Use defensive error handling to catch the entry of any invalid input values, and write one exception handler that catches any exceptions that occur.

5. Write a Visual Basic .NET program that will perform the basic cooking measurement conversions in the following list. The user should be able to enter a number and a measurement from the left side of the conversion (for example, tablespoon). The program should convert the measurement to the measurement in the right side of the conversion (for example, tea-spoon). Do not include any defensive error handling. Try to anticipate any errors that might occur and write exception handling code for these situations.

   ❏ 1 tablespoon = 3 teaspoons

   ❏ 1 cup = .5 pint

   ❏ 1 gallon = 4 quarts

   ❏ 1 fluid ounce = 1 tablespoon

6. Write a Visual Basic .NET program that will calculate the total cost of printing a given number of pages and envelopes using the business rules listed below. Business rules are standards that have been defined and should be followed throughout a company or even an entire industry. Users should be able to specify the color of paper they want and whether the order is a rush order. Do not provide any defensive code routines. Try to anticipate any exceptions that might be thrown and write exception handling code for those exceptions.

   ❏ If the total quantity of envelopes is less than 100, the cost to print each envelope is $.05. If the total quantity is greater than or equal to 100, the cost to print each envelope is $.04. The cost for quantities greater than or equal to 1,000 is $.03 per envelope.

   ❏ If the total quantity of pages is less than 100, the cost to print each page is $.10. If the total quantity is greater than or equal to 100, the cost to print each page is $.08. The cost for quantities greater than or equal to 1,000 is $.06 per page.

   ❏ There is no extra charge for white paper. There is an extra charge of $.01 per envelope and $.01 per page for any color other than white.

   ❏ The extra charge for a rush order is .02 percent of the total printing cost if the total quantity of envelopes and pages combined is less than 2,000. If the total quantity is 2,000 or greater, the extra charge is .01 percent of the total printing cost.

CHAPTER 9
ADO.NET

Accessing data stored in databases or other structures might be the most common task in many of your programs. Microsoft ADO.NET is a technology that allows access to various data sources to enable users to retrieve, manipulate, and update the data stored in those sources. The data source can be a fully functional database, such as a Microsoft Office Access or Microsoft SQL Server database, or even a plain text file.

In this chapter, we will cover the basics of ADO.NET, including accessing data stored in relational databases such as Access and SQL Server. For a more in-depth look at ADO.NET, check out the many other publications that cover ADO.NET in much more detail, including *Microsoft ADO.NET Step by Step*, by Rebecca Riordan.

Upon completion of this chapter, you will be able to:

■ Learn about the main objects that make up the ADO.NET object model.

■ Create Connection and DataAdapter objects by using the Data Adapter Configuration Wizard.

■ Use Command objects to build the table structures that will be added to a dataset.

■ Generate a dataset and populate the dataset with data at run time.

■ Bind controls to tables and columns in a data table.

■ Create simple SQL (Structured Query Language) statements.

■ Use an Access database in place of a SQL Server database.

RELATIONAL DATABASES AND ADO.NET

Before tackling the mechanics and components of ADO.NET, you need to understand databases. Data can be stored in many forms, including plain text files, spreadsheets, or fully functional relational databases. In this textbook, we will be using a relational database because that is the most widely used source of data for Microsoft Visual Basic .NET applications.

What Is a Relational Database?

A **relational database** is a collection of one or more tables of information that relate to each other in some way. Taking a simple College database as an example, we might have a table that stores information on each student (the Students table), another table that stores data on each of the classes that are offered (Classes) and perhaps another table that stores data on each of the classrooms (Classrooms). We could construct the database in such a way that data in the Classes table would relate to the Students table, and we could store and retrieve information on the classes a particular student or group of students are enrolled in. Adding the Classrooms table would allow us to include information on the particular classrooms that would be used to conduct the courses. Figure 9-1 shows the relationships between tables in our hypothetical College database.

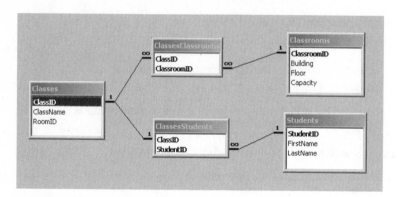

Figure 9-1   The tables of the College database and how they relate to each other

From Figure 9-1, you can see that this database has three primary tables and two linking tables. The primary tables are Students, Classes, and Classrooms. The linking tables ClassesStudents and ClassesClassrooms are used to link the Classes table with the Students table and the Classes table with the Classrooms table, respectively. A **linking table** provides a relational link between two tables that have no columns in common. If you want to relate two tables, they each must have a column in common. Looking at Figure 9-1, we can see that there is no column in either the Students table or the Classes table that we could relate intelligently. The ClassesStudents table provides the relationship between classes and students.

You might have used a relational database at one time or another, even if you didn't know it. Maybe you have browsed the Internet to get information about a particular film. You can view such information as the description or synopsis of the film and perhaps a list of actors. You might spot a particular actor in the list and decide to look up the filmography for that actor. You have just used a relational database. There is probably a films table that is related to an actors table. These linked tables enable you to retrieve a list of actors for a particular film or get a list of films that an actor starred in.

A well-constructed database minimizes the duplication of information, which helps to maintain the integrity of the data and also improves performance when users retrieve and update data. In this chapter, we will provide several examples of relational databases to help you familiarize yourself with them.

Database Terminology

It really helps to know the lingo when using databases. In this section, we will go over the various terms that are used when discussing databases, using the Students table in a hypothetical database named College. Figure 9-2 shows the Students table. Refer to this figure as you read through the following list of terms.

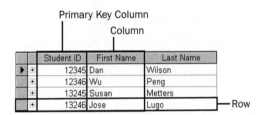

Figure 9-2   The Students table, showing the row (record), column (field), and primary key column

- **Table**   A table is an object composed of rows and columns. The intersection of a row and a column holds one piece of data related to the entity that the row represents. In this case, the entity is a student, and each row contains details for a single student.

- **Row**   A row is an object that stores the details of a single occurrence of an entity, which in this case is a student. A row is also referred to as a **record**.

- **Column**   A column is an object that represents an attribute or characteristic of the entity, such as a student's name or birth date. A column is also referred to as a **field**.

- **Primary key**   The primary key column is used to ensure that each row in the table is unique. If you refer to Figure 9-1, you can determine which column is the primary key for that table because it appears in boldface type. Although a primary key is not always required in a database table, it is strongly recommended that you provide one. In our Students table, the StudentID column is used as the primary key. A student can only have one StudentID, and two students cannot have the same StudentID. When constructing a table, we look for a column for which the value will always be unique for each record and use that field as the primary key. If there is no such field, we might create an identity or autonumber column that will provide a unique numeric value for each row added to the table. Keep in mind that most database systems allow two or more columns to be joined together to make up the primary key for a table. Such a key is called a **composite primary key**. You can see that the

ClassesStudents table and the ClassesClassrooms table in Figure 9-1 both have composite primary keys.

- **Foreign key**   A foreign key is used to relate two tables. The foreign key does not need to be unique for each record in a table, and in a one-to-many relationship, it never is. If we were to assume that a student can register for only one class, we could include a ClassID column as a foreign key in the Students table that would allow us to relate the Students table to the Classes table by joining the foreign key of the Students table to the primary key of the Classes table (assuming that the primary key of the Classes table is ClassID). This relationship would allow us to retrieve information on the student along with details of the class that the student is enrolled in. Looking at Figure 9-1, we see a more realistic relationship. The Students table is actually related to the Classes table through the ClassesStudents linking table. With this arrangement, we can now provide for a situation in which a student can enroll in many classes.

- **Constraint**   A constraint is basically a rule that defines data that can be typed into a field. An example of this is a primary key constraint. The primary key constraint is applied when a column is designated as the primary key and therefore requires that a value must be typed (*null* values are not allowed in a primary key column) and that the value must be unique in that column.

- **DDL**   Data Definition Language (DDL) is used for the construction and design of the tables in a database.

- **DML**   Data Manipulation Language (DML) is used to manipulate the data in a database table.

- **SQL**   Structured Query Language (SQL) is used to retrieve and update data in a database table.

- **One-to-many relationship**   This type of relationship between two tables is perhaps the most common of the various types of relationships. The table on the "one" side of the relationship will have one row with a particular value in its primary key. The table on the "many" side will have one or more rows with the same value in its foreign key. An example of a one-to-many relationship would be a customer-order table relationship in which the customer table is on the one side and the order table is on the many side. A customer can have many orders, but an order can have only one customer. Figure 9-1 shows the relationships between the tables. Notice that a one-to-many relationship is displayed as 1 (on the one side) to   (on the many side).

- **One-to-one relationship**   This type of relationship is less common and is used when a single row in one table relates to a single row in another table.

- **Many-to-many relationship**   This type of relationship between two tables requires the use of a third table to link the two primary tables. For example, an author might have written several books, and a book might have several authors. By creating a table linking authors to books, you can create a many-to-many relationship.

ADO.NET and Databases

Now that you have a basic understanding of databases, we can take a look at ADO.NET's role in programming for them in Visual Basic .NET.

Connected and Disconnected Data Access Models

Although there is no easy way to explain ADO.NET, we can start by saying that ADO.NET is a technology built around the concept of the disconnected data access model. What this means is that a subset of the data located in a remote database can be downloaded and stored on a local computer such as a laptop computer. At that point, the laptop can be disconnected from the network or server that runs the remote database. Users can interact with the data locally just as if they were connected to the remote database. At a later time, the laptop can be reconnected to the network and the remote database can be updated with all the changes, additions, and deletions.

To help you understand the disconnected data access model, it might help if you first understand the connected data access model and its inherent limitations.

The **connected data access model** requires the user to be connected to the database at all times. The database must be able to support that connection, and it does so quite well. Now consider a situation in which a thousand people are accessing the same database. Can the database support that number of connections? Enterprise database technologies such as SQL Server and Oracle certainly can support that number and more. However, as the number of connected users increases, there will be a relative decrease in performance. The disconnected data access model addresses this performance issue.

The **disconnected data access model** permits the user to connect to the database whenever data needs to be refreshed or updated. The concept is quite simple really: connect to the database, retrieve or update the data, and then disconnect from the database. Transactions are typically fast, and resource usage is kept to a minimum. The Internet is the ultimate disconnected model. ADO.NET is designed around the disconnected data access model, making it an important part of your programming tool kit.

The ADO.NET Object Model—A Simplified View

Figure 9-3 shows the ADO.NET object model. The providers are the objects that retrieve the data from the database. The consumers are the objects (forms and form controls, variables, and other objects) that use or display the data. The databases are not actually part of the model, but they are included to show where the providers get the data to pass to the consumers. Let's look at the connection and data provider portions of this model in a bit more detail.

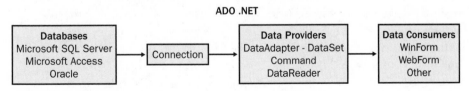

Figure 9-3   A simplified ADO.NET object model

The *Connection* object comes in four basic varieties:

- **SQLConnection**   Used exclusively for SQL Server databases
- **OracleConnection**   Used exclusively for Oracle databases
- **OleDbConnection**   Used for all OLE DB–compliant databases
- **OdbcConnection**   Used for all other databases

To retrieve and update information in a database, you must be able to connect to it. The *Connection* object provides this important function. To connect to a database such as a SQL Server database, you must provide the connection information required by the database. This information typically would include the name of the server that the database is running on (*Data Source*), the name of the database (*Initial Catalog*), a valid user name (*User ID*) and a password (*Password*).

The Data Provider objects use the *Connection* object to connect to the database and provide the necessary intelligence to ask for and retrieve the data. This data is then passed to the *data consumer*. The Data Provider objects shown in Figure 9-3 are:

- **DataAdapter**   The *DataAdapter* (*SQLDataAdapter*, *OracleData-Adapter*, *OleDbDataAdapter*, and *OdbcDataAdapter*) is the brains behind the *DataSet*. It is explicitly designed for the database you are connecting to and is used to translate your requests into the language the database uses. The *DataAdapter* object is most useful when implementing the disconnected data access model. A *DataAdapter* can be created at design time or at run time.

- **Command**   The *Command* object (*SQLCommand*, *OracleCommand*, *OleDbCommand*, and *OdbcCommand*) can be used independently of many of the objects in ADO.NET, with the exception of a *Connection* object. The *Command* object is used to run SQL statements (or stored procedures) to retrieve or update data in a database. A *Command* object can be created at design time or at run time.

    TIP   *Stored procedures are prepared and precompiled SQL statements that reside on the database. This type of SQL statement is fast because it doesn't need to be translated and compiled prior to being run by the database. In contrast, a SQL statement sent by the program must be translated and compiled each time it is sent. Oracle and SQL Server support the use of stored procedures in this way. Microsoft Access does not support this type of stored procedure.*

- **DataReader**   The *DataReader* object uses a *Command* object to retrieve data one row at a time. This limitation is actually a good thing because there is only one buffered row at a time in memory. This makes the *DataReader* very efficient, so it has little impact on available resources. The data returned (the result set) is a read-only, forward-only stream of data (sometimes referred to as a *firehose cursor*). Because the *DataReader* object is read-only, it cannot be used to update data in a database. Other than the fact that it cannot be used to update the database, the only downside of a *DataReader* is that it tends to hang on to a connection for a little while longer than a *DataAdapter* when filling a dataset. A *DataReader* object can only be created at run time.

■ ***DataSet***   The *DataSet* object supports the disconnected data access model. The *DataSet* is a memory-resident representation of the data that is passed to it by the *DataAdapter*. The *DataSet* can represent a complete set of data, including tables, constraints, and relationships between the tables. A *DataSet* object can be created at design time (*typed*) or at run time (*untyped*).

A typed dataset is a class that has an Extensible Markup Language (XML) schema associated with it. The schema represents the data structure of the table or tables that it is created from. When using a typed dataset, you can refer to each of the tables and columns by name. In addition, type mismatch errors will be caught when the code is compiled rather than at run time.

By contrast, an untyped dataset has no schema associated with it at design time but will have one when it is filled at run time. With untyped datasets, a type mismatch error will not be caught when the code is compiled but will, instead, throw an exception at run time that must be caught and handled at that time.

When it is created, a *DataSet* contains one or more *DataTable* objects in its *Tables* collection. You can add additional data tables by using the *Add* method of the *Tables* property. In addition, a *DataSet* has a *Relations* collection. A **relation** links one table to another to more accurately represent the structure of the database it is based on and to allow navigation between the parent table and the child table.

Although there are several other objects available for use in ADO.NET, we will discuss them when they are referred to in the text.

Creating a Database Program

Now that you have a basic understanding of databases and several important ADO.NET objects, you are ready to begin programming with ADO.NET. For all of the examples in this chapter, we will be using a SQL Server database named pubs. If you do not have SQL Server or MSDE (Microsoft Desktop Engine) available, you can use the Access database (Pubs.mdb) located in your student file. Instructions on how to set up Server Explorer to use the Access database are provided toward the end of the chapter under the section "Using Microsoft Access." After you are set up to use the Pubs.mdb database, you should return to this section to continue working through this example.

When you incorporate database access into a program, you need to design the interface carefully so that the information is displayed in a logical and understandable way. This is not as easy as it sounds, but it gets easier with practice. If the interface is designed for data entry by means of input controls such as text boxes or list boxes, the input controls should be arranged in a way that makes sense to the people entering the data. The TAB key is typically used to move from one control to the next in a logical order, so make sure that the tab order is set correctly. To make things simple, for the first example we will be using just the titles table from the pubs database.

▶ Creating a Windows application that uses ADO.NET

1. Create a new Microsoft Windows application called **Bookstore**. Use the information in Table 9-1 to create a basic form with one text box. You will add additional controls after you are satisfied that you have a good connection to the database and can retrieve data from the tables.

Table 9-1 **Bookstore Form Properties**

(Name)	Text
frmBooks	**The Book Store**
txtTitleID	\<blank\>

2. Make sure the form is displayed in the designer window, and then navigate through Server Explorer until the pubs database is displayed in the tree view. If Server Explorer is not visible, select Server Explorer from the View menu. Click the plus sign (+) next to each node to expand each nested list until you see the pubs database. If it is installed, the pubs database will be located under Servers\SQL Servers*NameOfSQLServerInstance* (typically the name of your computer). If the Server Explorer window is not visible in the integrated development environment (IDE), on the View menu, select Server Explorer.

3. Click the plus sign next to the pubs database to expand the list of tables, as shown in Figure 9-4.

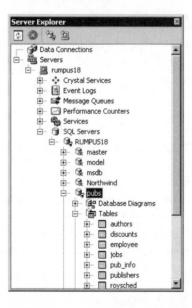

Figure 9-4   List of tables in Server Explorer

4. Click once to select the titles table and then drag the table onto the form. The *Connection* and *DataAdapter* objects will be created automatically and added to the component tray.

Although that didn't seem like too much work, be aware that Microsoft Visual Studio .NET did a lot behind the scenes. This isn't always a good thing because it doesn't allow you to see what's going on. If something should go wrong, it would be nice to know how it was all done so that you have a chance to correct it. In the next example, you will be using the Data Adapter Configuration Wizard to get a better idea about what just happened. Before you do that, though, you need to finish this example by adding and filling the DataSet, and then adding the controls to the form to bind to the data.

What Is Binding?

Binding is the programmatical linking of the data source to a control that can display the data. In the current example, you will be creating a dataset to act as the data source and then adding text boxes to the form to display the data. By binding each text box to a particular column in a table (in the dataset), you will be able to display the value defined by the intersection of the bound column with a particular row number. Remember that a table is a collection of rows and columns. A value is defined by the intersection of a row and a column (think of a spreadsheet). When a text box is bound to a column, it will display the value defined by the bound column and a row number that you will provide in code.

▶ **Continuing the Bookstore program**

1. Right-click SQLDataAdapter1 in the Component Tray, and then select Preview Data. The window shown in Figure 9-5 will appear.

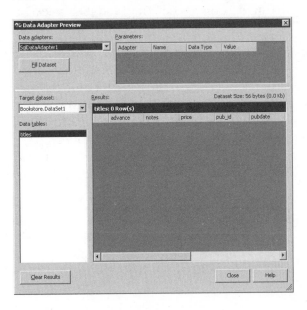

Figure 9-5   The Data Adapter Preview window

Notice that the Data Adapter Preview window shows the current *Data-Adapter*, the target dataset, and the data table that you will be using.

2. Click the Fill Dataset button to populate the Results window in the dialog box, as shown in Figure 9-6. This will allow you to establish the connection with the database and return a set of rows. All that is left to do now is add the real dataset, provide the code to fill the dataset, and then bind the data to the *Text* property of the text box that you added to the form.

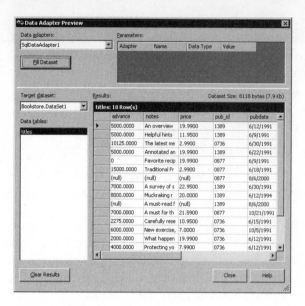

Figure 9-6   The Data Adapter Preview window populated with fields from the titles table

3. Close the Data Adapter Preview window.

4. Right-click SQLDataAdapter1 in the Component Tray, and then select Generate Dataset.

5. Click New (if it is not already selected) in the Generate Dataset dialog box shown in Figure 9-7, and accept the default name *DataSet1*. Remember that you only dragged over the titles table, so the table list only shows that table along with the *DataAdapter* associated with it. This method of creating a dataset creates a typed dataset. Make sure that the Add This Dataset To The Designer check box is selected. This will create an instance of DataSet1, which you just created, and add that instance to the Component Tray of the current application.

TIP   The new instance of *DataSet1* will be called *DataSet11*. If you had named the class *dsTitles* rather than using the default name of *DataSet1* when you created it, the new instance would be named *dsTitles1*. It is important to remember that whenever you need to reference the dataset in code, you must refer to it by its instance name (*DataSet11* or *dsTitles1*) and not by its class name.

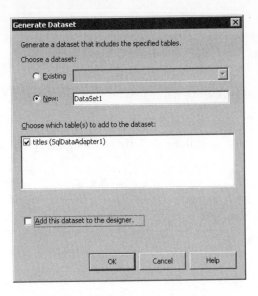

Figure 9-7   The Generate Dataset dialog box

6. Click OK to close the Generate Dataset dialog box. The new dataset will have the name *DataSet11* and will be added to the Component Tray. Also, a new file (DataSet1.xsd) will be created and added to Solution Explorer and to the project folder.

   In reality, when a typed dataset is created, three files are created and added to Solution Explorer and the project folder:

   ❑ DataSet1.xsd is the XML schema file that describes the dataset.

   ❑ DataSet1.vb is the class module that derives from the *DataSet* class. The code for this class (properties, methods, and events) is automatically generated.

   ❑ DataSet1.xsx contains the layout information for the *DataSet1* schema view. This information is used when the dataset is displayed in the designer window.

7. Double-click the form to add the form's *Load* event handler to the Code Editor.

8. Type the following line of code in the *Load* event handler:

```
SqlDataAdapter1.Fill(DataSet11)
```

   When the dataset is generated, a *DataTable* object is created and added to the *Tables* collection of the dataset for each database table specified in the Generate Dataset dialog box. Each of these *DataTable* objects contains the schema based on the table it was created from, but no data is brought over. The dataset will be empty until the *Fill* method of the *Data-Adapter* is executed.

9. Switch back to design view. Bind the data to the *Text* property of the text box on the form. Select the text box in the designer window and locate the *DataBindings* property in the Properties window. Make sure to scroll all the way to the top to see the *DataBindings* property.

10. Click the plus sign to expand the property.

11. Select the *Text* property, and then click the down arrow.

12. Click the plus sign next to Dataset11, and then click the plus sign next to titles.

13. Select title_id as the bound column, as shown in Figure 9-8.

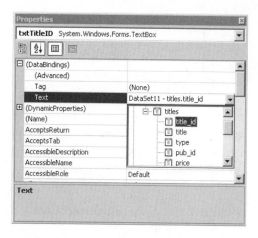

Figure 9-8   Properties for the txtTitleID field

14. Now let's run the program and see what happens. Press F5 to run the program. Your form should look like Figure 9-9.

Figure 9-9   The running Bookstore form

Although it doesn't seem like much right now, you have covered a lot of ground here. Of course, if it weren't for the automation provided by Visual Studio .NET, you would still be struggling to connect to the database. Let's review what you have done so far, and then you can add the additional controls and provide the ability to navigate the rows in the table.

- You located the pubs database in our list of SQL Server databases.

- By dragging the titles table onto the form, you were able to automatically create a *Connection* object and *DataAdapter*.

- You generated a typed dataset (after having previewed the data first).

- You then filled the dataset with data by using the *Fill* method of the *DataAdapter* object.

- Finally, you bound the *Text* property of the text box to the title_id column of the titles *DataTable*.

To continue, we need to add the rest of the controls to the form so that we can display the other columns in the titles table.

▶ **Adding the rest of the controls**

1. Add a text box to the form for each of the following columns in the titles table. Make sure that you name each text box properly. Include the txt prefix along with the name of the column. Do not include underscores when naming the controls, even if one is used in the name of the column. (For example, use txtPubID as the name for the text box that will bind to the pub_id column.)

   ❑ title

   ❑ pub_id

   ❑ price

   ❑ notes

   ❑ pubdate

2. Add labels to identify each of the text boxes on the form. It's not necessary to change the names of each of the labels because we won't be referring to them in code.

3. After all the text boxes and labels are added to the form, arrange the controls and set the tab order so that the tab sequence is logical. See Figure 9-10 for an example.

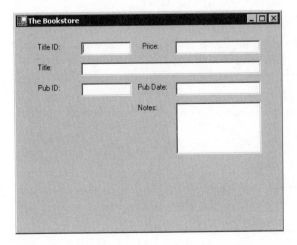

Figure 9-10   Bookstore application form showing all required controls

4. Set the *DataBindings* property for each of the text boxes to their respective columns in the titles table of *DataSet11*, and then run the program. When your program runs, it should look like Figure 9-11.

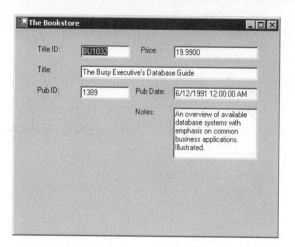

Figure 9-11 Bookstore application form displaying data from the titles *DataTable*

Navigating the *DataTable*

You have managed to bind the data in the titles *DataTable* of *DataSet11* to the text boxes and display it in a somewhat orderly fashion. The application would be complete if the user had a way to move from one row to another by using navigation buttons. It would be even better if we could display the current row number along with the number of rows that make up the table.

In this section, you will learn about the four objects that will provide the mechanism to allow you to navigate the rows of the *DataTable* and keep the data in each of the text boxes synchronized.

- **BindingContext** The *BindingContext* object manages a collection of *BindingManagerBase* objects. Every object that inherits from the *Control* class can have a single *BindingContext* object. When used in code, *Binding-Context* returns a *BindingManagerBase* object for a data source used by all the data-bound controls contained by that object.

- **BindingManagerBase** The *BindingManagerBase* object is used to synchronize all the controls that are bound to the same data source and data member. The *BindingManagerBase* class is abstract and cannot be directly instantiated. When used in code, the *BindingManagerBase* object will either be a *CurrencyManager* object or a *PropertyManager* object, depending on the data source and data member that is passed to the *Item* property of the *BindingContext* object. When passing ADO.NET objects to the *Item* property of the *BindingContext* object, a *CurrencyManager* object will always be returned.

- **PropertyManager** The *PropertyManager* object is a *BindingManager-Base* object that can only return a single value. We will not be using the *PropertyManager* object in this example.

■ ***CurrencyManager***   The *CurrencyManager* object (which has a somewhat confusing name that is not related in any way to money) is a *BindingManagerBase* object that is returned when ADO.NET objects are passed to the *Item* property of the *BindingContext* object. The *CurrencyManager* object is used to keep the displayed data synchronized. We will use *BindingContext* to return a *CurrencyManager* object and use that to navigate the *DataTable*. This will ensure that all the data-bound controls stay on the same row.

Because the form inherits from the *Control* class, we know it has a built-in *BindingContext* object. You will be using that *BindingContext* to return a *BindingManagerBase* (to be more specific, it will return a *CurrencyManager*) that you can use to synchronize the text box controls on the form and allow the user to navigate through the rows in the *DataTable*. The *BindingContext* object takes two arguments: the name of the *DataSet* object and the name of a *DataTable* in the dataset (the name of the *DataTable* must be enclosed in double quotation marks). These two arguments, used together, will identify the source of the data. To keep all the text boxes synchronized while navigating the table, you simply set the *Position* property of the *CurrencyManager* object. Because each of the text boxes is bound to the same source of data, when the position of the *CurrencyManager* changes, the values in the text boxes must also change to stay synchronized and thus display the correct values for the current row.

Let's look at this in code so that you can better understand what's happening. First you're going to use the *BindingContext* object of the form without explicitly creating a *CurrencyManager* object. You will find that the user can navigate the *DataTable* quite well because the *BindingContext* object implicitly returns the type of object that you need. After that, you will explicitly create a *CurrencyManager* object and use that object to perform the navigation duties. Before you can do that however, you need to add buttons to the form. These buttons will be used to run the code that changes the row.

▶ **Adding buttons to the form**

1. Add four Button controls to the bottom of your form, and set their *(Name)* and *Text* properties using the information in Table 9-2.

   Table 9-2   **Button Properties for the Bookstore Application**

(Name)	Text
btnFirst	**&First**
btnPrevious	**&Previous**
btnNext	**&Next**
btnLast	**&Last**

2. Double-click btnFirst to add the *btnFirst_Click* event handler to the Code Editor. Type the following line of code inside the *btnFirst_Click* event handler exactly as shown.

```
Me.BindingContext(DataSet11, "titles").Position = 0
```

3. Double-click each of the other buttons and code them using the information in Table 9-3.

Table 9-3 **Button *Click* Event Code**

Button	Code
btnPrevious	`Me.BindingContext(DataSet11, "titles").Position -= 1`
btnNext	`Me.BindingContext(DataSet11, "titles").Position += 1`
btnLast	`Me.BindingContext(DataSet11, "titles").Position = _` `    Me.BindingContext(DataSet11, "titles").Count - 1`

Now that you have coded the buttons, you need to provide information to users to let them know which row they are on and how many rows there are in total. You can display this information in a label.

4. Add a Label control beneath the buttons, name it **lblRecord**, and delete the contents of its *Text* property. The following code allows you to return the current position and display that in the label.

```
lblRecord.Text = (Me.BindingContext(DataSet11, _
    "titles").Position + 1).ToString()
```

Notice that you added 1 to the value of *Position*. You did this because the *Position* value starts at 0 (zero) and you want the information to be user friendly. Users might be disturbed if they saw that they were on the 0th row rather than the 1st row.

To make the application even better, you will display the total number of rows along with the current position. For the first row, this would be displayed as *Record 1 of 18*. Rather than show you an abstracted example, we will show a practical example by incorporating it into the current example.

5. Create a new method (Sub procedure) named **UpdateRecordNumber**. This method will be called from each of the four navigation buttons.

6. Place the following code inside the *UpdateRecordNumber* method:

```
lblRecord.Text = "Record " & _
    Me.BindingContext(DataSet11, "titles").Position + 1 & _
    " of " & Me.BindingContext(DataSet11, "titles").Count
```

As we mentioned earlier, the *Position* property starts at 0, so to display a row number that is meaningful to the user, you must add 1 to the value of *Position*. The value of the *Count* property is the same regardless of the value of the *Position* property.

7. Place the following line of code inside the event handler for each of the navigation buttons. Place the code below the existing code in each of the event handlers. You must also place this code inside the *Load* event handler of the form so that the current row and row count is displayed as soon as the form is displayed.

```
UpdateRecordNumber()
```

The completed form for the Bookstore application should look like Figure 9-12.

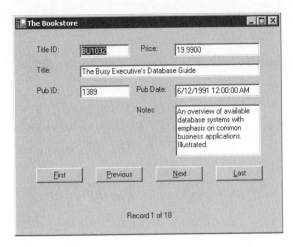

Figure 9-12 Completed form for the Bookstore application

Using *CurrencyManager*

You know that the *BindingContext* object returns a single *BindingManagerBase* for all the controls bound to the same data source. You also know that the *Binding-ManagerBase* object is either a *CurrencyManager* object or a *PropertyManager* object. Keep those two points in mind as you modify the example.

Up to now, you used *BindingContext* to implicitly return a *CurrencyManager* object. In this section, you will explicitly create a *CurrencyManager* object by assigning the returned value from the *BindingContext* object to it. The first step is to create an object variable that will store a *CurrencyManager* object. The next step is to explicitly convert the *BindingContext* object to a *BindingManagerBase* object. The last step is to assign the converted object to the declared *Currency-Manager* object variable.

▶ Adding a *CurrencyManager* object

1. Declare a *CurrencyManager* object variable. This will be declared at the class level because you will need it to be available in several of the procedures. Use the following line of code:

```
Private curMgrBooks As CurrencyManager
```

Next you need to convert the *BindingContext* object to a *BindingManager-Base* object and pass the converted object to the *CurrencyManager* object variable. This conversion can be performed by using one of two functions: *CType* or *DirectCast*. Although the *DirectCast* function is more efficient, there are specific rules governing its use, and it might fail when attempting some conversions. Although either function will work for this particular conversion, you will use the *CType* function. The following code will perform the required conversion and initialize the *Currency-Manager* object variable to the converted object.

2. Type the following code into the form's *Load* event handler. Place this code at the top of the procedure, above the existing code.

```
curMgrBooks = _
    CType(Me.BindingContext(DataSet11, "titles"), BindingManagerBase)
```

Now that you have a properly defined *CurrencyManager* object, you can use it instead of the *BindingContext* object for all of your routines.

3. In the event handler for each of the navigation buttons, and in the *Update-RecordNumber* Sub procedure, replace the following statement with the name of the object variable you created earlier: *curMgrBooks*.

```
Me.BindingContext(DataSet11, "titles")
```

When you have finished, the completed code should look as follows:

```
Public Class frmBooks
    Inherits System.Windows.Forms.Form

    Private curMgrBooks As CurrencyManager
    ' Windows Form Designer generated code

    Private Sub frmPubs_Load(ByVal sender As System.Object, _
            ByVal e As System.EventArgs) Handles MyBase.Load
        curMgrBooks = _
            CType(Me.BindingContext(DataSet11, "titles"), BindingManagerBase)
        SqlDataAdapter1.Fill(DataSet11)
        UpdateRecordNumber()
    End Sub

    Private Sub btnFirst_Click(ByVal sender As System.Object, _
            ByVal e As System.EventArgs) Handles btnFirst.Click
        curMgrBooks.Position = 0
        UpdateRecordNumber()
    End Sub

    Private Sub btnPrevious_Click(ByVal sender As System.Object, _
            ByVal e As System.EventArgs) Handles btnPrevious.Click
        curMgrBooks.Position -= 1
        UpdateRecordNumber()
    End Sub

    Private Sub btnNext_Click(ByVal sender As System.Object, _
            ByVal e As System.EventArgs) Handles btnNext.Click
        curMgrBooks.Position += 1
        UpdateRecordNumber()
    End Sub

    Private Sub btnLast_Click(ByVal sender As System.Object, _
            ByVal e As System.EventArgs) Handles btnLast.Click
        curMgrBooks.Position = curMgrBooks.Count - 1
        UpdateRecordNumber()
    End Sub

    Private Sub UpdateRecordNumber()
        lblRecord.Text = "Record " & curMgrBooks.Position + 1 & _
            " of " & curMgrBooks.Count
    End Sub
End Class
```

Using the Data Adapter Configuration Wizard

If you recall, you created the *Connection* and *DataAdapter* objects for the preceding example by using the drag-and-drop functionality built into Visual Studio .NET. Although that was perhaps the simplest and quickest way to perform this task, many times you cannot do it that way. This is especially true if you need to provide a custom SQL statement when creating the *DataAdapter*. Using the Data Adapter Configuration Wizard will allow you to see the steps that happened behind the scenes when you did it the first way.

Modifying the Bookstore Program

In this next example, you will modify the Bookstore program to include two additional forms. The first form you will add, named Switchboard, will be used as a switchboard to provide an entry point to the other two forms. The switchboard will become the new startup object. The second form, named Authors, will be used to display a list of authors along with book information, but rather than displaying the data in text boxes, as you did with the Books form, you will display the information in a DataGrid control. We will start with the switchboard, and when we get to the Authors form we will discuss the DataGrid in more detail.

▶ Adding a switchboard

1. Right-click the project name in Solution Explorer, point to Add, and then select Add Windows Form.

2. Name the class **Switchboard.vb**, and then click Open.

3. Select the new form in the designer window and change its name from Switchboard to **frmSwitchboard** in the Properties window.

4. Set the font size of the form to 10 points.

5. Add a label to the form to display the title **Bookstore Switchboard**. Set the font size and style of the label to 14 points bold, and set the *TextAlign* property of the label to MiddleCenter.

6. Add two buttons to the form. One button will be used to load and display the Books form (the original form) and the other will be used to load and display the Authors form. Name the buttons and set the *Text* properties by using the information in Table 9-4.

Table 9-4   **Navigation Buttons and Properties**

Button name	Text
btnBooks	**&Books**
btnAuthors	**&Authors**

7. Before going any further, let's change the startup object for the project to this new form. Right-click the project name in Solution Explorer and select Properties. This will display the Project Properties dialog box.

8. In the Startup Object list, select frmSwitchboard as the new startup object.

9. Run the program. When running, your form should look like the form shown in Figure 9-13.

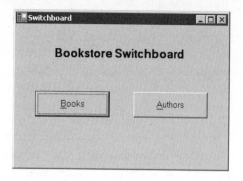

Figure 9-13   The Switchboard form

10. Add the boldface code shown here to the *btnBooks_Click* event handler. This code loads the books table.

```
Private Sub btnBooks_Click(ByVal sender As System.Object, _
        ByVal e As System.EventArgs) Handles btnBooks.Click

    Dim frmBooks As New frmBooks
    frmBooks.Show()

End Sub
```

Let's continue on and create the Authors form.

11. Right-click the project name in Solution Explorer, point to Add, and then select Add Windows Form.

12. Name the class **Authors.vb**, and then click Open.

13. Select the new form in the designer window and change its *(Name)* property from Authors to **frmAuthors** in the Properties window.

14. Set the font size of the form to 10 points.

15. Add a DataGrid to the form and size it so that it is slightly smaller than the client area of the form. The DataGrid should also be centered horizontally and vertically on the form.

16. Name the DataGrid **grdAuthors**. A little later you will be formatting the DataGrid so that the data is displayed correctly. Now that the Authors form is created, you can finish coding the Switchboard form.

17. Open the Switchboard form in the designer window and double-click btnAuthors. Add the following code to the *btnAuthors_Click* event handler.

```
Dim frmAuthors As New frmAuthors
frmAuthors.Show()
```

18. Test the program to ensure that the Switchboard form is displayed when the program runs. Test to make sure that frmBooks and frmAuthors appear when their respective buttons on the switchboard are clicked. Figure 9-14 shows frmAuthors.

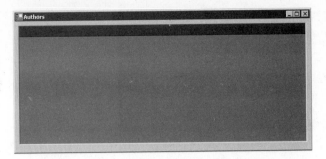

Figure 9-14   The frmAuthors form during execution

To return the information we need for the Authors form, we need to add a Data-Adapter to define and establish the data source.

▶ Adding a DataAdapter

1. Display the Authors form in the designer window.

2. Select the Data tab on the Toolbox to display the data components.

3. Double-click the SQLDataAdapter component in the Toolbox to add a new SQLDataAdapter to the Component Tray and display the Data Adapter Configuration Wizard, as shown in Figure 9-15. Click Next.

Figure 9-15   The Data Adapter Configuration Wizard welcome screen

4. Click the New Connection button to create a new connection, as shown in Figure 9-16. Although you have a Connection object on the Books form, you do not have one on this form. In reality, you would probably create a single Connection object as a common object and use the same one for all the forms, but for now you will create a separate one.

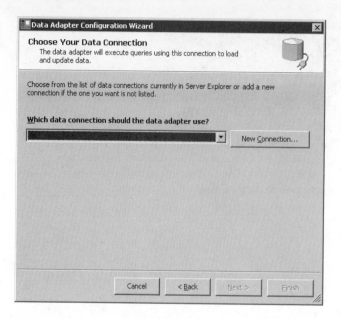

Figure 9-16 Choosing the data connection in the Data Adapter Configuration Wizard

5. In the Data Link Properties dialog box, select the Provider tab, as shown in Figure 9-17, to verify that SQL Server is the current provider. Because you added a SQLDataAdapter, SQL Server should be the default provider, but it generally pays to make sure. After you have confirmed this, click the Connection tab.

Figure 9-17 Data Link Properties dialog box for the Data Adapter Configuration Wizard

6. Select the server from the list of available servers, as shown in Figure 9-18.

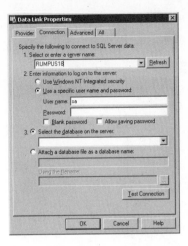

Figure 9-18   Selecting the server from the list of available servers

7. Enter **sa** in the User Name box, and leave the Password box blank.

Depending on how you set up your instance of SQL Server or MSDE, your user name and password might be different from the values stated above. For example, the latest version of MSDE does not allow blank passwords, therefore you will need to provide a password in addition to a user name. If you set up SQL Server to use Microsoft Windows NT Integrated Security, you must check the appropriate radio button in the Data Link Properties dialog box. Doing so will disable the User Name and Password text boxes. When using Integrated Security, a user name and password will not be required.

8. Click the Test Connection button to verify that you have established a good connection to the server. You should see the message box shown in Figure 9-19 if the connection succeeded.

Figure 9-19   Test connection succeeded message box

TIP   The Test Connection button tests whether you have successfully connected to the server, not the database.

9. Select pubs from the list of available databases on the server. If you do not see a list of databases, it is possible that you have not established a connection to the server. Check your user name and password again, or check whether you are using Windows NT Integrated Security. Click OK when you have finished to close the New Connection dialog box, and then click Next to move to the next step in the wizard.

10. Verify that Use SQL Statements is selected, as shown in Figure 9-20, and then click Next.

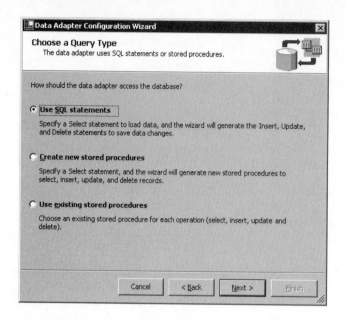

Figure 9-20   Choosing a query type in the Data Adapter Configuration Wizard

11. Click the Query Builder button, as shown in Figure 9-21.

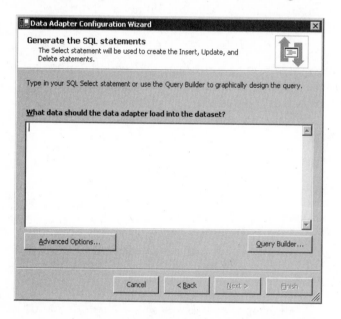

Figure 9-21   Generating the SQL statements in the Data Adapter Configuration Wizard

12. Add the following tables to the Query Builder window, as shown in Figure 9-22. To select all three tables at the same time, hold down the CTRL key and click each one in turn. Click Add.

- ❑ titles

- ❑ authors

- ❑ titleauthor

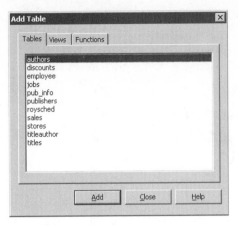

Figure 9-22   Adding tables to the Query Builder window

13. Click Close to close the Add Table dialog box.

14. Select the following columns from the tables, as shown in Figure 9-23.

- ❏ au_lname (from the authors table)

- ❏ au_fname (from the authors table)

- ❏ phone (from the authors table)

- ❏ title (from the titles table)

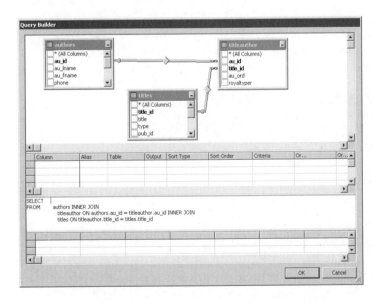

Figure 9-23   Adding the required columns to the Query Builder

You can see in Figure 9-23 that the SQL statement is almost complete. All you need to do now is establish the sort order.

15. Set the sort order for the columns. You want to order the data by the author's last name and then first name. Select the Sort Order column next to au_lname, and set the value to **1**. Then set the sort order for the au_fname column to **2**.

16. After that is done, you can display the results of the query in the grid at the bottom of the Query Builder window. Right-click a free area in the section that displays the tables, and then select Run from the context menu. The results of the query are displayed in the grid, as shown in Figure 9-24.

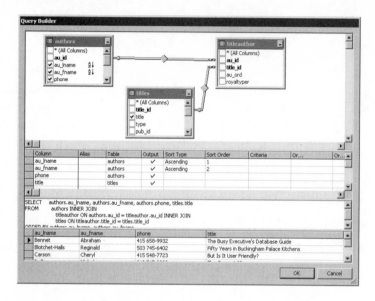

Figure 9-24   Query Builder displays the results of running the query

17. Click OK to close the Query Builder form, and then click Next. Because you haven't selected a primary key column in the SQL statement, the warning shown in Figure 9-25 appears.

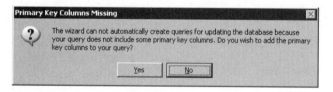

Figure 9-25   Primary Key Columns Missing warning message

18. In the warning message box, click No, and then click Finish, as shown in Figure 9-26. The message displayed in Figure 9-25 is telling you that the wizard cannot create the queries to add or update data in the database. Although your first instinct might be to click Yes and tell it to add the primary key columns to the query, in this case that would be a mistake. Remember that you only want to view the data and are not interested in updating it at this time. Another reason to click No is that the wizard will fail anyway. The query you have established spans three tables; the Data Adapter Configuration Wizard will not be able to create the additional commands for a query that is this complex.

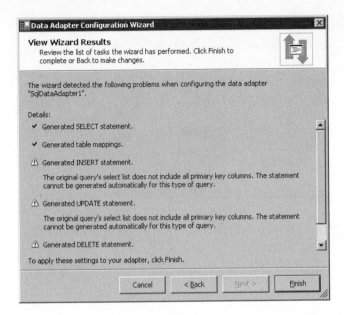

Figure 9-26   View Wizard Results in the Data Adapter Configuration Wizard

Your next task is to populate the dataset and establish the data source of the Data-Grid so the data will be displayed when the Authors form is loaded.

▶ **Populating the dataset and the DataGrid**

1. Ensure that the Authors form is displayed in the designer window.

2. Right-click SQLDataAdapter1 and then select Generate Dataset.

3. For the dataset, select the New option and accept the default name. In this case, the default name is DataSet2. Click OK.

4. Double-click the Authors form to add the form's *Load* event handler to the Code Editor. Verify that the form's *Load* event handler was created. If you double-clicked the DataGrid by mistake, the *Navigate* event handler for the DataGrid will have been created instead.

5. Type the boldface code shown below into the *Load* event handler.

```
Private Sub frmAuthors_Load(ByVal sender As System.Object, _
        ByVal e As System.EventArgs) Handles MyBase.Load
    SqlDataAdapter1.Fill(DataSet21)
End Sub
```

6. Switch back to design view for the Authors form. Select grdAuthors and then set the *DataSource* property in the Properties window to DataSet21. (Select from the list.)

7. Set the *DataMember* property in the Properties window to authors. (Select from the list.)

8. You're almost finished. Run the program and make sure that the Authors form displays correctly. The form should look like Figure 9-27.

Figure 9-27   The Authors form in the Bookstore application

For the last part of this example, you will be formatting the DataGrid and displaying the name of the author in the title bar of the DataGrid. This will add a nice touch to the form.

▶ **Formatting the DataGrid and finishing the form**

1. Select grdAuthors and then select the *TableStyles* property in the Properties window. Click the build button to display the DataGridTableStyle Collection Editor, as shown in Figure 9-28.

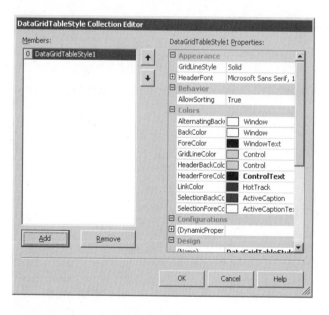

Figure 9-28   The DataGridTableStyle Collection Editor

2. Click the Add button to add a new style.

3. Scroll through the list of properties and select the *MappingName* property. Select authors.

4. Locate and select the *GridColumnStyles* property. Click the build button to display the DataGridColumnStyles Collection Editor. Click Add four times to add four column styles to the collection. Because you are displaying four columns in the grid, each of these styles will be mapped to the relevant column in the grid. Use Table 9-5 and Figure 9-29 to set each of the column styles. When you have finished, click OK to close the DataGridColumnStyle Collection Editor, and then click OK again to close the DataGridTableStyle Collection Editor.

Table 9-5 **Column Style Properties**

ColumnStyle	MappingName	Width
DataGridTextboxColumn1	**au_lname**	**75**
DataGridTextboxColumn2	**au_fname**	**75**
DataGridTextboxColumn3	**phone**	**90**
DataGridTextboxColumn4	**title**	**250**

Figure 9-29 Setting up the column styles in the DataGridColumnStyle Collection Editor

To display the name of the author in the header of the DataGrid, you need to write some code. When you select a row in the grid, you want to take the values from the two columns that store the first and last name. You will pass the name to the *CaptionText* property of the DataGrid. You will be using the *grdAuthors_Click* event handler to run the code.

5. Open the Code Editor and select grdAuthors in the Class Name list.

6. Select Click from the Method Name list. The *grdAuthors_Click* event handler will be added to the Code Editor.

7. Enter the boldface code shown below to the *grdAuthors Click* event handler.

```
Private Sub grdAuthors_Click(ByVal sender As Object, _
       ByVal e As System.EventArgs) Handles grdAuthors.Click

    Dim strFullName As String = _
        grdAuthors.Item(grdAuthors.CurrentRowIndex, 1).ToString() & " " & _
        grdAuthors.Item(grdAuthors.CurrentRowIndex, 0).ToString()

    grdAuthors.CaptionText = strFullName
End Sub
```

8. Run the program again and make sure everything works as it should. Did you notice one tiny problem? Although the name appears in the caption when you click a row in the DataGrid, no name is displayed when the form is first loaded. This is because you placed the code in the *Click* event handler of the DataGrid and, under normal circumstances, no *Click* events will occur until after the form is loaded and you have a chance to select a row with the mouse. How can you get the program to raise the *Click* event without the user having to do anything physically? The answer is to make a call to the *Click* event handler in code.

9. Add the boldface statements shown below to the *frmAuthors Load* event handler.

```
Private Sub frmAuthors_Load(ByVal sender As System.Object, _
       ByVal e As System.EventArgs) Handles MyBase.Load

    SqlDataAdapter1.Fill(DataSet21)
    grdAuthors_Click(sender, e)

End Sub
```

The above code calls the *grdAuthors_Click* event handler, passing the arguments *sender* and *e* to satisfy the requirements of the method.

You're just about done. The last thing to do is to change the DataGrid's default column headers to something a little more user friendly.

10. Reopen the TableStyles Collection Editor by selecting the DataGrid in design view and then selecting the *TableStyles (Collection)* property in the Properties window.

11. Display the DataGridColumnStyle Collection Editor.

12. Select each of the Members in turn, and set the *HeaderText* property for each column. The Header text should match the column name from the database table selected in the *MappingName* property.

13. After you have finished, click OK in each of the editors to close them. Save the project and run it again. Figure 9-30 shows the completed Authors form.

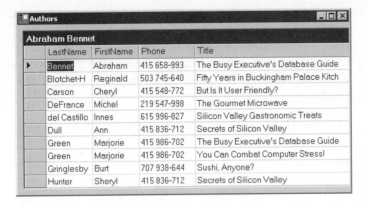

Figure 9-30   The completed Authors form

Try It

Modify the DataGrid to display the contract field from the authors table. Here are the general steps you need to follow:

1. Configure the DataAdapter to include the contract field from the authors table.

2. Generate the dataset to include the contract field.

3. Modify the *TableStyles (Collection)* property of the DataGrid to include the new field.

4. Resize the form as required to include the display of the contract field.

What Do You Think?

1. What are the advantages of storing information in a relational database?

2. What is the purpose of defining a primary key for a table?

3. Describe a one-to-many relationship between two tables.

4. How do the connected and disconnected data access models differ?

5. List the ADO.NET Data Provider objects.

6. How is binding used in Visual Basic .NET applications?

7. What objects are used to move through the rows of the *DataTable* object and keep the data in the bound controls synchronized?

USING SQL

In our initial discussion of databases, we said that SQL (Structured Query Language) is used to retrieve and update data in a database table. Although SQL provides a number of powerful statements for accessing and manipulating data, we will be using the four basic statements, which are *SELECT*, *UPDATE*, *INSERT*, and *DELETE*.

The *SELECT* statement is used to retrieve data from the database and to either display the data or use the data as part of an expression in code. The *SELECT* statement is the most widely used statement and is the basis for the other commands that were created when you included the DataAdapter object in your program. When setting up the DataAdapter for the Books form, you created a *SELECT* statement. From this statement, the Data Adapter Configuration Wizard was able to create the other statements.

The syntax for a simple *SELECT* statement looks like this:

```
SELECT column1, column2, column3, [additional columns as necessary]
    FROM tablename
```

The *UPDATE* statement is used to update existing data in a database table. When you are configuring a DataAdapter, the *UPDATE* statement is automatically created based on the *SELECT* statement. If the *SELECT* statement is too complex, the Data Adapter Configuration Wizard will not be able to create the *UPDATE* statement. To update the correct row, you must provide a *WHERE* clause. The *WHERE* clause is used to specify the row or rows that will be updated. Without a *WHERE* clause, the *UPDATE* statement will update the entire contents of the table. For example, if you wanted to update a specific row, you would provide the primary key column as the name of the column along with the value. Because that value must be unique, you can be sure that only that row will be updated. On the other hand, if you wanted to update all the rows in which the last name is Smith, the name of the column would be last_name and the value would be Smith.

The syntax for a simple *UPDATE* statement looks like this:

```
UPDATE tablename SET (column1 = value1, column2 = value2, …)
    WHERE column1 = value1
```

The *INSERT* statement is used to insert a new row in a database table. When you are configuring a data adapter, the *INSERT* statement is automatically created based on the *SELECT* statement. If the *SELECT* statement is too complex, the Data Adapter Configuration Wizard will not be able to create the *INSERT* statement. When creating and running an *INSERT* statement, you must provide values for the primary key column and any other column that does not allow the entry of *null* values.

The syntax for a simple *INSERT* statement looks like this:

```
INSERT INTO tablename (column1, column2, etc.) VALUES (value1, value2,…)
```

The *DELETE* statement is used to delete a row in a database table. To delete the correct row, you must provide a *WHERE* clause that is used to specify the row that will be deleted. Without a *WHERE* clause, the *DELETE* statement will delete the entire contents of the table. For example, if you wanted to delete a specific row, you would provide the primary key column as the name of the column along with the value. Because that value must be unique, you can be sure that only that row will be deleted. On the other hand, if you wanted to delete all the rows in which the last name is Smith, the name of the column would be last_name and the value would be Smith.

The syntax of a simple *DELETE* statement looks like this:

```
DELETE FROM tablename WHERE column1 = value1
```

Editing the Data and Updating the Database

The *DataAdapter* has an *Update* method that can be used to update the data in the database. This method examines the contents of the dataset and updates the appropriate rows in the tables of the database.

Take the Books form in the Bookstore program as an example. You can see that the controls you added are bound to the source of the data, which, in this case, is the dataset. When you look at the details of a record, you are really looking at the values stored in the *DataRow* (a row in a *DataTable*). If you change any of the values, you are changing the current value in that row. After you are done changing the values, you must not only accept the changes to the dataset; you must also propagate those changes to the database. This can all be done by running the *Update* method of the *DataAdapter*. To update the database and accept the changes in the dataset, run the following statement:

```
dataAdapterName.Update(datasetName)
```

To see this in action, you will need to add a button to the Books form that will be used to run the *Update* method.

▶ **Adding a button to the form**

1. Open the Books form in the designer window.

2. Add a new button to the form. You might have to adjust the size of the form and rearrange the other controls to keep the interface aesthetically pleasing.

3. Name the button **btnSave** and set the *Text* property to **&Save Record**. Remember that the ampersand (&) places an underscore representing the access key underneath the letter S.

4. Double-click btnSave to add the event handler to the Code Editor.

5. Type the boldface code shown here into the *btnSave_Click* event handler.

```
Private Sub btnSave_Click(ByVal sender As System.Object, _
        ByVal e As System.EventArgs) Handles btnSave.Click

    Dim intRowIndex As Integer = curMgrBooks.Position
    DataSet11.Tables("titles").Rows(intRowIndex).EndEdit()
    SqlDataAdapter1.Update(DataSet11)

End Sub
```

In the first statement, `Dim intRowIndex As Integer = curMgrBooks.Posi-tion`, you declared a variable to store the position of the current row. This is not really required because you could have just used *curMgr-Books.Position* as the value supplied to the *Rows* collection of the table.

The next statement, `DataSet11.Tables("titles").Rows(intRowIn-dex).EndEdit`, is quite interesting and warrants some explanation. If you change the value in the txtTitle text box, the value in the underlying row of the dataset is not *modified* but *proposed*. After you make any change to any value in a bound control, you are editing the underlying row, but the *RowState* of that row is not changed until you do one of two things:

- ❑ You could move to the next row. If you do this, the *RowState* property of the row you just edited will be changed from *unchanged* to *modified*. After the row is modified, the change will be made permanent in the database as soon as you run the *Update* method of the *DataAdapter*. Of course, moving to the next row just to update the *RowState* would be tedious and could get you into trouble if you didn't pay close attention to the row you were trying to update.

- ❑ You could use the *EndEdit* method (as you did in the previous example). The *EndEdit* method is used to change the *RowState* of the current row by notifying the row that editing is complete and that the row should now be placed in a modified condition.

The last statement, `SqlDataAdapter1.Update(DataSet11)`, is used to pass the modified row to the database. The form should now look like Figure 9-31.

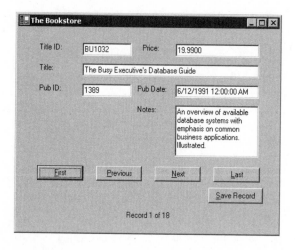

Figure 9-31   Bookstore application form displaying title record

▶ Testing the update

1. Run the program to test your additional work.

2. Open the Books form and navigate to any record.

3. Change the title and then click the Save button.

4. Close the Books form and then open it again.

5. Navigate back to the record that you just updated and verify that the changes you made are displayed.

6. Test other records in the same way, and verify that the changes were made permanent.

> **TIP**   When working with databases, do not attempt to change a value in a primary key column. The primary key usually has related foreign keys in other tables. Changing these values might corrupt the ability of the database to correctly relate the tables using these keys.

Adding and Deleting Records

A database application wouldn't be much good if you couldn't add new records and delete unwanted records. In this section you will be adding two more buttons and providing the functionality to add new rows and delete existing rows in the titles table.

Because the pubs database is relational, the titles table is related to other tables in the database. For this example, you need only be concerned with the relationship between the titles table and the publishers table. The column in question is pub_id. What this means to you is that when you add a new row to the titles table, you must be sure to enter a pub_id that already exists in the publishers table. In a real-world application you would provide additional functionality to insert a new publisher if this was required. If you wanted to make this a little more robust, you could replace the pub_id text box with a bound combo box and only allow the user to select the pub_id from a predefined list.

▶ **Completing the Books form**

To complete the application, you will add two more buttons to the Books form.

1. Use the information in Table 9-6 to name and set the *Text* properties of the buttons.

Table 9-6   **Books Buttons and Properties**

Button name	Text property
btnDelete	**&Delete Record**
btnAddNew	**&Add New Record**

2. Double-click btnAddNew to add the *btnAddNew_Click* event handler to the Code Editor.

3. Type the boldface code shown here into the *btnAddNew_Click* event handler.

```
Private Sub btnAddNew_Click(ByVal sender As System.Object, _
     ByVal e As System.EventArgs) Handles btnAddNew.Click

     curMgrBooks.SuspendBinding()
     m_blnAddNew = True
     For Each ctl As Control In Me.Controls
```

```
           If TypeOf (ctl) Is TextBox Then
               CType(ctl, TextBox).Clear()
           End If
       Next

       txtTitleID.Focus()
   End Sub
```

4. Double-click the Delete button to add the *btnDelete_Click* event handler to the Code Editor.

5. Type the boldface code shown here into the *btnDelete_Click* event handler.

```
Private Sub btnDelete_Click(ByVal sender As System.Object, _
        ByVal e As System.EventArgs) Handles btnDelete.Click
    If m_blnAddNew = True Then
        CurMgrBooks.ResumeBinding
        m_blnAddNew = False
    Else
        DataSet11.titles.Rows(curMgrBooks.Position).Delete
        SqlDataAdapter1.Update(DataSet11, "titles")
    End If
End Sub
```

6. Change the code in the *btnSave_Click* event handler to allow for updates in addition to inserts. The updated code is shown here. The boldface code is what you will be adding to (or modifying in) the event handler.

```
Private Sub btnSave_Click(ByVal sender As System.Object, _
        ByVal e As System.EventArgs) Handles btnSave.Click

    Select Case m_blnAddNew
        Case True
            Dim newRow As DataRow
            Dim rowValues(9) As String

            rowValues(0) = txtTitleID.Text
            rowValues(1) = txtTitle.Text
            rowValues(2) = "business"
            rowValues(3) = txtPubID.Text
            rowValues(4) = txtPrice.Text
            rowValues(8) = txtNotes.Text
            rowValues(9) = txtPubDate.Text

            newRow = DataSet11.titles.Rows.Add(rowValues)

        Case False
            Dim intRowIndex As Integer = curMgrBooks.Position
            DataSet11.Tables("titles").Rows(intRowIndex).EndEdit()

    End Select

    SqlDataAdapter1.Update(DataSet11, "titles")

    curMgrBooks.ResumeBinding()
    If m_blnAddNew = True Then
        curMgrBooks.Position = curMgrBooks.Count - 1
        UpdateRecordNumber()
    End If

    m_blnAddNew = False

End Sub
```

IMPORTANT If you are using the Pubs.mdb Microsoft Access database, setting the values for each of the elements for the new row may cause a problem as it is written. The order of the columns in the table inside the dataset will be different for the MS Access database. If you experience any problems attempting to insert a new row, review the section "Using Microsoft Access" later in the chapter.

7. Declare a new class-level *Boolean* variable named *m_blnAddNew* at the top of the Code Editor. This variable will be used to determine whether you will be saving an updated row or a new row. Use the following line of code:

```
Private m_blnAddNew As Boolean
```

8. Save your work and run the program once again.

9. Add a new row to the table by clicking the Add New Record button and entering the appropriate information. Remember that the pub_id must be a value that already exists in the publishers table.

10. After all the values are entered, click Save Record to save the new row. The new row will be added to the dataset and to the database.

11. Test the delete function by navigating to an existing record and clicking Delete Record. The record will be removed from the dataset and from the database. The completed form should look like Figure 9-32.

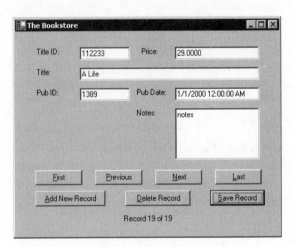

Figure 9-32 The completed Bookstore form

Inside the Code

We have introduced a few new coding structures that require some explanation. Let's look at the *btnAddNew_Click* event handler first.

- *curMgr.SuspendBinding*, as its name implies, is used to temporarily suspend data binding. When controls are bound to columns in a table, they normally display the piece of data that they are bound to. When you need to add a new row, you need the text box to be temporarily free so that the new data can be entered.

- The `For Each ctl As Control In Me.Controls` block allows you to loop through each of the text boxes and clear the current values. *ctl* represents a control that is too generic for you to use as it is, so you must use the *CType* function to convert it to a TextBox object to run the *Clear* method.

- The last line of code in this event handler places the cursor in the Title ID text box to make it easier for the user to start entering data.

In the *btnDelete_Click* event handler, you have provided code to see if the user is currently in the process of adding a new record (`m_blnAddNew = True`). The reason for this code is that the user might start to add a new record, which clears the text boxes and suspends the binding. This is okay so far, but what if users decide that they don't want to continue adding the new record, or what if they had clicked the Add New button by mistake? How would they back out of the operation without closing the Books form and reopening it again? The solution to this problem is to provide a means to delete the new record and resume binding.

Of course the *Delete* method still serves its original purpose: to delete the current record. The code inside the *Else* block runs the *Delete* method of the *Rows* collection of the current table to remove the row from the collection. The second line of code updates the database.

The code you have written so far hasn't been too earth-shattering. Moving on to the *btnSave_Click* event handler, we have some code that needs a lot of explanation.

There is no way to add a new row directly to a *DataTable* in a dataset. Instead, you must create a *DataRow* and define its structure to be the same as an existing row in the table. The *NewRow* method of the *DataTable* adds a detached row with the same schema (the same number and type of columns) as the table. After the *DataRow* is created and the values are added to it, it is added to the collection of data rows that currently exist in the *DataTable*.

The first thing you must do is determine what you are saving; you can do this by using the variable *m_blnAddNew*. Using this variable in a *Select Case* structure enables you to determine whether the save is occurring as a result of adding a new row or as a result of updating an existing row.

You will use these two object variables:

- **newRow**   Represents the new row that will be added to the collection.

- **rowValues**   Represents an array of values that will be used to populate the new row. We will be covering arrays in some detail in Chapter 11, but for now think of an array as a smart variable that can hold a number of values, with each value stored in its own separate compartment, or *element*. Each element is identified by a unique index. The starting element has an index value of 0, and the topmost (upperbound) index is always one less than the total number of elements.

Next you must set the values for the new row:

- Because you have 10 columns in the table, you have initialized the array to 10 elements. Remember that the value inside the parentheses of the array variable represents the upperbound index of the array. If there are 10 elements, the value is 9 because the first index is always 0.

- Although you are not providing values for each of the columns, you must explicitly specify the element that you are providing a value for. If you do not do this, the update might fail, and you might also be in danger of passing incorrect information to the database. In the previous code sample, notice that you have not specified any values for array elements 5 through 7. (rowValues(5) through rowValues(7) are missing from the list of value assignments.) These three elements represent columns for which we chose not to provide values.

- You have text boxes for most of the values you need to enter, but you have not provided a text box for the type column. Because that column does not allow *null* values, you must provide a value in order to success-fully save the row. For this reason, you have set that value in code. In a real application, you would obviously provide a means to enter this value.

- The statement newRow = DataSet11.titles.Rows.Add(rowValues) adds the new row to the collection of rows in the *titles DataTable*.

- If the save is the result of an update to an existing row, running the *EndEdit* method in the *Case False* block sets the *RowState* of the row you just edited to *Modified*.

Let's look at the last few code statements:

- Run the *Update* method of the *DataAdapter*.

- *curMgr.ResumeBinding* reattaches the text boxes to the columns that they were bound to at design time.

- The *If* block is used to again determine whether the update was the result of a new row being added or the result of an existing row being updated. This is necessary for two reasons. The first reason is that, when added to the collection, a new row is always added to the end of the collection. Because you should always leave the user on the new row, you should navigate to that row automatically. The second reason to use the *If* block is that if the user is just updating an existing row, the user wants to stay on that row and not move to the end of the collection.

- Setting the *Boolean* variable *m_blnAddNew* to *False* prepares the *DataSet* for another update or insert.

AcceptChanges Method

There might be times when the user does not want to make changes permanent in the database but still needs to have the changes updated in the dataset. The *AcceptChanges* method of the dataset will allow the user to do that. The following code will update the dataset:

```
DataSet11.AcceptChanges()
```

> **TIP** When the *AcceptChanges* method of the *DataSet* runs, the *RowState* property of all rows is set to *Unchanged*. Attempting to run the *Update* method of the *DataAdapter* after running *AcceptChanges* will fail to update the database because the *DataAdapter* cannot determine if any rows have changed.

Using Microsoft Access

If you do not have SQL Server or MSDE installed, or if the pubs database is not listed as one the installed databases, you can use the Pubs.mdb database that came in your student file. This is a Microsoft Access database. You do not need to have Access on your computer, because Microsoft Visual Studio .NET includes the Jet database engine.

▶ **Setting up Server Explorer to use Pubs.mdb**

1. Display the Books form in the designer window.

2. Display Server Explorer by selecting Server Explorer on the View menu.

3. In Server Explorer, right-click Data Connections and then select Add Connection from the context menu, as shown in Figure 9-33.

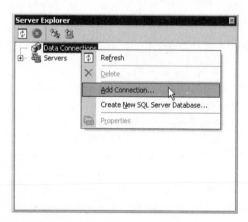

Figure 9-33   Adding a new connection

4. In the Data Link Properties dialog box, click the Provider tab and then select Microsoft Jet 4.0 OLE DB Provider, as shown in Figure 9-34.

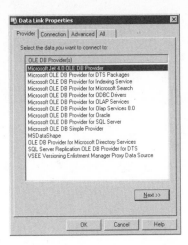

Figure 9-34   Selecting the Microsoft Jet 4.0 OLE DB Provider to use an Access database

5. After you have selected a provider, click Next to display the Connection tab.

6. Click the Build button next to the Select Or Enter a Database Name text box.

7. Navigate to the bin folder for the current project. You should see the Pubs.mdb file that you saved there, as shown in Figure 9-35.

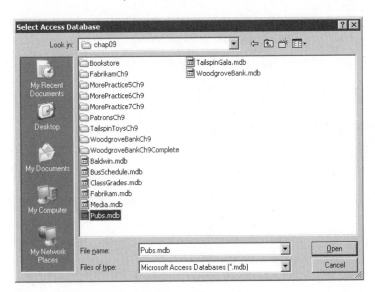

Figure 9-35   Selecting the Pubs.mdb database file

8. Select the file and click Open.

9. If it is not already entered for you, type **Admin** in the User Name box, and then click Test Connection, as shown in Figure 9-36.

Figure 9-36   Selecting the database, setting the user name, and testing the connection

10. If the connection is successful, you will see the message box shown in Figure 9-37.

Figure 9-37   Successfully connecting to the pubs database

11. Click OK to close the message box and again to close the Data Link Properties dialog box. The new data connection will be added to Server Explorer, as shown in Figure 9-38.

Figure 9-38   Adding the new data connection

12. Click the node next to the new data connection to expand the list, and then click the node next to Tables to expand the list of tables. Server Explorer should look like Figure 9-39.

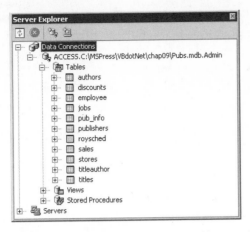

Figure 9-39   Displaying the list of tables

13. Select the titles table in Server Explorer and drag it onto the Books form. When prompted to include the password in the connection string, click the Include Password button. The OleDbConnection1 and OleDbDataAdapter1 objects will be added to the Component Tray.

14. Right-click on OleDbDataAdapter1 in the Component Tray and select Configure Data Adapter from the context menu to open the Data Adapter Configuration Wizard.

15. Click the Next button three times to display the *SELECT* statement that was created when you dragged over the titles table.

Figure 9-40   The default *SELECT* statement

Notice that the order of the columns is alphabetical rather than in the order they appear in the database (refer to Figure 9-40). This is a feature of the OleDbData-Adapter, and once understood, it is easy to make the necessary corrections. If the order of the columns is left the way they are and you attempt to insert a new row in the table using the method described in the "Completing the Books form" section, an exception may be thrown as you would be attempting to insert values into the incorrect columns. To prevent this problem from occurring, you need to change the order of the columns in the *SELECT* statement so that they match the table in the database.

Change the *SELECT* statement so that the columns are in the following order.

1. title_id
2. title
3. type
4. pub_id
5. price
6. advance
7. royalty
8. ytd_sales
9. notes
10. pubdate

After making the necessary changes, the *SELECT* statement should look like Figure 9-41.

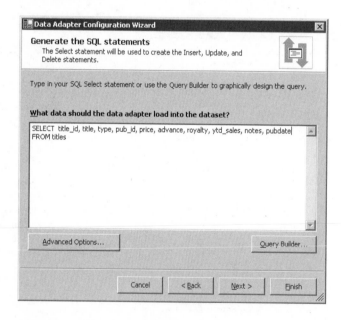

Figure 9-41   The corrected *SELECT* statement

Now that you have set up Pubs.mdb (MS Access) as the database and have the columns in the correct order, you can continue with the example that we started earlier in the chapter in the section "Creating a Database Program."

Try It

Add another button to the Books form that can be used to cancel changes that have been made to the data on the form before they have been saved. Use the *CancelEdit* method to do this.

What Do You Think?

1. List the four SQL statements discussed in this chapter, and include a brief description of the purpose of each.

2. What is the purpose of the *Update* method of the *DataAdapter* object?

3. How can you update the *RowState* property of a row that has just been edited?

4. How do you add a new row to a *DataTable* in a dataset?

5. Can you make changes to data in a dataset but not in the database itself?

6. What OLE DB provider should you use when you want to define a connection to an Access database?

Q&A

Q. When you use the Data Adapter Configuration Wizard and specify a *SELECT* statement that includes more than one related table in a database, why is the wizard not able to create the necessary update, insert, and delete commands?

A. The answer is **referential integrity**. This is basically the rule that ensures that rows are not inadvertently orphaned when they are added to a table. For example, let's say you have a child table that relates to a parent table. Referential integrity states that you cannot add a row to the child table if it does not have a corresponding row in the parent table. The Data Adapter Configuration Wizard is not able to produce a complex SQL statement that can update all the tables defined in the *SELECT* statement.

Q. You mentioned that *BindingManagerBase* is an abstract class and that it cannot be directly instantiated. Can you explain this in a little more detail?

A. An **abstract class** is defined with only methods and properties. Let's say we have a blueprint for a car, but the blueprint only defines the shell of the car. There are places to put the seats, but no seats are actually drawn. There is a place to put an engine, but no engine is there. There are places to put wheels, but no wheels are included. If you were to give this blueprint to a car manufacturer, they wouldn't be able to do much with it because a great amount of detail is missing from the blueprint. In programming terms, the abstract class has a *shell* that is loosely defined by the methods and properties of the class but that is devoid of the implementation code (the *details*) that is necessary to create an instance of the class.

Q. When I created the Switchboard form and coded the *Click* event handler for each of the buttons, I had to declare and instantiate the other forms before I could run the *Show* method. I didn't have to do that with other Microsoft Windows applications. Why did I have to do it there?

A. Actually, you did have to do it with other Windows applications, or, rather, Visual Basic .NET did it for you behind the scenes. Whatever you designate as the startup object becomes the entry point of the program. This entry point can be a form or an entry-point Sub procedure called *Main*. The startup object is set in the vbproj file and, when compiled, is set in the executable file for the program.

WRAPPING UP

- The connected data access model is required if users are to have immediate access to the database. The disconnected data access model allows users to be disconnected from the database and use the DataSet as a virtual representation of the database that they want to work with.

- Several objects make up the ADO.NET model:

  - The Connection object (SQLConnection, OracleConnection, or OleDbConnection) allows you to connect to a database by setting a connection string that specifies the name of the server (Data Source) and the database (Initial Catalog). You must also provide a user ID and password if you are not using Windows NT Integrated Security.

  - The *DataAdapter* object (*SQLDataAdapter, OracleDataAdapter, OleDbDataAdapter,* or *OdbcDataAdapter*) is used to pass data to and from the database. The *DataAdapter* has the ability to retrieve, update, insert, and delete data in the database through the use of *Command* objects. The *Fill* method of the *DataAdapter* is used to populate the dataset with the selected data. The *Update* method of the *DataAdapter* is used to permanently update the database with the changes made in the dataset.

  - The *Command* object (*SQLCommand, OracleCommand, OleDbCommand,* or *OdbcCommand*) is used to create a customized SQL statement to retrieve, update, insert, or delete data in a database. The *Command* object can be executed independently and only requires a valid *Connection* object to work.

  - The *DataReader* object is used when you want a read-only, forward-only stream of data from a database. The *DataReader* is lightweight and quite efficient. It cannot be used to update data in a database, and it tends to hang on to the *Connection* object a little longer than other methods of data retrieval.

- One way of creating and setting up *Connection* and *DataAdapter* objects is to drag a table onto a form. A second way is to add a *DataAdapter* object to the Component Tray of the form and use the Data Adapter Configuration Wizard to establish both objects.

■ The *Update* method of a *DataAdapter* makes updating a database easy. The *AcceptChanges* method of a *DataSet* will update the *DataSet* but will set the *RowState* property of all the rows to Unchanged, thus preventing any changes from being passed to the database.

KEYWORDS

abstract class	binding
column	composite primary key
connected data access model	constraint
disconnected data access model	field
foreign key	linking table
many-to-many relationship	one-to-many relationship
one-to-one relationship	primary key
record	referential integrity
relation	relational database
row	SQL
table	

REVIEW QUESTIONS

1. Which of the following is a type of information that might be required if you want to connect to a database? (Choose all correct answers.)

   a. Name of server

   b. Name of database

   c. Valid user name

   d. Operating system

2. A _____ is a collection of one or more tables that relate to each other in some way.

   a. primary key

   b. column

   c. record

   d. relational database

3. Each occurrence of an entity in a table is called a row or a _____.

   a. record

   b. field

   c. primary key

   d. connection

4. The column that uniquely identifies each record in a table is called the _____.

   a. foreign key

   b. relationship

   c. primary key

   d. row

5. When you drag a table from Server Explorer to your form, the *Connection* and *DataAdapter* objects are created and added to the _____.

   a. Toolbox

   b. property window

   c. Code Editor

   d. Component Tray

6. Which method of the *DataAdapter* is used to populate a table with data?

   a. *Fill*

   b. *Get*

   c. *Refresh*

   d. *Link*

7. Which property of the *BindingContext* object is used to navigate a table in a database?

    a. *Position*

    b. *CurrentRecord*

    c. *Move*

    d. *Locate*

8. Which tool can be used to easily configure a *DataAdapter*?

    a. Code Editor

    b. Toolbox

    c. Data Adapter Configuration Wizard

    d. Properties window

9. Which type of control is used to easily display multiple fields of information from a database table on a form?

    a. TextBox control

    b. DataGrid control

    c. ListBox control

    d. Label control

10. Which SQL statement should you use to add a new row to a database table?

    a. *SELECT*

    b. *UPDATE*

    c. *INSERT*

    d. *DELETE*

11. A well-designed relational database will duplicate information when possible, which improves performance and maintains integrity of the data. True or false?

12. The connected data access model requires that the user of the data be connected to the database at all times. True or false?

13. The DataAdapter object is defined to work with the type of database to which you are connecting and provides the intelligence behind the DataSet object. True or false?

14. SQL is used to retrieve and update data in a database table. True or false?

15. If you want to access information stored in an Access database from your Visual Basic .NET application, you must have Access installed on your computer. True or false?

16. A(n) _____ is composed of rows and columns.

17. Linking a control to a data source so that the data can be displayed is called _____.

18. The BindingManagerBase object that is responsible for keeping the displayed data synchronized is the _____.

19. The most widely used SQL statement, which retrieves data from a database, is the _____ statement.

20. The _____ method of the DataAdapter object can be used to modify data in a database.

STEP BY STEP

In this project for the Baldwin Museum of Science, you will create a form that will display all of the information for each of the patrons of the museum that are listed in the patrons table of the Baldwin.mdb database file that came with your student file. You will not be using a DataGrid for this exercise.

The completed form for this application will look like Figure 9-42.

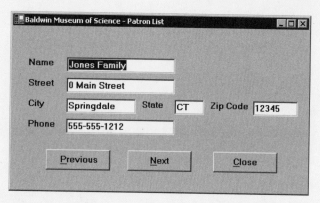

Figure 9-42   Completed Patrons form

▶ Creating a new project

1. Open Visual Studio .NET if it isn't already open.

2. Click the New Project button on the Start Page.

3. Click Visual Basic Projects under Project Types and Windows Application under Templates.

4. Type **PatronsCh9** in the Name box.

5. Browse to the location in which you are storing your projects.

6. Click OK.

▶ Configuring the form and changing the startup object

1. Right-click Form1.vb in Solution Explorer, and then rename Form1.vb as **Patrons.vb**. Press ENTER.

2. Click once in the title bar of the form, and then change the (Name) property of the form to **frmPatrons**.

3. Change the *Text* property of the form to **Baldwin Museum of Science – Patron List**, and then press ENTER.

4. Right-click the PatronsCh9 project name in Solution Explorer, and then click Properties.

5. Change the startup object to **frmPatrons**, and then click OK.

▶ Adding the required controls to the form

1. Add the controls listed in Table 9-7 to the form, and set their *(Name)* and *Text* properties as required.

Table 9-7   **Patrons Form Controls and Properties**

Control type	(Name)	Text
Label	**Label1**	**Name**
Label	**Label2**	**Street**
Label	**Label3**	**City**
Label	**Label4**	**State**
Label	**Label5**	**Zip Code**
Label	**Label6**	**Phone**
TextBox	**txtName**	\<blank\>
TextBox	**txtStreet**	\<blank\>
TextBox	**txtCity**	\<blank\>
TextBox	**txtState**	\<blank\>
TextBox	**txtZipCode**	\<blank\>
TextBox	**txtPhone**	\<blank\>
Button	**btnPrevious**	**&Previous**
Button	**btnNext**	**&Next**
Button	**btnClose**	**&Close**

2. Arrange the controls on the form so that your form looks like Figure 9-40.

▶ Creating the Connection

1. Open Server Explorer. Right-click Data Connections, and then select Add Connection.

2. Click the Provider tab.

3. Click Microsoft Jet 4.0 OLE DB Provider, and then click Next.

4. Click the build button next to Select or enter the database name and browser to find the Baldwin.mdb database file. Click OK to close the Select Access Database window.

5. Click Test Connection to verify your connection with the database.

6. Click OK.

▶ Adding Connection and DataAdapter objects

1. In Server Explorer, click the plus sign (+) next to the Baldwin.mdb database.

2. Click the plus sign next to Tables under the Baldwin.mdb database.

3. Click once to select the patrons table, and then drag the table to the form.

4. Click Include Password. You should now see OleDbConnection1 and OleDbDataAdapter1 in the Component Tray at the bottom of the window.

▶ Adding the Dataset

1. Right-click OleDbDataAdapter1, and then select Generate Dataset.

2. Click OK.

3. Double-click the form to open the form's *Load* event handler.

4. Type the following line of code in the *Load* event handler:

```
OleDbDataAdapter1.Fill(DataSet11)
```

▶ Binding the text boxes to the fields

1. Click the txtName text box on the form and then click DataBindings at the top of the Property window.

2. Click the drop-down arrow for the *Text* property under DataBindings.

3. Click the plus sign next to DataSet11.

4. Click the plus sign next to Patrons.

5. Click Name.

6. Repeat these five steps to bind the rest of the TextBox controls to the appropriate fields.

▶ Coding the Button controls

1. Double-click each of the Button controls and code them using the information in Table 9-8.

Table 9-8 **Button *Click* Event Code**

Button	Code
btnPrevious	Me.BindingContext(DataSet11, "patrons").Position -= 1
btnNext	Me.BindingContext(DataSet11, "patrons").Position += 1
btnClose	Me.Close()

▶ Saving and testing your project

1. On the File menu, select Save All to save your work.

2. On the Debug menu, select Start to run your project.

3. Test the program by clicking the Next button to move through the records. Then use the Previous button to move back to the beginning.

4. On the Debug menu, select Stop Debugging to end the program.

5. On the File menu, select Close Solution to close your project.

6. Close Visual Studio .NET.

FINISH THE CODE

To complete this exercise, you should open the WoodgroveBankCh9 project that came in your student file. This project contains a form for Woodgrove Bank that will be used to display records about the service performed on the ATM (Automatic Teller Machines) owned by the bank. You will be using the WoodgroveBank.mdb file that came with your student file.

▶ **Finish the project using the following requirements**

1. Open Server Explorer and add a new Connection that points to the WoodgroveBank.mdb database.

2. Click the Data tab on the Toolbox, double-click OleDbDataAdapter, and use the wizard to add a data adapter to the Component Tray.

3. Right-click the OleDbDataAdapter in the Component Tray, and then select Generate Dataset to add a dataset to the Component Tray.

4. Change the *DataSource* property of the DataGrid to **DataSet.Service**.

5. Change the *DataMember* property of the DataGrid to **Service**.

6. Click the *Table Styles (Collection)* property of the DataGrid to modify the column headings and column widths.

7. Add the required line of code to fill the dataset in the form's *Load* event handler.

8. Save the project and test it.

JUST HINTS

In this exercise, you will create an order entry form for Fabrikam, Inc. You will use the Fabrikam.mdb database file that came with your student file. You will use fields from the orders table in the database.

▶ **Creating the application**

1. Create the form as shown in Figure 9-43. The form will contain one Data-Grid control named grdOrders.

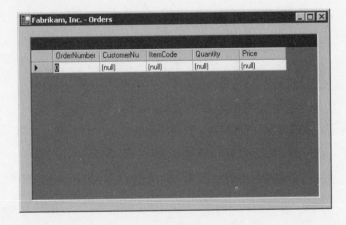

Figure 9-43   Completed Orders form for Fabrikam, Inc.

2. Populate the DataGrid with the fields from the orders table in the Fabrikam.mdb database.

3. Modify the column headers to display meaningful and clear labels.

4. Save and test the project. Try adding a new record to the database by using the DataGrid.

ON YOUR OWN

In this exercise, you will create a Visual Basic .NET application for Tailspin Toys that will be used to register guests for the annual Tailspin Toys Gala. Guests will need to provide the following information on the form:

- Name

- Street

- City

- State

- Postal code

- Phone

- Number of people attending

- Activities they want to participate in

- Whether they need a hotel room

The TailspinGala.mdb database has been created. It contains a table called attendees containing sample data for you to use to create and test the form. Buttons should be provided on the form to perform the following actions:

- Move to the first record

- Move to the last record

- Move to the previous record

- Move to the next record

- Add a new record

- Delete an existing record

- Close the form

MORE PRACTICE

1. Write the Visual Basic .NET code that will populate a *DataAdapter* called *daPayroll* with the records from a dataset called *dsNewChecks*.

2. Write the Visual Basic .NET code that will set the current position of a table called overtime in the *dsNewChecks* dataset to the last record in the table.

3. Write the Visual Basic .NET code to declare a *CurrencyManager* called *curPayrollDeductions*. Convert and assign the *BindingContext* for *dsPayroll*, and bind the deductions table to *curPayrollDeductions*.

4. Changes have been made to the current row in a table called deductions in a dataset called *dsNewChecks*. Write the Visual Basic .NET code that will save these changes to the database. The *DataAdapter* is called *SqlDataAdapter5*. Use a *CurrencyManager* called *curPayrollDeductions* to determine the position of the current row.

5. Write a Visual Basic .NET program that will open the ClassGrades.mdb database file that came with your student file, and create a form that will display all of the fields in the grades table. Do not use a DataGrid to display the data. Include buttons on the form to move to the next and previous records.

6. Write a Visual Basic .NET program that will open the Media.mdb database file that came with your student file, and create a form that will list all of the fields in the mycds table. Do not use a DataGrid to display the data. Include buttons on the form to add and delete records from the table, and to move to the next and previous records. You will also need a button to save any additions or changes to the table.

7. Write a Visual Basic .NET program that will open the BusSchedule.mdb database file that came with your student file, and create a form that will list all of the fields in the schedule table. Use a DataGrid to display all of the fields in the schedule table.

CHAPTER 10
PROCEDURES IN DETAIL

You have been using procedures for several chapters, so you should be quite familiar with them already. Procedures provide the basic grouping of code in all programs. They are used to provide flow to the program and, at the same time, to allow you to separate functionality. In this chapter, we will explain each type of procedure in detail and demonstrate how to use them. We will also describe when you should use one type of procedure over another.

Upon completion of this chapter, you will be able to:

- Learn about the four basic types of procedures: event procedures, Sub procedures, Function procedures, and Property procedures.

- Incorporate these four types of procedures into your programs.

- Pass arguments to procedures with parameters, by value.

- Pass arguments to procedures with parameters, by reference.

- Use Function procedures to return a value.

- Use Property procedures to add custom properties to a form.

EVENT, SUB, AND FUNCTION PROCEDURES

Event, Sub, and Function procedures can be incorporated into your programming to make your code more efficient. The increased efficiency comes from having code that is more readable and easier to maintain. Each type of procedure is used for a specific purpose, so it is important to understand when to use each and how to set them up. There is a fourth type of procedure called a Property procedure. Property procedures are quite different from event, Sub, or Function procedures, and they will be discussed later in the chapter. In this section, we will look at event, Sub, and Function procedures.

Event Procedures

We have talked about event procedures in some detail already, so we will not dwell on redundant details here. It is important to understand that each object (that is, each control or component) that you add to a program (including the form) has many events that are exposed by the original developer of the object class. When something significant occurs that affects the object, an event is raised. You, as a programmer, can take advantage of these events by providing code inside the event handlers associated with these events. The code you provide will run whenever one of these events is raised.

All event handlers are constructed in the same way. They are Sub procedures with two parameters: *sender* and *e*. An example of an event procedure (event handler) for the *Click* event of a Button control is shown in the following code sample:

```
Private Sub btnClose_Click(ByVal sender As System.Object, _
    ByVal e As System.EventArgs) Handles btnClose.Click
    ' provide code here to be executed whenever the button is clicked
End Sub
```

In this example, you can see the common elements of the event handler. Let's break this event procedure down and explain each of the elements in more detail.

- *Private*   This is a scope modifier and refers to the accessibility of the procedure. When an event procedure is private, it can only be accessed by other procedures within the same class.

- *Sub*   This tells you that this procedure runs the code inside the event handler and does not return a value.

- *btnClose_Click*   This is the name of the event procedure and has no effect on the event or how it is executed. The name could be anything, but why name it *Bernie* when *btnClose_Click* is so much more meaningful?

- *sender As System.Object*   This refers to the object that raised the event. You can use *sender* in your code to determine which control raised the event. In this example, the sender is *btnClose*.

- *e As System.EventArgs*   This is a standard parameter required in all event handlers. Although this parameter provides advanced information beyond the needs of most programmers, for some events, such as those dealing with the mouse or the keyboard, the *EventArgs* parameter provides such additional information as which mouse button was clicked or which key was pressed. You can incorporate this information into your code.

- **_Handles btnClose.Click_**   This provides the link between the event that was raised and the event handler.

- **_End Sub_**   This identifies the end of the procedure.

The examples in the following code sample show several event handlers so that you can see the common elements of each and also see why one might differ from another. The examples are based on the assumption that you have a form containing a label named lblMessage and a button named btnDisplayMessage.

```
' This event will be raised when the button is clicked...
Private Sub btnDisplayMessage_Click(ByVal sender As System.Object, _
    ByVal e As System.EventArgs) Handles btnDisplayMessage.Click

    lblMessage.Text = "The Display Message button was clicked"

End Sub

' This event will be raised when either mouse button is pressed and released.
' Notice that we still have the event args parameter but it is now declared as
' System.Windows.Forms.MouseEventArgs rather than System.EventArgs
Private Sub btnDisplayMessage_MouseUp(ByVal sender As Object, _
    ByVal e As System.Windows.Forms.MouseEventArgs) _
    Handles btnDisplayMessage.MouseUp
    If e.Button = MouseButtons.Left Then
        lblMessage.Text = "The left mouse button was clicked"
    ElseIf e.Button = MouseButtons.Right Then
        lblMessage.Text = "The right mouse button was clicked"
    End If

End Sub
' This event will be raised when the button has focus and a key is
' pressed and released. The event args parameter is declared as
' System.Windows.Forms.KeyEventArgs
Private Sub btnDisplayMessage_KeyUp(ByVal sender As Object, _
    ByVal e As System.Windows.Forms.KeyEventArgs) _
    Handles btnDisplayMessage.KeyUp

    If e.KeyCode = Keys.C Then
        lblMessage.Text = "The C key was pressed and released"
    End If

End Sub
```

You can see from the preceding code examples how event handlers are constructed and what each element means.

Event Sequencing

As you might expect, multiple events raised by the same control or object do not occur at the same time. There is a predetermined sequence for these events. For example, when a control such as a button is clicked, the order of the events is as follows:

1. _MouseDown_

2. _Click_

3. _MouseUp_

The sequence for keyboard events is:

1. *KeyDown*
2. *KeyPress*
3. *KeyUp*

Why is it important to know the sequence of events? Assume that you're displaying the results of a calculation in a label and have coded the calculation in the *Mouse-Down* event. If you then wanted to display other information in the same label by providing code in the event handler for the *Click* event, you would find that the results of the calculation would be missed because the *Click* event is raised immediately after the *MouseDown* event. You must ensure that you do not provide conflicting code in different events raised by the same control.

You need to be concerned not only with the sequence of events; you also need to understand which events are raised continuously and which events are only raised once for each occurrence. For example, the *MouseDown* event is only raised once for each occurrence, but the *KeyDown* event will continue to be raised as long as the key remains pressed. This is also true for the *KeyPress* event. In fact, if you coded the event handlers for both the *KeyDown* and *KeyPress* events, you would see that each event is raised continuously in an alternating fashion. The *KeyDown* event is raised first, followed by the *KeyPress* event. These two events will continue to be raised until the key is released. When the key is released, the *KeyUp* event will be raised once.

Using *EventArgs*

As we discussed earlier, all event handlers have two parameters: *sender* and *e*. Although *sender* always refers to the object that is raising the event, *e* represents event arguments (information that is sent when the event is raised). For some events, such as mouse and keyboard events, *e* provides additional information such as which mouse button or which key was pressed.

Let's look at another example of how to use *EventArgs* in code. The *MouseDown* and *KeyDown* event handlers in the following code sample show how you can use them with a text box. In the *MouseDown* event handler of the text box, we want to determine which button was pressed, and in the *KeyDown* event handler of the text box, we want to determine which key was pressed.

```
Private Sub txtMessage_MouseDown(ByVal sender As Object, _
        ByVal e As System.Windows.Forms.MouseEventArgs) _
        Handles txtMessage.MouseDown

    txtMessage.Text = e.Button.ToString()

End Sub

Private Sub txtMessage_KeyDown(ByVal sender As Object, _
        ByVal e As System.Windows.Forms.KeyEventArgs) _
        Handles txtMessage.KeyDown

    txtMessage.Text = e.KeyData.ToString()

End Sub
```

In this code sample, instead of the generic *EventArgs*, we have used a more specific *MouseEventArgs* for the *MouseDown* event handler and a more specific *KeyEventArgs* for the *KeyDown* event handler. In any event handler, if *e* is declared as anything other than *System.EventArgs*, it is probably safe to assume that additional information is provided that can be easily incorporated into the code you place inside the event handler.

In the preceding example, you can see that when the text box *txtMessage* has focus and the left mouse button is pressed, the text box will display the word *Left*. When the right mouse button is pressed, the text box will display the word *Right*. In addition, you will notice that any time the right mouse button is pressed and released while the mouse pointer is over a text box, the default context menu will be displayed for the text box. We will be discussing context menus more fully in Chapter 12.

Sub Procedures

Sub procedures, like event procedures, are methods that run one or more code statements when called. However, unlike event procedures, they do not run automatically in response to an event. Instead, Sub procedures must be explicitly called in order to run.

A Sub procedure is a custom method, which means that you, as the developer, will define the procedure, provide any required parameters, and provide the necessary code within the procedure that will run when the procedure is called. Let's work through some examples.

Calling a Sub Procedure

The scope (accessibility) of a Sub procedure can generally be defined as public or private. This means it can be made accessible to any code outside the class that it is defined in (public) or accessible only to code within the class (private).

In the example shown in the following code sample, we have created a Sub procedure called *DisplayMessage* that is designed to display a message. We will call this procedure from the *btnDisplayMessage_Click* event handler. For such a simple example, you might think that we have increased the complexity of our program unnecessarily by writing a Sub procedure that contains just one line of code. However, as your programs become more complex, you will find that providing this separation of functionality will greatly increase the readability and maintainability of your programs.

```
Private Sub btnDisplayMessage_Click(ByVal sender As System.Object, _
        ByVal e As System.EventArgs) Handles btnDisplayMessage.Click

    DisplayMessage()

End Sub

Private Sub DisplayMessage()

    lblMessage.Text = "The DisplayMessage Sub procedure was called"

End Sub
```

Using the Optional *Call* Keyword

When calling a Sub procedure, you might want to use the *Call* keyword, which is placed prior to the name of the procedure you are calling. This keyword is not required, but using it can make your code a little more understandable. The following code sample shows an example of this.

```
Private Sub btnDisplayMessage_Click(ByVal sender As System.Object, _
        ByVal e As System.EventArgs) Handles btnDisplayMessage.Click

    Call DisplayMessage()

End Sub
```

Running Common Code

You might be wondering why you need Sub procedures when you could just insert the code you want to run into an event procedure. The answer isn't always obvious, but, generally, you use Sub procedures when you want to run one or more code statements from more than one location in a program. Providing the same code in multiple places can lead to problems if you have to change the code. If you made a change in one event procedure but not in the others, you would introduce a bug into the program. Having the code in one place eliminates this kind of problem.

You have already used Sub procedures for common code in Chapter 9. In the database program, you provided a Sub procedure named *UpdateRecordNumber* to update the record number displayed in a label. This Sub procedure was called from the *Click* event handler of each of the navigation buttons. Take another look at part of that code to refresh your memory:

```
Private Sub btnFirst_Click(ByVal sender As System.Object, _
        ByVal e As System.EventArgs) Handles btnFirst.Click

    curMgrBooks.Position = 0
    UpdateRecordNumber()

End Sub

Private Sub btnPrevious_Click(ByVal sender As System.Object, _
        ByVal e As System.EventArgs) Handles btnPrevious.Click

    curMgrBooks.Position -= 1
    UpdateRecordNumber()

End Sub

Private Sub UpdateRecordNumber()

    lblRecord.Text = "Record " & curMgrBooks.Position + 1 & _
        " of " & curMgrBooks.Count

End Sub
```

Without this common Sub procedure (*UpdateRecordNumber*), you would have to provide the same code in each of the event handlers. By placing the code in one place, you have reduced the amount of code you have to write, and if you have to change the code for any reason, you only have to change it in one place.

Including Parameters in Sub Procedures

You can include **parameters** when you create Sub procedures. Parameters are variables that are declared inside the parentheses at the end of the Sub procedure declaration. Parameters are used to *catch* the arguments (*values*) that will be passed to the procedure when it is called. Let's say that you want to display a message that includes a text string entered into a text box. You could pass the contents of the *Text* property of the text box to the procedure when it's called rather than requiring the code in the procedure to retrieve the value. An example of how this can be done is shown in the following code sample.

```
Private Sub btnDisplayMessage_Click(ByVal sender As System.Object, _
        ByVal e As System.EventArgs) Handles btnDisplayMessage.Click

    ' Pass the contents of the text box as an argument...
    DisplayMessage(txtMessage.Text)

End Sub

Private Sub DisplayMessage(ByVal strMessage As String)

    ' Display the contents of the parameter in the label...
    lblMessage.Text = strMessage

End Sub
```

When you name parameters, it's not always necessary to use Hungarian notation. In the preceding example, we could just as well have named the parameter *message*. This is quite common, and many programmers choose not to use Hungarian notation when naming parameters. The IntelliSense built into Microsoft Visual Studio .NET will provide the correct data type when you are prompted for the argument. We will continue to incorporate Hungarian notation in this textbook to maintain consistency.

Passing Arguments by Value

In the preceding code sample, notice that the *strMessage* variable is declared *ByVal*. This means that a copy of the value will be passed to the parameter. If the called procedure changes the value that is passed, the original value is not changed. This is the default for all declared parameters, and the keyword *ByVal* will be added for you automatically if you do not include it when you declare the parameter. Take a look at the following code sample.

```
Private Sub btnDisplayMessage_Click(ByVal sender As System.Object, _
        ByVal e As System.EventArgs) Handles btnDisplayMessage.Click

    ' Call the procedure and pass the contents of the text box by value
    DisplayMessage(txtMessage.Text)

End Sub

Private Sub DisplayMessage(ByVal strMessage As String)

    ' Change the message...
    strMessage = "The message has been changed"
    ' Display the new message...
    lblMessage.Text = strMessage

End Sub
```

In this code sample, we have changed the message that was passed to the parameter when we called the procedure, and the label shows the new message. Figure 10-1 shows the form after the message has been changed. Notice that the original value in the text box has not changed.

Figure 10-1   Passing the message by value

Although passing by value using *ByVal* seems quite obvious, in the next section we will pass the message by reference with *ByRef*, and you will see something quite surprising.

Passing Arguments by Reference

Remember that when you pass an argument by value using *ByVal*, you are passing a copy of the value. If you pass the argument by reference, using *ByRef*, you are passing a reference to the object that holds the value. You could say that the parameter declared inside the called procedure is really just an alias for the object or property that is providing the argument. If you were to change the value of an argument passed by reference, you would be changing the original value. The following code sample shows that a seemingly inconsequential change to the way the parameter is declared has a major impact on the program.

```
Private Sub btnDisplayMessage_Click(ByVal sender As System.Object, _
        ByVal e As System.EventArgs) Handles btnDisplayMessage.Click

    ' Call the procedure and pass the contents of the text box by value
    DisplayMessage(txtMessage.Text)

End Sub

Private Sub DisplayMessage(ByRef strMessage As String)

    ' Change the message
    strMessage = "The message has been changed"
    ' Display the new message
    lblMessage.Text = strMessage

End Sub
```

In the preceding code sample, we have passed the message by reference (*ByRef*). We then changed the message just as we had done in the previous example. Figure 10-2 shows the form after the message has been changed. Notice that the original value in the text box has also changed.

Figure 10-2   Passing the message by reference

Why would you want to pass an argument by reference when changing it has this kind of effect? There are several reasons to pass arguments by reference. You might need to work with the original and perhaps change its value. Consider also that a copy will increase the use of memory. Remember that when you pass by value you are creating a copy of the original value and passing the copy. If you need to pass an object that is quite large, such as a *DataSet*, it might not be practical to pass it by value because that would increase the amount of memory that you're using by a significant amount. On the other hand, passing it by reference would have a negligible affect on memory usage.

> **TIP**   When you pass by reference using *ByRef*, if the value is changed in the called procedure, the original value is also changed.

Function Procedures

Function procedures are methods that run one or more code statements and return a value. You could consider the name of the Function procedure to be a variable that will store a value until it is returned to the method that called the function.

Although a Function procedure is similar to a Sub procedure in design, the keyword *Sub* is replaced with the keyword *Function*, and you should also provide a return data type to explicitly define the type of value that is being returned by the Function procedure.

Calling a Function Procedure

The scope (accessibility) of a Function procedure, as with a Sub procedure, can generally be defined as public or private. This means that the Function procedure can be made accessible to any code outside the class that it is defined in (public) or accessible only to code within the same class (private). In the following code sample, we are calling the function to return a message.

```
Private Sub btnDisplayMessage_Click(ByVal sender As System.Object, _
        ByVal e As System.EventArgs) Handles btnDisplayMessage.Click

    ' Call the GetMessage() function to display the returned value in the label
    lblMessage.Text = GetMessage()

End Sub
```

```
Private Function GetMessage() As String

    ' Return the text in the text box to the calling method
    Return txtMessage.Text

End Function
```

The code inside the *GetMessage* function will return the value to the code in the method that it was called from. Notice that the type of value we are returning is a *String*, so the function must be defined accordingly. If we wanted to, we could use the name of the Function procedure in place of the *Return* keyword, as shown in the following statement.

```
GetMessage = txtMessage.Text
```

Using the *Return* keyword is generally the more accepted method of returning a value from a Function procedure.

> **NOTE** The name of any Function procedure typically contains a verb, as in *Get-Message*, *CalculateTaxRate*, or *DisplayTotal*. Although it is not critical, using verbs in your Function procedure names is considered good programming practice.

Including Parameters in Function Procedures

Providing a value to the Function procedure when it is called can also be a more efficient way of coding. In the following code sample, we will pass two values to a Function procedure and return the result to the calling method.

```
Private Sub btnDisplayMessage_Click(ByVal sender As System.Object, _
        ByVal e As System.EventArgs) Handles btnDisplayMessage.Click

    lblMessage.Text = "The total price is " & _
        GetPrice(0.0825, 29.5).ToString()

End Sub

Private Function GetPrice(ByVal decTaxRate As Decimal, _
        ByVal decPrice As Decimal) As Decimal

    Dim decTax As Decimal = decPrice * decTaxRate
    Return decPrice + decTax

End Function
```

In this example, we provided the required **arguments** when we called the function. We must provide one argument for each parameter that is included in the function definition, and the arguments must have the same data type as the parameters. The order of the arguments must be the same as the order of the declared parameters. The function takes the values that are passed in and calculates the result, returning it to the calling method. When we defined this function, we specified the return type as *Decimal*.

> **NOTE** The label that is being used to display the message is expecting to receive a value of type *String*. To provide the required data type, we are converting the returned value by using the *ToString* method. This is a good programming practice, and it is required whenever you enforce strict data typing.

Using Optional Parameters

Including optional parameters provides greater flexibility when you create procedures. We would like to make the *decTaxRate* parameter in the previous example optional, meaning that we would like to provide the user with the ability to set a new tax rate or use a default tax rate. By making the *decTaxRate* parameter optional, we can provide that flexibility.

When including optional parameters, you must follow these requirements:

- A default value must be provided when the optional parameter is declared.

- An optional parameter must be placed at the end of the list of parameters.

Notice that in the following code sample, in addition to changing the code in the *Click* event handler, we have modified the parameter declaration in the *GetPrice* Function procedure so that *decTaxRate* is declared as the second parameter.

```
Private Sub btnDisplayMessage_Click(ByVal sender As System.Object, _
        ByVal e As System.EventArgs) Handles btnDisplayMessage.Click
    ' If the tax rate is provided, pass it as an argument with the price
    If IsNumeric(txtTaxRate.Text) Then
        lblMessage.Text = "The total price is " & _
            GetPrice(29.5, 0.0825).ToString()
    Else
        ' The tax rate is not provided so just pass the price
        lblMessage.Text = "The total price is " & GetPrice(29.5).ToString()
    End If
End Sub

Private Function GetPrice(ByVal decPrice As Decimal, _
        Optional ByVal decTaxRate As Decimal = 0.075) As Decimal
    ' The tax rate is optional, if an argument is not passed,
    ' use the default value
    Dim decTax As Decimal = decPrice * decTaxRate
    Return decPrice + decTax

End Function
```

The Sales Program

You will now put your knowledge of procedures to use in a more practical example. In this example, you will use a Microsoft Access database called Sales.mdb (included in the student file) to extract the names and prices of the items you will use in the Sales program. The completed form for the Sales program is shown in Figure 10-3.

Figure 10-3   The completed Sales form

▶ Creating the Sales application

1. Create a new Microsoft Windows application called **Sales**.

2. Name the form and add the following controls, naming each one as it is added. Use the information in Table 10-1 to set the properties for the controls added to the form.

Table 10-1   **Sales Form and Control Properties**

Control	(Name)	Text
Form	**frmSales**	**Sales**
ListBox	**lstItem**	
Label	**lblItem**	<blank>
Label	**lblPrice**	<blank>
Label	**lblTax**	<blank>
Label	**lblTotal**	<blank>
Label	Label1	**Item:**
Label	Label2	**Price:**
Label	Label3	**Sales Tax:**
Label	Label4	**Total Price:**
Label	Label5	**Select Item**

3. Copy the Sales.mdb file to the bin folder for the Sales project.

4. With Windows Explorer open and displaying the bin folder, right-click the Sales.mdb file and then select Properties.

5. If the Read-only check box is checked, click to clear it, as shown in Figure 10-4.

Figure 10-4   Removing the Read-only attribute

6. Click OK to save the change, and then close Windows Explorer.

7. In the Visual Studio .NET integrated development environment (IDE), display the form in the designer window.

8. Select the Data tab in the Toolbox.

9. Add an OleDbDataAdapter to the project.

10. In the Data Adapter Configuration Wizard, click New Connection.

11. In the Data Link Properties dialog box, click the Provider tab.

12. Select Microsoft Jet 4.0 OLE DB Provider, and then click Next, as shown in Figure 10-5.

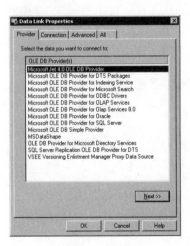

Figure 10-5   Setting the *Data Link Provider* property

13. Click the build button next to the text box to open the dialog box, and then navigate to the bin folder inside the Sales project folder, as shown in Figure 10-6.

Figure 10-6   Selecting the database

14. Select the Sales.mdb file, and then click Open.

15. In the User Name box, type **Admin** (if it is not already entered).

16. Select the Blank Password check box (if it is not already selected).

17. Click the Test Connection button to verify that you have a valid connection to the database.

18. Close the message box and then click OK to close the Data Link Properties dialog box.

19. Now that you are back in the Configuration Wizard, click Next twice.

20. Type the following SQL statement in the What Data Should The Data Adapter Load Into The Dataset? text box, as shown in Figure 10-7, or click Query Builder to open the QBE (Query By Example) dialog box. Note that Sales is the name of the database and Items is the name of the table in the database that you will be querying.

```
SELECT * FROM Items
```

Figure 10-7   Creating the SQL SELECT statement

Figure 10-8 shows the Items table in the Sales.mdb database file.

Figure 10-8   The Items table in the Sales.mdb database

21. Click Next.

22. Click Finish.

23. Click the Include Password button if a message box appears asking whether you want to include the password in the connection string.

24. Select the OleDbConnection1 component in the Components Tray (below the form), and then change the name in the Properties window to **cnnSales**.

25. Select the OleDbDataAdapter1 component in the Components Tray, and then change the name in the Properties window to **daSales**.

26. Right-click daSales (in the Components Tray), and then select Generate DataSet.

27. In the Generate DataSet dialog box (shown in Figure 10-9), make sure the New option button is selected and then type **dsSales** as the new name for the dataset.

28. Make sure the Add This Dataset To The Designer check box is selected, and then click OK.

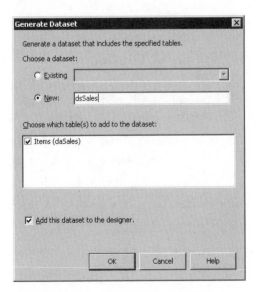

Figure 10-9   Creating the dataset

A new dataset called DsSales1 has now been added to the Component Tray.

29. Select the lstItems list box, and set the *Data Source* property to **DsSales1**.

30. Set the *DisplayMember* property to **DsSales1.Item**. The *DisplayMember* property is used to hold the list of user-friendly item names. Each item displayed in the list typically relates to a value in the *ValueMember* list.

31. Set the *ValueMember* property to **DsSales1.Price**. The *ValueMember* property is used to hold the list of values. In this case, the values are the prices of each of the clothing items. These values can be used in code and are not displayed in the list.

32. Double-click the form to open the Code Editor and add the *Load* event handler for the form.

33. Type the boldface code in the following code sample into the *Load* event handler for the form. This will fill the dataset with the data you will need for the program. The first line of code will fill the dataset. The second line will prevent the first item in the list box from being automatically selected when the form loads.

```
Private Sub frmSales_Load(ByVal sender As System.Object, _
        ByVal e As System.EventArgs) Handles MyBase.Load

    daSales.Fill(DsSales1)
    lstItem.SelectedIndex = -1

End Sub
```

Having done that, you will have a list of items in the list box when the form is loaded. Now you want to allow the user to select any item and display the appropriate information in each of the labels. This is a good time to write pseudocode to clearly define the functionality you want in the program.

- Select an item from the list.

- Display the selected item in the lblItem label. Use the *Text* property of the list box to retrieve the item.

- Display the price of the item in the lblPrice label. Use the *SelectedValue* property of the list box to retrieve the price.

- Display the tax in the lblTax label. The tax will be calculated by multiplying the price of the selected item by a constant value of 0.0825.

- Display the total price of the selected item in the lblTotalPrice label. Calculate the total price. The total price will be calculated by adding the original price to the tax.

Now that you have created the form and provided basic functionality by using properties, you need to write some code to finish the application.

You know what you want the program to do, so let's see if you can convert the pseudocode to real code to make it all happen.

▶ Coding the Sales application

1. Open the Code Editor and select lstItem in the Class Name list.

2. In the Method Name list, select Click. The *lstItem_Click* event handler will be added to the Code Editor.

3. Type the boldface code shown in the following code sample into the *lstItem_Click* event handler. You will see a blue wavy underline beneath LoadItemDetails when you finish the coding. This is expected because you haven't created that Sub procedure yet.

```
Private Sub lstItem_Click(ByVal sender As System.Object, _
        ByVal e As System.EventArgs) Handles lstItem.Click

    LoadItemDetails()

End Sub
```

4. Add a few blank lines below the *lstItem_Click* event handler and above the *End Class* statement.

5. Create the LoadItemDetails Sub procedure. Enter the code shown in the following code sample:

```
Private Sub LoadItemDetails()

    ' Retrieve the price and the tax for the selected item. Note that the
    ' SelectValue is explicitly converted to a decimal data type
    Dim decPrice As Decimal = CDec(lstItem.SelectedValue)
    Dim decTax As Decimal = GetTax(decPrice)

    ' Display the item, price, tax, and total
    lblItem.Text = lstItem.Text
    lblPrice.Text = FormatCurrency(decPrice)
    lblTax.Text = FormatCurrency(decTax)
    lblTotal.Text = FormatCurrency(GetTotal(decPrice, decTax))

End Sub
```

6. Next you will create a constant as a class-level declaration. Just below the Windows Forms designer–generated code region and outside any other procedure, declare the constant to be used as the tax rate. Use the following declaration:

```
Private Const m_decTAXRATE As Decimal = 0.0825D
```

7. Create the *GetTax* Function procedure to calculate the tax. Type the code exactly as shown in the following code sample.

```
Private Function GetTax(ByVal decPrice As Decimal) As Decimal

    ' Multiply the price by the tax rate and return the tax
    Return decPrice * m_decTAXRATE

End Function
```

8. Create the *GetTotal* Function procedure. Type the code exactly as shown in the following code sample.

```
Private Function GetTotal(ByVal decPrice As Decimal, _
    ByVal decTax As Decimal) As Decimal

    ' Add the price and the tax and return the total
    Return decPrice + decTax

End Function
```

9. Run the program, and verify that it works as expected by selecting various items in the list box and ensuring that the correct tax and total price are displayed.

10. To see what actually happens, set a breakpoint next to the following line of code inside lstItem's *Click* event handler.

```
LoadItemDetails()
```

11. Press F5 to run the program. It will stop at the statement on which you set the breakpoint. Press F11 to step into each line of code. Note the sequence of execution.

Inside the Code

Much of the code in the sales tax application is self-explanatory, but let's take a closer look at the *LoadItemDetails* Sub procedure to make sure that you understand what's going on.

In the first declaration, `Dim decPrice As Decimal = CDec(lstItem.SelectedValue)`, you are converting the list box's *SelectedValue* to a decimal by using the *CDec* function. Strict data typing requires that data be converted to the correct type before it is passed to the declared variable.

Although you have a declared parameter named *decPrice* in the *GetTax* and *GetTotal* Function procedures, the *decPrice* variable declared in this method is hidden from the other methods and will not cause any conflict.

The second declaration, `Dim decTax As Decimal = GetTax(decPrice)`, uses the value stored in the variable *decPrice* as an argument in the call to the *GetTax* Function procedure. This call will return the tax and, in turn, pass it back to the variable *decTax*.

The next statements display the selected item, price, and tax in the respective labels.

The last statement uses the price and the tax stored in the two variables and passes them as arguments to the *GetTotal* Function procedure. The total will be calculated, and the return value will be displayed in the appropriate label.

Notice that several of the statements use the *FormatCurrency* function. This function takes a value and converts it to a text format that displays the values to two decimal places and precedes the value with a dollar symbol.

We should point out a few things about the declaration and initialization of the constant *m_decTAXRATE*:

- Note the use of uppercase characters for the constant name. This is an accepted practice for naming constants. Many programmers avoid the use of Hungarian notation when naming constants, even when they use this notation for other variables and parameters. We have used it here because it is self-documenting and is consistent with the other declarations.

- Constants must be initialized to a value when they are declared. This might seem logical, but it can easily be missed. Fortunately, the compiler will notify you if you fail to initialize a constant.

- Finally, for this particular constant declaration, notice the use of the letter D at the end of the initializing value. This suffix is known as a *decimal literal*, and the letter D represents the *Decimal* type. This informs the compiler that the value being used to initialize the constant is a *Decimal* value. Once again, strict data typing requires that you explicitly define the type of data you are passing. For more information on literals, on the View menu, select Index, type **literals** in the Look For box, and then select *coercing data type* from the list of available topics.

Try It

Add two more labels to the form to display the discounted total amount. Create a new Function procedure named *CalculateDiscountedTotal*. The function should accept the original total (price + tax) as its parameter and then calculate and return the discounted total as 90 percent of the original total (a 10 percent discount). Call the *CalculateDiscountedTotal* Function procedure after the total is calculated. Display the discounted total on the form.

What Do You Think?

1. List the four kinds of procedures available in Microsoft Visual Basic .NET.

2. What are the two parameters used for event procedures?

3. Why is it important to know the sequence of events that occur for a control?

4. What is the main difference between a Sub procedure and a Function procedure?

5. Explain the difference between a parameter and an argument.

6. What is the difference between passing variables by value and passing variables by reference?

7. What are the two requirements for including optional parameters in procedure definitions?

PROPERTY PROCEDURES

You know that the controls you have been using have properties. These properties were created by the developer of the control. Surprisingly enough, you can create your own properties by using **Property procedures**. For example, you might want to create a custom *Title* property for a form and allow users to change the title at run time.

Property procedures can be read-only (cannot be written to at run time), write-only (cannot be read at run time), or read/write (can be written to and read at run time). The basic syntax of a read/write Property procedure is shown in the following code sample.

```
Public Property PropertyName() As String
    Get
        Return variableName
    End Get
    Set(ByVal Value As String)
        variableName = Value
    End Set
End Property
```

To use the new property, you need to provide a value that is passed to *Property-Name*. This is called *setting the property*. The parameter named *Value* in the *Set* block (also known as a *Set* method) is a keyword and is always included in any property procedure that can be written to. The value that is passed to the property is then stored in a private class-level variable. The value is then persisted until it needs to be read. When you want to read the value, you can just query the property as you normally would. The *Get* block (also known as a *Get* method) retrieves the value stored in the class-level variable and returns the value to the calling code. Let's look at this in action.

▶ **Setting up the CustomFormProperties application**

1. Create a new Windows application called **CustomFormProperties**.

2. Name the form and add a Label control, naming it as it is added. Use the information in Table 10-2 to set the properties of the form and control.

Table 10-2   **CustomFormProperties Controls and Properties**

Control	(Name)	Text
Form	**frmCustomProperties**	**Custom Properties**
Label	**lblTitle**	<blank>

3. Open the Code Editor and type the code shown in the following code sample to create the new *Title* property. When creating the property procedure, all you need to do is type in the declaration line of code, `Public Property Title() As String`, and then press ENTER. Visual Basic .NET will take care of creating the abstracted *Get* and *Set* methods. Of course you will have to complete the code by providing the class-level variable and adding the code to pass and return the value to and from the variable.

```
Private m_strTitle As String

Public Property Title() As String
    Get
        Return m_strTitle
    End Get
    Set(ByVal Value As String)
        m_strTitle = Value
    End Set
End Property
```

4. Display the form in design view, and then double-click it to again open the Code Editor and insert the *frmCustomProperties_Load* event handler.

5. Add the boldface code shown in the following code sample to the *frmCustomProperties_Load* event handler.

```
Private Sub frmCustomProperties_Load(ByVal sender As System.Object, _
        ByVal e As System.EventArgs) Handles MyBase.Load

    Title = "Using Custom Properties"
    lblTitle.Text = Title

End Sub
```

6. Run the program to see the results of your hard work. The displayed form should look like Figure 10-10.

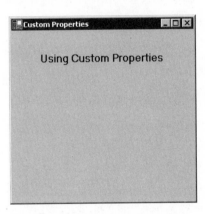

Figure 10-10   The custom Title property

Inside the Code

The new property you have created is known as a *read/write property*, which means that you can write a value to the property and you can also read the value from the property. The scope of the property is public, and, as such, the property will be accessible to any code that can refer to the class in which the property is created. The data type of the new property is declared as *String*, which means that it accepts a text value.

In the *frmCustomProperties_Load* event handler, you pass the string to the *Title* property.

```
Title = "Using Custom Properties"
```

This is then passed to the *Set* method and subsequently stored in the class-level variable *m_strTitle*.

You can return the string to the label's *Text* property by passing the value in the *Title* property to the label. Because the *Title* property cannot persist the value after it goes out of scope, it has to get the value from the class-level variable *m_strTitle* by using the code in the *Get* method.

To see what's actually happening, set a breakpoint next to the following line of code.

```
Title = "Using Custom Properties"
```

Press F5 to run the program, and, when it stops, press F11 to step into each line of code. Note the sequence of execution.

Read-Only Property Procedure

A read-only Property procedure is used when a property value can be read but cannot be written to or changed at run time. A definition of a read-only Property procedure uses the *Get* keyword. You would use such a property when you want the value of the property to remain constant throughout the lifetime of the program. The following code sample shows how a read-only property named *ApplicationName* is created.

```
Private m_strAppName As String

Public ReadOnly Property ApplicationName() As String
    Get
        Return m_strAppName
    End Get
End Property
```

Write-Only Property Procedure

A write-only Property procedure can be written to and changed but cannot be read at run time. You would use a write-only property when input is required but there is no need to recall the value in the property. The definition of a write-only Property procedure uses the *Set* keyword. You might use this type of Property procedure when you want the user to enter a user name or password. The value entered is used internally for access or validation. The following code sample shows how a write-only property named *UserName* is created.

```
Private m_strUserName As String

Public WriteOnly Property UserName() As String
    Set(ByVal Value As String)
        m_strUserName = Value
    End Set
End Property
```

In all cases, read-only and write-only Property procedures require the use of a class-level variable or other internal functionality to provide or store the value for use.

Try It

Add another Label control to the form in the CustomFormProperties application and call it lblSubtitle. Delete the contents of its *Text* property. Create a new read/write property called *Subtitle*, and populate this property with the string *Application Subtitle Goes Here* in the form's *Load* event. Run the application, and make sure the new label is displaying correctly.

What Do You Think?

1. When would you create a Property procedure in an application?

2. When are the *Get* and *Set* keywords used?

3. How do you set the property in the *Set* block of a Property procedure?

Q&A

Q. Is it better to implement Sub and Function procedures with or without parameters?

A. It really depends on the functionality you are providing in your program. Generally, if the calling procedure has already acquired data that must be used by the Sub or Function procedure that it is calling, it makes sense to pass the data rather than requiring the called procedure to have to extract the data a second time. This will become even more important when you create your own classes in Chapter 13.

Q. You mentioned using *Public* and *Private* scope modifiers. Aren't there three other scope modifiers named *Friend*, *Protected*, and *Protected Friend*?

A. Yes. We will discuss these scope modifiers in detail in Chapter 13 when we introduce classes and objects. Briefly, they would be used as follows:

- *Friend* Use *Friend* when you want the variable or procedure to be accessible to any code within the current project (assembly). Up to this point, you have generally been dealing with projects that contain only one file (the form class), so this has been of little importance to you. In more demanding programs, for which the project consists of multiple files, using the scope modifier *Friend* would allow the code in these other files to access the variables or procedures that you designate as "friends."

- *Protected* Use *Protected* when you want the variable or procedure to be accessible to classes derived from the current class. Because this is a key part of inheritance, it will become clearer to you when we discuss it further in Chapter 13.

- *Protected Friend* Use *Protected Friend* when you want the variable or procedure to be accessible to any code within the current project and to any class that is derived from the current class.

Q. Why did we use a database to get the items and prices in the Sales program? Couldn't we have provided these values in the code?

A. Absolutely, and it would have made the program much simpler. When you are dealing with a few items and prices that rarely change, it would make sense to provide a simpler solution. The problem is that the number and type of items might change, and of course you have to deal with inflation and the natural fluctuation of the economy. Before hard-coding any data inside a program's code, you need to carefully consider whether this is the best choice. Any changes to the data would require a change to the program and the subsequent headache of redistribution to your clients. On the other hand, if you have the data in an external database or file, the change is transparent to the users of the program.

Q. When I created the *Title* property in the CustomFormProperties project, why didn't I see it in the Properties window of the form?

A. Great question, and we are excited about the answer! Once again, we have to defer the details of this question until Chapter 13, but we will explain the answer a little here. It has to do with inheritance.

When you created the CustomFormProperties program (and all other Windows applications), you might have noticed the following class declaration for the form:

```
Public Class frmCustomProperties
```

Below that declaration there is another statement:

```
Inherits System.Windows.Forms.Form
```

What you see in the Properties window are the properties that were defined for the base class (the form that the form is inherited from). When you create your own base form class, you can inherit from it, and any new properties created in your base class will be available in the Properties window of the derived form. To clarify what we mean, let's add a new inherited form to the CustomFormProperties project.

1. Open the CustomFormProperties solution.

2. Right-click the project name in Solution Explorer, select Add, and then select Add Inherited Form. A dialog box will appear, as shown in Figure 10-11.

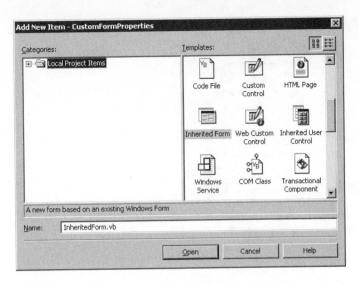

Figure 10-11   Creating an inherited form

3. Name the new form **InheritedForm.vb**, and then click Open. The Inheritance Picker dialog box will appear, as shown in Figure 10-12.

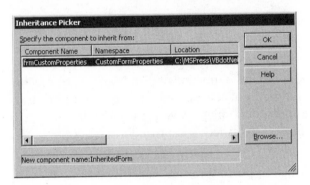

Figure 10-12   Using the Inheritance Picker

4. The original form is selected, so just click OK to create the inherited form.

5. The inherited form will then be added to the current project.

6. Select and open the inherited form in design view and look at the Properties window, as shown in Figure 10-13. Scroll down until you see the custom property named *Title* that we created in our original form. You could say that it is now an official property because it shows up in the Properties window at design time.

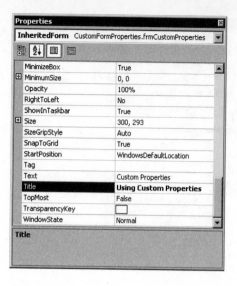

Figure 10-13   The Properties window for the inherited form

WRAPPING UP

- Event procedures are generally known as event handlers. An event handler runs one or more code statements when the event that it is linked to is raised.

- Sub procedures are used to separate functionality and provide blocks of common code that can be run from several different event handlers and other procedures. A Sub procedure might have parameters that accept arguments (values) when they are called. Sub procedures do not return a value to the calling procedure.

- Like Sub procedures, Function procedures are used to separate functionality. Function procedures generally are used to perform calculations or extrapolate data. Function procedures return a value to the calling procedure.

- When calling Sub or Function procedures with parameters, you can pass the arguments by value (*ByVal*) or pass the arguments by reference (*ByRef*). By default, all parameters are declared by value. This means that a copy of the value will be passed to the parameter when the procedure is called and, if the copy is changed, the original value is untouched. When passing by reference, you are providing a reference to the original value or object in memory. If the value is changed, the change is made to the original.

- Sub and Function procedures can have optional parameters. Optional parameters must be placed after any other parameters, and a default value must be provided when the optional parameter is declared.

■ Property procedures are used to create a custom property for a class or component. In our example, you created a custom *Title* property for the form. Property procedures can be read/write, read-only, or write-only. Custom properties will be displayed in the Properties window of any component derived from the component in which the property was originally created.

KEYWORDS

arguments

parameters

Sub procedures

Function procedures

Property procedures

REVIEW QUESTIONS

1. The _____ keyword in an event procedure provides the link between the event that was raised and the event handler.

   a. *e*

   b. *Handles*

   c. *sender*

   d. None of the above

2. Which type of procedure is created to run code when an event is raised?

   a. Event procedure

   b. Sub procedure

   c. Function procedure

   d. Property procedure

3. Which of the following mouse events is the first to be raised when the user clicks the mouse over a control?

   a. *Click*

   b. *MouseDown*

   c. *MouseUp*

   d. *MouseMove*

4. Which parameter of the *Click* event procedure provides additional information about the event occurrence?

   a. *e*

   b. *Private*

   c. *sender*

   d. None of the above

5. _____ are variables that are declared inside the parentheses at the end of a Sub procedure or Function procedure declaration.

   a. Arguments

   b. Parameters

   c. Return values

   d. Private values

6. Which type of procedure will always return a value to the statement that calls it?

   a. Event procedure

   b. Sub procedure

   c. Function procedure

   d. Property procedure

7. Which keyword is used to return a value in a Function procedure?

    a. *Callback*

    b. *Send*

    c. *Pass*

    d. *Return*

8. Property procedures can be created with which of the following characteristics? (Choose all correct answers.)

    a. Read-only

    b. Write-only

    c. Write/delete

    d. Read/write

9. Which keyword must you include when creating a new property that can be written to?

    a. *Set*

    b. *Build*

    c. *Get*

    d. *Write*

10. The scope of a Property procedure must be _____ if the property is to be accessible outside its class.

    a. Private

    b. Friend

    c. Class

    d. Public

11. A private event procedure can be accessed by procedures in all classes. True or false?

12. Programmers can control the sequence in which events occur for each type of object in their applications. True or false?

13. You can create a Sub procedure when you want to run one or more code statements from several locations in a program. True or false?

14. If you pass an argument using the keyword *ByRef*, you will be passing a reference to the object that holds the value. True or false?

15. If you use an optional parameter, you must include a default value for the parameter, and the optional parameter must be at the end of the list of parameters. True or false?

16. The _____ parameter of an event procedure refers to the object that raised the event.

17. The _____ of a Sub procedure can be public or private.

18. If you want a copy of a value to be passed as an argument, you should use the _____ keyword when declaring the parameter.

19. When you call a function or procedure, you must pass one _____ for each parameter that was defined for that function or procedure.

20. You must use the _____ keyword to create a read-only Property procedure.

STEP BY STEP

In this project for the Baldwin Museum of Science, you will create a form that will allow the user to click a picture of an animal on the form to have that animal's name displayed on the form. A Sub procedure will be created to display the animal's name.

The form for this application will look like Figure 10-14.

Figure 10-14   Animal name application for the Baldwin Museum of Science

▶ Creating a new project

1. Open Visual Studio .NET if it isn't already open.

2. Click the New Project button on the Start Page.

3. Click Visual Basic Projects under Project Types and Windows Application under Templates.

4. Type **AnimalsCh10** in the Name box.

5. Browse to the location in which you are storing your projects.

6. Click OK.

▶ Configuring the form and changing the startup object

1. Right-click Form1.vb in Solution Explorer, and rename Form1.vb as **Animals.vb**. Press ENTER.

2. Click once in the title bar of the form, and change the *(Name)* property of the form to **frmAnimals**.

3. Change the *Text* property of the form to **Baldwin Museum of Science**, and then press ENTER.

4. Right-click the AnimalsCh10 project name in Solution Explorer, and then click Properties.

5. Change the startup object to frmAnimals, and then click OK.

▶ Setting up the form

1. Add a Label control to the top of the form, and name it **lblAnimal-Clicked**. Delete the contents of its *Text* property. This label will display the name of the animal the user clicks.

2. Add six PictureBox controls to the form, and use the information in Table 10-3 to assign their *(Name)* and *Image* properties. The picture files to use for the animals are in your student file.

Table 10-3 **PictureBox Control Properties**

(Name)	*Image*
picTiger	**Tiger.jpg**
picElephant	**Elephant.jpg**
picMonkey	**Monkey.jpg**
picSnake	**Snake.jpg**
picGiraffe	**Giraffe.jpg**
picBird	**Bird.jpg**

3. Add to the bottom of the screen another label that instructs users to click the animal of their choice. You can use the default name for the label and set the *Text* property to the message shown in Figure 10-14.

▶ Adding code to the form

1. Open the Code Editor and type in the procedure that will be used to display the message at the top of the screen. This procedure is shown in the following code sample.

```
Private Sub DisplayMessage(ByVal strAnimal As String)

    Select Case strAnimal
        Case "Tiger"
            lblAnimalClicked.Text = "You picked the Tiger!"
        Case "Elephant"
            lblAnimalClicked.Text = "You picked the Elephant!"
        Case "Monkey"
            lblAnimalClicked.Text = "You picked the Monkey!"
        Case "Giraffe"
```

```
                lblAnimalClicked.Text = "You picked the Giraffe!"
            Case "Bird"
                lblAnimalClicked.Text = "You picked the Bird!"
            Case "Snake"
                lblAnimalClicked.Text = "You picked the Snake!"
        End Select
    End Sub
```

2. Double-click each of the picture controls, and type the following line of code into each of their *Click* event handlers. Substitute the correct animal name for *Tiger* as required.

```
DisplayMessage("Tiger")
```

▶ Saving and testing your project

1. On the File menu, select Save All to save your work.

2. On the Debug menu, select Start to run your project.

3. Test the program by clicking each animal picture on the form. A message stating which animal was clicked should appear.

4. On the Debug menu, select Stop Debugging to end the program.

5. On the File menu, select Close Solution to close your project.

6. Close Visual Studio .NET.

FINISH THE CODE

To complete this exercise, open the WoodgroveBankCh10 project that came in your student file. This project contains a form for Woodgrove Bank that is used to determine how much spending money users will have available after all of their bills are paid each month.

Finish the project by writing a procedure called *CalculateSpending*, and pass it amounts for monthly income and the costs of rent, food, insurance, clothing, utilities, gasoline, and savings as parameters. This procedure should subtract all costs from the monthly income and display the amount available for spending money in the lblSpendingMoney control on the form. Call the procedure from the *Click* event of the Spending Money button. Finally, add the required code to the Clear and Exit buttons.

JUST HINTS

In this exercise, you will create a reorder form for Fabrikam, Inc. The form will calculate shipping costs, taking into account the weight of the box being shipped and the shipping method to be used. Write a function that can be called to calculate the shipping cost, using weight and shipping method as parameters. Use the following information to develop this application:

- Next-day air costs $1.25 per pound.

- Two-day air costs $1.10 per pound.

- Ground shipping costs $.90 per pound.

Your completed form should look like Figure 10-15.

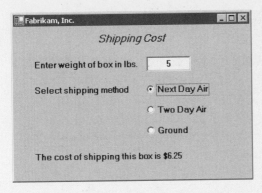

Figure 10-15   Shipping cost calculation for Fabrikam, Inc.

ON YOUR OWN

Create a form for Tailspin Toys that will be used to determine the average amount of time it will take to play a type of game, given a selected number of players. The user should be able to select the number of players from one list box and the type of game from another list box. Write a function that will be called when the user changes the selection in either list box and there is a selection made in each list box. The function should calculate total average playing time by using the selection from each list box and then display the result on the form. In your calculations, use the list of average minutes per player for each game type shown in Table 10-4.

Table 10-4   **Average Minutes Per Player**

Game type	Average minutes per player
Board Game (Adult)	25
Board Game (Child)	8
Card Game (Adult)	9
Card Game (Child)	3

MORE PRACTICE

1. Write the first and last statements of an event handler for the *btnClear_Click* event. Do not put any code inside the code block.

2. Write the Visual Basic .NET statements that will declare a Sub procedure called *ClearFields* that has no parameters. Do not put any code inside the code block.

3. Write the Visual Basic .NET statement that will call the *ClearFields* Sub procedure that was declared in the previous exercise.

4. Write the Visual Basic .NET statements that will declare a function called *CalcTax*, which uses an *Integer* parameter called *intAmount* and returns a *Decimal* value. Pass the parameter by value. Do not put any code inside the code block.

5. Write the Visual Basic .NET statement that will call the *CalcTax* function that was declared in the previous exercise. Use the variable *intSalesAmount* as the argument. Store the value returned by the function in a variable called *decSalesTax*.

6. Write the Visual Basic .NET statements that will create a read/write Property procedure for a property called *Color*. *Color* will use the *String* data type.

7. Write a Visual Basic .NET program that will allow the user to enter two numbers into text boxes, select a mathematical operator from a list box, and then click a button to see the result of the selected operation on the two numbers. Perform the calculation inside a function that takes the two numbers and the selected operator as parameters. Display the result in a message box in the form of an equation.

8. Write a Visual Basic .NET program that will calculate the diameter, circumference, or area of a circle. Create Sub procedures that will be called to use the formulas listed in Table 10-5 to calculate these values. Each Sub procedure should prompt the user to enter the information required for the calculation. Display the result of the selected calculation in a label on the form.

Table 10-5   **Circle Formulas**

Calculation type	Formula
Diameter	Radius * 2
Circumference	pi * Diameter (pi = 3.14)
Area	pi * Radius^2 (pi = 3.14)

9. Write a Visual Basic .NET program that will calculate the percentage growth of four categories of products for a company that bottles and sells beverages. Write a function that uses Last Year's Sales and This Year's Sales from Table 10-6 to return the growth percentage. The user should be able to select the category from a list box and see the calculated growth percentage for that category displayed on the form. The growth percentage is calculated by subtracting Last Year's Sales from This Year's Sales and then dividing the difference by Last Year's Sales.

Table 10-6   **Category Sales**

Category	Last Year's Sales	This Year's Sales
Juice	$565,000	$600,000
Soda	$600,000	$520,000
Water	$150,000	$325,000
Sparkling Water	$75,000	$82,000

CHAPTER 11
ARRAYS AND COLLECTIONS

Arrays and collections are objects that allow you to treat multiple items as a group rather than individually. Being able to do this adds efficiency to both the code writing process and the compilation process. Believe it or not, you have been using collections since Chapter 1. When you add controls to a form, you actually are adding them to the form's *Controls* collection. We briefly mentioned arrays and used one in Chapter 9, when we added values to a new row in a DataTable. In this chapter, we will discuss them in greater detail. Using arrays also makes it easier to handle multiple items at the same time, a need that arises frequently in practical programming. We will look at several other tools for handling lists of items, including queues, stacks, hash tables, and enumerations.

Upon completion of this chapter, you will be able to:

■ Learn what arrays are and when they are used.

■ Understand how to create and reference items in one-dimensional and multi-dimensional arrays.

■ Learn what collections are, and how they are created and used in Microsoft Visual Basic .NET programs.

■ Implement special collection objects: ArrayLists, Stacks, and Queues.

■ Use enumerations to provide a fixed list of values.

ARRAYS

An **array** is an object with one or more elements (placeholders) that are used to store multiple pieces of data of the same kind. The type of data can be any primitive type (such as *String*, *Integer*, *Long*, or *Double*) or even an object. The concept of arrays is sometimes difficult to grasp. For one thing, an array doesn't have a visual interface, so it isn't easy to see what's going on. A little later we will create a program that will allow you to compare a list box to an array. The list box will help you to visualize how an array works and what it would look like if it had a visual interface.

As we have already mentioned, an array is a variable, but, unlike a variable, which can only store a single piece of data, an array can store many pieces of data of the same type. Each piece of data is stored in an array element, and each array element is sequentially numbered, starting at the number 0 (zero). This sequential number is known as the **index** of the array and is used to identify the element in the array. To help you understand this concept a little better, consider a shelf that can store a single book. We will give it the name *bookshelf*. Although *bookshelf* is useful, it is somewhat limited unless you only own one book. If you were to stack a number of *bookshelf* objects together and call it *bookshelves*, you would have a more functional structure in which to store many books. If you number each shelf, you can provide a means of identifying which shelf is storing a particular book. Because arrays index their elements starting at 0, the first shelf would be referred to as *bookshelves(0)*. Assuming there are 10 shelves, the last shelf would be referred to as *bookshelves(9)*.

The naming convention used for the array declaration is the same as that used for any standard variable. For consistency, we will continue to use Hungarian notation when declaring arrays. We also advocate the use of the letter *m* or *g* to identify the array as class-level (private) or global (public), respectively. The fact that an array is an array and not a standard variable is apparent because of the inclusion of parentheses at the end of the name and a numeric value that determines the upper-bound element of the array.

Declaring and Dimensioning an Array

In this section, you will learn how to declare and dimension arrays. We have provided some examples to help you avoid some of the pitfalls you might encounter when using arrays in your programs.

Avoiding Terminology Confusion

There are a couple of terms that you need to know when dealing with arrays. We will explain them now, before we get started.

- **Declaration** As with any variable declaration, space is reserved in memory for the array. The amount of memory that is reserved is determined by the data type of the array and the number of elements specified. An array can be declared like this:

```
Dim strNames() As String
```

In the preceding declaration statement, we have not established the number of elements, so we cannot reference any element in code. For example, the following code will compile but will throw a run-time exception when we attempt to assign the first value.

```
Dim strNames() As String
strNames(0) = "Bernie"
strNames(1) = "Catherine"
```

- **Dimensioning**   The array is assigned a specific number of elements when it is dimensioned. After an array is dimensioned, you can assign and retrieve values to and from specific elements in the array. There are a number of ways to dimension an array and assign values to each of the elements.

```
Dim strNames(1) As String
strNames(0) = "Bernie"
strNames(1) = "Catherine"
```

In this example, we have declared the array and established the number of elements by setting the upperbound index of the array to 1. Remember that the array starts at index 0, so the upperbound index will always be one less than the total number of elements. After you have explicitly set the number of elements, you can assign a value to each one, as shown in the second and third lines of code.

Here is another way to declare an array:

```
Dim strNames() As String
ReDim strNames(1)
strNames(0) = "Bernie"
strNames(1) = "Catherine"
```

In this example, we have declared the array but have not specified the number of elements in the declaration statement. The second statement uses the *ReDim* statement to specify the number of elements. The *ReDim* statement allows us to specify the number of elements by resizing the array (in this case we are using it to resize the array from 0 elements to 2 elements). We will be revisiting the *ReDim* statement later in this chapter.

Here is a third way to declare an array:

```
Dim strNames() As String = {"Bernie", "Catherine"}
```

In this example, again we have declared the array without explicitly specifying the number of elements in the declaration, but we have provided what is known as a **value array**, which implicitly dimensions the array to a specific number of elements. In this example, we are dimensioning the array and also providing initializing values for each of the elements.

The Rules

An array, like any variable, can be used to store almost any kind of data, as long as the following simple rules are followed:

- First, you should specify the type of data that will be stored in the array. If the array is to hold text values, the array is declared as a *String* type. If it will hold integer values, it is declared as a *Short*, *Integer*, or *Long*, depending on the size of the numbers that will be assigned to any of its elements.

■ Second, the array must be dimensioned (sized) before any of its elements can be referenced in code. This means that you must specify the number of elements by assigning the index of the upperbound element or by assigning a value array to it when the array is declared.

Initializing an Array with Default Values

When an array is declared and dimensioned, each element is initialized to its default value. The following list shows the default initializing value for each type of array:

■ Numeric array: The default value is *0*.

■ String array: The default value is a *null* string.

■ Boolean array: The default value is *False*.

■ Object array: The default value is *x Nothing Nothing*. *Nothing* is a keyword in Visual Basic .NET that indicates an absence of value.

After the array is dimensioned, you can assign values to each of the elements. Any element not explicitly assigned a value will retain its default value.

You can also declare and initialize an array at the same time, like this:

```
Dim intPrices() As Decimal = {2.99, 1.99, 4.99}
```

As we discussed earlier, this is known as **implicit dimensioning**. The number of elements will be determined by the number of values being assigned to the array. In this case, the number of elements in the array will be 3, and the index of the upperbound element will be 2.

> **TIP**   Implicit dimensioning by assigning a value array can only be accomplished in the declaration statement and only when the number of elements is not explicitly set.

Dynamic Arrays—Using the *ReDim* Statement

All arrays declared in Visual Basic .NET are considered to be **dynamic arrays**. This means that you can resize the arrays at run time by using the *ReDim* statement. This capability is useful because you don't always know until run time how many items you want to place in an array. By using the *ReDim* statement, you can adjust the number of elements in the array at run time. For example, you might initially declare an array with a 0 index, meaning the array will contain one element. At run time, you can use the *ReDim* statement to change the index to 1, dynamically resizing the array so it contains two elements. Look at the following code to see just how easy it is to use the *ReDim* statement.

```
Dim intNumbers(0) As Integer    ' Create an array with one element
intNumbers(0) = 100             ' Assign the value 100 to the element
ReDim intNumbers(1)             ' Resize the array to have two elements
intNumbers(1) = 200             ' Assign the value 200 to the second element
```

There might be a problem with this code, depending on what you want to happen when the *ReDim* statement runs. By default, the *ReDim* statement deletes the contents of the array in addition to resizing it. If you have already assigned values to existing elements and want to preserve them when the array is resized, you must include the *Preserve* keyword along with the *ReDim* statement, as shown in the following code sample.

```
Dim intNumbers(0) As Integer
intNumbers(0) = 100
ReDim Preserve intNumbers(1) ' The value 100 in intNumbers(0) is preserved
intNumbers(1) = 200
```

> **TIP** If an array is resized to fewer elements than the number of elements that already exist in the array, you will lose any data in the elements that are discarded.

Use caution when using the *ReDim* statement. When an array is resized, a new array is created. If the *Preserve* keyword is used, each element in the original array is copied over to the new array. After the new array is created and filled, the old one is de-referenced and left for disposal. In our example, we showed how to resize an array by increasing its size by one element. Now that you know what's happening behind the scenes, you can see that resizing an array uses a lot of memory. The number of times an array is resized should be kept to a minimum.

The *ReDim* statement can only be run inside a procedure. For example, the following attempt to redimension an array at the class level will result in a syntax error, and the code will not compile:

```
Private m_strNames() As String
ReDim m_strNames(9)  ' This statement will produce a syntax error
```

Scope of an Array

Like standard variables, arrays have a scope that defines the accessibility of the array in your code. The scope of an array is either public (global) or private (class level). If an array is declared inside a procedure or code block, it has local scope and you must use the *Dim* keyword.

List Box and Array—A Simple Comparison

As we mentioned earlier in the chapter, sometimes it's hard to visualize an array and how the data is stored inside it. Because of this, we will use a list box to demonstrate what an array looks like and how it works. This simple comparison should make arrays a little easier to understand and give you some practice in writing code for them.

▶ **Creating the Comparison application**

1. Open Visual Basic .NET and create a new Windows application named **Comparison**.

2. Add the controls shown in Table 11-1 to the form, and set the *(Name)* and *Text* properties for each one as indicated in the table. When you are done, the form should look like Figure 11-1.

Table 11-1   **Comparison Form Controls and Properties**

Control	(Name)	Text
Form	**frmComparison**	**ListBox and Array – A Simple Comparison**
ListBox	**lstItems**	
Button	**btnFillList**	**Fill List**
RadioButton	**radClothing**	**Clothing**
RadioButton	**radFood**	**Food**
Label	**lblArrayItem**	<blank>
Label	Label1	**Array Item:**

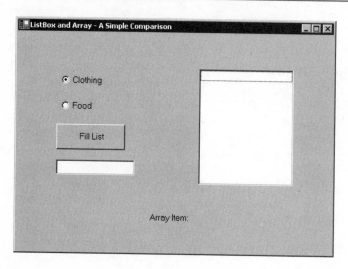

Figure 11-1   The completed Comparison form

3. Open the Code Editor and add the following class-level variables:

```
Private m_strClothing(9) As String
Private m_strFood(9) As String
```

4. You will be creating three event handlers to complete the application. Add the *Load* event handler for the form, and type in the boldface code shown in the following code sample.

```
Private Sub frmComparison_Load(ByVal sender As System.Object, _
      ByVal e As System.EventArgs) Handles MyBase.Load

    radClothing.Checked = True

    m_strClothing(0) = "Sports Jacket"
    m_strClothing(1) = "Polo Shirt"
    m_strClothing(2) = "Slacks"
    m_strClothing(3) = "Socks"
    m_strClothing(4) = "Shoes"
    m_strClothing(5) = "T-Shirt"
    m_strClothing(6) = "Belt"
    m_strClothing(7) = "Blouse"
    m_strClothing(8) = "Dress"
    m_strClothing(9) = "Skirt"

    m_strFood(0) = "Bread"
    m_strFood(1) = "Milk"
```

```
m_strFood(2) = "Cheese"
m_strFood(3) = "Sausage"
m_strFood(4) = "Butter"
m_strFood(5) = "Cereal"
m_strFood(6) = "Soup"
m_strFood(7) = "Turkey"
m_strFood(8) = "Chicken"
m_strFood(9) = "Oranges"

End Sub
```

5. Add the *btnFillList_Click* event handler, and type in the boldface code shown in the following code sample.

```
Private Sub btnFillList_Click(ByVal sender As System.Object, _
        ByVal e As System.EventArgs) Handles btnFillList.Click

    lstItems.Items.Clear()

    Select Case True
        Case radClothing.Checked
            Array.Sort(m_strClothing)
            For intIndex As Integer = 0 To m_strClothing.Length - 1
                lstItems.Items.Add(m_strClothing(intIndex).ToString())
            Next

        Case radFood.Checked
            Array.Sort(m_strFood)
            For intIndex As Integer = 0 To m_strFood.Length - 1
                lstItems.Items.Add(m_strFood(intIndex).ToString())
            Next

    End Select
End Sub
```

6. Add the *lstItems_Click* event hander, and type in the boldface code shown in the following code sample.

```
Private Sub lstItems_SelectedIndexChanged(ByVal sender As Object, _
        ByVal e As System.EventArgs) Handles lstItems.SelectedIndexChanged

    If radClothing.Checked Then
        lblArrayItem.Text = m_strClothing(lstItems.SelectedIndex)
    Else
        lblArrayItem.Text = m_strFood(lstItems.SelectedIndex)
    End If

End Sub
```

7. Save your work and test the application.

Inside the Code

When you created the two arrays, you dimensioned each of them to 10 elements by setting the upperbound index to 9 for each array. You then provided values for each of the elements in the *Load* event handler for the form.

By adding all the items in the array to the list box, you can see what is stored in the array. Any item displayed in the list box is a copy of the item stored in the array. By using the code in the *SelectIndexChanged* event handler, you can display the value stored in the current array by passing the index of the same item in the list box.

Note that you sorted the items in the array before you added them to the list box. The list box also has a *Sorted* property, but if you set that to True rather than sorting the array, the two collections would be out of synchronization.

Using the *DataSource* Property

Rather than using a loop to populate the list box, you could just as easily have passed the name of the array to the *DataSource* property of the list box. Let's look at how you can do that in the Comparison application.

Comment out (or delete) both *For...Next* loops in the *btnFillList_Click* event handler, and replace each by setting the *DataSource* property of the list box to each of the arrays, as shown in the boldface code in the following code sample. In addition, comment out or delete the code statement that clears the list box. The following code sample shows the event handler in its entirety. Retest the application.

```
Private Sub btnFillList_Click(ByVal sender As System.Object, _
        ByVal e As System.EventArgs) Handles btnFillList.Click
    With lstItems
        Select Case True
            Case radClothing.Checked
                Array.Sort(m_strClothing)
                .DataSource = m_strClothing

            Case radFood.Checked
                Array.Sort(m_strFood)
                .DataSource = m_strFood
        End Select
    End With
End Sub
```

Inside the Code

In this code you used a new coding technique that warrants some explanation, namely, the *With...End With* block. We will discuss this new statement type in the next section, so for now let's take a closer look at the rest of the code.

The *Select Case* structure checks the value of the radio buttons to determine which one is currently selected. When it finds the one that is selected, the code in that particular *Case* block runs. Once again, you sort the items in the array before you set the *DataSource* property of the list box. You then set the *DataSource* property of the list box to the name of the selected array, which is used to populate the list box.

With...End With

You use the *With...End With* block to specify the object at the start of the block so that you can reference any method or set any property for that object by just typing the period and then the name of the property or method. You don't have to specify the name of the object each time you reference one of its properties or methods. The *With...End With* statement might look somewhat strange, but it is more efficient than continually referencing the same object. Each time an object is explicitly referenced in code, the compiler must validate it. When using the *With* statement, you need to reference the object only one time. An added benefit is that it reduces the amount of code you have to type.

Using *With...End With* is more efficient because the compiler only has to verify once that the object exists, and this is done at the start of the code block rather than each time the object is referenced in code. You might not see a difference in the performance for small applications, but you will see an improvement in larger applications with a lot of references to objects.

Compare the preceding code with the following, in which we don't use the *With...End With* coding structure:

```
Select Case True
    Case radClothing.Checked
        Array.Sort(m_strClothing)
        lstItems.DataSource = m_strClothing
    Case radFood.Checked
        Array.Sort(m_strFood)
        lstItems.DataSource = m_strFood
End Select
lstItems.Refresh()
```

In the preceding example we have not significantly reduced the amount of typing, but it demonstrates the use of the technique and why you should incorporate *With...End With* statements into other programs that you create.

Multi-Dimensional Arrays

The arrays we have looked at so far are **one-dimensional arrays**. In this section, we will introduce **multi-dimensional arrays** and show you how to create and use a two-dimensional array, which is the simplest and most commonly used type of multi-dimensional array.

Let's return to the bookshelf analogy. We said that in a one-dimensional array, each shelf can hold only one book. If you constructed the shelves with partitions on each shelf, you could store many books on each shelf, each one in a different partition. This would be an example of a two-dimensional array. Looking at a worksheet in Microsoft Excel, you can see another example of a two-dimensional array structure. Each column in the worksheet represents the first dimension, and each row represents the second dimension. Taking that idea one step further, you can envision a three-dimensional array when you include multiple Excel worksheets as the third dimension.

As a further example, you could create a four-dimensional array that records the statistics of players in a basketball league. In Figure 11-2, we have used Excel to visually represent a four-dimensional array. The first dimension is represented by the column, the second dimension is represented by the row, the third dimension is represented by the worksheet, and the fourth dimension is represented by the workbook.

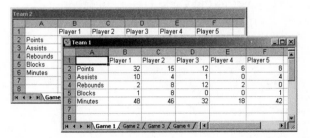

Figure 11-2   Using multiple workbooks to represent a four-dimensional array

The Baseball League Program

To demonstrate a two-dimensional array, you will create a program that uses an array to store the name of each team in a baseball league and the name of each player on each of the teams. For the sake of brevity, we will limit the league to two teams, but feel free to add more teams (and players) if you want.

In this sample application, you will create a form that will display the data stored in a multi-dimensional array, as shown in Figure 11-3.

Figure 11-3   The Baseball League application form

▶ Creating the Baseball League application

1. Open Visual Basic .NET, and create a new Windows application named **BaseballLeague**.

2. Add the controls, and set the *(Name)* and *Text* properties as shown in Table 11-2.

Table 11-2   **Baseball League Form Controls and Properties**

Control	(Name)	Text
Form	**frmBaseballLeague**	**The Baseball League**
DataGrid	**grdBaseballLeague**	

3. Set the *RowHeaderWidth* property of the DataGrid control to **0**, and set the *CaptionText* property of the DataGrid control to **Baseball League**.

4. Open the Code Editor and add the following class-level variable to the program.

```
Private m_strPlayer(8, 1) As String
```

5. Double-click the form (not the DataGrid) to add the *frmBaseballLeague_Load* event handler to the Code Editor, and then enter the boldface code shown in the following code sample.

```
Private Sub frmBaseballLeague_Load(ByVal sender As System.Object, _
        ByVal e As System.EventArgs) Handles MyBase.Load

    ' Assign the values to the array
    m_strPlayer(0, 0) = "Amy"
    m_strPlayer(1, 0) = "Brendan"
    m_strPlayer(2, 0) = "Brian"
    m_strPlayer(3, 0) = "Charlie"
```

```
        m_strPlayer(4, 0) = "Celia"
        m_strPlayer(5, 0) = "David"
        m_strPlayer(6, 0) = "Eric"
        m_strPlayer(7, 0) = "Evelyn"
        m_strPlayer(8, 0) = "Harriet"

        m_strPlayer(0, 1) = "Arnold"
        m_strPlayer(1, 1) = "Betty"
        m_strPlayer(2, 1) = "Carla"
        m_strPlayer(3, 1) = "Daniel"
        m_strPlayer(4, 1) = "Eleanor"
        m_strPlayer(5, 1) = "Frank"
        m_strPlayer(6, 1) = "George"
        m_strPlayer(7, 1) = "Mary"
        m_strPlayer(8, 1) = "Veronica"

        ' Create a DataTable and add the columns
        Dim dtPlayers As New DataTable
        dtPlayers.Columns.Add(New DataColumn("Batting", GetType(String)))
        dtPlayers.Columns.Add(New DataColumn("Yankees", GetType(String)))
        dtPlayers.Columns.Add(New DataColumn("Dodgers", GetType(String)))

        ' Assign the DataTable as the source of data for the DataGrid
        grdBaseballLeague.DataSource = dtPlayers

        ' Add the rows to the DataTable
        For intIndex As Integer = 0 To m_strPlayer.GetUpperBound(0)
            dtPlayers.Rows.Add(New String() {(intIndex + 1).ToString, _
                m_strPlayer(intIndex, 0).ToString(), _
                m_strPlayer(intIndex, 1).ToString()})
        Next
    End Sub
```

6. Save your work and test the application.

Using the *ReDim* Statement with a Multi-Dimensional Array

A multi-dimensional array can be resized just like a one-dimensional array. Use the *ReDim* statement, and specify the number of elements in each dimension. Look at the following array:

```
Dim strItems(1, 9) As String
```

We will now resize both dimensions of the array so that it contains 60 elements:

```
ReDim strItems(2, 19) As String
```

However, when you have an array that is already filled with data, there is a problem. You can only change the rightmost dimension when you redimension an array and the existing data is preserved.

For example, you can resize the array of players and preserve the contents as long as only the rightmost dimension is resized. The following code statement is therefore correct:

```
ReDim Preserve m_strPlayer(8, 2)
```

But the next line of code will result in a run-time exception being thrown, as shown in Figure 11-4.

```
ReDim Preserve m_strPlayer(17, 2)
```

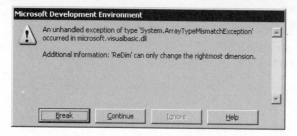

Figure 11-4 Run-time exception thrown when attempting to resize the first dimension of an array while preserving the existing data

Inside the Code

The array that you created for the Baseball League application has two dimensions. The first dimension has an upperbound index of 8, meaning that there are nine elements in the first dimension. The second dimension has an upperbound index of 1, meaning that there are two elements in the second dimension.

You have populated the array with the names of each of the players on the two teams. The first dimension of the array is the name of the player, and the second index value determines the team. Index 0 is the first team, and index 1 is the second team. If you wanted to display the fifth player on team 2 in a label, you could use the following code:

```
lblPlayer.Text = m_strPlayer(4, 1)
```

Because you are using a DataGrid to display the names of the players on the two teams, you must use an object that is acceptable to the *DataSource* property of the DataGrid. Any one of the following objects can be used as the data source:

- A DataTable
- A DataView
- A DataSet
- A DataViewManager
- A one-dimensional array

The array is a two-dimensional array, so you cannot use it as the DataSource. To accomplish the required task, you must create a DataTable object and set it up to accept the values in the array.

A DataTable is a collection of DataColumn and DataRow objects. You will be adding the rows a little later, but first you must establish the structure (schema) of the DataTable. You can do this by adding a DataColumn for each column you want in the DataTable. Let's look at the code that you used to create the DataTable.

```
Dim dtPlayers As New DataTable

dtPlayers.Columns.Add(New DataColumn("Batting", GetType(String)))
dtPlayers.Columns.Add(New DataColumn("Yankees", GetType(String)))
dtPlayers.Columns.Add(New DataColumn("Dodgers", GetType(String)))
```

The first line of code above declares a variable to accept a new instance of the *DataTable* class. The next three lines of code add three DataColumn objects to the columns collection of the DataTable object. The first column will be used to display the batting order for each player and has no reference to any value in the array. The second and third columns will be used for the players on each of the two teams.

The DataTable has a *Columns* collection, and to this you will add each new Data-Column. While you are placing *String* values in the columns, you must specify the type of value that you will be passing in. You use the *GetType* method and set it to *String*.

Notice that you have given names to each of the columns: Batting, Yankees, and Dodgers. When you run the program, you will notice that these names will appear in the header for each of the columns in the DataGrid.

The following line of code sets the *DataSource* property of the DataGrid to the new DataTable object:

```
grdBaseballLeague.DataSource = dtPlayers
```

The fact that you have set the DataSource before actually populating the DataTable is immaterial because the DataTable object exists even though no data has been added to it at this point.

The last block of code is the *For…Next* loop that is used to extract each of the names from the array and populate the *DataTable*. Notice that you also added values to the Batting column by using the current index value of the loop.

The *Add* method of the *Rows* collection requires an array of values. Each value will be placed in order. Because you have three columns, you provided three values. All that is required now is to loop through the first dimension of the array and pass the values to this method, as shown in the following code. Notice that the upper-bound index of the first dimension is established by running the *GetUpperBound* method of the array and passing the index value of the first dimension. Using this method is more flexible than specifying the actual index value and allows for the number of players in the array to be increased (or decreased) without having to change the loop.

```
For i As Integer = 0 To m_strPlayer.GetUpperBound(0)
    dtPlayers.Rows.Add(New String() {(i + 1).ToString(), _
        m_strPlayer(i, 0).ToString(), _
        m_strPlayer(i, 1).ToString()})
Next
```

Try It

Modify the Comparison application to allow the user to add one more item to the list box on the form. Your code should also add the items to the array so that the list box and the array always match.

1. Add a text box and a button to the form. Users will type the item they want to add into the text box and then click the button to add the item to the list box.

2. Use the *Add* method of the *Items* collection to add the item in the text box to the list box.

3. You will also need to add the item to the array. Redimension the array so there is room for the new item, and also make sure you include the *Preserve* keyword to retain the existing items in the array.

4. To prevent the user from adding any additional items to the list, disable the Add Item button.

5. Test the changes by adding a new item. You can verify that the array is also getting updated by setting a breakpoint in the code and viewing the contents of the array in the Immediate window.

What Do You Think?

1. What data types can be used to define the elements in an array?

2. What does it mean to redimension an array?

3. Why are dynamic arrays useful in Visual Basic .NET?

4. What is the benefit of using a *With…End With* statement block?

5. What is the difference between accessing an element in a one-dimensional array and accessing an element in a two-dimensional array?

ARRAYLISTS, QUEUES, STACKS, AND HASHTABLES

Arrays are not the only way to store and retrieve lists of items. In this section, we will look at other ways to store lists of items in a Visual Basic .NET program. We will briefly explain what a collection is and then introduce you to some of the more specialized collection classes, such as the *ArrayList*, the *Queue*, the *Stack*, and the *Hashtable*. Toward the end of the chapter, we will introduce the *Enumeration* collection, which is a defined collection of constants.

Each of these types has features that make it useful in one or more situations. We will talk about how and when they can each be incorporated into your programs.

Collections

As mentioned in the introduction to this chapter, we have been using collections for some time in this textbook. A form has a *Controls* collection, a list box has an *Items* collection, and an array is a collection of elements.

Using a **collection** makes life a lot simpler when you must deal with a group of items as a whole. For example, if you had a number of students and you wanted to dismiss all of them, it is much easier to refer to the students as a class and tell them the class is dismissed than it is to address and dismiss each student individually. *ArrayList*, *Queue*, *Stack*, and *Hashtable* are all specific kinds of collections, as we will see in the next sections.

ArrayList

One of the easiest collection classes to use is *ArrayList*. An ArrayList object is similar to an array in that it can store one or more values or objects. The two major differences between an array and an ArrayList are:

- When an ArrayList is created, you do not specify the number of elements.

- You never have to redimension an ArrayList to resize it.

Another important difference between an array and an ArrayList is that an ArrayList can store various types of data in each of its elements. For example, you could place a text value in one element and an object in another element.

An ArrayList is automatically sized to 16 elements when it is created. The size of an ArrayList is known as its *capacity*. If you add a 17th item to the ArrayList, it will automatically double in size and will have a capacity of 32 elements.

Following is a list of the more commonly used methods of ArrayList:

- ***Add***   Use the *Add* method of the ArrayList to add an item to the ArrayList. If the ArrayList is already filled to capacity, the capacity will automatically double to support the additional item.

  `ArrayListName.Add(nameOfItem)`

- ***Insert***   Use the *Insert* method of the ArrayList to insert an item to the array at a specified index. The elements following the item that was inserted will automatically be re-indexed when the item is inserted. If the ArrayList is already at capacity, the capacity will automatically double to support the additional item.

  `ArrayListName.Insert(4)`

- ***Remove***   Use the *Remove* method of the ArrayList to remove the first occurrence of an item from the array. The elements following the item that was removed will automatically be re-indexed when the item is removed. The capacity of the ArrayList is not automatically decremented when an item is removed, so you must use the *TrimToSize* method to resize the ArrayList.

  `ArrayListName.Remove(nameOfItem)`

- ***RemoveAt***   Use the *RemoveAt* method of the ArrayList to remove an item at a specified index. The elements following the item that was removed will be automatically re-indexed when the item is removed. The capacity of the ArrayList is not automatically decremented when an item is removed, so you must use the *TrimToSize* method to resize the ArrayList.

  `ArrayListName.RemoveAt(4)`

- ***TrimToSize***   If the capacity of the ArrayList is larger than required, running the *TrimToSize* method will eliminate the unused elements. You can also set the *Capacity* property to the number of elements that you require.

  `ArrayListName.TrimToSize()`

If all items are removed from an ArrayList and the *TrimToSize* method is executed, the ArrayList is automatically resized to its default capacity of 16 elements.

The Baseball League Application Using an ArrayList

In the next example, you will re-create the Baseball League program, but, rather than displaying the players in a DataGrid, you will use a list box and select the team by using radio buttons. The names of the players will be added to two one-dimensional arrays.

The completed form for the BaseballLeagueArrayList program is shown in Figure 11-5.

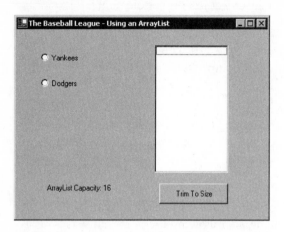

Figure 11-5 The completed BaseballLeagueArrayList form

▶ Creating the Baseball League application

1. Open Visual Basic .NET, and create a new Windows application named **BaseballLeagueArrayList**.

2. Add the controls to the form, and set the *(Name)* and *Text* properties for each one as shown in Table 11-3.

Table 11-3 **Baseball League Controls and Properties**

Control	(Name)	Text
Form	**frmBaseballLeague**	**The Baseball League - Using an ArrayList**
ListBox	**lstPlayers**	
RadioButton	**radYankees**	**Yankees**
RadioButton	**radDodgers**	**Dodgers**
Button	**btnTrimToSize**	**Trim To Size**
Label	**lblCapacity**	\<blank\>

3. Open the Code Editor and add the following class-level variables:

```
Private m_strYankees(8) As String
Private m_strDodgers(8) As String
Private m_arrlstTeams As ArrayList
```

4. Double-click the form to add the *frmBaseballLeague_Load* event handler to the Code Editor, and then enter the boldface code shown in the following code sample.

```
Private Sub frmBaseballLeague_Load(ByVal sender As System.Object, _
        ByVal e As System.EventArgs) Handles MyBase.Load

    m_arrlstTeams = New ArrayList

    m_strYankees(0) = "Amy"
    m_strYankees(1) = "Brendan"
    m_strYankees(2) = "Brian"
    m_strYankees(3) = "Charlie"
    m_strYankees(4) = "Celia"
    m_strYankees(5) = "David"
    m_strYankees(6) = "Eric"
    m_strYankees(7) = "Evelyn"
    m_strYankees(8) = "Harriet"

    m_strDodgers(0) = "Arnold"
    m_strDodgers(1) = "Betty"
    m_strDodgers(2) = "Carla"
    m_strDodgers(3) = "Daniel"
    m_strDodgers(4) = "Eleanor"
    m_strDodgers(5) = "Frank"
    m_strDodgers(6) = "George"
    m_strDodgers(7) = "Mary"
    m_strDodgers(8) = "Veronica"

    m_arrlstTeams.Add(m_strYankees)
    m_arrlstTeams.Add(m_strDodgers)

    DisplayCapacity(m_arrlstTeams.Capacity)

End Sub
```

In the *Load* event handler of the form, you initialized both arrays with their required values. You then added each array to the ArrayList collection. The call to the Sub procedure `DisplayCapacity(m_arrlstTeams .Capacity)` will be used to display the current number of elements of the ArrayList in a label. You will create the *DisplayCapacity* Sub procedure in the next step.

5. Add a new Sub procedure named *DisplayCapacity* to display the capacity of the ArrayList, as shown in the following code sample.

```
Private Sub DisplayCapacity(ByVal intCapacity As Integer)

    lblCapacity.Text = "ArrayList Capacity: " & intCapacity

End Sub
```

6. Next you will add the two *Click* event handlers for the radio buttons. Open the Code Editor and select radYankees from the Class Name box, and then select the *Click* event from the Method Name box. Type the boldface code shown in the following code sample.

```
Private Sub radYankees_Click(ByVal sender As Object, _
        ByVal e As System.EventArgs) Handles radYankees.Click

    With lstPlayers
        .DataSource = m_arrlstTeams(0)
    End With

End Sub
```

7. Add the code for the Dodgers radio button, as shown in boldface in the following code sample.

```
Private Sub radDodgers_Click(ByVal sender As Object, _
        ByVal e As System.EventArgs) Handles radDodgers.Click

    With lstPlayers
        .DataSource = m_arrlstTeams(1)
    End With

End Sub
```

When either of the two radio buttons is clicked, the *DataSource* of the list box will be set to the respective array stored in the *ArrayList*.

8. The last thing to do is to code the *Click* event handler for the button. Double-click the button in the design window. The button's *Click* event handler will automatically be added to the Code Editor. Add the boldface code shown in the following code sample.

```
Private Sub btnTrimToSize_Click(ByVal sender As System.Object, _
        ByVal e As System.EventArgs) Handles btnTrimToSize.Click

    m_arrlstTeams.TrimToSize()
    DisplayCapacity(m_arrlstTeams.Capacity)

End Sub
```

9. Save your work and test the application.

The code in the preceding code sample will trim the capacity of the ArrayList to the number of elements that are currently being used. In this case, the capacity will be 2 because that's the number of elements you have used. If you were to add another item to the ArrayList after you had trimmed it, what do you think the capacity would be? If you said 4, you are correct. An ArrayList that is already filled to capacity will always double in size when an item is added to it.

Queue and Stack

Queue and *Stack* are specialized collection classes that you can use when you want to add and remove items from a collection in a specific manner. A *Queue* collection class is used when you want to add items to the bottom of the list (*Enqueue*) and remove items from the top of the list (*Dequeue*). This is known as **FIFO** (First In, First Out). A *Stack* collection class is used to add items to the top of the list (*Push*) and remove items from the top of the list (*Pop*). This is known as **LIFO** (Last In, First Out).

To understand the implementation of *Queue* and *Stack*, consider a rack of sodas in a grocery store. If the rack is filled with cans from the back and a customer picks the first can at the front of the rack, the customer is using the FIFO method to pick from a queue. The first can that was added to the rack is the first can to be removed. If, on the other hand, the rack is filled from the front and a customer picks the first can from the front, the customer is picking from a stack by using LIFO. The last can that was added is the first one to be removed.

The next programming example will demonstrate the use of a Queue and a Stack. In this program, you will use one array that contains 18 elements, and each element will hold one player. You will add these players to a Queue and a Stack and demonstrate the *Dequeue* method of the Queue and the *Pop* method of the Stack.

The following list shows the Queue and Stack methods that you will be using in the program:

- **Enqueue** Adds an item to the back (or bottom) of the Queue.
- **Dequeue** Removes the item from the front (or top) of the Queue.
- **Push** Adds an item to the front (or top) of the Stack.
- **Pop** Removes the item from the front (or top) of the Stack.
- **Peek** Common to both the Queue and the Stack. It allows you to look at the next item to be removed from the Queue or the Stack.

Let's build an application using the *Queue* and *Stack* collections. The application will be named PickupGame. Figure 11-6 shows the completed form for this application.

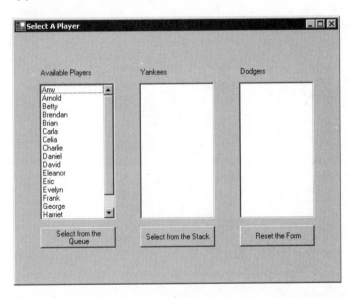

Figure 11-6   The Select A Player form in the PickupGame application

▶ Creating the PickupGame application

1. Open Visual Basic .NET, and create a new Windows application named **PickupGame**.

2. Add the controls shown in Table 11-4 to the form, and name each one as shown.

Table 11-4   **PickupGame Controls and Properties**

Control	(Name)	Text
Form	**frmBaseballLeague**	**Select A Player**
Label	Label1	**Available Players**
Label	Label2	**Yankees**

Table 11-4   **PickupGame Controls and Properties**

Control	(Name)	Text
Label	Label3	**Dodgers**
ListBox	**lstPlayers**	
ListBox	**lstYankees**	
ListBox	**lstDodgers**	
Button	**btnQueue**	**Select from the Queue**
Button	**btnStack**	**Select from the Stack**
Button	**btnReset**	**Reset the Form**

3. Open the Code Editor and add the following class-level variables:

```
Private m_strPlayers(17) As String
Private m_queuePlayers As New Queue
Private m_stackPlayers As New Stack
Private m_intPlayer As Integer
```

4. Double-click the form to add the *frmBaseballLeague_Load* event handler to the Code Editor, and then enter the boldface code shown in the following code sample.

```
Private Sub frmBaseballLeague_Load(ByVal sender As System.Object, _
    ByVal e As System.EventArgs) Handles MyBase.Load

    m_strPlayers(0) = "Amy"
    m_strPlayers(1) = "Brendan"
    m_strPlayers(2) = "Brian"
    m_strPlayers(3) = "Charlie"
    m_strPlayers(4) = "Celia"
    m_strPlayers(5) = "David"
    m_strPlayers(6) = "Eric"
    m_strPlayers(7) = "Evelyn"
    m_strPlayers(8) = "Harriet"
    m_strPlayers(9) = "Arnold"
    m_strPlayers(10) = "Betty"
    m_strPlayers(11) = "Carla"
    m_strPlayers(12) = "Daniel"
    m_strPlayers(13) = "Eleanor"
    m_strPlayers(14) = "Frank"
    m_strPlayers(15) = "George"
    m_strPlayers(16) = "Mary"
    m_strPlayers(17) = "Veronica"

    m_strPlayers.Sort(m_strPlayers)

    btnReset_Click(Nothing, Nothing)
End Sub
```

5. Double-click the Reset button in the design window. This will automatically add the *Click* event handler. Type in the boldface code shown in the following code sample.

```
Private Sub btnReset_Click(ByVal sender As System.Object, _
    ByVal e As System.EventArgs) Handles btnReset.Click

    For Each ctl As Control In Me.Controls
        If TypeOf (ctl) Is ListBox Then
            CType(ctl, ListBox).Items.Clear()
```

```
            End If
        Next

        m_queuePlayers.Clear()
        m_stackPlayers.Clear()

        For intIndex As Integer = 0 To m_strPlayers.Length - 1
            lstPlayers.Items.Add(m_strPlayers(intIndex))
            m_queuePlayers.Enqueue(m_strPlayers(intIndex))
            m_stackPlayers.Push(m_strPlayers(intIndex))
        Next

        lstPlayers.SelectedIndex = -1
    End Sub
```

6. You will now provide code in the *Click* event handlers for the Select From The Queue and Select From The Stack buttons. Double-click the Select From The Queue button in the designer window, and then type the bold-face code shown in the following code sample into the event handler.

```
Private Sub btnQueue_Click(ByVal sender As System.Object, _
        ByVal e As System.EventArgs) Handles btnQueue.Click

    If lstPlayers.Items.Count <> 0 Then
        lstPlayers.Items.Remove(m_queuePlayers.Peek.ToString())

        If m_intPlayer Mod 2 = 0 Then
            lstYankees.Items.Add(m_queuePlayers.Dequeue())
        Else
            lstDodgers.Items.Add(m_queuePlayers.Dequeue())
        End If

        m_intPlayer += 1
    End If

End Sub
```

7. Double-click the Select From The Stack button in the designer window, and then type the boldface code shown in the following code sample into the event handler.

```
Private Sub btnStack_Click(ByVal sender As System.Object, _
        ByVal e As System.EventArgs) Handles btnStack.Click

    If lstPlayers.Items.Count <> 0 Then
        lstPlayers.Items.Remove(m_stackPlayers.Peek.ToString())

        If m_intPlayer Mod 2 = 0 Then
            lstYankees.Items.Add(m_stackPlayers.Pop())
        Else
            lstDodgers.Items.Add(m_stackPlayers.Pop())
        End If

        m_intPlayer += 1
    End If

End Sub
```

8. Save your work and test the program to see how it works.

Inside the Code

Once again we have introduced some interesting code. Much of the code is probably familiar to you, but some of it requires explanation.

In the *btnReset_Click* event handler, the following code is used to clear the contents of all the list boxes:

```
For Each ctl As Control In Me.Controls
    If TypeOf (ctl) Is ListBox Then
        CType(ctl, ListBox).Items.Clear()
    End If
Next
```

You start by looping through all the controls in the form's *Controls* collection. You then evaluate each control to determine whether it is a list box. After you establish that, you can cast (convert from one object type to another) the generic control to a more specific type, in this case the list box.

Take a look at this next block of code:

```
For intIndex As Integer = 0 To m_strPlayers.Length - 1
    lstPlayers.Items.Add(m_strPlayers(intIndex))
    m_queuePlayers.Enqueue(m_strPlayers(intIndex))
    m_stackPlayers.Push(m_strPlayers(intIndex))
Next
```

Here you clear any existing items in the Queue and the Stack and then loop through each of the items in the array and add these items to the players list box, the Queue, and the Stack.

The code in the Queue and Stack button event handlers is quite similar, so we will discuss the code in just one of them.

```
If lstPlayers.Items.Count <> 0 Then
    lstPlayers.Items.Remove(m_queuePlayers.Peek.ToString())

    If m_intPlayer Mod 2 = 0 Then
        lstYankees.Items.Add(m_queuePlayers.Dequeue())
    Else
        lstDodgers.Items.Add(m_queuePlayers.Dequeue())
    End If

    m_intPlayer += 1
End If
```

The class-level variable *m_intPlayer* keeps track of which team will pick next. You can see that, at the end of the procedure, the value of *m_intPlayer* is incremented by 1.

You might be wondering why you need this variable in the first place. After a team picks a player, the selection should pass to the other team. You use the *Mod* operator to determine whether the value of *m_intPlayer* is an odd or even number. If it is an even number, there will be no remainder, so the result of the calculation will be 0. If the number is odd, there will always be a remainder of 1. If the number is even, the Yankees get the next player in the Queue or Stack; if the number is odd, the Dodgers get the next player.

Hashtable

A Hashtable is a way to store a reference to an object and a key value to locate the reference in an organized collection. The **reference** points to the location in memory where the object resides. The **key value** is a string key that is "hashed" to a unique number that is used to refer to the reference. For example, in the Baseball League application, you could store a reference to each team array and use the name of the team as the key value. The Hashtable is used to reference the objects that are added and also to prevent you from adding the same object twice using the same key. What makes a Hashtable so efficient in locating an object is the hashed key value. Lookups using hashed key values are extremely fast compared to lookups using raw string values because you are searching on integer values rather than on text values.

Let's look at the syntax for adding an object to a Hashtable:

```
HashtableName.Items.Add(key value as a string, objectName)
```

To practice using a Hashtable in code, you will copy the BaseballLeagueArrayList program that you created earlier and modify it to use a Hashtable rather than an ArrayList. The completed form for this program should look like Figure 11-7.

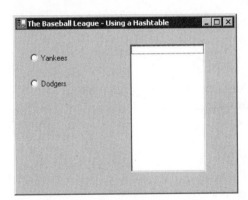

Figure 11-7   Using a Hashtable form for the BaseballLeagueHashtable program

▶ **Creating the BaseballLeagueHashtable application**

1. Open Windows Explorer and locate the BaseballLeagueArrayList program folder.

2. Right-click the folder name and then select Copy.

3. Right-click anywhere in the pane and then select Paste.

4. Right-click the new folder (now named Copy Of BaseballLeagueArrayList) and then select Rename.

5. Rename the new folder to **BaseballLeagueHashtable**.

6. Open the BaseballLeagueHashtable project in Microsoft Visual Studio .NET.

7. In Solution Explorer, right-click the solution and then rename it. You can use the same name: **BaseballLeagueHashtable**.

8. In Solution Explorer, right-click the project and then rename it. Once again, you can use the same name: **BaseballLeagueHashtable**.

9. Open the form in the designer and delete the Trim To Size button and the label next to it.

10. Open the Code Editor and locate and delete the following variable declaration and procedures:

   ❑ *m_arrlstTeams*

   ❑ *DisplayCapacity*

   ❑ *btnTrimToSize_Click*

11. Add the following variable declaration at the top of the code:

```
Private m_htTeams As Hashtable
```

12. In the *Load* event handler of the form, comment out the following code:

```
m_arrlstTeams = New ArrayList

m_arrlstTeams.Add(m_strYankees)
m_arrlstTeams.Add(m_strDodgers)

DisplayCapacity(m_arrlstTeams.Capacity)
```

13. In the *Load* event handler of the form, type the following code in place of the code that you just commented out:

```
m_htTeams = New Hashtable

m_htTeams.Add("Yankees", m_strYankees)
m_htTeams.Add("Dodgers", m_strDodgers)
```

14. In the *Click* event handler of the Yankees option button, replace the reference to the ArrayList with the following reference:

```
m_htTeams.Item("Yankees")
```

The procedure should now look as follows:

```
Private Sub radYankees_Click(ByVal sender As Object, _
        ByVal e As System.EventArgs) Handles radYankees.Click

    With lstPlayers
        .DataSource = m_htTeams.Item("Yankees")
    End With

End Sub
```

15. In the *Click* event handler of the Dodgers option button, replace the reference to the ArrayList with the following reference:

```
m_htTeams.Item("Dodgers")
```

The procedure should now look as follows:

```
Private Sub radDodgers_Click(ByVal sender As Object, _
        ByVal e As System.EventArgs) Handles radDodgers.Click

    With lstPlayers
        .DataSource = m_htTeams.Item("Dodgers")
    End With

End Sub
```

16. Save the project and test the program to make sure that everything works correctly.

Try It

Modify the BaseballLeagueHashtable application to include a selection of players from the Red Sox baseball team. To do this, you will have to add another RadioButton control for the Red Sox to the form and modify the code to support selection of this new button and Red Sox team members. You can make up your own names to use for the Red Sox team members.

What Do You Think?

1. What are the two major differences between an array and an ArrayList?

2. What is the default capacity of an ArrayList?

3. How do you add new items to an ArrayList and remove items that are no longer needed?

4. What is the purpose of the *TrimToSize* method of the ArrayList?

5. What is a Queue? What is a Stack? How are they different?

6. What is stored in a Hashtable?

7. What is the main benefit of using a Hashtable?

ENUMERATIONS

Enumerations are collections of integer values that are visually represented by names. The values assigned to the named constants in the enumeration must be integer data types (*Byte, Short, Long,* or *Integer*) or constant expressions that evaluate to integer values. You cannot declare and initialize an *Integer* variable and then assign it to the named constant. These values and the constant expressions that refer to these values cannot be changed at run time.

Enumerations are typically used when you want to provide a text representation of a numeric value in code. For example, you could create an enumeration that specifies the months of the year by using an underlying numeric value.

```
Private Enum Months
    January = 1
    February
    March
    April
    May
    June
    July
    August
    September
    October
    November
    December
End Enum
```

By default, the first constant in the list has a value of 0. Each constant added to the enumeration is sequentially numbered. By specifying the value for the first constant, you can predefine the starting value. By default, each constant that follows will have a value of one more than the previous constant. In the preceding example, the value of December will be 12.

You could also create an enumeration that provides more meaningful values, such as the boiling point of water expressed in degrees Fahrenheit or degrees Celsius. Take a look at the following example:

```
Private Enum BoilingPoints
    Celsius = 100
    Fahrenheit = 212
End Enum
```

To demonstrate enumerations, let's create an application that tracks student grades.

▶ Creating the GradeBook application

1. Create a new console application named **GradeBook**.

2. Type the boldface code shown here into the *Module* and *Main* Sub procedures.

```
Module Module1

    Private Enum Grades As Integer
        A = 90
        B = 80
        C = 70
        D = 60
        F = 59
    End Enum

    Sub Main()

        ' Loop until the word end is entered
        Do While True

            ' prompt to enter the percentage
            Console.Write("Enter the percentage: ")

            Dim strPercentage As String = Console.ReadLine()

            ' Exit the loop if the word "end" is entered
            If strPercentage.ToLower = "end" Then Exit Do

            ' Evaluate the percentage and compare it to the
            ' enumerated constants
            Select Case Integer.Parse(strPercentage)
                Case Is >= Grades.A
                    Console.WriteLine("You received an {0}", _
                        Grades.A.ToString())
                Case Is >= Grades.B
                    Console.WriteLine("You received an {0}", _
                        Grades.B.ToString())
                Case Is >= Grades.C
                    Console.WriteLine("You received an {0}", _
                        Grades.C.ToString())
                Case Is >= Grades.D
                    Console.WriteLine("You received an {0}", _
```

```
                              Grades.D.ToString())
                    Case Is <= Grades.F
                         Console.WriteLine("You received an {0}", _
                              Grades.F.ToString())
               End Select
          Loop

     End Sub

End Module
```

3. Save your work, and then press F5 to run the program. At the prompt, type **98**, and then press ENTER. The console window will display the results shown in Figure 11-8.

Figure 11-8   Using an enumeration to determine a grade

4. Continue entering various values to test the program. When you have finished testing, type the word **End** to terminate the program.

Inside the Code

Looking at the enumeration, you can see that it is declared as *Integer*. This is actually unnecessary because the default type for all enumerations is *Sytem.Int32*. Enumerations can be declared as any integer type (except *Char*), so you could just as well have declared it as *Byte*, *Short*, *Integer*, or even *Long*.

Each constant is created and provided with a value. If you had not specified any values, the first constant (*A*) would have the default value of 0 and the last constant (*F*) would have a default value of 4.

In *Sub Main*, you have created a *Do* loop that will make it easier to test various values without having to continually restart the program.

The expression in the *Select Case* statement takes the value that the user entered and that you passed to the *String* variable *strPercentage* and converts it from a *String* to an *Integer*.

```
Integer.Parse(strPercentage)
```

This conversion is required because comparing strings will generate incorrect results. For example, we know that 100 is greater than 99 when we compare them as numbers, but when comparing them as strings, each character, starting with the first one, is compared. The character 1 is less than the character 9, so the comparison will fail.

A Practical Enumeration Example

It is convenient that you can create a list of constants in an organized structure such as an enumeration, and although we have provided a couple of examples of how to create and use an enumeration, we haven't yet shown you a practical use. We will do that now.

Many of the properties that you set either in the Properties window or in code accept a numeric value that is represented as a constant. For example, if you set the *TextAlign* property of a text box, the listed values are displayed as constants that represent numeric values. The constant *HorizontalAlignment.Right* has a numeric value of 1, and the constant *HorizontalAlignment.Center* has a value of 2. If you were to run the following code, the text inside the text box would be aligned on the right side of the text box.

```
nameOfTextbox.TextAlign = 1
```

Visual Basic .NET provides these constants to make it easier for programmers to set these properties. Using the name of the constant rather than the value makes the code self-describing.

In the next example, you will create an application with a number of text boxes. You will then create a custom context menu and assign that menu to each of the text boxes. The context menu will list several menu items to allow the user to align the text in each of the text boxes.

Because the example you are going to create is of little use other than to demonstrate a more practical use of an enumeration, it will not be necessary to name the form or any of the controls that you will add to the form.

▶ Creating the UsingEnumerations program

1. Create a new Windows application named **UsingEnumerations**.

2. Display the form in the designer window and add four text boxes to the form. Lay out the form as shown in Figure 11-9. Don't worry about renaming the text boxes or deleting their *Text* properties.

Figure 11-9   The completed form for the UsingEnumerations program

3. Double-click the form in the designer window to add the *Form1_Load* event handler to the Code Editor.

4. Type the following code inside the *Form1_Load* event handler. This will be used to call the *CreateContextMenu* Sub procedure, which you will create shortly.

```
CreateContextMenu()
```

5. At the class level, create an enumeration called *Alignment*, and add the boldface constants and values to the enumeration, as shown in the following code sample.

```
Private Enum Alignment
    Left = 0
    Right = 1
    Center = 2
End Enum
```

6. At the class level, declare and instantiate the following context menu and menu items:

```
Private cmuFormat As ContextMenu
Private cmuFormatAlign As MenuItem
Private WithEvents cmuFormatAlignLeft As MenuItem
Private WithEvents cmuFormatAlignRight As MenuItem
Private WithEvents cmuFormatAlignCenter As MenuItem
```

7. Add a new Sub procedure named *CreateContextMenu*. Type the code as shown in the following code sample to create the context menu and assign it to each of the text boxes.

```
Private Sub CreateContextMenu()

    cmuFormat = New ContextMenu
    cmuFormatAlign = New MenuItem
    cmuFormatAlignLeft = New MenuItem
    cmuFormatAlignRight = New MenuItem
    cmuFormatAlignCenter = New MenuItem

    cmuFormat.MenuItems.Add(cmuFormatAlign)

    cmuFormatAlign.MenuItems.AddRange(New MenuItem() _
        {cmuFormatAlignLeft, cmuFormatAlignRight, cmuFormatAlignCenter})

    cmuFormatAlign.Text = "Align"
    For Each item As String In [Enum].GetNames(GetType(Alignment))
        Static intIndex As Integer
        cmuFormatAlign.MenuItems(intIndex).Text = item.ToString()
        intIndex += 1
    Next

    For Each ctl As Control In Me.Controls
        If TypeOf ctl Is TextBox Then
            CType(ctl, TextBox).ContextMenu = cmuFormat
        End If
    Next

End Sub
```

8. Select the menu item cmuFormatAlignLeft in the Class Name list, and then select the *Click* event in the Method Name list. The event handler will be added to the Code Editor.

9. Change the name of the event handler to *FormatAlign_Click*, and add the *Click* event for the other menu items to the *Handles* statement of the event handler.

10. Type the code shown in the following code sample inside the *FormatAlign_Click* event handler.

```
Private Sub FormatAlign_Click(ByVal sender As Object, _
     ByVal e As System.EventArgs) Handles cmuFormatAlignLeft.Click, _
   cmuFormatAlignRight.Click, _
   cmuFormatAlignCenter.Click

   Dim intAlignment As Integer = _
      [Enum].GetValues(GetType(Alignment))(CType(sender, MenuItem).Index)
   CType(cmuFormat.SourceControl, TextBox).TextAlign = intAlignment

End Sub
```

11. Press F5 to run the program.

12. Right-click any text box, point to Align, and then select Right from the context menu. Verify that the text in the text box is now right-aligned.

13. Do the same for the other menu options, and then test all of the other text boxes.

The completed form should look like Figure 11-10 when is it running. The figure also shows the context menu just before an item is selected in the menu.

Figure 11-10   The context menu to set the alignment of the text

Inside the Code

The values assigned to each of the named constants in the enumeration are required to set the alignment of the text in the text box.

```
Private Enum Alignment
   Left = 0
   Right = 1
   Center = 2
End Enum
```

You know that a named constant in the enumeration must be assigned an integer value or a constant expression that evaluates to an integer value. Rather than creating the enumeration as you did in the preceding example, you could create it like this:

```
Private Enum Alignment
    Left = HorizontalAlignment.Left
    Right = HorizontalAlignment.Right
    Center = HorizontalAlignment.Center
End Enum
```

Much of the code in this example should be familiar to you, so we will concentrate on the more cryptic statements and discuss them in detail. Let's look at the *For Each* loop block that sets the *Text* property of each of the menu items in the context menu.

```
For Each item As String In [Enum].GetNames(GetType(Alignment))
    Static intIndex As Integer
    cmuFormatAlign.MenuItems(intIndex).Text = item.ToString()
    intIndex += 1
Next
```

Starting with the declaration of the loop, `[Enum].GetNames(GetType(Alignment))`, there are several things here that we should explain:

- **[Enum]**   The word *Enum* is a reserved word that refers to the type *Enum* and not the enumeration class you have created. By including the square brackets, you are informing the compiler that you are referring to a declared enumeration and not the *Enum* type.

- **GetNames**   The *GetNames* method returns an array of the names of each of the constants in the enumeration.

- **GetType**   The *GetType* method requires the enumeration as an argument. (In this case, it is *Alignment*.)

The entire statement basically says *For Each item In* the collection of named constants in the enumeration. We can also say that the variable *item* will store a string representation of the name of each constant.

The name of the constant can then be used as the *Text* value of the menu item that refers to it. Look at the next statement.

```
cmuFormatAlign.MenuItems(intIndex).Text = item.ToString()
```

The value in *item* is passed to the *Text* property of the menu item you are referring to.

You know how to set the *Text* property of each menu item, so why are we using a static variable? Remember that a static variable will retain its value while the loop is running. The static variable *intIndex* refers to the index value of a particular menu item in the collection. Notice that you are incrementing this variable each time the loop runs. The first time through, the value of *intIndex* is 0 and will refer to the first menu item, *cmuFormatAlignLeft*; the second time through, the value will be 1 and will refer to the second menu item, *cmuFormatAlignRight*. Because this procedure runs only once, when the form loads, you do not care whether the value is retained after the procedure has run. There will be a problem though. If this procedure is called again, after the form is already loaded, an exception will be thrown.

Why will an exception be thrown? Look at the code again, and remember that the value in the variable *intIndex* refers to the index value of the menu item under the submenu *cmuFormatAlign*. You have only three menu items at that level, so the upperbound index value cannot be greater than 2. If you run the loop a second time, the static variable *intIndex* will have a value of 3, which would refer to a fourth menu item that you don't have.

As a good programmer, you would never call this procedure a second time, but, just in case, let's add some defensive programming to ensure that a situation like this could never arise.

To defend against this situation, let's start by looking at the statement that instantiates the context menu.

```
cmuFormat = New ContextMenu
```

When the procedure is run for the first time, the context menu object *cmuFormat* doesn't exist. After the statement to instantiate *cmuFormat* is run, the object is created and will exist.

Adding the following *If* statement as the first statement in the procedure will determine whether the context menu object exists. If it does exist, exit the Sub procedure. If it doesn't exist, run the rest of the code in the procedure.

```
If Not cmuFormat Is Nothing Then Exit Sub
```

Finally, we will look at the code in the *Click* event handler for the menu items.

```
Dim intAlignment As Integer = _
    [Enum].GetValues(GetType(Alignment))(CType(sender, MenuItem).Index)
```

The preceding statement declares a variable that will accept an integer. The value that you will pass to the variable must be the value of the constant that the menu item refers to.

The first part of the statement, `[Enum].GetValues(GetType(Alignment))`, refers to the array of values and works just like the *GetNames* method we looked at earlier. In this case, however, this part of the statement refers to the values assigned to each of the constants in the enumeration.

The second part of the statement, `(CType(sender, MenuItem).Index)`, gets the index of the menu item that the user clicked and passes that as an argument to the *GetValues* method. If you were to pass the value 2 to the *GetValues* method, you would be referring to the value in the constant named *Center*.

Wouldn't it have been easier to just pass the index value of the menu item to the *intAlignment* variable like this?

```
Dim intAlignment As Integer = CType(sender, MenuItem).Index
```

In this particular case, the answer is an emphatic *yes*, but that would only work when the values of each of the constants in the enumeration are 0, 1, and 2 and matched exactly with the index values of the menu items. If the values of the constants were 41, 42, and 43, they would not match, so when any menu item was clicked, an exception would be thrown.

The *GetValues* method of the enumeration returns an array of values. The order of the array is determined by the integer value of the constant and not by the order in which the constants are declared in the enumeration. If you change the order of the constants as shown in the following code sample, the code will still work as designed.

```
Private Enum Alignment
    Center = 2
    Left = 0
    Right = 1
End Enum
```

Try It

Modify the UsingEnumerations application to include an option to change the *ForeColor* property of the text box to red. Add the new menu item as a class-level variable. Modify the *CreateContextMenu* Sub procedure to add the new menu item. Add a new event procedure to handle the *Click* event of the new menu item. Change the *ForeColor* property of the selected text box in the event handler to Color.Red.

What Do You Think?

1. What is an enumeration?

2. List the data types supported by enumerations.

3. When is the *Enum* keyword used?

4. What is a static variable?

5. How is the order of values in an enumeration determined?

Q&A

Q.   Why would I choose to use an array when I could use an ArrayList, which has more functionality?

A.   It really depends on whether you need the functionality provided by the Array-List. Keep in mind that for lists of items that never change and are of the same type, an array is very efficient and is probably the better choice. On the other hand, an ArrayList is the better choice if the items are of different types or if the list will change frequently.

Q.   Why can I only resize the rightmost dimension of an array and preserve the existing data?

A.   The answer to that is quite simple when you think about it. Remember that when an array is redimensioned, a new array is created and sized to the new dimensions. The values in the existing array are then copied over. There is very little intelligence in the way the values are copied. By this we mean that the values are copied as a range and placed into the new array starting at the first element in the first dimension.

If you needed a two-dimensional array that stored the first and last names of some friends, the declaration would look like this:

```
Dim strFriends(1, 3) As String
```

The first dimension represents the columns, and the second dimension represents the rows. When the array is filled, it will look like Table 11-5.

Table 11-5   **Two-Dimensional Array**

Dan	Wilson
Pengw	Wu
Susan	Metters
Jose	Lugo

Now let's say that you wanted to add the telephone numbers in another column so that the results would look like Table 11-6 when you assigned the telephone numbers.

Table 11-6   **Adding a Column to the Array**

Dan	Wilson	555-0111
Pengw	Wu	555-0122
Susan	Metters	555-0121
Jose	Lugo	555-0199

You might think that by changing the value of the first dimension, you would be able to create the structure to add the telephone numbers and retain the existing values:

```
ReDim Preserve strFriends(2, 3)
```

Unfortunately, because of the way the values are copied over, the results would actually look like Table 11-7. As you can see, the results are somewhat less than perfect.

Table 11-7   **Array Contents After Redimensioning**

Dan	Wilson	Pengw
Wu	Susan	Metters
Jose	Lugo	

Q.   How could we accomplish what we wanted to do in the preceding example?

A.   If you really needed to do this, it is relatively simple. It's a matter of declaring two arrays and copying the values from the first array to the second array. The routine requires you to loop through each element in each dimension and pass the contained value to the same element in the new array. After that's done, assign the new values to each element in the new column. Take a look at the following code sample:

```
Dim strFriends(1, 3) As String
Dim strFriendsWithPhone(2, 3) As String
```

```
strFriends(0, 0) = "Dan"
strFriends(0, 1) = "Pengw"
strFriends(0, 2) = "Susan"
strFriends(0, 3) = "Jose"
strFriends(1, 0) = "Wilson"
strFriends(1, 1) = "Wu"
strFriends(1, 2) = "Metters"
strFriends(1, 3) = "Lugo"

For intIndex As Integer = 0 To strFriends.GetUpperBound(1)
    strFriendsWithPhone(0, intIndex) = strFriends(0, intIndex)
    strFriendsWithPhone(1, intIndex) = strFriends(1, intIndex)
Next

strFriendsWithPhone(2, 0) = "555-0111"
strFriendsWithPhone(2, 1) = "555-0122"
strFriendsWithPhone(2, 2) = "555-0121"
strFriendsWithPhone(2, 3) = "555-0199"
```

In the preceding code, we have dimensioned two arrays. The first one is filled with the first and last names of our friends. Next we created a loop that will iterate through the second dimension of the first array and pass the values to the same element in the second array. After that is done, we simply assign each telephone number to the appropriate element in the new column.

To see this in action, create a new console application and type the following code into the *Main* method.

```
Sub main()
    Dim strFriends(1, 3) As String
    Dim strFriendsWithPhone(2, 3) As String

    strFriends(0, 0) = "Dan"
    strFriends(0, 1) = "Pengw"
    strFriends(0, 2) = "Susan"
    strFriends(0, 3) = "Jose"
    strFriends(1, 0) = "Wilson"
    strFriends(1, 1) = "Wu"
    strFriends(1, 2) = "Metters"
    strFriends(1, 3) = "Lugo"

    For intIndex As Integer = 0 To strFriends.GetUpperBound(1)
        Console.WriteLine(strFriends(0, intIndex).ToString() & _
            " " & strFriends(1, intIndex).ToString())
    Next

    For intIndex As Integer = 0 To strFriends.GetUpperBound(1)
        strFriendsWithPhone(0, intIndex) = strFriends(0, intIndex)
        strFriendsWithPhone(1, intIndex) = strFriends(1, intIndex)
    Next
    Console.ReadLine()

    strFriendsWithPhone(2, 0) = "555-0111"
    strFriendsWithPhone(2, 1) = "555-0122"
    strFriendsWithPhone(2, 2) = "555-0121"
    strFriendsWithPhone(2, 3) = "555-0199"

    For intIndex As Integer = 0 To strFriendsWithPhone.GetUpperBound(1)
        Console.WriteLine(strFriendsWithPhone(0, intIndex).ToString() & _
            " " & strFriendsWithPhone(1, intIndex).ToString() & _
            " " & strFriendsWithPhone(2, intIndex).ToString())
```

```
    Next
    Console.ReadLine()

End Sub
```

This is the same code we showed you in the previous example, but we have added two additional loops. The first one will display the first and last names in the console window, and the second additional loop will display the first and last names along with the telephone numbers, as shown in Figure 11-11.

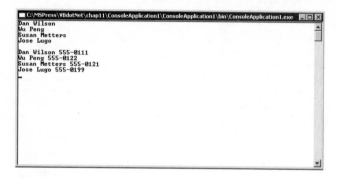

Figure 11-11 Displaying the first and last names from the first array and the first and last names along with the telephone numbers from the second array

WRAPPING UP

- The *With...End With* structure is used to reference an object once and then refer to any methods or properties of that object without having to repeat the name of the object again within the block. Using the *With...End With* block is more efficient because the compiler only has to verify the existence of the object once.

- Arrays are used to store lists of one or more items. A one-dimensional array is similar in concept to a list box. You can store a list of items in a single variable that has many elements. By specifying the array and the index value of an element, you can pass a value to or retrieve a value from the array.

- A two-dimensional array is similar in concept to an Excel worksheet. You can retrieve the value stored in an element by providing index values to the first and second dimensions. This would be analogous to providing the row and column numbers in a worksheet to locate the cell that stores the value you are looking for.

- Collections allow you to refer to many objects as a single item. A form has a collection of controls and a list box has a collection of items.

- An ArrayList is a specialized collection object. When using an ArrayList, you can easily add items to a collection. An ArrayList is automatically sized to 16 elements. You can resize an ArrayList by running the *TrimTo-Size* method. If the ArrayList is already at capacity, adding one more item to it will automatically double the current capacity.

- A Queue is also a specialized collection object. You can add items to a Queue by running the *Enqueue* method and remove them from the Queue by running the *Dequeue* method. A Queue is an FIFO collection, meaning that the first item in is the first item out.

- A Stack is similar to a Queue. You can add items to a Stack by running the *Push* method and remove them from the Stack by using the *Pop* method. A Stack is an LIFO collection, meaning that the last item in is the first item out.

- With both a Queue and a Stack, you can use the *Peek* method to see the next item that will be removed from the collection.

- A Hashtable is used to store a reference to an object and to retrieve that reference by specifying a key value that is hashed to an *Integer* value for fast lookups and retrieval.

- An enumeration allows you to create a finite list of constant values. The name of the constant represents a numeric value that cannot be changed at run time. By default, the first constant in the enumeration has a value of 0. By setting each constant to a specific number, you can provide more meaningful values.

KEYWORDS

array

dynamic arrays

FIFO

index

LIFO

one-dimensional array

collection

enumeration

implicit dimensioning

key value

multi-dimensional array

reference

REVIEW QUESTIONS

1. The value used to access a particular piece of data stored in an array is called the _____.

   a. index

   b. declaration

   c. data type

   d. element

2. The value of the starting index of an array is _____.

   a. –1

   b. 0

   c. 1

   d. 10

3. The default value of the *Object* data type is _____.

   a. *Null*

   b. 0

   c. an empty string

   d. *Nothing*

4. You can modify the size of an array at run time by running the _____ statement.

   a. *Resize*

   b. *NewSize*

   c. *DimSize*

   d. *ReDim*

5. You should use the _____ keyword when resizing an array at run time so that you don't lose any existing data in the array.

   a. *Save*

   b. *Preserve*

   c. *Keep*

   d. *Resize*

6. Which of the following types of statements can be used to specify an object once at the start of a statement block and then reference any property or method of that object without having to repeat the object's name?

   a. *If...Else*

   b. *Select...Case*

   c. *Do...While*

   d. *With...End With*

7. The name of the collection class that can store a list of items that can have different data types and that does not have to be resized with the *ReDim* statement is _____.

   a. *Array*

   b. *DataSource*

   c. *DataList*

   d. *ArrayList*

8. Which collection class is best used when you want to remove the first item from a collection by using the FIFO methodology?

   a. *Stack*

   b. *Array*

   c. *Queue*

   d. *ArrayList*

9. Which of the following are valid methods for the *Queue* or the *Stack* collections? (Choose all correct answers.)

   a. *Push*

   b. *Pop*

   c. *Peek*

   d. *Put*

10. Which of the following methods of the *Queue* and *Stack* collections is used to see the next item that will be removed from the collection?

    a. *Push*

    b. *Pop*

    c. *Peek*

    d. *Put*

11. Only numeric data can be stored in an array. True or false?

12. Every element in a one-dimensional array can be referenced by only one index value. True or false?

13. An array is a collection of elements. True or false?

14. An ArrayList is automatically sized to 24 elements when it is created. True or false?

15. A Hashtable will not allow the same key value to be used twice in one collection. True or false?

16. A collection object that is created to contain one or more values of the same type is called a(n) _____.

17. After you declare an array, you can use the _____ statement to define the size of the array.

18. The _____ method should be used to reduce the capacity of an ArrayList.

19. The _____ collection class should be used to remove the last item in a list. This is also known as LIFO.

20. A collection of integer values that are assigned names is called a(n) _____.

STEP BY STEP

In this project for the Baldwin Museum of Science, you will create a form that displays a list of dinosaurs and allows the user to click an item in the list to see more information about that type of dinosaur. The information about the dinosaurs will be stored in a two-dimensional array and loaded into the list box when the user clicks the Load Dinosaurs button.

The completed form for this application will look like Figure 11-12.

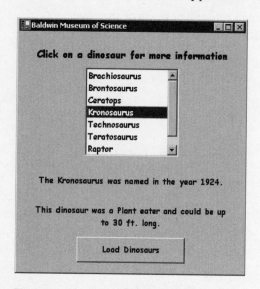

Figure 11-12   The completed Dinosaur form

▶ Creating a new project

1. Open Visual Studio .NET if it isn't already open.

2. Click the New Project button on the Start Page.

3. Click Visual Basic Projects under the Project Types, and then click Windows Application under Templates.

4. Type **DinosaurCh11** in the Name box.

5. Browse to the location in which you are storing your projects.

6. Click OK.

▶ Configuring the form and changing the startup object

1. Right-click Form1.vb in Solution Explorer, and then rename Form1.vb as **Dinosaur.vb**. Press ENTER.

2. Click once in the title bar of the form and change the *(Name)* property of the form to **frmDinosaur**.

3. Change the *Text* property of the form to **Baldwin Museum of Science**, and then press ENTER.

4. Right-click the DinosaurCh11 project name in Solution Explorer, and then select Properties.

5. Change the startup object to frmDinosaur, and then click OK.

▶ Setting up the form

1. Add a ListBox control to your form, and name it **lstDinosaurs**.

2. Add a Label control above the list box and change its *Text* property to **Click on a dinosaur for more information**. Set its *(Name)* property to **lblInstructions**, and then set the *Visible* property to False. You will make this label visible after the user has loaded the dinosaurs into the list box.

3. Add a Label control under the list box and change its *(Name)* property to **lblNameYear**. Delete the contents of its *Text* property.

4. Add a Label control under the other label and change its *(Name)* property to **lblEatSize**. Delete the contents of its *Text* property.

5. Add a Button control under the bottom label, and change its *(Name)* property to **btnLoadDinosaurs**. Change its *Text* property to **Load Dinosaurs**.

▶ Adding code to the form

1. Double-click any blank space on the form to open the Code Editor in the form's *Load* event handler.

2. Before you add the code to the *frmDinosaur_Load* event handler, you need to declare the array so that it can be used by any procedure in the form. To do this, click in the blank line above the line of code that begins with `Private Sub frmDinosaur_Load`, and then type the following line of code:

```
Public DinoArray(7, 3) As String
```

3. Type the following code in the *frmDinosaur_Load* event handler:

```
' Populate the DinoArray with information about the dinosaurs
Dim ArrayIndex As Integer

For ArrayIndex = 0 To 7
    Select Case ArrayIndex
        Case 0
            DinoArray(ArrayIndex, 0) = "Brachiosaurus"
            DinoArray(ArrayIndex, 1) = "1903"
            DinoArray(ArrayIndex, 2) = "Plant eater"
            DinoArray(ArrayIndex, 3) = "50 ft. tall"
        Case 1
            DinoArray(ArrayIndex, 0) = "Brontosaurus"
            DinoArray(ArrayIndex, 1) = "1879"
            DinoArray(ArrayIndex, 2) = "Plant eater"
            DinoArray(ArrayIndex, 3) = "90 ft. tall"
```

```
            Case 2
                DinoArray(ArrayIndex, 0) = "Ceratops"
                DinoArray(ArrayIndex, 1) = "1815"
                DinoArray(ArrayIndex, 2) = "Plant eater"
                DinoArray(ArrayIndex, 3) = "26 ft. long"
            Case 3
                DinoArray(ArrayIndex, 0) = "Kronosaurus"
                DinoArray(ArrayIndex, 1) = "1924"
                DinoArray(ArrayIndex, 2) = "Plant eater"
                DinoArray(ArrayIndex, 3) = "30 ft. long"
            Case 4
                DinoArray(ArrayIndex, 0) = "Technosaurus"
                DinoArray(ArrayIndex, 1) = "1984"
                DinoArray(ArrayIndex, 2) = "Plant eater"
                DinoArray(ArrayIndex, 3) = "4 ft. tall"
            Case 5
                DinoArray(ArrayIndex, 0) = "Teratosaurus"
                DinoArray(ArrayIndex, 1) = "1861"
                DinoArray(ArrayIndex, 2) = "Meat eater"
                DinoArray(ArrayIndex, 3) = "20 ft. long"
            Case 6
                DinoArray(ArrayIndex, 0) = "Raptor"
                DinoArray(ArrayIndex, 1) = "1932"
                DinoArray(ArrayIndex, 2) = "Meat eater"
                DinoArray(ArrayIndex, 3) = "30 ft. long"
            Case 7
                DinoArray(ArrayIndex, 0) = "Segnosaurus"
                DinoArray(ArrayIndex, 1) = "1979"
                DinoArray(ArrayIndex, 2) = "Meat eater"
                DinoArray(ArrayIndex, 3) = "30 ft. long"
        End Select
    Next
```

4. Type the following code in the *btnLoadDinosaurs_Click* event handler:

```
Dim ArrayIndex As Integer

For ArrayIndex = 0 To 7
    lstDinosaurs.Items.Add(DinoArray(ArrayIndex, 0))
Next

lblInstructions.Visible = True
```

5. Type the following code in *the lstDinosaurs_SelectedIndexChanged* event handler:

```
' Display related information about the selected dinosaur
lblNameYear.Text = "The " & lstDinosaurs.SelectedItem & _
    " was named in the year " & _
    DinoArray(lstDinosaurs.SelectedIndex, 1) & "."
lblEatSize.Text = "This dinosaur was a " & _
    DinoArray(lstDinosaurs.SelectedIndex, 2) & _
    " and could be up to " & _
    DinoArray(lstDinosaurs.SelectedIndex, 3) & "."
```

▶ Saving and testing the program

1. On the File menu, select Save All to save your work.

2. On the Debug menu, select Start to run your project.

3. Test the program by clicking the Load Dinosaurs button to populate the list box. Click several dinosaurs in the list and verify that the correct information is displayed for each dinosaur.

4. On the Debug menu, select Stop Debugging to end the program.

5. On the File menu, select Close Solution to close your project.

6. Close Visual Studio .NET.

FINISH THE CODE

To complete this exercise, open the WoodgroveBankCh11 project that came in your student file, and then complete the code to populate an array with a list of the bank's branch locations. The array should be populated in the *Click* event of the Load Branches button. Use the following list of branch locations to complete this task.

- Springfield
- Newburgh
- Huntington
- Rosemont
- Lakeville
- Stonington
- East Windsor

After the array is populated, complete the code for the Add Branch button, which should prompt the user to add another location name into an input box. Redimension the array and add this new location to the end of the array. Display to the user a message box confirming entry of the new location.

JUST HINTS

Fabrikam, Inc., has asked you to create a form that its employees can use to create a bill of materials for each of the company's products. A bill of materials is used to define all of the component parts that make up a product. The user should be able to enter the product ID, which will contain numbers and letters, a description of a subpart, the type of material used for the subpart, and the quantity of material used in the subpart. All fields should allow the entry and storage of alphanumeric characters. When users are finished entering all of the information, they should be able to click the Add Component button to add the component to the array and display it in the list box.

Each product can have a maximum of 10 components. Keep track of how many components have been added, and do not let the user add more than 10 components.

1. Create the form to enter the bill of materials information as shown in Figure 11-13.

2. Create an array to store the information as it is entered by users when they click Add Component.

3. After adding each component's information to the array, concatenate all of the fields together and add them to the list box on the form.

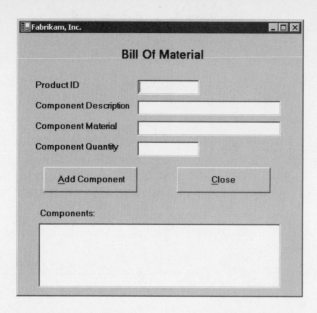

Figure 11-13   Fabrikam, Inc., bill of material entry form

4. Keep checking to make sure the maximum of 10 items has not been reached. When it is reached, disable the text boxes and the Add Component button.

ON YOUR OWN

You have been asked to create a Visual Basic .NET program for Tailspin Toys that will display a list of popular games along with a picture associated with the game. When users select a game from a list box, the picture associated with that game should be displayed in a picture box next to the list box. Store the list of game names and pictures shown in Table 11-8 in an ArrayList. The picture files for this project are in your student file.

Table 11-8   **Tailspin Toys Games and Pictures**

Game	Picture
Monopoly	Monopoly.bmp
Checkers	Checkers.bmp
Chess	Chess.bmp
Parcheesi	Parcheesi.bmp
Bingo	Bingo.bmp
Backgammon	Backgammon.bmp

MORE PRACTICE

1. Write a Visual Basic .NET statement that declares a private array called *strNames* that will hold 50 alphanumeric elements.

2. Write a Visual Basic .NET statement that declares a global array called *intValues* and at the same time initializes it to contain the numbers 0, 5, 10, 15, 20, and 25.

3. Write a Visual Basic .NET statement that will declare a private array called *intLowValues* that will hold 10 integer values. Populate the *intLowValues* array by using a *For...Next* loop to contain the numbers 1 through 10.

4. Write a Visual Basic .NET statement that will declare a private two-dimensional array called *intXYValues*, which will store 10 integer values in the first dimension and 100 integer values in the second dimension.

5. Write the Visual Basic .NET statements that will declare an ArrayList object called *intInOut*. Use a *For...Next* loop and an array called *intNumbers* to add the numbers 1 through 35 to the array list. Next, remove the last three numbers from the array list and use the *TrimToSize* method to resize the array list.

6. Write a Visual Basic .NET program that will create an array that contains the numbers 1 through 10 and the square and square root of each number. The array should be created and populated during the form's *Load* event. Display a list box on the form that contains the numbers 1 through 10. When the user clicks a number in the list box, look up the square and square root for that number in the array and display them in labels on the form.

7. Write a Visual Basic .NET program that will create a two-dimensional array to hold a deck of cards. When you load the array with the card values, load them in order, starting with the 2 of hearts, then the 3 of hearts, and on through the ace of hearts. Continue loading the diamonds, clubs, and then spades. Display a button that the user can click to enter the suit of a card and then the number associated with the card. Display the array indexes of that card to the user in a message box.

8. Write a Visual Basic .NET program that will allow the user to enter a sentence into a text box. Store that sentence in an array, with one character (including spaces) in each element of the array. Allow users to view the character stored at a particular location in the array by prompting them to enter a number representing a location in the array. Display the character in that location in a label on the form.

CHAPTER 12
MENUS AND TOOLBARS

Incorporating menus and toolbars into an application enhances it and provides an interface that most users are accustomed to. If a program's interface is busy, it makes sense to move the execution of some of the available functions to menus and/or toolbars. A good rule of thumb to follow when including menus and toolbars in an application is to provide a menu item for every function in the program and provide a toolbar button for the most significant ones.

Upon completion of this chapter, you will be able to:

■ Review examples of menus and toolbars in other applications.

■ Understand exactly what a menu is.

■ Learn how to create a menu by using the designer and at run time.

■ Learn how to create a context menu by using the designer and at run time.

■ Learn how to create a toolbar by using the designer and at run time.

■ Learn how to incorporate an ImageList as a repository for the images used by toolbar buttons.

MENUS

Before we get started, it might be helpful to look at the menus and toolbars used in the Microsoft Office suite of applications. When you look at them, you will start to see a commonality among them. This will help you when designing your own menus and toolbars.

The next several figures show menus and toolbars from each of the Office applications. While these menus and toolbars provide some advanced features that are beyond the scope of this textbook, they demonstrate the use of standardized menu and toolbar structures that users have come to expect.

In Figure 12-1, you can see the main menu and several toolbars used in Microsoft Office Word. In this figure, we have selected the Format top-level menu to display its submenu items.

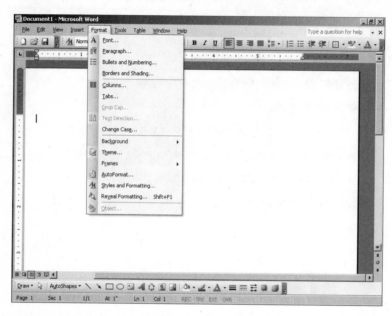

Figure 12-1   Menus and toolbars in Word

In Figure 12-2, you can see that many of the menus and toolbars used in Microsoft Office Excel are similar to those in Word.

In Figure 12-3, once again you can see that many of the menu items and toolbars used in Microsoft Office PowerPoint are similar to those in Word and Excel.

The preceding figures demonstrate the commonality of the menus and toolbars in each of these applications. This provides the user with a familiar interface. After the user has learned how to use one of these applications, that knowledge can be carried over to any application in the suite.

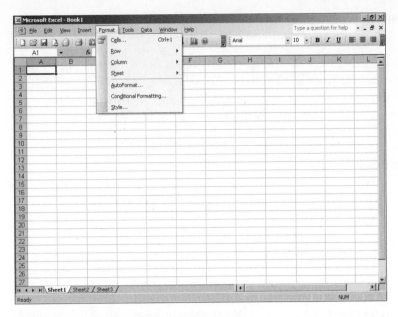

Figure 12-2   Menus and toolbars in Excel

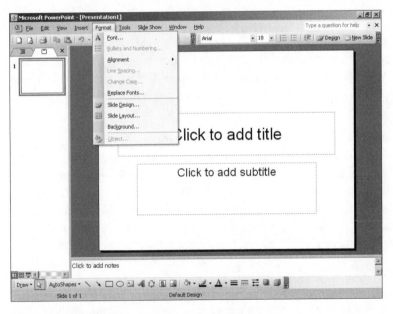

Figure 12-3   Menus and toolbars in PowerPoint

Creating Menus in Visual Basic .NET

To a programmer, a **menu** is a collection object. The collection in this case is called *MenuItems*. To create a menu, you add MenuItem objects to the menu's *MenuItems* collection. Each menu item is used to provide some functionality within the program. A **top-level menu item** is used to display one or more submenu items. A **submenu item** can be used to perform a task or to display another level of menu items, and so on.

To a user, a menu provides a way to interact with a program and perform tasks. The menu should therefore be logical and easy to use.

In the sections that follow, we will discuss two methods of creating menus: using the MainMenu component from the Toolbox and using the *MainMenu* class. You will also learn how to create a custom context menu. A **context menu** is a menu that appears when the right mouse button is clicked on an object such as a control or form.

Using the MainMenu Component

To create a menu from the Toolbox, the first step is to add a MainMenu component to the form. The component is actually placed in the component tray, which is located just below the form. The visual part of the MainMenu is automatically displayed at the top of the form and typically consists of several top-level menu items. Under each of the top-level menu items, there will be one or more submenu items. Each one of these submenu items might have additional submenu items under it.

How many levels of submenu items can you have? There is no real limit, but the practical limit is three or four levels. You might see some programs with more than four levels, but that is not common.

You can create as many MainMenu objects as you want, but only one of the MainMenu objects can be active on the form at any one time. The *Menu* property of the form can be set to the desired *MainMenu* object at design time or at run time. Setting the *Menu* property at run time allows you to designate which *MainMenu* is to be displayed at that time. This would be considered a *context-sensitive* menu system.

You will now create a menu by using the MainMenu component from the Toolbox. For this example, you will use the Bookstore program that you created in Chapter 9. Because you will be modifying the program, you should create a copy of the project folder. Rename the copy Bookstore_menu. You will add a MainMenu component to the program and create a menu for the Books form. The menu will replace the buttons that already exist on the form. After you are satisfied that everything works as intended, you will remove the existing buttons and delete the associated code.

IMPORTANT In this chapter, you will be creating two versions of the Bookstore application. You will also be switching from one version to another to complete each exercise. Switching between versions can sometimes lead to confusion because you might end up modifying the incorrect version. For this reason, when you are asked to create a copy of the program and rename it, make sure that you rename the copy as specified. In addition, verify that you are working with the version as specified in that section of the chapter.

You will be working with two versions of the original Bookstore program. In the Bookstore_menu version, you will be creating a main menu and a context menu by using the designer. In the Bookstore_menuclass version, you will be creating a main menu and a context menu by using the appropriate Microsoft .NET classes.

▶ Adding a main menu to the Bookstore application

1. Open the Bookstore program Bookstore_menu folder in Microsoft Visual Studio .NET.

2. Open the Books form in the designer window.

3. Add a MainMenu component from the Toolbox and name it **mnuBooks**. The MainMenu component will be added to the Component Tray below the form. A design view of the menu is placed at the top of the form, as shown in Figure 12-4.

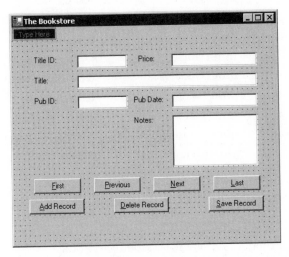

Figure 12-4   Bookstore_menu application with the main menu at the top of the form

4. A top-level menu item is automatically selected and prompts you to type in a menu label. Type **&File** as shown in Figure 12-5, but do not press ENTER or click the next menu item yet. You need to give the item a proper name.

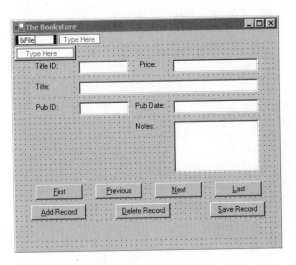

Figure 12-5   Labeling the menu

5. Locate the *(Name)* property in the Property window, type **mnuFile**, and then press ENTER.

6. Do the same thing for the other top-level menu items and for all submenu items. Use the information in Table 12-1 to create and define each menu item. To create a separator bar between menu items, add a menu item and place a hyphen in the *Text* property.

Table 12-1 **Menu Items for the Bookstore Application**

Top-level menu	Submenu item	(Name)	Text
File		**mnuFile**	**&File**
	Exit	**mnuFileExit**	**E&xit**
Data		**mnuData**	**&Data**
	Add New Record	**mnuDataAdd**	**&Add New Record**
	Save Record	**mnuDataSave**	**&Save Record**
	Separator	**mnuDataSep1**	-
	Delete Record	**mnuDataDelete**	**&Delete Record**
Navigate		**mnuNavigate**	**&Navigate**
	First Record	**mnuNavigateFirst**	**&First Record**
	Previous Record	**mnuNavigatePrevious**	**&Previous Record**
	Next Record	**mnuNavigateNext**	**&Next Record**
	Last Record	**mnuNavigateLast**	**&Last Record**
Help		**mnuHelp**	**&Help**
	About	**mnuHelpAbout**	**&About**

Figure 12-6 shows the Data menu as it will look when the Bookstore application is running, and Figure 12-7 shows the Navigate menu. If you used the Microsoft Office Access pubs database when you created the original application, you'll probably need to reconfigure the database connection to make this work. Rerun the DataAdapter Configuration Wizard and either reconfigure the connection or create a new connection.

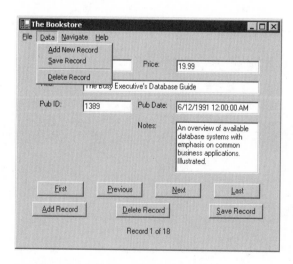

Figure 12-6 The Data menu

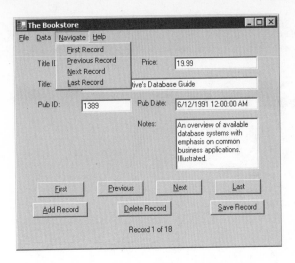

Figure 12-7   The Navigate menu

Editing Menu Item Names

Now that you have named each of the menu items the hard way, let's look at how to do it by using the designer.

▶ **Using the designer**

1. After adding all the menu items, right-click any one of the top-level menu items and then select Edit Names from the context menu, as shown in Figure 12-8.

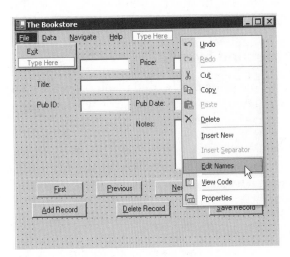

Figure 12-8   Selecting the Edit Names option

2. To change the name of any menu item, click once on the menu item to select it and then type the new name, as shown in Figure 12-9. If you inadvertently double-click the item, the Code Editor will open and the *Click* event handler for that menu item will be added. If this happens, delete the newly added event handler and switch back to the designer.

TIP A top-level menu item's only function is to display a list of submenu items. Although a top-level menu item has a *Click* event, this event should not be coded because it will never be called if there are menu items in the menu's *MenuItems* collection.

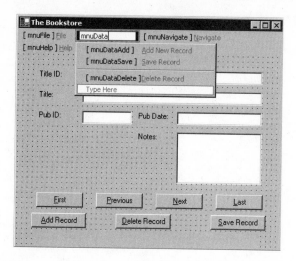

Figure 12-9   Clicking once on a menu item to change its name

Moving a Menu Item

You can move a menu item to another location in the menu structure by selecting it and dragging it to the new location. You can even move a menu item from one top-level menu list to another. Cutting the menu item and pasting it to another location achieves the same result.

Menu Properties, Methods, and Events

Tables 12-2, 12-3, and 12-4 list the most commonly used menu properties, methods, and events, along with a brief description of each one. You will be using some of these properties, methods, and events in the examples that follow.

It is important to know that a MainMenu and a ContextMenu are very similar in design and functionality. Both are containers for collections of MenuItem objects. We will discuss the ContextMenu a little later in this chapter.

Table 12-2   **Common Menu Properties**

Object	Property Name	Description
Menu	*IsParent*	Returns True if the menu contains menu items.
	MenuItems	A collection of menu items.
	MDIListItem	The *MenuItem* object that is used to display a list of MDI child forms.
ContextMenu only	*SourceControl*	The most recent control to display the context menu.

Table 12-2 **Common Menu Properties**

Object	Property Name	Description
MenuItem only	*Text*	The menu item's text.
	Enabled	Returns True if the menu item is enabled.
	Visible	Returns True if the menu item is visible.
	Checked	If this property is True, a checkmark will be displayed next to the text of the menu item.
	RadioCheck	If this property is True, a radio button will be displayed when the *Checked* property is set to True.
	Shortcut	The shortcut key associated with the menu item.
	ShowShortcut	If this property is True, the shortcut is displayed next to the text of the menu item.
	Mnemonic	Returns the character that is used as the access key.
	MDIList	If this property is True, the menu will list all the MDI child windows displayed within the parent form.
	Parent	Returns the parent menu for the menu item.
	Index	The position of the menu item within the menu.
	DefaultItem	Returns True if this is the default item for its menu. If a menu item is set to be the default item, when the user double-clicks the top-level menu, the action defined by the default menu item will be executed.
	Break	Returns True if this item is placed on a new line (main menu) or in a new column (submenu or context menu).
	BarBreak	Same as *Break*, except that a bar is displayed on the left edge of each menu item that is not a top-level menu item and has its *Break* property set to True.
	MergeType	The behavior of the menu item when its menu is merged with another menu (Add, Replace, Remove, or MergeItems).
	MergeOrder	The zero-based relative position of this menu item when its menu is merged with another menu.
	OwnerDraw	If this property is True, this menu item is drawn by code.

Table 12-3 **Common Menu Methods**

Object	Method name	Description
Menu	*GetMainMenu*	Returns the *MainMenu* object that contains this menu.
	GetContextMenu	Returns the *ContextMenu* object that contains this menu.

Table 12-3   **Common Menu Methods**

Object	Method name	Description
Menu	*MergeMenu*	Merges the items of another menu with the items of this menu. Items are merged according to the values of their *MergeType* and *MergeOrder* properties.
	CloneMenu	Returns an object that is a clone of the current item.
MainMenu only	*GetForm*	Returns the form that contains this menu.
ContextMenu only	*Show(control, point)*	Displays the context menu at the specified position.
MenuItem only	*MergeMenu-(menuitem)*	Merges this menu item with another *MenuItem* object.
	PerformClick	Generates a *Click* event for this menu item.
	PerformSelect	Generates a *Select* event for this menu item.

Table 12-4   **Common Menu Events**

Object	Method name	Description
ContextMenu only	*Popup*	The context menu is displayed.
MenuItem only	*Click*	The menu item is clicked or selected by means of the shortcut key or access key.
	Select	The mouse cursor is placed over the menu item, or the menu item is selected by means of the arrow keys.
	Popup	A menu's list of items is about to be displayed.
	MeasureItem	An owner-drawn menu needs to know the size of the menu item before drawing it.
	DrawItem	An owner-drawn menu is about to draw one of its menu items.

You will use some of these properties and methods to provide code in the appropriate event handlers for each of the menu items in the Bookstore_menu application. Because you are replacing the existing buttons with this menu, most of the code you will need is already written. You simply need to copy the code in the appropriate button's event handler and paste it into the event handler for the associated menu item. After you are sure that everything works correctly, you can delete the existing event handlers for the buttons.

▶ Adding code to menu items

1. In the designer, double-click the Exit menu item on the File menu. The *Click* event handler will be added to the Code Editor. Type the following code statement into the *mnuFileExit_Click* event handler:

```
Application.Exit()
```

The *Application.Exit* method terminates the program. Until now, you have used the statement *Me.Close* to terminate programs. *Me.Close* closes the current form and, if the current form is the only form open in the application, it also terminates the application. In contrast, *Application.Exit* terminates the program by closing all open forms. Because this program has multiple forms open, you need to use *Application.Exit* to close all the open forms and terminate the application.

2. Double-click the Add New Record menu item on the Data menu to add the *mnuDataAddNew_Click* event handler.

3. Locate the event handler for the Add New Record button (*btnAdd_Click*) and select the code in the event handler.

4. Right-click the selected code and select Copy from the context menu.

> **TIP** It's a good idea to copy the code rather than cutting it. That way you can verify that everything works as it should before deleting the event handlers for the buttons and deleting the buttons from the form. If you find that something does not work as expected, you can compare the code and locate the problem.

5. Return to the *mnuDataAddNew_Click* event handler and click between the upper and lower wrapper lines of the event handler. This will set the mouse cursor in the required position.

6. Right-click and then select Paste to place the copied code inside the event handler.

7. Repeat the previous two steps for the rest of the menu items.

8. When you have finished coding, test each menu item thoroughly to ensure that it works as it did when using the buttons.

Another Bug?

There is one small but significant bug that you might have found while testing. When you made a change to a value in a record and then clicked the Save Record menu item, you might have found that the new data was saved to the dataset but not to the database.

This bug could not have been found by comparing code. It has to do with where the focus is when the Save Record menu item is clicked. We'll explain this a bit more and show you how to resolve the problem, but before you correct the bug, let's look at the effect it has on the functionality of the application. After doing that, you'll be able to more clearly see why you need to correct it.

▶ Evaluating the bug

1. Run the application and open the Books form. Make a note of the record you are on.

2. Make a change to the title of any record, but do not tab out of the text box.

3. On the Data menu, select Save.

4. Move to the next record and then back to the record you just edited by using the Next Record and Previous Record menu items on the Navigate menu. Do not use the buttons on the form. It will become obvious why you can't use the buttons in a few moments.

Notice that the change you made to the title is still there. This means that the new title was saved in the dataset.

5. Now close the Books form and reopen it again.

6. Navigate back to the record you had previously edited and notice that the changes you made are not there.

Now let's see what happened and why the changes were not saved to the database.

Remember that each text box is bound to a field in the dataset and that any change to the value inside that text box is reflected in the dataset. That is not the case with the database. For the database to be updated, the *RowState* property for the current record must be changed from *Unchanged* to *Modified*.

In order for the *RowState* property of a record to be changed to *Modified* when the value in a text box is changed, the user must tab out of that text box and the *EndEdit* method must run. Running *EndEdit* on its own will not change the *Row-State* because the *EndEdit* method won't recognize that the value has changed until the control loses focus. You didn't actually tab out of the text box, so there was no change detected and, consequently, when the *EndEdit* method ran, the *RowState* was not changed to *Modified*. Forcing the user to tab out of the text box is not a practical solution, so you must provide a way to handle this that will be transparent to the user.

When a control such as a text box has focus and a menu item is clicked, the text box does not lose focus. You can test this by providing code to display a message in the *LostFocus* event handler of any of the text boxes, placing the cursor in that text box, and then clicking one of the menu items. The message does not appear because the text box never loses focus. Now select any other text box. The message will appear because the original text box does lose focus when you select another text box.

To correct the problem, you must force the text box to lose focus by providing code to shift focus to another control. This can be done in several ways. The method you will be using in this section is quite elegant, but you might find other ways to do the same thing.

▶ **Correcting the bug**

1. Add the boldface code in the following code sample to the last *Case* block of the *mnuDataSave_Click* event handler.

```
Case False
    Dim intRowIndex As Integer = curMgrBooks.Position

    Do
        Me.ActiveControl = Me.GetNextControl(Me.ActiveControl, True)
    Loop Until Me.ActiveControl. CanFocus

    DataSet11.Tables("titles").Rows(intRowIndex).EndEdit()
    txtTitleID.Focus()

End Select
```

Let's look a little closer at the code statement inside the *Do* loop. This statement is telling the program to shift the *ActiveControl* to the next control in the tab order.

```
Me.ActiveControl = Me.GetNextControl(Me.ActiveControl, True)
```

The *GetNextControl* method requires these two arguments:

❑ *Me.ActiveControl* sets the starting control for the search.

❑ *True* instructs the *GetNextControl* method to move forward in the controls collection. If you set this to *False*, you would be telling this method to move backwards.

The loop allows you to test the next control to ensure that it can receive focus before you attempt to set focus on it. Remember that text boxes and buttons are controls that can receive focus, but labels cannot receive focus. Attempting to set the focus on a control that cannot receive focus will throw an exception.

2. Test the program again to ensure that the problem has been corrected.

3. After you are satisfied that the program works as it should, open the form in the designer window and delete all the buttons. After the buttons are deleted, switch to the Code Editor and delete all the event handlers associated with the deleted buttons.

4. After the buttons are deleted, you should adjust the overall height of the Books form and, if necessary, reposition the remaining controls.

The form should now look like Figure 12-10 when it is running. The final code should look like the following code sample. Note that we have provided code samples for both SqlClient (Microsoft SQL Server) and OleDb (Access). Throughout the rest of this chapter, we will provide code samples for both when necessary.

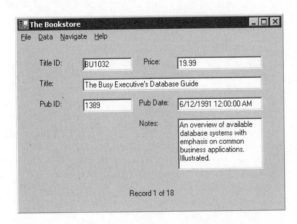

Figure 12-10   Using a menu on the Books form

The code sample using SqlClient components

```
Private Sub frmPubs_Load(ByVal sender As System.Object, _
        ByVal e As System.EventArgs) Handles MyBase.Load
```

```vb
        SqlDataAdapter1.Fill(DataSet11)
        curMgrBooks = _
            CType(Me.BindingContext(DataSet11, "titles"), CurrencyManager)
        UpdateRecordNumber()

    End Sub

    Private Sub UpdateRecordNumber()

        lblRecord.Text = "Record " & curMgrBooks.Position + 1 & " of " & _
            curMgrBooks.Count

    End Sub

    Private Sub mnuFileExit_Click(ByVal sender As System.Object, _
            ByVal e As System.EventArgs) Handles mnuFileExit.Click

        Application.Exit()

    End Sub

    Private Sub mnuDataAdd_Click(ByVal sender As System.Object, _
            ByVal e As System.EventArgs) Handles mnuDataAdd.Click

        curMgrBooks.SuspendBinding()
        m_blnAddNew = True
        For Each ctl As Control In Me.Controls
            If TypeOf (ctl) Is TextBox Then
                CType(ctl, TextBox).Clear()
            End If
        Next
        txtTitleID.Focus()

    End Sub

    Private Sub mnuDataSave_Click(ByVal sender As System.Object, _
            ByVal e As System.EventArgs) Handles mnuDataSave.Click

        Select Case m_blnAddNew
            Case True
                Dim newRow As DataRow
                Dim rowValues(9) As String

                rowValues(0) = txtTitleID.Text
                rowValues(1) = txtTitle.Text
                rowValues(2) = "business"
                rowValues(3) = txtPubID.Text
                rowValues(4) = txtPrice.Text
                rowValues(8) = txtNotes.Text
                rowValues(9) = txtPubDate.Text
                newRow = DataSet11.titles.Rows.Add(rowValues)

            Case False
                Dim intRowIndex As Integer = curMgrBooks.Position

                Do
                    Me.ActiveControl = Me.GetNextControl(Me.ActiveControl, True)
                Loop Until Me.ActiveControl.CanFocus

                DataSet11.Tables("titles").Rows(intRowIndex).EndEdit()
                txtTitleID.Focus()

        End Select
```

```
    SqlDataAdapter1.Update(DataSet11, "titles")
    curMgrBooks.ResumeBinding()
    If m_blnAddNew = True Then
        curMgrBooks.Position = curMgrBooks.Count - 1
        UpdateRecordNumber()
    End If
    m_blnAddNew = False

End Sub

Private Sub mnuDataDelete_Click(ByVal sender As System.Object, _
        ByVal e As System.EventArgs) Handles mnuDataDelete.Click

    DataSet11.titles.Rows(curMgrBooks.Position).Delete()
    SqlDataAdapter1.Update(DataSet11, "titles")

End Sub

Private Sub mnuNavigateFirst_Click(ByVal sender As System.Object, _
        ByVal e As System.EventArgs) Handles mnuNavigateFirst.Click

    curMgrBooks.Position = 0
    UpdateRecordNumber()

End Sub

Private Sub mnuNavigatePrevious_Click(ByVal sender As System.Object, _
        ByVal e As System.EventArgs) Handles mnuNavigatePrevious.Click

    curMgrBooks.Position -= 1
    UpdateRecordNumber()

End Sub

Private Sub mnuNavigateNext_Click(ByVal sender As System.Object, _
        ByVal e As System.EventArgs) Handles mnuNavigateNext.Click

    curMgrBooks.Position += 1
    UpdateRecordNumber()

End Sub

Private Sub mnuNavigateLast_Click(ByVal sender As System.Object, _
        ByVal e As System.EventArgs) Handles mnuNavigateLast.Click

    curMgrBooks.Position = curMgrBooks.Count - 1
    UpdateRecordNumber()

End Sub
```

The code sample using OleDb components

```
Private Sub frmPubs_Load(ByVal sender As System.Object, _
        ByVal e As System.EventArgs) Handles MyBase.Load

    OleDbDataAdapter1.Fill(DataSet11)
    curMgrBooks = _
        CType(Me.BindingContext(DataSet11, "titles"), CurrencyManager)
    UpdateRecordNumber()

End Sub
```

```vbnet
Private Sub UpdateRecordNumber()

    lblRecord.Text = "Record " & curMgrBooks.Position + 1 & " of " & _
        curMgrBooks.Count

End Sub

Private Sub mnuFileExit_Click(ByVal sender As System.Object, _
        ByVal e As System.EventArgs) Handles mnuFileExit.Click

    Application.Exit()

End Sub

Private Sub mnuDataAdd_Click(ByVal sender As System.Object, _
        ByVal e As System.EventArgs) Handles mnuDataAdd.Click

    curMgrBooks.SuspendBinding()
    m_blnAddNew = True
    For Each ctl As Control In Me.Controls
        If TypeOf (ctl) Is TextBox Then
            CType(ctl, TextBox).Clear()
        End If
    Next
    txtTitleID.Focus()

End Sub

Private Sub mnuDataSave_Click(ByVal sender As System.Object, _
        ByVal e As System.EventArgs) Handles mnuDataSave.Click

    Select Case m_blnAddNew
        Case True
            Dim newRow As DataRow
            Dim rowValues(9) As String

            rowValues(0) = txtTitleID.Text
            rowValues(1) = txtTitle.Text
            rowValues(2) = "business"
            rowValues(3) = txtPubID.Text
            rowValues(4) = txtPrice.Text
            rowValues(8) = txtNotes.Text
            rowValues(9) = txtPubDate.Text
            newRow = DataSet11.titles.Rows.Add(rowValues)

        Case False
            Dim intRowIndex As Integer = curMgrBooks.Position

            Do
                Me.ActiveControl = Me.GetNextControl(Me.ActiveControl, True)
            Loop Until Me.ActiveControl.CanFocus

            DataSet11.Tables("titles").Rows(intRowIndex).EndEdit()
            txtTitleID.Focus()

    End Select

    OleDbDataAdapter1.Update(DataSet11, "titles")
    curMgrBooks.ResumeBinding()
    If m_blnAddNew = True Then
        curMgrBooks.Position = curMgrBooks.Count - 1
        UpdateRecordNumber()
```

```
        End If
        m_blnAddNew = False

End Sub

Private Sub mnuDataDelete_Click(ByVal sender As System.Object, _
        ByVal e As System.EventArgs) Handles mnuDataDelete.Click

    DataSet11.titles.Rows(curMgrBooks.Position).Delete()
    OleDbDataAdapter1.Update(DataSet11, "titles")

End Sub

Private Sub mnuNavigateFirst_Click(ByVal sender As System.Object, _
        ByVal e As System.EventArgs) Handles mnuNavigateFirst.Click

    curMgrBooks.Position = 0
    UpdateRecordNumber()

End Sub

Private Sub mnuNavigatePrevious_Click(ByVal sender As System.Object, _
        ByVal e As System.EventArgs) Handles mnuNavigatePrevious.Click

    curMgrBooks.Position -= 1
    UpdateRecordNumber()

End Sub

Private Sub mnuNavigateNext_Click(ByVal sender As System.Object, _
        ByVal e As System.EventArgs) Handles mnuNavigateNext.Click

    curMgrBooks.Position += 1
    UpdateRecordNumber()

End Sub

Private Sub mnuNavigateLast_Click(ByVal sender As System.Object, _
        ByVal e As System.EventArgs) Handles mnuNavigateLast.Click

    curMgrBooks.Position = curMgrBooks.Count - 1
    UpdateRecordNumber()

End Sub
```

Using the *MainMenu* Class

When you add a MainMenu component from the Toolbox, it will remain in your computer's memory for the life of the form that it is associated with. It is instantiated when the form is loaded and isn't destroyed until after the form is closed. If the form requires a change in the menu, such as adding or removing various menu structures, you might need two or more MainMenu components for that form; you will switch between them at the appropriate times. In situations like this, it might be a good idea to use the *MainMenu* class and add the menu items at run time.

In the following example, you will recreate your menu by using the *MainMenu* class. This example will demonstrate how to create the menu at run time. If any of your future programs require the use of this technique, it will be easy to implement it by using this example as a guide.

▶ **Declaring and instantiating *MainMenu* and *MenuItem* objects**

1. Create a copy of the Bookstore program that you have been using in this chapter by copying the Bookstore_menu solution folder in Windows Explorer.

2. Rename the new folder from Copy Of Bookstore_menu to **Bookstore_menuclass**.

3. Open the copy in Visual Studio .NET, and then open the Books form in design view.

4. Select and delete the MainMenu component located in the Component Tray. Do not delete the code associated with the menu items; you will be able to use those event handlers again.

5. Open the Code Editor for the Books form.

6. At the top of the code window, just below the declaration for *m_blnAddNew*, add the following object variable declarations. Note that you are both declaring and instantiating the variables.

```
Private WithEvents mnuMain As New MainMenu
Private WithEvents mnuFile As New MenuItem
Private WithEvents mnuData As New MenuItem
Private WithEvents mnuNavigate As New MenuItem
Private WithEvents mnuHelp As New MenuItem
Private WithEvents mnuFileExit As New MenuItem
Private WithEvents mnuDataAdd As New MenuItem
Private WithEvents mnuDataSave As New MenuItem
Private WithEvents mnuDataSep1 As New MenuItem
Private WithEvents mnuDataDelete As New MenuItem
Private WithEvents mnuNavigateFirst As New MenuItem
Private WithEvents mnuNavigatePrevious As New MenuItem
Private WithEvents mnuNavigateNext As New MenuItem
Private WithEvents mnuNavigateLast As New MenuItem
Private WithEvents mnuHelpAbout As New MenuItem
```

We should point out that you declared and instantiated the *MainMenu* and *MenuItem* objects with the *WithEvents* keyword. Because you want to use the events for these objects, you need to expose them. Using the *WithEvents* keyword in the declaration will add these objects to the Class Name list in the Code Editor, and the events for each object will be listed in the Method Name list.

7. Create a new Sub procedure called **CreateMainMenu**, and then add the code statements shown in the following code sample to it. This procedure will create the structure of the menu.

```
Private Sub CreateMainMenu()

    mnuMain.MenuItems.AddRange(New MenuItem() _
        {mnuFile, mnuData, mnuNavigate, mnuHelp})
    Me.Menu = mnuMain

End Sub
```

8. Add a call to the *CreateMainMenu* Sub procedure at the end of the *frmBooks_Load* event handler. The *Load* event handler should now look like the following code sample.

The code sample using SqlClient components

```
Private Sub frmPubs_Load(ByVal sender As System.Object, _
        ByVal e As System.EventArgs) Handles MyBase.Load

    SqlDataAdapter1.Fill(DataSet11)

    curMgrBooks = _
        CType(Me.BindingContext(DataSet11, "titles"), CurrencyManager)
    UpdateRecordNumber()

    CreateMainMenu()

End Sub
```

The code sample using OleDb components

```
Private Sub frmPubs_Load(ByVal sender As System.Object, _
        ByVal e As System.EventArgs) Handles MyBase.Load

    OleDbDataAdapter1.Fill(DataSet11)

    curMgrBooks = _
        CType(Me.BindingContext(DataSet11, "titles"), CurrencyManager)
    UpdateRecordNumber()

    CreateMainMenu()

End Sub
```

9. Although you are a long way from finishing, go ahead and run the program to see the new menu. Start the program and open the Books form, which is shown in Figure 12-11.

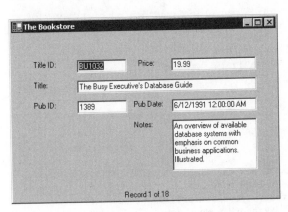

Figure 12-11 Books form with menu containing no menu items

It looks like you have a problem. The menu exists, but unfortunately you can't see it because you haven't provided any text for any of the menu items. You will do that now.

10. Type the boldface code shown here into the *CreateMainMenu* procedure.

```
Private Sub CreateMainMenu()
    mnuMain.MenuItems.AddRange(New MenuItem() _
```

```
        {mnuFile, mnuData, mnuNavigate, mnuHelp})
    Me.Menu = mnuMain

    mnuFile.Text = "&File"
    mnuData.Text = "&Data"
    mnuNavigate.Text = "&Navigate"
    mnuHelp.Text = "&Help"

End Sub
```

11. Run the program again to verify that the top-level menu is there, as shown in Figure 12-12.

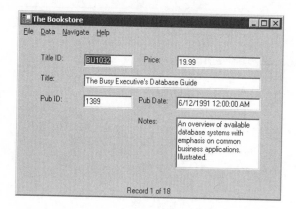

Figure 12-12   Books form displaying the menu

Adding all the submenu items is just as easy. Keep in mind that a menu is a collection of MenuItems. You just added the top-level menu items and can reasonably assume that each one must have a collection of MenuItems. These are the submenu items that you will add now.

12. Add the boldface code shown here to the *CreateMainMenu* procedure.

```
Private Sub CreateMainMenu()
    mnuMain.MenuItems.AddRange(New MenuItem() _
        {mnuFile, mnuData, mnuNavigate, mnuHelp})
    Me.Menu = mnuMain

    mnuFile.Text = "&File"
    mnuData.Text = "&Data"
    mnuNavigate.Text = "&Navigate"
    mnuHelp.Text = "&Help"

    mnuFile.MenuItems.AddRange(New MenuItem() {mnuFileExit})
    mnuData.MenuItems.AddRange(New MenuItem() _
        {mnuDataAdd, mnuDataSave, mnuDataSep1, mnuDataDelete})
    mnuNavigate.MenuItems.AddRange(New MenuItem() _
        {mnuNavigateFirst, mnuNavigatePrevious, mnuNavigateNext, _
            mnuNavigateLast})
    mnuHelp.MenuItems.AddRange(New MenuItem() {mnuHelpAbout})

    mnuFileExit.Text = "E&xit"
    mnuDataAdd.Text = "&Add New Record"
    mnuDataSave.Text = "&Save Record"
    mnuDataSep1.Text = "-"
    mnuDataDelete.Text = "&Delete Record"
    mnuNavigateFirst.Text = "&First Record"
```

```
        mnuNavigatePrevious.Text = "&Previous Record"
        mnuNavigateNext.Text = "&Next Record"
        mnuNavigateLast.Text = "&Last Record"
        mnuHelpAbout.Text = "&About"
```

```
End Sub
```

Now that you have a complete menu structure, you need to provide the functionality. The event handlers for each of the menu items already exist, so you don't have to do too much to get it all working.

When you deleted the MainMenu component, you left the code in place. Although the event handlers remain, the *Handles* statement was deleted from each of the event handlers. Remember that the *Handles* statement connects the procedure to the event that is raised when the menu item is clicked. To provide functionality, you must restore the *Handles* statement to each of the event handlers.

13. Locate the *mnuFileExit_Click* event handler. The event handler is now just a procedure that isn't connected to any event.

14. Add the boldface code statement in the following code sample to the end of the event handler declaration. Adding this statement connects the procedure to the event that is raised by the menu item when it is clicked. Don't forget to add the space and the underscore (line continuation character) at the end of the existing declaration.

```
Private Sub mnuFileExit_Click(ByVal sender As Object, ByVal e As EventArgs) _
        Handles mnuFileExit.Click
    Application.Exit()
End Sub
```

15. Add a *Handles* statement to each of the event handler procedures. Use Table 12-5 to help you add the event handler to the correct event.

Table 12-5　*Handles* **Statements for the** *Bookstore_menuclass* **Event Handlers**

Event handler	*Handles* statement
mnuFileExit_Click	Handles mnuFileExit.Click
mnuDataAdd_Click	Handles mnuDataAdd.Click
mnuDataSave_Click	Handles mnuDataSave.Click
mnuDataDelete_Click	Handles mnuDataDelete.Click
mnuNavigateFirst_Click	Handles mnuNavigateFirst.Click
mnuNavigatePrevious_Click	Handles mnuNavigatePrevious.Click
mnuNavigateNext_Click	Handles mnuNavigateNext.Click
mnuNavigateLast_Click	Handles mnuNavigateLast.Click

16. Run the program and check it thoroughly to make sure everything works as it should. After everything is tested, exit the program and close the solution in Visual Studio .NET.

Creating a Context Menu Using the Designer

As we mentioned at the beginning of the chapter, a context menu is a popup menu that appears when the right mouse button is clicked on an object such as a control or a form. A context menu typically appears when the user clicks the right mouse button while hovering over a form or control. For example, if there were text on the Clipboard and the user wanted to paste the text into a text box, right-clicking the mouse while hovering over the text box would display a context menu, and one of the menu items displayed would be Paste. Selecting the Paste menu item would place the text into the text box. Many controls (including forms) have a *ContextMenu* property. This property can be set at design time or at run time.

In this section, we will show you how to create a *ContextMenu* object by using the ContextMenu component, which is available in the Toolbox. The example involves creating a simple context menu that will be used to edit each of the text boxes. The menu will provide menu items to cut, copy, and paste text. By default, all text boxes come with a fully functional context menu, but there will be times when you do not want users to be able to use all of its choices. At those times, creating a custom context menu is the way to go. Our custom context menu will override the default as soon as you assign it to each of the text boxes' *ContextMenu* properties.

▶ Creating the context menu

1. Open the Bookstore program in the Bookstore_menu solution folder in Visual Studio .NET (the one for which you created the MainMenu by using the designer).

2. Display the Books form in design view.

3. Add a ContextMenu component from the Toolbox to the form. (You might have to scroll down the list of components in the Toolbox.)

4. Rename the ContextMenu from ContextMenu1 to **cmuEdit**.

   The new ContextMenu appears at the top of the form in place of the MainMenu, as shown in Figure 12-13. The top-level menu item will always be displayed as Context Menu. It has no properties and will not show at run time.

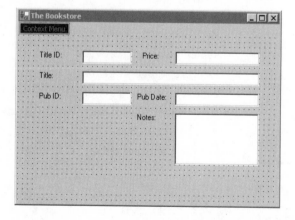

Figure 12-13   The ContextMenu is displayed at the top of the Books form

5. Click once to select Context Menu at the top of the form. A menu item (Type Here) will appear, prompting you to enter the text for the first menu item.

6. Type in the text for each of the menu items, and then change the names by using the Edit Names option. Refer to Table 12-6 for the names and text values to be used for each of the menu items.

Table 12-6   **Menu Item Names and Text Values for the Bookstore_menu Application**

Menu item name	Menu item text
cmuCut	**Cu&t**
cmuCopy	**&Copy**
cmuPaste	**&Paste**

Now that the structure of the context menu is created, you can assign the menu to each of the text boxes.

7. Select all the text boxes on the form, as shown in Figure 12-14.

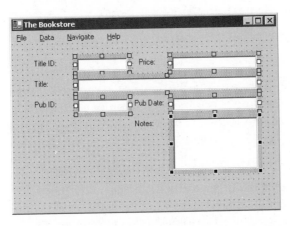

Figure 12-14   Selecting all TextBox controls on the Books form

8. When all the text boxes have been selected, locate the *ContextMenu* property in the Properties window. Click inside the property and select cmuContext from the dropdown list, as shown in Figure 12-15.

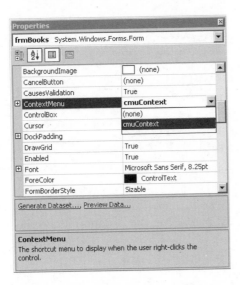

Figure 12-15   Assigning the *ContextMenu* property

The coding for the context menu is quite simple because each text box has *Cut, Copy,* and *Paste* methods that you can use in your code. The only challenge is finding out which of the text boxes caused the context menu to be displayed. Fortunately, this is not too difficult because the context menu has a built-in property that determines which text box prompted the context menu. This property is called *SourceControl,* and it will tell you which text box you are dealing with.

▶ **Coding the context menu**

1. Double-click the Cut menu item. The *cmuCut_Click* event handler will be added to the Code Editor.

2. Type the boldface code shown in the following code sample into the *cmuCut_Click* event handler.

```
Private Sub cmuCut_Click(ByVal sender As System.Object, _
        ByVal e As System.EventArgs) Handles cmuCut.Click

    CType(cmuEdit.SourceControl, TextBox).Cut()

End Sub
```

In the above code statement, you are casting the generic type *SourceControl* to a more specific type of *TextBox.* This is required in order to enable the *Cut* method. If you had used the following code, you would receive a syntax error and the code would not compile.

```
cmuEdit.SourceControl.Cut()
```

3. Do the same thing for each of the other menu items, using the *Copy* method for the Copy menu item and the *Paste* method for the Paste menu item. The final code should look like the following code sample.

```
Private Sub cmuCut_Click(ByVal sender As System.Object, _
        ByVal e As System.EventArgs) Handles cmuCut.Click

    CType(cmuEdit.SourceControl, TextBox).Cut()

End Sub

Private Sub cmuCopy_Click(ByVal sender As System.Object, _
        ByVal e As System.EventArgs) Handles cmuCopy.Click

    CType(cmuEdit.SourceControl, TextBox).Copy()

End Sub

Private Sub cmuPaste_Click(ByVal sender As System.Object, _
        ByVal e As System.EventArgs) Handles cmuPaste.Click

    CType(cmuEdit.SourceControl, TextBox).Paste()

End Sub
```

4. To test the functionality of the context menu, run the program and open the Books form.

5. Select some text in any of the text boxes. The text is highlighted when it is selected. Click the right mouse button, and select Cut from the context menu. The selected text is cut from the text box and placed on the Clipboard.

6. Click the right mouse button again, and select Paste from the context menu. The value is pasted back into the text box.

7. Continue testing until you are satisfied that everything is working as expected. Keep in mind that the *Cut* and *Copy* methods will work only when text is selected.

Using the *ContextMenu* Class

Just as you can create a *MainMenu* by using the class, you can do the same for a *ContextMenu*. To create a context menu by using the *ContextMenu* class, declare and instantiate a *ContextMenu* in the same way that you created the *MainMenu*.

■ Open the Bookstore program in the Bookstore_menuclass solution folder in Visual Studio .NET, and then open the Code Editor for the Books form.

We will start by declaring and instantiating the new context menu and each of the menu items that will be added to the menu. After that we will show you how to create the context menu structure. You will see that the entire process is identical to the process you used to create the *MainMenu*.

The following code shows how the context menu and each menu item are declared and instantiated in code.

```
Private WithEvents cmuEdit As New ContextMenu
Private WithEvents cmuEditCut As New MenuItem
Private WithEvents cmuEditCopy As New MenuItem
Private WithEvents cmuEditPaste As New MenuItem
```

Now we will construct the context menu. We have created a new Sub procedure called *CreateContextMenu*. This Sub procedure can be called from the *Load* event handler of the form or from any other suitable event handler, as shown in the following code sample.

```
Private Sub CreateContextMenu()

    cmuEdit.MenuItems.AddRange(New MenuItem() _
        {cmuEditCut, cmuEditCopy, cmuEditPaste})
    cmuEditCut.Text = "Cu&t"
    cmuEditCopy.Text = "&Copy"
    cmuEditPaste.Text = "&Paste"

    For Each ctl As Control In Me.Controls
        If TypeOf ctl Is TextBox Then
            CType(ctl, TextBox).ContextMenu = cmuEdit
        End If
    Next

End Sub
```

Try It

Modify the menu system you have set up for the Bookstore program in the Bookstore_menu solution folder to contain the top-level menu item Tools. The submenu items for Tools should be Verify Connection and Refresh Data. The Tools menu should appear to the left of the Help menu. Click Tools and drag it to the left of Help to move it. When users click Verify Connection, a message box stating "Connection is valid" should appear; when they click Refresh Data, a message box stating "Data is refreshed" should appear.

What Do You Think?

1. What is the primary difference between a regular menu and a context menu?

2. What are two ways to add a menu to a form?

3. What is the difference between the statements *Me.Close* and *Application.Exit?*

4. What is the *WithEvents* keyword used for?

5. If you do not create a custom context menu for a text box, what is displayed when the user right-clicks the text box at run time?

6. How can you determine which control was right-clicked to prompt the display of a context menu?

TOOLBARS

A **toolbar** typically appears at the top of the screen under the menu. Toolbars display icons that enable users to access commands. They provide a nice touch to any program, giving it a more professional look. Users have come to expect toolbars in the programs they use. Keep in mind that the inclusion of a toolbar should make sense and provide an easier way for the user to interact with the program. If a toolbar increases the complexity of the program and provides no added value, it should not be included.

Toolbars are provided to improve functionality in a program. Generally, you will provide a toolbar button for only the most used or significant functions in the program. Like a menu, a toolbar is a collection object; it has a collection of *ToolBarButtons*. You will now add a Toolbar component from the Toolbox and then add buttons to provide the functionality that you need.

In this example, you will be providing toolbar buttons to run all the actions currently run by the menu items in the Data menu.

▶ Adding a toolbar to the Bookstore application

1. Open the Bookstore application that is stored in the Bookstore_menu solution folder.

2. Display the Books form in design view.

3. Add a Toolbar component from the Toolbox to the form. (You might have to scroll down the Toolbox to find the Toolbar component).

4. Rename the toolbar from Toolbar1 to **tbrBooks**.

5. Locate the *ButtonSize* property and set it to **16, 16**. This reduces the size of the toolbar, as shown in Figure 12-16.

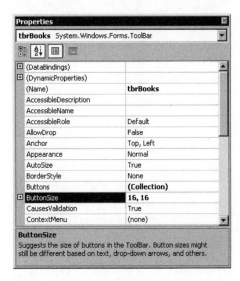

Figure 12-16   Setting the *ButtonSize* property

6. Click the *Buttons Collection* property to open the ToolBarButton Collection Editor, as shown in Figure 12-17.

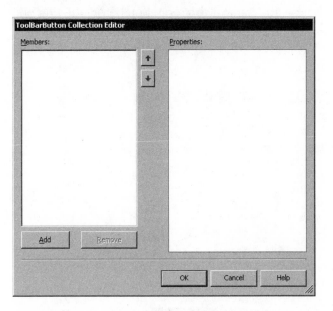

Figure 12-17   The ToolBarButton Collection Editor

7. Click the Add button to add the first toolbar button, as shown in Figure 12-18.

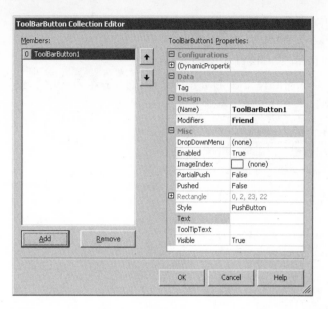

Figure 12-18   Adding a button to the *ToolBarButtons* collection

8. Rename the button from ToolBarButton1 to **tbbAddNew**, and then type **Add** in the *Text* property.

9. Add another toolbar button to save the record.

10. Rename the button from ToolBarButton1 to **tbbSave**, and then type **Save** in the *Text* property.

11. Add a third button to provide a space between the Save and the Delete buttons. Add a new button and name it **tbbSep1**, but, before moving on, locate the *Style* property in the Properties window and set the style to Separator, as shown in Figure 12-19. Do not provide a *Text* value for the separator.

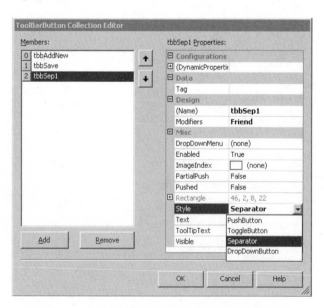

Figure 12-19   Setting the *Style* property

12. Add a fourth button, name it **tbbDelete**, and then type **Delete** in its *Text* property.

13. Click OK to close the ToolBarButton Collection Editor and run the program.

14. Open the Books form and admire your work. Notice the separation between the second and third buttons, as shown in Figure 12-20.

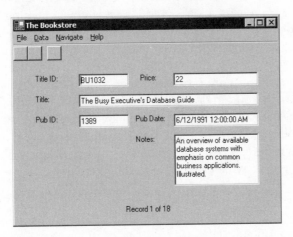

Figure 12-20   Displaying the toolbar on the Books form

Don't worry that the toolbar buttons are blank right now. We will add an ImageList control in a few moments that will be used to provide the images that the toolbar will use.

Coding the Toolbar Buttons

A toolbar does not work like a menu with respect to the collection. With a menu, you can code each of the menu items separately because each menu item has its own events. A toolbar button does not have its own events; it relies on the toolbar to provide that functionality.

To determine which button was clicked, you will use the additional information provided in the *ToolBarButtonEventArgs* parameter in the toolbar's *Click* event handler.

▶ **Adding code to toolbar buttons**

1. Double-click anywhere on the toolbar in design view to add the *tbrBooks_ButtonClick* event handler to the Code Editor.

2. Type the boldface code shown here in the *tbrBooks_ButtonClick* event handler.

```
Private Sub tbrBooks_ButtonClick(ByVal sender As System.Object, _
        ByVal e As System.Windows.Forms.ToolBarButtonClickEventArgs) _
        Handles tbrBooks.ButtonClick

    Select Case e.Button.Text
        Case "Add"
            mnuDataAdd_Click(Nothing, Nothing)
        Case "Save"
```

```
                mnuDataSave_Click(Nothing, Nothing)
            Case "Delete"
                mnuDataDelete_Click(Nothing, Nothing)
        End Select

    End Sub
```

You already have code written to perform the required actions, so calling the existing event handlers from each of the *Case* blocks makes sense. This is more efficient than providing specific code in each of the *Case* blocks, and it saves the extra typing. Remember that you should avoid writing duplicate code whenever possible. Having the code in one place makes code maintenance easier and, because there is less code to compile, there will be some improvement in the performance of the program. Notice that the two arguments you are providing when you call the existing event handler are *Nothing, Nothing*. You can do this because the current method call has no access to the *sender* object or the *EventArgs*. All you are doing is passing placeholders for the real arguments that will be picked up from the target event handler when it runs. Other books or references might code the calling statement by using `mnuDataAdd_Click(sender, e)`, which also is perfectly acceptable.

Using an ImageList

An ImageList is a repository for the images that you will use for the buttons on the toolbar. The ImageList has a collection of Images, and each image in the collection will be assigned to one of the buttons in the *ToolBarButtons* collection.

▶ Adding images to the toolbar buttons

1. Open the Books form in design view, and add an ImageList component to the form. (You might have to scroll down the Toolbox to find the ImageList component.) The ImageList will be added to the Component Tray below the form.

2. Select the ImageList and rename it from ImageList1 to **imglstBooks**.

3. Verify that the *ImageSize* property is set to 16, 16, as shown in Figure 12-21. This matches the value that you set in the toolbar's *ButtonSize* property.

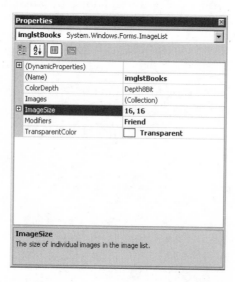

Figure 12-21   Renaming the ImageList and verifying the *ImageSize* property

4. Click the *Images Collection* property to display the Image Collection Editor, as shown in Figure 12-22.

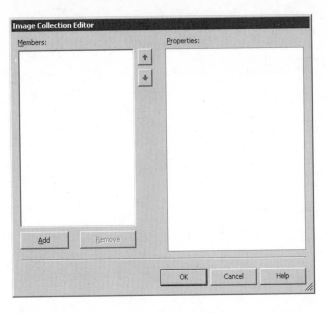

Figure 12-22   The Image Collection Editor

5. Click the Add button to add the first image. In the dialog box that appears, navigate to the folder that contains the images. You need images for the New, Save, and Delete buttons. The choice of images is up to you, but for now navigate to C:\Program Files\Microsoft Visual Studio .NET 2003\Common7\Graphics\bitmaps\Tlbr_W95 to select the images, as shown in Figure 12-23. (This assumes that you have installed Visual Studio .NET 2003 in its default location.)

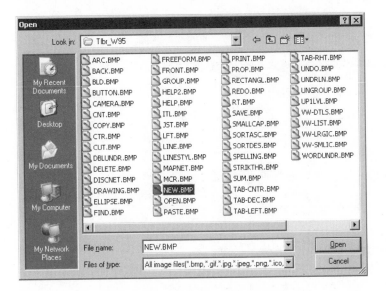

Figure 12-23   Selecting the images for the *ImageList*

6. Add two more images, one for the Save button (Save.bmp) and the other for the Delete button (Delete.bmp). The separator will not have an image.

7. After you have added the images, click OK, select the toolbar in the form, and then locate the *ImageList* property in the Properties window.

8. Click the *ImageList* property, and then select imglstBooks from the list, as shown in Figure 12-24.

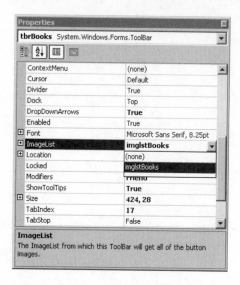

Figure 12-24   Setting the *ImageList* property

9. Locate the *Buttons Collection* property, and then click the build button to open the ToolBarButton Collection Editor.

10. Select the first button, tbbAdd, and then locate the *ImageIndex* property.

11. Click the down arrow and select the first image in the list. If you added the images in the correct sequence, it will have an index value of 0, as shown in Figure 12-25.

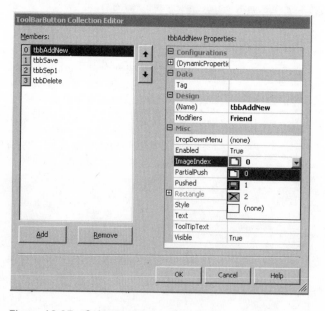

Figure 12-25   Selecting the *ImageIndex*

12. Select each button in turn, and set the *ImageIndex* as appropriate. Remember that the separator button does not have an image.

13. After you have finished, close the ToolBarButton Collection Editor. The toolbar should now display the correct images.

14. Run the program once again, and open the Books form.

15. Test the operation of the buttons to verify that everything works as expected.

Using the *Toolbar* Class

Creating the toolbar from the *Toolbar* class is a little different from creating a Main-Menu or a ContextMenu. You still have to declare and instantiate the Toolbar by using the *WithEvents* keyword, but that's where the similarity ends.

While you're creating the toolbar by using the *Toolbar* class, take the time to compare what you're doing now with what you did in the previous exercise when you used the Toolbar component. Although you will not set all of the properties, you'll see that the same properties that you saw in the Properties window are also available in code. Pay particular attention to how you set the size of the buttons on the toolbar.

▶ Using the *Toolbar* class

1. Open the Bookstore project in the Bookstore_menuclass solution folder in Visual Studio .NET.

2. Display the Books form in the Code Editor.

3. Type the following toolbar and toolbar button declarations below the existing declarations for the MainMenu.

```
Private WithEvents tbrBooks As New ToolBar
Private tbbAddNew As New ToolBarButton
Private tbbSave As New ToolBarButton
Private tbbSep1 As New ToolBarButton
Private tbbDelete As New ToolBarButton
```

4. Create a new Sub procedure named CreateToolbar, as shown in the following code sample. This procedure should be called from the *Load* event handler of the form. Be sure to add the calling statement directly after the call to create the MainMenu. Notice that in this procedure you are also creating an ImageList object from the *ImageList* class. This is done here because the ImageList is only required when the toolbar is created and properly configured.

In order for the ImageList to correctly locate the images that it needs, you must specify the location of each of the images. We know that the images are located in the default folder C:\Program Files\Microsoft Visual Studio .NET 2003\Common7 \Graphics\bitmaps\Tlbr_W95, but if we were to give this program to a user, that folder would not exist on their computer. To resolve this and make it easier to code, we should copy the required images to a new folder and include that folder in this solution. Complete the following steps to copy the images and place them in the appropriate location.

1. Open Windows Explorer and navigate to the bin folder for this solution.

2. Open the bin folder and create a new folder inside the bin folder and name it Images.

3. Navigate back to the folder that contains the images that we want to copy: C:\Program Files\Microsoft Visual Studio .NET 2003\Common7\Graphics \bitmaps\Tlbr_W95.

4. Select and copy the following images: NEW.BMP, SAVE.BMP, and DELETE.BMP.

5. Return to the Images folder that you just created and paste the copied images to that folder.

6. Once the images are in the proper location, close Windows Explorer.

Now you can write the code that will create the ToolBar. Notice that when we specify the location of the images, we include the code statement Application .StartupPath. This code statement is used to refer to the location of the executable file for the application. The .exe file will always be located in the bin folder and that is where you created the Images folder.

```vb
Private Sub CreateToolbar()

    ' Create the ImageList
    Dim imglstBooks As New ImageList

    ' Add the images to the Images collection. The bitmap files
    ' have been copied to a new folder called Images. This folder
    ' was created inside the bin folder for the project
    imglstBooks.Images.Add(Image.FromFile _
        (Application.StartupPath & "\Images\New.bmp"))

    imglstBooks.Images.Add(Image.FromFile _
        (Application.StartupPath & "\Images\Save.bmp"))

    imglstBooks.Images.Add(Image.FromFile _
        (Application.StartupPath & "\Images\Delete.bmp"))

    ' Add the toolbar to the controls collection of the form
    Me.Controls.Add(tbrBooks)

    ' Add the buttons to the button collection of the toolbar,
    ' set the ImageList property to the new ImageList and set
    ' the size of the buttons that will be added to the toolbar
    With tbrBooks
        .Buttons.AddRange(New ToolBarButton() _
            {tbbAddNew, tbbSave, tbbSep1, tbbDelete})
        .ImageList = imglstBooks
        .ButtonSize = New Size(16, 16)
    End With

    ' Set the ImageIndex assign the Text value
    ' for each of the buttons...
    With tbbAddNew
        .ImageIndex = 0
        .Text = "Add New"
    End With

    With tbbSave
        .ImageIndex = 1
        .Text = "Save"
    End With
```

```
' Set the style of the button to be used as a separator
With tbbSep1
    .Style = ToolBarButtonStyle.Separator
End With

With tbbDelete
    .ImageIndex = 2
    .Text = "Delete"
End With

End Sub
```

1. Select tbrBooks from the Class Name list, and then select ButtonClick from the Method Name list. This will add the event handler to the Code Editor.

2. Type the boldface code shown here inside the *tbrBooks_ButtonClick* event handler.

```
Private Sub tbrBooks_ButtonClick(ByVal sender As Object, _
        ByVal e As System.Windows.Forms.ToolBarButtonClickEventArgs) _
        Handles tbrBooks.ButtonClick

    Dim intButton As Integer = tbrBooks.Buttons.IndexOf(e.Button)

    Select Case intButton
        Case 0
            mnuDataAdd_Click(Nothing, Nothing)
        Case 1
            mnuDataSave_Click(Nothing, Nothing)
        Case 2
            ' this is the separator
        Case 3
            mnuDataDelete_Click(Nothing, Nothing)
    End Select

End Sub
```

3. Run the program. The toolbar will appear as shown in Figure 12-26.

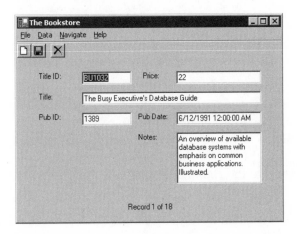

Figure 12-26   Displaying the toolbar created with the *Toolbar* class

4. Test the program to make sure that each toolbar button works as expected.

Inside the Code

As we mentioned earlier, creating the toolbar from the *Toolbar* class is a little different from creating either the main menu or the context menu.

```
Private WithEvents tbrBooks As New ToolBar
Private tbbAddNew As New ToolBarButton
Private tbbSave As New ToolBarButton
Private tbbSep1 As New ToolBarButton
Private tbbDelete As New ToolBarButton
```

From the declarations, you can see that the toolbar is declared and instantiated with events, but the buttons are not. Remember that, when you used the Toolbar component and coded the *Click* event handler for the toolbar, we explained that a toolbar button does not raise any events that you can use, but when the toolbar is clicked, additional information is provided from the *ToolBarButtonClickEventArgs* that tells you which button was clicked.

In the *CreateToolbar* procedure, you are declaring and instantiating an *ImageList* object by using the *ImageList* class, and then configuring the new toolbar. Much of the code is self-explanatory, but there are a few things that we should explain.

```
imglstBooks.Images.Add(Image.FromFile _
    (Application.StartupPath & "\Images\New.bmp"))
```

When adding the images to the *Images* collection of the *ImageList* object, you must add a fully formed image; just referencing the name of the file will not work. The statement *Image.FromFile* locates the image file and places the image in memory. The image is then added to the *Images* collection. Using the *Application.StartupPath* statement will allow you to locate the Images folder, which was created in the same folder as the program's executable file.

You might remember that when you created the toolbar by using the Toolbar component, you set the size of the buttons by using the *ButtonSize* property of the toolbar. Doing this in code is not too difficult, but it is different. Here is the code to size the buttons:

```
With tbrBooks
    ...
    .ButtonSize = New Size(16, 16)
End With
```

Size is a structure that is part of the *System.Drawing* namespace. The *Size* structure stores a pair of integers that represent the height and width of a rectangle. In this case, the rectangle is the button. You are creating a new *Size* structure and setting its height and width to 16 and 16, respectively. After the new *Size* structure is created, you assign the structure to the *ButtonSize* property. The values 16, 16 define the height and width in points.

The last piece of code we need to explain is in the *tbrBooks_Click* event handler. When you created this event handler by using the Toolbar component, you used the *Text* property of each button to determine which button was clicked. In this procedure, we will show you a different way of determining which button was clicked. Take another look at the code:

```
Private Sub tbrBooks_ButtonClick(ByVal sender As Object, _
        ByVal e As System.Windows.Forms.ToolBarButtonClickEventArgs) _
        Handles tbrBooks.ButtonClick

    Dim intButton As Integer = tbrBooks.Buttons.IndexOf(e.Button)

    Select Case intButton
        Case 0
            mnuDataAddNew_Click(Nothing, Nothing)
        Case 1
            mnuDataSave_Click(Nothing, Nothing)
        Case 3
            mnuDataDelete_Click(Nothing, Nothing)
    End Select
End Sub
```

In the preceding code, you're using the *IndexOf* method to retrieve the index of the button that was clicked. Using the *IndexOf* method is a little more efficient than evaluating the *Text* property because, as you already know, comparing integer values is always more efficient than comparing text values. The downside (there is always a downside) is that if you dynamically insert additional buttons into the toolbar, the indexing will change, which will result in a functional failure of the program.

Other than the slight improvement in efficiency, there is another reason to use the *IndexOf* method. If the toolbar emulates a particular menu structure, you can remove the *Select Case* statement and run a single line of code that will do exactly what you want. Take a look at the code:

```
Private Sub tbrBooks_ButtonClick(ByVal sender As Object, _
        ByVal e As System.Windows.Forms.ToolBarButtonClickEventArgs) _
        Handles tbrBooks.ButtonClick

    Dim intButton As Integer = tbrBooks.Buttons.IndexOf(e.Button)

    mnuData.MenuItems(intButton).PerformClick()
End Sub
```

Remember that for the preceding code to work, the index of each button must match the index of the menu item.

Using ToolTips

Another way to help users navigate the GUI for your application is to include **ToolTips** that briefly describe the purposes of buttons and controls on a form. The ToolTip for a button or control appears automatically when the user hovers the mouse pointer over the button or control. Let's look at how you can add ToolTips to the toolbar buttons on the Books form.

▶ **Adding ToolTips to buttons on the Books form**

1. Open the Books project in the Bookstore_menu solution folder.

2. Open the Books form in design view, and then click the *Buttons collection* property to display the ToolBarButton Collection Editor.

3. Select one of the buttons (not the separator) and locate the *ToolTipText* property.

4. Using the information in Table 12-7, provide a ToolTip for each of the buttons.

Table 12-7   **Tooltips for the Bookstore Application**

Button	*ToolTipText*
tbbAdd	**Add a new record**
tbbSave	**Save the current record**
tbbDelete	**Delete the current record**

5. Click OK to close the ToolBarButton Collection Editor.

6. Run the program again, and open the Books form.

7. Hover the mouse pointer over any one of the buttons for a moment, and the ToolTip will appear, as shown in Figure 12-27.

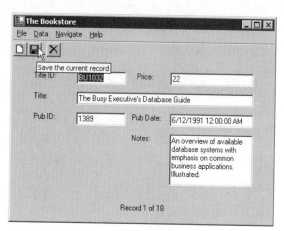

Figure 12-27   Testing ToolTips on the Books form

Try It

Add two buttons to the toolbar you created for the Books form in the Bookstore_menu solution folder that will perform the same actions as the Verify Connection and Refresh Data menu items that you added in the Try It exercise for the previous section in this chapter. The images for these two new buttons should come from the C:\Program Files\Microsoft Visual Studio .NET 2003\Common7\Graphics\bitmaps\Tlbr_W95 folder that you used earlier in this section. Select any image you would like to use for each of these two new toolbar buttons. Also add an appropriate ToolTip for each of these two new toolbar buttons.

What Do You Think?

1. What Toolbox component is used to add a toolbar to a form?

2. How can you determine which button on a toolbar was clicked?

3. How do you open the ToolBarButton Collection Editor when you are creating a toolbar for a form?

4. What is the purpose of the ImageList component?

5. What kind of information would you include in a ToolTip for a button?

6. When is a ToolTip displayed on a form?

Q&A

Q. How will I know that a menu is required in an application?

A. There is no clear answer to that. It really depends on the complexity of the program. If the user interface is cluttered with buttons and other controls, a menu is a good way to organize the functionality and at the same time clean up some of the clutter.

Q. I want to incorporate a menu, but I'm not sure what menu items to include. Where can I find examples to help me?

A. Most applications have menus. At the beginning of this chapter, we showed several examples of menu structures in Word, Excel, and PowerPoint. Look at the menu structures in other applications, and you will start to see commonalities among them. Providing a standardized menu structure allows the users of your program to quickly become comfortable with the interface and concentrate on learning the specific functionality that the program provides, rather than getting bogged down with trying to understand the menu.

Q. I have a top-level menu called Edit in my program that contains submenu items for Cut, Copy, and Paste. Is there some way to recreate this menu as a context menu without duplicating everything?

A. You can do this in a couple of ways. The first way, and probably the easiest way, is to use the *MergeMenu* method to merge an existing menu with the context menu you want to create. To add the new context menu to all the text boxes on the current form, declare and instantiate a class-level *ContextMenu* object. In the *Form_Load* event, or in another suitable event handler, add the code shown in the following code sample.

```
Private cmuEdit As New ContextMenu

Private Sub Form1_Load(ByVal sender As System.Object, _
      ByVal e As System.EventArgs) Handles MyBase.Load

    cmuEdit.MergeMenu(mnuEdit)
    For Each ctl As Control In Me.Controls
```

```
            If TypeOf ctl Is TextBox Then
                CType(ctl, TextBox).ContextMenu = cmuEdit
            End If
        Next
End Sub
```

The only disadvantage of using the *MergeMenu* method is that it adds all the menu items to the new context menu. If you want to add only selected menu items, you must use the second way, which is to clone each menu item and add it to the new context menu. This can be done by looping through each menu item in the existing menu as shown in the following code example, or, if you want only certain menu items, you have to address each one individually.

```
For intItem As Integer = 0 To mnuEdit.MenuItems.Count - 1
    cmuEdit.MenuItems.Add(mnuEdit.MenuItems(intItem).CloneMenu)
Next
```

Q. Why do I have to use a separate ImageList component to provide the images for toolbar buttons?

A. The ImageList component can be used to create a collection of images to be used with other controls that can accept an image, such as a PictureBox control. Just as you would refrain from providing duplicate functionality in your applications, Microsoft decided not to include an *Image* collection inside the Toolbar component. Instead, the ImageList component can be filled with images, and each image can be assigned to an individual toolbar button.

WRAPPING UP

- You can use any of the Microsoft Office applications, or any other program that contains a menu or a toolbar, to help you design your own menus and toolbars. Standardized menus and toolbars help your users by providing them with a familiar interface.

- A menu can be added to a form. MenuItem objects are added to the menu's *MenuItems* collection. Top-level menu items contain one or more submenu items. Submenu items are selected to perform a task or to display other submenu items.

- A MainMenu component can be placed in a form's Component Tray. It will appear at the top of the form at run time. A design-time view of the menu will appear on the form, allowing you to construct the menu.

- A context menu appears when the user clicks the right mouse button over a form or control. The *ContextMenu* property is used to determine what menu will appear, because the context menu and the ContextMenu object are used to define the context menu itself.

- The *MainMenu* and *ContextMenu* objects are similar. They have properties, methods, and events that you can use to configure them as needed.

- You can also add a main menu and a context menu to a form at run time by using the *MainMenu* and *ContextMenu* classes and instantiating them. Using the *MainMenu* and *ContextMenu* classes makes it easier to change the contents of the menu at run time.

- You can add a toolbar to a form by using the Toolbar component. The toolbar contains a collection of ToolBarButtons that define the functionality and appearance of the buttons on the toolbar.

- An ImageList is used to hold a collection of images that can be assigned to each of the buttons on a toolbar.

- You can add a *Toolbar* or an *ImageList* object to a form at run time by creating an instance of the *Toolbar* or *ImageList* class.

- ToolTips are used to provide hints to the user as to what a button or control is to be used for. You program ToolTips by using the *ToolTipText* property of the control.

KEYWORDS

context menu

submenu item

ToolTip

menu

toolbar

top-level menu item

REVIEW QUESTIONS

1. You insert a separator bar between menu items by adding a menu item and placing a(n) _____ in the *Text* property.

    a. underscore

    b. hyphen

    c. space

    d. asterisk

2. Which event of the *MenuItem* object is most commonly used to run code?

    a. *Popup*

    b. *Click*

    c. *Select*

    d. *Perform*

3. Which of the following statements will close all open forms and terminate the program?

    a. `Me.Exit`

    b. `Application.Close`

    c. `Me.Close`

    d. `Application.Exit`

4. The _____ property must be changed from *Unchanged* to *Modified* in order for a database to be updated to reflect changes made to data on a form.

    a. *DataChange*

    b. *RowState*

    c. *RowChange*

    d. *DataUpdate*

5. The control on a form that has focus is the _____.

    a. ActiveControl

    b. CurrentControl

    c. FocusControl

    d. ClickedControl

6. Which keyword must you include when an object is instantiated in order to expose the events for that object?

    a. *Handles*

    b. *WithEvents*

    c. *Using*

    d. *HandleEvents*

7. Which property is used to overwrite the default context menu that is assigned to each control on a form?

    a. *DefaultOverride*

    b. *OverrideContextMenu*

    c. *ContextMenu*

    d. *DefaultContextMenu*

8. Which parameter in a toolbar's *Click* event handler is used to determine which button on the toolbar was clicked?

    a. *ClickedButtonEvent*

    b. *ToolBarClicked*

    c. *ClickedToolBarArgs*

    d. *ToolBarButtonEventArgs*

9. Which component is used to hold the images that are displayed on the buttons in a toolbar?

    a. ImageList

    b. ToolbarImageList

    c. ToolbarImages

    d. ListImages

10. Which property of the Button control is used to enter a message that is displayed as a ToolTip for that button?

    a. *ToolTipText*

    b. *TipText*

    c. *Text*

    d. *ButtonToolTipText*

11. Submenu items should never be used to perform tasks. True or false?

12. You can change the text of a menu item by clicking it once in design view and then typing the new text value. True or false?

13. Although you can type code into the *Click* event for a top-level menu item, this is not recommended because the code will never be called. True or false?

14. If you want to change a menu for a form at run time, you should use the *MainMenu* class. True or false?

15. Each button on a toolbar has its own *Click* event handler to specify what action it should take when it is clicked. True or false?

16. The object that appears at the top of the form and that contains a collection of *MenuItem* objects is called the _____ collection object.

17. A top-level menu item is used to display one or more _____ items.

18. A(n) _____ menu appears when the user right-clicks a form or control.

19. A toolbar is a collection object that contains a collection of _____.

20. The message that appears when you hover the mouse pointer over a control is called a(n) _____.

STEP BY STEP

In this project for the Baldwin Museum of Science, you will create a form that will be used to register an event that will occur at the museum. The form will contain a menu system to help the user complete the form and manage existing events.

The form for this application will look like Figure 12-28.

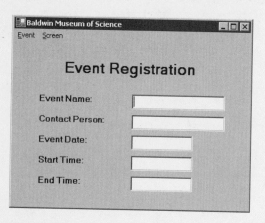

Figure 12-28   Completed Event form

▶ Creating a new project

1. Open Visual Studio .NET if it isn't already open.

2. Click the New Project button on the Start Page.

3. Click Visual Basic Projects under Project Types and Windows Application under Templates.

4. Type **EventCh12** in the Name box.

5. Browse to the location in which you are storing your projects.

6. Click OK.

▶ Configuring the form and changing the startup object

1. Right-click Form1.vb in Solution Explorer and rename Form1.vb as **Event.vb**. Press ENTER.

2. Click once in the title bar of the form and change the *(Name)* property of the form to **frmEvent**.

3. Change the *Text* property of the form to **Baldwin Museum of Science**, and then press ENTER.

4. Right-click the EventCh12 project name in Solution Explorer, and then select Properties.

5. Change the startup object to frmEvent, and then click OK.

▶ Setting up the form

1. Add the required Label controls and TextBox controls to the form, as shown in Figure 12-28. Assign the labels and text boxes appropriate *(Name)* and *Text* properties.

▶ Adding the menu to the form

1. Add a MainMenu control to the form from the Toolbox. Set its *(Name)* property to **mnuMainMenu**.

2. Click in the menu area at the top of the form where it says Type Here.

3. Type **&Event** and then set the *(Name)* property for this menu item to **mnuEvent** and press ENTER.

4. Continue this process to add the menu items shown in Table 12-8.

Table 12-8 **Event Form Menu Items**

Top-level menu	Submenu item	Name	Text
Event		**mnuEvent**	**&Event**
	New	**mnuEventNew**	**&New**
	Update	**mnuEventUpdate**	**&Update**
	Delete	**mnuEventDelete**	**&Delete**
	(Separator bar)	**mnuSep1**	–
	Find	**mnuEventFind**	**&Find**
Screen		**mnuScreen**	**&Screen**
	Clear	**mnuScreenClear**	**&Clear**
	(Separator bar)	**mnuSep2**	–
	Exit	**mnuScreenExit**	**&Exit**

▶ Saving and testing your project

1. On the File menu, select Save All to save your work.

2. On the Debug menu, select Start to run your project.

3. Test the program by clicking each menu item. You did not add any code to make the menus do anything in this exercise, so you will be verifying only that the menus look correct.

4. On the Debug menu, select Stop Debugging to end the program.

5. On the File menu, select Close Solution to close the project.

6. Close Visual Studio .NET.

FINISH THE CODE

To complete this exercise, open the WoodgroveBankCh12 project that came in your student file. This project contains a form that customers of the bank can use to make payments against outstanding loans they have with the bank. Complete the form by adding a toolbar that will contain buttons that perform the same actions as the menu items on the form. Also add ToolTips to the buttons on the toolbar.

JUST HINTS

In this exercise, you will create a form for Fabrikam, Inc., that will be used to calculate the shipping costs for a customer's order. The following fields should be displayed on the form:

- Order Number
- Shipping Method (ground, 2nd-day air, next day)
- Total Weight
- Value of Contents
- Shipping Cost
- Rush Charge
- Insurance Charge
- Total Cost

A toolbar with buttons to perform the following commands should be added to the form:

- Calculate shipping cost. Calculate the shipping cost by multiplying the total weight by $.25 for ground, $.50 for 2nd-day air, and $.75 for next day.
- Rush order. Add $10 to the shipping cost.
- Insurance. Add 1 percent of the value of the contents to the shipping cost.
- Recalculate total cost. Add the shipping cost, rush charge, and insurance charge, and display the total in the Total Cost field.
- Clear. Clear the contents of all fields on the form.

Include descriptive ToolTips for each button on the toolbar.

ON YOUR OWN

To complete this project for Tailspin Toys, copy the solution you created for Tailspin Toys in Chapter 9. Rename the solution folder to **TailspinToysCh12**. Open the project and replace the buttons on the form with a menu system. The menu items should perform the same operations as the buttons.

MORE PRACTICE

1. Design a menu system on paper for a form that has commands that allow the user to perform the following tasks: Open File, Save File, Close File, Print, Preview Output, Set Up Page, and Exit. Show the hierarchy of top-level menu items and submenu items.

2. Write the object variable declarations that would be required to create the menu system you designed in the previous exercise. Use the *MainMenu* class.

3. Design a toolbar on paper for a form that has the menu items shown in Table 12-9. For the purpose of this exercise, assume the toolbar buttons will display the name of the command they run rather than an image. Show separators as spaces between the commands.

Table 12-9   **Menu Items**

Top-level menu item	Submenu item
File	Open
	Save
	Close
Edit	Modify
	Undo
Tools	Option
Help	Index
	About

4. Write the ToolTips you would create for each of the buttons you added to the toolbar in the previous exercise.

5. Create a Microsoft Visual Basic .NET program that provides the user with a screen that can be used to create and edit a document. Include a menu system that provides the standard file and editing commands, such as those found in Notepad. You might want to use a large TextBox control to create the area in which users can type in their documents.

6. Create a Visual Basic .NET program that has one form with a toolbar that contains the buttons needed to play a bowling game. The form can be empty except for the toolbar, and there will be no actual code behind the buttons. You should include ToolTips for each toolbar button. Table 12-10 contains the button ToolTip text and the image files that should be used for the toolbar. The images can be found in C:\Program Files\Microsoft Visual Studio .NET 2003\Common7\Graphics\bitmaps\Tlbr_W95.

Table 12-10   **Toolbar ToolTips and Image Files**

ToolTip	Image file
Start a new game	new.bmp
Pause the game	prop.bmp
End the game	delete.bmp
Enter names of bowlers	smallcap.bmp
Reset score for one frame	undo.bmp
Print game scores	print.bmp
Calculate player average	sum.bmp
Call for lane assistance	help.bmp

7. Create a Visual Basic .NET program with one form that is used to set up a dental appointment for a patient. The user should be able to enter the patient's name and appointment time and date. The following commands should be provided in the menu and on the toolbar:

- ❑ Add appointment

- ❑ Modify appointment

- ❑ Delete appointment

- ❑ Print appointment reminder

- ❑ Close screen

When each menu or toolbar button is clicked, a message box should appear restating the purpose of that command. You should also include a context menu for each text box that contains the commands Add Appointment, Modify Appointment, and Delete Appointment.

CHAPTER 13
CLASSES AND OBJECTS

Believe it or not, you have been using classes and objects since Chapter 1. The console window and the forms you have used are classes. The TextBox and Label controls are classes. In fact, practically everything in Microsoft .NET is a class. When a class is instantiated, it becomes an instance of that class and is referred to as an *object*. In this chapter, we will present information that will help you to create classes that are robust and functional when used in your applications. We will also provide real-world analogies that will help you to understand the concepts we are discussing.

Upon completion of this chapter, you will be able to:

■ Learn the difference between a class and an object.

■ Understand the structure of classes.

■ Create a class, including the public and private interfaces.

■ Know what is meant by *encapsulation*.

■ Use a constructor to create an instance of a class.

■ Use a destructor to terminate an instance of a class.

■ Determine the expected lifetime of an object.

■ Find out what the garbage collector is.

■ Develop a class that inherits from a base class.

■ Understand visual inheritance.

■ Use polymorphism through inheritance.

BASIC CLASS CONCEPTS

The best place to start is to look at the difference between a class and an object. A **class** is the plan of an object, whereas an **object** is an instance of that plan. A class is analogous to a blueprint for a building, and an object is analogous to the building that is constructed from the blueprint. If you were constructing a house, you would draw up the plan for the house. This would be the creation of the class. You would then give the plan to a builder who would build the house. This would be the creation of the object. In other words, you would **instantiate** the class. The challenge is not the creation of the object; it is the design of the class.

Why Use Classes?

There are several advantages to creating and using classes in your applications:

- **Abstracting functionality.**   Classes help you to separate or *abstract* functionality away from the main part of the program. In our first example, the *Vehicle* class, you will see that the class, after it is instantiated, will be capable of functioning as a vehicle. When the Vehicle object is created, you will be able to refer to its public properties and run its public methods. Providing this kind of functionality within the main part of the program can sometimes lead to confusing code that might not work as you had intended it to.

- **Specializing.**   Classes should be specialized. This means that the class should be designed to be good at one thing and one thing only. Creating a class that can do many things generally results in a failure of the class to do anything right. For example, a class that is designed as a vehicle should not try to also act like a toaster.

- **Reducing complexity.**   A colleague of ours once said, "If your application is getting too complex, create more classes." What he meant was that it's easy to continue adding more and more functionality to a form's code module until you get to the point in which it becomes so cluttered that it's hard to follow the logic and flow of the program. This is like having a poorly organized cabinet that you use to store too many different kinds of things. Without some organization, it's easy for things to get lost or become useless because you can't access them.

- **Reusing code.**   Reusing code is important when you program for a living. If you write code that can be used in many programs, it makes sense to use it over and over again. Rather than having to type it into every program, you can compile it once and reference it in other programs.

The Structure of a Class

The structure of a class can be described in terms of:

- Its accessibility to the rest of the world, that is, whether it's public or private.

- The public interface. The public interface defines how the program will interact with the object. Properties, methods, and fields make up the public interface of the class.

- The private interface, that is, the inner workings of the class that are hidden from the rest of the world.

Public vs. Private

A class is generally public, which means that it can be accessed from outside the assembly in which it is placed.

A class has a **public interface** consisting of the public methods (Sub, Function, and Property procedures) and the public fields (variables). Internally, the class will have private fields and methods that provide the inner workings of the class. Remember that the user of the class will be the form or another class inside the assembly (the project). The user of the class will be able to access the properties and methods that are public but will not be able to access anything that is private.

To determine which properties, methods, and fields should be public and which should be private, you should think about what you want the user of the class to be able to access.

The inner workings of the class must be private if you don't want the user to be able to access the internal contents of the class. When creating a class, you need to analyze it to determine which of the properties, methods, and fields must be public for the class to work as desired. All other properties, methods, and fields should remain private. Note that, at any time during the development of the class, you can change the accessibility of any property, method, or field.

Properties and Methods

Remember that a property is an attribute of the object, for example, the *Text* property of a text box. A method is an action on the object, for example, to place the cursor inside a text box, use the *Focus* method of the text box.

With this in mind, you can think of a class as being an abstraction of a real-world thing. Let's use a vehicle as an example. If we were to design a class that represents vehicles, we would want to define its attributes (properties) and its actions (methods). Tables 13-1 and 13-2 show the proposed properties and methods of the *Vehicle* class, respectively.

Table 13-1 **Vehicle Class Properties**

Property	Scope/Accessibility	Description	Data type	Access
Manufacturer	Public	Maker of the vehicle	*Text*	Read and write
Type	Public	Type of vehicle (car, truck, and so on)	*Text*	Read and write
Model	Public	Model of the vehicle	*Text*	Read and write
Doors	Public	Number of doors	*Numeric*	Read and write
Color	Public	Color of the vehicle	*Text*	Read and write
Speed	Private	Current speed of the vehicle	*Numeric*	Read and write

Table 13-2 **Vehicle Class Methods**

Method	Scope/Accessibility	Procedure type	Action
EngineStart	Public	Sub	Start the vehicle
EngineStop	Public	Sub	Stop the vehicle
IsEngineRunning	Public	Function (return *Boolean*)	Determine whether the engine is running
Accelerate	Public	Sub	Increase speed of the vehicle
Decelerate	Public	Sub	Decrease speed of the vehicle
GetSpeed	Public	Function (return *Integer*)	Return the speed of the vehicle

The Vehicle Class

If you look at the *Vehicle* class described in Tables 13-1 and 13-2, you can see that properties such as *Manufacturer* and *Model* should be read and write enabled, meaning that the user of the class should be able to supply a value and read that value back. The user should not be able to access the *Speed* property directly, and the value of the *Speed* property should only be changed when the *Accelerate* and *Decelerate* methods are run (more on that later in the chapter).

Take a look at the methods. In a real vehicle, you perform the start and stop actions by turning the key in the ignition on and off. The *Accelerate* and *Decelerate* methods are used to change the current speed of the vehicle, as you do with the accelerator and brake pedals. Because the user cannot access the *Speed* property directly, we have also included a *GetSpeed* function that interrogates the *Speed* property internally and returns the speed of the vehicle.

Making Sense of the *Vehicle* Class

If the *Vehicle* class is to emulate a real vehicle, you need to make sense of the properties and methods you will be creating and understand how you need to implement them. For this you need to define the logic of the class. In doing so, your goal is to create an **abstraction** of a real vehicle. This means that you will cover the major functions of a real vehicle and not be concerned with insignificant details, such as whether the seats are electrically adjusted or whether the sun visor has a vanity light.

Let's look at each of the methods in logical terms:

- ***EngineStart***   Running the *EngineStart* method will set the instance variable *m_blnEngineRunning* to True.

  If the vehicle's engine is already started, you don't want to start it again.

- ***EngineStop***   Running the *EngineStop* method will set the instance variable *m_blnEngineRunning* to False.

  If the vehicle's engine is already stopped, you don't want to stop it again.

- ***Accelerate***   To increase the speed of the vehicle, you will call the *Accelerate* method of the class. The *Accelerate* method will contain code that increases the speed of the vehicle.

  If the vehicle is stopped (if the engine is not running), you don't want to accelerate. You could also set a maximum speed and prevent the *Accelerate* method from doing anything if you already are at maximum speed.

■ ***Decelerate*** To decrease the speed of the vehicle, you will call the *Decelerate* method of the class. The *Decelerate* method will contain code that allows you to decrease the speed of the vehicle.

If the vehicle is stopped (if the engine is not running) or if the current speed of the vehicle is at 0 (zero), you don't want to decelerate.

■ ***GetSpeed*** To return the current speed of the vehicle, you will call the *GetSpeed* method of the class. Remember that the *Speed* property is private and will be inaccessible to all classes outside of the *Vehicle* class. The *GetSpeed* method will interrogate the *Speed* property and return the value.

Creating the *Vehicle* Class

Although you could get into a lot more detail in this application, remember that you are creating an abstraction of a real vehicle and that you should include only those properties and methods that are important to the basic functional requirements of the class.

▶ Creating the VehicleDetails application

1. Create a new Windows application named **VehicleDetails**.

2. Select the Form1.vb file in Solution Explorer, and then change the name from Form1.vb to **VehicleForm.vb**.

3. Open the form in designer view, and change the name of the form from Form1 to **frmSelectVehicle**.

4. Open the Property Pages dialog box again by right-clicking the project name in Solution Explorer and reselecting the startup object. Remember that you changed the name of the form, so, if you attempt to run the program at this point, the compiler will not be able to find the startup object because it will be looking for *Sub Main*.

5. Change the *Text* property of the form to **Select Vehicle**.

6. Add a new class to the solution by right-clicking the project name in Solution Explorer, pointing to Add, and then selecting Add Class, as shown in Figure 13-1.

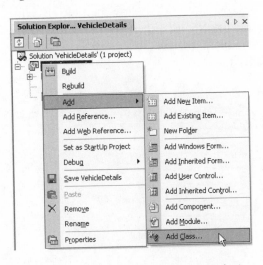

Figure 13-1   Adding a new class to a project

7. In the dialog box that appears, change the name of the class from Class1.vb to **Vehicle.vb**, and then click Open, as shown in Figure 13-2. The *Vehicle* class will be added to Solution Explorer, and the Code Editor will appear, showing the class declaration.

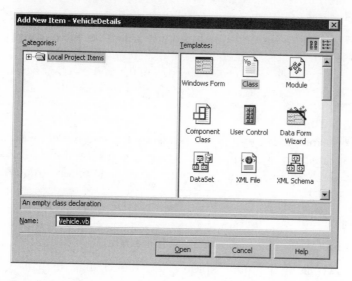

Figure 13-2   Renaming the class from Class1.vb to Vehicle.vb

8. Now you will add the fields (sometimes referred to as *instance variables*) to the *Vehicle* class. To do this, you need to create the private fields that will be used to persist (store) the property values. Add the boldface class-level variable declarations shown in the following code sample to the class.

```
Public Class Vehicle
    Private m_strManufacturer As String
    Private m_strType As String
    Private m_strModel As String
    Private m_intDoors As Integer
    Private m_strColor As String
    Private m_intSpeed As Integer
End Class
```

9. Next you will add the properties to the *Vehicle* class, starting with the *Manufacturer* property. Type the boldface code below the field declarations in the following code sample exactly as shown. The *Manufacturer* property will be read and write enabled. This will require the use of both the *Get* method and the *Set* method.

TIP   When you type the first line of code to create a new property and then press ENTER, the body of the property procedure will be completed for you. All you need to do then is type the implementation code.

```
Public Class Vehicle
    Private m_strManufacturer As String
    Private m_strType As String
    Private m_strModel As String
    Private m_intDoors As Integer
    Private m_strColor As String
    Private m_intSpeed As Integer
```

```
    Public Property Manufacturer() As String
        Get
            Return m_strManufacturer
        End Get
        Set(ByVal Value As String)
            m_strManufacturer = Value
        End Set
    End Property
End Class
```

10. Add the rest of the properties. Refer to Table 13-3 for the details required for each of these properties. Implement the *Get* and *Set* methods to read and write to the appropriate field variable. Review the *Manufacturer* property if you need to refresh yourself on what to enter. Notice that, unlike the rest of the property procedures, the scope of the *Speed* property is private.

Table 13-3 **Vehicle Class Property Details**

Property name	Scope	Return type	Accessibility
Type	Public	*String*	ReadWrite
Model	Public	*String*	ReadWrite
Doors	Public	*Integer*	ReadWrite
Color	Public	*String*	ReadWrite
Speed	Private	*Integer*	ReadWrite

11. Now that you have added the properties, it's time to add the methods (Sub and Function procedures). Start by creating the *EngineStart* and *EngineStop* methods. Type the following code below the property procedures you added in the previous steps. With the exception of the *GetSpeed* method, we are providing only the wrapper lines for the methods. You will be adding implementation code for each of these methods next.

```
Public Sub EngineStart()
End Sub
Public Sub EngineStop()
End Sub
Private Function IsEngineRunning() As Boolean
End Function
Public Sub Accelerate()
End Sub
Public Sub Decelerate()
End Sub
Public Function GetSpeed() As Integer
    Return Speed
End Function
```

12. Because the engine can never be running and stopped at the same time, you will need to add a class-level variable to persist the state of the engine. This will be a *Boolean* variable named *m_blnEngineRunning*, and it will be set to True if the engine is started and False if the engine is stopped. To do this, type the boldface line of code below after the other field declarations.

```
...
Private m_intSpeed As Integer
Private m_blnEngineRunning as Boolean
```

13. Type the boldface code shown in the following code sample inside the *EngineStart* method. This method is a Sub procedure that will set the value in *m_blnEngineRunning* to True.

```
Public Sub EngineStart()
    m_blnEngineRunning = True
End Sub
```

14. Type the boldface code shown in the following code sample inside the *EngineStop* method. This method is also a Sub procedure, but this time you will set the value in *m_blnEngineRunning* to False.

```
Public Sub EngineStop()
    m_blnEngineRunning = False
End Sub
```

To determine whether the engine is running, you will create a new function named *IsEngineRunning* that will be used to return the value in *m_blnEngineRunning*.

15. To create the new function, type the boldface code shown in the following code sample.

```
Public Function IsEngineRunning() As Boolean
    Return m_blnEngineRunning
End Function
```

16. In the *Accelerate* method, you must first make sure that the engine is running. If it is, you can increase the speed. Type the boldface code shown in the following code sample inside the *Accelerate* method.

```
Public Sub Accelerate()
    If IsEngineRunning Then
        Speed += 5
    End If
End Sub
```

17. The *Decelerate* method requires a little more thought. First you must determine whether the engine is running, and then you need to know what the current speed is. Because the vehicle will be decelerated by 5 mph each time the method is called, you must ensure that the current speed is greater than or equal to 5 mph. If the current speed is less than 5 mph, you will set the speed to zero. Type the boldface code shown in the following code sample inside the *Decelerate* method.

```
Public Sub Decelerate()
    If IsEngineRunning Then
        If Speed >= 5 Then
            Speed -= 5
        Else
            Speed = 0
        End If
    End If
End Sub
```

The VehicleDetails Program

The *Vehicle* class looks complete, so let's try it out. The user of the class will be the form shown in Figure 13-3. You will need to provide controls that will be used to create an instance of the *Vehicle* class, pass values to the various properties, and display that information.

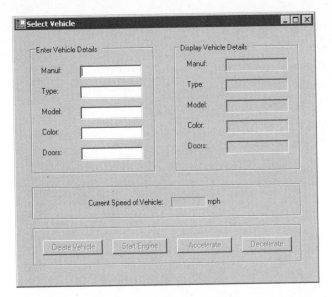

Figure 13-3   The form that is the user of the *Vehicle* class

▶ Adding group boxes to the form

1. Add the group boxes to the form, and name each one as shown in Table 13-4.

Table 13-4   **GroupBox Control Properties**

Control	Name	Text
GroupBox	**grpDetails**	**Enter Vehicle Details**
GroupBox	**grpDisplay**	**Display Vehicle Details**
GroupBox	**grpSpeed**	<blank>
GroupBox	**grpActions**	<blank>

2. Select the group box named grpDetails, and add the controls listed in Table 13-5 to it by dragging the controls from the Toolbox and dropping them in the group box.

Table 13-5   **GroupBox grpDetails Controls**

Control	Name	Text
TextBox	**txtManufacturer**	<blank>
TextBox	**txtType**	<blank>
TextBox	**txtModel**	<blank>
TextBox	**txtColor**	<blank>
TextBox	**txtDoors**	<blank>
Label	Label1	**Manuf:**
Label	Label2	**Type:**
Label	Label3	**Model:**
Label	Label4	**Color:**
Label	Label5	**Doors:**

3. Select the group box named grpDisplay, and add the controls listed in Table 13-6 to it by dragging the controls from the Toolbox and dropping them in the group box.

Table 13-6 **GroupBox grpDisplay Controls**

Control	Name	Text
TextBox	**txtDisplayManufacturer**	\<blank\>
TextBox	**txtDisplayType**	\<blank\>
TextBox	**txtDisplayModel**	\<blank\>
TextBox	**txtDisplayColor**	\<blank\>
TextBox	**txtDisplayDoors**	\<blank\>
Label	Label6	**Manuf:**
Label	Label7	**Type:**
Label	Label8	**Model:**
Label	Label9	**Color:**
Label	Label10	**Doors:**

4. In the Properties window, set the *ReadOnly* property for each of the text boxes in grpDisplay to True. This will allow the user to see the details but will not allow them to change or delete the values in them.

5. Set the *TabStop* property for each of the text boxes in grpDisplay to False. This will prevent the user from being able to tab to these text boxes.

6. Select the group box named grpSpeed, and add the controls listed in Table 13-7 to it by dragging the controls from the Toolbox and dropping them in the group box.

Table 13-7 **GroupBox grpSpeed Controls**

Control	Name	Text
Label	Label11	**Current Speed of Vehicle:**
Label	**lblCurrentSpeed**	\<blank\>
Label	Label12	**mph**

7. In the Properties window, set the *BorderStyle* property of lblCurrentSpeed to Fixed3D. This will give it the sunken look you see in the form in Figure 13-3.

8. Select the group box named grpActions, and add the controls listed in Table 13-8 to it by dragging the controls from the Toolbox and dropping them in the group box.

Table 13-8 **GroupBox grpActions Controls**

Control	Name	Text
Button	**btnCreateVehicle**	**Create Vehicle**
Button	**btnEngine**	**&Start Engine**
Button	**btnAccelerate**	**Accelerate**
Button	**btnDecelerate**	**Decelerate**

9. Set the *Enabled* property of each of the buttons in grpActions to *False*. You will be providing code to enable each of the buttons when it is appropriate.

Writing the Pseudocode

After the form is complete, it is time to code the program. Before doing that, however, you need to write pseudocode to gain a better understanding of how the program will work. The buttons on the form will remain disabled until the details are entered by the user.

1. Enable btnCreateVehicle when all the details are entered.

2. Create the Vehicle object by clicking btnCreateVehicle.

3. Display the details of the Vehicle object in the appropriate text boxes.

4. Start the engine by clicking btnEngine.

    a. Change the *Text* property of the btnEngine button to **Stop Engine**.

    b. Enable btnAccelerate.

5. Accelerate the vehicle by clicking btnAccelerate.

    a. Enable btnDecelerate.

    b. Disable btnEngine.

6. Decelerate the vehicle by clicking btnDecelerate.

    a. If the current speed is now at zero, disable btnDecelerate and enable btnEngine.

7. Stop the engine by clicking the btnEngine button.

    a. Change the *Text* property of btnEngine to **Start Engine**.

    b. Disable btnAccelerate.

    c. Disable btnDecelerate.

▶ Coding the VehicleDetails program

1. Open the form in design view, and double-click btnCreateVehicle.

2. Declare a class-level variable to store the Vehicle object. This variable is declared at the top of the code module, just below the Windows Form Designer–generated code region.

```
Private newVehicle As Vehicle
```

3. Type the boldface code shown in the following code sample inside the *btnCreateVehicle_Click* event handler.

```
Private Sub btnCreateVehicle_Click(ByVal sender As System.Object, _
        ByVal e As System.EventArgs) Handles btnCreateVehicle.Click

    Try
        newVehicle = New Vehicle
        With newVehicle
            .Manufacturer = txtManufacturer.Text
            .Type = txtType.Text
            .Model = txtModel.Text
            .Color = txtColor.Text
            .Doors = Integer.Parse(txtDoors.Text)
        End With

        DisplayDetails()
        btnEngine.Enabled = True
```

```
    Catch ex As SystemException
        MessageBox.Show(ex.Message, "Error in Vehicle Creation", _
            MessageBoxButtons.OK, MessageBoxIcon.Error)

    End Try
End Sub
```

After typing the code, you will notice a syntax error for the statement
`DisplayDetails()`. As you might have guessed, this is a call to a method
(Sub procedure) that you haven't created yet, so you will do that next.
Before you go further, we will explain the code just entered.

First you typed the line `newVehicle = New Vehicle`, which creates a single
instance of the *Vehicle* class and assigns it to the object variable you created earlier. After you have a reference to the actual object, you can
access its properties and, later on, its methods. The keyword *New* is interesting in that it is used to call the constructor of the *Vehicle* class. You
didn't provide an explicit constructor method when you created the class,
but the compiler provides a default constructor for you automatically. If
you had explicitly coded a constructor method, the compiler would not
have provided one. We will talk more about constructor methods a little
later in the chapter.

The next block of code assigns the values to the properties of the Vehicle
object. The *With...End With* block is used to make the code more efficient and to reduce the amount of typing.

```
With newVehicle
    .Manufacturer = txtManufacturer.Text
    .Type = txtType.Text
    .Model = txtModel.Text
    .Color = txtColor.Text
    .Doors = Integer.Parse(txtDoors.Text)
End With
```

The `DisplayDetails()` statement calls the Sub procedure *DisplayDetails*,
which you will create next. The last statement, `btnEngine.Enabled =
True`, enables the Start Engine button.

Notice that you have surrounded all of the above code in a *Try...Catch
...End Try* block. You have done this to catch any exception that will be
thrown if for some reason the object fails to instantiate or if you cannot
access any of the properties of the object.

4. Create the *DisplayDetails* Sub procedure by typing the code shown here
below the *btnCreateVehicle_Click* event handler.

```
Private Sub DisplayDetails()

    With newVehicle
        txtDisplayManufacturer.Text = .Manufacturer
        txtDisplayType.Text = .Type
        txtDisplayModel.Text = .Model
        txtDisplayColor.Text = .Color
        txtDisplayDoors.Text = .Doors.ToString()
    End With

End Sub
```

Again, using the *With...End With* block, you are assigning the property values from the object to the appropriate text boxes in the Display group box.

5. Switch to the designer, and double-click the Accelerate button. Type the boldface code shown in the following code sample into the *btnAccelerate_Click* event handler.

```
Private Sub btnAccelerate_Click(ByVal sender As System.Object, _
    ByVal e As System.EventArgs) Handles btnAccelerate.Click

    With newVehicle
        .Accelerate()
        lblCurrentSpeed.Text = .GetSpeed.ToString()
    End With

    btnDecelerate.Enabled = True

End Sub
```

When the user clicks the Accelerate button, the *Accelerate* method of the Vehicle object is called and the speed is read back. After the vehicle has accelerated, the speed is greater than zero, and you can enable the Decelerate button to allow deceleration.

6. Switch back to the designer, and double-click the Decelerate button. Type the boldface code shown in the following code sample into the *btnDecelerate_Click* event handler.

```
Private Sub btnDecelerate_Click(ByVal sender As System.Object, _
    ByVal e As System.EventArgs) Handles btnDecelerate.Click

    With newVehicle
        .Decelerate()
        lblCurrentSpeed.Text = .GetSpeed.ToString()
    End With

End Sub
```

In this procedure, you call the *Decelerate* method of the Vehicle object and read back the speed. You're probably wondering why you're not testing to see if the speed is at zero. Well, you could, but we have something much more powerful to show you when we get to the section entitled "Creating an Event in the *Vehicle* Class." Be patient; we will get to it soon.

7. Switch to the designer, and double-click the Start Engine button. Type the boldface code shown in the following code sample into the *btnEngine_Click* event handler.

```
Private Sub btnEngine_Click(ByVal sender As System.Object, _
    ByVal e As System.EventArgs) Handles btnEngine.Click

    If btnEngine.Text = "&Start Engine" Then
        newVehicle.EngineStart()
        btnAccelerate.Enabled = True
        btnEngine.Text = "&Stop Engine"
    Else
        newVehicle.EngineStop()
        btnAccelerate.Enabled = False
        btnDecelerate.Enabled = False
```

```
        btnEngine.Text = "&Start Engine"
    End If

    lblCurrentSpeed.Text = newVehicle.GetSpeed.ToString()

End Sub
```

This is a particularly interesting block of code because you are using the same button to start the engine that you are using to stop it. This is called a *toggle switch* because it toggles back and forth between two states (start and stop). The first time through, the *Text* property of the button is set to Start Engine. You know this because you set that value in the Properties window. After the user has clicked the button, the expression in the *If* statement will return True and the code inside the block will run. The *EngineStart* method of the Vehicle object runs, the Accelerate button is enabled, and the *Text* property of btnEngine is changed to Stop Engine.

As you might guess, the second time the button is clicked, the expression in the *If* statement will return False, code execution falls to the *Else* block, and the statements there will run.

The last statement displays the current speed in the current speed label, which should always be zero when the engine has just started.

When you are evaluating the *Text* property of the buttons, remember that you have provided an accelerator key for each of the buttons by including the ampersand (&) symbol. Because the *Text* property holds a literal value, you must include the ampersand symbol in the expression.

8. The next thing you need to do is to enable and disable the Engine button depending on current speed of the vehicle. If the vehicle's speed is greater than zero, you do not want to turn off the engine. Stay in the Code Editor, and select lblCurrentSpeed in the Class Name list. Then select the *TextChanged* event in the Method Name list. The event handler will be created for you. Type the following code into the *lblCurrentSpeed_TextChanged* event handler.

```
btnEngine.Enabled = Not CType(newVehicle.GetSpeed, Boolean)
```

The previous statement is interesting, but it is cryptic. This is another toggle switch, and it basically tests the value returned from the *GetSpeed* function of the Vehicle object. If the value is 0, the expression will return False. Because you want the Engine button to be enabled when the current speed is zero, you have to reverse the result of the expression by using the *Not* operator so that the overall result is True. If the current speed is greater than zero, the result of the expression will be True. This will be reversed if you use the *Not* operator, and the overall result will be False.

How is this done? In Microsoft Visual Basic .NET, a number can be converted to a *Boolean* value. The number zero will evaluate to False, and any number that is not zero will evaluate to True.

In the next statement, the *CType* function casts the *Integer* value to a *Boolean*. Remember that an *Integer* value of 0 will return False and an *Integer* value of something other than 0 will return True. Given this, when you are reducing the speed, you must not allow the vehicle's speed to go negative. If that happens, the result of the cast will be True, which might result in strange behavior.

```
btnEngine.Enabled = Not CType(newVehicle.GetSpeed, Boolean)
```

If you were to write this more fully, it would look like the following code:

```
If newVehicle.GetSpeed = 0 Then
    btnEngine.Enabled = True
Else
    btnEngine.Enabled = False
End If
```

There are just two more event handlers to code and then we will get to the coolest part of this example.

9. Switch to the designer, and double-click the txtManufacturer text box in the grpDetail group box.

10. Rename the event handler from *txtManufacturer_TextChanged* to **textboxes_TextChanged**. Do not delete the parameters.

11. Delete the *Handles* statement at the end of the event handler declaration. The event handler should now look like the following code:

```
Private Sub textboxes_TextChanged(ByVal sender As Object, _
    ByVal e As System.EventArgs)


End Sub
```

12. Type the boldface code shown in the following code sample into the *textboxes_TextChanged* event handler.

```
Private Sub textboxes_TextChanged(ByVal sender As Object, _
    ByVal e As System.EventArgs)

    If Trim(txtManufacturer.Text).Length > 0 AndAlso Trim(txtType.Text)
       .Length > 0 _
       AndAlso Trim(txtModel.Text).Length > 0 AndAlso Trim(txtColor.Text)
          .Length > 0 _
       AndAlso Trim(txtDoors.Text).Length > 0 AndAlso IsNumeric(txtDoors
          .Text) Then

       btnCreateVehicle.Enabled = True
    End If

    With txtDoors
       If Not IsNumeric(.Text) AndAlso .TextLength > 0 Then
          .SelectAll()
          .Focus()
       End If
    End With

End Sub
```

The preceding procedure will be used as a common procedure for all the text boxes in the grpDetail group box. Right now, this procedure is disconnected from the events that will eventually call it. You will provide the code to connect this procedure to the events a little later. For now, we'll explain the code that you will run.

The first *If* block tests to ensure that the user has typed a value in each of the text boxes. Note that you have used the *Trim* function to remove any blank spaces from each end of the text that is entered. This is considered a good programming practice. The code also tests whether the value in the Doors text box is numeric. If there is no value in the Doors text box, or if the user enters an alpha character, the result of the *IsNumeric* function will be False. The *AndAlso* operator is used to join the expressions. This operator is known as a logical operator. It requires that every expression connected by *AndAlso* must evaluate to True for the entire expression to return True. If any individual expression evaluates to False, the evaluation will terminate, the overall result will be False, and the code inside the *If* block will not run.

The second *If* block again tests the Doors text box. Although this is not absolutely required, we are using it to make the user interface a little friendlier. If the user accidentally types an alphabetical character in the Doors text box, the Doors text box will be selected and the text inside it will be highlighted. If you wanted, you could also display a message to users telling them that they must enter a numeric value.

Using *AddHandler*

The next step is to connect this event handler to the events that will be raised. To do this, you will use the *AddHandler* statement. The basic syntax of the *AddHandler* statement is:

```
AddHandler event, AddressOf eventhandler
```

The *AddHandler* statement associates an event with an event handler. The first argument, *event*, is the actual event that is raised, and in this case it will be the *TextChanged* event. In the second argument, the *AddressOf* operator returns a reference to the delegate that points to the event handler.

An event does not know which event handlers will run when the event is raised, and an event handler does not know which event is being raised. To provide the intelligence to link the two, you can use a delegate. A delegate knows both the event and the event handler and becomes the intermediary between an event and one or more event handlers. When using the *AddHandler* statement, you do not have to explicitly specify the *delegate* class because the *AddressOf* statement will always return a reference to the delegate.

You probably won't be too surprised to find out that there's also a *RemoveHandler* statement. You can use this statement if you want to prevent code in an event handler from running whenever the event is raised.

1. Switch to the designer, and double-click a free area of the form (not inside one of the group boxes). The *frmSelectVehicle_Load* event handler will be added to the Code Editor.

2. Type the boldface code shown in the following code sample into the *frmSelectVehicle_Load* event handler.

```
Private Sub frmSelectVehicle_Load(ByVal sender As System.Object, _
    ByVal e As System.EventArgs) Handles MyBase.Load
```

```
AddHandler txtManufacturer.TextChanged, AddressOf textboxes_TextChanged
AddHandler txtType.TextChanged, AddressOf textboxes_TextChanged
AddHandler txtModel.TextChanged, AddressOf textboxes_TextChanged
AddHandler txtColor.TextChanged, AddressOf textboxes_TextChanged
AddHandler txtDoors.TextChanged, AddressOf textboxes_TextChanged
```

```
End Sub
```

Now, when the form is loaded, the events are connected, and any time the text changes in any of the text boxes in the grpDetail group box, the code inside the event handler will run, which is exactly what you want.

Rather than using the *AddHandler* statement, you could have created the event handler as shown in the following example:

```
Private Sub textboxes_TextChanged(ByVal sender As Object, _
        ByVal e As System.EventArgs) _
        Handles txtManufactirer.TextChanged, _
                txtType.TextChanged, _
                txtModel.TextChanged, _
                txtColor.TextChanged, _
                txtDoors.TextChanged
```

```
End Sub
```

The *AddHandler* statement provides a little more flexibility than the *Handles* statement because you can:

- Connect or disconnect an event handler at run time

- Change the event handler at any time, when the program is running

- Connect multiple event handlers to the same event

Like the *Handles* statement, the *AddHandler* statement can connect events from multiple objects to a single event handler.

Creating an Event in the *Vehicle* Class

As we promised earlier, in the last part of this example, you will create an event in the class. This event will be raised when the vehicle is decelerated and the speed is zero.

Providing an event in a class allows the object to notify the user of the object when something happens, rather than requiring the user to query the object to determine the state. In the real world, if you had to continually ask someone if they were finished, it would be a pain. It would be easier if they had the ability to notify you when they were finished. In this example, you will enable the object to notify the user if the speed is zero when the *Decelerate* method is being executed.

▶ Adding an event to the *Vehicle* class

1. Open the *Vehicle* class in the Code Editor, and type the following event declaration at the top of the module, just below the other class declarations.

   ```
   Public Event Stopped()
   ```

2. Open the form's code module, and locate the declaration for the Vehicle object. Add the *WithEvents* keyword to the declaration. The declaration should now look like the following statement:

```
Private WithEvents newVehicle As Vehicle
```

3. Switch back to the *Vehicle* class, and locate the *Decelerate* method. Modify the existing code by inserting the boldface code shown in the following code sample. This will cause the *Stopped* event to be raised whenever the speed is zero.

```
Public Sub Decelerate()
    If IsEngineRunning Then
        If Speed >= 5 Then
            Speed -= 5
        Else
            Speed = 0
        End If
    End If
    If Speed <= 0 Then
        RaiseEvent Stopped()
    End If
End Sub
```

4. Now switch back to the form's code module.

5. In the Class Name list, select newVehicle.

6. In the Method Name list, select Stopped.

7. The event handler will be added to the Code Editor.

8. Insert the boldface code in the *newVehicle_Stopped* event handler, as shown in the following code sample.

```
Private Sub newVehicle_Stopped() Handles newVehicle.Stopped

    btnDecelerate.Enabled = False

End Sub
```

9. Run the program and enter the following data:

   ❑ Manufacturer: **Ford**

   ❑ Type: **Sedan**

   ❑ Model: **Taurus**

   ❑ Color: **White**

   ❑ Doors: **4**

10. Click the Create Vehicle button.

11. Click the Start Engine button, and then click the Accelerate and Decelerate buttons to ensure that everything works as expected. Remember that the

Start Engine button should be disabled when the vehicle's speed is greater than zero, and that the Decelerate button should be disabled when the vehicle's speed reaches zero. Figures 13-4 through 13-7 demonstrate the functionality of the program.

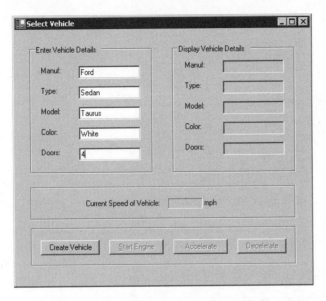

Figure 13-4   The Create Vehicle button is enabled after all of the data has been entered.

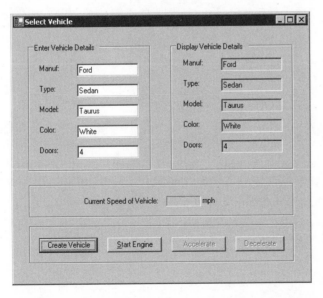

Figure 13-5   The Start Engine button is enabled after an instance of the *Vehicle* class is created.

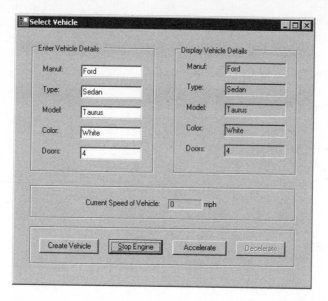

Figure 13-6 The engine is started: the Accelerate button is enabled and the Start Engine button's *Text* property is changed to Stop Engine.

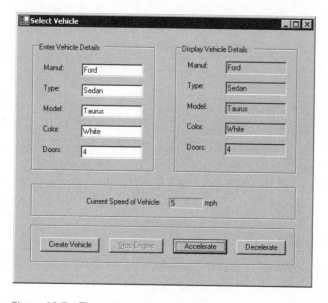

Figure 13-7 The vehicle's speed is greater than 0, so the Accelerate and Decelerate buttons are enabled, and the Stop Engine button is disabled.

Try It

Modify the *Vehicle* class you created in the previous exercise to include a property for air conditioning. The *Air Conditioning* property should be *Boolean*. Use RadioButton controls on the form to let the user specify whether the vehicle has air conditioning. The default setting for *Air Conditioning* should be Yes.

MORE WORK WITH CLASSES

There is much more to learn about working with classes. So far, you have learned how to create a simple class with properties, methods, and events. Now you are going to learn more about what was going on behind the scenes in the previous examples and add some more details to the process.

Encapsulation

Encapsulation is sometimes referred to as *data hiding*. When you hide the inner workings of a class, you are said to be *encapsulating* the data. When you employ encapsulation, any data required by the class is provided either by passing arguments when a method of the class is called or through explicit property procedures. You can provide code in the methods or properties that will evaluate the data being passed in before it can do any harm. If you were to provide public fields (public variables), you would be breaking the rules of encapsulation because any code that could access the object would be able to change the values without warning. Worse, if you could not evaluate the data being passed in and the data was invalid, it could cause a run-time exception to be thrown or a logic error in the program.

When you created the *Vehicle* class, you observed the rules of encapsulation by only allowing access to the class methods, fields, and events through the public interface. Data stored in the instance of the class (also known as *instance data*), such as the type of vehicle and the number of doors, can only be set or retrieved through the public properties. Direct access to the fields that persist the data is not allowed because those are marked *private*. Vehicle speed can only be changed by means of either the *Accelerate* method or the *Decelerate* method. And, of course, the speed can only be read by means of the *GetSpeed* function, which is also public. By setting these rules, you control how data flows in and out of the class, and you also provide the proper validation so that bad data cannot be introduced.

Object Lifetime

An object begins life when the constructor of the class is executed. The object will remain alive as long as a valid reference to the object is maintained. The validity of the reference depends on where the object is declared:

- If an object variable is declared and the object is instantiated inside a procedure, its reference will go out of scope when the procedure terminates. At that point, the object is no longer referenced and becomes unusable until the procedure is called again.

- If the object variable is declared at the class level, such as in a form, it has scope for the lifetime of the form. The properties and methods of the object can then be referred to from any procedure in that form.

If you look back at the form class for the VehicleDetails program, you can see that the object variable is declared at the class level, but the object is not instantiated until the user clicks the Create Vehicle button. If the form is closed, the object becomes unreachable because the variable that references the object has gone out of scope. Of course, this is a moot point if the form is the only form in the program because when it is closed, the entire program terminates. Even though the object is unreachable, it still exists in memory and will continue to exist until it is disposed of by the garbage collector.

Garbage Collection

Visual Basic .NET, along with the other languages supported by the .NET Framework, uses a memory management system known as **non-deterministic finalization**. What this means to you, as a developer, is that you are not required to explicitly destroy your objects after you are done with them. The garbage collector does it for you.

The **garbage collector** is responsible for managing the use of memory by the application, both when objects are created and when they are destroyed. The disadvantage of non-deterministic finalization is that you never know when the object is actually disposed of.

You could say that an object's effective lifetime starts when the constructor method of the class is executed and ends when the object variable goes out of scope. However, the actual lifetime of the object ends when the garbage collector disposes of the object.

The Constructor

An instance of a class is created when you use the *New* keyword in an object declaration or assignment statement.

```
Dim newObject As New MyClass
```

The preceding statement doesn't just declare the object variable; it also creates an instance of the class. The next code block shows the declaration and the creation of the instance of the class as two separate statements:

```
Dim newObject As MyClass
newObject = New MyClass
```

To create an instance of a class, the common language runtime will run a special method called a **constructor**. This method is named *New*. If the *New* method is not explicitly provided in code, the compiler will create one for you. This doesn't mean that the compiler adds the method for you in the Code Editor—it doesn't— but the presence of a constructor is always implied. The *New* method is used to instantiate new objects before any other code related to the object can run. You can use the constructor to open files, connect to databases, initialize variables, and take care of any other tasks that need to be completed before the object can be used.

The default constructor method looks as follows:

```
Public Sub New()
    MyBase.New()
    ' provide code here to perform any initializing tasks
End Sub
```

Implementation code is not required inside the constructor, but, as we said earlier, you can provide code if you need to initialize anything prior to object creation.

Visual Basic .NET also allows your classes to derive from other classes. This is known as **inheritance**. We will discuss the details of inheritance a little later in this chapter. One aspect of inheritance is worth pointing out now: when you create an instance of a class that is derived from another class, the constructor of the base class (the class you are inheriting from) is always executed first. This happens because the first line of code in a constructor uses the syntax *MyBase.New* to call the constructor of the class immediately above itself in the class hierarchy. If the base class is derived from another class, it will call the constructor in its base class. This will continue up the chain until all classes in the hierarchy are instantiated.

Unless you need to provide initializing code for the class, an explicit default constructor is not required, although it is good programming practice to explicitly create one.

▶ **Adding a constructor to the *Vehicle* class**

Open the *Vehicle* class in the Code Editor, and add a default constructor, as shown in the following code sample.

```
Public Sub New()
    MyBase.New()

End Sub
```

When you create a new instance of the *Vehicle* class, the constructor will be called and will make a call to its base class. Remember that the base class for the *Vehicle* class is *System.Object* and, as an instance of *System.Object*, already exists. Making an explicit call to *System.Object* is not required, but it is a good programming practice to include it.

The Destructor

Just as a class has a constructor, it can also have a **destructor**. If you find that you need a destructor, you must create it explicitly. (This is not the case for constructors.) The destructor method is named *Finalize*. Although creating a *Finalize* method might seem like a good thing, it comes with a price. There is a slight performance penalty when a *Finalize* method is explicitly created in the class. In addition, having a finalizer actually allows the object to stay in memory for a longer time.

If there is a penalty, why have a *Finalize* method at all? At times you might need to dispose of other objects and terminate references to objects that are outside the control of the common language runtime. These could be connections to databases or any open files that need to be closed. A destructor could be used for that.

There is never an implicit call to a *Finalize* method if one is not explicitly created in the class. The rule here is that if you don't have any specific cleanup tasks that must be completed prior to the object being disposed of, don't create a *Finalize* method.

To include a destructor, add the following code to the class:

```
Protected Overrides Sub Finalize()
    MyBase.Finalize()

    ' Provide cleanup code here
End Sub
```

Finalize is a protected method that overrides the destructor in its base class. This works even if the base class does not have an explicit *Finalize* method. The *Protected* scope modifier ensures that this method is visible to the current class and any derived classes but is not visible to any other module in the current assembly.

The *IDisposable* Interface

What if you want to perform cleanup tasks without the added overhead of using a *Finalize* method? You can implement the *IDisposable* interface and use its *Dispose* method to perform the cleanup.

Using the *Dispose* method of the *IDisposable* interface to dispose of managed or unmanaged resources is quite easy. In this section, you will modify the *Vehicle* class so that it will implement *IDisposable* and use its *Dispose* method to run some code. Although in the previous example you did not use any external resources, demonstrating the use of *IDisposable* will give you a little more insight into how it works so that you can incorporate it in programs that will use these resources.

Keep in mind that calling the *Dispose* method will not short circuit the garbage collector. The garbage collector will take some time to dispose of the object and reclaim the memory, but the *Dispose* method relieves you from having to put that cleanup code inside the *Finalize* method and still allows you to immediately run the cleanup code.

> **NOTE** When you include cleanup code inside the *Dispose* method, it is important that that method be called; if it is not called, the cleanup code will never run. Many programmers will include a *Finalize* method in their classes that explicitly calls the *Dispose* method just in case the garbage collector destroys the object before they have had a chance to run the cleanup code.

Although a detailed discussion of interfaces is beyond the scope of this textbook, we can say that an interface is like a class in that it is created with properties, methods, and events. It is unlike a class in that you cannot create an instance of an interface. Classes implement interfaces and, in doing so, they must implement the methods, properties, and events of the interface exactly as they were defined. The members of the interface (properties, methods, and events) are abstract method declarations that contain no implementation code. When you implement each of these properties, methods, and events, you will need to provide the implementation code for each one.

What's the catch? Ah yes, there's always a catch. The catch is that when you implement an interface, you are required to implement every property, method, and event of the interface. In this case, implementation could be as simple as coding the body of each property, method, and event but not providing any code within the body.

In the case of the *IDisposable* interface, there is only one member, and that is the *Dispose* method. You will use the *Dispose* method of the interface inside the *Vehicle* class to perform your cleanup chores.

▶ Implementing *IDisposable*

1. Open the VehicleDetails project in Visual Studio .NET (if it is not open already).

2. Display the *Vehicle* class in the Code Editor.

3. Add the boldface statement shown in the following code sample directly below the *Vehicle* class declaration.

```
Public Class Vehicle
    Implements IDisposable
    ...
End Class
```

As soon as you type in the *Implements* statement, you will notice a blue wavy line below the word *IDisposable*. This is not an error indication but a warning that tells you that you *must* implement the *Dispose* method of this interface. Any attempt to compile the code at that point will fail. Hovering the mouse pointer over the word *IDisposable* will display the message shown in Figure 13-8.

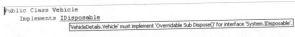

Figure 13-8   The warning message displayed to implement the *Dispose* method

4. To implement the *Dispose* method, select *IDisposable* from the Class Name list, as shown in Figure 13-9, and then select the *Dispose* method from the Method Name list, as shown in Figure 13-10.

Figure 13-9   Selecting *IDisposable* from the Class Name list

Figure 13-10   Selecting the *Dispose* method from the Method Name list

After you select the *Dispose* method, the procedure is automatically added to the *Vehicle* class module. All you have to do now is provide the code that will release any resources you might have been using.

Although you have no resources to clean up in this example, you will create another event in the class and raise that event when the *Dispose* method is called. This will demonstrate how running the *Dispose* method works.

5. Declare a new event named *Disposed* directly below the *Stopped* event that you declared earlier, as shown in the boldface line of code shown here:

```
Public Event Stopped()
Public Event Disposed()
```

6. Add the boldface statement shown in the following code sample to the *Dispose* method that you just created.

```
Public Sub Dispose() Implements System.IDisposable.Dispose
    RaiseEvent Disposed()
End Sub
```

7. Display the form's code module in the Code Editor.

8. Select newVehicle in the Class Name list, and then select the *Disposed* event in the Method Name list. The event handler will be inserted into the form's code module.

9. Type the boldface code shown in the following code sample into the *newVehicle_Disposed* event handler to display a message box when the event is raised.

```
Private Sub newVehicle_Disposed() Handles newVehicle.Disposed

    MessageBox.Show("Resources are being released", _
        "Releasing Resources", _
        MessageBoxButtons.OK, _
        MessageBoxIcon.Information)

End Sub
```

10. Now all you have to do is call the *Dispose* method from the form. You can do that by using the *Closing* event of the form. This event will always be raised just before the form closes. Select *(frmSelectVehicle Events)* in the Class Name list, and then select *Closing* in the Method Name list. The event handler for the *Closing* event will be added to the form's code module.

11. Type the boldface statement shown in the following code sample into the *frmSelectVehicle_Closing* event handler.

```
Private Sub frmSelectVehicle_Closing(ByVal sender As Object, _
        ByVal e As System.ComponentModel.CancelEventArgs) _
        Handles MyBase.Closing
```

```
newVehicle.Dispose()

End Sub
```

12. Run the program again. Create a new Vehicle object, and then close the form. Figure 13-11 shows the message that will appear when the *Closing* event is raised.

Figure 13-11   Releasing the resources message box

▶ Correcting a bug in the program

1. After testing the program a few times, you might have found a bug. Run the program again, but do not click the Create Vehicle button.

2. Click the close button in the upper-right corner of the window. An unhandled exception will be thrown, as shown in Figure 13-12.

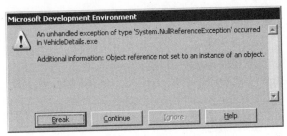

Figure 13-12   Unhandled exception message box

3. If you ran the program without debugging by pressing CTRL+F5, you should have seen the dialog box shown in Figure 13-13. If you received this message, you will need to run the program again with debugging.

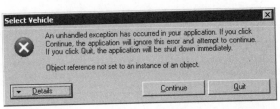

Figure 13-13   The exception message that appears if the program is run without debugging

4. Click Break to halt the program in break mode. The program statement `newVehicle.Dispose()` will be highlighted in yellow.

Remember that you are closing the form before you have created an instance of the *Vehicle* class. Because there is no object, you are attempting to run the *Dispose* method of a non-existent object. You can correct the situation by testing to make sure that there is an instance of the *Vehicle* class; if there isn't, don't run the *Dispose* method.

You will need to modify the code in the *frmSelectVehicle_Closing* event handler to include an *If* statement that will test to determine whether the object is *Nothing*. You will include the *Not* operator because you only want to run the *Dispose* method if the object exists.

5. Stop debugging by pressing SHIFT+F5.

6. Type the boldface code shown here into the *frmSelectVehicle_Closing* event handler.

```
Private Sub frmSelectVehicle_Closing(ByVal sender As Object, _
        ByVal e As System.ComponentModel.CancelEventArgs) _
        Handles MyBase.Closing

    If Not newVehicle Is Nothing Then
        newVehicle.Dispose()
    End If

End Sub
```

7. After making the change, run the program again and close it without creating a Vehicle object. Verify that the form closes without the exception being thrown.

Object Inheritance

Every class that you create supports inheritance. You could, for example, create a *Truck* class that inherits from *Vehicle*. The *Truck* class would inherit all of the properties, methods, and events of the *Vehicle* class. You could use the *Truck* class as is, or better yet, you could provide additional properties, methods, and events in the *Truck* class to support a truck's special requirements.

Class Hierarchy

Every class inherits from a base class. Even the *Vehicle* class has a base class: *System.Object*. The *Object* class can be considered the ancestor object for all objects created in Visual Basic .NET.

Although you didn't actually provide the statement *Inherits System.Object* in the class declaration of the *Vehicle* class, it is implied. You know this because of the additional methods that were provided when you created the class.

Here are a few examples of the properties and methods that you inherit from *System.Object* when you create a class:

■ **Equals**   Returns True if one instance of a class equals another instance of the same class

■ **GetHashCode**   Returns the hash-coded value of the object

■ **GetType**   Returns the type of the current instance of the class

■ **ReferenceEquals**   Returns True if the current object reference points to the same instance of the class as another object reference

■ **ToString**   Returns the *String* representation of the current object

To prove that the Vehicle object inherits from *System.Object*, type the boldface statement shown in the following code sample in the event handler of the Create Vehicle button.

```
Private Sub btnCreateVehicle_Click(ByVal sender As System.Object, _
        ByVal e As System.EventArgs) Handles btnCreateVehicle.Click

    Try
        newVehicle = New Vehicle

        MessageBox.Show("The Vehicle object is inherited from " & _
            newVehicle.GetType.BaseType.ToString(), "My Base")
    …
End Sub
```

Figure 13-14 shows the message that will appear when you click the Create Vehicle button.

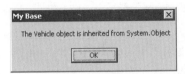

Figure 13-14   Message indicating inheritance from *System.Object*

Creating a *Truck* Class that Inherits from the *Vehicle* Class

You will now modify the VehicleDetails project by adding a new class named *Truck* that will inherit from the *Vehicle* class. This modification will also require a slight change to the user interface.

▶ Adding the *Truck* class

1. Using Windows Explorer, create a copy of the VehicleDetails project folder and rename it as **TruckDetails**.

2. Open the copy in Visual Studio .NET.

3. Right-click the project in Solution Explorer, and then select Properties.

4. In the VehicleDetails Property Pages dialog box, which is shown in Figure 13-15, change the Assembly name to **TruckDetails**, and then change the *Root Namespace* to **TruckDetails**. You will change the name of the form in a few moments and will have to come back to this dialog box to reset the startup object.

    TIP   The *Root Namespace* property cannot be changed if the form is open in design view.

5. Click OK, close the dialog box, and save the changes.

6. With the project name still selected in Solution Explorer, change the name from VehicleDetails to **TruckDetails** in the Properties window.

7. Select the solution name in Solution Explorer, and then change the name of the solution from VehicleDetails to **TruckDetails** in the Properties window.

8. Select the VehicleForm.vb file in Solution Explorer, and then change the name from VehicleForm.vb to **TruckForm.vb**.

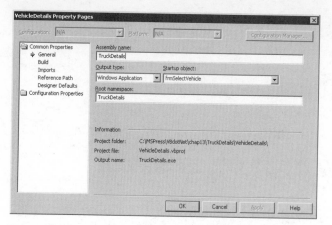

Figure 13-15   Changing the Assembly name and the *Root Namespace* in the property pages

9. Open the form in designer view, and change the name of the form from frmSelectVehicle to **frmSelectTruck**.

10. Open the Property Pages dialog box again by right-clicking the project name in Solution Explorer and reselecting the startup object. Remember that you changed the name of the form, so if you attempt to run the program at this point, the compiler will not be able to find the startup object because it will be looking for *Sub Main*.

11. Change the *Text* property of the form from Select Vehicle to **Select Truck**.

12. Change the name of the Create Vehicle button from btnCreateVehicle to **btnCreateTruck**.

13. Change the *Text* property of btnCreateTruck to **Create Truck**.

14. Change the *Text* property of the grpDetails GroupBox from Enter Vehicle Details to **Enter Truck Details**.

15. Change the *Text* property of the grpDisplay GroupBox from Display Vehicle Details to **Display Truck Details**.

16. Now that you are done with that, you will need to update the code. You will first replace any references to btnCreateVehicle with **btnCreateTruck**. Open the form's code module in the Code Editor and press CTRL+H. The Replace dialog box will appear.

17. Type **btnCreateVehicle** in the Find What box, and then type **btnCreateTruck** in the Replace With box, as shown in Figure 13-16.

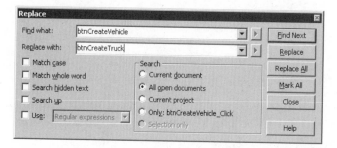

Figure 13-16   Replacing references to *btnCreateVehicle* with *btnCreateTruck*

18. Although you could click the Replace All button, you should really make the changes with a little more care. Click Find Next to locate the first reference to btnCreateVehicle.

19. The first reference to btnCreateVehicle will be highlighted in the code. Click Replace.

20. After you click the Replace button, the change is made and the next reference is located and highlighted. Make sure that this reference needs to be replaced, and then click Replace once again if it does.

21. Continue to click Replace until all references to btnCreateVehicle have been replaced with btnCreateTruck.

22. Back in Solution Explorer, right-click the project name, point to Add, and then select Add Class.

23. In the Add New Item dialog box, type **Truck.vb** in the Name box and then click the Open button. The new class will be added to Solution Explorer, and the Code Editor will display the code module for the *Truck* class.

24. Type the boldface statement shown in the following code sample directly below the *Truck* class declaration.

```
Public Class Truck
     Inherits Vehicle

End Class
```

25. Add a private field (class-level variable) named *m_strTruckType* to the *Truck* class by adding the boldface statement shown in the following code sample to the *Truck* class declaration.

```
Public Class Truck
     Inherits Vehicle
     Private m_strTruckType As String

End Class
```

26. Add a public property called *TruckType* to the *Truck* class by typing the boldface code shown in the following code sample.

```
Public Class Truck
     Inherits Vehicle
     Private m_strTruckType As String

     Public Property TruckType() As String
         Get
             Return m_strTruckType
         End Get
         Set(ByVal Value As String)
             m_strTruckType = Value
         End Set
     End Property
End Class
```

27. Open the form's code module, scroll to the top of the module, and place the insertion point at the top.

28. Press CTRL+H to open the Replace dialog box once again.

29. Type **Vehicle** in the Find What box, and then type **Truck** in the Replace With box.

30. Click Find Next to locate the first reference to *Vehicle*.

31. Click Replace.

32. Continue clicking Replace until all references to *Vehicle* in the form's code module are replaced by *Truck*. A word of warning: if you elected to search All Documents, the Replace dialog box also will locate and highlight the word *Vehicle* in the *Inherits* statement in the *Truck* class module. Do not replace this one.

33. In the *btnCreateTruck_Click* event handler, replace the *Type* property with the new property called *TruckType*.

```
With newTruck
    .Manufacturer = txtManufacturer.Text
    .TruckType = txtType.Text
    .Model = txtModel.Text
    .Color = txtColor.Text
    .Doors = Integer.Parse(txtDoors.Text)
End With
```

34. Make the same change in the *DisplayDetails* Sub procedure.

```
With newTruck
    txtDisplayManufacturer.Text = .Manufacturer
    txtDisplayType.Text = .TruckType
    txtDisplayModel.Text = .Model
    txtDisplayColor.Text = .Color
    txtDisplayDoors.Text = .Doors.ToString()
End With
```

35. Run the program and enter the following data:

- ❑ Manufacturer: **Ford**
- ❑ Type: **Stakebed**
- ❑ Model: **F250**
- ❑ Color: **Blue**
- ❑ Doors: **2**

36. Click the Create Vehicle button to create an instance of the *Truck* class. You should now see the message shown in Figure 13-17. Remember that you provided the code that will retrieve the name of the base class of the *Vehicle* class and display that in a message box. In this case, as you can see from Figure 13-17, the base class for the *Truck* class is the *Vehicle* class.

Figure 13-17   Message indicating inheritance from the TruckDetails.Vehicle object

Clicking OK on the message box will display the details of the truck in the appropriate text boxes, as shown in Figure 13-18.

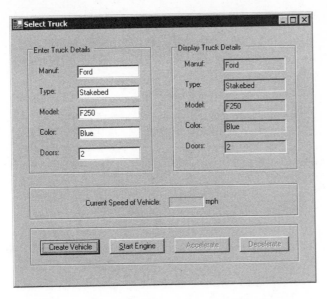

Figure 13-18   Displaying the details of the Truck object

As you can see, by adding a new class that inherits from a base class, you automatically inherit all the properties, methods, and events of the base class. You can also add properties, methods, and events to the derived class to further customize it.

How Inheritance Works

Inheritance works because the derived class actually creates an instance of the base class before the derived class is completely instantiated. When you refer to a property or method by referencing the instance of the derived class, you are really referring to the property or method of the instance of the base class. For example, when you create an instance of the *Truck* class, the class implicitly calls the constructor of the *Vehicle* class (the base class) and creates an instance of that class. If you then provide a value for one of the properties, such as the *Manufacturer* property, you are actually setting the property in the base class.

To prove this point, let's add a constructor to the *Truck* class and call the constructor of the base class.

▶ Adding a constructor to the *Truck* class

1. Open the *Truck* class in the Code Editor, and then add a default constructor, as shown in boldface code in the following code sample.

```
Public Class Truck
    Inherits Vehicle
    Private m_strTruckType As String

    Public Sub New()
        MyBase.New()
    End Sub
    …
End Class
```

2. Set a breakpoint next to the statement `Public Sub New()`.

3. Press F5 to run the program with debugging.

4. Type the appropriate values in each of the text boxes, and then click the Create Vehicle button.

5. The program will enter break mode and stop at the breakpoint you set previously.

6. Press F11 to step into the code, and watch what happens.

As you can see, after you press F11 to run *MyBase.New*, code execution switches to the constructor of the *Vehicle* class, creates an instance of the *Vehicle* class, and then returns to the *Truck* class to finish creating the instance of the *Truck* class.

Abstract Classes

Abstract classes are classes that generally contain only property, method, and event declarations with no implementation code. Abstract classes cannot be instantiated. You can create an abstract class to be a base class, knowing that you will inherit from it. You would then provide the implementation code in the derived class.

You can declare an abstract class by using the *MustInherit* keyword. You declare each property and method by using the *MustOverride* keyword. Note that you do not declare events by using the *MustOverride* keyword.

If you were to create the *Vehicle* class as an abstract class, your code would look like the following code sample:

```
Public MustInherit Class Vehicle
    Implements IDisposable

    Private m_strManufacturer As String
    Private m_strType As String
    Private m_strModel As String
    Private m_intDoors As Integer
    Private m_strColor As String
    Private m_intSpeed As Integer
    Private m_blnEngineRunning As Boolean

    Public Event Stopped()
    Public Event Disposed()

    Public MustOverride Property Manufacturer() As String
    Public MustOverride Property Type() As String
    Public MustOverride Property Model() As String
    Public MustOverride Property Doors() As Integer
    Public MustOverride Property Color() As String
    Public MustOverride ReadOnly Property Speed() As Integer
    Public MustOverride Function EngineStart() As Boolean
    Public MustOverride Function EngineStop() As Boolean
    Public MustOverride Sub Accelerate()
```

```
        Public MustOverride Sub Decelerate()
        Public MustOverride Sub Dispose() Implements System.IDisposable.Dispose
End Class
```

Creating an abstract class rather than a fully implemented class has the following benefits:

- You can provide partial implementation, or no implementation at all, in an abstract class. Because an abstract class cannot be directly instantiated, the derived class will have to provide the implementation code if none is provided in the base class.

- You are creating the class so that it will be inherited by other classes, and each of these other classes will implement the properties, methods, and events differently.

Sealed Classes

A **sealed class** is a class that cannot be a base class. It is at the end of the class hierarchy and cannot be inherited from. If we were to create the *Truck* class as a sealed class, it would look like the following code sample:

```
Public NotInheritable Class Truck
        Inherits Vehicle

        Private m_strTruckType As String

        Public Property TruckType() As String
            Get
                Return m_strTruckType
            End Get
            Set(ByVal Value As String)
                m_strTruckType = Value
            End Set
        End Property

End Class
```

Designating a class as sealed can provide the following benefits:

- It improves performance because the compiler understands that this object is the last in the hierarchical chain and will optimize the code at that point.

- A developer who uses your class cannot inherit from it and change the way the class performs. If you were to attempt to inherit from a *Truck* class that was sealed, you would get the syntax error shown in Figure 13-19.

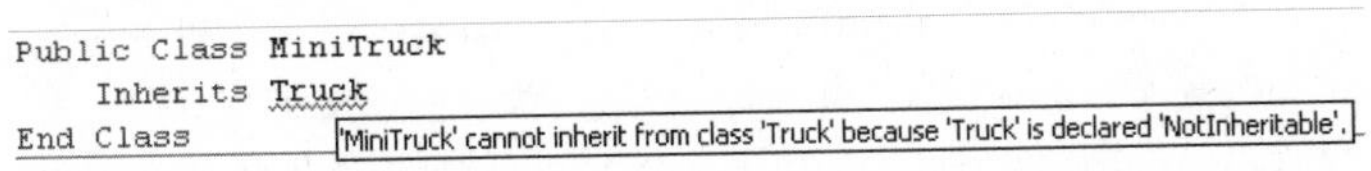

```
Public Class MiniTruck
    Inherits Truck
End Class        'MiniTruck' cannot inherit from class 'Truck' because 'Truck' is declared 'NotInheritable'.
```

Figure 13-19 Error message that appears when you try to inherit from a *NotInheritable* class

Visual Inheritance

What you have seen so far has been implementation inheritance. Now you will see that in addition to being able to inherit most .NET classes and base classes of your own design, you can also inherit from forms and other classes that have a visual interface. This is called **visual inheritance**.

If you were creating a program for a corporate client, you might want to ensure that all the forms in the program had a similar appearance and similar functionality. It can be annoying to users when they open a new form and it looks so different that they think they are in another program entirely. By using visual inheritance, you can create a base form class and place various elements on the form, such as logos or title labels or even other controls. You can then create all of the forms that will be used in the program and have each of them inherit from the base form. The inherited forms will have the same elements as the base form.

The best thing and the worst thing about using base forms are really the same. If you make a change to the base form, all the forms that derive from the base will also be changed. This is good because changes to the derived forms happen automatically, without a lot of development time and effort. It can also be bad because some changed elements might be acceptable in one form but not in another. In situations like this, you want to add to the base form only those elements that you know are acceptable in all forms, and then add custom elements to the derived forms.

So that you can see visual inheritance in action, you will add a base form to the VehicleDetails project and have the existing form, frmSelectVehicle, inherit from it. After you add the base form, you will add the following elements to the form:

- A label to display a title
- A picture box to display an image
- Two additional labels that will act as lines

▶ Using a base form in the VehicleDetails application

1. Open the VehicleDetails project in Visual Studio .NET.

2. Right-click the project name in Solution Explorer, point to Add, and then select Add Windows Form.

3. Type **BaseForm** in the Name box, and then click Open.

4. Open frmSelectVehicle in the designer.

5. Increase the height of the form by either dragging the bottom sizing handle or specifying the height size in the *Size* property of the form. The new height, which is the second number listed in the *Size* property of the form, is 552. You can use this as a starting point and adjust it from there as you need to.

6. Select all the controls on the form by drawing a marquee selection around them.

7. After all the controls are selected, on the Format menu, point to Center In Form, and then select Vertically. This will move the group of controls to the vertical center of the form.

8. Note the size of the form.

9. Open the new base form in the designer, and set the *Size* property so that it is the same as the size of frmSelectVehicle.

10. Add a label to the top of the form, and name it **lblTitle**.

11. Set the font size of the label to 12 points.

12. Add a PictureBox control to the bottom left side of the form, and name it **picImage**.

13. Select the picture box and locate the *Image* property in the Properties window.

14. Click the build button and locate an appropriate image (bitmap, .jpg, or .gif file) to display in the picture box. You can use the image car.bmp located in the student file or choose one of your own.

15. Set the *SizeMode* property of the PictureBox to StretchImage. This will shrink the image to the size of the picture box.

16. Add two additional labels to the bottom of the form (one above the other), and set the *Size* property of each of these labels to **452, 1**. This will set the width of the labels to 452 and the height to 1. You can adjust the width to fit the form.

17. Locate the *BackColor* properties of both of the line labels, and set the values to **ControlText**.

18. Rename these labels as **lblLine1** and **lblLine2**.

19. After the base form is complete, select Rebuild Solution from the Build menu.

20. The next step is where the magic happens. Open the frmSelectVehicle code module in the Code Editor.

21. Locate the statement just below the class declaration that says `Inherits System.Windows.Forms.Form`. Recode that statement so that it reads `Inherits BaseForm`.

You now have a base form (*BaseForm*) that inherits from *System.Windows.Forms.Form* and a derived form (frmSelectVehicle) that derives from *BaseForm*. If Microsoft were to update the *Form* class in Visual Basic .NET, you would be able to take advantage of those changes when you were working with the *BaseForm* (as long as you had installed the updates from Microsoft). Likewise, if you were to make changes to *BaseForm*, you would be able to take advantage of those changes when you were working with frmSelectVehicle.

> **TIP** When you make code modifications, such as changing the inherited base of a completed form, the event handlers might be disconnected from their associated events. If this happens, look at each event handler in the Code Editor and make sure that it has a *Handles* statement at the end of its declaration that references the required events.

Let's test the program to see if it actually works. You will create a *Title* property in the *BaseForm*. If everything works as you hope it will, you will see the new *Title* property in the Properties window of frmSelectVehicle. You can then set the value for *Title* in the Properties window of frmSelectVehicle and pass the value from *Title* to *lblTitle.Text* in code.

Although this might sound confusing, we will work through it slowly so that you can see what's happening at each step.

▶ Testing the BaseForm code

1. Open the BaseForm code module in the Code Editor.

2. You will add a class-level variable and a Property procedure for the new property called *Title*. Type the code shown in the following code sample just below the Windows Forms Designer–generated code region.

```
Private m_strTitle As String

Public Property Title() As String
    Get
        Return m_strTitle
    End Get
    Set(ByVal Value As String)
        m_strTitle = Value
    End Set
End Property
```

3. Now rebuild the solution by selecting Rebuild Solution on the Build menu.

4. Open BaseForm in design view, select the label (lblTitle), and locate the *Text* property in the Properties window.

5. Delete the text in the *Text* property and save the changes.

6. Close BaseForm and save the changes (if prompted).

7. Open frmSelectVehicle in design view, select the form, and then locate the new *Title* property in the Properties window.

8. Type **Two Programmer's Vehicle Sales** in the *Title* property of the form.

9. Open frmSelectVehicle in the Code Editor, and then type the boldface code shown in the following code sample in the *frmSelectVehicle_Load* event handler directly below the *AddHandler* statements.

```
Private Sub frmSelectVehicle_Load(ByVal sender As System.Object, _
        ByVal e As System.EventArgs) Handles MyBase.Load

    AddHandler txtManufacturer.TextChanged, AddressOf textboxes_TextChanged
    AddHandler txtType.TextChanged, AddressOf textboxes_TextChanged
    AddHandler txtModel.TextChanged, AddressOf textboxes_TextChanged
    AddHandler txtColor.TextChanged, AddressOf textboxes_TextChanged
    AddHandler txtDoors.TextChanged, AddressOf textboxes_TextChanged

    lblTitle.Text = Me.Title

End Sub
```

10. Run the program and make sure that everything works as expected.

    The completed SelectVehicle form should look like Figure 13-20 when it is running.

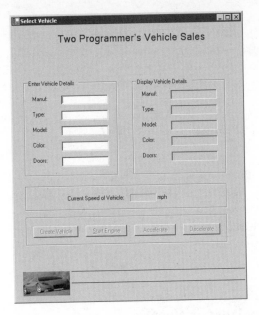

Figure 13-20   The completed SelectVehicle form

Try It

Add another Label control to the bottom of the BaseForm between the two lines. Display the current date and time in this label when the program is running. When you are testing the changes, make sure the date and time appear on the SelectVehicle form.

What Do You Think?

1. What is the purpose of encapsulation?

2. Describe the impact of non-deterministic finalization and garbage collection on programmers.

3. What is the difference between a constructor and a destructor?

4. How is a destructor created?

5. What is the purpose of the *IDisposable* interface?

6. What part does inheritance play in the development of new classes?

7. What is an abstract class?

8. How does visual inheritance work?

POLYMORPHISM

Polymorphism is a big word, but it's a simple concept when applied to object-oriented programming (OOP). *Polymorphism* is a Greek word that means *many forms*. In OOP, **polymorphism** means that an object can display different (polymorphic) behavior when it is implemented differently.

Let's take the *Vehicle* and *Truck* classes as examples. You know that the *Truck* class inherits from the *Vehicle* class, and therefore you can say that a Truck is a Vehicle and, as such, has all the behaviors of a Vehicle. For example, let's declare a Vehicle object variable and instantiate it as a Truck. You can see that, although you still have a Truck, it has all the behaviors of a Vehicle.

The interesting point of this is that when you declare the object as a Vehicle and instantiate it as a Truck, the new object can only behave like a Vehicle and will have none of the additional behaviors of a Truck.

So that you can practice using polymorphism, you will modify the TruckDetails program. This will require several changes to the *Vehicle* class and the *Truck* class. You will also modify the user interface and the code in the form. With the changes that you make, you will be able to select either a vehicle or a truck and run differ-ent implementation code depending on the type of vehicle you have selected.

▶ Implementing polymorphism

1. Using Windows Explorer, create a copy of the TruckDetails project folder and rename it as **VehicleDetails_Polymorphism**.

2. Open the copy in Visual Studio .NET.

3. Right-click the project in Solution Explorer and select Properties.

4. In the TruckDetails Property Pages dialog box, change the Assembly Name to **VehicleDetails** and then change the *Root Namespace* to **VehicleDetails**. As before, you will change the name of the form in a few moments.

5. Click OK to close the dialog box, and save the changes.

6. With the project name still selected in Solution Explorer, change the project name from TruckDetails to **VehicleDetails** in the Properties window.

7. Select the solution name in Solution Explorer, and change the name of the solution from TruckDetails to **VehicleDetails** in the Properties window.

8. Select the TruckForm.vb file in Solution Explorer, and change the name from TruckForm.vb to **VehicleForm.vb**.

9. Open the form in designer view, and change the name of the form from frmSelectTruck to **frmSelectVehicle**.

10. Open the Property Pages dialog box again by right-clicking the project name in Solution Explorer, and change the startup object.

11. Change the *Text* property of the form from Select Truck to **Select Vehicle**.

12. Change the name of the Create Truck button from btnCreateTruck to **btnCreateVehicle**.

13. Change the *Text* property of btnCreateVehicle from Create Truck to **Create Vehicle**.

14. Open the *Vehicle* class in the Code Editor.

15. Locate the *Speed* property, and change the scope modifier from *Private* to *Protected*, as shown in the boldface line of code in the following code sample.

```
Protected Property Speed() As Integer
    Get
        Return m_intSpeed
    End Get
    Set(ByVal value As Integer)
        m_intSpeed = value
    End Set
End Property
```

16. Locate the *Accelerate* method, and add the *Overridable* keyword between *Public* and *Sub*, as shown in the following code sample.

```
Public Overridable Sub Accelerate()
    If IsEngineRunning() Then
        Speed += 5
    End If
End Sub
```

17. Locate the *Decelerate* method, and add the *Overridable* keyword between *Public* and *Sub*, as shown in the following code sample.

```
Public Overridable Sub Decelerate()
    If IsEngineRunning() Then
        If Speed >= 5 Then
            Speed -= 5
        Else
            Speed = 0
        End If
    End If

    If Speed <= 0 Then
        RaiseEvent Stopped()
    End If

End Sub
```

18. Open the *Truck* class in the Code Editor.

19. Add the new *Accelerate* and *Decelerate* methods that will override the same methods in the *Vehicle* class, as shown in the following code sample.

```
Public Overrides Sub Accelerate()
    If IsEngineRunning() Then
        Speed += 2
    End If
End Sub

Public Overrides Sub Decelerate()
    If IsEngineRunning() Then
        If Speed >= 2 Then
            Speed -= 2
        Else
            Speed = 0
        End If
    End If

    If Speed <= 0 Then
        MyBase.Decelerate()
    End If

End Sub
```

▶ Modifying the user interface

1. Open VehicleForm in the designer.

2. Select and delete the txtType text box.

3. Replace the deleted text box with a combo box, name it **cboType**, and then delete the default *Text* property.

4. Align and size the combo box so that it's exactly the same size as the text box that it's replacing.

5. Select the combo box in the designer, and locate the *Items* property in the Properties window.

6. Click Collection to display the String Collection Editor dialog box.

7. Add the Truck and Vehicle items to the Items Collection by entering them into the String Collection Editor, as shown in Figure 13-21. After you type in the first item, press ENTER and type in the second item.

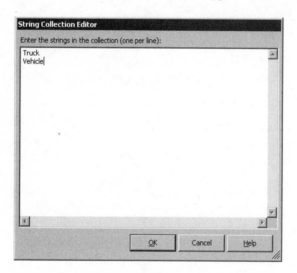

Figure 13-21   Adding the items to the String Collection Editor of the combo box

8. After you have entered both items, click OK to close the String Collection Editor.

9. With the form still displayed, on the View menu, select Tab Order to display the tab order of the controls.

10. Change the tab order of the combo box so that it follows immediately after txtManufacturer. You need to do this because the tab order was changed when you deleted the text box and added the combo box.

▶ Modifying the code in the form

1. Open VehicleForm in the Code Editor.

2. Locate the *frmSelectTruck_Click* event handler and change the name of the event handler to **frmSelectVehicle_Click**.

3. In the *frmSelectTruck_Load* event handler, locate the *AddHandler* statement for the *txtType.TextChanged* event. Change txtType.TextChanged to

cboType.TextChanged. The rest of the statement is correct because you will be linking the *TextChanged* event of the combo box to the event handler.

4. Locate the *btnCreateTruck_Click* event handler and change the name of the event handler to **btnCreateVehicle_Click**.

5. Inside the event handler, locate and delete the `newTruck = New Truck` statement.

6. In its place, add a *Select Case* statement, as shown in the following code sample.

```
Select Case cboType.Text
    Case "Truck"
        newVehicle = New Truck
    Case "Vehicle"
        newVehicle = New Vehicle
    Case Else
        Exit Sub
End Select
```

7. In the same event handler, locate the following assignment statement:

```
.Type = txtType.Text
```

8. Replace `txtType.Text` with **cboType.Text** so that the statement looks like this:

```
.Type = cboType.Text
```

9. Review the changes and compare them with the following code sample, which shows the event handler after all the changes have been made.

```
Private Sub btnCreateTruck_Click(ByVal sender As System.Object, _
        ByVal e As System.EventArgs) Handles btnCreateVehicle.Click

    Try
        Select Case cboType.Text
            Case "Truck"
                newVehicle = New Truck
            Case "Vehicle"
                newVehicle = New Vehicle
            Case Else
                Exit Sub
        End Select

        With newTruck
            .Manufacturer = txtManufacturer.Text
            .Type = cboType.Text
            .Model = txtModel.Text
            .Color = txtColor.Text
            .Doors = Integer.Parse(txtDoors.Text)
        End With

        DisplayDetails()

        btnEngine.Enabled = True

    Catch ex As SystemException
        MessageBox.Show(ex.Message, "Error in Truck Creation", _
            MessageBoxButtons.OK, MessageBoxIcon.Error)

    End Try

End Sub
```

10. Locate the *textboxes_TextChanged* event handler, and change the reference to txtType.TextLength to **cboType.Text.Length**, as shown in the following code sample.

```
Private Sub textboxes_TextChanged(ByVal sender As Object, _
    ByVal e As System.EventArgs)

    If Trim(txtManufacturer.Text).Length > 0 AndAlso cboType.Text.Length > 0 _
        AndAlso Trim(txtModel.Text).Length > 0 AndAlso Trim(txtColor.Text)
            .Length > 0 _
        AndAlso Trim(txtDoors.Text).Length > 0 AndAlso IsNumeric(txtDoors
            .Text) Then

        btnCreateVehicle.Enabled = True
    End If

    …
End Sub
```

To make the program a little easier to work with, whenever the user switches between vehicle types by using the combo box, you need to reset the form to its original configuration. To do this, you will add a new method to reset the form and call this method from the *cboType.SelectedValueChanged* event handler.

▶ Adding the *Form_Reset* method and testing

1. Open the VehicleForm in the Code Editor.

2. Add the method shown in the following code sample just below the *frmSelectTruck_Load* event handler.

```
Private Sub Form_Reset()

    With btnEngine
        .Enabled = False
        .Text = "&Start Engine"
    End With

    lblCurrentSpeed.Text = ""
    btnEngine.Enabled = False
    btnAccelerate.Enabled = False
    btnDecelerate.Enabled = False

End Sub
```

3. In the Class Name list, select cboType.

4. In the Method Name list, select SelectedValueChanged. The event handler will be added to the Code Editor.

5. Type the following statement inside the *cboType.SelectedValueChanged* event handler to call *Form_Reset*.

```
Form_Reset()
```

Now whenever the user selects a different vehicle, the form will be reset, but the original values in the text boxes will be retained. In a real-world application, you might want to clear all the text boxes in addition to resetting the buttons and clearing the speed label. Because we are just demonstrating polymorphism, we did not do that.

6. Press F5 to run the program.

7. Type the appropriate values in each of the text boxes, and then select Vehicle in the combo box.

8. Create a new Vehicle object by clicking Create Vehicle.

9. Start the engine by clicking Start Engine.

10. Click Accelerate several times to increase the speed of the vehicle. Notice that the speed increments by 5 after each click.

11. Click Decelerate several times. Notice that the speed decrements by 5 after each click. After the speed reaches 0, the Decelerate button is disabled.

12. Now select Truck in the combo box. All buttons except for the Create Vehicle button should be disabled.

13. Create a new Truck by clicking Create Vehicle. Remember that you are actually creating a Vehicle object that is displaying the behavior of a Truck.

14. Start the engine by clicking Start Engine.

15. Click Accelerate several times to increase the speed of the vehicle. Notice that the speed now increments by 2 after each click.

16. Click Decelerate several times. Notice that the speed now decrements by 2 after each click. After the speed reaches 0, the Decelerate button is disabled.

17. Figure 13-22 shows the running form. The vehicle selected is Truck.

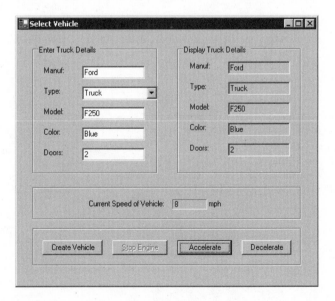

Figure 13-22   Displaying polymorphic behavior

Inside the Code

Let's take a closer look at the changes you have made, starting with the code for the *Speed* property in the *Vehicle* class.

```
Protected Property Speed() As Integer
   …
End Property
```

You changed the scope modifier from *Private* to *Protected*. The *Protected* modifier allows the current class and any derived class to access the method, but it does not allow access to any other class in the assembly. You needed to make this change to make the method accessible to the *Truck* class from which it is derived. If you didn't make this change, you could not have referred to the method in the *Truck* class. If you had made the method public, it would have been accessible to the form, and the speed could have been changed by just setting the value of the *Speed* property without running either the *Accelerate* or the *Decelerate* method. These methods are shown next, as defined for the *Vehicle* class.

```
Public Overridable Sub Accelerate()
   …
End Sub

Public Overridable Sub Decelerate()
   …
End Sub
```

By marking these methods as *Overridable*, you are saying that it is all right to override these methods in the derived class. Developers using the class as a base class might need to change the way these methods are implemented, and you are granting them permission to do so.

Here is the code for the *Accelerate* and *Decelerate* methods of the *Truck* class:

```
Public Overrides Sub Accelerate()
    If IsEngineRunning() Then
        Speed += 2
    End If
End Sub

Public Overrides Sub Decelerate()
    If IsEngineRunning() Then

        If Speed >= 2 Then
            Speed -= 2
        Else
            Speed = 0
        End If
    End If

    If Speed <= 0 Then
        MyBase.Decelerate()
    End If
End Sub
```

You have changed the implementation of these two methods. Instead of incrementing and decrementing by 5, as with the *Vehicle* class, you are now incrementing and decrementing by 2.

But the biggest change is how you are dealing with the *Stopped* event of the *Vehicle* class. Although a derived class inherits everything from the base class, you cannot raise an event created in a base class from code in a derived class. Remember that you are treating the Truck as a Vehicle, so even if you were to create a new event in the *Truck* class, you wouldn't be able to receive the event in the form. Instead, you will just call the *Decelerate* method of the base class and let that class raise the event.

Try It

Modify the *btnCreateVehicle_Click* event handler to display a message box that describes the properties and class type of the vehicle that was just created.

What Do You Think?

1. What does polymorphism mean in the context of OOP?

2. What is the purpose of the *Protected* scope modifier?

3. How can you allow developers to change the way methods inherited from the base class work inside their derived classes?

Q&A

Q. Would you ever have a *WriteOnly* property?

A. Yes. This would be useful if you wanted a user to enter a password or even a social security number. You would want to accept those values for verification purposes but would have no reason to need to read back those values.

Q. After I have created a class, is it okay to change the methods and properties if I feel that it makes the class more efficient?

A. Absolutely! As long as you do it before you distribute the application to your users. Remember that the public interface is a contract with the outside world, and that any changes to the existing interface will break that contract.

Changing the class is referred to as **refactoring**. This would be done to make the class more efficient or more effective. You might recall that, when we demonstrated polymorphism, you refactored the *Vehicle* class. Remember that you changed the modifier of the *Speed* property from *Private* to *Protected*, and that you also made the *Accelerate* and *Decelerate* methods *Overridable*.

Refactoring is a common practice because getting things exactly right the first time is rare.

Q. If I declare and instantiate a class inside a procedure and then run the procedure, what happens to the object after the procedure has completed?

A. The object is de-referenced and is considered unreachable. It will remain in memory until the garbage collector disposes of it.

Q. Referring to the last question, what if I ran the procedure a second time. Would this restore the reference to the same object and enable me to use it again?

A. No. When you run the procedure a second time, the old reference is destroyed and a new object is created.

Q. So what if I declare the object variable at the class level and create the instance of the class inside a procedure? Would I get the original object when I ran the procedure a second time?

A. Again, the answer is no. Each time you run `objectvariable = New MyClass`, you will get a new object. The only way to ensure that you have a reference to the same object is to instantiate it in a procedure that will run only once for the lifetime of the program. Such a procedure might be the *Form_Load* event handler or the constructor method of the form.

Q. I understand that OOP supports method overloading. What is method overloading, and how would I use it?

A. *Method overloading* refers to the ability to incorporate multiple methods with the same name but with different signatures in a class or a derived class. A *signature* is the list of parameters in the method declaration. To qualify as a different signature, the number of parameters in each overloaded method must be different, or the data type of the parameters must be different. Changing the names of any of the parameters would not qualify. Look at the following overloaded methods:

```
Private Overloads Function Calculate() As Double
    Dim dblNumber As Double
    Return dblNumber * 2
End Function

Private Overloads Function Calculate(ByVal dblNumber As Double) As Double
    Return dblNumber * 2
End Function

Private Overloads Function Calculate(ByVal dblNumber As Double, _
        ByVal intMultiplier As Integer) As Double
    Return dblNumber * intMultiplier
End Function
```

Notice that, when you overload a method, you must include the *Overloads* keyword in all the methods, including the original one.

If you added a fourth overloaded method but changed only the name of a parameter, you would receive a compile-time error.

```
Private Overloads Function Calculate(ByVal dblNumber1 As Double, _
        ByVal intMultiplier As Integer) As Double
    Return dblNumber1 * intMultiplier
End Function
```

Changing the order of the parameters as shown in the following example also results in a different signature, but that is considered a poor programming practice and should be avoided unless absolutely necessary.

```
Private Overloads Function Calculate(ByVal intMultiplier As Integer, _
        ByVal dblNumber1 As Double) As Double
    Return dblNumber1 * intMultiplier
End Function
```

You can also create an overloaded method in a derived class. The difference here is that the base class does not require that you include the *Overloads* keyword. Look at the following example, in which we are overloading the *GetSpeed* function of the *Vehicle* class inside the *Truck* class.

```
Public Overloads Function GetSpeed() As Integer
    Return Speed * 2
End Function
```

WRAPPING UP

- A class is a template or blueprint for an object. An object is an instance of a class.

- The public interface of a class is the public properties, methods, events, and fields of the class (the *public members*). When an instance of the class is created, code in the form or any other class can reference all the public members.

- When creating a class, decide which properties, methods, and events need to be public. All other properties and methods should be private and provide the internal workings of the class. Nothing outside the class that can refer to the instance of the class should be able to access anything that you have not made public.

- Encapsulation (data hiding) means that data is passed in and out of the class through its public interface (through its properties and methods). Instance fields should be private; making them public would break encapsulation by allowing potentially bad data to enter the class without warning.

- The constructor for a class is a special Sub procedure named *New*. A default constructor is not required because the compiler will create one for you if you have not provided one already. The constructor can be used to run any initializing code (such as code to open files or establish database connections) that must be run prior to the creation of the class.

- A destructor is a special Sub procedure named *Finalize*. The compiler will not create a default destructor if one is not provided in code. A destructor can be used to run cleanup code just before the object is destroyed by the garbage collector.

- Rather than implement the *Finalize* method, implement the *IDisposable* interface and provide cleanup code in the *Dispose* method. If you put cleanup code in the *Dispose* method, you must explicitly call that method to ensure that resources are released.

- The effective life of an object starts when the constructor is executed and ends when the object reference goes out of scope. The object remains in memory until the garbage collector destroys it.

- The garbage collector is a memory management system that manages the cleanup of what is referred to as the managed heap (a special memory area for storing objects). It uses a rather complex algorithm that determines when objects are unreachable and then destroys them, releasing the memory back to the application.

- A class can derive or inherit from another class. A derived class inherits all the properties, methods, events, and fields of the base class. All classes ultimately derive from *System.Object*.

- An abstract class is a base class that cannot be instantiated. Instead, you must inherit from it and create an instance of the derived class.

- A sealed class is the last class in the inheritance chain. You cannot derive from a sealed class. Creating a sealed class improves performance because the compiler can optimize the code when it can determine that there are no more subclasses to deal with.

- Visual inheritance allows you to create forms or controls to use as base classes for subclassed forms or controls. For example, you could create a base form, add whatever controls you want, and then include implementation code for those controls. When you inherit from that form, you will also inherit all of its functionality. Changes to the base form will affect all forms that derive from it.

- Polymorphism means that you can declare an object variable of a certain type and instantiate it as a derived type. In the VehicleDetails example, you declared a newVehicle object as a Vehicle but instantiated it as a Truck. Although the Truck can only be used as a Vehicle, you can provide implementation code to make it perform differently.

KEYWORDS

abstract class	abstraction
class	constructor
destructor	encapsulation
garbage collector	inheritance
instantiate	method overloading
non-deterministic finalization	object
polymorphism	public interface
refactoring	sealed class
visual inheritance	

REVIEW QUESTIONS

1. When you are going to create a new object from a class, you could say that you are going to _____ the object.

   a. inherit

   b. instantiate

   c. initialize

   d. construct

2. Classes should be _____, which means that they should be designed to do one thing only.

   a. inherited

   b. instantiated

   c. specialized

   d. encapsulated

3. The combination of multiple methods into one method is called _____.

   a. refactoring

   b. refining

   c. encapsulating

   d. constructing

4. Which methods are used to create attributes for classes? (Choose all correct answers.)

   a. *Sub*

   b. *Get*

   c. *Property*

   d. *Function*

5. You should add a(n) _____ to a class to let the object indicate that something has happened.

   a. property

   b. method

   c. value

   d. event

6. The .NET object that is responsible for managing an application's use of memory is called the _____.

   a. garbage collector

   b. constructor

   c. destructor

   d. object

7. A(n) _____ is used to open files, connect to databases, and perform other required tasks before a new object can be used.

   a. constructor

   b. destructor

   c. interface

   d. class

8. Classes that have properties, methods, and events but cannot be instantiated are called _____ classes.

   a. base

   b. sealed

   c. abstract

   d. inherited

9. A class that cannot be inherited from is called a(n) _____ class.

   a. base

   b. sealed

   c. abstract

   d. inherited

10. If you are using visual inheritance, you are creating a(n) _____ form class and then creating other forms that inherit from it.

    a. base

    b. sealed

    c. abstract

    d. inherited

11. A class is an instance of an object. True or false?

12. All methods and fields of a class should be available for the user to see and use. True or false?

13. In Visual Basic .NET, the number zero will always evaluate to True. True or false?

14. After an object goes out of scope, it can never be referenced again. True or false?

15. The destructor for a class must be explicitly created in an application's code. True or false?

16. The _____ of a class includes the methods and variables that can be accessed by the rest of the world.

17. The _____ statement is used to connect an event that will be raised by a class to an event handler.

18. _____ is the term that refers to the hiding of the inner workings of a class from the user.

19. The destructor method that is used in Visual Basic .NET is called _____.

20. If class B _____ from class A, class B will have all of the properties, methods, and events that class A has.

STEP BY STEP

In this project for the Baldwin Museum of Science, you will create a form that will be used to collect information about cats. The form will use the *Cat* class, and each cat entered will require the creation of another instance of the *Cat* class.

The *Cat* class will have the following properties:

- *Name*
- *Color*
- *Weight*
- *Age*

The *Cat* class will have the following methods:

- *Meow*
- *Sleep*
- *Wake Up*

When the new Cat object is created, a message will appear at the bottom of the screen containing all of the properties of the Cat object. A sound will be played when the user clicks the Meow button. The Sleep and Wake Up buttons will disable each other to limit their use. The form for this application will look like Figure 13-23.

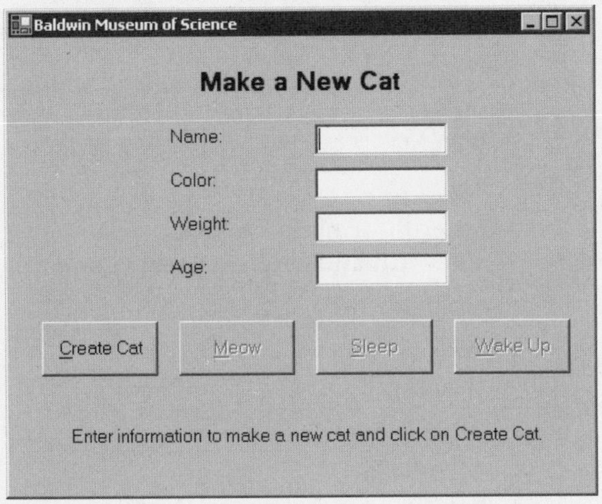

Figure 13-23   The completed frmNewCat form

▶ Creating a new project

1. Open Visual Studio .NET if it isn't already open.

2. Click the New Project button on the Start Page.

3. Click Visual Basic Projects under Project Types and Windows Application under Templates.

4. Type **CatsCh13** in the Name box.

5. Browse to the location in which you are storing your projects.

6. Click OK.

▶ Configuring the form and changing the startup object

1. Right-click Form1.vb in Solution Explorer, and rename Form1.vb as **NewCat.vb**. Press ENTER.

2. Click once in the title bar of the form, and change the *(Name)* property of the form to **frmNewCat**.

3. Change the *Text* property of the form to **Baldwin Museum of Science**, and then press ENTER.

4. Right-click the CatsCh13 project name in Solution Explorer, and then click Properties.

5. Change the startup object to frmNewCat, and then click OK.

▶ Setting up the form

1. Add the required Label controls and TextBox controls to the form, as shown in Figure 12-27. Assign the labels and text boxes *(Name)* and *Text* properties, as shown in Table 13-9.

Table 13-9   **frmNewCat Controls and Properties**

Control	(Name)	Text
Label	Label1	**Make a New Cat**
Label	Label2	**Name:**
Label	Label3	**Color:**
Label	Label4	**Weight:**
Label	Label5	**Age:**
Label	**lblNewCat**	**Enter information to make a new cat and click on Create Cat.**
TextBox	**txtName**	\<blank>
TextBox	**txtColor**	\<blank>
TextBox	**txtWeight**	\<blank>
TextBox	**txtAge**	\<blank>
Button	**btnCreateCat**	**&Create Cat**
Button	**btnMeow**	**&Meow**
Button	**btnSleep**	**&Sleep**
Button	**btnWakeUp**	**&Wake Up**

2. Set the *Enabled* properties of the btnMeow, btnSleep, and btnWakeUp controls to False.

▶ Creating the *Cat* class

1. Add a new class to the solution by right-clicking the project name in Solution Explorer, pointing to Add, and then selecting Add Class.

2. Change the name of the class in the dialog box from Class1.vb to **Cat.vb**, and then click Open.

3. Add the following fields to the *Cat* class.

```
Private m_strName as String
Private m_strColor as String
Private m_intWeight as Integer
Private m_intAge as Integer
Public m_blnAwake As Boolean
```

4. Add the properties shown in the following code sample to the *Cat* class.

```
Public Property Name() As String
    Get
        Return m_strName
    End Get
    Set(ByVal Value As String)
        m_strName = Value
    End Set
End Property

Public Property Color() As String
    Get
        Return m_strColor
    End Get
    Set(ByVal Value As String)
        m_strColor = Value
    End Set
End Property

Public Property Weight() As Integer
    Get
        Return m_intWeight
    End Get
    Set(ByVal Value As Integer)
        m_intWeight = Value
    End Set
End Property

Public Property Age() As Integer
    Get
        Return m_intAge
    End Get
    Set(ByVal Value As Integer)
        m_intAge = Value
    End Set
End Property
```

5. Add the methods shown in the following code sample to the *Cat* class.

```
Public Sub Meow()
    MessageBox.Show("The cat is trying to meow!")
End Sub

Public Sub Sleep()
    m_blnAwake = False
End Sub
```

```
Public Sub WakeUp()
    m_blnAwake = True
End Sub
```

▶ Coding the frmCat form

1. Open the form in design view, and then double-click the btnCreateCat button.

2. Declare a class-level variable to store the Cat object by typing the following line of code just below the Windows Forms Designer–generated code region.

```
Private newCat As Cat
```

3. Type the boldface code shown in the following code sample into the *btnCreateCat_Click* event handler.

```
Private Sub btnCreateCat_Click(ByVal sender As System.Object, _
        ByVal e As System.EventArgs) Handles btnCreateCat.Click

    Try
        newCat = New Cat
        With newCat
            .Name = txtName.Text
            .Color = txtColor.Text
            .Weight = CInt(txtWeight.Text)
            .Age = CInt(txtAge.Text)
        End With
        btnMeow.Enabled = True
        btnSleep.Enabled = True
        lblNewCat.Text = "Your new cat is called " & newCat.Name & _
            & " and it is " & newCat.Color _
            & ", weighs " & newCat.Weight & "lbs. and is " & newCat.Age _
            & " years old."

    Catch ex As Exception
        MessageBox.Show(ex.Message, "Error in Cat object creation", _
            MessageBoxButtons.OK, MessageBoxIcon.Error)
    End Try
End Sub
```

4. Return to the form design view, and then double-click the Meow button.

5. Type the following line of code inside the *btnMeow_Click* event handler.

```
newCat.Meow()
```

6. Return to the form design view, and then double-click the Sleep button.

7. Type the following code inside the *btnSleep_Click* event handler.

```
newCat.Sleep()
SleepMode()
```

8. Return to the form design view, and then double-click the Wake Up button.

9. Type the following code inside the *btnWakeUp_Click* event handler.

```
newCat.WakeUp()
SleepMode()
```

10. Add the new *SleepMode* Sub procedure by typing the code shown here in the Code Editor.

```
Private Sub SleepMode()
    If newCat.m_blnAwake = True Then
        btnWakeUp.Enabled = False
        btnSleep.Enabled = True
        lblNewCat.Text = "Your new cat is called " & newCat.Name & _
            & " and it is " & newCat.Color _
            & ", weighs " & newCat.Weight & " lbs. and is " & newCat.Age _
            & " years old. Your new cat is awake."
    Else
        btnWakeUp.Enabled = True
        btnSleep.Enabled = False
        lblNewCat.Text = "Your new cat is called " & newCat.Name & _
            & " and it is " & newCat.Color _
            & ", weighs " & newCat.Weight & " lbs. and is " & newCat.Age _
            & " years old. Your new cat is asleep."
    End If
End Sub
```

▶ **Saving and testing your project**

1. On the File menu, select Save All to save your work.

2. On the Debug menu, select Start to run your project.

3. Type information into the Name, Color, Weight, and Age boxes, and then click Create Cat. Notice the message that appears in the label at the bottom of the form. Click the Meow, Sleep, and Awake buttons to see how they work.

4. On the Debug menu, select Stop Debugging to end the program.

5. On the File menu, select Close Solution to close the project.

6. Close Visual Studio .NET.

FINISH THE CODE

To complete this exercise, you should open the WoodgroveBankCh13 project that came in your student file. This project contains a form for the Woodgrove Bank that is used to add a new banking transaction. When the user clicks the New Transaction button, a new instance of the *Transaction* class will be created. This new object will automatically be assigned a transaction number, which will be displayed in a text box on the form along with the current date. The user can add the rest of the information about the transaction, and then click Save Transaction to make changes to the properties of the Transaction object. In this exercise, you will finish the *Transaction* class that will be used in the program.

Finish the project by adding the following properties to the *Transaction* class:

- Transaction number
- Transaction date
- Transaction type
- Transaction amount
- Transaction initials

You might have to review the rest of the code in the program to determine the required names for the properties.

JUST HINTS

Now you are going to make a form that employees of Fabrikam, Inc., can use to enter expenses for which they should receive reimbursement from the company. Each expense entered will be an instance of the *Expense* class that you will create. The following information should be included in the *Expense* class.

- Employee number

- Submission date

- Expense date

- Expense amount

- Expense amount paid

- Expense description

- Expense status

You should also provide a method that can be used to approve the expense. The method should change the status of the expense to Paid, and change the Expense Amount Paid to be equal to the number in the Expense Amount field. Include a button on the form that can be used to call this method. Figure 13-24 shows the completed form.

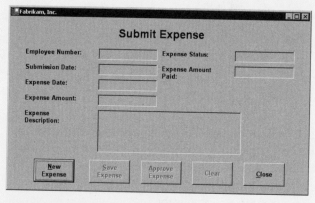

Figure 13-24   Completed project form

ON YOUR OWN

In this exercise, you will create a form for Tailspin Toys that will be used to create a new character for a computer game. Each new character will be an instance of the *Character* class that you will create. The form should include controls that enable the user to select or define the properties of the character. It should also include buttons that can be used to create a character and delete the character displayed on the form. The user should not be able to create a new character until all of the properties have been defined. Figure 13-25 shows an example of the type of form you might create.

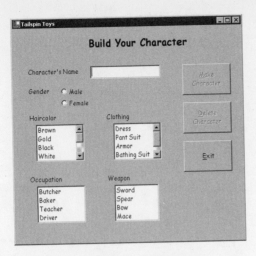

Figure 13-25   Sample character form

MORE PRACTICE

1. List some of the possible properties of a *Customer* class that could be used in an application for a company that sells and delivers furniture to its customers.

2. List the possible properties and methods of a *Storm* class that could be used in a weather-related application.

3. Write the code to declare fields and create the procedure for an *Integer* public property called *Height* that can be read and modified by the user.

4. Write the code to declare the fields and create the procedure for a read-only *String* public property called *Town*.

5. Write the code for a public method called *LandPlane* that returns a Boolean value representing the success of a landing. Return the value of the Boolean variable *blnOnGround* inside the method.

6. Write the code for a public method called *UpdateBalance* that will subtract the value in the *m_decTrxTotal* variable from the *m_decBegBalance* variable and store the result in the variable called *m_decNewBalance*.

7. Write the code that will instantiate a new object of the *Package* class and call it newPackage.

8. Write the code that will instruct the *Package* class to use the *txtDestination_TextChanged* event handler for the *NewDestination* *.TextChanged* event.

9. Write the code that will raise the *LostPackage* event when the *intDelivery-Days* variable is greater than 30.

10. Write the code that declares a public class called *Pet* that inherits from the class called *Dog*.

CHAPTER 14
INTRODUCTION TO ASP.NET

The Internet, the World Wide Web, HTML, DHTML, XML, ASP, and now ASP.NET. What does all this mean? The Internet has brought us many new technologies and even more acronyms; it's hard to keep everything straight. In this chapter, we will introduce you to the latest Internet development technology that Microsoft has to offer: ASP.NET. We will show you how Microsoft ASP.NET works with Microsoft Visual Basic .NET to enable you to develop Web applications.

Upon completion of this chapter, you will be able to:

■ Learn what ASP.NET is.

■ Find out what software is required to create ASP.NET Web pages.

■ Install Internet Information Server.

■ Understand the various types of applications that you can create by using ASP.NET.

■ See how Web applications work.

■ Use Hypertext Markup Language (HTML).

■ Differentiate between client-side controls (HTML controls) and server-side controls (Web Forms controls, or HTML controls created to run on the server).

BASIC ASP.NET CONCEPTS

ASP.NET is the next generation of ASP, but what is ASP? **ASP** (Active Server Pages) is a technology that enables the computer to which you are connecting to deliver the pages that are displayed in a Web browser.

You could think of ASP.NET as the ultimate client/server paradigm. The client in this case is the Web browser on your computer. The server is the computer that you are connecting to that is capable of sending pages of HTML code back to the Web browser. The Web browser (on the client) will interpret this code and display the content.

ASP.NET is the platform you use to create Web applications and services that run under **IIS** (Internet Information Services). Although you can create Web applications by using other technologies, ASP.NET allows you to take advantage of much of the Visual Basic .NET programming knowledge you have already learned when you produce Web content.

The following software must be installed and running on your computer before you can develop applications with ASP.NET:

- Microsoft Windows XP Professional, Windows 2000, or Microsoft Windows Server 2003
- Internet Information Services (IIS), or access to a server that is running IIS
- Microsoft Visual Studio .NET Professional or Visual Studio .NET Enterprise

Installing IIS

If you did not install IIS when you installed Visual Studio .NET, you will have to install it now. After IIS is installed, it will not work until it is registered correctly. The following steps will help you install and register IIS on your computer.

1. Click Start, point to Settings, and then select Control Panel.

2. When Control Panel opens, double-click Add Or Remove Programs to display the Add Or Remove Programs dialog box.

3. Click Add/Remove Windows Components.

4. Locate Internet Information Services (IIS), as shown in Figure 14-1, and then click the Details button.

5. Place checks next to FrontPage 2000 Server Extensions and World Wide Web Service, as shown in Figure 14-2, and then click OK.

6. Click OK. The wizard will now install IIS on your computer. You might be prompted to insert your Windows 2000 or Windows XP CD-ROM (or DVD) during the installation.

> **TIP**   If FrontPage 2000 Server Extensions and World Wide Web Service are already checked, IIS is already configured on your computer. Cancel the installation and close the dialog box.

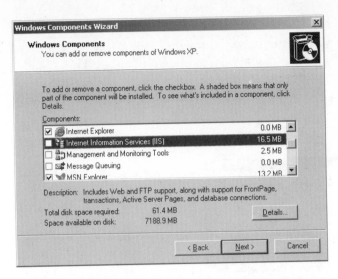

Figure 14-1   Installing IIS by using the Windows Components Wizard

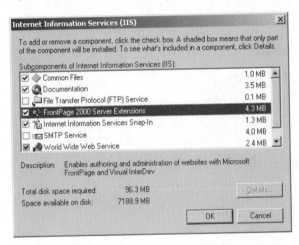

Figure 14-2   Selecting FrontPage 2000 Server Extensions and World Wide Web Service

Registering IIS with Visual Studio .NET and the .NET Framework

Ideally, IIS would be installed prior to Visual Studio .NET. This would ensure that IIS was properly registered. We assume that if you're following these instructions, you didn't install IIS when you installed Visual Studio .NET, so now you must repair the installation and register these new components. The next few steps will repair the installation and get everything working as it should.

1. Insert the Windows Component Update CD-ROM that came with Visual Studio .NET into your CD-ROM drive. (This CD-ROM might also be called the Prerequisites CD-ROM.) If your version of Visual Studio .NET came on DVD, this will be included on the DVD. If you are using CD-ROMs, ignore any message to insert Disk 1.

2. Click OK.

3. Click Start and then Run to open the Run dialog box

4. If your version of Visual Studio .NET came on CD-ROM, type the following command into the Run dialog box, as shown in Figure 14-3. (Note that to fit the code on this book's page, we had to break the single-line command. You should enter the text on one line.)

```
D:\dotNetFramework\dotnetfx.exe /t:c:\temp
    /c:"msiexec.exe /fvecms c:\temp\netfx.msi"
```

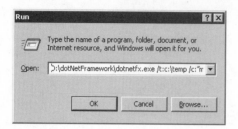

Figure 14-3   Entering the command to repair the IIS installation from CD-ROM

5. The previous statement will work if your CD-ROM drive is the D drive. If this is not the case, replace the letter D with the letter that corresponds to your CD-ROM drive.

6. If your version of Visual Studio .NET came on DVD, type the following command into the Run dialog box, as shown in Figure 14-4.

```
D:\wcu\dotNetFramework\dotnetfx.exe /t:c:\temp
    /c:"msiexec.exe /fvecms c:\temp\netfx.msi"
```

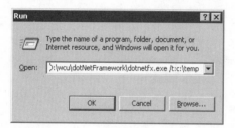

Figure 14-4   Entering the command to repair the IIS installation from DVD

7. Click OK, and then click Yes when prompted to install the .NET Framework package. After the installation and repairs are complete, you should be ready to build an ASP.NET Web application.

ASP.NET Applications

To create an ASP.NET application, you must have:

- A Web browser. Microsoft Internet Explorer or another browser, such as Netscape Navigator or Opera.

- A Web server. That is, a computer that is running IIS. This can be the computer you are developing on or any remote computer that you can connect to.

- A means to connect to the Web server.

There are four basic types of ASP.NET applications that you can develop:

- ***Web application*** Produces content that is displayed in a Web browser. The content is created on the server and is sent to the browser as plain HTML.

- ***Web service*** Provides a processing service for use with other applications over the Internet. Examples include a service that provides up-to-the-second stock quotes or a tax calculator.

- ***Internet-enabled application*** A standalone application that incorporates the use of the Internet within the application. An example of this is Help files that are located on the Microsoft Web site that you can connect to from within Visual Studio .NET.

- ***Peer-to-peer application*** A standalone application that uses the Internet to communicate with other users running their own instances of the same application. Instant Messenger is an example of this type of application.

In this chapter, you will be working with Web applications that are created with ASP.NET.

Understanding the Terminology

Before getting started, you should understand some of the terms that will be used in this chapter and in other references you might have a chance to read. As we progress through the chapter, we will provide additional discussion where necessary.

- **Static Web page** An .htm or .html file in which the content is made up of HTML code. The code is only changed when the developer has a need to change it. Until there is an explicit change to the code, the content will remain the same from one session to the next. Static pages are requested when the user types a page request into a browser and sends it to the Web server. The Web server locates the page and sends back an HTML stream that is interpreted and rendered by the browser.

  The following HTML code would be used to create a simple static Web page. The text is displayed in the browser. A static Web page can be created with a plain text editor such as Notepad and saved with an .htm or .html file extension.

  ```
  <html>
      <body>
          This is the text that is displayed in the browser.
      </body>
  </html>
  ```

- **Dynamic Web page** In contrast to a static Web page, a dynamic Web page can be one that you would produce by using Web Forms. The content of a dynamic Web page can change from one request to the next. The HTML code is produced on the Web server and sent back to the browser in response to the request.

- **Web site** One or more Web pages that are grouped together in an organized way.

- **Web browser**   An application that is capable of interpreting HTML code and rendering the page.

- **Web server**   A computer running software such as IIS. This computer might be local (the one you are currently developing on) or a remote computer that is many thousands of miles away.

How Web Applications Work

Web applications use Web browser/Web server architecture. The application resides on the server. When users connect to the application, the server responds to the various requests sent by the user's browser and serves up pages of plain HTML to the browser running on the user's computer.

The Web application actually runs under IIS. IIS manages the application and passes requests from the browser to the application. The requests are then processed by the application, and the responses are composed dynamically. Because the content is created dynamically, you can do many things that you could never do with static Web pages.

Creating a Simple Web Application

Visual Studio .NET provides Web-specific development tools to help you create Web applications quickly and easily. Creating a new Web application is similar to creating a Microsoft Windows application, but you select ASP.NET Web Application from the list of templates when creating the new project. You will create one now, and, afterwards, we will explain the various files that make up the application.

▶ **Creating the HelloInternet application**

1. Open Visual Studio .NET (if it is not open already).

2. Click New Project, and then select Visual Basic from the Project Types list and ASP.NET Web Application from the list of templates, as shown in Figure 14-5.

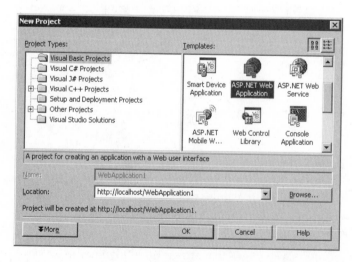

Figure 14-5   Selecting the ASP.NET Web Application template

Notice that, when you select the template, the Name box is immediately disabled and the Location list displays the location http://localhost/WebApplication1.

This is the default link to the application that you will create in a few moments. If you were to paste this link into the address box of a Web browser and press ENTER, you would be sending a request to the instance of IIS running on your computer. The application would then compose the response and send the required HTML back to your browser. Of course you will be changing the name of the application, so, by the time you have finished, the link will look like this: http://localhost/HelloInternet/HelloInternet.aspx.

3. Change the name of the application from WebApplication1 to **HelloInternet** by modifying the Location box entry, and then click OK. The wizard will create the Web application.

4. After the wizard has completed its task, the designer window will appear in Visual Studio .NET, and you can add controls to the interface.

5. Select the file WebForm1.aspx in Solution Explorer, and change the name of the file to **HelloInternet.aspx**.

6. Before adding controls, change the layout from Grid Layout to Flow Layout. Right-click Web Form in the designer window and select Properties.

7. In the DOCUMENT Property Pages dialog box shown in Figure 14-6, set the Page Title to **HelloInternet**, and then select Flow Layout from the Page Layout list. Click OK.

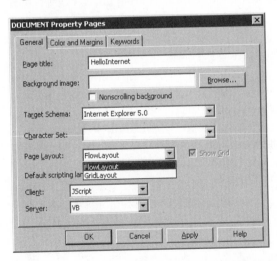

Figure 14-6   The DOCUMENT Property Pages dialog box

8. Locate the Toolbox and make sure that the Web Forms Toolbox is displayed.

9. Double-click the TextBox control to add it to the designer window.

10. Select the text box that you just added to the designer, and, using the standard Properties window, change the *ID* property of the text box from TextBox1 to **txtHello**.

11. Double-click the Button control in the Web Forms Toolbox to add it to the designer.

12. Select the button in the designer and change the *ID* property from Button1 to **btnHello**.

13. Change the *Text* property from Button to **Say Hello**.

14. Run the application by pressing F5. The application will display in your default browser. Nothing will happen when you click the button because you haven't added any code to the button's *Click* event.

15. Close the browser and double-click the button in the designer window. The Code Editor will display the code-behind module. This is different from what you have seen previously. We will explain it in a few moments.

16. Type the boldface code shown in the following code sample into the *btnHello_Click* event handler.

```
Private Sub btnHello_Click(ByVal sender As System.Object, _
        ByVal e As System.EventArgs) Handles btnHello.Click

    txtHello.Text = "Hello Internet"

End Sub
```

17. Press F5 to run the application again. Click the Say Hello button to see the results.

18. Next you will use the Response object to write directly on the Web form. Close the browser and display the code-behind module in the Code Editor.

    The Response object allows you to place information into the HTML output stream of the requested Web page. This information is included in the HTML that is sent back to the browser. The Response object is seldom used in ASP.NET development because it bypasses the common language runtime's ability to manage the response stream. For this reason, most developers use labels and other controls to display this kind of data. We're using it in this example to simplify the application so that you can more easily understand what's going on. For more information about the Response object, click Help, select Index, and then type **Response object [ASP.NET]** in the Look For list.

19. To test the Response object, comment out the first statement so that it will not run, and then add the boldface statement shown in the following code sample.

```
Private Sub btnHello_Click(ByVal sender As System.Object, _
        ByVal e As System.EventArgs) Handles btnHello.Click

    ' txtHello.Text = "Hello Internet"
    Response.Write("Hello from " & txtHello.Text)

End Sub
```

20. Run the application again. When the browser appears, type your name into the text box, and then click Say Hello. Figure 14-7 demonstrates the result of using the Response object.

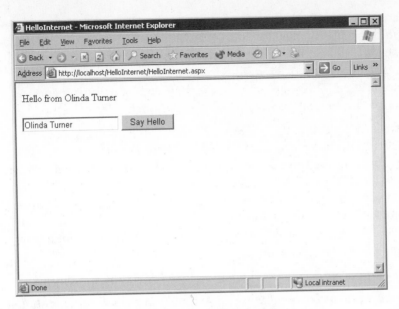

Figure 14-7   The form displaying the hello message

The Files That Make Up the Web Application

Figure 14-8 shows the Solution Explorer window for the HelloInternet application you just created. By default, some files are hidden. To show all the files in your project, click the Show All Files button at the top of Solution Explorer.

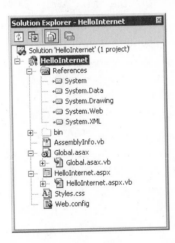

Figure 14-8   The files that make up the HelloInternet Web application

Let's look at the various files that make up a typical Web application:

- **References**   These files are similar to the references found in a standard Windows application. The difference is that a Web application references v*System.Web* instead of *System.Windows*.

- **AssemblyInfo**   The project is an assembly and, as such, includes an AssemblyInfo file that describes the assembly. The AssemblyInfo file for a Web application is functionally the same as the AssemblyInfo file for a Windows application. There is only one AssemblyInfo file per project.

- **Global.asax**   The Global.asax file is also known as the *ASP.NET application file*. This file is linked to the code-behind file (Global.asax.vb) and is responsible for responding to application-level events raised by ASP.NET. The Global.asax file resides in the root directory of an ASP.NET-based application. This is an optional file, but when a new Web application is created, a Global.asax file is included automatically.

- **Global.asax.vb**   This is the code-behind file for the Global.asax file. A code-behind file allows you to separate the displayed elements (HTML) from the functionality (programming logic). This is where you will write application-level and session-level code that responds to application-level and session-level events. The following event handlers are automatically provided when a new Global.asax file is added to an ASP.NET Web application. All you have to do is provide the code that you want to run when any of these events is raised.

  - *Application_Start*. Raised when an ASP.NET Web application starts.
  - *Application_End*. Raised when an ASP.NET Web application is shutting down.
  - *Session_Start*. Raised when a user's session begins.
  - *Session_End*. Raised when a user's session ends.
  - *Application_Error*. Raised when an unhandled exception occurs within an ASP.NET Web application.

- **HelloInternet.aspx**   This file contains the visual elements of the Web form.

- **HelloInternet.aspx.vb**   This is the code-behind module for HelloInternet.aspx. Besides the Web Forms Designer–generated code, the *Page_Load* event handler is also provided. Place code that you want to run when the page loads inside this event handler.

- **Styles.css**   This is the cascading style sheet used to define styles for the elements displayed in the browser when the Web page is rendered. A style sheet allows you to predefine how a page is formatted and displayed. Text is *styled* (font family, size, style, and so on) with a custom tag that is defined in the style sheet (.css). An HTML or an XML document is associated with a .css file. If the .css file is changed, the changes are automatically propogated to all the documents associated with it.

When you create a style sheet, you will specify tags or elements by name and set certain attributes, such as font family, font weight, and font size. You can think of a style sheet as a document that contains a set of instructions on how the data will be formatted and displayed or printed. When the HTML is produced, it refers to the style sheet that is downloaded and cached on the local computer. The Web page is then formatted per the instructions in the style sheet.

The following example shows a simple style sheet (named myStyles.css) that sets formatting instructions for the body of an HTML file and more specific instructions for the *<H1>* header tag.

```
body
{
    font-size: 12pt;
    vertical-align: baseline;
    color: black;
    direction: ltr;
    line-height: normal;
    font-family: Tahoma;
    letter-spacing: normal;
    background-color: olive;
    text-align: center;
    font-variant: normal;
}
H1
{
    font-weight: normal;
    font-size: 32pt;
    color: black;
    font-style: normal;
    font-family: Arial;
    font-variant: normal;
    text-align: center;
}
```

To link the myStyles.css file to a Web form, open the Web form (.aspx) in HTML view by clicking the HTML tab at the bottom of the designer window. Then add the following code to the *<HEAD>* section of the HTML page. The value for the *HREF* attribute assumes that myStyles.css is located in the same folder as the .aspx file.

```
<link Rel="stylesheet" HREF="myStyles.css" TYPE="text/css">
```

TIP   For more information on HTML, go to *http://www.w3c.org/MarkUp/*. For information on cascading style sheets, go to *http://www.w3c.org/Style/CSS/*.

■ **Web.config**   This file contains the settings that the Web server uses when processing the project. Among other things, these settings determine how errors are reported and what type of authentication to use. Authentication refers to the process of identifying whether the person accessing the Web site is who he or she claims to be. Authentication can be as simple as requiring a name and an e-mail address, or perhaps a username and a password. You can have only one Web.config file per folder within the Web site structure. You can use one Web.config file as a base file for other Web.config files in a Web site, allowing settings to be inherited whenever appropriate.

Try It

Open the HelloInternet Web application and change the layout from Flow Layout to Grid Layout in the Page Layout list in the Document Property Pages dialog box. Run the application and see if the format of the form is different than it was when Flow Layout was used.

Close the browser and return to design view. Click the HTML tab at the bottom of the screen and view the HTML code that was generated by the project. Notice that the *ms_positioning* attribute was added to the *<BODY>* tag.

Switch back to design view and change the layout back to Flow Layout.

What Do You Think?

1. What does ASP stand for, and what services does ASP technology provide?

2. List the three components you need to create an ASP.NET application.

3. Describe the four types of ASP.NET applications that you can develop.

4. What is the difference between a static Web page and a dynamic Web page?

5. How is the Response object used in the development of Web Forms?

THE MECHANICS OF WEB APPLICATIONS

By now you probably have lots of questions. In this section we will explain some of the more important details about your first Web application, including:

- What you are doing when you're using the Web Forms designer

- Why you changed from Grid Layout to Flow Layout

- Why we chose Web Forms controls rather than HTML controls, and what the difference is

- Why there is a code-behind file

- What happens when you run a Web application

- The lifetime of a Web application

Using the Web Forms Designer

The Web Forms designer is really a wizard that allows you to create the HTML that is required to produce a Web page. After you have more experience, you will generally spend most of your time designing in the HTML view of the Web page, where you have a little more control over what's being rendered. To switch to HTML view, click the HTML tab located in the lower-left corner of the design window.

Figure 14-9 shows the HelloInternet Web page as it really looks (in HTML view). If you have some experience with HTML, this should look familiar.

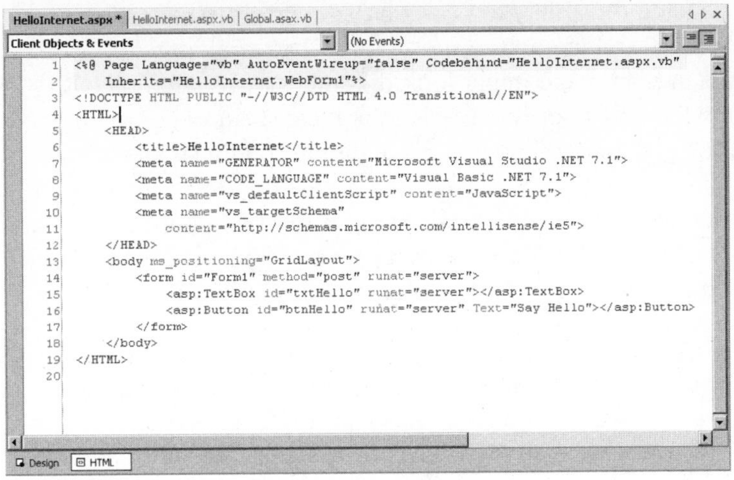

Figure 14-9   The HTML view of the Web page

Grid Layout vs. Flow Layout

When you format a Web Forms page in **Grid Layout** mode, you can preset the position of any Web Form control on the page by using a mouse. At design time, controls can be aligned and positioned where you want them. In Grid Layout, Visual Studio .NET adds a *style* attribute to each control that sets the **absolute position** of that control on the form. Take another look at Figure 14-9. You can see the *style* attribute for each of the controls that you added to the page.

When you format a Web Forms page in **Flow Layout** mode, you have no direct control over the positioning of the elements and how they are arranged on the page from top to bottom. You can use the spacebar and Enter keys to provide some spacing between the elements. In Flow Layout mode, the *POSITION* attribute is omitted because absolute positioning is not allowed and the browser takes care of the positioning of the elements when the page is rendered. Figure 14-10 shows the HTML view of the same page when Flow Layout is defined.

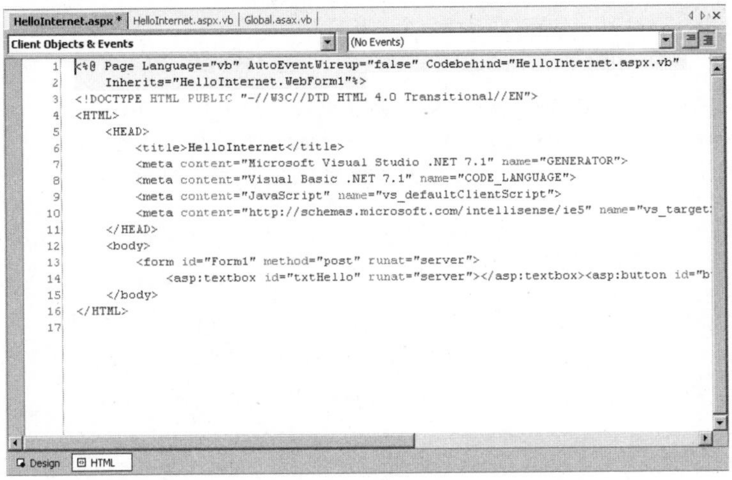

Figure 14-10   HTML view of the page in Flow Layout mode

You might think that having the ability to position the controls exactly where you want them is a good thing, and in some respects it is. The problem with using absolute positioning is that the page might look different or even completely wrong depending on which browser is rendering the page. Your pages might look good in Internet Explorer, but another browser might interpret a style attribute incorrectly or ignore it entirely. In Flow Layout mode, the controls are rendered one right after the other. Flow Layout is a World Wide Web Consortium (W3C) standard that all browsers comply with. Because of this compatibility issue, we used the Flow Layout mode in developing the HelloInternet application.

> **NOTE** The World Wide Web Consortium (W3C) develops specifications, guidelines, software, and tools. W3C is a forum for information, commerce, communication, and collective understanding. Browsers developed by Microsoft, Netscape, and other companies generally conform to the recommendations developed by the W3C.

Web Forms Controls and HTML Controls

Web Forms controls, also known as *server controls*, are a superset of HTML controls. In the HelloInternet application, you used Web Forms controls rather than HTML controls because of several advantages that they offer over HTML controls:

- Server controls trigger control-specific events—such the *Click* event of a button or the *SelectedIndexChanged* event of a list box—on the server, whereas HTML controls can trigger only page-level events through the use of client-side script—a script written in the Visual Basic Scripting Edition (VBScript) language or JScript—that is embedded in the HTML page.

- With server controls, data (known in ASP.NET as *_VIEWSTATE*) is persisted between requests (the _VIEWSTATE is buffered on the server and sent back to the browser with the new page), whereas with HTML controls, data must be saved and restored using page-level scripts (client-side script).

- Server controls automatically detect the browser and adapt the display as appropriate, whereas HTML controls cannot detect the browser, and code must be provided to do this.

- Server controls are .NET Framework classes and, as such, have a host of properties that can be set to customize the appearance and behavior of each control. HTML controls include only the basic attributes.

Despite the advantages of server controls, there are several reasons why you might want to use HTML controls in a Web application:

- When you upgrade an application from previous versions of ASP, HTML elements are converted to HTML controls. Changing all of them to Web Forms controls can be time-consuming and is not always necessary.

- Controls might not need to use the server-side events that are inherent with Web Forms controls.

- Persisting data (also known as *state management*) might not be necessary.

- HTML controls allow complete control over what is rendered. ASP.NET adjusts the appearance of Web Forms controls based on the browser being used. HTML controls are never adjusted because all browsers render them the same way.

- By default, HTML controls run on the Web browser and, as such, consume fewer resources. You can enable HTML controls to run on the Web server if you include the *runat="server"* attribute. To do this in the designer, right-click the HTML control and select Run As Server Control.

> **TIP** HTML controls and static elements can be used with Web Forms controls on the same page. Event handling for HTML controls must be provided in special *<script>* blocks. Raising these events will not require a round-trip to the server.

To prove our point, you will add a couple of HTML controls (a text field and a button) to the HelloInternet project that you worked on previously. You will also change the layout of the existing controls so that the button is placed below the text field.

1. Open the HelloInternet application in Visual Studio .NET.

2. Display the HelloInternet Web page in HTML view.

3. First you will change the layout of the existing controls on the Web page. You can easily do this by adding opening and closing paragraph tags around the existing code. The code should now look like this:

```
<form id="Form1" method="post" runat="server">
    <P><asp:textbox id="txtHello" runat="server" Height="30px"></asp:text-
box></P>
    <P><asp:button id="btnHello" runat="server" Height="28px"
        Width="148px" Text="Say Hello"></asp:button></P>
</form>
```

4. Create some space between the opening *<body>* tag and the opening *<form...>* tag, and insert the following HTML design code above the opening form tag. Refer to the code sample below step 20 in the "Creating the HelloInternet application" procedure above if you're not sure where to place this code.

```
<P><INPUT id="text1" style="WIDTH: 307px; HEIGHT: 22px" type="text"
    value="This is an HTML Text Field" size="45"></P>
<P><INPUT id="btnClientSide" style="WIDTH: 112px; HEIGHT: 24px"
    onclick="btnClientSide_ClickHandler"
    type="button" value="HTML Button"></P>
```

Notice that you provided a value for the text field. This is static text and will be displayed every time the page is loaded. For the button, you set a value for the caption on the button, and you also set a reference to an event handler (*btnClientSide_ClickHandler*). You will be creating the event handler next.

5. To create the event handler, insert the following code inside the *<HEAD>* section of the Web page.

```
<script language="vbscript">
    sub btnClientSide_ClickHandler()
        text1.innerText="The click event was raised from the HTML button"
    end sub
</script>
```

The following code sample shows the HTML code for the Web page.

```
<%@ Page Language="vb" AutoEventWireup="false"
    Codebehind="HelloInternet.aspx.vb" Inherits="HelloInternet.WebForm1"%>
<!DOCTYPE HTML PUBLIC "-//W3C//DTD HTML 4.0 Transitional//EN">
<HTML>
    <HEAD>
        <title>Hello Internet</title>
        <meta content="True" name="vs_showGrid">
        <meta content="Microsoft Visual Studio .NET 7.1" name="GENERATOR">
        <meta content="Visual Basic .NET 7.1" name="CODE_LANGUAGE">
        <meta content="VBScript" name="vs_defaultClientScript">
        <meta content=http://schemas.microsoft.com/intellisense/ie5
            name="vs_targetSchema">

        <script language="vbscript">
        sub btnClientSide_ClickHandler()
            text1.innerText="The click event was raised from the HTML button"
        end sub
        </script>
    </HEAD>

    <body>
        <P><INPUT id="text1" style="WIDTH: 307px; HEIGHT: 22px" type="text"
            value="This is an HTML Text Field" size="45"></P>
        <P><INPUT id="btnClientSide" style="WIDTH: 112px; HEIGHT: 24px"
            onclick="btnClientSide_ClickHandler"
            type="button" value="HTML Button"></P>
        <form id="Form1" method="post" runat="server">
            <P><asp:textbox id="txtHello" runat="server" Height="30px">
            </asp:textbox></P>
            <P><asp:button id="btnHello" runat="server" Height="28px"
                Width="148px" Text="Say Hello"></asp:button></P>
        </form>
    </body>
</HTML>
```

6. Save the changes and run the program by pressing F5. Figure 14-11 shows the form when it is first loaded.

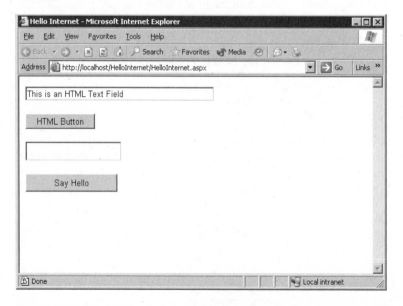

Figure 14-11   The Web page when it is loaded for the first time

7. Click HTML Button and notice that the text in the text field has changed, as shown in Figure 14-12. The event was raised on the browser and the code inside the scripted event handler was executed.

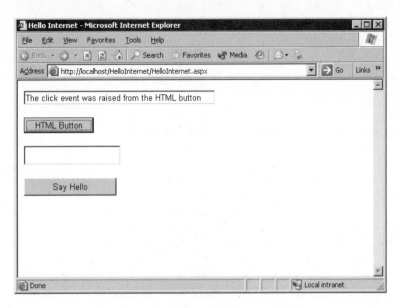

Figure 14-12   The Web page after HTML Button is clicked

8. Now type **Hello Internet** in the text box and click the Say Hello button. Figure 14-13 shows that the text in the Web Forms text box was changed, but also notice that the text in the text field was restored to its original value.

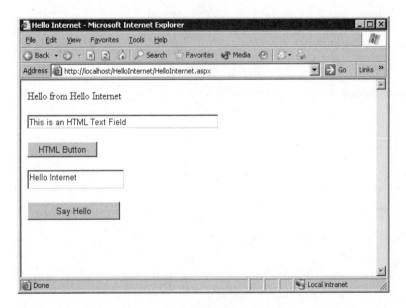

Figure 14-13   The Web page after the Say Hello button is clicked

As you can see from the previous example, it's easy to include HTML controls in a Web Form and provide functionality that doesn't require accessing the Web server.

The Code-Behind Module

Why is there a **code-behind module**? This has more to do with separation of functionality than anything else. The code-behind module (HelloInternet.aspx.vb) contains the Visual Basic .NET source code that is compiled and run on the server. The source code is never visible in the browser and, because it runs on the server, it is more secure. The Web form (HelloInternet.aspx) is the HTML that is interpreted and displayed in the browser along with the data (_VIEWSTATE) that is sent back from the server.

What Happens When You Run a Web Application?

After you have built a Web application and run it for the first time, Visual Studio .NET compiles the source code into an executable (DLL) file and places that file in the \bin folder. The user interface portion of the application remains as an .aspx or .html file.

When a browser requests the start page (*http://localhost/HelloInternet/HelloInternet.aspx*), IIS starts the application's executable file (HelloInternet.dll) and generates a response. The response (in this case) is to display the requested page. When text is entered into the text box and the button is clicked, another request is sent to IIS, and it in turn is handled by HelloInternet.dll, and another response is sent back to the browser. Note that the second response creates a new page. The value that appears in the text box is persisted on the server and returned with the new HTML.

The Lifetime of a Web Application

A Web application lives as long as it has active sessions. A session starts when the first request is sent to the application (*Session_Start*—the browser requests a start page) and ends when the session is closed (*Session_End*—the browser is closed or the user navigates to another Web site).

By using the HelloInternet application as an example, we can display the lifetime of the application and session in easy-to-understand steps.

1. The browser requests the start page.
2. The application starts.
3. The session starts.
4. The Web server starts the executable file, which then handles the request.
5. The executable file creates an instance of the requested Web Form and generates the HTML.
6. The Web server sends the HTML back to the Web browser and destroys the instance of the Web Form.
7. The user performs some tasks (enters text in the text box and clicks the button).
8. The request is sent to the Web server: a Post-back event (caused by the clicking of the button) sends the page's data (_*VIEWSTATE*) back to the server for event processing.

9. The executable file creates a new instance of the requested Web Form, fills in the data from the _VIEWSTATE_, and generates the HTML.

10. The Web server sends the HTML back to the Web browser and destroys the new instance of the Web Form.

11. The Web browser is closed, or the user navigates to a new Web site.

12. The session ends.

13. If this is the only session, the application ends.

Handling Events

Many events occur during the execution of our application. Following is a list of these events, along with a short description of what happens.

- Application and session events:
  - *Application_Start*. The first user visits the start page of the Web application.
  - *Application_End*. There are no more active sessions.
  - *Application_BeginRequest*. A browser navigates to any of the pages in the application, or a Post-back is raised.
  - *Application_EndRequest*. The request to the server ends.
  - *Session_Start*. A new user visits the start page of the application.
  - *Session_End*. A user leaves the application by closing the browser, navigating to a new Web site, or timing out.
- Web Form events:
  - *Page_Init*. The server controls are loaded and initialized from the Web Form's _VIEWSTATE_.
  - *Page_Load*. The server controls are loaded on the page; this is where you would provide code to change control settings or display text on the page.
  - *Page_PreRender*. The application is about to render the page.
  - *Page_Unload*. The page is unloaded from memory.
  - *Page_Error*. An unhandled exception is thrown.

Using a Session Variable to Welcome a User

Session variables are similar to the variables you are already familiar with. They're used to store a value, such as the name of the user or other information that you want to maintain. A session variable is typically declared in the *Session_Start* event handler and is available for the life of the session. In the next example, you will add to the HelloInternet Web application a session variable that stores the user's name and then displays the value when the page is loaded.

1. Open the Global.asax.vb code module in the Code Editor.

2. Add the boldface statement shown in the following code sample to the *Session_Start* event handler.

```
Sub Session_Start(ByVal sender As Object, ByVal e As EventArgs)

    Session("UserName") = "Bernie"

End Sub
```

3. Next you will display the value stored in the session variable. Open the HelloInternet.aspx.vb code module in the Code Editor.

4. Add the boldface statement shown in the following code sample to the *Page_Load* event handler.

```
Private Sub Page_Load(ByVal sender As System.Object, _
        ByVal e As System.EventArgs) Handles MyBase.Load

    Response.Write("Welcome " & Session("UserName"))

End Sub
```

5. Run the application and note the welcome message.

6. Enter some text in the text box, and then click Say Hello.

Notice that the hello message appears along with the welcome message. Because you have already welcomed the user, displaying the welcome message a second time is probably not the right thing to do. You need to find a way to post the welcome message only at the start of the session and suppress it for all subsequent page loads.

7. Add the boldface statement shown in the following code sample to the *Page_Load* event handler.

```
Private Sub Page_Load(ByVal sender As System.Object, _
        ByVal e As System.EventArgs) Handles MyBase.Load

    If Not (Page.IsPostBack) Then
        Response.Write("Welcome " & Session("UserName") & "<br>")
    End If

End Sub
```

8. Run the application again, and type your name into the text box. Click Say Hello and observe the message that appears on the Web form.

What you are saying here is to run the *Response.Write* statement only if the page being displayed is not the result of a Post-back event being raised. Remember that when you clicked the button you raised a Post-back event, so the server is obliged to respond with a fresh page. When the new page is sent back, the welcome message is not sent back as part of the HTML. You have essentially suppressed the message at the server.

Virtual Folders

When you create a new Web application or Web service, it automatically resides in the default root folder for IIS. This folder is called *wwwroot* and is located in the Inetpub folder. Projects created in this folder are automatically registered with IIS and will run when the start page of the Web application is opened in the browser.

Putting too many projects inside wwwroot can cause organizational problems because you are mixing development projects with production projects. You need to find a way to better organize these projects so that they can be stored correctly and run without too many problems.

Creating a separate folder on your hard drive to store your Web projects is one way to organize projects. The problem with storing projects in another location (not in wwwroot) is that IIS will not be able to locate the projects unless you provide a means to locate the storage area. **Virtual folders** allow you to do that.

In the next example, you will create a Web application that will access a database and allow you to display data in a DataGrid. You will create the project in a folder on your hard drive and point to it from a virtual folder that you will create in IIS.

The InternetPubs Web Application

There are three main steps required to complete this project:

■ Create a standard folder on your hard drive by using Windows Explorer.

■ Create a virtual folder using IIS that points to the Web application.

■ Create the Web application.

▶ **Creating a standard folder**

1. Open Windows Explorer, and create a new folder called **WebApplications** under the root drive.

2. Open the WebApplications folder, and create another new folder called **InternetPubs**, as shown in Figure 14-14.

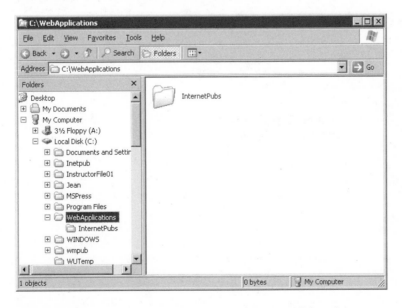

Figure 14-14   Creating a new folder structure to store Web projects

► **Creating a virtual folder**

1. To open IIS, click Start, point to Settings, and then select Control Panel. Select Administrative Tools, and then select Internet Information Services. You can also get to IIS by right-clicking My Computer on the desktop and selecting Manage. When the dialog box opens, click the plus sign next to Applications And Services to expand the list. IIS will be listed with the rest of the services.

2. When IIS opens, navigate to the Default Web Site folder in the left-hand pane by expanding the local computer and Web Sites icons, as shown in Figure 14-15.

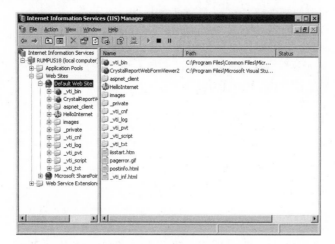

Figure 14-15 The Default Web Site folder

3. On the Action menu, point to New, and then select Virtual Directory to create a new virtual folder, as shown in Figure 14-16.

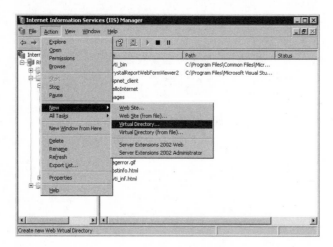

Figure 14-16 Creating a new virtual folder

4. This will start the Virtual Directory Creation Wizard.

5. Click Next.

6. Enter a name for the alias. This name can be the same as the name you gave to the folder for this Web application. Use the same naming conventions you would normally use for naming a folder. In this case, we used *InternetPubs* as the alias, as shown in Figure 14-17.

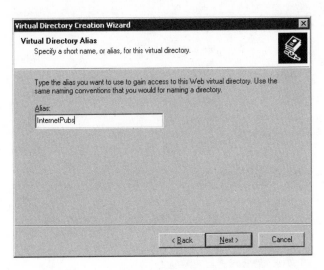

Figure 14-17   Creating an alias

7. Click Next.

8. Click the Browse button, as shown in Figure 14-18, and then navigate to the InternetPubs folder that you created in Windows Explorer. Click OK to close the Browse For Folder window, and then click Next.

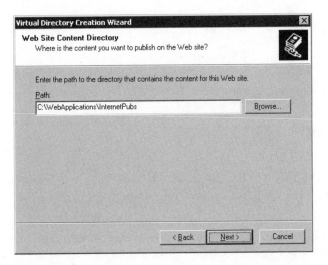

Figure 14-18   Click Browse to find the folder in which the Web application will be stored.

9. Keep the default Access Permissions shown in Figure 14-19. Click Next.

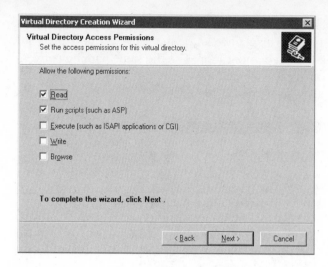

Figure 14-19   The default Access Permissions

10. Click Finish. This closes the wizard and brings you back to the IIS application window. Figure 14-20 shows the IIS window with the new virtual folder created.

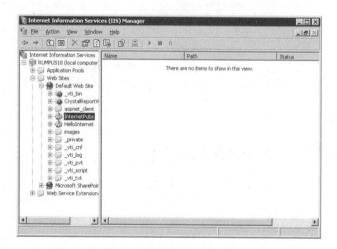

Figure 14-20   The new virtual folder

11. Close IIS Manager.

12. Open Visual Studio .NET (if it is not open already) and click the New Project button on the Start Page, or, on the File menu, point to New and then select Project.

13. In the New Project dialog box, select Visual Basic Projects in the list of Project Types, and select ASP.NET Web Application in the list of Templates.

14. Type **http://localhost/InternetPubs** in the Location box, and then click OK, as shown in Figure 14-21. The new Web application will be created, and the Web Form will be displayed in design view.

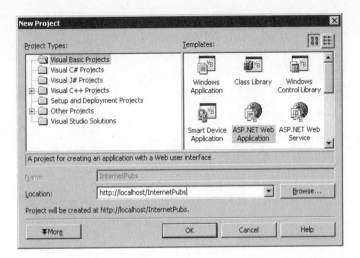

Figure 14-21 Setting the location of the new Web application

15. Switch to Flow Layout by using the Document Property Pages.

16. Select WebForm1.aspx in Solution Explorer, and rename it **Internet-Pubs.aspx**.

   TIP Rather than renaming the default Web Form, many developers choose to delete the default Web Form and add a new one to the solution, giving it the new name as it is created.

17. Add a DataGrid control to the Web Form from the Web Forms Toolbox.

18. Open the Properties window for the DataGrid control, and change the (*ID)* property to **grdPubs**.

At this point you could run the application, but the browser would be blank because you have not configured the DataGrid yet. You will do that as soon as you know what data and how many columns of data you will be displaying.

▶ **Adding the data classes**

The next step is to add the data classes to the application to provide the needed functionality. Although you could add data components to the designer, we prefer to use classes and instantiate them by using code. Using the classes will give you a little more flexibility, and you will also see that using the classes is quite easy.

Before you do that, however, you need to make sure that you have a copy of the Pubs.mdb file in the bin folder of the project.

1. Make a copy of the Pubs.mdb file from the student file and place the copy in the bin folder inside the InternetPubs project folder.

2. Open the InternetPubs.aspx.vb module in the Code Editor. Notice that the *Page_Load* event handler is already created for you.

3. In the Code Editor, change the name of the class from WebForm1 to **InternetPubs**. The class declaration should look like this:

```
Public Class InternetPubs
    Inherits System.Web.UI.Page
```

4. At the top of the class module (above the class declaration), add the bold-face *Imports* statements shown in the following code sample.

```
Imports System.Data.OleDb
Imports System.Text

Public Class InternetPubs
    Inherits System.Web.UI.Page
```

5. Add the following class-level declaration to the module.

```
Private m_cnPubs As OleDbConnection
```

6. Add the boldface code shown in the following code sample to the *Page_Load* event handler. This code will instantiate the connection class, assign a ConnectionString, and call a new Sub procedure named *BindGrid*, which you will create in a moment.

```
Private Sub Page_Load(ByVal sender As System.Object, _
        ByVal e As System.EventArgs) Handles MyBase.Load

    m_cnPubs = New OleDbConnection

    With m_cnPubs
        .ConnectionString = "Provider=Microsoft.Jet.OLEDB.4.0;Data Source=" & _
            Web.HttpRuntime.AppDomainAppPath & "bin\Pubs.mdb;User ID=admin"
    End With

    If Not IsPostBack Then
        BindGrid()
    End If

End Sub
```

7. Create a new Sub procedure named *BindGrid* with private scope.

8. Type the boldface code shown in the following code sample inside the *BindGrid* Sub procedure.

```
Private Sub BindGrid()

    Dim dsPubs As DataSet = New DataSet
    Dim daPubs As OleDbDataAdapter = New OleDbDataAdapter
    Dim strSQL As StringBuilder = New StringBuilder
    Dim cmSelect As OleDbCommand = New OleDbCommand

    strSQL.Append("SELECT au_lname, au_fname, titles.title_id, title, price ")
    strSQL.Append("FROM Authors, Titles, TitleAuthor ")
    strSQL.Append("WHERE authors.au_id = titleauthor.au_id AND ")
    strSQL.Append("titleauthor.title_id = titles.title_id ")
    strSQL.Append("ORDER BY au_lname, au_fname")

    With cmSelect
        .CommandText = strSQL.ToString()
        .CommandType = CommandType.Text
        .Connection = m_cnPubs
    End With

    daPubs.SelectCommand = cmSelect
    daPubs.Fill(dsPubs, "Authors")

    grdPubs.DataSource = dsPubs
    grdPubs.DataBind()

End Sub
```

Next you will add the appropriate columns to the DataGrid, and then format it so that it looks pleasing.

9. Display the InternetPubsWeb Form in design view.

10. Right-click the DataGrid and select Property Builder from the context menu.

11. On the left side of the dialog box, click the Columns icon.

12. Clear the Create Columns Automatically At Runtime check box. The check box is selected by default. Although leaving this selected will save you from needing to set up each column yourself, it displays the default column names in the header text and doesn't allow for custom formatting. The DataGrid would be functional but not user friendly.

13. Select Bound Column from the Available Columns list, and then click the arrow to add the column type to the Selected Columns list.

14. Add four more Bound Columns to the Selected Columns list, making a total of five columns.

15. Select each column in the Selected Columns list in turn, and set the properties using the information in Table 14-1. Figure 14-22 shows the completed DataGrid Properties dialog box.

Table 14-1   **Column Properties**

Header text	Data field	Data formatting expression
Title ID	**title_id**	<blank>
Last Name	**au_lname**	<blank>
First Name	**au_fname**	<blank>
Title	**title**	<blank>
Price	**price**	{0:C}

Figure 14-22   Setting the column properties of the DataGrid

16. Click OK to save the changes to the column properties.

17. To format the DataGrid, right-click it and then select Auto Format. Figure 14-23 shows the Auto Format dialog box.

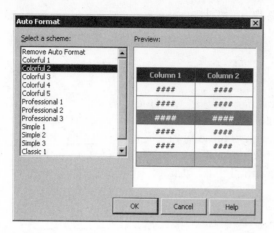

Figure 14-23   Setting the format of the DataGrid

18. Select any scheme that is pleasing to you, and then click OK.

19. Run the application to display the results. If everything works as designed, the data will appear in the browser as shown in Figure 14-24.

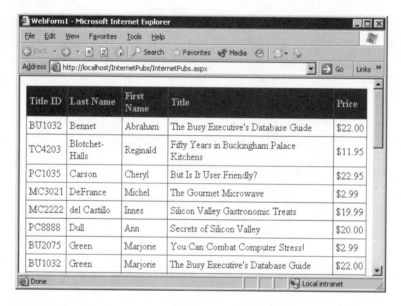

Figure 14-24   Displaying the data on the Web form

Inside the Code

Let's look at the first two statements:

```
Imports System.Data.OleDb
Imports System.Text
```

You can see that by using the *Imports* statement you are able to provide a shortcut when you deal with the *OleDb* data classes and the *StringBuilder* class. Without these *Imports* statements, when you refer to the *StringBuilder* class in code, you always have to use the fully qualified name, which would be *System.Text.StringBuilder*.

```
With m_cnPubs
    .ConnectionString = "Provider=Microsoft.Jet.OLEDB.4.0;Data Source=" & _
        Web.HttpRuntime.AppDomainAppPath & "bin\Pubs.mdb;User ID=admin"
End With
```

In the *Page_Load* event handler, you create an instance of the connection class and establish a connection string that allows you to connect to the database. The interesting thing about the connection string is the use of AppDomainAppPath. This provides you with a path to the project folder. The DLL resides in the bin folder, and that is where we placed the Microsoft Office Access database.

Let's look at the *Bind_Grid* Sub procedure. After having declared the DataSet, DataAdapter, Command, and StringBuilder objects, you provide the connection string by using the *StringBuilder* class and setting up the Command. You then set the *SelectCommand* property of the DataAdapter to the new command you have created. You can then fill the DataSet and set the DataSource of the DataGrid to the DataSet. After that is done, the call to the *DataBind* method of the DataGrid will enforce the binding.

Try It

Modify the HelloInternet Web application you made in this chapter to add another session variable that will be used to store a message of your choice. Modify the HelloInternet.aspx.vb code module to display this message instead of the previous message.

What Do You Think?

1. What is the difference between the Grid Layout mode and the Flow Layout mode when you are formatting Web forms?

2. What is a code-behind module?

3. How long is a Web application considered to be "alive"?

4. What is the purpose of session variables?

5. How are virtual folders used?

Q&A

Q. You talked about session variables. Can I also include application variables?

A. Yes, but remember that an application is global. That means that every user will see the same values that you assign to those variables. In contrast, the values assigned to session variables are only available to the user of that session.

Q. How long does a session last?

A. By default, a session will expire after 20 minutes if there is no user activity. You can specify a different session length by assigning the length of time (in minutes) to the *TimeOut* property of the session object.

Q. If the default layout is Grid Layout, and we switched to Flow Layout for compatibility reasons, when would it be okay to use Grid Layout?

A. Good question. The default is Grid Layout because Microsoft wanted Web Forms to emulate (as much as possible) Windows Forms. Designing a Web page is easier because you can place controls at set locations on a form. We would suggest that you use Grid Layout when you want the page to display exactly as designed and you have control over the browser that is being used to render the page. For example, you might want to do this on a corporate intranet because corporations generally specify the browser for all users.

WRAPPING UP

- ASP.NET applications run under IIS. When developing an ASP.NET Web application, you will generally install IIS on your local computer.

- IIS is typically installed prior to installing Visual Studio .NET. This ensures that IIS is properly registered with Visual Studio .NET. If you install IIS after Visual Studio .NET, you can repair the installation by running the dotnetfx.exe, as described at the beginning of this chapter.

- ASP.NET allows you to create Web applications, Web services, Internet-enabled applications, and peer-to-peer applications.

- To develop ASP.NET Web applications, you must have a Web browser, access to a Web server, and a means to connect to the Web server.

- A static Web page consists of plain HTML code. An ASP.NET Web application produces dynamic Web pages because the HTML is composed each time the server responds to a request.

- Web applications work because the application itself resides on the Web server. A request to the server starts the application and starts a session. The application composes the HTML and sends an HTML stream back to the browser. The browser reads and then renders the HTML.

- Web Forms controls are server controls. Events are raised on the server, and the application responds to those events when a Post-back is executed. On a Post-back event, the application will respond by sending back a fresh Web page. The following Web Forms controls execute a Post-back: Buttons, LinkButtons, ImageButtons, and HyperLinks. Other Web Forms controls have an *AutoPostBack* property that is set to False and so will not execute a Post-back. The events raised by these controls are buffered until there is an explicit Post-back. At that time, all the other events are handled.

- HTML controls can be used along with Web Forms controls on a Web page. HTML controls require page-level scripts to raise events. HTML controls are useful when you are providing functionality that does not require access to the Web server.

- You can use session variables when you want to store information for the duration of a session. After the session times out, the session variables are destroyed.

- You can use virtual folders to help organize your projects and to avoid cluttering up IIS by mixing applications that are under development with production applications.

- Displaying and interacting with data in a database is just as easy with Web applications as it is with Windows applications. Use all the normal data classes or add the data components from the Data Toolbox. You can easily customize the Web Forms DataGrid by using the Property Builder and the AutoFormat dialog box.

KEYWORDS

ASP	absolute position
code-behind module	Flow Layout
Grid Layout	IIS
virtual folders	Web application

REVIEW QUESTIONS

1. Which of the following do you need to develop Web Forms with ASP .NET? (Choose all correct answers.)

    a. Visual Studio .NET Professional or Visual Studio .NET Enterprise

    b. IIS

    c. FrontPage

    d. Windows XP Professional, Windows 2000, or Windows Server 2003

2. Where do you go to install IIS on your computer if it was not previously installed?

    a. Start, Settings, Control Panel, Add/Remove Programs

    b. Start, Accessories, Add/Remove Programs

    c. Start, Visual Studio .NET

    d. Start, Settings, IIS

3. Which two options should you check when installing IIS for use with ASP.NET application development? (Choose two answers.)

    a. FrontPage 2000 Server Extensions

    b. ASP.NET Extensions

    c. World Wide Web Service

    d. IIS ASP.NET Extensions

4. Which Visual Basic project template should you use to create a new ASP.NET Web application?

    a. ASP.NET Web Service

    b. ASP.NET Console Application

    c. ASP.NET Browser Application

    d. ASP.NET Web Application

5. Which type of layout should you use when you want the browser to handle the positioning of elements on the Web page when it is displayed on the user's screen?

    a. Grid Layout

    b. Form Layout

    c. Flow Layout

    d. Dynamic Layout

6. A Web application session starts when _____.

    a. the Web browser requests the start page

    b. the Web server requests the start page

    c. the Web browser displays the start page

    d. the user navigates to the application's Web site

7. Which of the following types of events are often used in Web applications? (Choose all correct answers.)

    a. Application events

    b. Session events

    c. Browser events

    d. Web Form events

8. The default root folder for IIS is called _____.

    a. Inetpub

    b. WebApplication

    c. WebService

    d. wwwroot

9. A(n) _____ folder is created to point to another location in which the files for a Web application project are stored.

    a. pointer

    b. alias

    c. virtual

    d. reference

10. Which of the following can you use in a connection string to reference the path to the project folder without explicitly typing the path?

    a. AppDomainAppPath

    b. ProjectPath

    c. AppProjectPath

    d. AppPath

11. In ASP.NET, a Web browser creates a Web page that is sent to the server to display in a browser. True or false?

12. You must have a Web browser available on your computer if you want to create ASP.NET applications. True or false?

13. Web pages created with ASP.NET for Web applications do not contain any HTML. True or false?

14. You should use the Grid Layout mode when you want to preset the position of any Web Forms control on the page at design time. True or false?

15. A Web Form can contain either Web Forms controls or HTML controls, but not both at the same time. True or false?

16. The Microsoft technology that allows a server to send a Web page to a Web browser to display is called _____.

17. The _____ object is used to write directly on a Web Form with ASP.NET.

18. The wizard that you use to create the HTML for a Web page when developing with ASP.NET is called the _____.

19. The file that contains the Visual Basic .NET source code that is compiled and runs on the server is the _____ module.

20. A(n) _____ variable is used to store information in a Web application created with ASP.NET.

STEP BY STEP

In this project for the Baldwin Museum of Science, you will create a Web form that will be used to display the hours the museum is open when the user selects a day of the week. The completed Web form is shown in Figure 14-25.

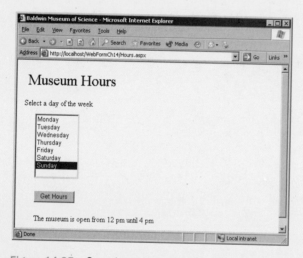

Figure 14-25   Completed Web form for the WebFormCh14 project

▶ Creating a new project

1. Open Visual Studio .NET, if it isn't already open.

2. Click the New Project button on the Start Page.

3. Click Visual Basic Projects under Project Types and ASP.NET Web Application under Templates.

4. Change the name of the application in the Location box to **WebFormCh14**.

5. Click OK.

▶ Configuring the Web form

1. Right-click the WebForm1.aspx file in Solution Explorer, and change the name to **Hours.aspx**. Press ENTER.

2. Right-click the form and select Properties.

3. Change the Page Title to **Baldwin Museum of Science**.

4. Click OK.

▶ Adding controls to the Web form

1. Make sure the Web Forms Toolbox is displayed.

2. Double-click the Label control to add it to the designer window. Position the label at the top center of the designer.

3. Select the label that you just added to the designer, and change the *ID* property to **lblTitle** and the *Text* property to **Museum Hours**.

4. Increase the *Font Size* property of the lblTitle control to **X-Large**.

5. In the Toolbox, double-click the Label control again to add another label to the designer window. Position this label on the left side of the designer under the first label you added, as shown in Figure 14-25.

6. Select the label that you just added and change the *ID* property to **lblSelection** and the *Text* property to **Select a day of the week**.

7. Double-click the ListBox control in the Toolbox to add a list box to the right side of the designer.

8. Select the list box, and change the *ID* property to **lstDays**.

9. Click the *Items* property for the list box and add the seven days of the week by using the List Item Collection Editor.

10. Double-click the Button control in the Toolbox to add a button under the list box, as shown in Figure 14-25.

11. Change the *ID* property of the button to **btnHours**, and change the *Text* property to **Get Hours**.

12. Add another Label control at the bottom of the form.

13. Select the new label, change the *ID* property to **lblHours**, and delete the contents of the *Text* property.

▶ Adding code to the Web form

1. In the designer, double-click the Button control to open the *btnHours_Click* event handler.

2. Type the boldface code shown in the following code sample into the *btnHours_Click* event handler.

```
Private Sub btnHours_Click(ByVal sender As System.Object, _
        ByVal e As System.EventArgs) Handles btnHours.Click
    ' Display the appropriate hours in the lblHours control based on the
    ' selection made by the user

    Select Case lstDays.SelectedIndex
        Case 0, 1, 2
            lblHours.Text = "The museum is open from 12 pm until 6 pm"
        Case 3, 4
            lblHours.Text = "The museum is open from 10 am until 7 pm"
        Case 5
            lblHours.Text = "The museum is open from 10 am until 8 pm"
        Case 6
            lblHours.Text = "The museum is open from 12 pm until 4 pm"
    End Select
End Sub
```

▶ Saving and testing your project

1. On the File menu, select Save All to save your work.

2. On the Debug menu, select Start to run the project.

3. Test the program by selecting various days in the list box and verifying that the correct hours are displayed in the label at the bottom of the form when you click Get Hours.

4. Close the browser when you are done testing.

5. On the File menu, select Close Solution to close your project.

6. Close Visual Studio .NET.

FINISH THE CODE

To complete this exercise, open the WoodgroveBankCh14 project that came in your student file and finish the Web Form. This form is to be used to display current rates that the certificates of deposits (CDs) offered by the bank are paying. The information about the CDs and their rates are in an Access database called Rates.mdb that also came in your student file. Display all fields in the CDRates table in the DataGrid control that is on the Web Form.

JUST HINTS

In this exercise, you will make a Web Form for Fabrikam, Inc., that can be used by customers to subscribe to the company's mailing list. The customers should be able to enter the following items of information:

- Name
- Phone number
- E-mail address

There should also be a button labeled Subscribe. When users click this button, the information they entered should be stored in session variables and a message should be displayed on the Web Form thanking them for subscribing.

▶ Creating the application and finishing the Web Form

1. Set up a virtual folder to store the application. Name the folder Subscribe.

2. Create a new Web application, and save it in the Subscribe virtual folder.

3. Add three Label controls and three TextBox controls to the Web Form. Set their *ID* and *Text* properties.

4. Add a Button control to the form, and set the *ID* and *Text* property of the button as required.

5. Create three session variables in the *Session_Start* event handler.

6. In the *Click* event of the button, assign the contents of the three text boxes to the appropriate session variables. Also include a statement using the Response object to display the message "Thank you for your subscription!"

ON YOUR OWN

In this exercise for Tailspin Toys, you will create a Web application that will display the current players in an online game and allow the user to join a room as a character. The information to display is in an Access database called Players.mdb that came in your student file. You should also include fields that allow users to enter a character name and select a room they want to enter from a list of available rooms. There should be a button called Join that users will click after entering these two pieces of information. The information entered should be saved in session variables when users click the Join button. A message verifying the character name and the room they want to join should also be displayed when they click the Join button.

MORE PRACTICE

1. Write the Visual Basic .NET statement that will use the Response object to display the message "Your account balance is $0.00" on a Web Form.

2. Write the Visual Basic .NET statement that will create a session variable called *AccountStatus* and assign it the value Open.

3. Write the Visual Basic .NET statement that will use the Response object to display the contents of the session variable called *CurrentBalance* on a Web Form.

4. Write a Visual Basic .NET Web application using ASP.NET that can be used to display a survey indicating levels of satisfaction for service received at a restaurant. The form should contain a Level Of Satisfaction field that allows the user to select Very Satisfied, Somewhat Satisfied, Not Satisfied, or Very Unsatisfied. Users should also be able to enter comments into a text box to further describe their feelings regarding the service. Include a button at the bottom of the form that is labeled Submit. When the user clicks the Submit button, all input and selections made on the form should be stored in session variables.

5. Write a Visual Basic .NET Web application using ASP.NET that will use a DataGrid control to display the contents of a train schedule on a Web Form. Use the Access database called TrainSchedule.mdb that came with your student file to complete this exercise. Create a virtual folder to store this project.

6. Write a Visual Basic .NET Web application using ASP.NET that can be used to make a seat selection for an event at a theatre. The Web Form should display a picture of the theatre seating arrangement and allow users to select the type of seat they would like. The form should also display a list of the seating types, along with the cost of each type of seat. Use the Seating.mdb Access database file from your student file to display the seat types and prices. The file Seating.bmp, which also came with your student file, can be used to display the seating arrangement in the theatre. Also include a button labeled Purchase that will display a confirmation message by using the Response object.

APPENDIX A
MICROSOFT DESKTOP ENGINE 2000

Microsoft Desktop Engine (MSDE) 2000 is a database management system (DBMS) designed to be used during application development. It ships with all versions of Microsoft Visual Studio .NET and can be used to create the databases that you will need to develop applications that require the use of a relational database.

The following are some of the engine's capabilities:

- Is fully compatible with Microsoft SQL Server 2000. You can develop an application that uses MSDE as the database. When the application is ready to deploy (distribute to the end user), just change the name of the data source (the server).

- Is royalty-free and can be packaged and deployed with any application. This allows you to create a fully functional application without your users having to provide their own DBMSs.

- Can have five concurrent batch updates to a single database before performance degrades.

- Has a limit of 2 gigabytes (GB) for each database file.

- Uses OSQL.exe as a command-line interface.

- Allows up to 16 named instances of MSDE running on a single computer.

INSTALLING MSDE 2000

MSDE can be copied from the student file or downloaded from Microsoft. We have included MSDE in the student file, along with the SQL files for installing the Pubs database. The version in the student file was the latest version when this textbook went to press. You should check the Microsoft website to make sure you have the latest version. To download MSDE from Microsoft, follow the step-by-step instructions below.

▶ **Download MSDE 2000 from Microsoft**

1. Open Microsoft Internet Explorer, and type the following URL in the address bar:

   http://www.microsoft.com/sql/msde/downloads/download.asp

2. Select the language version in the list under Downloads, and then click Go.

3. Click the link Download Files Below, or scroll to the bottom of the page to locate the file.

4. Click the link MSDE2000A.exe to download MSDE.

5. Click the Save button to open the Save As dialog box. Navigate to a suitable location on your hard drive, and then click Save. We recommend that you create a new folder under the root (C:\) called MSDE and save it to that folder.

6. Click the link ReadmeMSDE2000A.htm to view the documentation. If you have access to a printer, you might want to print the document and review it as you work your way through the steps.

   MSDE2000A.exe is a self-extracting file that contains all the files required to install MSDE 2000 Release A.

7. Open Microsoft Windows Explorer, and navigate to the folder in which you saved MSDE2000A.exe.

8. Double-click the file to extract the contained files. As shown in Figure A-1, the default location for the installed files is a folder named C:\MSDERelA. Click Finish to accept the default folder, or enter (or browse to) a new location, and then click Finish. If the folder does not exist, you will be notified with a prompt. Click Yes and the folder will be created for you.

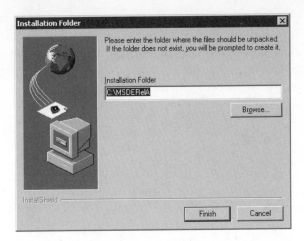

Figure A-1   Setting the installation folder

▶ Setting Up MSDE for Installation

1. Open Windows Explorer and navigate to the new folder.

2. Locate and open the Setup.ini file in Notepad.

3. Assuming that this is the first instance of MSDE (or SQL Server) on your computer, type the following parameter (exactly as shown) underneath *[OPTIONS]*.

```
[placeholder]=password
```

NOTE   If you are installing a second or subsequent instance of MSDE (or SQL Server), you must specify a *named instance* in the Setup.ini file along with the password. The first instance is known as the *default instance* and, when installed, it will have the default name MSSQLSERVER. Each subsequent instance will have the name MSSQL$*InstanceName* (where *InstanceName* is the name you specified in the Setup.ini file).

Following is an example of how to set the *InstanceName* parameter. We chose VSdotNET as the name of the instance:

```
INSTANCENAME=VSdotNET
```

Setting the Security Mode

You can set up MSDE 2000 to use one of two security modes.

- Windows NT Security. This is sometimes referred to as *Windows NT Integrated Security* or *Windows Authentication*. It grants access to the database based on the Microsoft Windows NT account.

- SQL Server Security. This security mode requires the user to log on to the database by using a separate account set up by the DBA (database administrator).

Under normal circumstances, Windows NT Security is all that will be required. The user will log on to the computer and be allowed access to the database without having any additional credentials. If you have a situation in which you want everyone to have access to the computer but you want only select groups of individuals to have access to the database, use SQL Server Security.

1. To create an instance of MSDE 2000 that uses SQL Server Security, type the following parameter (exactly as shown) below the previous parameters in the Setup.ini file.

    `SECURITYMODE=SQL`

    NOTE No additional parameter is required if you want to use Windows NT Security.

2. Save the changes and close Notepad.

▶ **Running the MSDE 2000 Installer**

1. Double-click Setup.exe to run the installer. The installation might take several minutes.

2. When MSDE 2000 is installed, click the Start button, point to Programs, and then locate and select Microsoft SQL Server.

3. Click Service Manager to open the Service Manager dialog box.

4. In the Services box, type the name of your computer followed by a back-slash and the name of the instance of MSDE 2000. For example, if the name of your computer is RUMPUS18 and the name of the instance you specified in the Setup.ini file is VSDOTNET, type **RUMPUS18\VSDOTNET**.

5. To locate the name of your computer, right-click My Computer and then select Properties. Click the Computer Name tab. The full computer name is listed, which will include the domain name (if any), followed on a separate line by the computer name. All that is required for the SQL Service is the computer name.

6. Click Refresh Services. Notice that SQL Server is automatically placed in the Services list, as shown in Figure A-2.

Figure A-2   Using the SQL Server Service Manager to start the service

7. Click Start/Continue to start SQL Server. The SQL Server Service Manager display changes, as shown in Figure A-3, to emphasize that the SQL Server service is now running.

NOTE *SQL Server must be running in order to connect to any SQL Server database from your applications.*

Figure A-3 **The service has started**

ADMINISTERING MSDE 2000 USING OSQL

MSDE 2000 is only a database server. To use it, you need to create or install a database. You will do that now by using a command-line utility called Osql.exe, which was included when you installed MSDE 2000.

What Does Osql Do?

Osql.exe allows you to interactively enter Transact-SQL statements in a command window environment. You can use this utility to create a new database, to make changes to an existing database, to query a database to update existing data, to insert new data, or to simply return data.

NOTE *Transact-SQL (or T-SQL) is a language that is specific to SQL Server. To learn more about T-SQL, go to http://msdn.microsoft.com, enter **T-SQL** in the Search MSDN For box, and then click Go. When the results show, click the hyperlink Using Transact-SQL With SQL Server, and then click the hyperlink Transact-SQL Overview.*

▶ **Installing the Pubs Database Using Osql.exe**

The Pubs database is the database of a fictitious book publishing company. It is used in several examples in this textbook.

IMPORTANT *The instance of MSDE 2000 that you created must be running before you can install the Pubs database.*

1. Locate the file INSTPUBS.sql in the student file, and copy it to the MSDERelA folder or the folder into which you downloaded MSDE 2000.

2. Open a command window by clicking the Start button and then click on Run. Type the word **cmd** and then click OK.

3. Type the following command, exactly as shown, into the command window.

```
osql -E -S RUMPUS18\VSDOTNET -i C:\MSDERelA\INSTPUBS.SQL
```

The preceding command is written for the situation in which the stored procedure file, INSTPUBS.SQL, is located in the MSDERelA folder and the instance name of MSDE 2000 is VSDOTNET. The name of the computer, RUMPUS18, must be changed to the name of your computer.

> **NOTE**   If you used SQL Security when you installed MSDE 2000, you must include the user name and password in the command. You can use the sa (System Administrator) account and use password as the password. The command would look as follows. (Be sure to enter all of the information on a single line.)

```
osql -U sa -P password -S RUMPUS18\VSDOTNET
  -i C:\MSDERelA\INSTPUBS.SQL
```

4. Press ENTER to create the database. This process might take a few minutes.

Inside the Command

osql is the name of the command window utility. *-E* assumes that you installed MSDE 2000 using Windows NT Security. *-S* is the name of the instance of MSDE 2000, along with the name of your computer. *-i* is the name of and the full path to the input file (the stored procedure).

▶ **Testing the Installation by Using Osql.exe**

Although you can create a new project using Visual Basic .NET to make sure you are connecting to the Pubs database and are able to retrieve data from it, you can use Osql.exe to do the same thing. This will confirm that MSDE 2000 is running correctly and that the Pubs database was properly installed.

1. Open a command window.

2. Type the following command and press ENTER.

```
osql -E -S RUMPUS18\VSDOTNET
```

> **NOTE**   The preceding command is written for the situation in which the instance of MSDE 2000 is VSDOTNET and Windows NT Security was selected during installation. The name of the computer, RUMPUS18, must be changed to the name of your computer. In addition, if SQL Security was selected during installation, you will need to use the –U and –P flags in place of the –E flag, as discussed earlier in this section.

3. Type the following command and press ENTER.

```
USE Pubs
```

4. Type **GO** and press ENTER.

5. Type the following SQL statement and press ENTER.

```
SELECT title FROM titles
```

6. Type **GO** and press ENTER.

The query results, which consist of 18 book titles, will appear in the command window.

APPENDIX B
MICROSOFT .NET FRAMEWORK

So, just what is the Microsoft .NET Framework? To make a long story short, the .NET Framework is a set of standards that are used to generate applications and XML Web services. The .NET Framework provides a multilanguage environment that makes it easier to develop applications for both Microsoft Windows and Web environments. The .NET Framework consists of three main parts:

- The common language runtime
- A hierarchical set of class libraries (FCL)
- A componentized version of Active Server Pages (ASP) called Microsoft ASP.NET

CONTENTS OF THE .NET FRAMEWORK

Let's first look at the languages supported by Microsoft Visual Studio .NET and the .NET Framework, and then we'll talk about the common language runtime and the class hierarchy.

Languages Supported by Visual Studio .NET

When you install Visual Studio .NET on your computer, the tools required to create programs using the following languages are automatically installed:

- Microsoft Visual Basic .NET
- Microsoft Visual C++ .NET
- Microsoft Visual C# .NET
- Microsoft Visual J# .NET

Each of these languages has its own features and capabilities that you should take into consideration when determining which language to choose. Perhaps one of the most important things to keep in mind is your familiarity with a particular language. If one developer is familiar with Visual Basic and another is familiar with Visual C#, it is possible to have each of them create his or her pieces (components) of the application in the respective languages and put them together at the end. We'll talk more about how this works later in this appendix. First let's look at the highlights of each of these four languages.

Visual Basic .NET, although still a robust and extensive language, is perhaps the easiest of the Visual Studio .NET languages to learn. Applications created in earlier versions of Visual Basic can be upgraded to Visual Basic .NET, although this upgrade can produce some strange code and might require some extensive rework after the conversion.

Visual C++ .NET is a systems-level language that is used to create high-performance applications while still integrating the use of the familiar GUI-based integrated development environment (IDE) in Visual Studio .NET. Visual C++ has the distinction of being able to access what is called unmanaged C++ code from its applications. This means that other programs written in the C++ language outside of Visual Studio .NET can be run from within Visual C++ .NET.

Visual C# .NET is a new language that should look familiar to C++ or Java programmers. You can think of C# as being a hybrid language because it incorporates the best features of both C++ and Visual Basic and would be the preferred language if you were moving from any curly-braced language.

Visual J# .NET provides the ability for Java programmers to develop applications by using Visual Studio .NET and the .NET Framework. Visual Studio .NET provides the tools needed to migrate existing Java applications into Visual J# .NET.

Common Language Runtime

The common language runtime is the part of the .NET Framework that manages and runs code written for the .NET Framework. The common language runtime manages all aspects of code execution, including:

- Just-In-Time compilation of methods.

- Handling the memory requirements of the managed code.

- Ensuring type safety for the code the runtime is running.

- Handling errors in managed code by using a common error handling framework based on exceptions. This is called *structured exception handling*, and it uses the *Try...Catch* methodology originally developed for C++.

The common language runtime is layered over the operating system and provides an environment for hosting managed applications. Code that runs in the common language runtime is referred to as *managed code*. Code that runs outside the runtime is called *unmanaged code*. Some languages, such as Visual C++ .NET, are designed to interface with unmanaged code.

Common Type System

The common type system (CTS) is a specification that defines how supported languages use common types in the common language runtime. The *String* type used in Visual C# is identical to the *String* type used in Visual Basic .NET. The common type system is important in that it allows the .NET Framework to support multiple languages. The common type system also provides an object-oriented model that programming languages can use to ensure they are 100 percent compatible with the other languages that use the .NET Framework.

Common Language Specification

The common language specification (CLS) is a subset of the CTS. The CLS provides rules that define features that must be common to all languages supported by the .NET Framework. Developers working within the .NET Framework can assume that any language will support the features defined by the CLS. If a component is developed within the .NET Framework and adheres to the rules defined by the CLS, it is said to be a *CLS-compliant* component.

Compiling a Program

Programs written in any of the languages supported by the .NET Framework can compile into the same intermediate language—Microsoft Intermediate Language (MSIL)—which is then turned into machine code. This capability provides distinct advantages over older compilers that required extensive rework to create cross-platform applications. Let's look at how a program is compiled in the .NET Framework.

Microsoft Intermediate Language

The code that you write in Visual Basic .NET is called the source code (language-specific code). Visual Basic .NET source code is easy to understand, but the computer can't do much with it until it is compiled into a set of instructions that is native to the computer's CPU. The common language runtime compiles source code into MSIL code (pronounced *missile*). MSIL code is a set of instructions that is CPU-independent. MSIL code is not machine readable and must be converted (compiled) into something that the processor can understand. Just-In-Time (JIT) compilers are used to perform this last step.

Just-In-Time Compiler

The JIT compiler is used to translate the MSIL code into a set of instructions that a particular CPU can process. This CPU-specific code, most often called *native code*, is the set of instructions that the computer will actually run. This JIT compiling must be done once for each method before the code can run on a computer. After the JIT compiling is complete and the native code has been generated, the native code is cached in memory and can be run repeatedly without further recompilation.

The .NET Framework Class Library

The .NET Framework comes with a set of class libraries called the Framework Class Library (FCL). The FCL is a collection of reusable classes and types approved by the common language runtime for use in managed applications. There are more than 7000 types, which include classes, structures, interfaces, enumerations, and delegates that are integrated in the .NET Framework.

The .NET Framework Class Library is organized in a hierarchical structure that uses namespaces to group related types together. At the top of the structure is the *System* namespace, which contains types that can be used by any language that supports the .NET Framework. All other namespaces descend from the *System* namespace.

Learning about all the types included in the FCL is not trivial. Some classes in the FCL contain as many as 100 methods (or more). The good news is that you don't have to learn them all. Most people pick up on the basic ones and learn others as they go. Knowing where to find them and how to use them in your applications is half the battle.

System.Object

The .NET Framework is built on the concept of inheritance, and every object inherits in some way or another from *System.Object*. The hierarchical chain in the .NET Framework Class Library is quite extensive and complex; however, Microsoft has made it easier by dividing the hierarchy into namespaces. When we refer to *System.Object*, *System* is the namespace and *Object* is the name of the object. This is known as the *fully qualified name*.

Namespaces

Namespaces are nothing more than groupings of classes or types. Namespaces provide a way to logically categorize these classes and types so they are easier to locate and use. Each namespace contains types that you can use in your program. As we mentioned earlier, these types can be categorized as classes, structures, enumerations, delegates, and interfaces. The code that defines and implements the namespaces and types is stored in .dll and .exe files.

Namespaces provide scope. This means that two classes with the same name can be used in your program as long as they are in different namespaces, and as long as you use the fully qualified names to reference them.

To illustrate our point here, recall the console-based Hello World program that you created in Chapter 1. When you typed in the line of code `Console.Write-Line("Hello World")`, you were actually specifying the *WriteLine* method of the *Console* class. You didn't use the fully qualified name for the class, which is *System.Console*, but we know that *Console* is a member of the *System* namespace. How did Visual Studio .NET know where to locate the *Console* class? The answer is in the references.

References

A number of references are already included in the projects you have created so far. We have discussed many of these references in detail in several of the chapters. To review the references, open Solution Explorer and click the References node (click the plus sign (+) next to the word *References*).

Using the *Imports* Statement

If you do not want to type the fully qualified names for the types used in your code, you can use the *Imports* statement. In the following code sample, see how Visual Basic .NET uses the *Imports* statement to provide the fully qualified name:

```
Imports System.Console
Module Module1
    Sub Main()
        WriteLine("Hello")
        ' Without the Imports statement, you would have to use
        ' System.Console.WriteLine("Hello").
    End Sub
End Module
```

Notice that after you have added the *Imports System.Console* statement, you no longer have to place the word *Console* in front of the *WriteLine* method.

All namespaces shipped by Microsoft begin with one of two names: "System" or "Microsoft." To find the fully qualified name (namespace and type name) containing the type you want to use, you can use any of the following utilities:

- Windows Class Viewer (WinCV.exe)

- Intermediate Language Disassembler (Ildasm.exe)

- Type Finder (FindType.exe)

Windows Class Viewer – WinCV.exe

The Windows Class Viewer utility is a Windows application that allows you to view information about any type. Figure B-1 shows how you can use it to find information about the *String* type.

▶ **Running WinCV.exe and locating information on any .NET Framework class or type**

1. Open Windows Explorer and browse to find the C:\Program Files\Microsoft Visual Studio .NET 2003\SDK\v1.1\Bin folder.

2. Double-click the WinCV.exe file to run the program.

3. Type the name of the class you are looking for—in this case **String**—in the Searching For box, and then press ENTER.

   The results of the search will be displayed in the Class Viewer, as shown in Figure B-1.

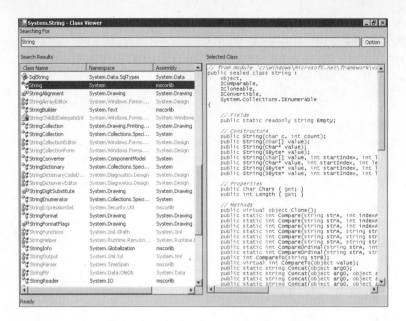

Figure B-1 The *String* class displayed in the Class Viewer

Notice that the left pane shows the class name, the namespace, and the assembly that the class is defined in. The right pane shows the class definition and all the members, including fields, properties, and methods, along with the interfaces that the class implements.

Intermediate Language Disassembler – Ildasm.exe

The Intermediate Language Disassembler can be difficult to use when you know only the name of the class or type that you want to find information about. Ildasm.exe requires that you know both the name and the location of the assembly in which the class is defined. After you know the correct assembly and have opened it with the Intermediate Language Disassembler, you will be able to view more detailed information on the members of the class that the Class Viewer was not able to provide.

▶ Running Ildasm.exe and locating information on any .NET Framework class or type

1. Open Windows Explorer and browse to find the C:\Program Files\Microsoft Visual Studio .NET 2003\SDK\v1.1\Bin folder.

2. Double-click the Ildasm.exe file to run the program. After a few moments, the IL Disassembler dialog box will appear.

    To demonstrate using the Intermediate Language Disassembler, we can get more information on the *String* class that you researched by using WinCV.exe. We know that there is a definition of the *String* class under the *System* namespace and that this is defined in an assembly called *mscorlib*. This .dll file is located in the folder C:\Windows\Microsoft.NET\Framework\v1.1.4322\mscorlib.dll.

3. To use the Intermediate Language Disassembler to find information about the *String* class, select the File menu and then select Open.

4. In the Open File dialog box, browse to the location of the mscorlib.dll file listed above, and open it by clicking it and then clicking the Open button.

Note that the version number (v1.1.4322) might be different on your computer, depending on the version of the .NET Framework that you have installed. In addition, if your operating system is Windows 2000 rather than Windows XP, the primary folder will be Winnt rather than Windows.

The IL DASM window displays a tree-view of the classes and types in the mscorlib.dll assembly. By clicking the plus sign to the left of the class name, you can expand the view to see more detailed information. Figure B-2 shows detailed information about the selected class.

Figure B-2   *String* class information displayed in the IL DASM window

Double-clicking any one of the fields, properties, or methods will bring up another dialog box that shows the implementation code for that item, as shown in Figure B-3. Notice that the code is not quite what we are used to because it is already compiled into Intermediate Language code.

```
String::Format : string(string,object[])                              _ □ ×
.method public hidebysig static string  Format(string format,
                                                object[] args) cil managed
{
  .param [2]
  .custom instance void System.ParamArrayAttribute::.ctor() = ( 01 00 00 00 )
  // Code size       9 (0x9)
  .maxstack  8
  IL_0000:  ldnull
  IL_0001:  ldarg.0
  IL_0002:  ldarg.1
  IL_0003:  call       string System.String::Format(class System.IFormatProvider,
                                                     string,
                                                     object[])
  IL_0008:  ret
} // end of method String::Format
```

Figure B-3   An overloaded Format method of the *String* class

You can use the Intermediate Language Disassembler to view details on any assembly, even assemblies that you have created yourself. For example, you can locate the HelloWorldWindows.exe file for the HelloWorldWindows application that you created in Chapter 1 and open it in Ildasm.exe. Figure B-4 shows the assembly that is displayed in the IL DASM window.

Figure B-4   HelloWorldWindows.exe assembly information displayed in the IL DASM window

Type Finder – FindType.exe

The Type Finder utility is a sample application that is included when you install Visual Studio .NET. There are two versions of this sample application: one created in Visual Basic .NET and another created in Visual C# .NET. Both of these sample applications can be located in the folder C:\Program Files\Microsoft Visual Studio .NET 2003\SDK\v1.1\Samples\Applications\TypeFinder.

▶ **Using the Type Finder utility**

1. To create the FindType.exe application file, open Windows Explorer and navigate to the TypeFinder folder. Open the vb folder and then double-click the Build.bat file. The application file will be created and placed in the same folder. If the creation of the application file fails, the compiler vbc.exe is not in your current search path. At this point, open the Type Finder solution in Visual Studio .NET and build it from there.

2. To use the TypeFinder application, open a command window and change to the folder that contains the FindType.exe application file. At the prompt, type the following command statement (all on one continuous line) and then press ENTER. Don't be concerned if the statement wraps to the next line, but make sure that there is a space between NET and 2003.

```
cd "C:\Program Files\Microsoft Visual Studio .NET
2003\SDK\v1.1\Samples\Applications\TypeFinder\vb"
```

3. To display a list of the namespaces that refer to the *String* class (or that have the word *String* in the class name), type the following command statement at the prompt and then press ENTER.

    `FindType String`

    The results are displayed in a window containing two columns. The first column shows the type (class, structure, or interface) and the second column displays the fully qualified name.

Table B-1 contains a list of the more common namespaces provided by the .NET Framework Class Library. For a more complete list, on the Help menu, select Index, and then type **.NET Framework Class Library** in the Look For list box.

Table B-1   **Common Namespaces**

Namespace	Description
Microsoft.VisualBasic	Contains classes that support compilation and code generation using the Visual Basic .NET language.
Microsoft.Win32	Provides two types of classes: those that handle events raised by the operating system and those that manipulate the system registry.
System	Contains fundamental classes and base classes that define commonly used value and reference data types, events and event handlers, interfaces, attributes, and processing exceptions. Other classes provide services supporting data type conversion, method parameter manipulation, mathematics, remote and local program invocation, application environment management, and supervision of managed and unmanaged applications.
System.Collections	Contains interfaces and classes that define various collections of objects, such as lists, queues, bit arrays, hashtables, and dictionaries.
System.ComponentModel	Provides classes that are used to implement the run-time and design-time behavior of components and controls. This namespace includes the base classes and interfaces for implementing attributes and type converters, binding to data sources, and licensing components.
System.Data	Consists mostly of the classes that constitute the Microsoft ADO.NET architecture. The ADO.NET architecture enables you to build components that efficiently manage data from multiple data sources. In a disconnected environment (such as the Internet), ADO.NET provides the tools to request, update, and reconcile data in multiple-tier systems. The ADO.NET architecture is also implemented in client applications, such as Windows Forms or HTML pages created by ASP.NET.
System.Data.Common	Contains classes shared by the .NET Framework data providers. A .NET Framework data provider describes a collection of classes used to access a data source, such as a database, in the managed space.

Table B-1   Common Namespaces (continued)

Namespace	Description
System.Data.Odbc	Encapsulates the .NET Framework Data Provider for ODBC. A .NET Framework data provider describes a collection of classes used to access a data source, such as a database, in the managed space. By using the *OdbcDataAdapter* class, you can fill a memory-resident *DataSet*, which you can use to query and update the data source. For additional information about how to use this namespace, see the *OdbcDataReader*, *OdbcCommand*, and *OdbcConnection* classes.
System.Data.OleDb	Encapsulates the .NET Framework Data Provider for OLE Database (OLE DB). The .NET Framework Data Provider for OLE DB describes a collection of classes used to access an OLE DB data source in the managed space.
System.Data.OracleClient	Encapsulates the .NET Framework Data Provider for Oracle. The .NET Framework Data Provider for Oracle describes a collection of classes used to access an Oracle data source in the managed space.
System.Data.SqlClient	Encapsulates the .NET Framework Data Provider for Microsoft SQL Server. The .NET Framework Data Provider for SQL Server describes a collection of classes used to access a SQL Server database in the managed space.
System.Data.SqlTypes	Provides classes for native data types within SQL Server. These classes provide a safer, faster alternative to other data types. Using the classes in this namespace helps prevent type-conversion errors caused in situations in which loss of precision could occur. Because other data types are converted to and from *SqlTypes* behind the scenes, explicitly creating and using objects within this namespace results in faster code as well.
System.DirectoryServices	Provides easy access to the Active Directory directory service from managed code. The namespace contains two component classes, *DirectoryEntry* and *DirectorySearcher*, which use the Active Directory Services Interfaces (ADSI) technology. ADSI is the set of interfaces that Microsoft provides as a flexible tool for working with a variety of network providers. ADSI gives the administrator the ability to locate and manage resources on a network with relative ease, regardless of the network's size.
System.Drawing	Provides access to GDI+ basic graphics functionality. More advanced functionality is provided in the *System.Drawing.Drawing2D*, *System.Drawing.Imaging*, and *System.Drawing.Text* namespaces.
System.Drawing.Drawing2D	Provides advanced two-dimensional and vector graphics functionality. This namespace includes the gradient brushes, the *Matrix* class (used to define geometric transforms), and the *GraphicsPath* class.

Table B-1 **Common Namespaces (continued)**

Namespace	Description
System.Drawing.Imaging	Provides advanced GDI+ imaging functionality. Basic graphics functionality is provided by the *System.Drawing* namespace.
System.Drawing.Printing	Provides print-related services. Typically, you create a new instance of the *PrintDocument* class, set the properties that describe what to print, and call the *Print* method to actually print the document.
System.Drawing.Text	Provides advanced GDI+ typography functionality. Basic graphics functionality is provided by the *System.Drawing* namespace. The classes in this namespace allow users to create and use collections of fonts.
System.IO	Contains types that allow synchronous and asynchronous reading and writing on data streams and files.
System.Messaging	Provides classes that allow you to connect to, monitor, and administer message queues on the network and send, receive, or peek messages.
System.Text	Contains classes representing ASCII, Unicode, UTF-7, and UTF-8 character encodings; abstract base classes for converting blocks of characters to and from blocks of bytes; and a helper class that manipulates and formats *String* objects without creating intermediate instances of *String*.
System.Windows.Forms	Contains classes for creating Windows-based applications that take full advantage of the rich user-interface features available in the Windows operating system.

GLOSSARY

absolute position   In Grid Layout, absolute positioning is used to control where elements are placed on a Web Form.

abstract class   An abstract class is created to be a base class and provide the properties, methods, and events that are common to any class that inherits from it. An abstract class cannot be instantiated directly and must be inherited from. For example, a car and a truck have many things in common, but they are specific types of vehicles. It would make sense to create a *Vehicle* class to provide the common functionality and then create a *Car* class and a *Truck* class that inherit from the base *Vehicle* class.

abstraction   A class is considered an abstraction of a real-world entity. For example, a *Car* class would have properties that define a car, such as model and color, and it would also have methods that act on the car, such as accelerate and decelerate.

application file   A simple program can be compiled into a single application file (.exe). More complex programs might consist of an application file along with one or more support files. In Microsoft ASP.NET, the Global.asax file is considered the application file.

argument   A value that you provide when calling a method that contains a parameter that will accept the value being passed.

array   A collection of elements that store values or references of the same type. You can read or write to each value by specifying the name of the array along with an index number (inside parentheses) that represents the element that is storing the value.

ASP.NET   The latest version of ASP (Active Server Pages)—a set of technologies in the Microsoft .NET Framework for building Web applications and XML Web services.

assembly   One or more files in a project that are versioned and deployed as a single unit.

auto hide   Any window in the Microsoft Visual Studio .NET IDE that has its *Auto Hide* property set to True will retract automatically when the mouse pointer is moved away from it.

base exception object   The base object for all exceptions that are thrown. Although the base exception object can be thrown, it is typically too generic to be useful.

binding   The programmatical linking of a data source to a control that can display the data. For example, you might want a text box to display the name of a person. By using binding, you can link the *Text* property of the text box to the data source and, more specifically, to the column that stores the name value.

Boolean expression   An expression that evaluates to True or False.

breakpoint   A debugging tool. When you set a breakpoint, program execution will hold and enter break mode when execution reaches the code statement marked with the breakpoint. You can customize breakpoints by including special conditions when the breakpoint is created.

bug   An error in programming code or logic.

Call Stack   A debugging tool. The Call Stack displays a list of method calls leading up to the current method. The current method is always displayed at the top of the Call Stack window.

casting   The transformation of one type to another. Also known as *coercion*.

class   A class is a blueprint or template for an object.

code   A grouping of one or more keywords and/or expressions that performs a task within a program when compiled and run.

code editor   A text editor that allows you to edit text or code. When you are editing code, the language-specific service checks for syntax and usage errors.

code module   A single file containing the code for one or more types (classes, structures, enumerations, or interfaces).

code-behind module   A code module that is associated with a Web Form.

collection   A group of one or more objects of the same type. A collection class has an *Item* property that, along with an index number or key value, can be used to refer to an object at a specific location in the collection. A collection typically has methods that add and remove items from the collection. It will also have a *Count* property to determine how many objects are currently in the collection.

column   In a database table, a column represents an attribute of the entity. For example, in a students table, the *first_name* column stores the first name data values of individual students.

comment   A statement preceded by a single quotation mark that is used to describe code.

comparison operator   An operator that is used to compare each side of an expression. For example, the greater than operator (>) is used to check whether the operand on the left side of the operator is greater than the operand on the right side. If it is, the result of the expression is True.

compilation error   Typically a syntax error caused by misspelled keywords that prevents the code from being compiled.

composite primary key   Two or more columns that, when joined together, make up the unique value that defines a primary key. For example, in a linking table called titleauthors (used to link the titles table to the authors table), the two columns *titleid* and *authorid* would make up the primary key. An author can write more than one book and, as a result, might show up more than once in the titleauthors table. Likewise, a book can be written by more than one author and again might show up more than once. By designating these two columns as the primary key, you are saying that the combination of *titleid* and *authorid* can only occur once and is therefore unique.

concatenation   Used to join two or more strings into one longer string. The ampersand symbol (&) is used to perform concatenation.

condition   Criteria that is used to determine the result of an expression. In a SQL statement, it would be the value that is defined in the *WHERE* clause of the statement.

conditional expression   An expression that evaluates to True when one or more of the conditions evaluates to True.

connected data access model   A data model whereby an application has immediate access to the underlying database. The database might be on a network share that the user has access to, or the database might be on the local computer.

console application   An application that runs in an MS-DOS–style window.

constant   A variable that is assigned a value when it is declared. The value cannot be changed at run time and remains constant throughout the life of the program.

constraint   A property assigned to a table column that prevents certain types of invalid data from being placed in that column. For example, a primary key constraint would prevent a value from being entered in a particular row if the same value existed in another row of that column.

constructor   A special method called *New* that creates an instance of a class. A default version of the constructor is implicitly created if the developer of the class does not provide one.

container control   A control, such as a form or a group box, that is used to contain other controls.

context menu   A popup menu that appears when the user clicks the right mouse button when the mouse pointer is over a control that has a menu associated with the *ContextMenu* property of that control.

controls   Visual components placed on a form, such as a button or a text box.

debug version   A version of the compiled application that includes debugging information.

declaration   A line of code that sets aside memory to store the object or value defined by the declaration.

default button   The button in a dialog box that has focus when the dialog box is first displayed.

default event   An event that the original developer of the component has designated as the default. When the programmer using the component double-clicks the component at design time, the wrapper lines for the event are automatically inserted into the code module.

defensive programming   Code that consists of one or more expressions that will be used to determine whether the code that is to be run will be successful before it is run.

design   The visual and functional design of a program.

destructor   Can be used to dispose of resources when an object is no longer required. A destructor (or finalizer) must be explicitly created; it is not provided by default. You should only create a destructor if there is a specific need for one.

disconnected data access model   A data model whereby an application runs on a portable computer or a computer that is disconnected from the network and does not have immediate access to the underlying database. The application uses a virtual copy of the database known as a *DataSet* that is created and populated from the original data source when the computer is connected. Data can be added to the dataset, existing data can be updated in the dataset, and data can be deleted from the dataset. After the computer is reconnected, the database can be updated with the changed data from the dataset.

docked   A window, when docked, is placed against the side, top, or bottom of the container window.

dynamic array   An array that can be sized at run time. All arrays in Microsoft Visual Basic .NET are dynamic.

encapsulation   The process of ensuring that all access to the data that an object can store or work on is obtained through predefined properties and methods. For example, providing a public field in a class would break encapsulation by providing an access point that cannot be controlled or monitored.

enumeration   A defined collection of constant values represented by a numeric value.

event   A user- or system-initiated action, such as when a user clicks a button on a form. The event is said to be *raised* when an action occurs.

event handlers   The methods that are linked to an event. The *Handles* statement is used to link a method to an event.

exception   An object that is thrown when an error occurs at run time.

exception bubbling   A condition in which the code inside a method causes an exception to be thrown but the method is not able to handle the exception, and the exception is thrown back to the preceding method. Exception bubbling continues back up the Call Stack until a method is found that can handle the exception. If no method is found, an unhandled exception is thrown, which might result in the termination of the application.

execution errors   A run-time error that causes an exception to be thrown.

field   A public variable that a class exposes. A field can be used in place of a Property procedure, but access to the data will be lost. A field breaks encapsulation.

field (database table)   Another name for a column.

FIFO   First In, First Out. Describes the manner in which items are added to a collection of objects when you are using a *Queue* collection.

File I/O   A means to write to and read from files located on a disk or a network share.

floating window   A window that you can move by clicking its title bar and dragging it to a new position.

Flow Layout   When a Web Form's *pageLayout* property is set to FlowLayout, the Web browser will arrange elements in the order in which they occur on the page, from top to bottom.

flowchart   A diagram that visually explains the flow of a process.

focus   A control that *has focus* is the active control.

foreign key   A column in a table that relates to the primary key in another table.

form   A container control that provides the background for an application.

Function procedure   A method that returns a value when it is called.

garbage collector   A utility that is designed to clean up unused objects that are still in memory. The garbage collector typically runs when the CPU is idle or when resources are critically low. Garbage collection is also known as *non-deterministic finalization.*

grid   Used to align controls on a form. A grid is a series of horizontally and vertically displayed dots that form a pattern on the form at design time.

Grid Layout   When a Web Form's *pageLayout* property is set to GridLayout, absolute positioning attributes are inserted into each element that is added to the Web Form.

IIS   Internet Information Services. A service that runs on the computer that hosts a Web application or XML Web service. IIS is used to compile the application and respond to HTTP requests from the Web browser running on the remote computer. Responses are sent as plain HTML or XML.

implicit dimensioning   The process of dimensioning an array by assigning values as part of the declaration statement.

index   The numeric value that refers to an item in an array or collection.

infinite loop   A loop that has no logical end point.

inheritance   The process of automatically obtaining all the properties, methods, and events from a base class.

instantiate   To create an instance of a class. To create an instance of a class, you use the *New* keyword when you declare or assign the variable. The *New* keyword calls the constructor of the class to create the instance.

integrated development environment (IDE)   A workspace that provides the means to design and code an application.

IntelliSense   Intelligent, context-sensitive Help that appears when you're typing code into the Code Editor.

intrinsic controls   Controls that are provided by default in the Toolbox.

key value   The value that you provide when you are using a Hashtable to set and get an item in a collection.

keywords   Also known as reserved words. Keywords are language-specific words that have specific meaning and functionality.

LIFO   Last In, First Out. Describes the manner in which items are added to a collection of objects when you are using a Stack collection.

line-continuation character   A space followed by the underscore character. The line continuation character allows long lines of code to be broken up into multiple lines to make the code easier to read.

linking table   A table that joins two other tables. You would typically do this because the two tables that you want to join have no common column.

logic error   An error that produces unwanted results when the code is run.

logical operator   An operator that is used to join inclusionary or exclusionary operands (expressions). The And operator is used to join two operands and requires that both operands evaluate to True. The Or operator is used to join two operands and requires that at least one of the operands evaluate to True. The Xor operator, known as an Exclusive Or, is used to evaluate two operands and requires that only one of the operands evaluate to True.

many-to-many relationship   A relationship in which many rows in one table match many rows in a related table.

menu   An object that has top-level and sub-level menu items.

method   An action on an object. A method can be a Sub procedure or a Function procedure.

method overloading   A situation in which two or more methods with the same name exist in the same code module. The signature of each method must be different from the others. The signature of a method refers to the number, type, or order of the parameters in the method declaration.

modules   A file containing Visual Basic .NET code.

multi-dimensional array   An array with two or more dimensions. A two-dimensional array is similar in concept to a worksheet in Microsoft Excel.

non-deterministic finalization   Another name for garbage collection.

object   A single instance of a class.

object-oriented programming (OOP)   A programming and development technique that provides for the separation of functionality by creating functional code modules called classes. Each class is specifically designed to emulate a real-world entity. OOP promotes code reuse.

one-dimensional array   An array with one dimension that contains a number of elements. Similar to a list.

one-to-many relationship   A relationship in which one row in one table matches many rows in a related table.

one-to-one relationship   A relationship in which one row in one table matches one row in a related table.

outlining   Allows regions of code to be collapsed, so that only the header text will appear, or expanded to show the entire contents of that region. Outlining displays a plus sign (+) or a minus sign (–) symbol next to the header text, denoting whether the region is collapsed or expanded.

parameters   Variables declared as part of a method signature that will accept values (arguments) when the method is called.

placeholder   A parameter is a placeholder for a value. In the *Console.WriteLine* method, a number starting at 0 when placed inside curly-braces serves as a placeholder for the string literal that is provided as one of the arguments.

polymorphism   Object-oriented programming provides for polymorphism based on inheritance by allowing a method in a derived class to override the same method in the base class and run different implementation code.

primary key   A column or field for which each row under that column cannot contain a null value and must be a unique value.

primitive data types   Primitive types are defined through keywords. These keywords are aliases for the predefined types in the System namespace. The primitive type Integer refers to the structure System.Int32.

procedure   A Property, Method, or event procedure that, when called, runs the code inside the procedure.

project   A project in Visual Studio .NET helps you organize and perform common tasks on the items included in the project. These items include the files, references, and folders that make up the application. The project can be considered an assembly and, when deployed, will become an executable file (.exe), a dynamic-link library (.dll), or a module. *See also* assembly.

proper casing   The capitalization style in which the first letter of each significant word is uppercase and all subsequent letters in each word are lowercase.

Property procedures   Read-only, write-only, and read/write properties. Use Set and Get accessor methods within the Property procedure to write and read the value.

pseudocode   Natural language code that describes a part of a process.

public interface   The properties, methods, events, and fields of a class that are marked as public.

Quick Watch   Provides a fast way to evaluate variables and expressions at any point.

rapid application development (RAD)   A term that describes the use of pre-built controls and components to aid the developer in quickly producing a functional application.

record   *See* row.

refactoring   The art of making code cleaner and more elegant without changing the final outcome. For example, to return the circumference of a circle, you could provide code that would multiply the diameter by 3.14159265358979323846. To refactor this process and make the code a little more elegant, you could just use the pi constant that is available in the System.Math namespace.

reference   A value that points to the location of an object in memory.

referential integrity   A set of rules governing how related data is managed. For example, a titles table has a foreign key called pubid that is used to relate the titles table to the publishers table. The rules that define referential integrity require that pubid must exist in the publishers table in order to be a valid value in the titles table. In addition, referential integrity will prevent the inadvertent deletion of a row in the publishers table if related rows exist in the titles table.

relation   The joining of two tables based on a common column.

relational database   A collection of information organized into tables. Each table models an entity, such as a student or book. Each column in each table models an attribute of the entity. Tables are related through matching columns. For example, the primary key in one table will relate to a foreign key in another table.

release version   A version of a compiled application that does not include debugging information.

row   A row is an instance of an entity. For example, in a students table, each row describes a single student. Also known as a record.

run-time error   An error that causes an unhandled exception to be thrown. A run-time error might cause a program to stop responding.

scope   Defines the visibility and lifetime of a variable, method, or class, and refers to the accessibility of the variable, method, or class to other code within a procedure, code module, or assembly, or even outside the assembly.

sealed class   A class that cannot be inherited from. Marking a class as sealed can improve performance because the compiler knows that there will be no subclasses below that level.

short-circuiting   The short-circuiting operators AndAlso and OrElse are logical operators that allow a second or subsequent expression is to be ignored if the prior expression has already determined the overall result. If the first expression in an AndAlso operation evaluates to False, the second expression is not evaluated and the overall result is False. If the first expression

in an OrElse operation evaluates to True, the second expression is not evaluated and the overall result is True.

sizing handles   Nodes placed at the corners and sides of a control that allow you to resize the control by using a mouse. To resize a control, you place the mouse pointer over the sizing handle and, with the left mouse button depressed, move the mouse.

solution   A group of one or more projects within the same instance of Visual Studio .NET.

specification   A list of one or more requirements. A visual design specification sets the number of forms and the number, type, and location of the embedded controls.

splash screen   A form that displays momentarily when an application is started. A splash screen typically provides information to the user while the application is being loaded into memory.

SQL   Structured Query Language

statements   A grouping of one or more keywords and expressions designed to perform a task.

strongly typed   When referring to a language, strongly typed means that strict rules are enforced regarding the type and use of variables, constants, classes, and structures used in the program. Visual Basic .NET enables you to enforce these rules by setting the Option Strict On attribute at the top of each code module. When referring to datasets, a strongly typed dataset is one in which an XML schema file is created that stores information on the tables and columns in the dataset. This information includes the names of the tables and columns along with the data types, relations, constraints, and other pertinent information.

structured exception handler   Exception handling code that uses a *Try...Catch* structure. The code that could potentially throw an exception is placed in the *Try* block. Any exception that is thrown because of a failure of the code in the *Try* block is caught in the *Catch* block and handled there.

Sub procedure   A method used to run code.

submenu item   An item in the Menu-Items collection of a menu. Clicking the submenu item will run code to perform the desired task

syntax error   An error in the spelling or use of one or more keywords or program statements that causes the keyword or statement to be unrecognizable by the compiler. The program will fail to compile. The language-specific service performs syntax checking before compilation takes place.

tab order   The sequence in which each control receives focus when the user presses the TAB key.

table   A collection of rows and columns

test   The process during which code is subjected to a series of analyses to determine whether it functions as designed.

toolbar   A component that has a collection of toolbar buttons.

ToolTip   A message that appears when the user rests the mouse pointer over a control that has a message associated with its Tool-Tip property.

top-level menu item   A menu item whose function is to display a collection of one or more submenu items.

unhandled run-time exception   An exception that is thrown when an error occurs during code execution and there is no acceptable Try…Catch in any method that can handle the exception and allow the program to continue.

variable   A named location in memory that is designed to store a value or reference.

virtual folders   Used when developing Web applications or XML Web services. A virtual folder is registered under IIS (Internet Information Services) and points to the location of the files that make up the application or service. The physical files reside in another location on the computer or on a network share. Using virtual folders allows you to better organize your Web applications during development.

Visual Basic .NET   A language supported by the Microsoft .NET Framework.

visual inheritance   Allows you to create a form as a base and then create another form that inherits from it. Controls that are added to the base form will also be in the derived form.

Visual Studio .NET   A common development environment that can be used to develop applications. Visual Studio .NET can be used to develop applications in multiple languages, including Visual Basic .NET, Visual C# .NET, Visual C++ .NET (with managed extensions), and Visual J# .NET.

Watch   One of up to four windows that can be used to monitor a variable or expression while code is being run.

Web application   An application that is built on the Microsoft ASP.NET platform and runs under IIS (Internet Information Services) on a Web server. The Web server can be the development computer that you are working on or a computer that is thousands of miles away. The application is compiled on the server and, when run, serves HTML code dynamically to the browser that sent the request.

Windows application   An application that provides a graphical user interface from which the user can interact with the application through the use of a mouse and a keyboard.

Windows Forms Designer   Allows you to add controls to a form, arrange them, and provide the necessary code for the events that they raise. The Windows Forms Designer also allows you to add components and other non-visual components. Non-visual components are added to the Component Tray located below the form at design time.

wrapper lines   The first and last lines of a method that declare and set the boundaries of the method. Code that runs when the method is called is placed between the wrapper lines of the method.

INDEX

Symbols

& (ampersand), 56, 60, 98, 102, 140, 496
= (assignment operator), 194, 229
* (asterisk), 94
\ (backslash), 241
&= (concatenation operator), 249
{} (curly braces), 228
"" (double quotation marks), 19, 102, 245
= (equals sign), 102, 194, 195, 229
> (greater than operator), 195
>= (greater than or equal to operator), 195
- (hyphen), 440
+= (increment operator), 237
< (less than operator), 195
<= (less than or equal to operator), 195
<> (not equal to operator), 195
 () (parentheses), 101, 141, 337, 361, 390
. (period), 396
+ (plus sign), 176, 306
? (question mark), 177
' (single quotation mark), 54, 95, 121
 [] (square brackets), 58, 419

A

absolute position, Web Form control, 555
abstract classes, 516, 521
abstract functionality, classes and, 484, 486, 503
abstract method declarations, 507
accelerator keys, 496. *See also* keyboard
AcceptChanges method, DataSet object, 338
Access
    connecting to databases, 343
    databases, 299. *See also* OLE DB providers; OleDb components
    example database, 305, 335
    stored procedures, 304
access keys. *See also* keyboard
    creating, 60
    GUI design, 55
access permissions, virtual folder, 565
accessibilty. *See* scope
Active Server Pages (ASP), ASP.NET vs., 544
ActiveControl object, 447
Add method
    ArrayList object, 403
    controls, 101
    Items collection, 401
    ListBox control, 203
    Rows collection, 401
    Tables property, 305

AddHandler statement, 498–499
AddRange method, ListBox control Items collection, 228–230, 249
AddressOf statement, 498
ADO.NET, 299–353
    adding and filling DataSet objects, 307–311
    adding Button controls to forms, 313–315
    adding controls to applications, 311
    binding, 307, 329
    Bookstore database application. *See* Bookstore database application
    connected and disconnected data access models, 303, 329
    creating Windows applications, 306–307
    CurrencyManager objects, 315–316
    Data Adapter Configuration Wizard, 317, 319–325
    Data Provider objects, 329
    formatting DataGrid controls, 326–328
    navigating DataTable objects, 312–313
    object model, 303–305
    populating DataSet objects and DataGrid controls, 325
    relational databases, 300–302
    SQL and, 330–342
    switchboard forms, 317–319
alias, virtual folder, 565
alignment, control
    using Format menu, 89–91, 92
    using grid, 88, 92
ALT key, 56, 60
ALT+CTRL+X key combination, 79
ALT+O key combination, 82
ampersand (&), 56, 60, 98, 102, 140, 496
And operator, 204, 205
AndAlso operator, 205, 206–207, 498
application development, 47–54. *See also* applications
    comments, 54
    flowcharts, 50–53, 54
    ideal development cycle, 48–49, 54
    pseudocode, 53, 54
    real development cycle, 49
    user interface design. *See* GUI (graphical user interface) design
Application objects, 444, 460, 468
Application_BeginRequest event, 561
Application_End event, 552, 561
Application_EndRequest event, 561
Application_Error event, 552